SPIRITUAL MARRIAGE

SPIRITUAL MARRIAGE

SEXUAL ABSTINENCE
IN MEDIEVAL WEDLOCK

Dyan Elliott

PRINCETON UNIVERSITY PRESS

PRINCETON, NEW JERSEY

26934816

LIBRARY OF CONGRESS CATALOGING-IN-PUBLICATION DATA

ELLIOTT, DYAN, 1954–
SPIRITUAL MARRIAGE : SEXUAL ABSTINENCE IN MEDIEVAL WEDLOCK / DYAN
ELLIOTT.
P.   CM.
INCLUDES BIBLIOGRAPHICAL REFERENCES AND INDEX.
ISBN 0-691-08649-4
1. MARRIAGE—RELIGIOUS ASPECTS—CHRISTIANITY—HISTORY OF
DOCTRINES.   2. SEXUAL ABSTINENCE—RELIGIOUS ASPECTS—CHRISTIANITY—
HISTORY OF DOCTRINES.   3. MARRIAGE—RELIGIOUS ASPECTS—
CHRISTIANITY—HISTORY OF DOCTRINES—MIDDLE AGES, 600–1500.
4. SEXUAL ABSTINENCE—RELIGIOUS ASPECTS—CHRISTIANITY—HISTORY OF
DOCTRINES—MIDDLE AGES, 600–1500.   5. EUROPE—SOCIAL LIFE AND
CUSTOMS.   6. EUROPE—CHURCH HISTORY—MIDDLE AGES, 600–1500.
I. TITLE.

BV835.E424   1993
306.7—DC20   92-35220 CIP

To my parents, Helga and George

*In our day, it is true, no one perfect in piety
seeks to have children except spiritually.*

AUGUSTINE, *On the Good of Marriage* 17.19

CONTENTS

ACKNOWLEDGMENTS

THE FRIENDSHIP, generosity, and guidance of a number of people made this study possible. I have been fortunate to have had a series of gifted mentors. The late John Brückmann was the first to inspire me with a love for medieval studies when I was still an undergraduate. Though we rarely agreed about anything that touched on women or the church, the disagreement was always interesting. I also wish to thank Penelope Doob, invaluable friend and adviser of my entire academic life. Michael Sheehan, superb teacher and scholar, supervised this study in its earlier dissertation form. His recent death is a sad loss to me and his many other devoted students. Nor can I fail to mention the influence of my friend Leonard Cohen who, over the years, has never ceased to agitate this study with real, if exasperating, questions, including the crucial one: "why chastity?"

Others have offered assistance at crucial stages along the way. In particular, I am indebted to Robert Clark, Marsha Groves, Virginia Picchietti, Martha Vinson, Callie Williamson, and especially Arthur Field (for their help with arcane languages); Martha Zuppan (for her help with still more arcane computer languages); Deborah Schlow (for her insight into *my* language); and Michael Dobson (for his insight into Shakespeare's language). I am also grateful for the support and encouragement I received from Lauren Osborne and Joanna Hitchcock, my editors at Princeton University Press, and from Lauren Lepow, my manuscript editor.

Finally, many thanks to my colleague and friend Paul Strohm who read and commented on the entire manuscript, offering invaluable criticism and insight.

ABBREVIATIONS

AA SS	*Acta Sanctorum.* Paris and Rome, 1865–.
AB	*Analecta Bollandiana.* Brussels, 1882–.
Acta . . . Birg.	*Acta et Processus Canonizacionis Beate Birgitte.* Ed. Isak Collijn. Samlingar utgivna av Svenska Fornskrifsällskapet, ser. 2, Latinska Skrifter, vol. 1. Uppsala, 1924–1931.
ACW	Ancient Christian Writers. Westminster, Md., 1946–.
Akten . . . Dorotheas	*Die Akten des Kanonisationsprozesses Dorotheas von Montau von 1394 bis 1521.* Forschungen und Quellen zur Kirchen- und Kulturgeschichte Ostdeutschlands, vol. 12. Ed. Richard Stachnik. Cologne and Vienna, 1978.
ANL	Ante-Nicene Christian Library. Edinburgh, 1867–1903.
BS	*Bibliotheca Sanctorum.* 13 vols. Rome, 1961–1970.
Canonisation de Dauphine	*Enquête pour le procès de canonisation de Dauphine de Puimichel, Comtesse d'Ariano.* Ed. Jacques Cambell. Turin, 1978.
Caterina. Biog.	*Biografia.* In *Edizione critica dei manoscritti Cateriniani.* Vol. 2 of *S. Caterina Fieschi Adorno.* Ed. Umile Bonzi da Genova. Turin, 1962.
CCCM	Corpus Christianorum, Continuatio Mediaeualis Turnholt, 1966–.
CCSL	Corpus Christianorum, Series Latina. Turnholt, 1953–.
CSEL	Corpus Scriptorum Ecclesiasticorum Latinorum. Vienna, 1866–.
DMA	*Dictionary of the Middle Ages.* 13 vols. New York, 1982–1989.
DS	*Dictionnaire de spiritualité.* Under the direction of Marcel Viller, et al. 15 vols. to date. Paris, 1937–.
DTC	*Dictionnaire de théologie catholique.* Ed. A. Vacant et al. 1930–1950. 13 vols.

EETS	Early English Text Society. London, 1864–.
FC	Fathers of the Church. New York and Washington, D.C., 1947–.
GCS	Die griechischen christlichen Schriftsteller der ersten drei Jahrhunderte. Leipzig, 1897–1841; Berlin and Leipzig, 1953; Berlin, 1954–.
LNPNFC	A Select Library of Nicene and Post-Nicene Fathers of the Church. New York, 1887–1892. Oxford, 1890–1900.
MGH	Monumenta Germaniae Historica. Hanover (etc.), 1826–.
MPH	Monumenta Poloniae Historica. Lvov and Cracow, 1864–1893.
Narratione . . . Lucia	G. Marcianese, *Narratione della nascita, vita, e morte della B. Lucia da Narni*. Ferrara, 1616.
NCE	*New Catholic Encyclopaedia*. 14 vols. and index. New York, 1967.
PG	Patrologia Graecia. Ed. J. P. Migne. 162 vols. Paris, 1857–1866.
PL	Patrologia Latina. Ed. J. P. Migne. 221 vols. Paris, 1844–1864.
Processi . . . Francesca	*I Processi inediti per Francesca Bussa dei Ponziani (1440–1453)*. Ed. Tommaso Placido Lugano. Studi e Testi, 120. Vatican City, 1945.
Rev.	*Revelaciones.* (Bks. 1, 5, 7, and *Extravagantes* appear in Samlingar . . . , ser. 2, Latinska Skrifter. Uppsala, 1956–; bks. 2, 3, 4, 6, and 8 in *Revelationes*. Ed. Florian Waldauf von Waldenstein. Nuremburg, 1500).
SC	Sources Chrétiennes. Paris, 1940–.
Vie . . . Auzias	*Vies Occitanes de saint Auzias et de sainte Dauphine*. Ed. Jacques Cambell. Bibliotheca Pontificii Athenai Antoniani, 12. Rome, 1963.
Vie . . . Dauphine	Ibid.
Vita Brig.	*Vita b. Brigide prioris Petri et magistri Petri*, in *Acta . . . Birg*.
Vita Dorotheae	*Vita Dorotheae Montoviensis Magistri*

Johannis Marienwerder, Ed. Hans West-pfahl. Forschungen und Quellen zur Kirchen- und Kulturgeschichte Ost-deutschlands, vol. 1. Cologne and Graz, 1964.

SPIRITUAL MARRIAGE

INTRODUCTION

> Beauty, truth, and rarity,
> Grace in all simplicity,
> Here enclosed in cinders lie.
>
> Death is now the phoenix' nest;
> And the turtle's loyal breast
> To eternity doth rest,
>
> Leaving no posterity:
> 'Twas not their infirmity,
> It was married chastity.
> (Shakespeare, *The Phoenix and the Turtle*)

IN THESE STANZAS, Shakespeare invoked a model of conjugal love that is undoubtedly foreign to modern sensibilities. His strange birds seem to have participated in what in the medieval period would have been designated a "spiritual marriage"—a legally binding marriage in which sexual relations have been remitted by the consent of both parties for reasons of piety. If his verses seem somewhat cryptic, it is because Shakespeare does not pause to align them with the appropriate antecedents. This may imply that his audience was positioned at the end of a tradition: the last group for which a detailed explanation was unnecessary. The tradition to which these verses alluded will be the subject of this study, which traces the history of spiritual marriage in the West from the time of Christ up until approximately the year 1500.

The term "spiritual marriage" is not without ambiguity since it has been used to describe any number of quasi-nuptial situations. This designation has frequently been applied to syneisaktism: the domestic relations under which two self-professed ascetics of different sexes decide upon chaste cohabitation. It has also been used for a number of different allegorically charged scenarios. The bishop's marriage with his see, Christ's union with the church, or the mystical marriage of God with the soul are all described as spiritual marriages.

Despite this confusion, I can think of no more appropriate way to characterize intramarital chastity. "Chaste marriage" was a strong contender, but, in fact, chaste marriage was a designation frequently used by medieval authorities, especially in the high and late Middle Ages, to designate a union in which the individuals were true to their marriage vows. "Celibate marriage," another possibility, was too anomalous: although occasionally a married couple's transition to chastity is described as a transition to the celibate life, the word *celibate*, by and large, retains its pristine meaning, which is single.[1]

Each of the different arrangements characterized as a spiritual marriage is, in its own right, deserving of separate study. My focus, chaste cohabitation in the context of licit marriage, is particularly intriguing for the way in which it exposes the interaction of a theoretical paradigm of marriage with an actual practice. From a theoretical standpoint, the possibility of such behavior engages the contradictions of the Christian theory of marriage that were already in place by the end of the fourth century. Most of the church fathers were apprehensive of human sexuality, as sexual relations were generally considered to be a reminder of humanity's fallen state. Therefore, the leaders of the church sought protection behind a functionalist view of human sexuality. At the risk of oversimplifying their oversimplification, one might say that they tended to see women for their sexual potential, sex for its procreative potential, and marriage as the institution created for housing these two most essential, but rather dangerous, components of society. But the patristic ambivalence toward carnal relations was ultimately destabilizing to this convenient view of marriage. In their elevation of virginity, the church fathers also, wittingly or unwittingly, opened the door to a spiritualized definition of marriage that allowed the institution to exist independent of sex. Because these same authorities were in favor of restricting those possessed of a spiritual vocation from all superfluous contact with the opposite sex, since such contact was perceived as a potential threat to spiritual development, unconsummated marriage emerged as a challenging and problematical possibility.

Despite its distinguished theoretical framework, the emergence of spiritual marriage as a frequently chaotic and unregulated practice

---

[1] The assignation of the term "chastity" to normal conjugal relations is discussed later in the Introduction. Jacques de Vitry's *Vita Mariae Oigniacensis* demonstrates some of the other alternatives. Her husband's conversion to chastity is described as the achievement of not simply a celibate but even an angelic way of life ("visitatus est a Domino, ut non solum coelibem et vere Angelicam vitam continendo promereretur"), while the couple is later described as united by the bond of spiritual matrimony ("matrimonii spiritualis nexu") (see *AA SS*, June, 5:550).

could be construed as a spontaneous and complex reaction against society's expectations: a revolt against the reproductive imperative and a pious rebellion against the prevailing view that the call to a higher level of spirituality implied the separation of women and men. Of equal interest is the challenge spiritual marriage presented to patriarchal authority. The move to chastity was most frequently associated with female initiative: very often a woman's struggle for a spiritual marriage appears to be no less than a fight for physical autonomy and self-definition. Release from sexual duties, moreover, is often perceived as potentially altering traditional gender-dictated roles and challenging normative concepts like female submission. From the perspective of the hierarchy of sexes, spiritual marriage may then have posed a parallel threat to both husband and society.

On the other hand, it is not merely difficult but impossible to attempt too exacting a distinction between the theoretical paradigm and the practice. Practice is produced within an ideology, and ideology is likewise realized through practice. What we have, then, is a complex reciprocity between theory and practice in which each refers to and, in turn, modifies the other. The theoretical paradigm is undoubtedly more accessible to modern historians through the written record. Its realization in actual practice may often be in doubt—but this occasionally fictive quality does not undermine the historicity of purported occurrence and particular social use.

All the different kinds of sources used in this study have special problems, but a certain problem common to all is that of semantics. A reference to matrimonial chastity does not necessarily mean that absolute chastity is observed in marriage. It may just mean that the couple practiced sexual fidelity, a usage already alluded to above. It may also signify that during the extensive penitential periods of the church, sexual continence was observed. Or it could indeed mean that the couple in question had mutually agreed to forgo sexual relations perpetually. A few examples should suffice to demonstrate this problem in terminology.[2] With respect to Ida of Bologne (d. 1113), we are told that she preserved her marriage chastely "servato nempe caste conjugio"—a phrase that would be ambiguous if the *vita* did not go on to speak of her children.[3] According to the life of Salome of Galicia (d. 1268), she lived not only retaining purity of mind, but chastity as well ("sed eciam obtenta castitate"), and in her case we

---

[2] A number of these semantic problems are taken up by Duane J. Osheim's "Conversion, *Conversi*, and the Christian Life in Late Medieval Tuscany," *Speculum* 58 (1983): 368–390.

[3] *AA SS*, April, 2:142.

learn that her marriage was never consummated.[4] Robert Grosseteste's *Templum Dei* lists the preservation of chastity as one of the licit ends of marriage, but it is unclear from the context what level of chastity he is referring to.[5] If I have erred in assessing the degree of chastity ascribed to a couple, it is on the conservative side. I have not assumed that any union could be designated a spiritual marriage unless absolute sexual continence was purportedly observed, as opposed to matrimonial chastity.

The many different kinds of sources in this study are intended to provide a textured and varied treatment of spiritual marriage. They are basically three-tiered: expressions of theory, channels by which this theory reached the laity, and alleged testimony to actual practice. The theoretical side is derived almost exclusively from Scripture, theology, and canon law. The treatment of theology and canon law, moreover, is selective, highlighting important developments in the early church up to the time of Augustine and again tracing the development of the theology of marriage during the high Middle Ages. Chapter 5 also examines the rules of certain lay penitential orders—sources that are theoretical but also contribute to our understanding of practice.

These erudite formulations were erratically transmitted to the laity. I have sought to recognize this communicative unevenness by isolating some of the most obvious means of popularization through written sources, either aimed at the laity or representing possible protocols for lay behavior.[6] The increasing popularity of certain hagiographical genres is one of the most basic routes. A number of saints' lives that portray spiritual marriage gained increasingly wide circulation in the course of the Middle Ages, as illustrated by the wild success of Jacobus de Voragine's *The Golden Legend* (between 1261 and 1265). In fact, Jacobus's arsenal of spiritual marriages is almost entirely dependent on late antique or very early medieval cults.[7] Cer-

---

[4] W. Kętrzyński, ed., *Vita sanctae Salomeae reginae Haliciensis, MPH*, vol. 4 (Lvov, 1884), p. 778.

[5] "Castitas: quando contrahunt ne impetantur uel sollicitentur ab aliis, set caste adinuicem simul uiuant" (Robert Grosseteste, *Templum Dei*, ed. J. Goering and F.A.C. Mantello [Toronto, 1984], p. 60).

[6] Iconography, on the other hand, a potentially valuable source, has not been included in this study. For an idea of the kind of information that can be extracted from iconography, see Sixten Ringbom's, "Nuptial Symbolism in Some Fifteenth-Century Reflections of Roman Sepulchral Portraiture," *Temenos* 2 (1966): 68–97.

[7] On *The Golden Legend*'s popularity, see Sherry L. Reames, *The "Legenda Aurea": A Reexamination of Its Paradoxical History* (Madison, Wis., 1985), pp. 3–5. The saints in this collection who participated in spiritual marriages are discussed in chapter 4 in the section entitled "Vows of Continence and Channels to the Laity."

tain specific legends, such as the *passio* of St. Cecilia or the life of St. Alexis, are especially central to this study because they were frequently evoked as paradigms. Thus, I both examine the early history of these legends and attend to certain pivotal reintroductions through the obvious route of popularization, and also through the more subtle form of renarration that occurs when the hagiographer of a later saint makes reference to his subject's conscious efforts at exemplification.

The early Middle Ages could be considered something of a pastoral wasteland, at least from a historian's perspeċtive. There were sermons, but they were largely intended for a monastic audience; there were penitentials, but not much evidence regarding their application; there were saints' lives, but it is impossible to say who read them. With respect to the high and later Middle Ages, however, pastoral care seemingly becomes more uniform while the amount of *pastoralia* produced is likewise on the increase. In chapter 4, I analyze a number of confessors' manuals, most of which are written in the wake of Lateran IV in response to the canon *Omnis utriusque sexus*—a canon stipulating that Christians confess at least once a year. These works were intended for the parochial clergy and give some indication of what the priest was expected to know about marriage generally, and about vows of chastity in particular, for the purpose of hearing confession. Some of this information would have been communicated to the laity. Nevertheless, this is an oblique method of acquainting oneself with lay understanding. Not only were confessors' manuals in no way directed immediately to a lay audience, but many of these volumes were too large, too expensive, and very often too sophisticated for circulation and widespread usage among the clergy. Therefore, I also examine popular theological works expressly intended for the laity, such as *Handlyng Synne* and the *Lay Folks' Catechism*. Obviously, sermons, another genre of *pastoralia* of which there is an abundance remaining from this period, were an even more direct means of transmitting information regarding marriage and chastity. Because medieval preaching and sermon literature is so vast a field and necessarily beyond the scope of this study, I tend to rely on D. L. d'Avray's recent work on marriage sermons.[8] Popular works in the vernacular, such as Arthurian romance, Ramon Lull's *Blanquerna*, and the Mira-

---

[8] See, for example, "The Gospel of the Marriage Feast of Cana and Marriage Preaching in France," in *The Bible in the Medieval World: Essays in Memory of Beryl Smalley*, ed. Katherine Walsh and Diana Wood, Studies in Church History, Subsidia, 4 (London, 1985), pp. 207–224, and d'Avray and M. Tausche, "Marriage Sermons in *ad status* Collections of the Central Middle Ages," *Archives d'histoire doctrinale et littéraire du moyen âge* 47 (1980): 71–119.

cles of the Virgin are likewise consulted to garner information about representations of marriage—specifically, spiritual marriage.

With the actual "practice" of spiritual marriage, one must proceed with considerable caution. Most of the evidence for spiritual marriage is derived from hagiography, which is notoriously difficult to enlist on behalf of a historical enterprise. Saints' lives are always partisan: they are written with a view to promoting the cult of their subject. Sanctity is, by definition, extraordinary: a saint's relationship with the social milieu in which he or she was produced is a complex one. Finally, as Hippolyte Delehaye has so amply demonstrated, hagiography possesses its share of the attendant evils common to all legendary material: borrowings (many of the most popular saints' lives are indebted to Hellenistic romances), the use of topoi, credulous acceptance of the miraculous, oversimplification, and lack of specific detail are some of the most obvious.[9]

These difficulties appear insurmountable if one is only concerned, or even most concerned, with the historical referentiality of these accounts. Is this a reliable account of the individual's marriage? was she or was she not sexually active? But this narrowly positivistic thinking prematurely forecloses other forms of legitimate historical inquiry. The "extraordinary" nature of the men and women in this study is undeniable, but it may be harnessed to the scholar's advantage. The margins of society can work in inverse relation to the culture itself: they invariably tell us more about what nestles safely within these limits, as well as suggesting the level of deviation that was deemed tolerable. A more direct relationship between the saint and society is also discernible. Saints embodied certain values that medieval men and women have gone on record as admiring. The hagiographer's bias may lead him to claim any number of fictional deeds on behalf of his holy candidate, but his very partisanship ensures that these pious fictions conform to patterns of sanctity which are revered by society. The "inside-outside" nature of saints is evinced by the fact that, though often deviating from socially sanctioned norms, saints also frequently provide valuable role models that pious individuals, consciously or unconsciously, pattern their own religious expression upon. What I am then taking to be historical about these sources is precisely their imaginary function, a function exercised in relation to the very particular circumstances that gave rise to their creation and deployment, and shaped their usage.

Even so, some figures are, of course, more "historical" than others

---

[9] On distortions and borrowings in legendary saints' lives, see Hippolyte Delehaye's *The Legends of the Saints*, trans. Donald Attwater (New York, 1962), esp. chaps. 1–3.

in the sense that they actually existed. A distinction between figures that were historical in this sense and those that were "legendary" or even fictive, is made in the study proper and in the appendixes. Occasionally, I have also been able to indicate the point in an individual's posthumous career when he or she was first aligned with the spiritual marriage tradition. Yet even in the high and later Middle Ages, when all of the individuals in question are "historical" and the sources are themselves improved in both quality and quantity, sanctified behavior is still realized and recorded in terms of a powerful tradition. Although in the last two chapters I have attempted to reconstruct the way in which the sexuality of these individuals was portrayed as interacting with their spirituality, "portrayed" remains the operative word. Whether examining the renarrated life of an individual who lived or a wholly fictive life, these sources are most securely historical when construed as repositories for social values and ideology.

Although saints' lives seem to be the most fruitful, and certainly the most prolix, source for spiritual marriage, chronicles and related documents occasionally make mention of such relations and are likewise included in this study. These accounts are valuable, since the writer often has no investment in "proving" the individual's claims to sanctity but rather presents the saint matter-of-factly within a context of ecclesiastical or secular politics—a juxtaposition that frequently gives us a clear sense of the political ends to which a purportedly spiritual union might be put. But the temporal backdrop and the slight, seemingly disinterested, notice of such unions should not beguile us: the chronicler is no less interested than the hagiographer. A highly inflected view of an institution can, needless to say, be projected within an incidental or seemingly "thrown away" remark.

When a couple agreed on a vow of chastity, they were, according to the theory that had evolved by the high Middle Ages, supposed to register such a commitment with the bishop to forestall backsliding. Soundings taken of the bishops' registers are, however, disappointing.[10] I have also examined the printed ecclesiastical court records for England without much success.[11] And yet we know that instances of

[10] One instance of a *votum continencie* occurs before William Melton by William de Sibbilton' and his wife Isolde in 1321 (Rosalind M. T. Hill, ed., *The Register of William Melton: Archbishop of York, 1317–1340*, vol. 1, Canterbury and York Society Ser., vol. 70 [Torquay, 1977], no. 30, p. 11) Also see the case of Margery Kempe discussed below.

[11] I attempted no such survey for Continental sources, although a few examples have come to my attention, which are cited in chapter 4. Possibly Continental ecclesiastical sources, although not nearly as abundant as English records, would prove more lucrative, as these countries seem to have been more profoundly influenced by the penitential movement.

spiritual marriage are not simply restricted to saints' lives. Several disputes involving vows of chastity are included in Gregory IX's *Decretales*. Moreover, eyewitnesses, such as Jacques de Vitry, testify to the presence of spiritual marriage in pious lay communities.

The relative silence of the ecclesiastical records is, to a large extent, owing to the disposition of the pious subjects themselves. Couples were understandably reluctant to make public an agreement of chastity. After all, chastity was, and is, an extremely private matter. We will see below how chastity and secrecy often operate as inseparable leitmotivs in hagiographical sources, and for good reason. When the vow of chastity that Margery Kempe made with her husband, John, became known, the slander and mockery they endured eventually induced them to separate.[12] Some of the couples discussed in chapter 6 endured similar trials. Reluctance to register an intention of sexually abstaining may also be related to fear of backsliding. Finally, the ecclesiastical authorities may well have been less than careful about recording seemingly noncontentious matters such as vows of chastity—especially if these vows did not imply formal separation. Margery and John, for example, made their vow formally before Philip Repyngdon, bishop of Lincoln. We also know that this vow must have taken place between 23 June 1413 and 19 February 1414. The register for these years is still intact, yet no record of such a vow was kept.[13]

Spiritual marriage is often a transitional stage in which the couple is on their way to a more complete renunciation of the world—a kind of gray zone that may not be reported because it is not made known. The hagiographer of Edmund Rich (d. 1240), archbishop of Canterbury, for example, paints an unforgettable picture of his subject's pious progenitors, Mabel and Reynold, but especially of Mabel. Edmund's mother wore two steel breastplates in order to make her hair shirt sink further into her flesh; when her two sons went to study at Paris, she gave them hair shirts as a parting gift with instructions on how to use them.[14] While still cohabiting, Reynold and Mabel's life was austere. We are told that they eventually separated by mutual consent: she remained in the world to raise their five children, while he professed as a monk at Evesham where he allegedly was happy to find that the regimen was less tasking than at home. Mabel, for her

---

[12] Margery Kempe, *The Book of Margery Kempe* 1.76, ed. Sanford Brown Meech and Hope Emily Allen, *EETS*, o.s., no. 212 (London, 1940; reprt. 1960), pp. 179–180.

[13] Ibid. 1.15, pp. 33–35; 273–274n.33.

[14] Bertrand of Pontigny, *Vita beati Edmundi Cantuariensis archiepiscopi*, in *Thesaurus novus anecdotorum*, ed. E. Martène and U. Durand (Paris and Florence, 1717; reprt. 1968), 3:1775, 1778.

part, was glad of his departure, as she was then able to increase her own and the children's austerities. Did they observe a period of chastity before Reynold left to enter a monastery? Such a supposition would not be out of keeping with what we know about other pious couples, or even with the canonical conceptions of an authority like John Andreas that a private vow between couples precedes a solemn vow. But the situation is complicated by the fact that, in this case, the parents are evoked to create a context for Edmund's piety and are not treated for their own sake. Moreover, of the two, Mabel receives the lion's share of attention. Factors such as these demonstrate just how elusive a vow of chastity between husband and wife might be.

The history of spiritual marriage is a testament to social creativity. My goal is to show how this widely known collective construct acts as a vehicle for human thought and action. The isolation of spiritual marriage as a subject and its diachronic analysis throughout the Middle Ages demonstrates its availability for varied social use, including frequent appropriations on behalf of competing interests. Spiritual marriage is itself a highly malleable construct, no more stable than the shifting historical circumstances that give rise to its different evocations. For this reason, I have attempted to ground my study in the context of larger issues that shaped its varied historical representations. Issues such as the church's repeated engagements with dualism, the Gregorian reform, and important developments in the theology and canon law of marriage are all examined in detail. The changing intellectual and social climates are contextually represented against the backdrop of changing patterns in sanctity.

The flexibility of spiritual marriage recommends it as a sensitive gauge for measuring social aspirations and expectations. In particular, this study provides a special window into two separate but related issues that figure prominently in contemporary women's studies: the history of marriage and sexuality, and the history of female spirituality. Balanced precariously at the crossroads of the theory and practice of marriage, spiritual marriage permits us to eavesdrop on the frequently tense dialogue between the two. For example, as an orthodox exemplar that was thought to be frequently enacted as a heretical practice, spiritual marriage demonstrates the way in which the realization of an ideal could actually test the limits of orthodoxy. On the other hand, its persistence as an exemplar evokes the unflattering light in which orthodox theorists regarded normal conjugal relations.

Although theoretically available to either sex, spiritual marriage was most frequently identified as a female religious practice. In particular, women seem to have availed themselves of this model as a means of attaining autonomy in marriage through chastity, which is represented as a way of more closely aligning themselves with celestial favor. While "the supernatural provides the legitimacy that enables women to leave the domestic sphere," as Judith Hoch-Smith and Anita Spring have suggested,[15] spiritual marriage is of particular interest in that it focuses on those women who do not or have not yet effected this separation. As such, it points to some of the ways in which a husband's authority intrudes upon the wife's spirituality and the manner in which a transition to chastity might erode his authority. However, women did not control the medium through which their personal histories were represented. Thus, this study traces the means by which different restatements of this same model could be wielded ideologically against women not only to contain female spirituality but, through an interesting paradox, actually to enforce submission to patriarchal authority.

Despite the potential treachery of the tradition, a thorough examination of the sources, particularly the evidence of female saints' lives, suggests that representations of spiritual marriage were much more central to an understanding of the female religious vocation than anyone has hitherto supposed. Indeed, many medieval authors assume that the impulse toward chastity was not an idiosyncratic fancy restricted to a handful of saints but was shared by "ordinary" wives with pious leanings as well. Did, then, the possibility of a spiritual marriage operate as a psychological placebo or even a coercive device that collaborated with the common formulas of thwarted vocation and forced marriage, so familiar to the women of this age? It is impossible to test the "truth" quotient of the hagiographer's representation of chastity's appeal for the average woman. But its very articulation not only draws attention to the power and importance of the phenomenon; it also lends insight into how a tradition could emancipate or coerce—depending on how it is used.

A number of different studies have already dealt explicitly with aspects of spiritual marriage, as well as with related subjects. The earliest literature in this field focused on the church hierarchy's attitude toward syneisaktism—the chaste cohabitation of two ascetics of opposite sexes. In his work *Virgines Subintroductae* (1902), Hans Achelis traced the church's battle with syneisaktism up until the end of the sixth century and sparked off a lively debate among scholars by his underlying thesis that St. Paul condoned syneisaktism and that later church condemnations deviated from the practice of the ancient church. In "Le 'mariage spirituel' dans l'antiquité chrétienne," Pierre

---

[15] *Women in Ritual and Symbolic Roles* (New York and London, 1978), introd., p. 15.

de Labriolle refutes Achelis's thesis, reexamining much of the same material from the more traditional point of view that the church always regarded these ascetical men and their *virgines subintroductae* as dangerous fanatics (1921).[16] Recently, a number of excellent studies have provided a clearer context for such behavior. Scholars such as Jo Ann McNamara, Elaine Pagels, Aline Rousselle, and particularly Peter Brown have made considerable strides in interpreting the impulse toward chastity in light of changing social and intellectual conditions in late antiquity.[17]

Other scholars have interpreted isolated aspects of spiritual marriage's social deployment. Baudouin de Gaiffier's ground-breaking *"Intactam sponsam relinquens* à propos de la vie de S. Alexis" (1947) sheds light on the situation of the young *malmarié* by isolating two basic motifs associated with forced marriage in saints' lives: flight on the wedding night or the conversion of the spouse to spiritual marriage. More recently, Jo Ann McNamara has drawn attention to how, prior to the Gregorian reform, the church tried to impose chastity on its married priesthood in an effort to develop a celibate clergy.[18]

For the later period, complementary developments in social history and the history of ideas, emphasizing subjects such as marriage, sexuality, and popular piety, have considerable bearing on my subject and have occasionally conspired to draw spiritual marriage into the limelight. The work of James Brundage, in particular, underscores the way in which the ascetic orientation of many canonists and theologians was frequently at odds with the acknowledged purpose of marriage. Brundage and others have highlighted the consensual, spiritualized view of marriage that became more prominent in the high Middle Ages. Jean Leclercq emphasizes what twelfth-century monastic theologians contributed to the theory of the spiritual bond between spouses. Georges Duby traces the development of a definition of marriage that he perceives as disembodied. Penny S. Gold describes the way in which twelfth-century canonists and theologians adjusted the theory of marriage to accommodate the spiritual marriage of Mary

[16] Hans Achelis, *Virgines Subintroductae: ein Beitrag zum VII. Kapitel des I. Korintherbriefs* (Leipzig, 1902). For Labriolle's debunking, see *Revue historique* 137 (1921): 204–225.

[17] Jo Ann McNamara, *A New Song: Celibate Women in the First Three Christian Centuries* (New York, 1983); Elaine Pagels, *Adam, Eve, and the Serpent* (New York, 1988); Aline Rousselle, *Porneia: On Desire and the Body in Antiquity*, trans. Felicia Pheasant (Oxford and New York, 1988); Peter Brown, *The Body and Society: Men, Women, and Sexual Renunciation in Early Christianity* (New York, 1988).

[18] De Gaiffier, *AB* 65 (1947): 157–195; McNamara, "Chaste Marriage and Clerical Celibacy," in *Sexual Practices and the Medieval Church*, ed. Vern L. Bullough and James A. Brundage (Buffalo and New York, 1982), pp. 22–33, 231–235.

and Joseph. John Noonan and Charles Donahue stress the resurfacing of the consensual theory of marriage in the twelfth century, while Michael Sheehan's work has delineated the penetration of the consensual theory to the masses.[19]

A number of important sociological studies of medieval sanctity have strongly influenced this present work. André Vauchez's *La sainteté en occident* and, more recently, his *Les laïcs au moyen âge* contain insightful analyses of changing patterns in sanctity, exposing trends like the democratization of sanctity in the high Middle Ages and the the rise of the lay saint. The latter work, in particular, draws attention to the virginal marriage of the fourteenth-century Provençal nobles Elzear and Dauphine. Donald Weinstein and Rudolph Bell's study *Saints and Society* provides statistical evidence that establishes a number of gender-based differences in religious practice. Chastity emerges as particularly central to the female religious vocation. Richard Kieckhefer's *Unquiet Souls* is an especially illuminating analysis of the penitential spirituality of fourteenth-century saints, creating an appropriate context for understanding their rigorous asceticism.[20]

Especially germane to my focus is the recent interest in female spirituality, in particular efforts to comprehend what is distinct in women's religious experiences. Caroline Walker Bynum has made an immense contribution in this area. Her work *Holy Feast and Holy Fast* not only emphasizes but sensitively contextualizes the centrality of food in female religious expression, ultimately challenging the

---

[19] For Brundage, see especially *Law, Sex, and Christian Society in Medieval Europe* (Chicago and London, 1987); for Leclercq, see *Monks on Marriage: A Twelfth-Century View* (New York, 1982); for Duby see *The Knight, the Lady, and the Priest: The Making of Modern Marriage in Medieval France*, trans. Barbara Bray (New York, 1983), pp. 177–185; for Gold, see "The Marriage of Mary and Joseph in the Twelfth-Century Ideology of Marriage," in *Sexual Practices and the Medieval Church*, ed. Bullough and Brundage, pp. 102–117, 249–251; for Noonan see "Power to Choose," *Viator* 4 (1973): 419–434; for Donahue, see "The Policy of Alexander III's Consent Theory of Marriage," in *Proceedings of the Fourth International Congress of Canon Law*, Toronto, 21–25 August 1972, ed. Stephan Kuttner, Monumenta Iuris Canonici, ser. C: Subsidia, vol. 5 (Vatican City, 1976), pp. 251–281; for Sheehan, see "Marriage Theory and Practice in the Conciliar Legislation and Diocesan Statutes of Medieval England," *Mediaeval Studies* 40 (1978): 408–460.

[20] Vauchez, *La sainteté en occident aux derniers siècles du moyen âge d'après les procès de canonisation et les documents hagiographiques*, Bibliothèque des Ecoles Françaises d'Athènes et de Rome, fasc. 241 (Rome, 1981), esp. pp. 410–418; idem, *Les laïcs au moyen âge: pratiques et expériences religieuses* (Paris, 1987), pp. 211–224; Weinstein and Bell *Saints and Society: The Two Worlds of Western Christendom, 1000–1700* (Chicago and London, 1982), pp. 42–44, 234–235; Kieckhefer, *Unquiet Souls: Fourteenth-Century Saints and Their Religious Milieu* (Chicago and London, 1987).

hitherto dominant view that female asceticism was grounded in a hatred of the body.[21] The association of chastity with the female vocation has become an area of considerable interest that has produced a number of stimulating works. Scholars such as Rosemary Radford Ruether, Elizabeth Clark, and Jo Ann McNamara have emphasized the importance of virginity in patristic writing as a mechanism for female empowerment by means of transcendence of rigid gender distinctions.[22] Parallel findings are made by Clarissa Atkinson in her work *Mystic and Pilgrim*—a study focusing on the fifteenth-century mystic Margery Kempe, who participated in a spiritual marriage and whose chastity was an important part of her religious calling.[23]

This study is clearly indebted to the work of these authors on a number of levels. Chapter 1, in particular, which is intended to provide some context for the phenomenon of spiritual marriage in the early Christian tradition, touches on many of the same issues discussed at greater length by scholars such as Peter Brown, Jo Ann McNamara, and Elaine Pagels. And yet the emphasis of this study, shaped by its syncretic approach and its focus on the *longue durée*, distinguishes it from the others in both method and contribution. As an analysis of the relation between theory and practice, of the interaction among tradition, social use, and seemingly "spontaneous" spirituality over time, it seeks to produce a closer understanding of how an exemplary pattern of female behavior can be manipulated to the gain or detriment of ordinary women.

[21] *Holy Feast and Holy Fast: The Religious Significance of Food to Medieval Women* (Berkeley and Los Angeles, 1987), esp. chaps. 8–10.

[22] See Ruether, "Misogynism and Virginal Feminism in the Fathers of the Church," in *Religion and Sexism: Images of Woman in the Jewish and Christian Traditions*, ed. Ruether (New York, 1974), pp. 150–183; Elizabeth Clark, "The Virginal *Politeia* and Plato's *Republic*: John Chrysostom on Women and the Sexual Relation," in *Jerome, Chrysostom, and Friends: Essays and Translations*, Studies in Women and Religion, vol. 1 (New York and Toronto, 1979), pp. 1–34, and "John Chrysostom and the *Subintroductae*," *Church History* 46 (1977): 171–185.

[23] *Mystic and Pilgrim: The Book and the World of Margery Kempe* (Ithaca, N.Y., 1983). For a discussion of virginity and autonomy in Visigothic Spain, see Joyce E. Salisbury, "Fruitful in Singleness," *Journal of Medieval History* 8 (1982): 97–106.

ONE

"A PLACE IN THE MIDDLE": INTRAMARITAL CHASTITY AS THEORETICAL EMBARRASSMENT AND PROVOCATION

> Gray is a mixture of black and white
> Life and death have no middle ground between them,
> But I do not know whether to put the *syneisaktoi*, as
> everyone calls them,
> Among the married or single, or save them a place
> somewhere in the middle. . . .
> Marriage is a legitimate and honorable condition; but
> still it belongs to the flesh:
> Liberty from the flesh is a better condition by far.
> Yet if marriages are non-marriages, O "beloved ones,"
> You will live in ambiguous unions.[1]

FROM ITS INCEPTION, the Christian message allowed for a two-tiered group of adherents.[2] The elite corps was celibate—free from any ties that might hinder total devotion to God. By rejecting reproduction, such a group implicitly challenged the centrality of the conjugal family, which was not only the cornerstone of patriarchal society, but the ultimate generator of gender roles that subordinated women to men. It is little wonder that Christianity was initially characterized as a religion of women and slaves—individuals who had little to gain from the status quo. But this potential radicalism was cushioned and, eventually, all but dispelled by the provision for a second tier of adherents. After the celibate elite came the larger community of the married, still implicated in the world, still essential links in the interminable chain of sex and reproduction, still subject to prescribed gender roles. Such individuals were allotted an honorable, albeit a lesser, position in the faith. Yet their very inclusion limits the possibilities for a comprehensive social change.

[1] Gregory of Nazianzus, *Epig.* 15, *PG* 38, cols. 89–90. Unless otherwise indicated, all translations are mine.
[2] Cf. Pagels, *Adam, Eve, and the Serpent*, p. 22.

Spiritual marriage, or total sexual abstinence in wedlock, is somewhat of an anomaly because it occasions a blurring of what were widely perceived as two discrete groups: the continent and the married.[3] From the standpoint of social cohesion, there are very sound reasons for keeping these two categories separate. Since the purpose of marriage was to harness the sex urge, either toward the production of legitimate offspring or, according to Paul's reformulation, as a remedy to sin, the suspension of sexual intercourse removed the institution's very raison d'être and had the potential for disrupting gender roles. For this reason, married individuals who were committed to absolute chastity represent a kind of "fifth column" in the otherwise patriarchal institution of marriage. How the chill, but liberating, touch of chastity entered marriage, why church authorities vacillated between actively encouraging and coolly tolerating this hybrid, and its ultimate impact on the conjugal unit generally, and gender roles, in particular, are problems that stalk the history of Christian marriage.

Marriage versus Continence: The New Testament Kerygma

The distinction between the married and the celibate was implicit in the teaching attributed to Christ by the synoptic Gospels. To the married majority, his central message was one of reform, upholding marriage as a stable, indissoluble institution. In response to the Saduccees' questions regarding divorce (Matt. 19.3–12), Christ answers with an uncompromising reference to Genesis 2. Husband and wife become one flesh: what God joins, mere mortals should not attempt to separate. When the apostles despair of the married state if the liability is so great, Christ answers with his fleeting remarks regarding voluntary celibacy.

> "All men take not this word, but they to whom it is given. For there are eunuchs who were born so from their mother's womb; and there are eunuchs who were made so by men; and there are eunuchs who have made themselves eunuchs for the kingdom of heaven. He that can take it, let him take it." (Matt. 19.11–12)[4]

Mention of a third type of eunuch may have been a reference to the Essenes, a Jewish ascetical sect whose inner core abstained from mar-

[3] McNamara makes this point in "Chaste Marriage," p. 33.

[4] Biblical citations accord with the Latin Vulgate. When Vulgate citations are at variance with modern usage (as, for example, with Kings or Psalms) both forms are given. Quotations are from the Douay translation of the Vulgate, unless otherwise indicated.

riage and to whom Christ may have been indebted for some of his teaching. Perhaps he was even a member of the sect.[5] The emphasis of the passage could be seen as more descriptive than prescriptive, but Christ is at the very least affirming this way of life that was so at odds with mainstream Judaism, and he seems to have ranked celibacy higher than marriage, considering the former a singular and peculiar vocation.[6]

Other passages of tantalizing obscurity, but with a long history in Christian exegesis, are Christ's projections into the human race's future. His emotional outburst regarding the end of the world: " 'But woe to them that are with child and give suck in those days!' " (Luke 21.23) could read as a grim condemnation of procreation to the eschatologically inclined primitive church.[7] Moreover, his response to the Sadducees that both marriage and death cease to exist after the resurrection but humans will live as angels sets up an ugly equation between marriage and death for those predisposed to criticize marriage (Matt. 22.30).

[5] Only the elite corps of the Essenes seem to have been celibate. See Jean Daniélou, *The Theology of Jewish Christianity*, vol. 1 of *The Development of Christian Doctrine before the Council of Nicaea*, trans. John A. Barker (London, 1964), pp. 373–374. Josephus also speaks of a second order of Essenes who married purely for procreative purposes (*Jewish War* 2.160–161, trans. H. St. J. Thackeray in *Josephus*, Loeb Classical Library [London, 1927], 2:384–385). There is no mention in the Gospels of Christ's possible affiliation with the Essenes, but since the discovery of the Dead Sea Scrolls, many scholars have speculated on the degree of Christ's involvement or contact with the sect. Martin A. Larson believes that Christ was an Essene and the core of the early Christian community consisted of defected Essenes (*The Essene Heritage: Or the Teacher of the Scrolls and the Gospel Christ* [New York, 1967], pp. 172–174). A. Dupont-Sommer believes that Christ was greatly influenced by Essenism but intentionally modified much of their teaching. Nevertheless, early Christianity is still indebted to the Essenes (*The Essene Writings from Qumran*, trans. G. Vermes [Oxford, 1961], pp. 370–378). Arthur Vööbus points out that the followers of Jesus represent most of the groups current in Judaism at the time and posits that a group of Essene ascetics were drawn to Christ's teachings and formed an Aramaean Palestinian corps in the primitive church that was important for the transmission of asceticism (*History of Asceticism in the Syrian Orient* [Louvain, 1958], 1:26–31).

[6] Unlike the Essene community at Qumran, neither Christ nor Paul presents celibacy as an obligation, but as a gift of the spirit (Willy Rordorf, "Marriage in the New Testament and the Early Church," *Journal of Ecclesiastical History* 20 [1969]: 194).

[7] Ton H. C. Van Eijk stresses, however, with respect to the Lucan text, especially in the old Syriac versions, that it can legitimately be read that abstinence is a condition for partaking of the resurrection. Likewise, the text could favor the reading that by anticipating the resurrection through remaining continent, one is already partaking of the next world. These are two standard Encratite interpretations ("Marriage and Virginity, Death and Immortality," in *Epektasis: Mélanges patristiques offerts au Cardinal Jean Daniélou*, ed. Jacques Fontaine and Charles Kannengiesser [Paris, 1972], p. 215).

Christ's advocacy of the superiority of the single state had pragmatic moorings. The celibate was freer to devote him or herself to God's work. It is undoubtedly for this reason that he required that his apostles leave their wives in order to follow him. Indeed, Christ showed considerable disregard for family ties and concerns, a disregard that at times bordered on hostility. Comments such as " 'Who is my mother and who are my brethren?' " or " 'If any man come to me, and hate not his father and mother and wife and children . . . he cannot be my disciple' " (Matt. 12.48; Luke 14.26) posed an undeniable challenge not only to Jewish values, but to Roman patrician ones as well.[8]

Paul's explicit ranking of celibacy over marriage was less ambiguous and more systematic than Christ's fleeting remarks. At times encouraging and at times holding in check the fervent eschatology of the primitive church, Paul juggles the doctrinal tensions implicit in his own personal background and his era. As a Jew, it was his responsibility to affirm marriage and procreation as positive goods, the legacy of a beneficent creator. Even so, Judaism, especially Essenism, possessed a doctrine of two conflicting spirits or *yeserim* that coexist in human hearts: one good, one evil, and both struggling for mastery.[9] As a hellenized Jew, moreover, he was influenced by various contemporary intellectual and spiritual trends that tended to reinforce the idea of humanity at war with itself, but contributed a dualistic element, which sharpens the distinction (and, hence, the conflict) between spirit and matter. Thus the principle of the two *yeserim* was compounded by various Stoical, Pythagorean, Neoplatonic, and Gnostic influences. As a result, Paul identifies the abode of humanity's propensity for evil, not as the heart, but as the flesh.[10] He, accordingly, asserts: "I see another law in my members, fighting against

---

[8] Also see Luke 8.19–21, 18.29–30; cf. Mark 10.29; Matt. 19.29–30. The Gospels are silent regarding Christ's marital status. In view of his insistence on his followers' renunciation of family, however, one might assume that he too was single. Geza Vermes explains Christ's putative celibacy by examining the rabbinic tradition that assumes the incompatibility of marriage and prophecy (*Jesus the Jew: A Historian's Reading* [New York, 1973], pp. 99–102). Jerome is likewise aware of this tradition (*Adversus Jovinianum* 1.20, 1.33, *PL* 23, cols. 249, 267–268). Daniélou also points to the link between prophecy and virginity in the Jewish Christian tradition (*The Theology of Jewish Christianity*, p. 351). Also see Brown, *The Body and Society*, p. 41.

[9] Daniélou, *The Theology of Jewish Christianity*, pp. 357–358; Brown, *The Body and Society*, pp. 34–37.

[10] Norman Powell Williams, *The Ideas of the Fall and of Original Sin: A Historical and Critical Study* (London, 1927), pp. 152–153. According to Williams, it is in keeping with Paul's "twice-born" temperament to associate the hereditary propensity toward sin with natural appetites (p. 156). Also see Brown, *The Body and Society*, pp. 46–48.

the law of my mind and captivating me in the law of sin that is in my members" (Rom. 7.23); and again: "the flesh lusteth against the spirit; and the spirit against the flesh. For these are contrary one to another; so that you do not the things that you would" (Gal. 5.17).

Paul's physical pessimism may have fed his preference for celibacy. But both of these instincts complemented a longing for a total transformation of the social order that was abroad in Christian circles. This is perhaps most explicit in the early baptismal formula that Paul invokes: "There is neither Jew nor Greek; there is neither bond nor free; there is neither male nor female. For you are all one in Christ Jesus" (Gal. 3.28). The "double threat" of continence and egalitarianism clearly marks this vision as millenarian and potentially harmful to both marriage and the family, which are institutions that support social rank and maximize the distance between the sexes.[11] And indeed, this is how Paul is remembered in the popular apocryphal gospels that circulated in the early church. But so radical a kerygma spawned considerable sexual confusion among new converts and, in the face of this chaos, Paul and his immediate successors retreated.[12] Paul's first letter to the Corinthians is the antidote to many symptoms of sexual disorder: the problems suggest just how far Paul may once have gone, and the solutions he provides outline the safe way back. The fledgling church of Corinth was unstrung by its new freedoms: individuals were unclear as to the significance or even licitness of marriage; women were challenging traditional gender signs; fornication and even incest were indulged in.

Paul responded by sharpening, perhaps inadvertently, the two-tiered modus vivendi already present in Christ's vision of society. Celibacy was preferable to marriage, but for reasons that were, by his own admission, pragmatic and eschatological. Marriage carries with it incumbent "tribulation of the flesh" (1 Cor. 7.28). It also requires time and energy, which are better spent in service to God (1 Cor. 7.32–33). Both of these reasons are distinct from a yearning for a moral or

[11] John G. Gager, *Kingdom and Community: The Social World of Early Christianity* (Englewood Cliffs, N.J., 1975), pp. 33–34. W. A. Meeks argues that Gal. 3.28 was regarded by some as signifying the abolition of biological differences between the sexes and that Paul later reacted against this interpretation ("The Image of the Androgyne: Some Uses of a Symbol in Earliest Christianity," *History of Religions* 13 [1974]: 165–208). Elisabeth Schüssler Fiorenza, however, criticizes Meeks's reading, instead interpreting these passages as an attack on the patriarchal household ("Justified by All Her Children: Struggle, Memory, and Vision," in *On the Threshold of the Third Millennium*, ed. P. Hillyer, special issue of *Concilium* [London and Philadelphia, 1990], pp. 29–32).

[12] See Brown, *The Body and Society*, pp. 49–57.

cultic purity, which will loom so large in the early church fathers.[13] Instead, they are generated from Paul's view that "the time is short"; in these last times of last times Christians should train their minds on heaven as much as possible: "it remaineth that they also who have wives be as if they had none" (1 Cor. 7.29).[14] At no time, however, does Paul suggest that celibates enjoy a heightened intimacy with Christ or a special reward that was denied the married.[15]

But even though Paul's response privileges chastity over marriage, he nevertheless attempts to restore order by a strengthening of marriage and gender roles. Following Christ, Paul maintains the strict indissolubility of the marriage bond (1 Cor. 7.10–11), with the possible exception of a pagan spouse abandoning a Christian (1 Cor. 7.15). Female subordination was also at issue. Women in the Corinthian church were refusing to wear veils: a symbolic shorthand that, by challenging traditional gender distinctions, imperiled the sociosexual hierarchy and ultimately permitted women to assume certain leadership functions.[16] While Paul acknowledges women's gift of prophecy (1 Cor. 11.5) and, both in this letter and elsewhere, either he or his successors confirm female ministry in the church,[17] he nevertheless lays down a strict hierarchy of submission of Christ to God, man to Christ, woman to man.[18] Moreover, Paul reminds his audience of the Jewish requirement that women's heads be covered as a symbol of female subjection and further insists that women keep silence in church.[19]

[13] With regard to cultic purity, Paul, as the Apostle to the Gentiles, in fact did away with many of the taboos associated with the Old Law (see his dismissal of circumcision in Gal. 5.2–6). In all probability, the Levitican prohibitions surrounding the emission of seed and menstruation would have been, likewise, set aside.

[14] Philippe-H. Menoud believes that Paul's preference for celibacy is generated more from the practical difficulties for Christians in that specific period than from eschatological motives, which Menoud tends to downplay ("Mariage et célibat selon saint Paul," *Revue de théologie et de philosophie* 1 [1951]: 24). Cf. Robin Scroggs, "Paul and the Eschatological Woman," *Journal of the American Academy of Religion* 40 (1972): 297.

[15] Menoud, "Mariage et célibat selon saint Paul," p. 25.

[16] Elisabeth Schüssler Fiorenza, "Word, Spirit, and Power in Early Christian Communities" in *Women of Spirit: Female Leadership in the Jewish and Christian Traditions*, ed. Rosemary Radford Ruether and Eleanor McLaughlin (New York, 1974), p. 37; Constance Parvey, "The Theology and Leadership of Women in the New Testament," in *Religion and Sexism*, pp. 123–125.

[17] For example, see 1 Cor. 16.19; Rom. 16.1–6; and the Ps.-Pauline 2 Tim. 4.19; cf. Fiorenza, "Word, Spirit, and Power in Early Christian Communities," pp. 33–36; Meeks, "The Image of the Androgyne," pp. 197–198; Scroggs, "Paul and the Eschatological Woman," pp. 293–294.

[18] 1 Cor. 11.3; cf. Eph. 5.22–24; Col. 3.18.

[19] 1 Cor. 11.2–16, 14.34–36. Of the two reasons that Paul gives for women's head-

But if Paul's treatment of marriage is traditional from the point of view of sexual hierarchy, on another level it is profoundly innovative in that it signifies a distinct break with the Old Testament mandate to "increase and multiply" (Gen. 1.28).[20] The avoidance of all sexual contact is pronounced a positive good (1 Cor. 7.1), yet Paul, like Christ, recognized that celibacy was a vocation that not all possessed. Those who cannot contain are urged to marry, thereby limiting their sexual activity to one partner (1 Cor. 7.2 and 9). The reproductive function of marriage is thus obliterated and marriage is narrowly defined as a prophylactic measure against incontinence. The couple's sexual bondage is described in striking terms: husband and wife no longer have complete physical autonomy but each is under the power of the other (1 Cor. 7.4). This forms the basis of the canonical conjugal debt that will figure so prominently in the issue of spiritual marriage.

Paul's exclusively remedial vision of marriage places the sex act squarely at the center of the conjugal bond, thus reinforcing the natural barrier between the married majority and the celibate elite. His general admonition that each individual remain in the state in which he or she was called would fortify this boundary. Even so, there is sufficient emphasis on chastity to facilitate its later seepage into marriage. Paul recommended that the couple abstain for brief periods for the purpose of prayer (1 Cor. 7.5), a recommendation that would go ill for the married at the hands of the patristic fathers.[21] His recom-

---

covering, the first is based on the order of creation in Gen. 2.22–23. The second is potentially even more damaging for women in that Paul makes an oblique reference to what is supposed to be the earlier and original version of humanity's Fall: the seduction of human women by fallen angels (Gen. 6.1–4; see Williams, *Ideas of the Fall and of Original Sin*, pp. 19–29). Except for this one allusion, as Williams notes, Paul unequivocally opts for the Adam-and-Eve story of the Fall, and it is his authority that more or less dislodges all competing theories in the Christian tradition (pp. 113–122). Elsewhere, Paul obliquely refers to the apocryphal tradition whereby Eve's seduction by the serpent resulted in the Fall (2 Cor. 11.2–3; also see 1 Tim. 2.14; Williams, *Ideas of the Fall and of Original Sin*, p. 122; cf. John Bugge, *"Virginitas": An Essay in the History of a Medieval Ideal*, Archives internationales d'histoire des idées, series minor, 17 [The Hague, 1975], pp. 9–11). For an alternative reading of 1 Cor. 11.2–16 in which it is argued that the female head-covering is not a symbol of subjection but of authority (albeit sexually distinguished from male authority), see Scroggs, "Paul and the Eschatological Woman," pp. 297–302. Needless to say, Scroggs rejects 1 Cor. 14.33b-36 as Pauline. Likewise, Meeks denies that Paul is advocating female subjection, but is rather concerned that the symbols which distinguish male from female are retained ("The Image of the Androgyne," pp. 199–202).

[20] See Pagels, *Adam, Eve, and the Serpent*, pp. 15–16.

[21] Scholars such as Robin Scroggs view this letter as a response defending marriage against a radically ascetic contingent in the Corinthian community. Paul's statement that couples may separate only for prayer is a concession to their asceticism. Moreover,

mendation that those "who have wives be as if they had none" (1 Cor. 7.29), when wrested from its millenarian context, could read as a stern counsel to abstain. Modern scholars have also construed Paul's ambiguous instructions involving the marriage of a virgin (1 Cor. 7.36–38) as a possible approbation for an unconsummated marriage.[22]

Scroggs contends that it becomes clear contextually that Paul understands sexual enjoyment as the primary end of marriage and does not denigrate this function ("Paul and the Eschatological Woman," pp. 295–296; cf. John Coolidge Hurd, The Origin of I Corinthians [London, 1965], p. 163). If Scroggs is correct, it may mean much for the modern church, but little for the history of Christian sexuality in that Paul's meaning was, by Scroggs's own admission, almost immediately reinterpreted (p. 302).

[22] This passage involves a man's query about the licitness of a virgin's marriage. How the petitioner stands in relation to the woman is what generates the confusion: is he someone who can marry her or someone who is responsible for her marriage (a parent or guardian)? The problem is compounded when Paul switches from the singular and answers the question in the elliptical plural "let them marry" (v. 36, as rendered in the Revised Standard Version). For a summary of the textual difficulties presented by the ambiguity of the pronouns used in the Greek, see R. Kugelman, "Virgines Subintroductae," NCE, 14:698; also see Hurd, The Origin of I Corinthians, pp. 171–176; Roland H. A. Seboldt, "Spiritual Marriage in the Early Church: A Suggested Interpretation of 1 Cor. 7:36–38," Concordia Theological Monthly 30 (1959): 103–107.

While many scholars think the text refers to a father's query regarding the marriage of his virgin daughter, an alternative reading is that this is an apostolic sanction for syneisaktism, a practice that will be discussed later in this chapter. This theory was pioneered by Eduard Grafe's "Geistliche Verlöbnisse bei Paulus," Theol. Arbeiten aus dem rheinischen wissenschaftlichen Prediger-Verein N.F. 3 (1899): 57–69, and then followed by Hans Achelis's monograph Virgines Subintroductae, which traces the history of syneisaktism until the sixth century. Also see A. Jülicher, "Die geistlichen Ehen in der alten Kirche," Archiv für Religionswissenschaft 7 (1904): 373–386. This reading has also found favor more recently. Derrick Sherwin Bailey (The Man-Woman Relation in Christian Thought [London, 1959], pp. 34–35), Hurd (The Origin of I Corinthians, pp. 179–180), and John Gager, for example, all attest to the apostolic sanction for the institution, though differing in particulars. Gager, moreover, unquestioningly assumes that Paul was condoning chaste cohabitation, as such a practice was in keeping with the minimization of sexual barriers and abandonment of marriage that characterize millenarian movements (Kingdom and Community, p. 36). Jo Ann McNamara also accepts this reading (A New Song, pp. 39–40). Indeed, the Revised Standard Version translation of the Bible favors this interpretation.

Others are, however, skeptical and point out that there is little evidence that early exegetes understood Paul this way. Among those who reject the syneisaktism interpretation of 1 Cor. 7.36–38 are Pierre de Labriolle, "Le 'mariage spirituel,'" pp. 205–208; R. Kugelman, "1 Corinthians 7:36–38," Catholic Biblical Quarterly 10 (1948): 63–71; Roger Gryson, The Ministry of Women in the Early Church, trans. Jean LaPorte and Mary Louise Hall (Collegeville, Minn., 1976), pp. 206–208; J. J. O'Rourke, "Hypotheses regarding 1 Corinthians 7, 36–38," Catholic Biblical Quarterly 20 (1958): 292–298. O'Rourke, however, while debunking the syneisaktism theory, also finds considerable problems with the most common alternative reading: namely, that this is a father who is arranging the marriage of his virginal daughter. He posits that the male in question is a master who wishes to dispose of a female slave in marriage.

Paul's uncertain appeals to tradition were magnified by his successors. They amended Paul's vision of marriage, shaping it to the contours of the pagan patriarchal family.[23] Female subordination is corroborated, while the traditional reproductive function of marriage is, in turn, reinstated. The author of Ephesians even sets a sacred seal on female submission by equating the husband with Christ and the wife with the church (Eph. 5.22–25). Drawing on the unity of husband and wife as one flesh, evoked by Christ from Genesis 2, husbands are exhorted to love their wives as their own bodies, thus equating man with the Christ/spirit and woman with the church/body. The post-Pauline texts relentlessly drive home the association between woman and the lower physical realm. Special attention is given to female dress and modesty (1 Tim. 2.9). Women are even promised salvation through motherhood (1 Tim. 2.15).[24] This emphasis on women's reproductive capacity is a double blow: not only did antique medical theory assign the female an ancillary role in conception,[25] but childbearing itself was implicated in Eve's curse, as articulated in Genesis 3. Moreover, an explicit invocation of Genesis would ultimately force women out of the ministry: they are again ordered to be silent in church and denied the right to teach or hold any authority over men. These injunctions are justified by the reminder that woman was second in the order of creation, but the first to be deceived (1 Tim. 2.11–14). In short, these later epistles mark the beginning of the end of orthodox Christianity as a millenarian movement. The liberating spirit of Galatians, dissolving all distinctions between believers and uniting them in Christ, is forgotten. Equality in Christ is implicitly transferred to a spiritual/supernatural plane.[26]

[23] The blueprint for this remodeling is found in the so-called household codes—most fully articulated in Col. 3.18–4.1 and Eph. 5.22–6.9, but also present in the Ps.-Pauline pastoral epistles and elsewhere. New Testament scholarship now recognizes that these codes, which not only uphold the husband's rule over the wife but also that of master over slave and parent over child, are most indebted to Aristotelian politics and ethics—possibly with a Stoical overlay. See Elisabeth Schüssler Fiorenza's historical-critical analysis of these codes in *Bread Not Stone: The Challenge of Feminist Biblical Interpretation* (Boston, 1984), pp. 70–79. Also see *In Memory of Her: A Feminist Theological Reconstruction of Christian Origins* (New York, 1983), pp. 251–270.

[24] Parvey, "The Theology and Leadership of Women," pp. 136–137.

[25] See, for example, Rousselle, *Porneia*, pp. 29–32; John T. Noonan, *Contraception: A History of Its Treatment by Catholic Theologians and Canonists* (Cambridge, Mass., 1966), p. 89; Vern Bullough, "Medieval Medical and Scientific Views of Women," *Viator* 4 (1973): 486–489.

[26] Parvey, "The Theology and Leadership of Women," p. 146. This trend seems to mark the beginning of the distinction between "the order of creation" and "the order of redemption," so commonly appealed to by the clergy throughout the church's history to justify the subordination of women. Fiorenza points out that neither of these expressions is used in the New Testament ("Justified by All Her Children," p. 27).

Experimentation with Gender Roles: Gnostics, Encratites, and *Virgines Subintroductae*

Such a reinstatement of reproduction and reminder of traditional gender roles was both timely and multifunctional. On the most obvious level, the third generation of Christians who were responsible for the pastoral epistles no longer perceived Christ's coming as imminent, so they were ensuring the continuity of the faith. But the affirmation of reproduction also constructed a bulwark against two related problems: dualism and a disruption in gender roles. Paul's words regarding sexual continence were sown on fertile ground, as many, influenced by various philosophical currents of the day, were inclined to reject the material world and procreation as the means through which its hold was perpetuated.[27] Closely aligned with this rejection was the concomitant assumption that the separation between the sexes was a reflection of the material taint, that marriage maximized this separation, and that men and women could meet on a freer and easier footing outside of the strictures of marriage. Moreover, by anticipating the future kingdom where none would marry or be given in marriage, the movement toward chastity was a partial realization of the eschaton. That women had much to gain from and eagerly embraced this potentially egalitarian platform has been well-documented in modern scholarship.[28] Indeed, the writers of the pastoral epistles make no secret of the fact that their emphasis on procreation and female subordination was in response to a crisis among their female adherents (2 Tim. 3.6–7).

The crisis was precipitated by the second-century Gnostics, who saw procreation as a grim mechanism by which "true" creation, which was spiritual, was entrapped in diabolical matter. The female element was identified with false material creation;[29] the male with

---

[27] For a discussion of how this ties in with the widespread sense of alienation in this period, see E. R. Dodds, *Pagan and Christian in an Age of Anxiety* (Cambridge, 1965). Although Peter Brown criticizes Dodds for concentrating too exclusively on individual neuroses and thus creating too static a picture (*Religion and Society in the Age of Saint Augustine* [London, 1972], pp. 75–81), Dodds's first chapter, "Man and the Material World" (pp. 1–36), is still an excellent introduction to the widespread sense of alienation from the world in this period. Cf. Rosemary Ruether's *Sexism and God-Talk: Toward a Feminist Theology* (Boston, 1983), pp. 79–80.

[28] See, for example, McNamara, *A New Song*, pp. 44–50; Elaine Pagels, *The Gnostic Gospels* (New York, 1979), pp. 59–66; Elizabeth Castelli, "Virginity and Its Meaning for Women's Sexuality in Early Christianity," *Journal of Feminist Studies in Religion* 2 (1986): 61–88, esp. 78–84; also see Michel Verdon, "Virgins and Widows: European Kinship and Early Christianity," *Man*, n.s., 23 (1988): 488–505, esp. 500–504.

[29] This is clearly expressed in *The Apocryphon of John* (James A. Robinson, ed., *The*

the pristine, spiritual realm: indeed, Gnostic cosmology delineated the primal cosmic disaster in terms of the division of the sexes, a lamentable rift that was perpetuated through the procreative act. The restoration of order required the total obliteration of the female element.[30] The Valentinian Gnostics achieved this obliteration on a symbolic level through a ritualized marriage ceremony by which a woman "became male," which meant nothing less than for a woman to achieve spiritual personhood.[31] The rejection of carnal marriage and the allegorical rapprochement between the sexes may have allowed men and women to interact with equality and unaccustomed familiarity much in the spirit of Galatians 3.28—conditions that were becoming so unusual to mainstream Christianity that Gnostic coreligionists were repeatedly accused of sexual promiscuity by mainstream Christians.[32]

Concurrent with Gnosticism was the Encratite movement, which held sway over the Syrian church. The ascetical elite, like the Gnos-

---

Nag Hammadi Library [San Francisco, 1977], p. 104); see also *The Sophia of Jesus Christ* (pp. 219–220, 221, 225), *Second Treatise of the Great Seth* (p. 330), *Letter of Peter to Philip* (p. 396), *Trimorphic Protennoia* (p. 464), and the Valentinian Ptolemaeus's account of Sophia's (i.e., the truant female element's) defiance (Robert M. Grant, trans., *Gnosticism: A Source Book of Heretical Writings* [New York, 1961; reprt. 1978], 2.2, p. 165). For a thoroughgoing analysis of this theme, see Jorunn Jacobsen Buckley, *Female Fault and Fulfilment in Gnosticism* (Chapel Hill, N.C., 1986).

[30] In the *Dialogue of the Savior*, Christ exhorts his disciples to " 'Destroy [the] works of femaleness,' " while *Zostrianos* reads "Flee from the madness and the bondage of femininity, and choose for yourselves the salvation of masculinity" (Robinson, ed., *Nag Hammadi*, pp. 237, 393).

[31] *Gospel of Philip*, Robinson, ed., *Nag Hammadi*, pp. 139, 141, 142, 143, 145, 149, 150, 151; also see *The Gospel of Thomas*, p. 130. Cf. the *Exegesis on the Soul* in which the female soul is androgynously united with the bridegroom, a concept bearing close parallels with the Origenist soul marriage (pp. 183–184). Irenaeus describes the Marcosian rite as suspiciously requiring an actual bedroom, along with certain "profane" formulas of consecration: "Quidam enim ex ipsis sponsale cubiculum quoddam adaptant, et quasi mysticum conficiunt cum quibusdam profanis dictionibus his qui sacrantur, et spiritales nuptias dicunt esse id quod ab eis fit, secundum similitudinem supernarum coniugationum" (*Contre les hérésies* 1.21.3, ed. Adelin Rousseau and Louis Doutrelau, *SC*, no. 264 [Paris, 1979], 1:298). The bedroom is convenient to Irenaeus's reports of Marcus's womanizing. He alleges, for example, that a certain female follower was not content with a spiritual union, desiring nothing less than complete physical satisfaction ("sed secundum corporis copulationem et secundum omnia unire ei cupit, uti cum eo descendat in unum" [1.13.3, p. 196]). Fiorenza suggests that Irenaeus is, in fact, failing to recognize the cosmic ritual ("Word, Spirit, and Power," pp. 49–50); cf. Meeks, "The Image of the Androgyne," pp. 188–191. Brown, on the other hand, thinks that the misunderstanding was willful (*The Body and Society*, p. 106).

[32] See Brown, *The Body and Society*, pp. 118–120; McNamara, *A New Song*, p. 67. Also see the above note.

tics, eschewed marriage and procreation. Sexual renunciation became a precondition for baptism: married individuals were urged to abstain sexually and to raise their children as virgins. Often Encratite imagery parallels Gnostic usage by associating the material world with the transitory female element. Thus, according to the Pseudo-Clementine homily: "the present world is female, as a mother bringing forth the souls of her children, but the world to come is male, as a father receiving his children from their mother."[33] The tenor of this teaching seems to have generated two rather conflicting responses. On the one hand, much of the literature produced in Encratite circles suggests that their rigid asceticism did not mitigate the distance between the sexes, but in fact alienated women and men further as potential threats to one another's chastity. The second letter on virginity by the Pseudo-Clement, for example, is addressed to a group of priests whose function it is to travel in order to minister to the needs of fellow Christians. The letter is a very meticulous account of the possible situations in which one might encounter a woman, and the circumstances under which one might be permitted to accept female hospitality. Such situations are very few indeed. This is stated at the outset and then reiterated as regularly as a mantra throughout the epistle:

> With maidens we do not dwell, nor have we any thing in common with them; with maidens we do not eat, nor drink; and, where a maiden sleeps, we do not sleep; neither do women wash our feet, nor anoint us; and on no account do we sleep where a maiden sleeps who is unmarried or has taken the vow: even though she be in some other place [if she be] alone, we do not pass the night there.[34]

Likewise, a Syrian homily intended for male heads of households suggests that the Encratite emphasis on physical purity in fact bolstered patriarchal control over family members.[35]

---

[33] Thomas Smith, trans., *The Clementine Homilies*, in *Ante-Nicene Fathers*, ed. Alexander Roberts and James Donaldson, vol. 8 (Buffalo, 1886), 2.15, p. 231; (critical edition, *Die Pseudoklementinen I. Homilien*, ed. Bernhard Rehm, *GCS*, vol. 42 [Berlin and Leipzig, 1953], pp. 40–41].

[34] B. L. Pratten, trans., "The Second Epistle of Clement on Virginity" c. 1, in *ANL*, ed. Alexander Roberts and James Donaldson, vol. 14 (Edinburgh, 1869), p. 382.

[35] The author is particularly adamant with regard to the daughter's isolation. The father is warned to guard her carefully. If the daughter suffers as a result of his vigilance, this is ultimately propitious, as she is suffering for Christ. All masculine company is a potential threat, from which she must be protected. For this reason, religious ceremonies are vetoed. Finally he is enjoined to search her bed for evidence of wrongdoing and anxiously watch her every expression for unseemly attitudes. See David Amand and M.-C. Moons, eds. "Une curieuse homélie grecque inédite sur la virginité adressée aux

In the Apocryphal Acts, however, which were produced in an Encratite milieu in the second and third century but were also extremely popular in orthodox circles,[36] the flight from "the Other" is
not so categorical. New converts are required to define themselves in
terms of a spiritual community consisting of both men and women.
The difference in perspective may be attributable to a difference in
readership and, perhaps, even authorship. It is possible that these
works were produced for or even by women, who, as a number of
scholars have recently argued, may be less inclined to define their
spirituality in terms of rigid gender dichotomies.[37] Certainly the authors of these works took pains to simulate a woman's point of view.
Each of the Apocryphal Acts traces the impact of its apostle's missionizing on a pagan community. The standard kerygma advances
that only the chaste can be saved and that marriage bonds should be
rejected—unilaterally, if need be. Moreover, this message is clearly
directed to wellborn women: the ones upon whom the pressures of
family and perpetuation of lineage rested most heavily.[38] For these
women, all of whom are either married or betrothed, conversion to
Christianity is identical with a conversion to chastity.[39] Conjugal

---

pères de famille" c. 1–2, *Revue Bénédictine* 63 (1953): esp. 2.19–43, pp. 38–44; Vööbus,
History of Asceticism in the Syrian Orient, 1:78.

[36] Augustine found it necessary to remind his readers that they were not canonical
works. See *De natura et origine animae* 1.10; as cited by Mary Ann Rossi, "The Passion
of Perpetua, Everywoman of Late Antiquity," in *Pagan and Christian Anxiety: A
Response to E. R. Dodds,* ed. Robert C. Smith and John Lounibos (Lanham, Md. 1984),
p. 65.

[37] Stevan L. Davies posits that a community of chaste women (the majority of
whom were widows) was responsible for the writing of the Apocryphal Acts. He bases
his conclusions on the number of positive female role models in the Acts, the high
premium placed on chastity, and the sensitivity of men concerning the woman's difficulties in fulfilling her spiritual vocation (see *The Revolt of the Widows: The Social
World of the Apocryphal Acts* [Carbondale, Ill., 1980], pp. 50–73). As compelling as
Davies's argument is in many respects, he dismisses Tertullian's testimony (that the
Acts of Paul were composed by a presbyter in Asia Minor, who was later deposed for his
trouble) too summarily (p. 108; Tertullian, *De baptismo* c.17). Davies's thesis, more-
over, relies rather heavily on the *Acts of Paul.* Cf. Virginia Burrus's folkloric analysis,
which posits a community of female storytellers (*Chastity as Autonomy: Women in
the Stories of Apocryphal Acts,* Studies in Women and Religion, vol. 23 [Lewiston and
Queenston, 1987], esp. pp. 67–77). Also see McNamara, *A New Song,* p. 78.
On women's less dichotomous attitude toward gender, see especially Bynum, *Holy
Feast and Holy Fast,* pp. 292–294; cf. "Women's Stories, Women's Symbols: A Critique
of Victor Turner's Theory of Liminality," in *Anthropology and the Study of Religion,*
ed. Robert L. Moore and Frank E. Reynolds (Chicago, 1984), pp. 110–112. Also see
Burrus, *Chastity as Autonomy,* pp. 73–74.

[38] Brown, *The Body and Society,* p. 99.

[39] Ross S. Kraemer, "The Conversion of Women to Ascetic Forms of Christianity,"
Signs 6 (1980): 300.

relations are described in the most vile terms and, as with the Gnostics, nuptial imagery is transferred to an allegorical plane. In the *Acts of Thomas*, for example, Christ, in the likeness of the apostle, preaches continence to a newlywed couple on their wedding night, promising:

> "If ye abstain from this foul intercourse, ye become holy temples, pure, being quit of impulses and pains, seen and unseen, and ye will acquire no cares of life or of children, whose end is destruction. . . . Ye shall be without care, leading a tranquil life without grief or anxiety, looking to receive that incorruptible and true marriage, and ye shall be therein groomsmen entering into that bride-chamber which is full of immortality and light."[40]

Accepting his counsel, the bride is grateful that the " 'mirror (veil) of shame is removed from me. . . . I have set at nought this husband and this marriage that passeth away from before mine eyes, . . . because I am yoked unto a true husband' " while the groom gives thanks to God " 'who hast rid me of this disease that is hard to be healed and cured and abideth for ever.' "[41] This, however, is one of the few instances of a joint conversion between spouses that was amiably resolved by a chaste marriage.[42] Generally, hostility between the sexes is maximized from the perspective of the converted women and their consanguinal and affinal relations, and the carnal family is replaced by a spiritual network within which women achieve distinction, if not parity, with the apostles and their disciples through chastity. Often the women's singular postconversion status is expressed through transvestism, signifying a rejection of their biological destiny and possibly an assertion of equivalence with men.[43]

Neither the Encratites nor the Gnostics offer fully developed alternatives to traditional gender roles.[44] Both reject marriage and procreation as antithetical to a life in the spirit, yet their programs for reform are embedded with implicitly patriarchal assumptions. The Gnostics require that women be transformed into males; the Encratites require that women redefine themselves spiritually in terms

[40] M. R. James, trans., *The Apocryphal New Testament* (Oxford, 1924; reprt. 1966), pp. 369–370.

[41] Ibid., p. 370.

[42] The few peaceable spiritual marriages in the Acts are only mentioned in passing. In general, such couples were either converted simultaneously, or the initiative was taken by the husband (see *Acts of Thomas*, ibid., pp. 422, 425, 430). The tale of the youth who slew his betrothed because she did not want to live in chastity with him presents something of an exception (pp. 388–389).

[43] Castelli, "Virginity and Its Meaning," pp. 75–76.

[44] Cf. ibid., pp. 84–88; McNamara, *A New Song*, p. 69; Burrus, *Chastity as Autonomy*, pp. 94–99.

of a spiritual, but male-dominated, family.[45] A mystical marriage with a higher male spirit is the means by which the spiritual alchemy is achieved, in either case. Even so, these flawed symbolic solutions provided a temporary meeting ground for the sexes in the practical realm that the pastoral epistles denied. At a time when mainstream orthodoxy was calling for a cessation of the female ministry, Gnostic and Encratite women were still actively engaged in missionizing. Furthermore, both faiths accommodated experiments in heterosexual cohabitation whereby two like-minded ascetics would contract chaste, stable relationships to facilitate their devotions.[46]

Many of these suspect trends were also present in what will eventually be regarded as orthodox asceticism, albeit in a muted form. Orthodox ascetics were equally quick in elaborating on the pragmatic reasons that were the underpinnings of New Testament chastity. But, like their heretical counterparts, they too went far beyond Paul in devising explanations for why chastity was deserving of extra merit[47]—also relying on imaginative reconstructions of prelapsarian humanity. The Eastern fathers, in particular, saw the division of humanity into two sexes as a mutation in God's original plan, and chastity as a mechanism for reuniting humanity and partially realizing the eschaton.[48] Gregory of Nyssa's early writings describe unfallen humanity as androgynous,[49] while in his later works, we find a full articulation of the negative cycle of birth, procreation, and death.

> Therefore, just as the power which destroys what is born is begotten along with physical birth, so it is clear that the Spirit bestows a life-giving power upon those born through it. . . . Separating ourselves from life in the flesh which death normally follows upon, we must seek a kind of life which does not have death as its consequence. This is the life of virginity.

---

[45] See esp. Ruether, *Sexism and God-Talk*, pp. 100–101, 196; Kraemer, "The Conversion of Women," pp. 303–304.

[46] See Vööbus, *History of Asceticism in the Syrian Orient*, 1:78–79; Brown, *The Body and Society*, p. 100.

[47] See, for example, Elizabeth Clark's analysis of Chrysostom's deviation from Paul in her introduction to his *On Virginity. Against Remarriage*, trans. Sally Rieger Shore, Studies in Women and Religion, vol. 9 (lewiston, Lampeter, and Queenston, 1983), pp. xix–xxi, xxvii.

[48] This is especially true of Origen's work. See Henri Crouzel, *Virginité et mariage selon Origène*, Museum Lessianum, section théologique, no. 58 (Paris and Bruges, 1962), pp. 18, 26, 44–58, 82. Williams points out, however, that in Origen's earlier work he seems drawn to the idea of a historic, sexual Fall involving Eve's seduction by the serpent (*Ideas of the Fall and of Original Sin*, pp. 226–227).

[49] *De hominis opificio* c. 16, *PG* 44, cols. 185c, 189d, as cited by Van Eijk, "Marriage and Virginity," p. 231. Williams, *Ideas of the Fall and of Original Sin*, pp. 272–273.

And again:

> For the bodily procreation of children (let no one be displeased by this argument) is more an embarking upon death than upon life for man. Corruption has its beginning in birth and those who refrain from procreation through virginity themselves bring about a cancellation of death by preventing it from advancing further because of them, and, by setting themselves up as a kind of boundary stone between life and death, they keep death from going forward.[50]

Some also applied masculine imagery to female virgins as a symbol of their renunciatory achievement.[51]

But what ultimately distinguishes orthodoxy from dualism was that the church fathers had appointed themselves as guardians of marriage and procreation and this sponsorship had a number of potent results. There was a growing awareness that marriage and procreation were best defended if they were admitted as a part of God's original plan. So rather than the imposition of a sexless, Edenesque order on earth, we eventually find a reversal of this trend. Gregory of Nyssa, for example, ultimately disavowed his earlier belief in a pristine, androgynous human.[52] The tendency to reconstruct prelapsarian humanity on the basis of temporal gender roles is even more characteristic of the West, which was less influenced by Gnosticism and more inclined to take Genesis literally, and culminates in Augustine's works.[53] Orthodox attempts to validate marriage and procreation thus eventually sanctioned the division between the sexes. Ascetical efforts to transcend sexual boundaries and gender roles could be construed as willful interference with God's plan.

The second century witnessed the rise of the clergy, whose ultimate success, as Peter Brown has pointed out, was owing to their acceptance of preexisting social structures, which included marriage.[54] In the course of the struggle for mastery over splinter groups,

[50] Gregory of Nyssa, On Virginity 13.3 and 14.1, in Ascetical Works, trans. Virginia Woods Callahan, FC, vol. 58 (Washington, D.C., 1967), p. 48; for a critical edition see Traité de la virginité, ed. Michel Aubineau, SC, no. 119 (Paris, 1966), pp. 428–433.

[51] See Clark, "Friendship between the Sexes: Classical Theory and Christian Practice," in Jerome, Chrysostom, and Friends, pp. 55–58; cf. "The Virginal Politeia and Plato's Republic: John Chrysostom on Women and the Sexual Relation" ibid., pp. 15–20, also Ruether, "Misogynism and Virginal Feminism," p. 176. Even Augustine, less given to this kind of imagery, praises his mother by describing her as being female in appearance, but male in faith ("muliebri habitu, uirili fide" [Confessionum Libri XIII 9.4.8, ed. Martin Skutella and Lucas Verheijen, CCSL, vol. 27 (Turnholt, 1981), p. 137]).

[52] According to Williams, Gregory dropped the idea of androgynous humanity in the later Oratio catechetica (Ideas of the Fall and of Original Sin, p. 274).

[53] Ibid., pp. 246–247, 361.

[54] Brown, The Body and Society, pp. 143–144.

the "orthodox" camp focused many of their attacks on the easy and unstructured relations between the sexes—indeed, dangerous familiarity between the sexes will from this point on be consistently identified as one of the hallmarks of heretical doctrines throughout the history of Christianity. The orthodox priesthood, on the other hand, while securing the rights of the married majority, increasingly sought to distinguish themselves from their more worldly brethren through celibacy.

The twofold division between the celibate clergy and the married laity was somewhat simplistic: it failed to assimilate the growing number of celibate women, now a familiar fixture in both orthodox and heretical circles, since women were quick to take advantage of the freedom implicit in the New Testament kerygma. There was, understandably, a natural affinity between the clergy and celibate women.[55] But this affinity was eventually construed as problematical. In the third century, certain members of the orthodox clergy had begun to experiment in chaste, heterosexual cohabitation, setting up housekeeping with female ascetics. The female companions came to be referred to among their critics as *syneisaktoi* in the East and *virgines subintroductae* in the West—both terms implying illicit cohabitation.[56] The crisis of syneisaktism ultimately ensured that, differing from heretical initiative, orthodox asceticism defined itself not only in terms of its chastity but in the strict separation from the opposite sex, which had the effect of strengthening gender roles.

Cyprian (d. 258), bishop of Carthage, was the first to raise the outcry against syneisaktism. He was responding to an appeal of a certain Pomponius, who had recently excommunicated a deacon for cohabiting with consecrated virgins. The accused parties allegedly even shared the same bed, while maintaining that they preserved their purity. Cyprian censures this practice, and approves Pomponius's disciplinary measures.[57] But such experiments persisted.

---

[55] Ibid., pp. 145–146.

[56] The term *virgines subintroductae* (literally, "virgins surreptitiously brought in [to a man's home]") seems to have derived from a fourth-century translation of the canons of Nicaea, cited below, which condemned the practice. The women were also sneeringly referred to as *agapētae*, or "beloveds." For a quick overview, see Hans Achelis, "Agapētae," in *Encyclopaedia of Religion and Ethics* (New York, 1961), 1:177–180.

[57] Cyprian then stipulates that such couples should be separated, and the women must undergo physical examinations in order to clear their names. If they are no longer virgins, they must do penance. If, moreover, they refuse to forgo the association, they are to be permanently expelled from the congregation (Ep. 4, "To Pomponius," *S. Thasci Caecili Cypriani opera omnia*, ed. W. Hartel, *CSEL*, vol. 3,2 (Vienna, 1871), pp. 472–478).

The growing emphasis on clerical celibacy encouraged members of the clergy to reject traditional marriage, and some resorted to these less conventional unions.[58]

Treatises began to circulate condemning the practice and legislation soon followed, carefully listing which women were permitted to live in a clerical household.[59] The third canon of the Council of Nicaea forbade a cleric to shelter any woman except a mother, sister, aunt, or some such person who was above suspicion. It became standard practice for this canon to be reiterated at all councils touching on clerical discipline in both the East and the West.[60] Even so, syneisaktism seems to have continued as late as the sixth century, and it may have persisted in isolated areas such as Ireland until a much later date.[61]

Although there are no remaining defenses of syneisaktism, scholars such as Pierre de Labriolle and Elizabeth Clark have attempted to reconstruct the positions of its practitioners on the basis of their critics' attacks.[62] The individuals in question perceive their way of life as a continuation of the apostolic age,[63] but their main line of

[58] Achelis, *Virgines Subintroductae*, pp. 61–66.

[59] Labriolle cites twenty-four councils and synods between 267 and 787 that forbid clerics (and occasionally laymen) to cohabit with unrelated women. These restrictions were reiterated by Gratian in D. 32 c. 16 and D. 81 c. 23–31; ("Le 'mariage spirituel,'" p. 222 n. 1; also see M. Dortel-Claudot, "Le prêtre et le mariage: évolution de la législation canonique des origines au XIIe siècle," *L'année canonique* 17 [1973]: 327–328).

[60] "Interdixit per omnia magna synodus, nec episcopo nec presbytero nec alicui prorsus, qui est in clero, licere subintroductam habere mulierem, nisi forte matrem aut sororem aut amitam vel eas tantum personas quae suspicionem effugiunt," Nicaea, c. 3 (*Conciliorum oecumenicorum decreta*, ed. G. Alberigo, et. al. [Freiburg, 1962], p. 6; see Achelis, *Virgines Subintroductae*, pp. 69–70). Nor is the attention syneisaktism received restricted to ecclesiastical legislation, as Justinian also censured the practice (*Nov.* 123.29).

[61] Achelis ends his study in the sixth century. For evidence in Ireland, see Kuno Meyer, "*An Crīnōg*: ein altirisches Gedicht an eine Syneisakte," *Sitzungsberichte der königlich preussischen Akademie der Wissenschaften: Sitzung der philosophisch-historischen klasse* 18 (1918): 362–374.

[62] See Elizabeth Clark for a careful analysis of Chrysostom's treatises and a reconstruction of the arguments of the clerics and their *agapētae* ("John Chrysostom and the *Subintroductae*," esp. pp. 176–184) and Pierre de Labriolle's discussion of Chrysostom as well as the Ps.-Cyprian's *De singularitate clericorum* ("'Le mariage spirituel,'" esp. pp. 216–221). Clark translates both of Chrysostom's treatises addressing the subject in *Jerome, Chrysostom, and Friends*. See *Instruction and Refutation Directed against Those Men Cohabiting with Virgins* (pp. 164–208) and *On the Necessity of Guarding Virginity* (pp. 209–248). The critical edition for these works is edited by Jean Dumortier in *Saint Jean Chrysostome: Les cohabitations suspectes. Comment observer la virginité* (Paris, 1955).

[63] On occasion, biblical precedents are cited as a means of defense: there is the case of Elijah who lived with a widow, the women who administered to Christ, the ones who

defense is based on practical considerations. The women were un-protected and needed someone to look after their property;[64] the men, on the other hand, needed domestic services.[65] But although their respective domestic functions are portrayed as conventionally gendered, the milieu was probably conducive to the relaxation of traditional roles. Elizabeth Clark argues cogently that syneisaktism provided a couple with a rare opportunity for friendship between the sexes.[66] As with the heretical experiments, this movement toward friendship was facilitated by common ascetical practices, most par-ticularly chastity, which in turn softened gender distinctions by ren-dering women less subordinate to men. The more astute of the ortho-dox critics were sensitive to the role that sexual intercourse played in fueling the gender system. John Chrysostom, for example, who wrote two treatises against syneisaktism, was also a powerful advocate for female virginity, which he occasionally presented as a means of es-caping Eve's curse of subordination. Nevertheless, while John Chry-sostom can fathom the appeal of an easy rapport between the sexes based on shared concerns and increased intimacy, he judged the net

---

accompanied the apostles on their travels, and the example of the Virgin Mary living with St. John after Christ's death (Ps.-Cyprian, *De singularitate clericorum* c. 20, in *S. Thasci Caecili Cypriani opera omnia*, ed. W. Hartel, *CSEL*, vol. 3,3 [Vienna, 1871], p. 196; cf. Ps.-Basil, *Sermo de contubernalibus* c. 2, *PG* 30, col. 814). Indeed, the use of Mary's cohabitation with John as ammunition was considered so offensive by certain orthodox polemicists that a refutation of this claim forms the bulk of Epiphanius's attack on the "heresy" of syneisaktism (Epiphanius, *Adversus octoginta haereses* 78.11, *PG* 42, cols. 715–738). The Ps.-Jerome, on the other hand, denies outright that Mary followed any of the apostles on their travels, adding that the apocryphal Thecla was also prohibited by Paul from accompanying him on his missionizing because of the temptation she afforded (Ep. 42, *Ad Oceanum* c. 5, *PL* 30, col. 290).

[64] Chrysostom, *Against Those Men Cohabiting with Virgins* c. 6, trans. Clark, pp. 179–182; ed. Dumortier, pp. 63–66. *On the Necessity of Guarding Virginity* c. 4, trans. Clark, pp. 221–222; ed. Dumortier, pp. 109–110; Ps.-Basil, *Sermo de contubernalibus* c. 9, *PG* 30, col. 823; Jerome, Ep. 117, "To a Mother and Daughter Living in Gaul" c. 1, ed. I. Hilberg, *Epistulae, CSEL*, vol. 55 (Vienna and Leipzig, 1912), p. 423.

[65] Chrysostom, *Against Those Men Cohabiting with Virgins* c. 9, trans. Clark, p. 190; ed. Dumortier, p. 76; Ps.-Cyprian, *De singularitate clericorum* c. 19, *CSEL*, 3,3:194. The Ps.-Cyprian added the perhaps less credible motive that cohabitation with a member of the opposite sex provided one with a daily opportunity to triumph over Satan and that the couple would undoubtedly have an opportunity to make up for any wrongdoing through martyrdom (c. 9; 35; pp. 183–184; 210–211). It seems more proba-ble, however, that such absurdist rationales were created by the orthodox opposition in an effort to discredit the *subintroductae* and their companions.

[66] Clark, "John Chrysostom and the *Subintroductae*," pp. 183–185; cf. Rosemary Rader, *Breaking Boundaries: Male/Female Friendship in Early Christian Commu-nities* (New York, Ramsey, and Toronto, 1983), pp. 70–71.

result as pernicious.[67] Men become womanish in their ways,[68] while women become lordly, aggressive and domineering.[69]

But for John, these disruptions of gender roles are more apparent than real. Gender boundaries were as implacable as sexual desire itself. He thus maintains that living with a woman is gratifying, whether intercourse is involved or not, and argues that these spiritual couples "would not enjoy such a despicable reputation nor would there be so many scandals, if a violent and tyrannical pleasure were not found in their cohabitation."[70] Certainly, there were a number of contemporary examples that endorsed his view. Athanasius, for example, tells of a certain priest named Leontius who castrated himself so that he could continue to cohabit with the virgin Eustolium.[71] A seventy-year-old priest who was cohabiting with a woman turned a deaf ear to Basil the Great's threats of suspension.[72] The anonymous *On the Singleness of the Clergy* describes syneisaktism as an "unfriendly friendship" promoted by the Devil.[73] The temporary freedom from gender roles and sexual tension is nothing but a satanic ploy. While the Devil is seducing the couple with visions of perfect sanctity, they are troubled by no libidinous desires: these only come

[67] See Elizabeth Clark's excellent discussion of this in "John Chrysostom and the *Subintroductae*," pp. 181–182.

[68] "Christ wants us to be stalwart soldiers and athletes. He has not furnished us with spiritual weapons so that we take upon ourselves the service of girls worth only three obols, that we turn our attention to matters which concern wool and weaving and other such tasks, that we spend all day having our souls stamped with women's habits and speech" (*Against Those Men Cohabiting with Virgins* c. 10, trans. Clark, p. 195; ed. Dumortier, p. 82. Also see c. 11, trans. Clark, pp. 196–197; ed. Dumortier, p. 83, and *On the Necessity of Guarding Virginity* c. 10, trans. Clark, p. 241; ed. Dumortier, p. 131).

[69] *Against Those Men Cohabiting with Virgins* c. 10, trans. Clark, p. 193; ed. Dumortier, p. 82. Cf. Ps.-Chrysostom, *Ascetam facetiis uti non debere*, PG 48, cols. 1058–1059.

[70] *Against Those Men Cohabiting with Virgins* c. 1, trans. Clark, p. 165; ed. Dumortier, p. 46.

[71] Athanasius, *Apologie pour sa fuite* c. 26, in *Apologie à l'empereur Constance. Apologie pour sa fuite*, ed. J.-M. Szymusiak, SC, no. 56 (Paris, 1958), pp. 164–165; *Historia Arianorum* c. 28, PG 25, cols. 723–726. Because of imperial favor, however, Leontius nevertheless rose to become bishop of Antioch (Roger Gryson, *Les origines du célibat ecclésiastique du premier au septième siècle* [Gembloux, 1970], pp. 69–70).

[72] Basil, Ep. 55, "To the Priest, Gregory," *Saint Basile: Lettres*, ed. Yves Courtonne (Paris, 1957), 1:142; trans. Agnes Clare Way, notes by R. J. Deferrari, *Saint Basil: Letters*, FC, vol. 13 (New York, 1951), 1:144–145. Deferrari points out that though the authenticity of this letter has been called into question, it is supported by the manuscript tradition (1:144 n. 1).

[73] "Donec diutius inter ambos inimicam nutriat amicitiam" (Ps.-Cyprian, *De singularitate clericorum* c. 19, CSEL, 3,3:194).

up suddenly like tempests when they are in the middle of the sea, far from help.[74]

So from the orthodox perspective, syneisaktism simply created the illusion of dissolving gender boundaries, and this illusion prevented its practitioners from perceiving their own concupiscence until it was too late. An easy familiarity between the sexes was a pleasure that, according to John Chrysostom, had to be deferred until the next life.[75] The author of *On the Singleness of the Clergy* likewise says that only in paradise will women cease to be a danger to men, but his begrudging tone does not seem to anticipate this future contact as a pleasure.[76]

Many of the treatises denouncing syneisaktism were addressed to a clerical audience and availed themselves of antifeminism to win their point. The unknown writer of *A Sermon on Concubines* describes woman as the root of every evil.[77] He provides a number of Old Testament examples to underline women's destructive powers[78] and compares them at length with wild beasts, especially dragons and serpents.[79] This recourse to antifeminism, in turn, helped to solidify the conviction that true piety is only manifested in isolation from the other sex. A passage from Proverbs was frequently cited in support of this position: "Can a man hide fire in his bosom, and his garments, not burn? Or can he walk upon hot coals, and his feet not be burnt?" (Prov. 6.27–28).[80] Again and again orthodox antagonists tried to con-

[74] Ibid. c. 19, pp. 194–195.

[75] "For when bodily passions are henceforth undone and tyrannical desire has been quenched, there will be no hindrance in the next world to prevent man and woman from being together" (*Against Those Men Cohabiting with Virgins* c. 13, trans. Clark, p. 204; ed. Dumortier, pp. 93–94). Basil of Ancyra upholds one of the most radical views regarding the realized eschatological state of virgins (wherein virgins no longer exist as male and female; they are incorruptible and free from passion and lust), yet a female virgin is still crippled by her body (*On Virginity*, PG 30, col. 772; as cited in Van Eijk, "Marriage and Virginity," p. 226).

[76] Ps.-Cyprian, *De singularitate clericorum* c. 4, CSEL, 3,3:177. He also suggests that sexual distinctions are to some extent dissolved in church during the administration of the sacraments ("in conuentu uero sacrorum, ubi spiritus dominatur, ancilla semet ipsam cognoscens perdit suae uoluptatis usum, perdit et luxum dum tractantur caelestia, dum celebrantur sancta mysteria: tota humanitas occupatur, ubi non humana sed diuina sunt omnia," c. 14, p. 188).

[77] Ps.-Basil, *Sermo de contubernalibus* c. 2, PG 30, col. 814.

[78] Ibid., col. 815.

[79] Ibid. c. 3, col. 818; cf. Ps.-Cyprian, *De singularitate clericorum* c. 6, CSEL, 3,3:179–180; Ps.-Jerome, Ep. 42, *Ad Oceanum* c. 3, PL 30, col. 289.

[80] For example, see Ps.-Cyprian, *De singularitate clericorum* c. 2, p. 175; Ps.-Jerome, Ep. 42, *Ad Oceanum* c. 3, PL 30, col. 289; Ps.-Chrysostom, *Ascetam faceiis uti non debere*, PG 48, col. 1057; Jerome, Ep. 22, "To Eustochium" c. 14, CSEL, 54:161–162. In the early Middle Ages, a strange dramatization of Prov. 6.27–28 will be used as proof of chastity. See pp. 90 and 272, below.

vince their opponents of the general superiority of same-sex cohabitation, while resistance was ascribed to lustful motives.[81] Pseudo-Jerome asks, "If anyone were to see a cleric living with women, he would not believe that he is chaste. If you seek modesty, why are you living with women?" One of Gregory of Nazianzus's epigrams rather elliptically avows that the separation of man and woman inspires greater hope.[82] Basil the Great seems to concur: "The honor of celibacy lies in this—namely, in the separation from companionship with women."[83] Indeed, one of the most powerful arguments produced by the author of *On the Singleness of the Clergy* against syneisaktism depends on the model provided by married couples who, having decided on a life of chastity, part company by mutual consent so that the presence of the other will not act as an irritant which might erode one or both parties' resolve.[84]

The crisis over syneisaktism was a symptom of the church's growing institutionalization and ever-increasing need to have clearer rules and more distinct boundaries. The church fathers understood what wives were and they understood about concubines: but they did not know where the *subintroductae* fit into their scheme of things and this evidently troubled them. The author of *On the Singleness of the Clergy*, for example, comments caustically on the strange *caritas* that makes virgins into wives and wives into virgins.[85] Nor were such murky characterizations atypical. The urgent need for clarification would inspire men like Gregory of Nazianzus to press for an unnuanced, overwhelmingly carnal definition of marriage. Yet Gregory knew better. In his funeral oration for his sister Gorgonia he had praised her for the adroit mixing of celibacy with marriage.[86] Even so,

---

[81] John Chrysostom refutes the men requiring *subintroductae* for household needs by pointing out that a male companion would be stronger, less extravagant, and ultimately more economical (*Against Those Men Cohabiting with Virgins* c. 9, trans. Clark, pp. 191–192; ed. Dumortier, pp. 77–78. *On the Necessity of Guarding Virginity* c. 4, trans. Clark, pp. 219–222; ed. Dumortier, pp. 107–110.).

[82] "Si aliquis senserit clericum habitare cum feminis, non credit eum esse castum. Si pudicitiam quaeris, quare habitas cum feminis?" (Ps.-Jerome, Ep. 42, *Ad Oceanum* c. 4, *PL* 30, col. 289); Gregory of Nazianzus, *Epig.* 12, *PG* 38, cols. 87–88; cf. Ps.-Basil, *Sermo de contubernalibus* c. 9, *PG* 30, col. 823).

[83] Basil, Ep. 55, "To the priest, Gregory," *Saint Basile: Lettres*, ed. Courtonne, 1:141–142; trans. Way, *Saint Basil: Letters*, FC, vol. 13, 1:144.

[84] Ps.-Cyprian, *De singularitate clericorum* c. 31–32, *CSEL*, 3,3:207–208.

[85] "Grande miraculum, ut uirginum caritas uirgines faciat uelut coniuges credi et coniugum caritas coniuges faciat uelut uirgines aestimari" (ibid. c. 32, p. 207); cf. Chrysostom, *Against Those Men Cohabiting with Virgins* c. 1, trans. Clark, p. 164; ed. Dumortier, p. 45.

[86] "In laudem sororis suae Gorgoniae" (*Orat.* 8, c. 8, *PG* 35, col. 798). On Gorgonia, see Rader, *Breaking Boundaries*, pp. 90–92. Rader also translates the passage in question.

his engagement with the *subintroductae* led him to present marriage and celibacy as diametrically opposed, like black and white—a characterization that serves as the epigraph for this chapter. To the *subintroductae* and their clerical companions, he assigns a somber and essentially flawed middle ground between these two poles.

Spiritual Marriage and the Church Fathers

According to the orthodox mind-set, marriage was the only admissible context for heterosexual cohabitation. But this meeting ground was hopelessly compromised. The conjugal act was at the center of orthodox perceptions of marriage, and this generated a revulsion among certain theorists that was reinforced by contemporary philosophical currents. Arguing from a Platonic standpoint, Origen presented conjugal relations as a heightened form of humanity's flawed corporeal state. Sex was possessed of a stain or impurity that negated prayer,[87] while original sin was identified as the first sexually transmitted disease.[88] The church fathers also inherited a Stoical mistrust of passion as an obstruction to reason. Prelapsarian humanity was thought to possess a Stoic immovability or *apatheia*, an ideal that stood in stark contrast to the vitiated sex act.[89] Paul's view that a spouse sought primarily to please his or her mate, while a celibate was free to please the Lord (1 Cor. 7.32) was exaggerated by a parallel prejudice in pagan circles which outlined the irreconcilability of marriage and philosophy.[90] Arguments were borrowed from the pagan philosophers to buttress this view.[91]

[87] Henri Crouzel, "Le célibat et la continence dans l'église primitive: leurs motivations," in *Sacerdoce et célibat: études historiques et théologiques*, ed. J. Coppens, Bibliotheca ephemeridum theologicarum Lovaniensium, 28 (Gembloux and Louvain, 1971), p. 358; idem, *Virginité et mariage selon Origène*, pp. 60–62, 82.

[88] Williams, *Ideas of the Fall and of Original Sin*, pp. 226–231.

[89] This application of Stoic criteria is especially true of, and was in fact initiated by, Clement of Alexandria, who speaks with conviction of the mastery of the stomach and especially the genitals as being essential for the Christian sage (*Le Pédagogue* 2.10.90, ed. H.-I. Marrou, trans. Claude Mondésert, SC, no. 108 [Paris, 1965], pp. 174–177; cf. 2.10.83, 2.10.95, 2.10.100; pp. 164–167, 182–183, 190–191). In the *Stromata*, moreover, Clement says that the Divinity is passionless and that continence means to never go against reason (*Les Stromates* 2.18.80–81, ed. and trans. Claude Mondésert, introd. and notes by Th. Camelot, SC, no. 38 [Paris, 1954], pp. 97–99). See J. P. Broudéhoux, *Mariage et famille chez Clément d'Alexandrie*, Théologique historique, 2 (Paris, 1970), pp. 77–78; 121–136; Brown, *The Body and Society*, pp. 133–134; Noonan, *Contraception*, pp. 76–81. The Stoical standard was also readily embraced by the Western fathers, particularly Ambrose and Augustine. See William Joseph Dooley, *Marriage according to St. Ambrose* (Washington, D.C., 1948), pp. 43–50.

[90] See Crouzel, "Le célibat," pp. 352–356.

[91] See, for example, John Chrysostom, *La virginité* 40.1–4, ed. Herbert Musurillo,

If virginity was an anticipation of the future kingdom, marriage was hopelessly bound to the temporal order—a constant reminder of our fallen state. The nuptial bond would be dissolved with the resurrection, as would family ties.[92] Thus energetic defenders of marriage, such as Clement of Alexandria, tended to ratify, as opposed to challenging, the status quo of so limited an institution, while the spirit of Galatians 3 entirely yielded to the conservative tone of the pastoral epistles.

Because of the uncontestedly pro tem nature of marriage, its symbolic value was raided by traffickers in allegory who, paralleling Gnostic and Encratite exegetes, attempted to detach the idea of marriage from the institution, thus leaving the institution an empty husk devoid even of self-referentiality. Clement of Alexandria was the first to use the nuptial imagery of Ephesians 5 as a means of dignifying marriage,[93] but the image was reapplied by his student Origen as a figure of virginity. Although Origen grants that the example of Christ and the church is prescriptive for behavior between spouses, real marriage is only a distant image of this celestial union, while virginity is its realization.[94]

SC, no. 125 (Paris, 1966), pp. 232–237; idem, Sur le mariage unique c. 1, 5–6 (in A une jeune veuve. Sur le mariage unique, trans., introd., and notes, B. Grillet; ed. G. H. Ettlinger, SC, no. 138 [Paris, 1968], pp. 160–163, 186–193); Gregory of Nyssa, Traité de la virginité 4.1–6, SC, no. 119, pp. 302–323; Ambrose, De virginibus 1.6.25–29, ed. Otto Faller, Florilegium Patristicum, fasc. 31 (Bonn, 1933), pp. 29–30. This line of thinking achieved classical expression in Jerome's Against Jovinian, and it is significant that Jerome was heavily dependent on Porphyry's On Abstinence for much of his vituperation, despite the fact that the latter was deeply hostile to Christianity. Jerome claims his source for this material is the no longer extant treatise On Marriage, by the Greek philosopher Theophrastus (Adversus Jovinianum 1.47, PL 23, col. 289).

[92] See, for example, Clement of Alexandria, who also sees the division of the sexes as part of the temporal order only. The disappearance of the sexes signifies the disappearance of desire (Le Pédagogue 1.4.3, ed. H.-I. Marrou, trans. M. Harl, SC, no. 70 [Paris, 1960], pp. 128–129; Broudéhoux, Mariage et famille chez Clément, p. 87). Also see Gregory of Nyssa, Traité de la virginité 14.4, SC, no. 119, pp. 442–443. Tertullian, though admitting that there is no marriage in the coming kingdom, nevertheless speaks of a strengthening of the ties between husband and wife, largely to support his argument against remarriage (see De monogamia 10.5–6, in Tertulliani opera, pt. 2, ed. E. Dekkers, CCSL, vol. 2 [Turnholt, 1954], p. 1243.

[93] Clement of Alexandria, Stromata 3.12.84, trans. John E. L. Oulton and Henry Chadwick, in Alexandrian Christianity, Library of Christian Classics, vol. 2 (London, 1954), p. 80; critical edition by O. Stählin, revised by L. Früchtel, Clemens Alexandrinus: Stromata, GCS, vol. 15 (Berlin, 1960), pp. 234–235; Broudéhoux, Mariage et famille chez Clément, p. 86 n. 83.

[94] See Crouzel, Virginité et mariage selon Origène, pp. 30–37. The soul-marriage is dependent on the nuptial imagery of Christ and the church. Rosemary Ruether analyzes the way in which the latter demonizes female sexuality and maternity, while the former imparts a sadomasochistic quality to the mystical relationship (Sexism and God-Talk, pp. 143–149). Intense nuptial imagery is more characteristic of the Eastern

The deprecation of marriage in favor of continence became something of an elite discourse that fostered social cohesion among the celibate. Thus already toward the end of the second century Tertullian could exclaim: "How many men and women there are whose chastity has obtained for them the honor of ecclesiastical orders!"[95] And yet the prestige of celibacy also implied an alternative practice, which was chastity in marriage. Orthodox references to total matrimonial chastity are comparatively modest, although they begin as early as the second century. The authorized collection of the *Sentences* by Sextus encourages married continence, while Hermas, in his visionary work *The Shepherd*, relates that he is told by an angelic guide to treat his wife as a sister.[96] Toward the end of the century, Clement of Alexandria (though generally inclined to minimize the differences between virginity and marriage) praises chastity in marriage, touting it as a realization of the resurrection on earth.[97] In the third century, Methodius registers the continent couple in his vision of the elect.[98]

And yet the church fathers bear little in common with the wandering apostles of the Apocryphal Acts and their radical interference with the marriage bond. Orthodox eulogies on matrimonial chastity are not intended as denials of the sex drive or as a blitzkrieg on procreation. The disparate authorities all presupposed that chastity in

---

fathers but also penetrated the West. Ambrose and Jerome are the best representatives for this tradition in the West. (See Ambrose, *De virginitate, Liber unus* 12.69–70, ed. E. Cazzaniga, Corpus Scriptorum Latinorum Paravianum [Turin, 1954], pp. 32–33, and Jerome, *Adversus Jovinianum* 1.30, PL 23, cols. 263–266). Ambrose is especially eloquent on the subject of the virgin as the *sponsa Christi* and was probably responsible for the assimilation of the *velatio conjugalis* with the dedication of a consecrated virgin in the West. See Raymond D'Izarny, "Mariage et consécration virginale au IVe siècle," *La vie spirituelle* supp. 6 (1953): 92–118.

[95] "Quanti igitur et quantae in ecclesiasticis ordinibus de continentia censentur" (*Exhortation à la chasteté* 13.4, ed. C. Moreschini, SC, no. 319 [Paris, 1985], p. 116; translated by W. P. Le Saint in *Tertullian: Treatises on Marriage and Remarriage, ACW,* no. 13 [Westminster, Md., 1951], p. 64). The reference to women in ecclesiastical orders could be to the orders of widows or deaconesses in the early church. Since this work was written subsequent to Tertullian's break with orthodoxy in favor of the Montanist church, it could also refer to the office of female prophet (see Jean LaPorte, *The Role of Women in Early Christianity,* Studies in Women and Religion, vol. 7 [New York and Toronto, 1982], pp. 109–130, 53).

[96] Henry Chadwick, ed. and trans., *The Sentences of Sextus* 230a (Cambridge, 1959), pp. 38–39; also see the notes for 230a, pp. 172–173. Hermas, *The Shepherd* vis. 2.2.3, trans. Kirsopp Lake, in *The Apostolic Fathers,* vol. 2, Loeb Classical Library (London and New York, 1913), pp. 18–19.

[97] See Broudéhoux, *Mariage et famille chez Clément,* pp. 105–106, 109.

[98] See Methodius, *Le banquet* 9.4, ed. Herbert Musurillo, SC, no. 95 (Paris, 1963), pp. 278–279.

the context of marriage not only would but should follow a period of normal sexual activity, a period that corresponds with the couple's youth. The transition to marital chastity was not intended to be abrupt or violent but to correspond with the individuals' life cycle.[99] Thus Ambrose will remark, when discussing Elizabeth's embarrassment over her late conception of John the Baptist, that there is a season for everything and that a transition from sexual activity to abstinence is a natural one which occurs with age.[100] Few would encourage a couple to contract for such a life precipitously, and no one would encourage two people who were intent on retaining their chastity to marry.[101] Such a situation is too perilously close to syneisaktism.

Although orthodox authorities by no means sought to eliminate the conjugal act, they did contrive to discipline it. Christian apologists prided themselves on the sexual restraint of the married: Justin Martyr and Athenagoras both tend to slight the remedial function of marriage in favor of the Stoically flavored argument that Christians only engage in sex with a view to procreation, while some refrain from marriage altogether.[102] Clement of Alexandria's insistence on sexual abstinence during pregnancy and lactation was likewise inspired by a Stoical ethic.[103] Cultic purity further restricted marital usage. The alleged incompatibility of prayer and normal conjugal relations gave rise to regulations that forbade sexual relations on feast days or before receiving the Eucharist.[104]

But there was a world of difference between the practical use of continence as a means of restraining marital usage and the ambitious transition to total continence. Disciplined sexuality was still contained by marriage; total sexual abstinence was more ambiguous. It was clearly a spiritually vertical move; what was unclear was whether husband and wife ascended in tandem or alone. Supposing that they had no children or that their childen were grown. What then was the fabric of the couple's bond? Unfortunately, the authorities

---

[99] See Brown, *The Body and Society*, pp. 79, 135, 149–150, 378.

[100] Ambrose, *Traité sur l'Evangile de S. Luc* 1.43–44, ed. Gabriel Tissot, SC, no. 45 (Paris, 1956), pp. 68–69.

[101] Possible exceptions are Paulinus of Nola (see chapter 2, the section entitled "A Golden Moment: Early Realizations") and, for the twelfth century, Hugh of St. Victor (see chapter 4, "The Defense of Marriage").

[102] Justin Martyr, 1 *Apologia* 29 in *S. Iustini Apologiae duae*, ed. Gerhard Rauschen, rev. ed., Florilegium Patristicum, fasc. 2 (Bonn, 1911), pp. 56–57; Athenagoras, *Legatio pro Christianis* c. 33, *PG* 6, cols. 965–966; cf. Minucius Felix, *Octavius* 31.5, ed. Jean Beaujeu (Paris, 1964), pp. 53–54.

[103] Broudéhoux, *Mariage et famille chez Clément*, pp. 132–134; Brown, *The Body and Society*, p. 149.

[104] Noonan, *Contraception*, p. 70.

seem to fail us here. Rather than the theological development of a
spiritual bond between spouses which in some way promoted the
unified salvation of husband and wife (no incredible leap insofar as
Paul stated explicitly in 1 Cor. 7.14 that the unbelieving spouse is
sanctified by the believing), the common tendency was to see the
conjugal debt as a shackle that linked husband and wife and impeded
the salvation of either or both. John Chrysostom gives a lurid, but not
atypical, description of husband and wife as two slaves chained together, each inhibiting the other's pace.[105] The church fathers' emphasis on the conjugal debt, whether defending or decrying it, inhibited them from developing a coherent vision of the institution that
could exist independently of sex. All of the authorities agree that such
a couple should remain together, especially prior to the rise of monasticism. But the reasons are probably pragmatic: women were regarded
as more frequently agitating for such a change, and they must be
controlled; men wishing to join the increasingly celibate priesthood
must not leave their wives destitute.

At root, the orthodox mentality which affirmed and protected gender boundaries and upheld the view that pious pursuits were best
undertaken in isolation from the opposite sex was naturally incapable of articulating how such a couple would benefit spiritually by
remaining together. Paul's comment that a spouse lived primarily for
his or her mate, while the celibate could live for God (1 Cor. 7.32–34),
buttressed by parallel prejudices in pagan philosophy, dwarfed their
imaginations.[106] Clement of Alexandria, for example, was the first to
stress the sanctity of marriage, arguing that if the law was holy, marriage was holy.[107] He was also one of the first, perhaps the first, to
apply to the family unit Christ's words regarding his presence when
two or three are gathered together in his name (Matt. 18.20).[108] Yet he

[105] John Chrysostom, *La virginité* 41.2, *SC*, no. 125, pp. 236–239. Likewise, Origen
contrasts the liberty of the celibate with the slavery of the married, describing the
couple as semiliberated when they part for prayer (Crouzel, *Virginité et mariage selon
Origène*, pp. 160–161). Tertullian describes the joy that awaits spouses when they are
finally freed from the conjugal debt by the death of their mate (Tertullian, *A son épouse*
1.7.1, ed. Charles Munier, *SC*, no. 273 [Paris, 1980], pp. 114–115; and especially idem,
Exhortation à la chasteté c. 10, *SC*, no. 319, pp. 102–107). This is in spite of the fact that
Tertullian, on occasion, displays quite an optimistic view of the spiritual community
of husband and wife. See F. Forrester Church, "Sex and Salvation in Tertullian," *Harvard Theological Review* 68 (1975): 83–101, esp. 94–96.

[106] On pagan misogamic influences, see Crouzel, "Le célibat," pp. 352–356.

[107] Clement of Alexandria, *Stromata* 3.12.84, trans. Oulton and Chadwick in *Alexandrian Christianity*, pp. 79–80; ed. Stählin, *GCS*, 15:234–235.

[108] Clement of Alexandria, *Stromata* 3.10.68, trans. Oulton and Chadwick in *Alexandrian Christianity*, p. 71; ed. Stählin, *GCS*, 15:226–227; Broudéhoux, *Mariage et
famille chez Clément*, p. 84. Cf. Tertullian's closing for *A son épouse* 2.8.7–9, *SC*, no.

is at a loss to propose how the wife is a helpmate to her husband, apart from the conjugal debt.[109] Still, Clement went further than some were prepared to go. Chrysostom, who ultimately had greater impact on the development of marriage in the Eastern church, explicitly denies that there is any spiritual succor in marriage, stating that woman is no longer a helper to her husband insofar as procreation is no longer necessary.[110] Even Julian of Eclanum, Augustine's great opponent who had positioned himself as the defender of marriage against its ascetical detractors, seems to have construed marriage almost exclusively in terms of the sex act.[111]

Augustine may rightly be considered the architect of spiritual marriage in the West since he was the first to develop a full and coherent theory of marriage that was not dependent on the conjugal debt. Moreover, his ethereal conception of marriage eventually became definitive, securing spiritual marriage an honorable place at the heart of an elaborate theoretical structure. But his solution emerged over the course of the late fourth and early fifth century, which was a trying time for the conjugal unit. Orthodox asceticism was, for the first time, making substantial inroads into the institution of marriage. The cessation of persecutions and the conversion of the Empire inspired more and more individuals to choose ascetic chastity as a means of distinguishing themselves from superficial converts. A multiplication of treatises on virginity corresponded with the active recruitment of virgins.[112] Over the course of the fourth century, increasing emphasis was placed on the necessity of clerical celibacy. The secondary place of marriage had never been more apparent in an orthodox context.

The situation came to a head in the late fourth century when the vocal panegyrists on the excellence of virginity inspired a reaction. We know the names of three members of the antiascetic resistance. Vigilantius, Jovinian, and Helvidius all attempted to debunk the conventional ranking, whereby virginity was deserving of extra merit in

---

273, pp. 148–150. Jo Ann McNamara, however, rightly points out that Clement's familial rhetoric reinforces traditional Roman-patriarchal norms (*A New Song*, pp. 93–94).

[109] Clement of Alexandria, *Stromata* 3.18.108, trans. Oulton and Chadwick, in *Alexandrian Christianity*, p. 91; ed. Stählin, *GCS*, 15:246.

[110] John Chrysostom, *La virginité* c. 46–47, *SC*, no. 125, pp. 256–271. He refutes the argument that marriage deserves any extra merit for the obstacles encountered in that this burden was assumed voluntarily (c. 45, pp. 254–257).

[111] See Michel Meslin, "Sainteté et mariage au cours de la seconde querelle Pélagienne," in *Mystique et continence*, Travaux scientifiques du VIIe congrès international d'Avon, Les études Carmélitaines, 31 (Bruges, 1952) pp. 293–307, esp. 298–302.

[112] See Th. Camelot, "Les traités *De virginitate* au IVe siècle," in *Mystique et continence*, pp. 273–292.

both this life and the next,[113] and the latter two used the example of
Mary and Joseph's union as a vindication of their views. They were
shouted down by Ambrose and Jerome—the two most zealous advocates of virginity.[114] But Jerome's characteristically overenergetic reaction was particularly problematical. His notorious treatise *Against
Jovinian* was so adamant in its denunciation of marriage and created
such a scandal that his friends attempted to suppress it.[115] Other,
more subtle, problems also arose in the course of this controversy.
Helvidius had claimed that the various references to "Christ's brethren" (Luke 8.19; Mark 3.31; Matt. 12.46) made it clear that Mary had
children subsequent to Jesus and therefore marriage should be accorded a higher position than virginity, insofar as Christ's mother saw
fit to take part in it. Jerome vigorously refuted this position, dismiss-
ing the brethren of the Lord as Christ's cousins,[116] and arguing that
Joseph was really Mary's guardian and only putatively her husband.[117]

Augustine stepped into the fray of the marriage debate to refute
Jovinian, while at the same time to correct some of Jerome's excesses.[118] Although he agreed that virginity deserved to be ranked
above marriage, he did not believe that the elevation of the one re-

---

[113] See Jerome, *Adversus Jovinianum*, esp. bk. 1, *PL* 23, cols. 221–296. Jerome popularized what became the classic maxim that virgins reap a hundredfold reward, chaste
widows a sixtyfold, and the married a mere thirtyfold, based on a peculiar exegesis of
Matt. 13.8 (see 1.3, cols. 222–224; see also Ep. 49, "To Pammachius" c. 2–3, *CSEL*,
54:353–354). In the letter Jerome defends himself against charges of depreciating marriage by stressing that his assessment of marriage is less extreme than that of others
who claimed a hundredfold reward for martyrs, sixty for virgins, and thirty for widows,
leaving nothing for the married. He may have been referring to Origen and Cyprian (see
St. Jerome: Letters and Select Works, ed. and trans. W. H. Fremantle, *LNPNFC*, 2d ser.,
vol. 6 [Oxford and New York, 1893], p. 67 n. 3). Also see Ep. 123, "To Geruchia" c. 8,
CSEL, 56:82.

[114] See Noonan, *Contraception*, p. 116; Brown, *The Body and Society*, pp. 359–361,
377.

[115] See Eps. 48 and 49, "To Pammachius," *CSEL*, 54:347–387.

[116] *Adversus Helvidium* c. 9–17, *PL* 23, cols. 201–212.

[117] Ibid. c. 3–4, cols. 194–197. We learn later, however, that Joseph also remained
a virgin (c. 19, col. 213). Ambrose concurred in Jerome's assessment of Mary's virginity, yet unlike Jerome, he did not describe Joseph as merely a guardian but—in line
with Roman law, which considered consent alone necessary for a marriage, not
consummation—as a full-fledged husband. This assumption did not lead Ambrose to
dwell on the implications of chaste marriage, as he clearly considered the circumstances around Mary's marriage to be unique (Dooley, *Marriage according to St. Ambrose*, pp. 1–3, 6–7). Even so, his formulations undoubtedly influenced Augustine.

[118] For a more detailed treatment of Augustine's background and the way it informed his thinking on sexuality, see Brown, *The Body and Society*, pp. 387–395. Also
see Brown's account of Augustine's life (*Augustine of Hippo: A Biography* [Berkeley
and Los Angeles, 1967]).

quired the vilification of the other.[119] But in order to ensure an honorable place for marriage, he had both to affirm reproduction and to distance himself from the sexually oriented mentality which had led Jerome to deny that Mary and Joseph were, in fact, married—a position that could, by implication, destabilize any union where sexual relations had ceased.

As Elaine Pagels has forcefully shown, Augustine took his cue from the temporal order and projected it backward on paradise.[120] Marriage and procreation were part of God's original intention for humanity. In a radical break from traditional exegesis, Adam and Eve are envisaged as two sexually differentiated incarnate beings who were created for sexual activity.[121] The sexual hierarchy is likewise transplanted; thus marriage is described as "a kind of friendly and genuine union of the one ruling and the other obeying."[122] Since woman was created as man's subordinate, and sexual intercourse was now interpreted as part of the divine plan for humanity, the heady rhetoric of virginity, whereby women achieve equivalence with men through sexual abstinence, is entirely undercut.

Although Augustine carved out an honorable place for sex in Eden, his courage went no further: Adam and Eve sinned before their union

[119] Augustine's *Retractationes* (2.22–23) clarify the relation between the treatises *De bono coniugali* and *De sancta virginitate* and the Jovinian heresy, as well as his purpose in writing them (ed. A. Mutzenbecher, *CCSL*, vol. 57 [Turnholt, 1984], pp. 107–109).

[120] Pagels, *Adam, Eve, and the Serpent*, chap. 5, "The Politics of Paradise," esp. pp. 113–114; cf. Ruether, *Sexism and God-Talk*, pp. 94–95.

[121] In Augustine's earliest treatments of the subject, he was still influenced by the Eastern belief that Adam and Eve possessed purely spiritual bodies, and that God's injunction to multiply was made with reference to exclusively spiritual works (Emile Schmitt, *Le mariage chrétien dans l'oeuvre de saint Augustin: une théologie baptismale de la vie conjugale* [Paris, 1983], pp. 84–87). Later on, however, he was compelled by the naturalism of the Pelagians to assume a more realistic position, and he thus not only admitted that unfallen humanity was incarnate, but even conceded that, had Adam and Eve not transgressed God's commandment, they would have brought forth children in paradise in the fulfillment of God's plan. At the time that he wrote *De bono coniugali* (401) Augustine refused to take a stand on this point but offered a number of allegorical interpretations of God's injunction to multiply (in *Opera sancti Aureli Augustini*, ed. J. Zycha, *CSEL*, vol. 41 [Prague, Vienna, and Leipzig, 1900], p. 188). The change to a more concrete interpretation of Genesis and of Adam and Eve's reproductive potential is first perceptible in *De Genesi ad litteram* (9.36.6, 9.19.36) written between 401 and 414 (as cited by Schmitt, *Le mariage chrétien*, pp. 91–94). Cf. *De civitate Dei* 14.21, ed. B. Dombart and A. Kalb, *CCSL*, vol. 48 (Turnholt, 1955), p. 443. Also see Brown, *The Body and Society*, pp. 399–401.

[122] "Alterius regentis, alterius obsequentis amicalis quaedam et germana coniunctio" (*De bono coniugali* 1.1, *CSEL*, 41:188; trans. Charles T. Wilcox, in *Saint Augustine: Treatises on Marriage and Other Subjects*, FC, vol. 27 [New York, 1955], p. 9).

was consummated.[123] Their insubordination to God was fittingly punished by a parallel revolt on the part of the very bodies that had been created to serve them. Humanity was thenceforth the victim of concupiscence—a basic disruption in an individual's chain of command that rendered the flesh no longer subservient to the will.[124] The genitals were the most deeply afflicted area and thus sexual activity was blighted by passion, in addition to acting as a conduit for original sin.[125]

By granting marriage a tenuous foothold in Eden, Augustine elevated his fantasy union just high enough to cast a shadow over its temporal counterpart. Particularly damaging is his nostalgia for Edenesque purity, which prompts him to explore the character of prelapsarian intercourse—virgin terrain for theological speculation. Augustine hypothesizes that the sex act would have been free from all the pernicious tensions of passion, rendering sex as voluntary and rational as the movement of a hand or a foot.[126] Liberated from the violence of lust, the woman would have retained her virginity, as the male seed would have entered her with the same ease with which the menstrual flow is dispelled.[127]

Although stripped of its pristine luster, the solid dignity of marriage is not entirely effaced. But new, less lofty, functions are annexed to and merged with the old. It remains the first bond of human society, but it takes on a new role as a mechanism for channeling the perversity of the flesh. Postlapsarian marriage safely harnesses concupiscence in the service of procreation, which was ever regarded as marriage's true end and its major good.[128] But in addition to this good,

[123] Augustine, *De civitate Dei* 14.21, 14.26, *CCSL*, 48:443, 449–450.

[124] The body's defiance of reason is best articulated in *On Marriage and Concupiscence*, the purpose of which was to differentiate the evil of carnal concupiscence from the essential goodness of marriage ("carnalis concupiscentiae malum, propter quod homo, qui per illam nascitur, trahit originale peccatum, discernamus a bonitate nuptiarum" [*De nuptiis et concupiscentia* 1.1.1, in *Opera sancti Aureli Augustini*, eds. C. F. Urba and J. Zycha, *CSEL*, vol. 42 (Prague, Vienna, and Leipzig, 1902), p. 212]).

[125] On the genitals' susceptibility, see ibid. 1.7, pp. 218–219; cf. *De civitate Dei* 14.19, *CCSL*, 48:441–442; on the transmission of sin, see *De nuptiis et concupiscentia* 1.21–23, 1.25–27, *CSEL*, 42:233–236, 237–240. On the evolution of Augustine's thinking with respect to original sin, see Williams, *Ideas of the Fall and of Original Sin*, pp. 326–380. As Williams notes, not only did Augustine place new emphasis on original sin (eternal hellfire for the unbaptized), but he also developed the concept of original guilt (pp. 330, 360–365).

[126] *De civitate Dei* 14.23–24, *CCSL*, 48:445–448.

[127] Ibid. 14.26, p. 449.

[128] Augustine, *De bono coniugali* 1.1, 3.3, 9.9, *CSEL*, 41:187, 190–191, 199–201. On procreation as the true end of marriage, as distinguished from the other goods, see B. A. Pereira, *La doctrine du mariage selon saint Augustin*, 2d ed., Etudes de théologie historique (Paris, 1930), pp. 41–65.

Augustine isolates two others: faith (which is basically sexual fidelity) and indissolubility.[129] If these three goods seem somewhat compromised by new unsavory potentials, Augustine is quick to reallocate the blame: what is sinful in marriage is not the fault of the institution itself, but the fault of those who make evil use of it. Moreover, Augustine is careful to assert that marriage is not simply good because it saves the couple from the evil of fornication (which was more or less the position of Jerome) but good in and of itself, albeit a lesser good than continence.[130]

Despite his endorsement of procreation, Augustine's definition of the nature of the marriage bond was not to be found in the debt-oriented Pauline tradition, but in the Roman conception of the institution. The Roman free marriage was a private act, based solely on the consent of the parties involved (which of course included parents or guardians), and requiring no further external gesture.[131] Consummation had no role in determining whether or not a marriage had occurred. If the nature of the relationship was called into doubt, the sole means of discerning the existence of a marriage was the presence of *affectio maritalis*: a rather formless term which designated, without describing, the proper attitude that one spouse should have toward the other.[132]

In line with this secular framework, Augustine distinguishes between the end of marriage (which is procreation) and the essence of marriage, which is the agreement between spouses.[133] Marriage provides a natural society between the sexes that is not dissolved by sterility or when the couple is past their reproductive years.[134] Likewise, mutual consent to contain does not dissolve the marriage bond. On the contrary, after a couple has ceased to have sexual relations, "the order of charity still flourishes between husband and wife."[135] In fact, the chaste bond is stronger insofar as the couple's marital pledge "will have to be kept by an especial endearment and concord,—not by the voluptuous links of bodies, but by the voluntary affections of

[129] Augustine, *De bono coniugali* 4.4, 7.6–7, 29.32, CSEL, 41:191–193, 196–197, 226–228.

[130] Ibid. 5.5, 8.8, pp. 194, 198.

[131] *Dig.* 50.17.30; P. E. Corbett, *The Roman Law of Marriage* (Oxford, 1930), pp. 91–93; K. Ritzer, *Le mariage dans les églises chrétiennes du Ier au XIe siècle* (Paris, 1970), pp. 218–219. See also Paul Veyne, "The Roman Empire," in *History of the Private Life*, ed. Paul Veyne, trans. Arthur Goldhammer (Cambridge, Mass., 1987), 1:33–34.

[132] Corbett, *Roman Law of Marriage*, p. 95; John T. Noonan, "Marital Affection in the Canonists," *Studia Gratiana* 12 (1967): 482–489.

[133] Pereira, *La doctrine du mariage selon saint Augustin*, p. 51.

[134] Augustine, *De bono coniugali* 1.1, CSEL, 41:187–188.

[135] "Uiget tamen ordo caritatis inter maritum et uxorem" (ibid. 3.3, p. 190; trans. Wilcox, FC, 27:12).

souls."[136] The example he uses to demonstrate the superiority of such unions is the ever-virginal marriage of Mary and Joseph, who were truly married and possessed of all of the three goods of marriage.[137] Their union is upheld as an ideal.[138]

Augustine's solution was an impressive one, but nevertheless riddled with problems and contradictions. Although he attempts to defend the institution, he still presents it as otiose in light of the New Testament mandate. Thus in answer to those who murmur that if everyone abstained, the human race would come to an end, Augustine responds optimistically that this would be a felicitous outcome, as the City of God would be achieved all the sooner.[139] The exemplary union of Mary and Joseph and their miraculous possession of all three goods was not only an impossible model, but a potentially dangerous one in that Augustine further specifies that Mary was chosen as the mother of God for her ongoing commitment to virginity.[140] But it was hardly in Augustine's mind that a couple should resolve to marry and remain virgins: in fact groups that had done this and adopted children, such as the Abelites, had been condemned as heretics by Augustine's own pen.[141]

But Augustine's preoccupation with concupiscence presents still greater hurdles for the married. Even as concupiscence had the effect of alienating an individual from his or her body, the proposed stratagems for coping with it would likewise divide husband and wife.[142] Augustine differentiated a sex act that was motivated by desire for offspring from one that was motivated by lust alone. The first act was deemed sinless, while the second was sinful—but only venially so, by virtue of the sanctity of marriage.[143] Such careful scrutinizing of

[136] "Immo firmius erit, quo magis ea pacta secum inierunt, quae carius concordiusque seruanda sunt, non uoluptariis corporum nexibus sed uoluntariis affectibus animorum" (*De nuptiis et concupiscentia* 1.11.12, *CSEL*, 42:224; Peter Holmes and Robert Wallis, trans., *Saint Augustin: Anti-Pelagian Writings*, LNPNFC, vol. 5 [New York, 1887], p. 268); cf. *De sermone Domini in monte* 1.14.39, *PL* 34, col. 1249.

[137] Augustine, *De nuptiis et concupiscentia* 1.11.12–1.12.13, *CSEL*, 42:224–226.

[138] Augustine, *De consensu Evangelistarum* 3.1, as cited by Pereira, *La doctrine du mariage selon saint Augustin*, p. 54.

[139] Augustine, *De bono coniugali* 9.9–10.10, *CSEL*, 41:199–202.

[140] Augustine, *De sancta virginitate* 4.4, ed. Zycha, *CSEL*, 41:238.

[141] This African group had entirely disappeared by the time Augustine gives us our sole notice of them (R. Vander Plaetse and C. Beukers, eds., *De haeresibus* 1.87, *CCSL*, vol. 46 [Turnholt, 1969], pp. 339–340; Labriolle, "Le 'mariage spirituel,'" p. 225). Other groups such as the Adamites and Euchites, both of which were first mentioned in the fourth century, were also practitioners of chaste cohabitation (Epiphanius, *Adversus octoginta haereses* 2.1.52, 3.2.80; *PG* 41, cols. 953–960, *PG* 42, cols. 755–774).

[142] See Brown, *The Body and Society*, p. 418.

[143] Augustine, *De nuptiis et concupiscentia* 1.12.13, 1.14.16, 1.15.17, 1.23.25; *CSEL*, 42:226, 228–230, 237–238.

libidinous urges is even more divisive when applied to the actors: the initiating party would be guilty of a venial sin as opposed to the complying party, who is sinless.[144]

Augustine implicitly contrasts the divisive sex act with the unitive transition to chastity. Marriage is most holy when deflected from its true end. Yet, despite his declaration that the bond is strengthened with a transition to chastity, his inability to fathom any way in which women were helpmates to men, apart from procreation, seems to undermine the possibilities of a spiritually companionate marriage.[145] Augustine, in fact, says explicitly that for all purposes aside from procreation, a male companion is to be preferred.[146] The "absentee" essence of Augustine's bond is strikingly brought to the fore by a hypothetical conversation with a good Christian husband. When asked if he wants his wife in heaven with him, he would correctly answer no. When asked if he would like her with him to share in that "angelic transformation which is promised to saints," he would answer yes.

> From this it is evident that in the same woman a good Christian loves the being that God has created, and that he wishes her to be transformed and renewed, while he hates the corruptible and mortal relationship and marital intercourse. . . . He loves her insofar as she is a human being, but . . . he hates her under the aspect of wifehood.[147]

[144] Augustine, *De bono coniugali* 6.6–7.6, *CSEL*, 41:195–196.

[145] Ibid. 13.15, pp. 207–208. Elizabeth Clark's "'Adam's Only Companion': Augustine and the Early Christian Debate on Marriage" discusses Augustine's failure to develop a theory of companionate marriage in terms of the position he was driven to assume in the course of his many polemical battles—most particularly, the Pelagian controversy (in *The Olde Daunce: Love, Friendship, Sex, and Marriage in the Medieval World*, ed. Robert R. Edwards and Stephen Spector [Albany, N.Y., 1991], pp. 15–31, notes on pp. 240–254).

[146] Augustine, *Ad Genesi ad litteram* 9.5.9; *De gratia Christi et de peccato originali* 2.35.40; as cited by Schmitt, *Le mariage chrétien*, p. 92; cf. Ruether, "Misogynism and Virginal Feminism," p. 156.

[147] "Itaque si aliquem bene christianum, qui tamen habet uxorem, quamvis cum ea adhuc filios generet, interrogem, utrum in illo regno habere velit uxorem; memor utique promissorum Dei et vitae illius, ubi corruptibile hoc induet incorruptionem, et mortale hoc induet immortalitatem (1 Cor. 15.53–54); jam magno vel certe aliquo amore suspensus, cum exsecratione respondebit, se vehementer id nolle. Rursus si interrogem, utrum uxorem suam post resurrectionem accepta angelica immutatione quae sanctis promittitur, secum ibi vivere velit; tam vehementer se id velle quam illud nolle respondebit. Sic invenitur bonus christianus diligere in una femina creaturam Dei, quam reformari et renovari desiderat: odisse autem conjunctionem copula-tionemque corruptibilem atque mortalem: hoc est, diligere in ea quod homo est, odisse quod uxor est" (*De sermone Domini in monte* 1.15.41, *PL* 34, col. 1250; trans. Denis J. Kavanagh, *Commentary on the Lord's Sermon on the Mount, FC*, vol. 11 [New York, 1951], pp. 61–62).

Moreover, in the course of the Pelagian controversy, Augustine's awareness of concupiscence grew to such alarming proportions that the wisdom of remaining together for a couple who had made the difficult transition to chastity was seriously in doubt. In *Against Julian*, for example, he tells of a man of eighty-three who, after living in chastity for twenty-five years with his wife, took a concubine.[148]

Augustine's efforts to uphold the traditional hierarchy resulted in a definition of marriage that simultaneously evoked heretical practice and female initiative to elude male mastery. It arrested female insubordination by projecting the husband's authority into paradise and, ironically, by emphasizing the very spiritual bond that, in heretical and Encratite contexts, had created the occasion for equality. Even so, Augustine's vision of marriage ultimately dominated the West, thus allowing for a protected, but uncomfortable, middle ground between celibacy and marriage in Christian practice.

---

[148] *Contra Julianum* 3.20.22, as cited by Brown, *The Body and Society*, p. 419.

TWO

SPIRITUAL MARRIAGE AS INSOLUBLE PROBLEM

OR UNIVERSAL NOSTRUM?

A Golden Moment: Early Realizations

WHY WASN'T Augustine more cautious? Peter Brown describes the immense comfort that Augustine drew from the example of Paulinus and his wife Therasia,[1] his contemporaries and correspondents, who renounced their conjugal rights around 390 and founded a community at Nola near Naples—one that lent substance to Augustine's ambitious construction of the spiritual bond between spouses. Possibly, Paulinus and Therasia were the human material which proved that the superimposition of Mary and Joseph's surreal union on the world was not totally impracticable. Carmen 21 (written by Paulinus in 407) creates a memorable frieze of a remarkable cast. Turcius Apronianus ("a boy in years but old towards the motions of the flesh")[2] and his wife Avita are two permanent members of the community.[3] Avita was the sister of Melania the Elder—the renowned widow who traveled widely in the Holy Land. The latter was instrumental in the conversion of Apronianus to the chaste life.[4] Their daughter, Eunomia, is described as "a maiden now pledged to eternal marriage in heaven."[5] As for Asterius, their son, "his devoted parents with true affection together appointed him a child consecrated to Christ."[6]

[1] Brown, *The Body and Society*, p. 403.

[2] "Aetate puerum sensibus carnis senem" (line 211, *Opera sancti Pontii Meropii Paulini Nolani*, ed. W. Hartel, *CSEL*, vol. 30 [Prague, Vienna, and Leipzig, 1894], p. 165; P. G. Walsh, trans., *The Poems of St. Paulinus of Nola*, *ACW*, no. 40 [New York, 1975], p. 179).

[3] Carm. 21, line 283 (*CSEL*, 30:167). Also see Palladius, *Lausiac History* 41.5, trans. Robert T. Meyer, *ACW*, no. 34 (Westminster, Md., 1965), pp. 118–119; critical edition, ed. C. Butler (Cambridge, 1904), 2:128–129.

[4] Palladius refers to this incident but mistakenly speaks of Melania the Elder and Avita as cousins (Meyer, trans., *Lausiac History* 54.4, *ACW*, no. 34, p. 135; Butler, ed., 2:146–148); see Walsh, trans., *Poems of St. Paulinus*, *ACW*, no. 40, p. 386 n. 12.

[5] "Et simul Eunomia aeternis iam pacta uirago / in caelo thalamis" (Carm. 21, lines 66–67, *CSEL*, 30:160; Walsh, trans., *Poems of St. Paulinus*, *ACW*, no. 40, p. 175).

[6] "Quem simul unanimes uera pietate parentes / infantem Christo constituere sacrum" (Carm. 21, lines 314–315, *CSEL*, 30:168; Walsh, trans., *Poems of St. Paulinus*, *ACW*, no. 40, pp. 182–183).

The poem also commemorates the presence of two eminent visitors: Melania the Younger, granddaughter to the older Melania and second cousin to Eunomia, and her husband Valerius Pinian—who at his wife's urging embraced a life of religious chastity around 403 when she was but twenty and he was twenty-four.[7] Hence, "conquering his own body, he expelled the devil's dominion from his limbs, and now in peace of spirit the chaste freedom of his faithful soul wears away the yoke of sin."[8] These two are accompanied by Albina, the mother of Melania, who was recently widowed and is now also converted to chastity. Thus the community is connected by both blood and purpose.[9] There is no place for regret over the former humiliation of conjugal relations. Marriage, chastity, and even virginity interlock to produce this tranquil vision.

If Paulinus's way of life incarnates Augustine's ideal, his actual experience of marriage corrects some of Augustine's pessimism. In contrast to the grim view that the only purpose for marrying is procreation and that otherwise male company is preferable, we have Paulinus's epithalamium for Julian of Eclanum (of *Against Julian* fame) and his wife Titia. Paulinus concludes by invoking Christ to

> aid the pure hearts through his [the bishop's] chaste hands, so that they may both agree on a compact of virginity, or be the source of consecrated virgins. Of these prayers, the first condition is preferable, that they keep their bodies innocent of the flesh. But if they consummate physical union, may the chaste offspring to come be a priestly race.[10]

Hyperbole? Perhaps. But this is one of the few instances for the entire period under surveillance where an orthodox authority is complacent about the entrance into a marriage that has perpetual chastity as a possible end. Moreover, there is reason to believe that Julian and his

[7] Carm. 21, lines 72–78, 836–847, *CSEL*, 30:160–161, 185–186.

[8] "Corporis victor sui, / pulsoque regno diaboli e membris suis / iam spiritali pace peccati iugum / fidelis animae casta libertas terit" (ibid., lines 247–250, p. 166; Walsh, trans., *Poems of St. Paulinus*, ACW, no. 40, pp. 180–181).

[9] "Prima chori Albina est cum pare Therasia; / iungitur hoc germana iugo, ut sit tertia princeps / agminis hymnisonis mater Auita choris. / matribus his duo sunt tribus uno pignora sexu, / flos geminus, Melani germen et Eunomia. / haec eadem et nobis maribus sunt pignora; nam quos / discernit sexus, consociat pietas. . . . / ergo cohors haec tota simul, tria nomina matres, / quattuor in natis, in patribus duo sunt" (Carm. 21, lines 281–287, 292–293, *CSEL*, 30:167).

[10] "Perque manus castas corda pudica iuua, / ut sit in ambobus concordia uirginitatis / aut sint ambo sacris semina uirginibus. / uotorum prior hic gradus est, ut nescia carnis / membra gerant; quod si corpore congruerint, / casta sacerdotale genus uentura propago" (ibid. Carm. 25, lines 232–237, p. 245; Walsh, trans., *Poems of St. Paulinus*, ACW, no. 40, pp. 252–253).

bride took the hint to leave the marriage unconsummated or at some point made a transition to chastity.[11]

But Paulinus's epithalamium speaks enthusiastically about other changes that Augustine would find even less laudatory: the chaste spouse who has achieved the status of sister is no longer subject to her husband.[12] The application of the ancient and optimistic rhetoric of virginity to marriage permeates his correspondence with like-minded chaste couples and permits him to present husband and wife, now equals, as more positive spiritual aids to one another, and this, in turn, encourages him to project marriage into paradise. In a letter to Aper and Amanda, Paulinus speaks with warm approval of Amanda's assumption of Aper's secular responsibilities, which served to encourage him to lead the monastic life. Hence, Paulinus describes her as "confront[ing] worldly needs as a tower founded on unbudging rock confronts storms . . . so that you [Aper] may be shielded from the sea."[13] The bond between them is likewise metamorphosed.

[11] Julian was made a deacon, a position requiring chastity, in 409, between six and nine years after the marriage. He became a bishop in 416, and Augustine (ca. 421) describes him as a man vowed to continence (Contra Julianum 3.21.50, PL 44, cols. 727–728; Brown, The Body and Society, p. 409). The second option articulated by Paulinus, namely, that Julian's potential children be consecrated to chastity, is a natural expectation in view of Paulinus's milieu: of the characters described in Carm. 21, all of the surviving offspring (Eunomia, Apronianus, and Melania) embraced chastity as did their progenitors.

[12] "Grande sacramentum, quo nubit eclesia Christo / et simul est domini sponsa sororque sui. / sponsa quasi coniunx, soror est, quia subdita non est. . . . / hinc soror et coniunx, quoniam sine corporis usu / mente coit cui uir non homo sed deus est . . . / nubere uel nubi fragilis iam deserit aetas / omnibus aeterno corpore conpositis. / ergo mei memores par inuiolabile semper / uiuite. . . . / et uobis fratres sponso concurritte Christo, / sitis ut aeterni corporis una caro" (Carm. 25, lines 167–169, 173–174, 189–192, 195–196, CSEL, 30:243–244; Walsh, trans., Poems of St. Paulinus, ACW, no. 40, pp. 250–251). Jerome writes in a similar mode to a chaste couple, claiming that their spiritual relationship has transformed a wife into a sister, a woman into a man, a subordinate into an equal: "Habes tecum prius in carne, nunc in spiritu sociam, de coniuge germanam, de femina uirum, de subiecta parem, quae sub eodem iugo ad caelestia simul regna festinet" (Ep. 71, "To Lucinus" c. 3, CSEL, 55:4). Cf. Gregory of Nazianzus's funeral oration for his sister Gorgonia wherein she is praised for winning her husband to chastity—a change that transformed him from master to companion in service ("In laudem sororis suae Gorgoniae," Orat. 8, c. 8, PG 35, cols. 797–798).

[13] "Se necessitatibus saeculi pro te uelut quaedam procellis in immobili scopulo stabilita turris opposuit. . . . ut tu seclusus a pelago" (Ep. 44, "To Aper and Amanda" c. 4, CSEL, 29:373; trans. P. G. Walsh, Letters of St. Paulinus of Nola, ACW, no. 36 [Westminster, Md., 1967], 2:237. Also see Ep. 39, c. 1–2, CSEL, 29:334–336, in which Paulinus discusses the pressures Aper felt as a landowner, prior to his withdrawal from the world. Eucher (later bishop of Lyons) and Galla also followed Paulinus's and Therasia's lead in embarking on an ascetical path: they retired to the island of Sainte Marguerite near the monastic foundation of Honoratus (see Letters of St. Paulinus, trans.

He [God] transforms not only souls but also feelings, changing the transient into the eternal. See how you remain the married couple you were, yet not coupled as you were. You are yourselves yet not yourselves. Now you know each other, as you know Christ, apart from the flesh.[14]

The community at Nola, while unique, was not an isolated experience for this period. It seems that the fifth-century poet Sedulius was a member of a similar group.[15] But I have dwelt on Paulinus's *familia*, immediate and extended, at some length because we know so much about it and because parallel experiments—spiritual marriage as a community undertaking—were not again attempted in the West for over six hundred years. Once monasticism gained a firmer foothold, it became the natural forum for asceticism—not only providing an alternative for the pious couple who might formerly have lived out their vocation in a spiritual marriage, but also institutionally canonizing the position that salvation is best pursued in isolation from the other sex. This new state of affairs can be measured by the fact that when Gregory the Great speaks of a number of couples who abstain by mutual agreement, this is described as a temporary ar-

---

Walsh, *ACW*, no. 35, 1:9, introd.). Paulinus's designation of them as perpetual consorts ("perpetui coniuges") is probably an oblique reference to their chastity (Ep. 51, "To Eucher and Galla" c. 4, *CSEL*, 29:425). According to Ado's martyrology (compiled 858), Eucher lived in a cave while Galla brought him food. When the people of Lyons wished to appoint him bishop, they broke down the wall and led forth the reluctant Eucher. Then it was his wife's turn to live in the cave, while her saintly daughters, Consortia and Tulla—both consecrated virgins—ministered to her needs (*Sancti Adonis Martyrologium*, *PL* 123, col. 398; also see Lenain de Tillemont, who clears up the misconception that there were two Euchers, both believed to be bishops of Lyons, in "Notes sur saint Eucher," in *Mémoires pour servir à l'histoire ecclésiastique des six premiers siècles* [Paris, 1711], 15:848–857).

[14] "Conuertit non solum animas sed et affectus, temporalia in aeterna. manetis ecce idem coniuges ut fuistis, sed non ita coniuges ut fuistis; estis ipsi nec ipsi; et sicut Christum, ita et uosmet ipsos iam secundum carnem nostis" (Ep. 44, "To Aper and Amanda" c. 4, *CSEL*, 29:372–373; Walsh, trans., *Letters of St. Paulinus*, ACW, no. 36, 2:237).

[15] Little is known of Sedulius except through his letter to the priest Macedonius, who was the leader of a small Christian community of which Sedulius was a member. The group is an assortment of people of different ranks, married and celibate, clerical and lay. Sedulius perceives the young noble matron Perpetua's union as next in excellence to the palm of virginity: "proximam uirginitatis continet palmam in coniugii foedere manens pudica" ("Epistola ad Macedonium," *Sedulii opera omnia*, ed. J. Huemer, *CSEL*, vol. 10 [Vienna, 1885], pp. 10–11). His praise seems to imply absolute continence, but Patrick Corbet notes that the same phrase is borrowed to describe the marriage of Empress Mathilda, wife of Henry the Fowler. In this latter instance it refers to conjugal chastity in the less exacting sense (*Les Saints Ottoniens: Sainteté dynastique, sainteté royale, et sainteté feminine autour de l'an Mil* [Sigmaringen, 1986], p. 187).

rangement while the couple was basically en route to the monastery.[16]

Pastoral Problems: Some Late Antique Tensions

Chastity was as appealing to orthodox women as it was to the women in the Apocryphal Acts: they were generally the ones who agitated for spiritual marriage. The husband's relative foot-dragging bespoke his closer association with social position and public life, which a change to chastity undercut, while a woman's eagerness bespoke resistance to her physical implication in a system where the dividends were, admittedly, low. But the husband generally only complied with his wife's request after his will had been broken by external forces. Undoubtedly this kind of "psychic emasculation" contributed to the destabilization of his authority and the construction of new roles. Paulinus himself was born to wealth, privilege, and an active career in public life. Only after experiencing the death of his newborn son, and difficulties surrounding his brother's murder (which endangered Paulinus's life and property), did he yield to his wife's promptings by renouncing the world and conjugal relations.[17] His voluntary withdrawal from secular affairs and liquidation of considerable properties were the scandal of the late antique world.[18]

Among those attracted to Paulinus's community was Melania the Younger, who had been married against her will at fourteen. She begged her young husband, Pinian, to take a vow of chastity with her, even offering him all her wealth if he would cease to exact the conjugal debt.[19] But Pinian demurred, insisting upon two children to

[16] "Et multos sanctorum nouimus cum suis coniugibus et prius continentem uitam duxisse et postmodum ad sanctae ecclesiae regimina migrasse" (Reg. 11, 27, "To Theoctista," *Registrum epistularum*, ed. Dag Norberg, *CCSL*, vol. 140a [Turnholt, 1982], p. 909).

[17] Joseph T. Lienhard, *Paulinus of Nola and Early Western Monasticism* (Cologne and Bonn, 1977), pp. 28–29, 50. Carm. 21 (lines 414–420, *CSEL*, 30:171–172) makes an oblique reference to the death of Paulinus's brother and his subsequent conversion.

[18] In the late 380s or early 390s Paulinus was baptized and renounced conjugal relations. He was then ordained in 394. He and his wife Therasia sold off much of their property and settled near Naples in the town of Nola, where they gathered together a community that was devoted to asceticism. See Lienhard, *Paulinus of Nola*, pp. 24–30; cf. Peter Brown, *The Cult of the Saints: Its Rise and Function in Latin Christianity* (Chicago, 1981), pp. 53–54.

[19] Denys Gorce, ed., *Vie de sainte Mélanie* c. 1, *SC*, no. 90 (Paris, 1962), pp. 130–133. This life has been translated into English by Elizabeth Clark (*The Life of Melania the Younger*, Studies in Women and Religion, vol. 14 [Lewiston, Lampeter, and Queenston, 1984] pp. 27–28). Melania's life is thought to have been written by the priest Gerontius

whom they could entrust their estates. The cost of delay was high. The first child was a daughter, who was promptly dedicated to God. But Melania nearly died in childbirth with the second child, the awaited son was stillborn, and their young daughter died soon after. Pinian was sufficiently shaken that he gave in to his wife's request[20] and probably, if asked, would have reasoned like Melania that if God had intended them to have children, he would not have taken them away so soon.[21] Melania clearly emerged as both Pinian's spiritual guide and the dominant party in the relationship.[22] But their problems were by no means over: Melania's relatives were so resistant to her and her husband's conversion to chastity (particularly as there was no living heir) that the young couple made plans to flee the city.[23] The family also resented the couple's liberal use of their huge resources and made repeated efforts to wrest the property from their control.[24]

But by the late fourth century, the church was growing progressively less sympathetic toward female efforts to act autonomously. Melania, for example, considered flight to escape her marriage, but the holy men she consulted advised her to wait, confident that she would be able to bring her husband around to chastity.[25] Although female patronage was ardently encouraged by ecclesiastical authorities, many pious women, autonomous by virtue of widowhood or spiritual marriage, were criticized by these same authorities for their injudicious use of their considerable funds.[26] Moreover, spiritual

---

(d. 485), who knew her well. Also see Palladius's account (Meyer, ed., *Lausiac History* 61.12, *ACW*, no. 34, pp. 141–142; Butler, ed., 2:155–156).

[20] Gorce, ed., *Mélanie* c. 5–6, *SC*, no. 90, pp. 134–139; trans. Clark, pp. 29–30.

[21] Ibid. It should be added, however, that Melania insisted on attending an all-night vigil near the end of her term that brought on early labor (Gorce, ed., *Mélanie* c. 5, pp. 134–135; trans. Clark, p. 29). This is not the last instance that we will find of a reluctant mother deliberately neglecting herself (and, of course, the child) during pregnancy or lactation.

[22] The subtlety of Pinian's dependence on his wife and the shift in their respective roles is evident when Melania wishes to upbraid him gently over the senseless finery of his clothes. After she questioned him as to how he regarded her, he answered, " 'From the time when we gave our word to God and entered the chaste life, I have looked on you in the same way as your holy mother Albina.' Melania then exhorted him, saying, 'Then be persuaded by me as your spiritual mother and sister' " (Gorce, ed., *Mélanie* c. 8, *SC*, no. 90, pp. 142–143; trans. Clark, p. 32).

[23] Gorce, ed., *Mélanie* c. 6, *SC*, no. 90, pp. 138–139; trans. Clark, p. 30.

[24] For an analysis of Melania's struggle with her relatives over property rights, see Elizabeth Clark's "Commentary," in *The Life of Melania*, pp. 99–102; also see Brown, *The Body and Society*, p. 410.

[25] Gorce, ed., *Mélanie* c. 4, *SC*, no. 90, pp. 132–135; trans. Clark, p. 29. Cf. Palladius, *Lausiac History* 61.3, trans. Meyer, *ACW*, no. 34, p. 142; ed. Butler, 2:155.

[26] For female patronage, see Brown, *The Body and Society*, pp. 150, 344–345, and

marriage presented serious disciplinary problems. Even though orthodox efforts to transform the conjugal unit by ascetic chastity begin as early as the second century and are stepped up in the fourth century, nevertheless we are still in a time when the theology of marriage and the Christian rites surrounding it are at best ill-defined, while the guidelines regarding an agreement to live chastely are even more ephemeral.[27] All orthodox writers, in conformity with Paul's desire to protect the spouse's right to the conjugal debt, are agreed that such a decision must be mutual. Even Jerome, perhaps the most tireless advocate for chastity, both within and outside marriage,[28] was mindful of Paul's injunction that couples remain together: his proposed gloss was that if a man was only patient, his wife would eventually become his sister.[29] But women in particular got tired of waiting. Both Augustine and Chrysostom, the two major theorists of marriage for late antiquity, were aware of the female predilection for chastity and the danger of wives who attempted to act unilaterally.[30]

Augustine's letter to the noble matron Ecdicia lays bare his ultimate pastoral nightmare, combining all of the public and private complications that could potentially ensue as a result of chaste marriage. Ecdicia made a vow precipitously but was fortunate enough to win her husband over to chastity as well.[31] Yet Ecdicia construed

---

idem, *The Cult of the Saints*, pp. 46–48; for the ambivalence of church authorities over female use of rank and wealth, see Elizabeth Clark, "Ascetic Renunciation and Feminine Advancement: A Paradox of Late Ancient Christianity," in *Ascetic Piety and Women's Faith: Essays on Late Ancient Christianity*, Studies in Women and Religion, vol. 20 (Lewiston and Queenston, 1986), pp. 175–208, esp. 182, 188–189, 190–191.

[27] For conflicting customs in the late antique West, see Ritzer, *Le mariage dans les églises chrétiennes*, pp. 81–123, 217–266. Note that both Augustine and Ambrose were reluctant to permit priests or bishops to preside over or even be present at wedding festivities (p. 100). In Italy, the nuptial blessing was generally reserved for the clergy until the eleventh century (pp. 234–236).

[28] Jerome wrote two letters on the education of virgins (Ep. 107, "To Laeta," *CSEL*, 55:290–305; cf. Ep. 130, "To Demetria," *CSEL*, 56:175–201). He also focused much of his energy urging recently bereaved widows (many of whom he'd never met!) not to remarry (Eps. 54, "To Furia," *CSEL*, 54:466–485; 79, "To Salvina," *CSEL*, 55:87–101; 123, "To Geruchia," *CSEL*, 56:72–95). His most spectacular success was with Blaesilla, the young widowed daughter of his intimate friend Paula. Under his encouragement, she embarked upon so strenuous an ascetic regime that she was dead in three months. See his letter of condolence to her mother (Ep. 39, "To Paula," *CSEL*, 54:293–308).

[29] *Adversus Jovinianum* 1.11, *PL* 23, col. 236, and Ep. 48, "To Pammachius" c. 6, *CSEL*, 54:359.

[30] Augustine states explicitly that continence is more pleasing to women: "Placuit continentia mulieri, uiro non placet" (*De adulterinis coniugiis* 1.4.4, ed. J. Zycha, *CSEL*, 41:351). Cf. John Chrysostom, who reprimands the many wives who behave this way for instigating sin rather than justice (*In epistola I ad Corinthios homilia XIX* c. 1 ad 7.5, *PG* 61, col. 153).

[31] Ep. 262, "To Ecdicia" c. 3–4, *Epistolae*, ed. A. Goldbacher, *CSEL*, vol. 57 (Vienna

chastity as radical freedom. She immediately assumed financial independence by giving away a large percentage of their fortune to two traveling monks during her husband's absence[32] and advertised her personal autonomy by the assumption of a widow's garb against her husband's will.[33] The frustrated husband retaliated by breaking his vow through adultery. Augustine blamed Ecdicia's arrogance for her husband's fall and was quick to remind her that "he did not cease to be your husband because you were both refraining from carnal intercourse; on the contrary you continued to be husband and wife in a holier manner because you were carrying out a holier resolution, with mutual accord."[34] A sermon on the consensual nature of marriage, buttressed by the example of Mary and Joseph, clearly reiterates the moral behind this painful affair: release from the conjugal debt in no way impairs the husband's authority over the wife. In fact, Augustine goes so far as to state that the more subjected a woman is, the more chaste she is.[35]

A return to former intimacies was also a disturbing possibility. Augustine's letter to Armentarius and Paulina, a couple whose pledge of chastity he had *heard* about (they did not come to him themselves) and who later came to regret their decision, is gracefully poised between encouragement and warning. He states that he would happily spend his time praising chastity in marriage, but that their decision now imposes a more urgent set of responsibilities:

> But, as you have now made the vow, as you have now bound yourself, you are not free to do anything else. . . . Now that your promise binds you

---

and Leipzig, 1911), pp. 623–624. Also see Brown, *The Body and Society*, pp. 403–404. A parallel situation arises in a letter, spuriously attributed to Paulinus of Nola, that upbraids a noble matron for vowing chastity without consulting her husband. The author asserts that chastity was not hers to vow and claims that he knows many marriages that have been broken through this kind of ignorance and which often end in the neglected party's adultery (Ep. 2, "To Celancia" c. 28, *CSEL*, 29:456). If the neglected husband commits adultery, the wife will be equally at fault, if not more so. As she is bound by two conflicting debts, the author admits that the only real solution is to convert her husband to chastity as well, making the two in one flesh into two in one spirit. In the interim, however, he counsels her to honor the debt to her husband.

[32] Ep. 262, "To Ecdicia" c. 5, *CSEL*, 57:624–625.

[33] Ibid. c. 9, pp. 628–629.

[34] "Non enim, quia pariter temperabatis a commixtione carnali, ideo tuus maritus esse destiterat; immo uero tanto sanctius inter uos coniuges manebatis, quanto sanctiora concorditer placita seruabatis" (ibid. c. 4, p. 624; trans. Sr. Wilfrid Parsons, *Letters*, *FC*, vol. 32 [New York, 1956], p. 263).

[35] "Nonne sunt coniuges qui sic vivunt, non quaerentes ab invicem fructum carnis, non exigentes ab invicem debitum concupiscentiae corporalis? Et tamen illa subjecta est viro, quia sic decet; et tanto subjectior, quanto castior" (Serm. 51, 13.21, *PL* 38, col. 345).

before God, I do not invite you to great perfection, I warn you to avoid a great sin. If you do not keep what you have vowed, you will not be the same as you would have been if you had not made the vow. For, in that case, you would have been less perfect, not worse; whereas now—which God forbid!—you will be as much worse off if you break your word to God as you will be more blessed if you keep it.[36]

He does offer the couple one possible out. Perhaps the wife's agreement was in some way flawed: "If there has been inconsidered haste, there is a question of making amends for rashness rather than of keeping a promise. God does not exact of us what is vowed at another's expense." In short, flawed intention is all that can save them from the implications of so important a pledge to God. Yet Augustine comments on the unlikeliness that this release clause applies because he has, again, *heard* that the wife had long since been eager for this step.[37]

Orthodox authorities are generally very severe with regard to broken vows of chastity: especially if they concern consecrated virgins.[38] When addressing vows of chastity in the context of marriage, Augustine states that, once the vow is made, both marital and extramarital sexual relations are denied.[39] But the complexity of these pastoral problems resulted from the fact that not one but two souls were at stake.[40] The situations only came to light because of the parties'

---

[36] "Sed quia iam uouisti, iam te obstrinxisti, aliud tibi facere non licet. . . . nunc uero, quia tenetur apud deum sponsio tua, non te ad magnam iustitiam inuito, sed a magna iniquitate deterreo. non enim talis eris, si non feceris, quod uouisti, qualis mansisses, si nihil tale uouisses. minor enim tunc esses, non peior; modo autem tanto—quod absit—miserior, si fidem deo fregeris, quanto beatior si persolueris" (Ep. 127, "To Armentarius and Paulina" c. 8, *CSEL*, 44:27–28; trans. Parsons, *FC*, 18:363).

[37] "Si praepropere factum fuerit, magis est corrigenda temeritas quam persoluenda promissio. neque enim deus exigit, si quis ex alieno aliquid uouerit" (Ep. 127, "To Armentarius and Paulina" c. 9, *CSEL*, 44:28; trans. Parsons, *FC*, 18:364). Cf. Jerome's Ep. 122, "To Rusticus," who took a vow with his wife but wavered in his steps, as would a person on high sea, and finally fell ("tuaque rursum uestigia quasi in salo posita fluctuasse, immo—ut apertius loquar—esse prolapsa" [c. 4, *CSEL*, 56:69]). The couple agreed to do penance by a pilgrimage to the Holy Land, a vow that the wife fulfilled. Jerome writes to remind the husband of his promise.

[38] According to Roman law, abductors of nuns received capital punishment (*Nov.* 123.43). Even in the Germanic kingdoms, secular authorities upheld the holiness of such vows by applying strict penalties to trangressors. See, for example, the laws of the Lombard king Liutprand (30.I; 94.XII, *The Lombard Laws*, trans. Katherine Fischer Drew [Philadelphia, 1973], pp. 159–160, 185).

[39] Serm. 132, c. 3, *PL* 38, col. 736.

[40] Boniface, count of the Household and of Africa, for example, was moved to vow chastity by the loss of his wife but then, soon after, married for a second time. Augustine reproaches him for breaking his vow but grants that he cannot abstain sexually without his wife's consent. Hence his new job is to gain this consent. In this instance of

failure to synchronize their disparate spiritual capacities. What succor does Augustine offer to a married woman desirous of a life of chastity who is married to a husband wishing to enjoy matrimony's conventional prerogatives? The answer is unrelenting. The desires of the stronger (i.e., more spiritual) party must invariably yield to the requirements of the weaker[41]—a solution that conjures up Chrysostom's grim depiction of the marriage bond as a shackle, restricting the able stride of one to the limping pace of the other. Her only consolation is this: reward will ultimately be meted out on the basis of worthy intentions, not simply actions. Thus Augustine reproaches Ecdicia for her initially hasty vow as follows:

> How much more fitting would it have been for you, to whom subjection was more appropriate, to yield to his will in rendering him the debt in this way, since God would have taken account of your intention to observe continence which you gave up to save your husband from destruction![42]

Such an attribution is party to Augustine's view that the initiator of sexual relations is guilty of a venial sin, while the respondent performs a meritorious act.

The dangers of intramarital chastity are exacerbated by the fact that chastity in marriage was more often than not a well-guarded secret—a factor that is too easily forgotten in view of the celebrated members of Paulinus's community. Both Jerome and Augustine

---

a unilateral vow, spiritual marriage is the only honest solution (Ep. 220, "To Boniface," *CSEL*, 57:431–441). This letter was written ca. 427. Augustine's protection of the marriage, and of the innocent spouse, against the irresponsible behavior of the one who is forsworn is complemented by his reluctance to pronounce such unions invalid—though he declares that the guilty party is, in fact, worse than an adulterer: "Quapropter non possum quidem dicere a proposito meliore lapsas, si nupserint, feminas adulteria esse, non coniugia, sed plane non dubitauerim dicere lapsus et ruinas a castitate sanctiore, quae uouetur domino adulteriis esse peiores" (*De bono uiduitatis* 11.14, *CSEL*, 41:320).

[41] Even though Augustine upholds the husband's unequivocal authority, he nevertheless believes that Ecdicia, as the spiritually stronger, was rendered all the more responsible for her husband's welfare. Augustine's critique of Ecdicia is thus that she disturbed her husband with her presumption rather than supporting him with her love ("Infirmus enim erat et ideo tibi, quae in communi proposito fortior uidebaris, non erat praesumptione turbandus sed dilectione portandus" [Ep. 262, "To Ecdicia" c. 5, *CSEL*, 57:625]).

[42] "Quanto magis te, quam magis subiectam esse decuerat, ne ipse quoque in adulterium diabolica temptatione traheretur, in reddendo huius modi debito uoluntati: eius obtemperare conuenerat, cum tibi uoluntatem continendi acceptaret deus, quia propterea non faceres, ne periret maritus!" (ibid. c. 2, p. 623; trans. Parsons, *FC*, 32:262–263).

claim that they know many couples who sexually abstain, but it is unlikely that their abstinence was known to the community at large.[43] A couple's natural taciturnity about matters relating to the marriage bed was reinforced by spiritual counsel. In his famed letter to Polycarp, Ignatius (d. ca. 107) writes that couples who are able to abstain should avoid boasting of it: otherwise they are lost.[44] The virtue of concealment underlies Paulinus's praise of Rouen for sheltering husbands and wives who secretly live in chastity.[45] Only very rarely have epitaphs divulged such secrets. A late fifth-century monument at Aosta, though badly damaged, seems to make a rather startling claim:

> Here [rest] in peace the faithful servant of God, Ampelius, and Singenia who lived in conjugal affection and love [. . .] for about sixty [or seventy?] years without interruption. Faithful they abided in the peace of the Lord. Their life was such that the wife relinquished her husband and lived for more than twenty years in perpetual chastity.[46]

[43] Augustine describes the couple's transition to chastity as restraining carnal concupiscence, but not conjugal charity ("Et multos novimus fratres nostros fructificantes in gratia, in nomine Christi ex consensu ab invicem continere concupiscentiam carnis, non autem continere ab invicem charitatem conjugalem" [Serm. 51, 13.21, *PL* 38, col. 345]). Jerome uses the example of the many married women who voluntarily abstain (either after baptism or just after their nuptials) in his campaign against second marriages ("Si multae in coniugio uiuentibus adhuc uiris intellegunt illud apostoli . . . et castrant se propter regna caelorum uel a secunda natiuitate post lauacrum ex consensu uel post nuptias ex ardore fidei . . ." [Ep. 123, "To Geruchia" c. 10, *CSEL*, 56:83]).

[44] "To Polycarp" c. 5 (*Ignace d'Antioche. Polycarpe de Smyrne. Lettres. Martyre de Polycarpe*, ed. Th. Camelot, 3d. rev. ed., *SC*, no. 10 [Paris, 1958], pp. 174–177).

[45] In an erotically charged passage, Paulinus describes the way in which the chaste couple (now secret siblings) mingles in their bed with Christ and the saints: "subiugatorum deo coniugum arcana germanitas, quae orationibus sedulis laetum in operibus suis Christum ad uisitationem non iam maritalis tori sed fraterni cubilis inuitat, cum ipso sanctisque eius uicissim mixta concubitu castitatis spiritibus uisitantium immaculato amore confunditur" (Ep. 18, "To Vitricius" c. 5, *CSEL*, 29:132–133).

[46] "IN HVC LOC[o requiescunt] / IN PACE FEDELIS FAMV[lus dei ampeliu] / S ET SINGENIA QVI VIXER[unt in coniu-] / GALI ADFECTV ET CARITA[te . . .] / ANNIS CIRCITER LX AVT [LXX?] AN[nos. . .cont-] / INVOS IN PACE DOMINICA F[idi perman-] / SERVNT QVORUM VITA TALIS F[uit ut lin-] / QVENS CONIVX MARITVM XX AN[nos] / EXCEDENS IN CASTITATE PERPET[ua] / PERDVRARET" (Otto Hirschfeld, ed. *Corpus Inscriptionum Latinarum*, vol. 12, *Inscriptiones Galliae Narbonensis Latinae* [Berlin, 1888], no. 1724). For the sake of legibility, I did not indicate the full extent of the damage in my translation. Clearly in such a case, any reading can be only a hypothesis. Others, such as H. Leclercq, have, however, also interpreted the inscription in this way (see n. 47, below). A monument at Avignon, belonging to Casaria (d. 586 or 587) and raised by her husband Valens implies that they converted to chastity after the death of their child. A tradition dating back at least as far as the eleventh century alleges that their marriage was virginal, that Valens became bishop of Avignon, and that Casaria ended her life as recluse (ibid., no. 1045; also see

The fact that the wife was responsible for the inscription and the oddity of its disclosure has since raised scholarly eyebrows.[47]

Secrecy was an essential element in most narratives treating spiritual marriage, and practical considerations reinforce natural discretion. For example, after eighteen years of virginal cohabitation, the wife of Amon of Nitria (d. ca. 350) suggested that they separate because " 'it is unspeakable that you hide such virtue as yours living together with me in virginity.' "[48] Or so Palladius tells us. But another source alleges that they only separated after the death of their parents.[49] The mimes Theophilus and Marie, though for all the world appearing as debauched souls, had secretly pledged chastity and never consummated their marriage. But their secrecy was initially necessary, and it was only after their parents' deaths that they were free to sell their substantial property and take up their peripatetic life.[50] In view of the familial resistance, Melania and Pinian would have done well to keep their pious resolve a secret.

The risks of spiritual marriage were admittedly high, but the church fathers had boxed themselves into an interesting corner—the unusual proportions of which require careful soundings. The threat of dualism dictated that orthodoxy stand guardian over marriage and procreation. Although all Western authorities were agreed that procreation was the chief end of marriage,[51] the ascetic milieu made it impossible to construct a defense of marriage that was grounded in the conjugal act.[52] Had they been prepared to do so, the marriage of the Virgin and the mention of "Christ's brethren" would have been

---

J.-H. Albanès, "Inscription de sainte Casarie," *Revue des sociétés savantes* 1 [1875]: 158–163, esp. 162; *BS*, vol. 3, cols. 893–894. Cf. the tomb of Cassius [d. 538], bishop of Narni and his wife Fausta, n.159, below).

[47] H. Leclercq, "Aoste," in *Dictionnaire d'archéologie chrétienne et de liturgie*, vol. 1, pt. 1 (Paris, 1924), col. 2494.

[48] Palladius, *Lausiac History* 8.4, trans. Meyer, *ACW*, no. 34, pp. 42–43; ed. Butler, 2:26–29.

[49] Rufinus, *Historia monachorum*, *PL* 21, cols. 455–456; as cited in de Gaiffier, "*Intactam sponsam*," pp. 166–167.

[50] John of Ephesus, *Lives of the Eastern Saints* c. 52, ed. and trans. E. W. Brooks, *Patrologia Orientalis*, vol. 19, fasc. 2, pt. 3 (Paris, 1925), pp. 175–177; see de Gaiffier, "*Intactam sponsam*," pp. 171–172. The same pattern is apparent in ahistorical hagiographical accounts: when both sets of parents of the chaste couple Julian and Basilissa die, they separate and found religious communities (*AA SS*, January, 1:577).

[51] This is not necessarily true of the Eastern church. Chrysostom tended to dissociate sex and reproduction—a distinction that may explain why the Slavic church had a number of saints who were miraculously born of virgins (see n. 137, below).

[52] John Noonan points out that Eph. 5 would have been the natural starting place for constructing a positive ethos for sexual relations, had the church fathers been so inclined (*Contraception*, p. 73).

the obvious way to go. Instead Mary's virginal union, buttressed by the Roman notion of *consensus*, became an essentially separate issue that would have been better excluded from mainstream discussions of marriage. It was, nevertheless, the scaffolding that supported Augustine's theoretical elaboration of spiritual marriage, thus dissociating marriage and the conjugal act. Yet this definition evoked an actual practice that was probably pioneered by women who were, more often than not, hostile to the husband's rule, which was above all symbolized by his sexual claims. Augustine, aware of this contradiction and anxious to contain female insubordination, attempted to make the husband's authority as transcendent as the bond itself: the transition to chastity theoretically strengthened both. Thus, Augustine attempted to supplant the link between chastity and freedom with his own link between chastity and subjection.

And yet, since mistrust of human nature made patristic writers ambivalent about experiments in chaste heterosexual cohabitation, the Western fathers were ultimately unprepared to embrace the consequences of their own theory, and, in fact, the more cautious writers, like Ambrose or even Augustine later in his career, did not openly exhort their flocks to attempt spiritual marriage.

The Universal Nostrum

Despite official trepidation, spiritual marriage was simply too adaptable to be suppressed and too useful to be ignored. Although written sources are scant from the sixth to the eleventh centuries, a number of uses can be discerned in the sources that do exist. The model is first appropriated by hagiographers, primarily with a didactic intent.[53] Thus the usual criticisms of saints' lives for the purpose of historical inquiry—be they biases, borrowings, or their formulaic nature— present no difficulty for our present aims. The hagiographic model is, in turn, appropriated by chroniclers to accommodate certain changes in the marriage laws. Concurrent with these two social uses is the appropriation by the clergy for the purposes of clerical discipline.

Virginal Marriage and Didactic Hagiography: The Affirmation of the Spiritual Bond

Unlike the gradual evolution of chastity within marriage envisioned by authorities like Ambrose, the spiritual marriages of the early Mid-

[53] Thomas J. Heffernan, *Sacred Biography: Saints and Their Biographers* (Oxford, 1988), p. 19.

dle Ages were normally more aggressively conceived as virginal unions that were never consummated. In the *passio* of St. Cecilia, the theme of the virgin spouses achieves its most popular expression.[54] The pious Cecilia was forced to marry the youth Valerian, whom she proceeded to convert on their wedding night by telling him that there was an angel who would kill him if he made any sexual advances toward her. When Valerian asks how he too may see the angel, she sends him to Pope Urban, who baptizes him. On his return home, not only does he see the angel, but he and Cecilia are crowned with two wreaths in token of their commitment to chastity: lilies for Cecilia and roses for Valerian. These wreaths will never diminish in fragrance and are visible only to those who serve chastity.[55] The story then unfolds with a series of conversions (beginning with Valerian's brother) and a series of martyrdoms, culminating in Cecilia's.

The Cecilia legend and its many analogues would score poorly on the scale of referentiality. Although the *passio* purports to be set in the third century during the time of the persecutions, there is no evidence for such a figure from this period, while the legend itself seems to date from the end of the fifth century. It is almost certainly a pious fiction that was embroidered around the honorable burial place accorded to the foundress of a church who, according to an inscription, was named Cecilia.[56] The Cecilia legend also shows many parallels with the purportedly true stories of Maxima and Martinian, as reported by Victor of Vita. Both tales involve forced marriage, a vow of chastity on the wedding night, and great success in missionizing leading up to an eventual martyrdom.[57] The Cecilia story has even

---

[54] For Cecilia's *passio*, see Bonino Mombrizio, *Sanctuarium seu Vitae sanctorum* (Paris, 1910), 1:332–341.

[55] Ibid., pp. 333–334.

[56] On the development of her cult, see especially Hippolyte Delehaye, *Etude sur le légendier romain: les saints de novembre et de décembre*, Subsidia Hagiographica, 23 (Brussels, 1936), pp. 73–96.

[57] *Historia persecutionis Africanae provinciae* 1.30–38, ed. M. Petschenig, *CSEL*, vol. 7 (Vienna, 1881), pp. 13–17; de Gaiffier, "*Intactam sponsam*," p. 169. Maxima, however, was not martyred but was still living in a monastery in 488, when Victor was writing. The nonhistorical *passiones* of Chrysanthus and Daria (*AA SS*, October, 11:476–483; de Gaiffier, "*Intactam sponsam*," p. 174 n. 2) and Julian and Basilissa (*AA SS*, January, 1:576–579,582–587; de Gaiffier, "*Intactam sponsam*," pp. 173–174) also share the features of the virginal *passiones* outlined above. The arguments used by Julian's parents in favor of marriage were later borrowed for a version of the Alexis legend (see B. de Gaiffier, "Source d'un texte relatif au mariage dans la vie de S. Alexis, BHL. 289," *AB* 63 [1945]: 49–52, for the appropriate passages). Alexis will be discussed in the next chapter.

Victor of Vita's account of Maxima and Martinian—two Christian captives who were forced by their Vandal masters to marry—also resembles Jerome's allegedly true

borrowed certain sections that describe the chaste bond between the couple.[58]

But although such legends are often pious fabrications, they are no less culturally "true"—true to the beliefs, yearnings, and fantasies of their writers and readers. Whether representative of actual situations or not, they struck a responsive chord. Baudouin de Gaiffier's seminal article *"Intactam sponsam relinquens*: à propos de la vie de S. Alexis"* isolates two groups of aspirant virgins who were coerced into marriage: those who manage to convert their spouses and thereafter remain with them in virginal purity and those who flee before the marriage can be consummated.[59] The legends of Cecilia and Alexis are representative of the course of action that each sex is depicted as most inclined to take: women stayed, men fled.[60] The extreme popularity of the Cecilia story is a tacit recognition of a woman's particular vulnerability in the marriage game. Her socially enforced passivity inclined her to comply in the hope that she could convert her husband to chastity, as witnessed in the life of Melania the Younger. Moreover, Cecilia, like Melania, becomes the dominant party in the marriage and the missionizing nucleus for the community.

The Cecilia legend possesses three irreducible elements that are common to most hagiographical depictions of virginal marriage: reluctance to marry, conversion of the spouse on the wedding night, and a secret resolve to preserve virginity.[61] These points possess a number of historical resonances subordinated to hagiographical ends. For example, as clerical asceticism came to dominate the hagiographical discourse of the early Middle Ages, the number of lay saints

---

story of the captive monk Malchus. The latter was married against his will by his Saracen masters and was about to kill himself when the woman suggested a spiritual marriage (*Vita Malchi monachi captivi* c. 6, ed. and trans. Charles C. Mierow, in *Classical Essays Presented to James A. Kleist*, ed. Richard E. Arnold [St. Louis, Mo., 1946], pp. 44–49).

[58] Victor of Vita, *Historia persecutionis Africanae provinciae* 1.30–32, *CSEL*, 7:14.

[59] De Gaiffier, *"Intactam sponsam,"* p. 182.

[60] A number of the fleeing men did, however, first persuade their spouses to live out their lives as consecrated virgins—an element that de Gaiffier notes was a later addition to the Alexis motif (ibid., p. 163). De Gaiffier also observes that he knows of no occasion when a female saint fled from her nuptials (p. 184 n. 1), but fails to comment on the female agency apparent in the unions that developed into spiritual marriages. This second pattern is implicit in the series of legends he summarizes—although he tends to conflate the flight and the conversion models (pp. 164–181). The pattern emerges clearly in my more comprehensive lists of spiritual marriages in appendixes 1, 3, and 4.

[61] These elements are parallel to de Gaiffier's analysis of the Alexis legend, except that secrecy supplants flight (see ibid., p. 163).

declined—especially married ones. The hagiographer is at pains to explain why somebody of peculiar sanctity would be married in the first place, and compulsion plays a central role in this context.[62] Likewise, the *vitae* would invariably have it that the revelation of a secret desire to remain chaste occurs in the bedroom on the night of the wedding—a situation that was both dramatic and titillating. And yet, in point of fact, the nuptial chamber was often the first place in which the young couple had ever been alone together.[63] Likewise, the vow of virginity is safeguarded by secrecy—certainly a symptom of both the private and the pragmatic considerations alluded to above, and yet a useful claim that is impossible to refute—barring the appearance of embarrassing offspring.[64]

Perpetual virginity reinforced the hierarchy of merit in heaven and was an important expression of the values of the postconversion church. But this very emphasis on virginity ultimately dwarfs Augustine's assurances that God credits the chaste intentions of a reluctant spouse who is still required to honor the conjugal debt. Indeed, the realm of intentionality seems to have receded along with the Roman world. The stark tariffs of Germanic code and penitential alike favor actions over intentions.[65] Early hagiography shares in this tendency: its psychological dimensions are relatively flat. One picture is valued more than many words.[66]

---

[62] See Laurent Theis, "Saints sans famille? Quelques remarques sur la famille dans le monde franc à travers les sources hagiographiques," *Revue historique* 255 (1976): 12–13.

[63] De Gaiffier, "*Intactam sponsam*," pp. 182–183 n. 2.

[64] Cf. the example of Gumbert and Bertha discussed in this chapter in the section entitled "Consummated Marriages: The Transitional Model and the Clergy."

[65] See John F. Benton, "Consciousness of Self and Perceptions of Individuality," in *Renaissance and Renewal in the Twelfth Century*, ed. Robert L. Benson and Giles Constable (Cambridge, Mass., 1982), pp. 263–295; esp. 272, 284–285, 288.

[66] Cf. Heffernan, *Sacred Biography*, pp. 4–5. One might further speculate that admonitions for extended periods of continence in normal marital life had become very commonplace, thanks to penitential literature (see Pierre J. Payer, *Sex and the Penitentials: The Development of a Sexual Code, 550–1150* [Toronto, 1984], esp. pp. 23–28; idem, "Early Medieval Regulations concerning Marital Sexual Relations," *Journal of Medieval History* 6 [1980]: 364–370; Brundage, *Law, Sex, and Christian Society*, pp. 52–61). Penitents guilty of severe sins were ordered to abstain sexually from their spouses altogether, and this was often a question of years (see the "Penitential of Finian" c. 37 and 38, in John T. McNeill and Helena M. Gamer, trans., *Medieval Handbooks of Penance* [New York, 1979], pp. 94, 95]. Finian also recommends perpetual continence in the event of sterility (c. 41, p. 95; cf. the "Penitential of Cummean" c. 22 and 23, p. 104; the "Pentitential of Theodore" c. 4, p. 196; the "Penitential of Columban" c. 18, pp. 254–255). Moreover, the combination of liturgical and physiological limitations (intercourse was forbidden during menstruation, pregnancy, and lactation) might restrict a highly fertile, not to mention highly observant, couple's

But the emphasis on chastity should not eclipse the fact that these stories are primarily about marriage. Furthermore, because they are richly encoded with church kerygma to that effect, their didactic possibilities are immense. The virginal marriage realizes some of the most ambitious expectations that St. Paul placed upon the married. It complies with his injunction to have wives as if you had them not (1 Cor. 7.29), and reflects the brother-sister relationship that the apostles theoretically achieved with their wives (1 Cor. 9.5). The instigator also fulfills St. Paul's expectation that the unbelieving spouse would be sanctified by the believing (1 Cor. 7.14), without contravening the right to the conjugal debt. Women are more frequently presented as the instrument of the process of santification. In the case of Cecilia and Valerian this end was soon realized, first in baptism, then ultimately in martyrdom. But in the lives of confessor saints the development was often slower and more graphic. Guthland, the virginal spouse of Bertilia (d. ca. 687), was initially described in negative terms: lacking in both his wife's embraces and her religious convictions. Yet he made daily strides in sanctity and faith through the intervention of his wife's prayers and was eventually liberated from all carnal temptation. Their mutual sanctification expressed itself in a life of almsgiving and tending the sick.[67]

Most notably, virginal marriage demonstrates how the couple in question could become two in one flesh (Eph. 5.31–32) on the basis of consent to marry as opposed to the commingling of bodies, and this union is represented as indissoluble. These points were not so easily carried. The flip side of the Roman consensual theory of marriage was divorce by mutual consent, which, despite its inconsistencies with ecclesiastical imperatives, would continue to be permitted in the Byzantine Empire. Justinian also allowed unilateral repudiation in the event that either spouse wished to enter a monastery.[68] Anec-

---

sexual activity to as little as 21.5 times a year or 1.8 times a month. See especially Jean-Louis Flandrin, *Un temps pour embrasser: aux origines de la morale sexuelle occidentale (Ve–XIe siècle)* (Paris, 1983), pp. 41–71; also see James Brundage, " 'Better to Marry than to Burn?' The Case of the Vanishing Dichotomy," in *Views of Women's Lives in Western Tradition: Frontiers of the Past and the Future*, ed. F. R. Keller, Women's Studies, vol. 5 (Lewiston, Queenston, and Lampeter, 1990), pp. 195–216, esp. 200–201 and tables 1 and 2; cf. idem, *Law, Sex, and Christian Society*, pp. 59–60. Perhaps nonconsummation alone retained the power to impress.

[67] "Porro ipse memoratus juvenis desideratis seu religiosis ejus amplexibus tandem potitus, coepit quotidie in sanctitate, nec non religione Christi pedetentim succrescere: quod meritis seu precibus B. Bertiliae actum fore, remota omni titubatione verissime credendum est, videlicet ne ejus pudicitiae violator existeret" (AA SS, January, 1:156; cf. the seventh-century life of Sigolena of Albi, AA SS, July, 5:631–632).

[68] Brundage, *Law, Sex, and Christian Society*, pp. 114–117.

dotes celebrating the heroics of Eastern asceticism, which continued to circulate in the West after the Germanic invasions, give striking examples of unilateral repudiation and frequently depict the cessation of sexual activity as equivalent to the dissolution of the marriage bond.[69] The drama of female sexual renunciation in the Apocryphal Acts implied as much, and the behavior of Augustine's correspondent Ecdicia suggests that these attitudes were also current in the West. Various polemicists had frequently exacerbated the tendency to equate marriage and the conjugal act. The author of *On the Singleness of the Clergy* refers to spiritual marriage as "coniugalitas castrata" and suggests that the very love which the couple shared in marriage induces separation,[70] while Jerome had argued, on the basis of their chastity, that Mary and Joseph were not actually married. But both consensuality and indissolubility were further jeopardized by Teutonic influence, since coitus was essential to the Germanic definition of marriage and repudiation was the norm.[71]

Hagiographical depictions of spiritual marriage attempted to correct these errors. Sometimes the message is explicit. Hence, Gregory of Tours tells us that Riticius (Rheticius, d. 314), bishop of Autun, was joined to his virginal spouse by the embrace of spiritual love (*spiritualis dilectionis conhibentia*), not by lust.[72] Likewise, despite the un-

---

[69] This cavalier attitude toward the marriage bond is epitomized in the so-called sayings of the desert fathers (*Apophthegmata patrum*), which were probably collected by the end of the fifth century and circulated widely in both the East and the West. See Johannes Quasten, *Patrology* (Westminster, Md., 1960), 3:187–189, for discussion of and bibliography on this genre.

John Cassian gives the example of a young Egyptian named Theonas who, having heard Abbot John's counsels of perfection, returned home with the intention of converting his wife to chastity. When the wife remained unmoved by his arguments in favor of chastity, he left her to become a monk (*Conférences* 21.8–10, ed. E. Pichery, *SC*, no. 64 [Paris, 1959], 3:82–86). Cf. Palladius's account of a certain Innocent, a priest of the Mount of Olives, who abandoned his wife and son after his conversion (*Lausiac History* c. 44, trans. Meyer, *ACW*, no. 34, p. 120; ed. Butler, 2:131). There is a possibility that this was none other than Pope Innocent I (*ACW*, no. 34, p. 204 n. 392). Also see *Verba seniorum* 5.34 (the systematic collection translated by Pelagius and John, in *PL* 73, cols. 882–883) for other instances of unilateral repudiation. Monks were also frequently tormented by memories of their estranged wives. One individual combated his concupiscence by digging up the wife's rotting corpse and carrying a part of it around (5.22, cols. 878–879; cf. 5.40, col. 886).

[70] Ps.-Cyprian, *De singularitate clericorum* c. 32, *CSEL*, 3,3:208; "Ecce sancta dilectio quae coniugalibus ad communem laudem inducit absentiam" (p. 207).

[71] Brundage, *Law, Sex, and Christian Society*, pp. 134–137.

[72] "Transacta adulescentia, uxorem simili morum honestate praeclaram sortitus est, cum qua spiritalis dilectionis conhibentia, non luxoria copulatur" (Gregory of Tours, *Liber in gloria confessorum* c. 74, ed. Bruno Krusch, in *MGH, Scrip. Rer. Merov.*, vol. 1,2 [Hanover, 1885], p. 792).

conventional circumstances surrounding the marriage of Amator (d. 418), bishop of Auxerre, (the well-meaning but aged Bishop Valerian precipitated the couple's vow of chastity by reading the Levitican consecration of priests over the couple as opposed to the intended marriage blessing), his wife Martha's agreement to chastity is grounded in a vision of verbal consensus: " 'For already, most beloved brother, we depend on one judgment, and on that account I gladly embrace what things are pleasing to you, with God's favor.' "[73] Upon their agreement to remain chaste, Julian and Basilissa immediately "began to be fruitful in spirit, not in flesh."[74] Their "*proles*" took the form of ministering to the poor and the eventual foundation of monasteries.

But not trusting to words or even charitable acts alone, the hagiographer frequently looked to the physical world for the corroboration of spiritual truths. In the *vitae* of both SS. Cecilia and Amator, the virginal couples are miraculously crowned by twin wreaths. The Cecilia legend states explicitly that the flowers are roses and lilies—well-known symbols of virginity and martyrdom. The wreaths also evoke classical marital rites, which involve the double crowning of the bride and groom—a practice that still persists in the Eastern church.[75] Hence the wreaths function as symbols of both virginity and marriage—once again providing a dramatization of the consensual nature of the bond.[76]

On the other hand, the hagiographers of spiritual marriage also responded to a deep emotional craving that ran counter to the actual theology of marriage. The dissolution of the marriage bond with death was too harsh. If virginity was a vehicle for transcending the

[73] " 'Jam enim, dilectissime frater, ex uno dependemus arbitrio, et ideo quae tibi Deo favente sunt placita libenter amplector'" (*AA SS*, May, 1:54).

[74] "Coeperunt esse spiritu, non carne, fructificantes" (*AA SS*, January, 1:577).

[75] Mombrizio, *Sanctuarium*, 1:333–334; *AA SS*, May, 1:54. Also see the *passio* of Julian and Basilissa in which the nuptial chamber itself is redolent of lilies and roses and the discussion of this scent acts as a catalyst for their conversion (*AA SS*, January, 1:577). No crowns materialize, however. Cf. the Eastern legend of Theophanus the Chronographer (d. 817, *AA SS*, March, 2:216). For the ritual crowning of newlyweds, see Ritzer, *Le mariage dans les églises chrétiennes*, pp. 135–137, 206–209. Robinson discusses the significance of the crowns in the context of the "Second Nun's Tale" (see F. N. Robinson, ed., *The Works of Geoffrey Chaucer*, 2d ed. [Boston, 1957], p. 758 n. 220; also see pp. 821–822 n. 1735).

[76] There are frequent reminders in these tales that the marital bond is complete. Hence Cecilia tells her brother-in-law that God's love is the source of her marriage, and assumes the intimate footing with him that marriage would entitle her to, as is evident in her familiar kiss: "Sancta Cecilia osculata est pectus eius et dixit: hodie te uere mecum fateor esse cognatum. Sicut enim amor dei fratrem tuum coniugem fecit: ita te mihi cognatum contemptus faciet idolorum" (Mombrizio, *Sanctuarium*, 1:334).

temporal realm and experiencing something of eternity, it could likewise be used to purify and transform the marriage bond into something eternal. This view, all but a gentle murmur in Paulinus's correspondence, is represented with growing assurance in hagiographical discourse. Thus a contemporary *vita* reports that when Wandrille (d. 668), founder and abbot of Fontenelle, attempts to convert his wife to virginity on their wedding night (not yet aware that she has the same end in mind), he promises her that " 'those who are joined in one flesh here would be joined without end in the glory of the saints.' "[77] The combination of virginity and martyrdom doubled the potential for projecting marriage beyond the grave. Thus, the popular *passio* of Daria and Chrysanthus hints at timeless consummation: "They were made companions in blood in their passion, just as they had been husband and wife [*coniuges*] in mind; as if in one bed, so they remained in one pit."[78]

Although the emotional need to dress marriage in an eternal cloth is implicit in all of the *passiones* of virginal spouses, it is nevertheless most explicit in the *vitae* of the confessor saints. And this is fitting. The confessors' triumph over death grew incrementally and modestly out of day-to-day existence, and was not focused on the sharp glory of death itself. Often their death is as unspectacular as their life. Their virtue is modestly shrouded by secrecy. But the grave divulges their secret more marvelously and surely than the anomalous epitaph of Ampelius and Singenia. Their merits are not revealed by death but from somewhere beyond death.

Gregory of Tours is the unquestionable master of these graveside miracles. He tells us that the virginal spouse of Riticius tearfully implored her husband on her deathbed that they be placed in the same tomb so that " 'as the love of a single chastity preserved them in one bed, it would maintain them in the fellowship of one grave.' "[79] When Riticius died, it was impossible to move the funeral bier until one old-timer remembered Riticius's promise.[80] When they reached the

---

[77] " 'Qui hic in una carne coniuncti fuerant, in gloria sanctorum sine fine copularentur' " (*Vita Wandregiseli* c. 4 in *Passiones vitaeque sanctorum aevi Merovingici*, ed. B. Krusch and W. Levison, *MGH, Scrip. Rer. Merov.*, vol. 5 [Hanover and Leipzig, 1910], p. 15).

[78] "Facti sunt in passione sociati sanguine, sicut fuerant etiam mente coniuges; quasi in uno lectulo, ita in una fovea durantes" (*AA SS*, October, 11:483).

[79] " 'Ut quos unius castitatis dilectio uno conservavit in thoro unius reteneat sepulchri consortio' " (*Gloria confessorum* c. 74, *MGH, Scrip. Rer. Merov.*, 1,2:792).

[80] The immovable body of a saint is a common motif since, as Patrick J. Geary points out, saints were believed to have control over the disposition of their bodies even after their death (*Furta Sacra: Thefts of Relics in the Central Middle Ages*, rev. ed. [Princeton, N. J., 1990], pp. 111–112).

tomb, Riticius was miraculously restored to life, but only long enough to reveal their purity: " 'Remember, sweetest spouse, what you had solicited from me. Now accept your long-awaited brother, to join with unpolluted limbs those which lust did not pollute but true chastity cleansed.' " And her virgin bones moved to one side.[81]

Gregory's portrayal of the chaste union of Injuriosus and Scholastica evokes the same motif but is even more lovingly painted. Scholastica converted her husband to ascetic chastity on their wedding night. The wife was the first to die, and the touching events surrounding her interment deserve to be cited in full:

> After he had performed all her funeral rites and had placed her in the tomb, her husband said: "I thank you, Lord Jesus Christ, Master, and eternal God, for granting that I may hand back to Your loving care this treasure as unsullied as when I received her from Your hands." As he spoke, she smiled up at him. "Why do you say that," she said, "when no one asked you to?" Not long after she was buried her husband followed her. Although their two tombs were placed by different walls, a new miracle occurred which proved their chastity. When morning dawned and the people came to visit the place, they found the two tombs side by side, although they had left them far apart. This shows that when heaven unites two people the monument which covers their buried corpses cannot hold them apart. Down to our own times the inhabitants of the place have chosen to call them "the Two Lovers."[82]

---

[81] " 'Recordare, dulcissima coniux, quae nobis fueras deprecata. Nunc suscipe expectatum diu fratrem et coniungere artubus inpollutis, quos non luxoria polluit, sed castitas vera mundavit' " (*Gloria confessorum* c. 74, *MGH, Scrip. Rer. Merov.*, 1,2:792). Cf. the tenth- or eleventh-century *vita* of Bishop Severus of Ravenna (d. ca. 390), whose wife predeceased both him and his virginal daughter. When he went to bury his daughter, he rather querulously ordered his wife's bones to move (" 'O mulier, cur mihi molesta es?' "), and her bones shifted obediently to one side to make room for the daughter (*AA SS*, February, 1:85). He was later buried between the two women. His allegedly sharp tone was probably owing to her nagging prior to his elevation to the bishopric and her initial disbelief when she heard the reports of his elevation (p. 83).

[82] "Peracto vir funeris officio cum puellam in sepulchro deponeret, ait: 'Gratias tibi ago, domine Iesu Christe, aeternae domine deus noster, quia hunc thesaurum, sicut a te commendatum accepi, ita immaculatum pietati tuae restituo.' Ad haec illa subridens: 'Quid,' inquid, 'loqueris quod non interrogaris?' Illamque sepultam ipse non post multum insequitur. Porro cum utriusque sepulchrum e diversis parietibus collocatum fuisset, miraculi novitas, quae eorum castitatem manifestaret, apparuit. Nam facto mane cum ad locum populi accederent, invenerunt sepulchra pariter, quae longe inter se distare reliquerant, scilicet ut, quos tenet socios caelum, sepultorum hic corporum non separet monumentum. Hos usque hodie Duos Amantes vocitare loci incolae volurunt" (Gregory of Tours, *Libri Historiarum X* 1.47, ed. Krusch and Levison, *MGH, Scrip. Rer. Merov.*, vol. 1, pt. 1, rev. ed. [Hanover, 1951; reprt., 1965], p. 31; idem., *The History of the Franks*, trans. Lewis Thorpe [Harmondsworth, Middlesex, 1974; reprt.

The tender and humorous miracle at the graveside, the fact that the husband died soon after the wife, and the miraculous movement of the graves proclaim that the strength of their union endured into the next world. Finally, the name given them by the populace is a ready acknowledgment of this.

The "Two Lovers" slept in the same bed, hand in hand, maintaining "laudable chastity."[83] Their exceptional purity was rewarded by uninterrupted intimacy. Only once does Gregory extend a similar favor to a nonvirginal couple: a couple who had made the seasonal transition to ascetic chastity, after a perfunctory period of childbearing. The husband was the first to die and the wife followed him within a year. When she was placed in the tomb, the husband's arm went around her neck in an eternal embrace. And the wondering populace realized "what chastity is for them, what fear in God, and also what love there was between them in the world, who embrace each other in the tomb."[84] The less dazzling, but more accessible, instance of conjugal chastity brings the promise of unending union closer to the average Christian.

This triumphal and antitheological aspect of spiritual marriage is peculiarly Western and affords no correlative in the Eastern church. As Peter Brown has demonstrated for the West, the saint's tomb was the place where heaven and earth met and the place where proof of his or her sanctity was manifested. For the East, the locus of sanctity was the living saint.[85] Their lives were hidden sources of God's grace and their death was open-ended. Eastern instances of virginal marriages were thus evidence of God's manifold grace in unlikely recipients— the married. They were revealed by God to his chosen ascetics, as

---

1982], p. 97). Gregory also tells their story in *Gloria confessorum* c. 31 (*MGH, Scrip. Rer. Merov.*, 1,2:767), only he adds that the two had separated to become religious after many years of secret chastity. Cf. Flodoard's account of Gumbert and Bertha (d. late seventh century), in which the dead Bertha appears to her late husband's nephew to ask that her husband's body be moved to her grave (*Historia Remensis ecclesiae* 4.47, ed. J. Heller and G. Waitz, *MGH, Scrip.*, vol. 13 [Hanover, 1881], p. 596). It is unclear whether this was a virginal marriage, although later authors claim that it was.

[83] "Et datis inter se dextris, quieverunt, multos postea in uno strato recumbentes annos, sed cum castitate laudabili" (Gregory of Tours, *Libri Historiarum X* 1.47, *MGH, Scrip. Rer. Merov.*, 1, 1:31).

[84] "Cognovitque, quae eis castitas, quae timor in Deum, quae etiam inter ipsos dilectio fuisset in saeculo, qui se ita amplexi sunt in sepulchro" (*Gloria confessorum* c. 41, *MGH, Scrip. Rer. Merov.*, 1,2:774). This story was told of Hilary of Dijon.

[85] See Peter Brown, *The Cult of the Saints*, esp. pp. 9–11, 75–85; idem, "The Holy Man in Late Antiquity," in *Society and the Holy in Late Antiquity* (Berkeley and Los Angeles, 1982), pp. 139–140, 151–152; "Eastern and Western Christendom in Late Antiquity: A Parting of the Ways," ibid., pp. 180–186, 190–192, 225–227.

much to keep them humble as to edify them. Thus when two desert fathers questioned God as to their spiritual progress, he answered that they trailed behind the Egyptian shepherd Eucharistos and his wife Mary. The fathers found and questioned the shepherd, who answered their questions with great reluctance.

"Behold, we got these sheep from our parents, and whatever God would give to me from them, we make that into three parts: a part for the poor, a part for receiving pilgrims, and a third part for our own use. Moreover, from the time that I took my wife, I have not been polluted, nor has she, but she is a virgin. We each sleep apart, and at night we wear sackcloth, but in the day, our clothes. Nobody knew these things up until now."[86]

So different a perspective availed no "grave" disclosures.

In the hands of Western hagiographers, virginal marriage became the vehicle of complex theological doctrine, while expressing a less orthodox, perhaps popular belief, which projected the marriage bond beyond the grave. This motif virtually dominated hagiographical depictions of marriage until the eleventh century. Nor should it surprise us that such unions, shorn of concupiscence, are among the most positive portrayals of marital unity and concord over the entire course of the Middle Ages. While a more holistic idealization of heterosexual love will have to await the rise of vernacular literature, here we find the belief in a profound intimacy and companionship between the sexes that is in no way contingent on sexual intercourse.[87]

---

[86] " 'Ecce istas oves habemus a parentibus nostris, et quidquid ex eis donaverit mihi Deus', facimus illud tres partes: partem unam pauperibus, et unam partem in susceptione peregrinorum, et tertiam partem ad usum nostrum. Ex quo autem accepi uxorem, neque ego pollutus sum, neque illa, sed virgo est, singuli autem remoti a nobis dormimus; et noctu quidem induimus saccos, in die vero vestimenta nostra. Et usque nunc nemo hominum haec cognovit' " (Verba seniorum 3.2 [the systematic collection], translated from the Greek by Pelagius and John, PL 73, col. 1006). The mimes Theophilus and Marie likewise enlightened chosen ascetics by the revelation of their chastity, but each revelation was underlined by weighty injunctions for secrecy (John of Ephesus, Lives of the Eastern Saints c. 52, esp. pp. 165–166, 170, 174, 176–177, 178). Cf. John Cassian's story of a virtuous rustic who, having been forced into marriage, preserved his chastity with his wife for twelve years (Conférences c. 7, SC, no. 54, 2:187–189). This story, attributed to Abbot John, was intended to evoke admiration, not emulation. This distinction will be discussed at greater length in chapters 4 and 5.

[87] A step is, however, taken in eleventh-century Ottonian Saxony toward validating the conjugal act through proles. See Vita Mahthildis reginae c. 5–6, ed. G. H. Pertz, MGH, Scrip., vol. 4 (Hanover, 1841), pp. 286–287 and Corbet, Les Saints Ottoniens, pp. 184–207, esp. 187–188. These attempts foundered due to the rising ascetical climate, which will be discussed in chapter 3.

Virginal Marriage and Historical Narrative: The Negation of the Spiritual Bond

Chroniclers also enshrined a different form of spiritual marriage in which the protagonist, invariably female, fails to convert her husband to chastity but refuses to consummate her marriage, much to his chagrin. Moreover, from the chroniclers, this motif worked its way back into hagiographical discourse. Heretical circles aside, there are early notices of such behavior in Eastern Christianity. St. Magna (d. after 420) lived in a community of two thousand consecrated virgins, but Palladius remarked on her unusual status: "I do not know what to call her, whether virgin or widow, for she was forcibly married to a man by her mother, but she deceived him and kept putting him off, as many say, so that she remained intact."[88] St. Olympias, Chrysostom's friend and patron, was another such figure.[89] These women had little to wish for from marriage except the death of their spouses—a situation hardly conducive to marital *caritas*.

Even so, such a motif had a great future in the West where the anomalous virgin-widow becomes something of a stock figure. It was particularly popular in the Anglo-Saxon kingdoms. Bede's well-known example of Queen Æthelthryth (d. 679) demonstrates a successful policy of sexual evasion through the course of not one, but two marriages. The first husband died about three years after the marriage, but it was only after twelve years of chaste cohabitation with her second husband, Egfrid of Northumbria, that the king reluctantly permitted her to enter a monastery.[90] Later hagiographical versions of her life depict Egfrid as regretting his decision, incorporating dramatic chase scenes in which the very tides act as a safeguard to her chastity.[91]

---

[88] Palladius, *Lausiac History* 67.1, trans. Meyer, *ACW*, no. 34, p. 148; ed. Butler, 2:163.

[89] Both Palladius and the anonymous life, written in the fifth century, report that though she was the bride of Nebridius, prefect of Constantinople, the marriage lasted less than a year and was never consummated. She heroically withstood efforts to remarry her, theoretically using the same argument as did Melania with regard to her children: namely, that if God had intended her to remarry, he would not have called her first husband so soon (Clark, trans., "Life of Olympias" c. 2–3, in *Jerome, Chrysostom, and Friends*, pp. 128–129; also see Palladius, *Lausiac History* 56.1, trans. Meyer, *ACW*, no. 34, p. 137; ed. Butler, 2:149–150; and the *Dialogue of Palladius Concerning the Life of Chrysostom* c. 61, trans. Herbert Moore [London and New York, 1921], pp. 150–151; critical edition *Paladii dialogus de vita S. Joannis Chrysostomi*, ed. P. R. Coleman-Norton [Cambridge, 1928], pp. 110–111).

[90] Bede, *Ecclesiastical History of the English People* 4.19, ed. and trans. Bertram Colgrave and R.A.B. Mynors [Oxford, 1969], pp. 390–397.

[91] See the *Acta prolixiora*, written in the mid-twelfth century by Thomas, a monk at Ely (*AA SS*, June, 5:431).

Bede is adamant about the truth of his story, having heard it directly from Wilfrid, bishop of York and Æthelthryth's spiritual adviser.[92] Bede also draws attention to the fact that her body withstood the grave's ravages as proof of her virginity. Similar stories are told of other Anglo-Saxon queens, but the traditions are considerably more muddled and often much later. Cyneswitha and Cyneburga, purportedly daughters of the seventh-century king Penda of Mercia, were alleged to have kept their virginity through their respective royal marriages—at least according to some accounts.[93] They eventually retired to Cyneburga's religious foundation at Castor. A contemporary notice implies that Cuthburga, queen of Northumbria and eventual abbess of Wimborne (d. ca. 725), also kept her royal husband at arm's length—although later embellishments erroneously credit his conversion to chastity and entrance into monasticism to her.[94] The

[92] Bede's account is also corroborated by the contemporary *The Life of Bishop Wilfrid* by Eddius Stephanus (ed. and trans. Bertram Colgrave [Cambridge, 1927; reprt. 1985], c. 19, p. 40).

[93] In 963, Cyneburga and Cyneswitha's relics (along with those of their kinswoman Tibba) were translated at Peterborough. There is considerable confusion surrounding their marriages, much of which was fostered by William of Malmesbury. While Bede mentions Cyneburga's marriage to Alfrid, son of King Oswy of Northumbria (*Ecclesiastical History* 3.21, pp. 278–279), Malmesbury claims that Cyneburga hated sex and took the veil. Yet elsewhere he alleges that she remained a virgin. (In a possibly spurious donation of 680, however, her brother Æthelred refers to her as one who preserved her virginity [*AA SS*, March, 1:444, 441]). According to Goscelin of Canterbury's *vita* of St. Mildrith, Cyneswitha was married to Offa, probably king of the East Saxons (though Goscelin says West Saxons) and kept her virginity through the assistance of the Virgin Mary (D. W. Rollason, ed., "Vita Deo dilectatae virginis Mildrethae," in *The Mildrith Legend: A Study in Early Medieval Hagiography in England* [Leicester, 1982], appendix C, p. 115; see p. 162 n. 25). Bede tells us that Offa eventually abdicated (709) and died in Rome as a monk (*Ecclesiastical History* 5.19, pp. 516–517). But if this same Offa was Cyneswitha's husband, she would have been fifty-four or fifty-five at the time of her marriage (*AA SS*, March, 1:444).

[94] The Bollandists are skeptical about Cuthburga's virginity, but the tradition is old: it is mentioned in an early version of the Usuard martyrology. There is some doubt as to whom she married: Aldfrid, king of Northumbria (d. 705), seems the most likely candidate, but other sources call her husband Egfrid or Osred (who was Aldfrid's son— she might have been his mother! see *AA SS*, August, 6:696–698). The Bollandists give Capgrave's life, which claims that she converted her husband to virginity and that he eventually entered a religious community as well. The editor, however, thinks that this is inaccurate (p. 698, see note e). Also see the fourteenth-century life of Cuthburga, in which she convinces her husband to permit her to remain a virgin and soon after enters a religious foundation. No mention, however, is made of his conversion. This life has been edited and translated by J.M.J. Fletcher, who posits that John of Tynemouth (d. 1366) was the probable author ("The Marriage of St. Cuthburga, Who Was Afterwards Foundress of the Monastery at Wimborne," *Proceedings of the Dorset Natural History and Antiquarian Field Club* 34 [1913]: 167–185. See esp. pp. 172–179 for the wedding night-conversion debate).

same pattern is repeated by St. Osyth (d. ca. 700), this time purportedly a granddaughter of King Penda, whose *vita* (though possibly representing the murkiest tradition yet) has the advantage of giving details as to how she escaped marriage intact.[95] When her husband, Sigerius, king of the East Saxons, finally grew impatient of her many evasions and excuses and was prepared to take her by force, divine intervention saved her. A messenger burst into the royal bedroom to announce the discovery of a marvelous white stag. The king went off hunting and the queen availed herself of the chance to be consecrated as a virgin by two East Anglian bishops. When Sigerius returned, he was confronted with a fait accompli. He released Osyth, who went off to establish a monastic foundation at Chich.[96]

The Continent affords some later and darker analogues. The nobly born Phairaildis (d. ca. 745), purportedly the daughter of Theodoric (duke of Lotharingia) and his saintly wife Amalberga,[97] was beaten daily by her frustrated husband and she eventually prayed to Christ that her husband be visited with a divine illness.[98] He was soon wounded nearly fatally in a hunting accident. The motif takes a still more chilling turn in the case of the empress Richardis (d. ca. 895), wife of Charles the Fat. For the year 887, Regino of Prüm's contemporary *Chronicon* reports that the empress was accused of adultery with Liudward, bishop of Vercelli, who served as her husband's chancellor.[99] Richardis denied the charges and surprised the assembly by

---

[95] As Christopher Hohler has definitively shown, much of the confusion surrounding St. Osyth results from the conflation of two different saints: one from Essex and one from Aylesbury in Buckinghamshire ("St. Osyth and Aylesbury," *Records of Buckinghamshire* 18 [1966]: 61–72, esp. 62–63, 67–68). None of her extant lives can be dated prior to the late eleventh or early twelfth century. The virginal marriage is intrinsic to all the versions of the legend, however. See Denis Bethell, "The Lives of St. Osyth of Essex and St. Osyth of Aylesbury," *AB* 88 (1970): 75–127, for the dating and comparison of four twelfth-century manuscripts; esp. pp. 86–87. Also see Susan J. Ridyard, *Royal Saints of Anglo-Saxon England: A Study of West Saxon and East Anglian Cults* (Cambridge, 1988), pp. 134–135.

[96] See the early twelfth-century life from Bury St. Edmunds, edited by Bethell, "The Lives of St. Osyth," appendix 1, pp. 112–113; cf. *AA SS*, October, 3:942. The latter is Capgrave's fifteenth-century account, based on the lost *Sanctilogium* of John of Tynemouth, which is, in turn, based on a twelfth-century source. Also see A. T. Baker, ed., "An Anglo-French Life of St. Osith," *Modern Language Review* 6 (1911): 487–491, lines 380–726.

[97] There are problems with this attribution, as Lotharingia did not exist as a territory until the division of Charlemagne's empire by his grandsons in 843.

[98] "'Christi Dei fili, quaeso, ne sim tibi vili, / Pro prece servili, moveare Dei pie fili: / Quae prece devota tibi fundo, suscipe vota. / Hunc morbo vel peste grava, qui verbera prava / Dat mihi, meque ferit, feriens me perdere quaerit'" (*AA SS*, January, 1:171). This life is derived from a tenth-century Flemish manuscript.

[99] Regino, *Chronicon* 887, ed. G. H. Pertz, *MGH, Scrip.*, vol. 1 (Hanover, 1876), p.

maintaining that, although married more than ten years, she was still a virgin, and she offered to demonstrate her virginity through an ordeal. It would seem that this severe proof was not exacted and that Richardis was permitted to retire from court and enter her monastic foundation at Andlau. Posterity was reluctant to let so dramatic an opportunity slip by and assigned her a grisly ordeal in which she was wrapped in a large cloth, doused with flammable liquid, and set alight at its four corners. The empress emerged unscathed.[100]

While still presented as emblems of female merit, these stories represent the antithesis of the spiritual model described above. They delineate an explicit denial of Pauline and Augustinian theology— undermining the mutuality of the debt, depicting the failure of the believing spouse to sanctify the unbelieving, and undercutting the spiritual bond between the couple by calling into question the validity of a marriage devoid of consummation. Far from symbolizing the unity and concord of the couple in question, these marriages show husband and wife as implacable stumbling blocks to the other's salvation.

The question arises as to why a model so hostile to biblical and patristic teaching was tolerated. And here we see the other face of the virginal marriage topos: the relative instability of marriage in this period enabled chroniclers, jurists, and statespersons to manipulate spiritual marriage in a freer and more plastic way to achieve other ends. While consensuality and indissolubility were never entirely forgotten, they were only successfully upheld in the twelfth century. In the sixth and seventh centuries particularly, the church had very little control over marriage and seemed content with a laissez-faire policy.[101] Divorce by mutual consent and even unilateral repudiation

---

597. For similar charges of adultery used against unwanted wives in this period, see Siegmund Hellmann, "Die Heiraten der Karolinger," in *Ausgewählte Abhandlungen zur Historiographie und Geistesgeschichte des Mittelalters* (Weimar, 1961), pp. 348–352. Liutward was not chosen arbitrarily: Charles was being pressured by the magnates to get rid of his chancellor (see Karl Brunner, *Oppositionelle Gruppen im Karolingerreich* [Vienna, Cologne, and Graz, 1979], pp. 155–156).

100 According to the Bollandists, the details for the ordeal are a later tradition that emerges in the *Annales Mettenses apud Chesnium*. No official *vita* was produced for Richardis, only an *oratio* for her feast day (the Bollandists cite a fifteenth-century breviary). But the cult is old and certainly well-established by the eleventh century, as Leo IX formally translated her relics in 1049 (see *AA SS*, September, 5:793–794, 796–797; also Ernst Dümmler, *Geschichte des ostfränkischen Reiches* [Leipzig, 1888; reprt. Hildesheim, 1960], 3:283–285). For the use of ordeals in clearing the reputations of queens, see Robert Bartlett, *Trial by Fire and Water: The Medieval Judicial Ordeal* (Oxford, 1986), pp. 13–19, esp. 16–17.

101 See Jo Ann McNamara and Suzanne F. Wemple, "Marriage and Divorce in the

seem to have been tolerated. Rules governing the entrance into religion were likewise relaxed. In 601 Gregory the Great had written vehemently against certain "heretics" who proclaimed that religious conversion dissolved a marriage. He also argued that since the two were of one flesh, it was impossible that one part should go over to continence and the other remain in pollution. Thus, a conversion to monasticism must be mutual and simultaneous.[102] The fact is, however, that such separations became common practice. The Frankish Council of Compiègne (757) even explicitly permitted the party who remained in the world to remarry.[103]

Little was done to supervise the actual formation of the bond. Occasional church interventions in matrimonial matters were limited to established unions that conformed to local customs.[104] It was only in the latter part of the eighth century that the church became more actively involved in efforts to regulate marriage, but it did not actually begin to assert jurisdiction until the tenth or eleventh century.[105] On the other hand, when Archbishop Hincmar of Rheims (d. 882) made an effort to articulate what constituted a valid marriage, consummation was included as an essential component.[106] So a "thinning-out" of the Roman-patristic vision of consensus obtained in both clerical and lay circles.

The insecurity of marriage in the early Germanic kingdoms explains the popularity of the virgin-widow motif in Anglo-Saxon En-

---

Frankish Kingdom," in *Women in Medieval Society*, ed. Susan Mosher Stuard (Philadelphia, 1976), pp. 95–124, esp. 100–101. The Anglo-Saxon clergy, on the other hand, were perhaps more active in denouncing the morality of local kings but had little impact until the late Anglo-Saxon period (see Margaret Ross, "Concubinage in Anglo-Saxon England," *Past and Present* 108 [1985]: 24–29; Pauline Stafford, "The King's Wife in Wessex," *Past and Present* 91 [1981]: 7–10, 13–14).

[102] Reg. 11, 27, "To Theoctista," *Registrum epistolarum, CCSL,* 140a:908–909. This decretal was used by both Gratian (C.27 q.2 c.19) and Peter Lombard (*Sent.* 4.27.7.1). Cf. Reg. 6, 49, "To Urbicus" (*CCSL,* 140:422), also cited by Gratian (C.27 q.2 c.21), and Reg. 11, 30, "To Adrian" (*CCSL,* 140a:918–920; Gratian, C.27 q.2 c.26; Peter Lombard, *Sent.* 4.27.7.2).

[103] McNamara and Wemple, "Marriage and Divorce," p. 103; Gérard Fransen, "La rupture du mariage," in *Il matrimonio nella società altomedievale,* 22–28 aprile 1976, Settimane di Studio del Centro italiano di studi sull'alto medioevo, 24 (Spoleto, 1977), 2:627.

[104] Fransen, "La rupture," pp. 606–609; Ritzer notes the absence of any legislation on the formation of the bond before 755 (*Le mariage dans les églises chrétiennes,* p. 286).

[105] Brundage, *Law, Sex, and Christian Society,* p. 137; Fransen, "La rupture," p. 609.

[106] Brundage, *Law, Sex, and Christian Society,* pp. 136–137; Suzanne F. Wemple, *Women in Frankish Society: Marriage and the Cloister, 500 to 900* (Philadelphia, 1985), pp. 83–84.

gland. All of these legends were purportedly set in the seventh or early eighth centuries when Christianity was still in early days. Early Anglo-Saxon customary law permitted unilateral repudiation to either party.[107] Frankish marriage practices, on the other hand, were more prejudicial to women than their Anglo-Saxon counterparts, as the example of the long-suffering Phairaildis might suggest. Repudiation was a male prerogative—hence the infrequency of the motif on the Continent.[108] Clearly for the hagiographers, be they contemporaries or those who modeled their narrative on what they believed to be contemporary practice, the prospect of one spouse retiring to a monastery while the other remained in the world—and even remarried—presented no problem. Perhaps the virgin bride was perceived as not quite a wife; thus the flawed union was easily overlooked. Whatever the rationale, the clergy's apparent flexibility in these cases bears the unmistakable impression of secular mores. But who stood to gain by this flexibility—the husband, the wife, or the clergy?

If we accept these narratives at face value, the women and the clergy were the obvious beneficiaries. The women purportedly implicated in these virginal marriages were not only queens but great patrons of the church. Certain members of the clergy might support female endeavors to resist consummation, if this resulted in the women's loyalty.[109] Stoical resistance was easily sculpted into a model of female heroism. From the standpoint of self-interest, the lack of heirs was undoubtedly advantageous to the church. Æthelthryth gave Wilfrid an estate at Hexham, where he founded a church, and she later went on to found her own monastery at Ely. Moreover, her second husband, Egfrid, clearly believed that Bishop Wilfrid was the driving force behind Æthelthryth's resolve to retain her virginity, since he promised the cleric estates and money if he

---

[107] This seems to be true for the earliest code, that of Æthelbert of Kent (601–604). See c. 79–80, in *The Laws of the Earliest English Kings*, ed. and trans. F. L. Attenborough (New York, 1963), p. 14. Also see Ross, "Concubinage in Anglo-Saxon England," pp. 11–13; cf. Rebecca Colman, "Abduction of Women in Barbaric Law," *Florilegium* 5 (1983): 62–75; Anne L. Klinck, "Anglo-Saxon Women and the Law," *Journal of Medieval History* 8 (1982): 110.

[108] Although Clovis's mother allegedly repudiated her husband in favor of a more advantageous union, generally repudiation was the privilege of men alone (Wemple, *Women in Frankish Society*, p. 42). This explains the bishop of Noyon's trepidation about consecrating Radegund, wife of Chlotar I.

[109] Jane Tibbetts Schulenburg's analysis of the varying ratios of female saints over the centuries also indicates that women generally fared best in the Germanic kingdoms in the seventh and eighth centuries ("Sexism and the Celestial Gynaeceum—from 500 to 1200," *Journal of Medieval History* 4 [1978]: 117–133, esp. 121–122, 128).

would convince her to consummate the union.[110] The Anglo-Saxon female saints of royal birth generally operated as an essential link between church and state, both before and after their retirement to the cloister.[111] In fact, Susan Ridyard has demonstrated that virtually all the cults of Anglo-Saxon royal women, including the ones described above, were promoted by the monastic foundations that these women favored, either in life with their endowments or in death with their relics.[112] The cults of kings were, on the other hand, generated in secular circles for political ends. In contrast to the male model of the martyr-king who earned his sanctity through death in defense of the faith, the profile for female sanctity in Anglo-Saxon England required the rejection of royal prerogative during a woman's lifetime. Virginity and retreat from the world were central to the construct.[113] The general eclipse of the virgin consort motif coincides with Christianity's entrenchment in England and a concomitant waning of queenly influence, dating from the mid-eighth century.[114] But this trend is also concurrent with the familiar paradox of improvement in the condition of the average woman, which probably had the effect of making the flight to the cloister less central.[115]

But if we adopt the more skeptical view that the women in question were sterile, as some scholars have suggested, the dissolubility of these virginal marriages ultimately benefits the husband.[116] Richardis's trial is the most compelling example. As in the Anglo-Saxon model, Richardis is a queen and a great patron of the church. Furthermore, as Pauline Stafford has pointed out, the fact that a cleric was named as her codefendant, a charge that would recur in parallel situations of inconvenient royal wives, indicates the ongoing coalition between royal

---

[110] Eddius, *The Life of Bishop Wilfrid* c. 22, p. 44; Bede, *Ecclesiastical History* 14.19, pp. 392–393.

[111] See Joan Nicholson, "*Feminae gloriosae*: Women in the Age of Bede," in *Medieval Women*, ed. Derek Baker, Studies in Church History, Subsidia, 1 (Oxford, 1978), pp. 15–29.

[112] Ridyard, *Royal Saints*, pp. 248–249.

[113] Ibid., pp. 82–83, 235–247.

[114] See Stafford, "The King's Wife in Wessex," pp. 3–7.

[115] Klinck traces the process of amelioration over the Anglo-Saxon period, arguing against the common perception that Anglo-Saxon women consistently enjoyed a higher status than was true after the Norman Conquest ("Anglo-Saxon Women and the Law," pp. 107–121).

[116] Pauline Stafford, for example, assumes that Æthelthryth—a veteran of two childless marriages—was sterile (*Queens, Concubines, and Dowagers: The King's Wife in the Early Middle Ages* [Athens, Ga., 1983], pp. 74, 81). It should be noted that Æthelthryth was much older than her second husband (see Eddius, *The Life of Bishop Wilfrid*, p. 165, note for c. 19).

women and the clergy.[117] And yet, in an incident set later than its Anglo-Saxon counterparts—at a time when Christianity was relatively entrenched and the Carolingian reformers had turned their attention to upholding the indissolubility of marriage[118]—Charles charged his wife with adultery, intending to repudiate her. There was an important precedent in the not too distant past for what was probably a trumped-up charge. In 858, Lothar II, ruler of Lotharingia, accused Theutberga, his childless wife of two years, of incest and adultery, hoping to marry his concubine. The combined efforts of Hincmar of Rheims and the papacy defeated Lothar's attempt.[119]

This celebrated defeat was only the most jarring incident in a series of church interventions, which gradually reacquainted the Frankish empire with a more exacting standard of marriage. Once again, this standard was hardly new, but it had slumbered fitfully until the reign of Louis the Pious. Adultery was ceasing to be considered legitimate grounds for the dissolution of a marriage.[120] Likewise, monasticism was no longer as effectual a tool for resolving matrimonial differences: it was firmly reasserted that if one spouse withdrew to a monastery, the other could not remain in the world—much less remarry.[121] On the other hand, the less exacting standard, though gradually falling into disgrace, had not been forgotten. The canonical

---

[117] Stafford, *Queens, Concubines, and Dowagers*, p. 96; eadem, "The King's Wife in Wessex," p. 13. Also see Bartlett, *Trial by Fire and Water*, p. 17. Cf. the situation of Hadeloga, allegedly the daughter of Charles Martel (d. 741), who was supported by the ruler's chaplain in her efforts to resist marriage. Charles accused them of fornication and threw them out of court. Fortunately, the chaplain was wealthy because of the many offerings he had received. They "eloped" and cofounded a monastery in Franconia (*AA SS*, February, 2:309–310).

[118] Wemple, *Women in Frankish Society*, pp. 76–88.

[119] Hincmar's efforts to come to terms with the innumerable complications of this case take the form of a treatise *De divortio Lotharii et Tetbergae, PL* 125, cols. 623–772. For a detailed discussion of Lothar's divorce and its wider significance, see Jane Bishop, "Bishops as Marital Advisors in the Ninth Century," in *Women of the Medieval World: Essays in Honor of John Mundy*, ed. Julius Kirshner and Suzanne F. Wemple (Oxford, 1985), pp. 53–84; also see Wemple, *Women in Frankish Society*, pp. 84–87.

[120] Efforts to eliminate adultery as grounds for a divorce and remarriage date from the late eighth century. On the other hand, this trend was not absolute. Pope Eugenius II had permitted the innocent party in an adultery case to remarry in 826, and this had been incorporated into a capitulary by Lothar I. The penitentials (still circulating in this period despite Carolingian efforts to suppress them) permitted divorce and remarriage. As late as 1031, the Council of Bourges confirmed the practice (Brundage, *Law, Sex, and Christian Society*, pp. 84, 164, 201; McNamara and Wemple, "Marriage and Divorce," pp. 108–111; Wemple, *Women in Frankish Society*, p. 85; Fransen, "La rupture," p. 624).

[121] Bishop, "Bishops as Marital Advisors," pp. 77–79.

collection of Regino of Prüm (not only important in its own right but of special interest in that it was Regino who provided us with the contemporary account of Richardis's trial) disallows remarriage in the case of adultery but cites conflicting canons concerning the right to remarry if one party enters a monastery.[122]

If the gradual stabilization of marriage was beneficial to a majority of women, it carried disadvantages, perhaps lethal ones, for a minority. Indissolubility made the men of a progressively lineage-conscious nobility desperate. Hincmar himself is acutely aware of the incumbent dangers for women. He claims that certain savage men "kill their earlier wives out of a suspicion of adultery: this they do by no law, reason, or trial, but out of their own animosity and cruelty alone or out of grasping lust for another wife or concubine."[123] The tenth and eleventh centuries would see a rise in the number of female saints who were murdered by their husbands—all of them martyrs to the rule of indissolubility.[124] Richardis's dilemma is a muted prefiguration of this gloomy type.

Richardis's trial is probably best understood in terms of her husband's persistent anxiety over the succession—an anxiety that was undoubtedly compounded by the morbid working of his increasingly infirm brain. According to Hincmar, Charles married Richardis around 862.[125] After over ten years, it became clear that there were no children forthcoming. In 873, during the course of a violent epileptic attack, Charles expressed a desire to retire from the world and to

---

[122] For canons condemning remarriage on the grounds of adultery see *De ecclesiasticis disciplinis et religione Christiana* 2.101, 103, *PL* 132, cols. 303–304. Of the canons that permit remarriage on the entrance of one party into religion, one is from the Council of Compiègne (2.107–108, col. 305); those against remarriage are largely from Nicholas I's intervention in Lothar's divorce (2.109, 113, cols. 305–306; cf. c. 110).

[123] This outburst, however, is but a part of Hincmar's larger complaint against those savage ("immites") men (". . . ut prioribus uxoribus ex suspicione adulterii, nulla lege, nulla ratione, nullo judicio, sed sola sua animositate et crudelitate, vel libidine ad aliam uxorem vel concubinam tendente, occissis" [*De divortio Lotharii et Tetbergae*, *PL* 125, col. 658]) who refuse to do penance before approaching the altar.

[124] See Georges Duby's account of St. Godelive (*The Knight, the Lady, and the Priest*, pp. 130–135). Cf. the predicament of St. Geneviève of Brabant, whose husband also attempted to kill her (Agnes B. C. Dunbar, *A Dictionary of Saintly Women* [London, 1904], 1:336–338). St. Gangulf was martyred by his wife and her lover and was supposedly invoked by unhappily married men (see *AA SS*, May, 2:645–646; Marc Glasser, "Marriage in Medieval Hagiography," *Studies in Medieval and Renaissance History*, n.s. 4 [1981]: 18 n. 35). The martyrdom of the husband was not a common motif.

[125] See *Annales Bertiniani* 862 (ed. G. Waitz, *MGH, Scrip. Rer. Germ. in usum scholarium*, vol. 5 [Hanover, 1883], pp. 59–60).

abstain sexually from his wife.[126] While hardly a solution to his problems, this episode at least bears witness to Charles's frustration. In 885, Charles convened a council in order to legitimize his bastard son, Bernard. His efforts failed.[127] But Richardis's trial of 887 would seem to indicate that Charles, although mentally and physically ill, was by no means reconciled to his heirless plight.[128]

In attempting to obtain a divorce for adultery, Charles was swimming against the tide—even if his wife were to enter a monastery. What undoubtedly ensured that he achieved his ends was Richardis's claim of virginity. Hincmar's pronouncement that consummation was essential to a valid marriage not only went unchallenged at the time (ca. 860) but had a fresh ring to it. This consideration raises a number of intriguing questions as to where the plea of nonconsummation originated. Regino claims that at the time Richardis revealed her virginity, the couple had been married for more than ten years. A later source specifies twelve.[129] But if the marriage occurred around 862, it had endured for more than twenty years. This discrepancy brings to mind Charles's impotent ravings of 873 when he allegedly resolved to abstain from his wife. Perhaps he had. Perhaps Richardis's original line of defense was that she had remained chaste for over ten years.[130] The attribution of virginity was probably a clerical masterstroke that shaped spiritual marriage—a distinctive mode of female spirituality—to serve purely masculine ends. The repudiated wife, on the other hand, manages to escape with her life and is posthumously rewarded with sainthood.

Consummated Marriage: The Transitional Model and the Clergy

Voluntary transitions from normal conjugal relations to chastity were the only type of spiritual marriage that had been endorsed, however cautiously, by the church fathers. And yet this kind of union was often eclipsed by two more compelling models. The flamboyant virginal union was, as we have observed, the darling of hagiographers and

---

[126] Ibid. 873, p. 122.

[127] See Dümmler, *Geschichte des ostfränkischen Reiches*, 3:243–245.

[128] According to the eleventh-century chronicler Herimann, Charles had undergone some kind of surgery on his head in 887. He was later deposed in the same year and died miserably, strangled by some of his own followers, in 888 (Herimann of Reichenau, *Chronicon* 887 and 888, ed. G. H. Pertz, *MGH, Scrip.*, vol. 5 [Hanover, 1844; reprt. Leipzig, 1925], p. 109).

[129] Ibid.

[130] Cf. Hellmann, "Die Heiraten der Karolinger," p. 350.

chroniclers alike, while the constrained movement to chastity had become a central feature of clerical discipline.[131]

The hagiographer frequently wielded the virginal marriage motif as a kind of a philosophers' stone, constantly seeking to transform matrons into virgins. At times, however, he overreached himself. The allegedly virginal marriage of Gumbert and Bertha (d. late seventh century) is undercut by the fact that the latter was murdered by her stepchildren, which at the very least implies a previous marriage for someone.[132] The contemporary author of the *vita* of the seventh-century St. Sigolena of Albi had more promising material to work with since there were no children. He reports that she and her husband lived happily, and chastely, for about ten years.[133] The question of when the actual conversion to chastity occurred and whether she was a virgin at the time is, however, probably purposefully sidestepped.[134] (One would assume that if she were a virgin, her hagiographer would make the most of it.) But this slight ambiguity sufficed, for a number of martyrologies, as warrant to classify or perhaps reclassify her as a virgin.[135]

[131] In the Eastern church, however, Theodore the Studite's (d. 826) funeral oration for his mother, Theoctista, gives a rare and stirring portrait of this kind of transitional union. After having a number of children, she won her husband over to chastity. For five years, they slept together chastely in the same bed. Eventually they separated to live as ascetics (*Laudatio funebris in matrem suam* c. 4, PG 99, cols. 885–890; also see the monk Michael's *Vita S. Theodori Studitae* c. 1, PG 99, cols. 115–118, and Bishop, "Bishops as Marital Advisors," p. 64).

[132] On the other hand, Flodoard claims that Bertha's body was uncorrupted after one hundred years, which is usually interpreted as a sign of virginity (*Historia Remensis ecclesiae* 4.47, MGH, Scrip., 13:596). Flodoard's account is based on *acta* written one hundred years after the couple's death. See AA SS, April, 3:630, and AA SS, May, 1:117–118.

[133] AA SS, July, 5:632; see Wemple, *Women in Frankish Society*, p. 151. Sigolena is one of the few saints that I know of who actually mourned the death of her husband; she is probably the only one for this early period.

[134] We are told that after her marriage some time elapsed ("transeunte igitur spatio temporis") before she raises the question of chastity with her husband. He stalls for time ("Adhuc paulisper sustine, et cum voluntas Dei fuerit, ita postea fiet") but is then suddenly converted by God—much to his wife's joy (AA SS, July, 5:631). The editor of her *vita* tends to doubt her virginity but says that no clear answer can be arrived at (p. 629).

[135] Ibid., pp. 628–629. With respect to the Belgian St. Aye (d. 691?) and her husband Hidulph, their respective lives were sufficiently late that a posthumous attribution of virginity presented little problem. AA SS summarizes a seventeenth-century Gallican life (April, 2:575–578; also see June, 5: 495–496). See Félix Hachez, "Du culte de sainte Aye," *Annales du cercle archéologique de Mons* 7 (1867): 357–365. As is clear from the Cecilia legend, spiritual marriage is an especially useful accolade when little is known of a saint, but the hagiographer is anxious to flesh out his or her history. Thus St. Serena of Spoleto (d. late third century), who was said to have ministered to the martyrs of Cordoba, is later credited with a virginal union (see AASS, January, 3:642–644).

When a gradual transition to chastity is described, it is usually a small part in the much larger economy of fertility. For example, a sterile couple frequently sought divine assistance in conception and, in return, consecrated the child to God.[136] Occasionally, a couple would also pledge marital chastity in return for a child, as was true of the parents of both SS. Alexis and Nicholas.[137] Both scenarios reflect the Old Testament recognition that God was the opener and sealer of wombs, augmented by the Christian corollary that the divine gift of fertility is only duly recompensed by chastity. But such contracts are not the focus of a saint's life: they are generally made by the parents of the saints. The divinely solicited offspring is invariably chaste.[138]

[136] This pattern seems to be based on an Old Testament model, particularly the conception of Samuel (see 1 Sam. 1.11–28 [= Kings]; cf. Gen. 21.1–2, 29.31, 30.2, 30.22; Judg. 13.2–24). It is picked up in the apocryphal events surrounding Mary's nativity (see the second-century Book of James, or Protevangelium, in The Apocryphal New Testament, trans. James, pp. 39–40). For Latin instances, see the life of St. Genulph, who, according to apocryphal tradition, was the first bishop of Cahors (d. ca. 250; vita ca. 900; AA SS, January, 2:446), the life of St. Donatus, bishop of Besançon (d. ca. 660; contemporary vita; AA SS, August, 2:197–198), and the life of Arnoul, bishop of Tours (fl. early sixth century; vita before the eleventh century; Bollandists, eds., Vita S. Arnulphi c. 2, in Catalogus codicum hagiographicorum latinorum antiquiorum saeculo XVI qui asservantur in Bibliotheca Nationali Parisiensi [Brussels, 1889], 1:416).

[137] For Alexis, see AA SS July, 4:251. There are no early lives of St. Nicholas, the legendary bishop of Myra who purportedly died in the fourth century. Though there are references to him from as early as the mid-sixth century, the first Greek life dates from the mid-ninth century. See the Latin thirteenth-century account of his birth in Jacobus de Voragine's The Golden Legend, trans. Granger Ryan and Helmut Ripperger (New York, 1941), p. 16. For a history of Nicholas's cult, see Charles W. Jones, Saint Nicholas of Myra, Bari, and Manhattan: A Biography of a Legend (Chicago and London, 1978). Cf. the contemporary vita for the Greek saint Euphraxia (d. 420), whose legend also circulated in the West (AA SS March, 2:261). The Latin church reserved the phenomenon of the virgin birth for Christ. This was not true for the East, particularly the Slavic church, where a number of saints were said to have been born of chaste unions (see Eve Levin, Sex and Society in the World of the Orthodox Slavs, 900–1700 [Ithaca, N.Y., 1989], pp. 61–65). This discrepancy may devolve from differing theological perspectives. John Chrysostom, for example, tended to dissociate sex and reproduction, seeing children as gifts from God that could have been procured by extrasexual means, if humanity had not been so weak as to need marriage in order to control concupiscence. See Chrysostom, La virginité c. 15–19, SC, no. 125, pp. 144–159; idem, In illud: Propter fornicationes uxorem . . . 1.33, PG 51, col. 213, as cited by L. Godefroy, "Mariage," DTC, vol. 9, col. 2094.

[138] Alexis's parents, Euphemianus and Aglae, seemed unaware that a child conceived by divine help must be dedicated to God: their own chastity was not an adequate compensation. Alexis's famous flight from the marriage bed and subsequent life as an ascetic demonstrate that the cycle of repayment was more than his parents bargained for (AA SS July, 4:251–252. Alexis's life is discussed in chapter 3 in the section entitled "St. Alexis and the Masculine Calling"). Cf. the Greek legend of St. Galaction, who was likewise conceived with divine help but was married to Episteme against his will. He convinced her to leave the marriage unconsummated (AA SS, November, 3:33).

Related to this transactional view is the tendency to interpret the loss of a child as a divinely willed act, precipitating a movement to conjugal chastity. Fortunatus speaks of this pattern,[139] while the examples of Paulinus and Melania suggest that when such a transition did occur, the movement to chastity provided a positive reconstruction for their loss. Their decision seemed complicit with God's will.[140]

But if spontaneous transitions to chastity are modest in number, constrained ones abound.[141] With the church's growing drive to develop a chaste priesthood in the West, pressure was placed upon an aspiring candidate to the priesthood not to marry, while those who were married were first encouraged and later ordered to abstain sexually.[142] As Jo Ann McNamara notes, this represents a reversal in the general trend whereby women are the main instigators of chastity in marriage.[143] It also eliminates the secrecy motif. If anything was to be secret, it would be conjugal relations after ordination.

Although clerical continence had basically become a prerequisite in the West from the fifth century, the church continued to ordain

[139] Wemple, *Women in Frankish Society*, p. 151.

[140] The inscription on the tomb of Casaria also indicates that the loss of a child precipitated the move toward chastity (see n. 46, above). Yet tragedy did not necessarily cement the marriage bond. St. Monegonde, for example, a contemporary of Gregory of Tours, was inconsolable after the death of her daughters and left her husband in order to become an anchoress. See Gregory of Tours, *Liber vitae patrum* 19.1, ed. B. Krusch, *MGH, Scrip. Rer. Merov.*, 1,2:736; cf. *Gloria confessorum* c. 24, ibid., pp. 763–764. The Greek legend of Athanasia and Andronicus shows a similar pattern. The couple's conversion to chastity is prompted after twelve years of marriage when both their children die on the same day. The couple part to join separate religious foundations, where they remain for another twelve years. She eventually enters her husband's monastery, disguised as a monk, but her identity is revealed only after her death. Thus the bond between the couple endures but undergoes considerable change (*AA SS*, October, 4:998–1000).

[141] See McNamara, "Chaste Marriage," pp. 22–33, 231–235, and Wemple, *Women in Frankish Society*, pp. 127–148. I am especially indebted to these works for the following.

[142] Especially since Vatican II, there has been a wealth of material on the church's struggle to achieve clerical celibacy. For the period prior to the Gregorian reform, see especially Roger Gryson, *Les origines du célibat ecclésiastique*; Charles A. Frazee, "The Origins of Clerical Celibacy in the Western Church," *Church History* 41 (1972): 149–167, esp. 149–158; A. M. Stickler, "L'évolution de la discipline du célibat dans l'église en occident de la fin de l'âge patristique au concile de Trente," in *Sacerdoce et célibat*, pp. 373–442, esp. 375–394; M. Dortel-Claudot, "Le prêtre et le mariage," pp. 319–344, esp. 319–337; John E. Lynch, "Marriage and Celibacy of the Clergy: The Discipline of the Western Church; an Historical-Canonical Synopsis," *The Jurist* 32 (1972): 14–38. H. C. Lea's *History of Sacerdotal Celibacy in the Christian Church*, 3d rev. ed., 2 vols. (London, 1907) is still basic to this field. See vol. 1, esp. chaps. 8–11.

[143] McNamara, "Chaste Marriage," pp. 28–29.

married men until the end of the tenth century.[144] What was to be done with the wives? *The Apostolic Canons*,[145] Leo I, and Gregory the Great all forbade clerics to abandon their wives but insisted they live with them chastely.[146] This solution would prove to be completely impracticable.

The problem of clerical wives seemed particularly critical in the newly converted Frankish kingdom, probably because the local church was not overly nice about gaining the consent of the wife to her husband's ordination. In the Gallo-Roman church a clerical wife had been required to take a vow of chastity known as a *conversio*—in essence consenting to her husband's ordination.[147] The wife would receive a blessing and a distinct costume at the time of the ordination.[148] But Suzanne Wemple indicates that this custom had fallen into disuse in the course of the sixth century and was only reintroduced in the Carolingian period.[149] Given the pastoral problems that a spontaneous and mutual vow engendered, little imagination is required to predict the complications devolving from a constrained and probably one-sided vow. The Frankish councils did their best to

[144] Dortel-Claudot, "Le prêtre et le mariage," pp. 332–337.

[145] The *Apostolic Canons* are an apocryphal collection that was produced in the second half of the fourth century and enjoyed great popularity in the Eastern and Western churches. They were translated into Latin ca. 500 by Dionysius Exiguus and included in the famed *Dionysiana*, which served as a font for the influential Carolingian *Hadriana* (see J. Rambaud-Buhot, "*Dionysiana Collectio*," *NCE*, 4:876). Canon 6 reads: "episcopus aut presbiter uxorem propriam nequaquam sub obtentu relegionis abiciat. si uero rei⟨e⟩rit, excommunicetur, sed si perseuerauerit, deponatur" (*Die Canonessammlung des Dionysius Exiguus in der ersten Redaktion*, ed. A. Strewe [Berlin, 1931], p. 4).

[146] Leo I, Ep. 167, "To Rusticus of Narbonne" c. 3, *PL* 54, col. 1204; Gregory I, "To Romanus, Fontinus, Savinus et al.," Reg. 9, 3, *CCSL*, 140a:663–664. See Dortel-Claudot, "Le prêtre et le mariage," p. 328; Gryson, *Les origines du célibat ecclésiastique*, pp. 101, 162, 166.

[147] See the Council of Orange, 441, c. 21 (*Concilia Galliae*, ed. C. Munier, *CCSL*, vol. 148 [Turnholt, 1963], p. 84); Arles II, 524, c. 2 (ibid., p. 114). The Council of Agde (506, c. 16) also requires the wife to take a vow and then enter a convent (ibid., p. 201).

[148] M. Andrieu, ed., *Les Ordines Romani* (Louvain, 1956), 4:140–141 (as cited by Lynch, "Marriage and Celibacy of the Clergy," p. 30). There are no details concerning this blessing.

[149] Wemple, *Women in Frankish Society*, pp. 132–133. Even in the earlier period, wives do not seem to have always been consulted. The *vita* for Germanus of Auxerre (d. 448), written about thirty years after his death, reports that he was forced to assume the bishopric very much against his will ("invitus, coactus, addictus"). This prompted a conversion that induced him to give up the world. Among other things, his wife was transformed into his sister ("uxor in sororem mutatur ex coniuge" [Constantius, *Vita Germani Episcopi Autissiodorensis* c. 2, ed. W. Levison, *MGH, Scrip. Rer. Merov.*, vol. 7 (Hanover and Leipzig, 1920), p. 252]).

monitor the clerical couple. They tried to enforce separate rooms or, failing that, separate beds, often threatening degradation or deposition for incontinence,[150] while at least one council insisted that clerics separate from their wives.[151]

Suzanne Wemple's study *Women in Frankish Society* traces the way in which tensions resulting from the drive to develop a chaste priesthood resonate throughout Frankish sources. In contrast to the clerical couples in Paulinus's circle whose elevation to the priesthood was preceded by a couple's mutual commitment to chastity,[152] spiritual marriage is but an enforced means to an institutional end. Chastity coincides with ordination, and thus the movement is abrupt, awkward, and frequently unsuccessful. Moreover, wives bear the brunt of the blame for these failures.[153] So it is with Gregory of Tours's account of Urbicus (d. ca. 312), bishop of Clermont-Ferrand, who lived apart from his wife after his elevation to office. Their transition to chastity was deceptively smooth: both gave themselves over to prayer and good works. And yet one night "the woman was filled with the Devil's own malice . . . for he inflamed her with desire for her husband and turned her into a second Eve." She came to his house and pitifully reproached him for rejecting her, citing Paul's counsel that husband and wife return to one another, lest they be tempted by Satan (1 Cor. 7.5). His resolve broke down and his wife was admitted.[154] Both Urbicus and others like him were rewarded with sainthood for eventually abandoning their wives.[155]

[150] Regarding separate beds, see Auxerre, 561–605, c. 21 (*CCSL*, 148a:268); Orleans, 541, c. 17 (ibid., p. 136). The Council of Tours in 567 (c. 20), probably following the sanctions of Spanish councils, deprived the priest who resisted the presence of a third party in the bedroom of a month's communion and imprisoned a cleric who refused to play this role (ibid., p. 184). See Dortel-Claudot, "Le prêtre et le mariage," pp. 330–331; Lynch, "Marriage and Celibacy of the Clergy," p. 29. For other sanctions see, Orange, 441, c. 22 (*CCSL*, 148:84); Tours, 461, c. 2 (ibid., p. 144); Orleans, 549, c. 4 (*CCSL*, 148a:149); Tours, 567, c. 20 (ibid., pp. 183–184); Mâcon, 581–583, c. 11 (ibid., p. 225); Lyons, 583, c. 1 (ibid., p. 232); Auxerre, 561–605, c. 20 (ibid., pp. 267–268).

[151] The Council of Lyons in 583 tried to make priests separate from their wives (c. 1, *CCSL* 148a:232).

[152] Paulinus, Pinian, and Eucher were all converted to chastity before their ordination. Cf. the eighth-century account of Lupus of Troyes (d. 478) and his wife, Pimeniola, who, after seven years of marriage mutually exhorted one another to make the change ("se ad conversionem hortatu mutuo contulerunt" [*Vita S. Lupi Episcopi Trecensis* c. 2, ed. B. Krusch, *MGH, Scrip. Rer. Merov.*, 7:296]).

[153] See Wemple, *Women in Frankish Society*, pp. 133–136.

[154] "Libor inimici . . . conmovetur in femina; quam in concupiscentiam viri succendens, novam Evam effecit" (Gregory of Tours, *Libri Historiarum X* 1.44, (*MGH, Scrip. Rer. Merov.*, 1, 1:29; trans. Thorpe, *History of the Franks*, pp. 93–94).

[155] Cf. the career of Genebaud (d. ca. 555), bishop of Laon and a contemporary of St. Remy's, who impregnated his wife in the course of the visits he made for the sake of her

Only occasionally does one catch a glimpse of a peaceful and uncomplicated clerical union. The near contemporary *vita* of St. Germanus of Auxerre (d. 448) presents the priest Senator and his wife Nectariola as models of hospitality and piety. But this life predates Frankish efforts to supervise clerical marriages, and neither this couple nor their union is of central importance in the narrative.[156] Generally, the unions that do sustain the painful transition to chastity are fraught with sexual anxiety. Thus Gregory of Tours reports that a certain bishop's wife (who seemingly continued to share her husband's bed after his ordination) was frustrated by his sexual reserve and became convinced that he was unfaithful. She burst into the bedroom during his siesta only to discover a lamb sleeping on his chest—a miraculous testimony to his chastity.[157] One has little doubt that the antiuxorial milieu of the Frankish church informed Fortunatus's life of Hilary, bishop of Poitiers (d. 368). Hilary is depicted as successfully praying for the death of both his daughter and his wife—a drastic but effective solution to the Frankish clergy's dilemma.[158]

Spiritual marriage among the clergy is most successful when graced by the virginal underpinnings of the unconsummated marriage. Thus with Amator and Martha or with Riticius and his wife, there are no painful differences to reconcile, no impossible synchronizations to achieve.[159] But very often the virginal model goes awry, if

---

religious instruction. He named his unwelcome son "Latro" (robber) as a reminder of his guilt. But since the bishop was fearful that the cessation of these visits would generate suspicion, the visits continued and a daughter soon followed. This one was likewise penitentially named "Vulpecula" (little fox). See Flodoard's *Historia Remensis ecclesiae* 1.14, *MGH, Scrip.*, 13:425. Both Urbicus and Genebaud are entered in some versions of Usuard's *Martyrologium*, printed in *AA SS*, June, vol. 6. For Urbicus, see the *Auctaria* for March 20 (p. 151); for Genebaud, see the *Auctaria* for December 8 (p. 663). Flodoard also refers to Genebaud as a saint.

[156] Constantius, *Vita Germani Episcopi Autissiodorensis* c. 22, *MGH, Scrip. Rer. Merov.*, 7:267. This couple is introduced only to augment Germanus's prestige. When he was a guest in their house, his pious hostess hid straw in his bed, which she later used to cast out demons.

[157] *Gloria confessorum* c. 77, *MGH, Scrip. Rer. Merov.*, 1:794.

[158] Venantius Fortunatus, *Vita sancti Hilarii* 13.46–50, ed. B. Krusch, *MGH, Auct. Ant.*, vol. 4,2 (Berlin, 1885), p. 6. Hilary's prayer for his daughter's death was linked to his determination that she remain chaste. He allegedly wrote her an exhortation to chastity during his exile over Arianism (6.18–20, p. 3). This letter is undoubtedly spurious, and some attribute it to Fortunatus himself (see *Epistola ad Abram filiam suam, PL* 10, cols. 549–552). Cf. the legend of St. Peter's daughter, Petronilla, whom he kept in a state of paralysis so that her chastity would not be threatened. This episode is described in the spurious, but ancient, Acts of SS. Nereus and Achilleus (*AASS*, May, 3:6–13; see p. 10).

[159] Cassius, bishop of Narni (d. 538) is also popularly believed to have had a virginal

only because the stakes are much higher than simply mutual sanctification in wedlock. As Peter Brown notes, "laymen eyed their new
leaders anxiously. They instantly denounced priests who continued
to beget children with their wives once ordained to serve at the altar."[160] This vigilance was too impatient for the sweet disclosures of
the grave.[161] In the case of Simplicius (d. ca. 420) and his wife, although they had secretly preserved their virginity in marriage, they
were forced to prove it after his elevation to the bishopric of Autun.
First the wife and then the husband stood for an hour in front of the
crowd with burning coals in their garments—a dramatic affirmative
to the rhetorical question in Proverbs 6.27–28: "Can a man hide fire
in his bosom, and his clothes not burn? Or can he walk upon hot
coals, and his feet not be burnt?"[162] It would seem that when spiritual
marriage is entrusted with an agenda other than simple edification
through the revelation of conjugal chastity—be it sacerdotal purity or
affairs of state—the proofs become crueler and more immediate, as is
clear from the trial of Empress Richardis.

Often, virginal marriages are but feeble disguises for unilateral repudiation. This is clear from the lives of two alleged disciples of St.
Remy. Theodoric had little luck in converting his wife to virginity on
his wedding night: "The spouse, languishing with love of carnal desire, spurned the health-giving warnings of her spouse and answered
with bitterness of spirit when she saw herself despised." Theodoric
left her and never looked back.[163] Arnoul, bishop of Tours, suc-

---

marriage with his wife, Fausta. But little is known of Cassius, apart from stray references from Gregory the Great (*Dialogues* 3.6.2, ed. Adalbert de Vogüé, and trans. Paul
Antin, *SC*, no. 260 [Paris, 1979], 2:276–278). The inscription on his tomb mentions
that he is buried by a certain Fausta, who is presumed to have been his wife. The fact
that he was a bishop gave rise to the expectation that they lived as brother and sister
which, in turn, fostered the virginal-marriage legend (*AA SS*, June, 7:445–447).

[160] Brown, *The Body and Society*, p. 443.

[161] Riticius and his wife were permitted the luxury of a grave-side miracle since his
elevation to the priesthood occurred only after her death.

[162] Gregory of Tours, *Gloria confessorum* c. 75, *MGH, Scrip. Rer. Merov.*, 1,2:792–
793. The Irish clergy and their female ascetic companions repeatedly had recourse to
this proof of chastity (see Roger E. Reynolds, "*Virgines Subintroductae* in Celtic Christianity," *Harvard Theological Review* 61 [1968]: 559–560). It is unclear, however,
whether this severe test of chastity is an insular influence or how this practice relates
to the Germanic ordeal.

[163] "Sed sponsa tabescens amore carnalis desiderii, spernit salutaria monita sponsi
et amaro animo respondet, dum se despectam videt" (Flodoard, *Historia Remensis
ecclesiae* 1.24, *MGH, Scrip.*, 13:443). The two lives printed in *AA SS* are based on
Flodoard. The second and later life tries to remedy the situation slightly by having
Remy send Theodoric back to fetch his spouse, who is then converted to chastity (July,
1:59). There is no further mention of her, however. Cf. the example of St. Leobard
(Gregory of Tours, *Liber vitae patrum* c. 20, *MGH, Scrip Rer. Merov.*, 1,2:741–742).

cessfully converted his wife, Scaribourge, to chastity, with some help from St. Remy.[164] But Arnoul's eventual murder by members of his estranged wife's household points to an underlying conflict which is not mitigated even by the fact that he supposedly died in her arms.[165]

All of these incidents underline the practical difficulties of institutionalizing the charismatic gift of chastity. But they have an important didactic message as well. They are grim reminders of the implacable nature of concupiscence. Even age and shared vocation are ultimately insufficient safeguards against the dangers of the opposite sex. Hence, Gregory the Great tells of a priest who "from the moment of his ordination to the priesthood, . . . loved his wife as a brother loves his sister, but he avoided her as he would an enemy." When he is on his deathbed, and his wife puts her ear near his face to listen for his breathing, he rasps at her " 'Go away from me, woman. The fire is still flickering. Take away the tinder.' "[166]

Despite the multivalence of spiritual marriage, a binary division can be discerned. When entrusted with the patristic vision of consensus and indissolubility, manifested primarily in saints' lives, spiritual marriage becomes a shorthand for the elimination of concupiscence and occasionally heralds a modest suspension of traditional gender roles. These qualities, in turn, impart an eschatological significance to the marriage bond. The more historically circumstantial exponents, be they chroniclers or clerical reformers, not only argue to the opposite purpose, but also demonstrate how a spiritual practice refined by women can be appropriated and turned against them. Whether functioning as a screen for unilateral repudiation or an instrument for achieving sacerdotal celibacy, spiritual marriage is a cryptogram for marriage as a terminal affair with temporal and spiritually delimiting ends, and women are eminently expendable.

The coexistence of these two visions corresponds to the painful process of Christianization. Once Christianity is sufficiently entrenched, spiritual marriage, for a time, subsides. With the exception of Empress Richardis, the incidents of spiritual marriage discussed above, real or purported, are generally said to have occurred prior to the ninth century. That the phenomenon continued to intrigue is evident from the continued circulation of these legends, yet ninth- and tenth-century churchmen were reluctant to attribute such mer-

---

[164] Bollandists, eds., *Vita S. Arnulphi* c. 3, in *Catalogus codicum hagiographicorum latinorum antiquiorum*, 1:416.

[165] Ibid. c. 23–24, pp. 426–427.

[166] Gregory cannot resist adding that as soon as she stepped back, his strength seemed to return (*Dialogues* 4.12.2–3, *SC*, no. 265, 3:48 and 50; trans. O. J. Zimmerman, *FC*, vol. 39 [New York, 1959], pp. 203–204).

itorious behavior to their contemporaries. This reluctance corresponds to both institutional and attitudinal changes.

Naturally, the rise of monasticism would offer an option to many couples who might otherwise have lived out their vocation in the world. But the link between spiritual marriage and female spirituality must also be placed in this balance. In the process of converting a given area, the church invariably courted women and supported their religious vocation. This is as true for the conversion of the Germanic kingdoms as it was for the late Roman Empire.[167] Moreover, a relatively high number of female saints corresponds to the early years of Christianity in the different regions of Western Europe. The number of female saints tapers off from the mid-eighth century, as do representations of spiritual marriage.[168] Both of these trends correspond to church intervention in matrimony and the relative stabilization of marriage.[169] But the amelioration of marriage laws cuts both ways: if the average woman was ensured of more security, there was less scope for female heroism. Indeed, Suzanne Wemple indicates that the Carolingian period corresponds with women's loss of influence in the church.[170] What is at play, then, is the domestication of female heroism.

Carolingian reforms were also leveled against clerical incontinence.[171] Although their success was perhaps only marginal and undoubtedly short-lived, the holy cleric living in chastity with his wife was no longer a suitable topic for the hagiographer.[172] But clerical attempts at spiritual marriage had undoubtedly muddied the waters. Because the theoretical chastity of a clerical couple's common life had been repeatedly abused to the extent that such an arrangement

[167] See Brown, *The Body and Society*, pp. 150, 344–345; idem, *The Cult of the Saints*, pp. 46–48; Schulenburg, "Sexism and the Celestial Gynaeceum," p. 128. Cf. Schulenburg's "Women's Monastic Communities, 500–1100: Patterns of Expansion and Decline," in *Sisters and Workers in the Middle Ages*, ed. Judith M. Bennett et al. (Chicago, 1989), pp. 217–220.

[168] See Schulenburg, "Sexism and the Celestial Gynaeceum," pp. 122–123. According to Joseph-Claude Poulin, there are no female saints in Carolingian Aquitaine (*L'idéal de sainteté dans l'Aquitaine carolingienne d'après sources hagiographiques, 750–950* [Quebec City, 1975], p. 42).

[169] Schulenburg, "Sexism and the Celestial Gynaeceum," p. 123.

[170] For the Carolingian reforms' impact on monasticism, see Wemple, *Women in Frankish Society*, pp. 165–174; cf. Stafford, "The King's Wife in Wessex," p. 7, and Schulenburg's "Women's Monastic Communities," pp. 224–225.

[171] See esp. Wemple, *Women in Frankish Society*, pp. 143–148.

[172] Poulin's study of hagiography in Aquitaine further suggests that the saintly bishop of Merovingian times was eclipsed by the monastic saint (*L'idéal de sainteté*, pp. 34–35).

was eventually forbidden by the church, this disciplinary defeat inevitably colored the way in which similar lay efforts would be regarded. Where the clerical "cream" had failed, what chance had the humble laity of succeeding? Conversely, why accentuate clerical humiliation by trumpeting lay successes?

THREE

ELEVENTH-CENTURY BOUNDARIES:
THE SPIRIT OF REFORM AND THE CULT
OF THE VIRGIN KING

*The idea of society is a powerful image. It is potent in its
own right to control or to stir men to action. This image
has form: it has external boundaries, margins, internal
structure. Its outlines contain power to reward
conformity and repulse attack. There is energy in its
margins and unstructured areas.*[1]

THE ELEVENTH CENTURY was responsible for the construction of ambitious formulations of society that attempted to
raise rigid boundaries between its various constituents. The
latter part of the century is dominated by the struggle of the Gregorian reformers to separate the clergy from the laity, using sexual
activity as the point of demarcation.[2] Georges Duby has further examined the rise of a new vision of society based on its purportedly
trifunctional orders of men: those who pray, those who fight, and
those who work the land—a clearly vexed description insofar as it
ignores both the rising merchant class and women altogether.[3] This
second omission is especially indicative of the misogynist climate of
the time: Jo Ann McNamara has astutely noted that the exclusion of
women from all three orders corresponds with the clergy's flight from

---

[1] Mary Douglas, *Purity and Danger: An Analysis of the Concepts of Pollution and
Taboo* (London, 1966), p. 114.

[2] Georges Duby, *The Three Orders: Feudal Society Imagined*, trans. Arthur Goldhammer (Chicago, 1980), pp. 81, 108, 209–210, 255–256.

[3] For the origins of the concept of *ordines*, see ibid. esp. pp. 82–83; also see Yves
Congar, "Les laïcs et l'ecclésiologie des *ordines* chez les théologiens des XIe et XIIe
siècles," in *I laici nella 'Societas Christiana' dei secoli XI e XII*, Atti della terza
Settimana internazionale di studio, Mendola, 21–27 agosto 1965. Pubblicazioni
dell'Università Cattolica del Sacro Cuore. Miscellanea del Centro di Studi Medioevali,
vol. 5 (Milan, 1968), pp. 83–117, esp. 91–92. On the failure of this model to accommodate women, see Duby, *The Three Orders*, p. 81. This exclusion inspired Shulamith
Shahar to entitle her study *The Fourth Estate: A History of Women in the Middle Ages*
(trans. Chaya Galai [London and New York, 1983]).

women in their drive to develop a celibate priesthood, and has interpreted both these complementary ideological constructs as symptoms of a crisis in masculine identity.[4]

The feasibility of these models relied on an unrealistic estimate of society's complicity. But, in fact, powerful formulations are generally developed in response to what are perceived as threats against an inchoate status quo. Its positive articulation as a canonized standard is invariably reactionary and, in fact, inspires more transgressions.[5] Because the clergy presented celibacy as the most compelling instrument of demarcation, it naturally became the most obvious vehicle for lay transgression. The many crossings and recrossings between these two rather artificially polarized states—between sexual activity and celibacy—not only tended to blur these boundaries but also gave rise to some notable hybrids. The cult of the virgin king, the last instance of boundary crossing to be considered in this chapter, was just such an anomaly.

Popular Heresy

Monastic asceticism, particularly the reformed order of Cluny, made considerable inroads into lay consciousness, which resulted in the rise of popular heresy around the year 1000.[6] The various heresies

[4] "The *Herrenfrage*: The Restructuring of the Gender System, 1050–1150," presented at Fordham University's Conference "Gender and Society II: Men in the Middle Ages (9–10 March 1990). Dr. McNamara kindly sent me a copy of this paper, which will shortly appear in print in a collection entitled *Medieval Masculinities*, ed. Clare A. Lees. Much of this chapter is indebted to her bold formulations.

[5] It is not surprising that R. I. Moore identifies the eleventh century as a pivotal one in *The Formation of a Persecuting Society: Power and Deviance in Western Europe, 950–1250* (Oxford, 1987).

[6] Marc Bloch discredited the idea that the year 1000 was widely held to signal the end of the world (*Feudal Society*, trans. L. A. Manyon [Chicago, 1961], 1:84–85). For a more recent assessment, see Georges Duby, *L'An mil* (Paris, 1967), and idem, *The Three Orders*, pp. 144–145.

There are a number of recent and responsible efforts to relate heresy to social change. Brian Stock explores the relation between the revival of heresy and the impact of texts on both literate and nonliterate individuals (*The Implications of Literacy: Written Language and Models of Interpretation in the Eleventh and Twelfth Centuries* [Princeton, N.J., 1983], pp. 88–151, esp. 145–151). Janet L. Nelson relates the growth of heresy to assaults on society's belief structure as well as to fundamental social changes ("Society, Theodicy, and the Origins of Heresy: Towards a Reassessment of the Medieval Evidence," in *Schism, Heresy, and Religious Protest*, ed. Derek Baker, Studies in Church History, no. 9 [Cambridge, 1972], pp. 65–77). R. I. Moore argues against the assignation of any single origin for heresy but notes society's sense of the failure of the Carolingian church (*The Origins of European Dissent* [New York, 1977], esp. pp. 42–

generally tended to reject marriage altogether. In fact, the first articulations of the tripartite society were framed in response to precisely this threat.[7] Particularly germane to our interest is the heresy reported at Monforte ca. 1028, of which the countess of Monforte was allegedly one of the leaders. According to Landulf's *History of Milan*, the heresiarch Gerald told Bishop Aribert of Milan: "'We esteem virginity above all else, although we have wives. He who is virgin keeps his virginity, but he who has lost it, after receiving permission from our elder [*nostro maiori*], may observe perpetual chastity. No one knows his wife carnally, but carefully treats her as his mother or sister.'"[8] When asked by the bishop how the human race would perpetuate itself if all practiced virginity, he answered that once humanity was free of corruption it could reproduce itself sinlessly like bees.[9]

---

45). C. Violante analyzes heresy in terms of the relation between rural and urban ("Hérésies urbaines et hérésies rurales en Italie du 11e au 13e siècle," in *Hérésies et sociétés dans l'Europe pré-industrielle, 11e–18e siècles*, ed. Jacques Le Goff, Civilisations et Sociétés, 10 [Paris, 1968], pp. 171–197).

For the relation between monastic spirituality and the rebirth of popular heresy, see H. Taviani, "Naissance d'une hérésie en Italie du Nord au XIe siècle," *Annales ESC* 29 (1974): 1232–1233, 1247; Violante, "Hérésies urbaines et hérésies rurales en Italie," p. 178; Moore, *The Origins of European Dissent*, pp. 40–41; Karl F. Morrison, "The Gregorian Reform," in *Christian Spirituality*, ed. Bernard McGinn and John Meyendorff, vol. 16 of *World Spirituality* (New York, 1985), pp. 188–191; André Vauchez, *La spiritualité du moyen âge*, Collection Sup., L'historien, 19 (Rome, 1975), pp. 53–57. For eschatological aspects in Cluniac spirituality around the year 1000, see Dominique Iogna-Prat, "Continence et virginité dans la conception clunisienne de l'ordre du monde autour de l'an mil," *Académie des inscriptions et belles-lettres. Comptes rendus*, January–March (1985): 127–143, and Kassius Hallinger, "The Spiritual Life of Cluny in the Early Days," in *Cluniac Monasticism in the Central Middle Ages*, ed. Noreen Hunt (Hamden, Conn., 1971), pp. 40–41.

[7] See Duby, *The Three Orders*, pp. 19, 29–36.

[8] "Virginitatem prae ceteris laudamus; uxores habentes, qui virgo est virginitatem conservet, qui autem corruptus, data a nostro maiori licentia castitatem perpetuam conservare licet" (Landulf the Senior, *Mediolanensis historiae libri quatuor* 2.27, ed. Alessandro Cutulo in *Rerum Italicarum Scriptores*, vol. 4,2, rev. ed. [Bologna, 1942], p. 68); trans. Walter L. Wakefield and Austin P. Evans, trans., *Heresies of the High Middle Ages* (New York and London, 1969), p. 87.

[9] This kind of animal lore was quite common in the medieval period. It was popularized in works like the *Physiologus* (fourth century) in the early years of the church and the *Etymologiae* of Isidore of Seville (d. 636), as well as in the bestiaries of the high Middle Ages (see F. McCulloch, *Mediaeval Latin and French Bestiaries*, University of North Carolina, Studies in Romance Languages and Literatures, no. 33 [Chapel Hill, N.C., 1960], pp. 15–28). For a discussion of Neoplatonic influence, see Moore, *The Origins of European Dissent*, pp. 34–35; also see Stock, *The Implications of Literacy*, pp. 102–103. Peter Damian makes a similar observation about the perpetual virginity of bees when discussing the natural chastity of the animal world: "Apes sobolem successurae posteritatis enutriunt, ut virgines perseverent" (bk. 1, Ep. 8, *PL* 144, col. 232). Also see his analogy between the Virgin Birth and the way worms grow sponta-

The appearance of the various heresies suggests that the times were auspicious for a forceful resurfacing of spiritual marriage among the laity. Indeed, they were in many respects: in contemporary matrimonial theory, the patristic vision of the sufficiency of consent in the formation of marriage was making a comeback, simultaneously with the resurfacing of the cult of the Virgin.[10] And yet the official church resisted the practice because fruitful lay marriage was important to other ecclesiastical objectives. The few instances in which women seem to have initiated a spiritual marriage were discreetly downplayed.[11] Meanwhile, the reform movement, which had begun in the

---

neously in wood (or were thought to) without sexual intervention (Serm. 46, c. 20; Serm. 67, c. 4 in *Sermones*, ed. John Lucchesi, *CCCM*, vol. 57 [Turnholt, 1983], pp. 289–290, 410).

[10] Peter Damian was at the forefront of both these trends. His treatise *De tempore celebrandi nuptias* is one of the few treatises addressing marriage directly that had been written since the time of Augustine. This work attacks the misconception that there can be no marriage without coupling, instead alleging that a couple is truly united by the marriage contract (*dotali foedere jungitur*). He invokes two examples in support of this view: the marriage of Mary and Joseph, and the incident at the marriage at Cana, when John the Evangelist was purportedly called away from his virginal marriage by Christ—a tradition that seems to have originated with Bede (Op. 41, c. 2, *PL* 145, col. 662). Damian's views anticipate the consensual theory of marriage formulated by the twelfth-century theologians, as discussed in chapter 4. Both approaches deemphasize the importance of sexual relations in the formation of the bond. On the other hand, Damian focuses on certain legal formalities, particularly the transmission of dowry, rather than the consent of the parties. Despite so strong a testimonial on behalf of the nonphysical nature of the marriage bond, however, it would be wrong to see this work as a deliberate promotion of spiritual marriage. As the title itself suggests, the treatise was not written to inspire the laity to greater heights of perfection, but to contradict the error that a marriage solemnized in Lent is invalid because of the required suspension of sexual activity (see Burchard of Worms, *Decretorum libri viginti* 19.75, *PL* 140, col. 1000. Also see Brundage, *Law, Sex, and Christian Society*, pp. 188–189).

On Damian's promotion of the cult of the Virgin, see *In nativitate Beatissimae Virginis Mariae* (Serms. 45 and 46, *CCSL*, 57:265–290). Also see Etienne Delaruelle, *La piété populaire au moyen âge* (Turin, 1975), pp. 58–61, and Owen J. Blum, *St. Peter Damian: His Teaching on the Spiritual Life*, Catholic University of America, Studies in Mediaeval History, n.s., vol. 10 (Washington, D.C., 1947), pp. 157–160.

[11] As Jo Ann McNamara has pointed out, Beatrice of Tuscany and her daughter Mathilda, both instrumental in the Gregorian reform movement, were ambitious for lives of chastity but only marginally supported in this quest ("Chaste Marriage," p. 32). Beatrice's vow of chastity with her husband was only reluctantly countenanced by Peter Damian, who queried both her husband's commitment and her own decision to forgo future offspring: "De mysterio autem mutuae continentiae, quam inter vos, Deo teste, servatis, diu me, fateor, duplex opinio tenuit, ut virum quidem tuum arbitrarer hilariter hoc pudicitiae munus offerre; te vero gignendo prolis desiderio non hoc libenter admittere" (bk. 8, Ep. 14, *PL* 144, col. 452). Scholars such as Blum have noted that Damian generally shows no inclination to encourage members of the laity to higher

monasteries, had spread to the secular clergy. Over the course of the eleventh century, a series of reforming popes (some of them Cluniac monks) declared war on clerical marriage in an effort to restructure society according to the strict binary division between clergy and laity referred to above. From this perspective, the laity's sexual activity was as important as the clergy's sexual abstinence. The reformers' masterstroke was temporarily to harness the elements of lay asceticism on behalf of their program, providing them with a vicarious purity through the priesthood.[12] In the second half of the eleventh century and for the first few decades of the twelfth century, there are no further heresies.[13]

The War on Clerical Marriage: Celibacy versus Marriage, Clergy versus Laity, Men versus Women

The measures taken against the marriage of clerics (styled "nicolaitism" after the heretics described in Rev. 2.6 and 14–15) have been

---

levels of asceticism (*St. Peter Damian*, pp. 191–194). Mathilda, on the other hand, made two political marriages in order to further the ends of the papal party. The first marriage (probably between 1069 and 1071) was to Godfrey the Hunchback, duke of Lower Lorraine. There are a number of rumors surrounding this marriage: some sources say that the marriage was never consummated, and that Mathilda stipulated from the outset that it was a marriage of state (see Nora Duff, *Matilda of Tuscany: La gran donna d'Italia* [London, 1909], pp. 104–109). Other sources claim that after one child, who did not survive infancy, Mathilda abstained sexually due to the pains of childbirth (see the anonymous *Vita comitissae Mathildis* c. 7, ed. G. G. Leibnitius, *Rerum Italicarum Scriptores*, vol. 5, [Bologna, 1724], p. 392). At any rate, the marriage was not a success and the couple separated (Duff, *Matilda of Tuscany*, pp. 111–113, 136–137). After Godfrey's death, Mathilda was persuaded to make a second marriage to Guelf V of Bavaria. This was undertaken purely out of obedience to the Holy See, which needed support against the imperial party. This motive collapsed when the imperial party no longer presented a threat, and the couple separated in 1095 (Duff, *Matilda of Tuscany*, pp. 191–194, 216–218). The rather ambivalent anonymous biographer also claims that she was briefly married to the duke of Normandy but, impatient with a husband's rule, had him murdered while he was defecating (Leibnitius, ed., *Vita comitissae Mathildis* c. 7, p. 393). On the extent of Beatrice's and Mathilda's support of the papal party, see Demetrius B. Zema, "The Houses of Tuscany and of Pierlone in the Crisis of Rome in the Eleventh Century," *Traditio* 2 (1944): 157–169.

[12] According to R. I. Moore, the laity attached increasing importance to the priesthood with the fragmentation of the family unit that resulted from the settlement of new land. The priest came to symbolize community and stability in a time of shifting fortunes ("Family, Community, and Cult on the Eve of the Gregorian Reform," *Transactions of the Royal Historical Society*, ser. 5, 30 [1980]: 56–57).

[13] Moore, "The Origins of Medieval Heresy," *History* 55 (1970): 33–34; cf. Jeffrey Burton Russell, *Dissent and Reform in the Early Middle Ages* (Berkeley and Los Angeles, 1965), pp. 5–7.

well-documented elsewhere.[14] For the purposes of this study, it will suffice to isolate a number of factors that have bearing on this subject. Despite the many efforts at separating priests and their wives, clerical marriage had been tolerated until the eleventh century. Couples were permitted to remain together with the understanding that they would remain chaste. Indeed, Leo the Great's injunction that priests not abandon their wives is reiterated in all the principal canonical collections such as *Dionysio-Hadriana, Hispana,* Regino of Prüm, and Burchard of Worms. Yet, from the time of the Council of Bourges in 1031, priests were required to send away their wives.[15] The implications of such a change were shocking indeed and excited considerable controversy from both factions.[16] Up until this point it was customary for clerical marriages to be celebrated in church and to receive the nuptial blessing. The wives were properly dowered, according to their rank, as would be the case with any other marriage contract.[17] Although in theory no one in major orders was permitted to marry after ordination, these marriages were still judged valid but were considered illicit. It was not until Lateran II in 1139 that holy orders universally were considered to be an impediment to marriage.[18] The Gregorian reformers, however, denied the validity of all marriages of clerics in major orders, no matter when they were contracted, and made no distinction between wives and concubines.[19] Indeed, Peter

[14] H. C. Lea still provides one of the most thorough overviews (see *History of Sacerdotal Celibacy,* 1:206–286).

[15] Dortel-Claudot, "Le prêtre et le mariage," pp. 336, 340.

[16] For a summary and discussion of the pamphlet warfare produced by each side, see Anne Llewellyn Barstow, *Married Priests and the Reforming Papacy: The Eleventh-Century Debates,* Texts and Studies in Religion, vol. 12 (New York and Toronto, 1982), pp. 107–171.

[17] Gregory VII's letter of complaint to William the Conqueror about the bishop of Dol describes just such a public ceremony, although he professes shock and disgust over it—especially the way in which the bishop used church property to dower his daughters (see P. Jaffé, ed., *Epistolae collectae,* Ep. 16, in *Monumenta Gregoriana, Bibliotheca Rerum Germanicarum,* vol. 2 [Berlin, 1865], pp. 541–542). This letter is a reminder that the Gregorian reform was not wholly given over to issues of purity but was also animated by economic self-interest. For a fascinating analysis of the church as a corporate entity, which assesses its policies on the basis of money and power as opposed to spiritual concerns, see Jack Goody's controversial work, *The Development of the Family and Marriage in Europe* (Cambridge, 1983). Also see Frazee, "The Origins of Clerical Celibacy in the Western Church," pp. 159–160.

[18] This position was first affirmed by Innocent II at Pisa in 1135 and then reissued at Lateran II (Barstow, *Married Priests and the Reforming Papacy,* pp. 102–103; Dortel-Claudot, "Le prêtre et le mariage," pp. 343–344; Stickler, "L'évolution de la discipline du célibat," p. 406). The marriage of clerics in minor orders continued to be both valid and licit throughout the Middle Ages.

[19] Dortel-Claudot, "Le prêtre et le mariage," p. 338; Barstow, *Married Priests and the Reforming Papacy,* p. 43.

Damian (1007–1072), one of the most influential reformers and most prolific of propagandists, cruelly mocks clerical wives for their part in what he holds to be a meaningless marriage ceremony.[20] And thus, at a time when the church was making progressive strides in enforcing upon the laity the indissolubility of marriage, it also embarked on its last and most virulent round of marriage breaking among its own ranks. It was a blow from which marriage, already under attack by fanatical lay contingents, would be slow to recover.[21]

Despite the Draconian legislation, the coercive arm of the reformers was still short. They needed to convince the laity of what they themselves already firmly believed: that the boundaries between clergy and laity were real, sacrosanct, and essential to the well-being of Christendom. This was inevitably done at the expense of the lay condition. As Robert Bultot has shown, for Peter Damian, secularity and sin were virtually indistinguishable concepts. In Damian's writings, words like *profane*, *lay*, and *immoral* were rendered synonymous.[22] The possibility of confusing the two ways of living or of one's appropriating the functions proper to the other was presented as a real danger.[23] To live *more laicorum* was the hallmark of a bad priest.[24] And yet, while Damian made the occasional discreet appeal to certain nobles to suppress clerical marriage by force,[25] common sense in conjunction with his contempt for the laity made him fearful of its full-scale mobilization.[26]

But Ariald (d. 1066), one of the clerical leaders of the popular Pa-

[20] Damian provokingly says—when addressing clerical wives in a hypothetical conversation—that despite seemingly careful legalities, their unions were essentially empty and worthless: "Nec vos terreat, quod forte, non dicam fidei, sed perfidiae vos annulus subarrhavit: quod rata et monimenta dotalia notarius quasi matrimonii jure conscripsit; quod juramentum ad confirmandam quodammodo conjugii copulam utrinque processit. Totum hoc, quod videlicet apud alios est conjugii firmamentum, inter vos vanum judicatur et frivolum" (Op. 18, 2.7, *PL* 145, col. 412).

[21] A hint of prejudice, which favored chastity over the marriage bond, remained throughout the Middle Ages. Thus canon law permitted an unconsummated marriage to be dissolved for an entrance into religion, as will be seen in chapter 4.

[22] Robert Bultot, *Christianisme et valeurs humaines. A. La doctrine du mépris du monde, en Occident, de S. Ambroise à Innocent III*, vol. 4, *Le XIe siècle*, vol. 1, *Pierre Damien* (Louvain and Paris, 1963), pp. 54–58.

[23] "Sed plerumque conversatione conjugatorum vita confunditur virginum, cum et illi ultra habitum assumunt opera, et isti juxta ordinem proprium non excitant corda" (Serm. 46, *PL* 144, col. 759).

[24] Bultot, *Pierre Damien*, p. 60.

[25] See, for example, his appeal to the widowed Adelaide of Savoy, who controlled parts of northern Italy and Burgundy (Op. 18, *PL* 145, cols. 418–419).

[26] See, for example, his denunciation of the revolt of the Florentines against their bishop under the leadership of John Gualdboldi, in Op. 30, *PL* 145, cols. 523–530; cf. Carm. 22, 974–977.

tarene reform movement in Milan, felt otherwise.[27] His delineation of the essential difference between the clergy and the laity was intended to incite rebellion. Andrew of Strumi, Ariald's follower and eventual hagiographer, vividly re-creates one of his sermons in which the present priesthood, originally entrusted with illuminating the world with the light of the Scripture, is presented as betraying their mission by assuming a lay way of life. " 'Just like laymen they [i.e., clerics] openly marry wives, like wicked laymen they follow lust, and they are the more capable of carrying out this impious work the less they are oppressed by terrestrial work: by living, namely, off of the gift of God.' "[28] Ariald's message had the desired effect. At the conclusion of the sermon, a certain Nazarius (a man "whose life was laudable in all things, although he was married") played the proverbial dog to Ariald's Pavlov: " 'Who is so stupid as not to be able to consider lucidly that the life of those whom I call upon to bless my house ought to be different and more elevated than mine.' "[29]

By impressing their vision of the church on lay society, the Patarene leaders molded the laity into an instrument that would realize the reformers' ends. The masses of married priests were boycotted. Clerical couples were violently separated and their houses plundered.[30] Despite protests from certain members of the curia, all of the Patarene methods received papal sanction. In 1059, Nicholas II adopted the lay boycott of masses for general use in Christendom—a measure that smacked of Donatism and would henceforth encourage the laity

---

[27] For a concise overview of the movement and its significance, see H.E.J. Cowdrey, "The Papacy, the Patarenes, and the Church of Milan," *Transactions of the Royal Historical Society*, ser. 5, 18 (1986): 25–48.

[28] " 'Sicut laici palam uxores ducunt, stuprum quemadmodum scelestes laici secuntur atque ad nefandum hoc opus patrandum tanto sunt validiores, quanto a terreno labore minus oppressi, videlicet viventes de dono Dei' " (Andrew of Strumi, *Vita sancti Arialdi* c. 4, ed. F. Baethgen, *MGH, Scrip.*, vol. 30,2 [Leipzig, 1934], p. 1052). For a detailed analysis of this sermon, see Stock, *The Implications of Literacy*, pp. 217–223.

[29] " 'Quis tam insipiens est, qui non lucide perpendere possit, quod eorum vita esse altius debeat a mea dissimilis, quos ego in domum meam ad benedicendum eam voco' " (Andrew of Strumi, *Vita sancti Arialdi* c. 6, *MGH, Scrip.*, 30,2:1053; Stock, *The Implications of Literacy*, p. 223; also see Moore, "Family, Community, and Cult," pp. 68–69).

[30] Arnulf of Milan is considered to be the most reliable source for the Patarene uprising. On the lay boycott and the ensuing mob violence, see *Arnulfi gesta archiepiscoporum Mediolanensium* 3.11–13, 3.17, 3.20–21 (ed. L. C. Bethmann and W. Wattenbach, *MGH, Scrip.*, vol. 8 [Hanover, 1848; reprt. Leipzig, 1925], pp. 19–20, 22, 23). Landulf the Senior, himself a married priest who was deeply opposed to the reform's objectives, gives a more partisan account in *Mediolanensis historiae libri quatuor* 3.10, 3.15, 3.28, pp. 93, 99, 119. Also see Andrew of Strumi, *Vita sancti Arialdi* c. 6, *MGH, Scrip.*, 30,2:1053.

to sit in judgment of the clergy, promoting anticlericalism.[31] The lay leader, Erlembald, who dominated the movement after Ariald's murder, received the papal banner to carry into battle.[32] All of the Patarene leaders were eventually canonized.

Women were the "matter" that was out of place in the reformer's vision; the "dirt" that imperiled sacerdotal purity.[33] And so, like dirt, they were ruthlessly swept to one side. Many scholars have noted that clerical wives bore the brunt of the reformers' abuse. This is certainly true on a legislative level. Before the Gregorian reform "proper," the reform-minded emperor Henry II ordered that wives and children of priests should become slaves of the church (Pavia, 1022). Leo IX later ordered that wives and concubines of priests become slaves of the Lateran Palace (Rome, 1050). These canons, or slight variations thereof, were reissued at fairly regular intervals.[34] The priests, on the other hand, were, at very worst, threatened with excommunication or deposition. But it is inevitable that with a campaign which aimed at nothing less than completely purging a male clergy of their female companions, women in general would become the enemy. Although Peter Damian corresponded and seems to have developed friendships with several women,[35] he often presented the clerical wives, not the priests themselves, as the real trangressors.[36]

[31] This revolutionary piece of legislation, forbidding the laity to attend the mass of any priest who had a concubine or a *subintroducta* (the designation "wife" is, significantly, withheld), was first promulgated under Nicholas II in 1059: "Ut nullus missam audiat presbyteri, quem scit concubinam indubitanter habere, aut subintroductam mulierem" (Council of Rome, 1059, c. 3; G. D. Mansi, *Sacrorum conciliorum nova et amplissima collectio*, vol. 19 [Florence, 1797], col. 897). It was not really enforced, however, until it was reissued by Gregory VII in 1074 (see Lea, *History of Sacerdotal Celibacy*, 1:228). Note that Burchard of Worms's *Corrector*, written between 1007 and 1012, still chastised members of the laity who dared to refuse a sacrament administered by a married priest, assigning a year's penance to the recalcitrant. This is in accordance with canons from the earliest years of the church: "*De irreligiositate. . . .* Sprevisti missam vel orationem, vel oblationem conjugati presbyteri, ita dico ut nolles tua peccata sibi confiteri, vel ab eo accipere corpus et sanguinem Domini, ob hoc quia peccator tibi esse videretur? Si fecisti, unum annum per legitimas ferias poeniteas" (*Decretorum libri viginti* 19.5, *PL* 140, col. 963). Also see Vauchez, *La spiritualité*, p. 52.

[32] Arnulf, *Arnulfi gesta* 3.17, *MGH*, *Scrip.*, 8:22.

[33] See Douglas, *Purity and Danger*, p. 40.

[34] Barstow, *Married Priests and the Reforming Papacy*, pp. 43–44; Stickler, "L'évolution de la discipline du célibat," pp. 403–405; Lynch, "Marriage and Celibacy of the Clergy," p. 189; Dortel-Claudot, "Le prêtre et le mariage," p. 341.

[35] See Jean Leclercq, "S. Pierre Damien et les femmes," *Studia Monastica* 15 (1973): 48–49.

[36] Like Jerome, Damian also found himself attracted to women, and believed it was not safe for him to be around young ones—or so he writes to a young countess (Ep. 7, c. 18, *PL* 144, col. 458). On the psychological factors that provided a frame for his anti-

I speak to you, O you the clerics' charmers, Devil's choice tidbits, expulsion from paradise, virus of minds, sword of souls, wolfbane to drinkers, poison to companions, material of sinning, occasion of death. You, I say: I mean the female chambers of the ancient enemy, of hoopoes, of screech owls, of night owls, of the she-wolves, of the bloodsuckers, which say: Give, give! without ceasing (Prov. 30.15). And so come, hear me whores, prostitutes, lovers, wallowing pools of greasy hogs, bedrooms of unclean spirits, nymphs, sirens, lamiae, followers of Diana . . . For you are the victims of demons destined to the fall into eternal death.[37]

Both active hostility and manifest indifference to women's material and spiritual welfare correspond to the pivotal place sexuality, and thus women, occupied in the reformers' vision of society. Pivotal but marginal.[38] Women were not only a source of temptation that must be shunned but perhaps a source of envy to the newly reformed priesthood. Sexual purity was the cornerstone to their claims of sacerdotal ascendancy, and the reformers still recognized women's virtuosity in this area. Peter Damian himself acknowledged that male chastity was more fragile.[39]

But the reformers' attitudes toward women were inseparable from wider social and intellectual trends. The expulsion of clerical wives corresponds to a general marginalization of female spirituality in this period. The monasteries that were reformed along Cluniac lines, even if originally double monasteries of monks and nuns, were changed into male houses, so as a result there were fewer religious options for women than there had formerly been. Much of this had to do with the augmentation of the priest's role and the increased importance of monastic masses—factors that inhibited the foundation of female

---

feminism, see Lester K. Little's "The Personal Development of Peter Damian," in *Order and Innovation in the Middle Ages: Essays in Honor of Joseph R. Strayer*, ed. William C. Jordan et al. (Princeton, N.J., 1976), pp. 317–341, 523–528; cf. Mary Martin McLaughlin, "Survivors and Surrogates: Children and Parents from the Ninth to the Thirteenth Century," in *The History of Childhood*, ed. Lloyd deMause (New York, 1974), pp. 103–105.

[37] "Vos alloquor, o lepores clericorum, pulpamenta diaboli, projectio paradisi, virus mentium, gladius animarum, aconita bibentium, toxica convivarum, materia peccandi, occasio pereundi. Vos, inquam, alloquor gynecaea hostis antiqui, upupae, ululae, noctuae, lupae, sanguisugae, Affer, affer sine cessatione dicentes (Prov. 30.15). Venite itaque, audite me, scorta, prostibula, savia, volutabra porcorum pinguium; cubilia spirituum immundorum, nymphae, sirenae, lamiae, dianae . . . Vos enim estis daemonum victimae ad aeternae mortis succidium destinatae" (Op. 18, 2.7, *PL* 145, col. 410; also see Op. 17, cols. 379–387).

[38] Cf. Moore, "Family, Community, and Cult," p. 67.

[39] Leclercq, "S. Pierre Damien et les femmes," pp. 49, 53.

houses.[40] Indeed, the only foundation for women that Cluny was responsible for was Marcigny—developed as a refuge for women whose husbands had separated from them to become monks at Cluny.[41] Thus, even had the expelled wives of priests had sufficient means to enter a Benedictine house (which required a substantial dowry) this alternative was limited. Hence, Georges Duby speculates that clerical wives were probably one of the groups which joined the wandering preachers and became a part of the itinerant poor.[42]

St. Alexis and the Masculine Calling

Many scholars have noted that the flight from the world was a peculiarly masculine pattern in this period.[43] The sources by and large support this, although one should bear in mind that this age was little inclined to extol female spirituality. But from a psychological standpoint, a male flight seems to ring true. The masculine laity, who had assisted the clergy in achieving their new purified standard, could hardly remain impervious to the disadvantages or even dangers of remaining in their *ordo*. Their "transgressive desires" are most fittingly represented by the legend of St. Alexis—the young Roman nobleman who abandoned his bride on his wedding night for his own

[40] R. W. Southern, *Western Society and the Church in the Middle Ages* (Harmondsworth, Middlesex, 1970), pp. 310–312; Schulenburg, "Sexism and the Celestial Gynaeceum," pp. 124–125. Schulenburg estimates that for every four foundations for men there was one for women. Cf. "Women's Monastic Communities," pp. 226–232. In this latter work, however, Schulenburg points out that patterns of donation, which implicate both laymen and laywomen, are equally prejudicial to female religious (pp. 232–237). Also see Vauchez, *La spiritualité*, pp. 116–117, and Penelope D. Johnson, *Equal in Monastic Profession: Religious Women in Medieval France* (Chicago and London, 1991), pp. 251–264. Johnson pursues these trends into the thirteenth century.

[41] Southern, *Western Society*, pp. 310–311; Noreen Hunt, *Cluny under Saint Hugh, 1049–1109* (London, 1967), pp. 186–194.

[42] "Les pauvres des campagnes dans l'occident médiéval jusqu'au XIIIe siècle," *Revue d'histoire de l'église de France* 52 (1966): 28.

[43] See Vauchez, *La spiritualité*, p. 118; Christopher N. L. Brooke, *The Medieval Idea of Marriage* (Oxford, 1989), p. 69; cf. Nicolas Huyghebaert, "Les femmes laïques dans la vie religieuse des XIe et XIIe siècles dans la province ecclésiastique de Reims," in *I laici nella 'Societas Christiana' dei secoli XI e XII*, p. 370. Guibert of Nogent, on the other hand, depicts religious enthusiasm as affecting both sexes of all ages and rank. He speaks explicitly of noblewomen rejecting their husbands and their children for their vocation: "feminae itidem insignes maritorum celebrium jugalitate deserta, et a piis cordibus liberorum caritudine abstenta, ecclesiasticis se stipendiis contradebant" (*Histoire de sa vie* 1.11, ed. Georges Bourgin, Collection de textes pour servir à l'étude et à l'enseignement de l'histoire, fasc. 40 [Paris, 1907], p. 36).

idiosyncratic spiritual destiny.[44] The chronology of the cult is of interest. The Alexis story probably originated in the latter half of the fifth century with the anonymous "Man of God" tale, which was of either Syrian or Greek provenance.[45] His cult developed in the Byzantine Empire, where, over the course of the eighth or ninth century, he received the name Alexis.[46] The cult of Alexis reached the West only toward the end of the tenth century when Sergius, archbishop of Damascus, fled to Rome with his followers. Sergius established an important intellectual center at the church of St. Boniface on the Aventine, and it is from there that Alexis's cult spread.[47] Versions of the legend reached Spain and Italy in the late tenth century. One of the earliest traces of his cult is a homily that Bishop Adalbert of Prague wrote while visiting Rome between 989 and 996.[48] It was not until the eleventh century that his cult became widespread, and at this point a standard Latin version seems to have developed.[49] It was

[44] Originally the anonymous protagonist died in Edessa, far from his native Rome (Arthur Amiaud, ed. and trans., *La légende syriaque de saint Alexis, l'homme de Dieu* [Paris, 1889], pp. 3–4, 7–8). Cf. parallel patterns outlined by de Gaiffier for the brother of St. Syncletica (*"Intactam sponsam,"* p. 168), Macarius the Roman (p. 170), Abraham Kidunaia (p. 171), Leobard (p. 173), and Maximus (p. 175).

[45] Amiaud favored the Syrian explanation, as this manuscript was earliest. Carl J. Odenkirchen convincingly summarizes the scholarship for a Greek origin insofar as the Greek version is clearly more primitive (*The Life of St. Alexius, In the Old French Version of the Hildesheim Manuscript* [Brookline, Mass., and Leyden, 1978], introd., pp. 31–32).

[46] There are a number of significant additions made to the legend during this period that soften Alexis's unilateral repudiation of his bride. Rather than fleeing immediately after the ceremony, Alexis converts his spouse to chastity in the nuptial chamber. He also gives her some gifts: a ring, a belt, and a veil, according to most versions of the legend (*AA SS*, July, 4:252). These gifts emphasize that the couple is married (hence showing a consensual understanding of the bond) and further bind the bride to chastity. Alexis also returns home after his sojourn in the East to die pitifully under his father's staircase. His identity is revealed only after his death (for these later additions, see de Gaiffier, *"Intactam sponsam,"* pp. 163–164). Concerning the significance of Alexis's gifts to the bride, see de Gaiffier, *"Intactam sponsam,"* pp. 186–190; Ulrich Mölk, "Saint Alexis et son épouse dans la légende latine et la première Chanson française," in *Love and Marriage in the Twelfth Century*, ed. W. Van Hoecke and A. Welkenhuysen, Mediaevalia Lovaniensia, ser. 1, studia 8 (Leuven, 1981), pp. 163–167. The veil, in particular, seems to be the traditional *velatio conjugalis* or *flammeum* (see D'Izarny, "Mariage et consécration virginale," pp. 94–97, and Ritzer, *Le mariage dans les églises chrétiennes*, pp. 217–219).

[47] Odenkirchen, *The Life of St. Alexius*, introd., pp. 33–34; *BS*, vol. 1, cols. 814–823.

[48] Adalbert emphasizes Alexis as a type of apostolic poverty and speaks of the hundredfold reward that he received, and that those like him will receive, for spurning carnal marriage in favor of virginity ("Homilia in natale S. Alexii Confessoris," *PL* 137, cols. 897–900).

[49] Aleksander Gieysztor, *"Pauper sum et peregrinus.* La légende de saint Alexis en

probably in the mid- or late eleventh century that the Old French version was written—the first work produced in vernacular French.

I have emphasized the spread of Alexis's cult in the West because it seems to correspond with the rise of lay piety as a side effect of the reform movement. Moreover, for the religious fervor of the masculine laity (whether heretical or orthodox in expression) as well as for clerical opponents to nicolaitism, the legend was peculiarly expressive of the age: an age in which purity was found outside rather than inside of marriage and in which this purity was portrayed as primarily the province of the male. It is significant that Alexis's sacrifice is prefigured by the vow of chastity taken by his parents after his conception.[50] Nor is it surprising that the cult was promoted by the Cluniac order and fostered by Peter Damian.[51]

Contemporary reenactments of the Alexis legend seem to have been occurring all over Europe, only the cloister replaced his voluntary exile and anonymous ignominy. The social status of the participants was a match for the alleged nobility of Alexis. The conversion of Simon of Crépy (d. between 1080 and 1082), count of Valois, is notable in this respect. Not only was he one of the most powerful men of his day, although still in his early twenties, but, as his biographer asserts, he surpassed Alexis when he converted his *sponsa* to monasticism in their nuptial chamber. A number of men and women were converted by his preaching.[52]

This retreat from the world seems to have been prompted by fear,

---

occident: un idéal de pauvreté," in *Etudes sur l'histoire de la pauvreté*, ed. Michel Mollat, Publications de la Sorbonne, Sér. "Etudes," vol. 8 (Paris, 1974), pp. 125–128. Ulrich Mölk traces Alexis's cult by examining breviaries, missals, and other liturgical books to assess to what extent Alexis's feast was celebrated in France ("La diffusion du culte de S. Alexis en France aux XIe et XIIe siècles et le problème de la genèse de la Chanson de S. Alexis," in *Littérature et société au moyen âge*, ed. Danielle Buschinger, Actes du colloque des 5 et 6 mai 1978, Université de Picardie, Centre d'études médiévales [Paris, 1978], pp. 231–238). The "canonical" version of the legend, which is thought to be close to its eleventh-century form, is printed in *AA SS*, July, 4:251–254.

[50] *AA SS*, July, 4:251.

[51] Mölk, "Saint Alexis et son épouse dans la légende latine," p. 164; idem, "La diffusion du culte de S. Alexis," p. 235. In his sermon on Alexis, Peter Damian talks at length about his parents' piety and the way in which a good marriage renders good fruit. He does not, however, directly address their vow of chastity, though he describes their marriage as chaste: "Dignum itaque fuit ut de tam casto, tam sancto, tam denique immaculato coniugalis pudicitiae thalamo, tam praeclara soboles nasceretur" (Serm. 28, c. 1, *CCSL*, 57:162). We know from the legend that they did take a vow of chastity after Alexis's birth—otherwise Damian's meaning might have been unclear.

[52] Guibert of Nogent, *Histoire de sa vie* 1.10, pp. 27–29; *AA SS* September, 8:744–751; also see Duby, *The Knight, the Lady, and the Priest*, pp. 125–127; cf. the timely flight of Simon's noble contemporary Bernard of Mount Joy (*AA SS*, June, 3:550).

which in turn gave rise to devotion. A dynastic example from an anonymous monastic chronicle, written in Brabant some time after 1122, will suffice to demonstrate this.[53] In 1091 a rich man named Heribrand had a most terrifying dream while sleeping beside his wife Adele—"quite a religious and virtuous woman" (admodum religiosa et honesta femina). It seems that God had damned him to eternal torment and that he was only saved by the intercession of St. Peter. After waking up his wife and telling her about the dream, he proposed that they give up the world in favor of the religious life, and she willingly agreed. He was just in time, as he died about a month later. All of their five sons were eventually drawn into the monastic vortex, though all at different times. Some were married; some were widowed; some brought their children; all donated their property. Three of the youngest ones went first; then the eldest, named Folcard. On-ulf, the last brother remaining in the world, was vehemently opposed to Folcard's conversion, no doubt frightened of what would come next, "and among other words of objection and pride, affirmed by oath that he would never become a monk even if he knew while [still] alive that he was going to hell."[54] Soon after this show of spirit, he was seized by a grave illness, and the rest is predictable: he took the habit along with his wife and three children just in time to make a good end.

Fear of death was no new thing, nor were deathbed conversions to the monastic life, for which parents would often impoverish their heirs on behalf of their own immortal souls.[55] Nevertheless, something new had happened. The laity's spiritual awakening was a rude one. They almost instantly began to question, and ultimately to doubt, whether they could be saved while continuing in their station.[56] The story of the conversion of the monkish chronicler Heri-mann's parents is expressive in this context. His father, Radulf, suffered a serious illness and, during his convalescence, secretly went to see his brother-in-law, Walter, a monk. He told him that when he had thought that he was dying, he had made a clean confession and had received the last rites. But as soon as he felt better, he once again felt bound by his sins. He asked Walter's advice, who answered: " 'In truth . . . I say to you that as long as you were to live in the world just as you

---

[53] G. H. Pertz, ed., Chronicon Affligemense c. 12–13, MGH, Scrip., vol. 9 (Hanover, 1851), pp. 412–414; see Huyghebaert, "Les femmes laïques," pp. 367–368.

[54] "Atque inter alia contradictionis et elationis verba se nunquam monachum futurum, etiamsi sciret se vivum ad tartara deducendum, cum iuramento affirmavit" (Pertz, ed., Chronicon Affligemense c. 13, p. 414).

[55] See Goody, The Development of the Family and Marriage in Europe, pp. 81–102.

[56] Cf. Vauchez, La spiritualité, pp. 55–56.

lived up until now, I do not see how you can be saved, but if in fact you wish to be saved, abandon the world and take up the monastic life.' "[57] When Radulf asked how Walter could offer such advice to his sister's husband, the latter cited Luke 14.26 about hating one's wife and children. Radulf's soul should by no means be imperiled for his wife's sake. Her permission should be asked, but if she withheld it, she should be abandoned.[58]

Such merciless reasoning, such indifference to a spouse's well-being, evokes the unilateral repudiations of Eastern ascetics. One might expect an equally grim outcome. But when Maisend, his wife, discovers Radulf weeping and learns the reason, it turns out that she too had been fearing for her soul and wanted to abandon the world. In the meantime, she suggests that they live chastely and, in response to Radulf's questioning, resolves that their three sons likewise be dedicated to God. Radulf is overjoyed and wants to embark immediately upon their new life, only to learn that his wife is pregnant. They will give up the world as soon as she has given birth:

> After this, just as they told me many times, for an entire year and a half they remained in the world and lay together in one bed. Nevertheless they did not do anything carnal, not by their own strength, but with the grace of Christ protecting them.[59]

Maisend was only twenty-four when her fourth son, Radulf was born. Nevertheless, she placed his cradle on the altar of the church and took the veil as onlookers wept.[60] As is generally the case, Radulf and Maisend's conversion sparked a chain reaction, and a number of people in their community likewise abandoned the world.[61] Radulf and Maisend could be satisfied only by a complete break with their past, despite very pressing familial claims. Spiritual marriage was a temporary measure.[62]

---

[57] " 'In veritate . . . dico vobis, quod, quamdiu in seculo vixeritis sicut hactenus vixistis, non video, quomodo salvari possitis, sed si re vera salvus esse vultis, seculum relinquite et monasticam vitam assumite' " (Herimann of Tournai, *Liber de restaura-tione S. Martini Tornacensis* c. 61, ed. G. Waitz, *MGH, Scrip.*, vol. 14 [Hanover, 1883], p. 302).

[58] " 'Numquam consulam vobis, ut pro sorore mea animam vestram perdatis. Licentiam tantum ab ea querite; quam si illa noluerit dare, consulo, ut, ea relicta, parteque substantie vestre ei dimissa, ad Deum fugiatis' " (ibid.).

[59] "Post hec, sicut ipsi multociens mihi retulerunt, anno integro et dimidio in vita seculari manserunt, in uno lecto indivisi iacuerunt, nec tamen aliquid carnale gesserunt, non sua fortitudine, sed Christi gratia eos protegente" (ibid.).

[60] Ibid. c. 63, p. 304.

[61] Ibid. c. 65–66, p. 305.

[62] Maisend's situation is also of interest in that it again demonstrates the dearth of

The Blurring of Boundaries: A Tentative Sketch
of Female Spirituality

The Alexian model, though transgressive in its way, was easily assimilated into the division between clergy and laity insofar as the men in question actually left their respective *ordo*. More threatening, however, were attempts to blur such boundaries, as the fledgling peniten tial movement was wont to do. It is rather precocious at this stage to identify categorically the flight from the world with male spirituality and the blurring of boundaries with female. On the other hand, by the thirteenth century women will have irrefutably left their mark on the penitential movement and won begrudging acceptance for a religious vocation pursued in the world. Moreover, already in the eleventh century, the most conspicuous sponsors of female spirituality appeared indifferent to many of the newly sanctioned divisions in society. The mission of the wandering preacher Robert of Arbrissel is a case in point. He was portrayed by his biographer, Baldric, as one of the most Christlike men of his day,[63] and his perfection is epitomized in the dissolution of all canonized boundaries. Baldric's insistence on this point speaks for itself.

A great multitude of vagabonds clung to him. . . .

Many of both sexes were joined to him because he dared deny no one on whom God breathed.

He led the mixed soldiers of Christianity hither.

Lay and clerics walked together. . . . all joined together in brotherly love.

religious options for women in this period. The group surrounding St. Martin of Tournai originated with the conversion of Odo of Orleans, who attracted both clergy and laity to the monastic life. But when Maisend made her conversion, there was no monastic house for women in this area. So great was the need that the abbot of St. Martin's had to found two female houses. The one in which Maisend was destined to live was a house that Radulf had donated. There were already sixty women to fill this new foundation (ibid. c. 69, pp. 306–307; Huyghebaert, "Les femmes laïques," pp. 366–367).

[63] Baldric, bishop of Dole, *Vita B. Roberti de Arbrissello* 4.23, *PL* 162, col. 1055. For a summary of some of the conflicting views regarding Robert and especially his relations with women, see Jacqueline Smith, "Robert of Arbrissel: *Procurator Mulierum*," in *Medieval Women*, ed. Baker, pp. 175–184. Robert's efforts on behalf of women should be compared with the twelfth-century foundations of Prémontré by Norbert of Xanten, which originally included both sexes (Herimann of Laon, *De miraculis B. Mariae Laudunensis* 3.7, ed. R. W. Wilmans, *MGH, Scrip.*, vol. 12 [Hanover, 1856], p. 659), and especially that of St. Gilbert of Sempringham (*The Book of St. Gilbert* c. 9, ed. and trans. Raymonde Foreville and Gillian Keir [Oxford, 1987], p. 307).

Many *publicani* and *publicanae* clung to him.

The multitude of those renouncing sins grew in such a degree that the number was almost countless; he did not wish them to be designated by any name except the poor of Christ. Many men assembled of every condition; women gathered: poor and noble ones, widows and virgins, young and old, prostitutes and man-haters.

They accepted the poor and did not repel the weak, nor did they refuse incestuous women, or concubines, or lepers or the powerless.

He in fact preached to the poor, he called the poor, he gathered the poor. Yet, if any woman of the nobility hurried to him, to one who discerns, he then resembled Jesus with Nicodemus, Peter with Cornelius the Centurion. Since the abundance of God's grace attracts all, he repelled no one.[64]

Robert's universal call to the "Poor of Christ" had the effect of legitimizing the marginal and marginalizing the great. His critics bitterly reproached him for the confusion ensuing from his lack of discrimination.[65] Indeed, Robert's vision of redemption extended to the dark-

---

[64] "Adhaerebat ei tanta convenarum multitudo" (2.15, *Vita B. Roberti Arbrissello, PL* 162, col. 1051).

"Sexus utriusque plures adjuncti sunt ei, quia neminem, cui Deus aspirasset, audebat repellere" (3.16, col. 1051).

"Promiscuos Christianitatis tirones illuc induxit" (3.16, col. 1052).

"Laici et clerici mistim ambulabant. . . . omnes amore fraterno conglutinabantur" (3.17, col. 1052).

"Multi publicani et publicanae ipsi adhaeserint" (3.18, col. 1053).

"Intantum peccatis abrenuntiantium crevit examen, ut numerus pene fuerit innumerus: quos alio nolebat censeri vocabulo, nisi pauperes Christi. Multi confluebant homines cujuslibet conditionis; conveniebant mulieres, pauperes et nobiles, viduae et virgines, senes et adolescentes, meretrices et masculorum aspernatrices" (3.19, col. 1053).

"Suscipiebant pauperes, ac debiles non repellebant; nec incestas, nec pellices refutabant, leprosos, nec impotentes" (4.22, col. 1055).

"Iste revera pauperibus evangelizavit, pauperes vocavit, pauperes collegit. Nam si qua mulier ad eum de nobilitate maturavit, illi qui sapit, ibi Nicodemum et Jesum, ibi Cornelium Centurionem et Petrum assimilabat, affluentia siquidem gratiarum Dei omnes allicit, neminem repellit" (4.23, col. 1055).

[65] Marbod, the bishop of Rennes, alleges that under Robert's influence, poor priests were deserting their flocks, mobs were forming whose proper place was with their respective pastors, and that most of this rabble were attracted by a love of novelty, rather than religion. Marbod is intensely suspicious of the hasty conversions that

est reaches of the flesh: to the lepers and the "prostitutes" (probably a number of these were the repudiated wives of clerics).[66] These outcasts mixed freely with the morally and physically sound. It was not the cult of the pure Virgin that Robert emphasized, but the cult of Mary Magdalene: the holy whore.[67] The fact that Robert was repeatedly accused of syneisaktism—in this context meaning that he slept in chastity with his disparate sisterhood—suggests that he was experimenting with the limits of gender boundaries themselves.[68]

Robert eventually founded the double monastery of Fontevrault in order to provide a more settled life for his following.[69] But the foundation itself ran counter to contemporary norms. Although accommodating both sexes, Fontevrault was peculiarly designed to meet women's spiritual needs and was governed by an abbess. The brothers were there to serve the sisters.[70] Furthermore, the first elected abbess of Fontevrault was not a stainless virgin, but a matron—and one who may have been a repudiated wife with a living husband.[71] And so,

---

Robert had the gift of inspiring, and claims that many return to their old lives and thus incur damnation. Worse still is the situation of young women who come to miserable ends, giving birth in poor houses (Marbod of Rennes, Ep. 6, "To Robert," *PL* 171, cols. 1484–1486).

[66] Duby, "Pauvres des campagnes," p. 28.

[67] See Jacques Dalarun, "Robert d'Arbrissel et les femmes," *Annales ESC* 39 (1984): 1151–1154.

[68] Marbod refers to the scandal that had arisen around the fact that, at the end of a day's journeying, Robert would stretch out to sleep between the two sexes while watch was set: "Has etenim solum communi accubitu per noctem, ut referunt, accubante simul et discipulorum grege, ut inter utrosque medius jacens, utrique sexui vigiliarum et somni leges praefigas" (Ep. 6, "To Robert," *PL* 171, col. 1481). Even after the foundation of Fontevrault, Robert's sleeping arrangements were called into question, this time by Geoffrey of Vendôme. Geoffrey claims that Robert himself perceives sleeping with women in chastity, and thus overcoming the fires of lust, as taking up the cross of Christ. But to Geoffrey, this is a novel and fruitless kind of martyrdom: "Feminarum quasdam, ut dicitur, nimis familiariter tecum habitare permittis, quibus privata verba saepius loqueris, et eum [sic] ipsis etiam, et inter ipsas noctu frequenter cubare non erubescis. Hinc tibi videris, ut asseris, Domini Salvatoris digne bajulare crucem, cum exstinguere conaris male accensum carnis ardorem. Hoc si modo agis, vel aliquando egisti, novum et inauditum, sed infructuosum genus martyrii invenisti" (*Epist.* bk. 6, 47, *PL* 157, col. 182).

[69] On the foundation and constitution of Fontevrault, see Penny S. Gold, "Male/Female Cooperation: The Example of Fontevrault," in *Distant Echoes*, vol. 1 of *Medieval Religious Women*, ed. John A. Nichols and Lillian Thomas Shank, Cistercian Studies Series, no. 71 (Kalamazoo, Mich., 1984), pp. 151–168.

[70] Ibid., pp. 153–154, 156–160.

[71] Baldric makes frequent reference to the marital status of the abbess, Petronilla (see *Vita B. Roberti de Arbrissello* Prologue, c. 1, cols. 1043–1044; 4.21, col. 1054). Dalarun analyzes the background of the early female members of Fontevrault and concludes that the majority of these women were casualties of the eleventh-century

Robert's sensitivity to the female spiritual vocation was at odds with eleventh-century patterns of monastic foundation, while anticipating future trends.[72] His inclusion of both sexes in Fontevrault stayed the flight from the other. His insistence that women should rule over men and matrons over virgins further challenged both sexual and moral hierarchies.

Although Fontevrault lost much of its pioneering spirit after the death of its founder, Robert and his early following had challenged the sharp dichotomy between the cloister and the world as effectively as any of the early eleventh-century heresies had done. He even wrote a short rule of life for Ermengarde, countess of Brittany, which outlined the path of redemption in the midst of court life.[73]

There is also evidence from this period, albeit sparse, for groups of pious laypeople who were married and remained in the world. In 1091, Bernold of Constance fleetingly enumerates three divisions of converted laypeople (*conversi*) who live a common life but do not take orders or become religious: single men, women, and married individuals.[74] Unmarried men attach themselves to monasteries and serve the monks; unmarried women depend on a collegial church or abbey for religious instruction, and are vowed to its service, perhaps living in a nearby village. These two divisions pledge celibacy. But the married couples live the common life in the world, wearing some sort of

---

marriage crisis: either noble women repudiated for their sterility or clerical wives ("Robert d'Arbrissel et les femmes," pp. 1143–1145; idem, *Robert d'Arbrissel: fondateur de Fontevraud* [Paris, 1986], pp. 82–84).

[72] On the parallel work of Norbert of Xanten and Gilbert of Sempringham, see n. 63, above. There may have been a tendency to overestimate Robert's concern for women, however. A number of scholars have recently pointed out that Fontevrault developed more out of necessity than from Robert's conscious planning. See Smith, "Robert of Arbrissel," pp. 179–180. Dalarun also argues that Robert's promotion of women was actually a side effect of his own peculiar asceticism—they were purely instrumental as a source of temptation ("Robert d'Arbrissel et les femmes," pp. 1147–1151; idem, *Robert d'Arbrissel*, pp. 64–78).

[73] Ermengarde fled to Fontevrault for a year, attempting to escape her marriage, but was forced to return to her husband. Robert's compassionate letter (ca. 1109) alternates between sympathy (he clearly believed her marriage to be consanguinous) and admonishments to submit to the judgment of the church and her duties to her husband (René Nidurst, ed., "Lettre inédite de Robert d'Arbrissel à la comtesse Ermengarde," *Bibliothèque de l'Ecole des Chartes* 3,5 [1854], esp. pp. 227–230). This letter is of particular significance since, apart from his name on a few charters, it is the only extant document by Robert. For the rule, see pp. 232–235.

[74] G. Meersseman and E. Adda, "Pénitents ruraux communautaires en Italie au XIIe siècle," *Revue d'histoire ecclésiastique* 49 (1954): 343–346; also see Vauchez, *La spiritualité*, pp. 138–140. Such groups probably evolved from pious confraternities or guilds. See Susan Reynolds, *Kingdoms and Communities in Western Europe, 900–1300* (Oxford, 1984), p. 69.

distinct penitential costume, and swearing obedience to external religious authority who undertake their spiritual direction. Although
there have always been penitents, expiating their sins in isolation,
what is original about these lay associations is the fact that whole
villages were dedicating themselves and their land en masse. Bernold
tells us that there are a number of such associations in Germany, but
we have no other evidence for them until the twelfth century, when
similar movements emerge in the Italian countryside.[75] Extended
periods of continence played a sufficiently large part in their discipline that these groups warranted the name *continentes*[76]—a clear
challenge to all orders, be they binary or tertiary.

The Virgin King

One of the most dramatic examples of the fluidity of lay spirituality,
of the "slippage" between orders and functions, is the emergence of
the confessor king—kings who earned their religious stripes not
through glorious martyrdom, actively fighting for the faith, but
through persevering in a life of asceticism.[77] The first "full-blown"
confessor king, Robert the Pious, was eyed nervously during his lifetime by one of the more conservative ecclesiastics of his circle.[78]
Adalbero, bishop of Laon, launched his famous vision of the three
orders of society through the medium of a satiric poem that was
intended to arrest Robert's dangerous asceticism.[79] He vividly depicts a world of chaos in which peasants are crowned,[80] bishops
are stripped naked,[81] uxorious monks boisterously go to war,[82] and

[75] "Set et ipsi coniugati nichilominus religiose vivere et religiosis cum summa
devotione non cessaverunt obedire. Huiusmodi autem studium in Alemannia pot-
issimum usquequaque decenter effloruit, in qua provincia etiam multae villae ex integro se religioni contradiderunt seque invicem sanctitate morum praevenire inces-
sabiliter studuerunt" (as cited in Meersseman and Adda, "Pénitents ruraux," p. 344).

[76] Vauchez, *La spiritualité*, p. 142.

[77] See Robert Folz, *Les saints rois du moyen âge en occident* (Brussels, 1984), p. 69. A
masculine precedent for the confessor king may be discerned, however, in Odo of
Cluny's life of the noble Gerald of Aurillac, who is portrayed as particularly monastic
in his devotions. According to Poulin, this is the first substantial effort to reconcile lay
life with conceptions of sanctity (*L'idéal de sainteté*, pp. 82–89, 95–98, 127–28).

[78] See Duby, *The Three Orders*, pp. 44–55.

[79] Adalbero describes the house of God as threefold—some pray, some fight, others
labor: "Triplex ergo Dei domus est quae creditur una. / Nunc orant, alii pugnant aliique
laborant" (*Poème au roi Robert*, lines 295–296, ed. Claude Carozzi [Paris, 1979], p. 22).

[80] Ibid., lines 37–38, p. 4.

[81] Ibid., lines 41–42, p. 4.

[82] Ibid., lines 77–79, p. 6; lines 94–114, p. 8; lines 131–148, pp. 10–12.

cowled taciturn knights refuse to copulate.[83] But Adalbero's warning seemingly went unheard. Both bishop and king died in 1031, and the poem remained unfinished. At the hands of his monastic hagiographer, Helgaud of Fleury, Robert is depicted as an ascetic, indeed almost anemic, king: virtually a monk on a throne.[84]

Robert's matrimonial problems, not to mention his progeny, were too well known for him to be a plausible candidate for the crowning virtue of Christian asceticism: sexual purity.[85] But the lives of other monarchs, especially those who died without heirs, were more readily recast in this monkish mold. And thus in a period when reformers and antireformers alike were straining to emphasize the legitimate boundaries of society, the anomaly of the royal virginal marriage resurfaces.

Virginal monarchs are both old and new: old in that there is ample evidence that such a model of sanctity was both highly esteemed and eminently expedient in the early Germanic kingdoms; new in that the eleventh-century avatar seems to have broken many of the rules implicitly encoded in the prototype. The most profound deviation is that it is the chastity of men and not women that is extolled.[86]

There is an early precedent for these virginal kings. Alfonso II (d. 842), commonly known as "the Chaste," ruled the small Christian kingdom of Asturias in northern Spain in critical times. He was the first king to begin a coherent offensive against the Muslims, he was responsible for establishing the court at Oviedo, and he founded a number of important churches and monasteries.[87] From a religious

[83] Ibid., lines 39–40, p. 5; lines 68–76, p. 6; cf. the king's resolve to correct this disorder by stamping out the nobility's excessive piety (lines 420–421, p. 32).

[84] See Joel T. Rosenthal, "Edward the Confessor and Robert the Pious: 11th Century Kingship and Biography," *Mediaeval Studies* 33 (1971): 7–20, esp. pp. 12–16; also see Claude Carozzi, "Le roi et la liturgie chez Helgaud de Fleury," in *Hagiographie, Cultures, et Sociétés, IVe–XIIe siècles*, Actes du Colloque organisé à Nanterre et à Paris (2–5 mai 1979), Centre de Recherches sur l'Antiquité tardive et le haut Moyen Age, Université de Paris-X (Paris, 1981), p. 417; on the different worldviews of Helgaud and Adalbero, see esp. pp. 426–428.

[85] For a discussion of Robert's marriages, see Duby, *The Knight, the Lady, and the Priest*, pp. 75–85.

[86] F. Graus, for example, notes that the chaste marriage conforms with traditional hagiographical models, but does mention the gender change ("La sanctification du souverain dans l'Europe centrale des Xe et XIe siècles," in *Hagiographie, Cultures, et Sociétés*, p. 561).

[87] See Antonio Ubieto Arteta, ed., *Crónica de Alfonso III*, Textos Medievales, 3 (Valencia, 1971), pp. 42–45; and *Chronicon Albeldense* c. 58, in H. Florez, *España Sagrada*, vol. 13 (Madrid, 1756), app. 6, pp. 451–452 (also called *Epitome Ovietensis*). These earliest accounts of Alfonso II's reign date to the second-to-last decade of the ninth century. See esp. Román Menéndez Pidal, ed., *España Cristiana, 711–1038*, vol. 6 of *Historia de España*, 3d ed. (Madrid, 1971), introd., pp. vii–xii for a discussion of the

standpoint, Alfonso was pivotal in promoting the cult of St. James (whose body was apparently discovered during his reign) and in beginning the construction of the important church of Santiago de Compostella.[88] He died without issue. Rumors concerning his chastity began to circulate soon after his death: one late ninth-century chronicle reports that "chastely, soberly, immaculately, piously, and gloriously . . . beloved by God and men, he sent forth his glorious spirit to heaven."[89] A coeval source provides more information still regarding the nature of his remarkable purity: "He lived a most chaste life without a wife; and thus he passed over from the Kingdom of earth to the Kingdom of Heaven."[90] This king was not only chaste, but celibate—a different, although equally unsettling, kind of anomaly.[91]

But leaving aside the enigma of Alfonso's holy bachelorhood, the concept of a "virgin king" was something of a false start—too strange and perhaps even too irresponsible a notion to inspire widespread veneration in a kingdom that was struggling for its life. His cult remained exclusively local, revolving around the church of Oviedo,

---

sources, and pp. 41–60 for an account of his reign. Also see L. Barrau-Dihigo, "Recherches sur l'histoire politique du royaume Asturien (718–910)," *Revue Hispanique* 52 (1921): 152–169, 223, 235, 246–250, and Florez, *España Sagrada*, 37:130–152. For Alfonso as a possible precedent for the ethos of the Reconquest, see Augustin Fliche, "Alphonse II le Chaste et les origines de la reconquête chrétienne," in *Estudios sobre la Monarquia Asturiana*, Instituto de Estudios Asturianos (Oviedo, 1949), pp. 119–134.

[88] There is no mention of the discovery of James's body in the *Crónica de Alfonso III* or in the *Chronicon Albeldense*—the earliest sources. But see Munio Mondoñedo, Hugo Porto, and Gerard the Presbyter's *Historia Compostellana* 1.2.1, *PL* 170, col. 894. Also see T. D. Kendrick, *St. James in Spain* (London, 1960), pp. 18–19. The famous battle of Clavijo (834), in which St. James appeared before the Christian troops, seems to fall chronologically within Alfonso's reign, but scholars attribute this victory to one of his successors—either Ramiro I or Ordoño I (Kendrick, *St. James in Spain*, pp. 19–23; also see Menéndez Pidal, *Historia de España*, 6:104 n. 70). The confusion may have originated as a result of Alfonso's importance in promoting the cult of James, and this association continues to mislead scholars. T. C. Akeley attributes the battle to Alfonso (*Christian Initiation in Spain, c. 300–1100* [London, 1967], p. 40).

[89] "Kaste, sobrie inmaculate, pie ac gloriose . . . , amabilis Deo et hominibus gloriosum spiritum emisit ad caelum." The chronicler goes on to suggest that his body was venerated: "corpus uero eius cum omni ueneratione exequiarum reconditum in supradicta ab eo fundata ecclesia Sancte Mariae saxeo tumulo quiescit in pace" (Ubieto Arteta, ed., *Crónica de Alfonso III*, from the Oviedo version, p. 44).

[90] "Absque uxore castissimam vitam duxit: sicque de Regno terrae ad Regnum transiit Caeli" (*Chronicon Albeldense* c. 58, in Florez, *España Sagrada*, vol. 13, app. 6, p. 452).

[91] Unmarried kings are not unknown, but generally their situation presented the opposite problem to Alfonso's enigmatic behavior. The Anglo-Saxon Æthelbald was reproached by Boniface for his numerous concubines and his refusal to take a legitimate wife (see Stafford, *Queens, Concubines, and Dowagers*, p. 71).

which he had constructed and where he was buried. His memory was kept alive by royal chroniclers. No independent *vita* was produced to celebrate his virtues. His sanctity was a modest appendix to his political and ecclesiastical policy, and a tribute to the relative stability of his fifty-two-year reign. Yet it was also an apology for the succession problems that inevitably followed the childless monarch's death.[92] The cult of the apostle St. James, which was destined to become a rallying point for all of Europe, ultimately had more to offer than that of the chaste king.

It is in the eleventh century that the "virgin king" comes into his own, in line with the infiltration of ascetic values into lay life. In recently converted Hungary, the early cults of the national saints were intended to provide legitimization for the new religion and the new regime—a situation not unlike that of Asturias. Thus the cult of St. Stephen (d. 1038), the first king of Hungary, corresponds with the reign of Ladislaus, the monarch responsible for the consolidation of both church and state.[93] But Ladislaus hedged his bets. Stephen had died a confessor king—his marriage to Gisela, sister of the German emperor Henry II, was widely known, as were their children.[94] Moreover, Stephen had responded to insurrection in an effective but unsaintly way: the conspirators had their hands cut off and their eyes put out.[95] The elevation of Stephen's relics in 1083, the visible act that

[92] For the civil wars following Alfonso's death, see Barrau-Dihigo, "Recherches sur l'histoire politique du Royaume Asturien," pp. 218–221.

[93] Stephen's *Legenda minor* and *Legenda maior* are both edited by E. Bartoniek and printed in *Scriptores Rerum Hungaricarum*, vol. 2, ed. E. Szentpétery (Budapest, 1938), pp. 393–400, 377–392. The *Legenda minor* is the source for the *Legenda maior* and was probably written immediately after the canonization in 1083. The *Legenda maior* was, in turn, the foundation for Hartvic's extremely popular *Legenda S. Stephani regis* (before 1116, Bartoniek, ed., ibid., pp. 401–440). See C. A. Macartney, *The Medieval Hungarian Historians: A Critical and Analytical Guide* (Cambridge, 1953), pp. 161–170. Also see Folz, *Les saints rois*, pp. 76–77. For Stephen's work on behalf of the church and his political significance, see, in Folz, *Les saints rois*, pp. 79–82; for Ladislaus's legend and later canonization, see pp. 101–107. Also see Karol Gorski, "Le roi-saint: un problème d'idéologie féodale," *Annales ESC* 24 (1969): 374, and Gábor Klaniczay, "From Sacral Kingship to Self-Representation: Hungarian and European Royal Saints," in *The Uses of Supernatural Power in the Middle Ages*, trans. Susan Singerman (Cambridge, 1990), pp. 86–91.

[94] For his marriage to Gisela, see Bartoniek, ed., *Legenda maior* c. 9, *Scriptores Rerum Hungaricarum*, 2:384 (the author calls her Gilla); Hartvic, *Legenda S. Stephani regis* c. 10, ibid., p. 415. The *Legenda minor* mentions Stephen's marriage to a relative of the German emperor but does not further specify the relationship (c. 2, ibid., p. 394).

[95] See the *Legenda minor* c. 7, ibid., p. 399. Graus notes that the Hungarian hagiographers seem to have had less difficulty in reconciling the punitive function of their kings with the expectations of sainthood than is the case with other countries ("La sanctification du souverain," p. 563). Even so, the blinding incident is omitted altogether in the *Legenda maior*, while Hartvic relates the offense of the conspirators and

officially confirmed an individual's sanctity, coincided with the raising of two other holy bodies: that of Prince Emeric (d. 1031, also called Henry), Stephen's last remaining child and heir, who was said to have retained his virginity in marriage, and that of Bishop Gerard of Csanád (d. 1046), Hungary's first martyr, who, according to Gerard's *Legenda maior*, was also Emeric's tutor.[96] Flanking Stephen like the two sides of a venerable triptych, these secondary saints mitigated Stephen's deficiencies. The solemn translation was performed with the collaboration of Gregory VII.[97]

Emeric's *vita* is an early twelfth-century effort that is considered to be of little historical value.[98] It bases his claims to sanctity on his asceticism, most particularly his purported chastity.[99] This predilec-

---

says that they were punished appropriately, but tactfully refrains from describing their punishment (*Legenda S. Stephani regis* c. 21, *Scriptores Rerum Hungaricarum*, 2:430). This suggests a slight change in consciousness since the writing of the *Legenda minor* that seems to be borne out by the addition of a vision in the later two lives which was not present in the *Legenda minor*. It was miraculously announced to Stephen's father, Geza, that his as-yet-unborn son would have to complete his father's work of Christianization because Geza had too much blood on his hands (*Legenda maior* c. 3, ibid., p. 379; Hartvic, *Vita S. Stephani regis* c. 2, ibid., p. 404). So it would seem that if the Hungarians were initially oblivious to the conflicting demands of sanctity and royal justice, they did not long remain so. At any rate, the triple canonization undoubtedly smoothed the way for a veneration that might otherwise have been problematical.

[96] Gerard's *Legenda minor* dates from the late eleventh or early twelfth century. It is edited by E. Madzsar and printed in *Scriptores Rerum Hungaricarum*, 2:471–479. This life may have served as the foundation for the *Legenda maior*, which exists in a fourteenth-century manuscript (see pp. 480–506; the original date of its composition is uncertain). For the relationship between the two texts, see Macartney, *Medieval Hungarian Historians*, pp. 154–161, and Z. J. Kosztolnyik, *Five Eleventh Century Hungarian Kings: Their Policies and Their Relations with Rome*, East European Monographs, no. 79 (New York, 1981), pp. 35–36. For Gerard's tutorship to Emeric, see Gerard's *Legenda maior* c. 5, p. 488; cf. the Bollandist commentary to Emeric's life in *AA SS*, November, 2:483. Macartney notes that although there is no mention of Gerard's tutorship in the more reliable *Legenda minor* or any other source, such a relationship is not impossible (*Medieval Hungarian Historians*, p. 157). Kosztolnyik thinks it unlikely, however, given what can be reconstructed concerning the chronology of Gerard's life (*Five Eleventh Century Hungarian Kings*, pp. 16–17). For Gerard's work in the conversion of Hungary, see, in Kosztolnyik, pp. 24–35; for his efforts to restore the Arpádian dynasty (of which Stephen and Ladislaus were members) that eventually cost him his life, see pp. 26–27, 68–71.

[97] For an account of the triple canonization, see the Bollandist commentary for Emeric's life in *AA SS*, November, 2:485, and Folz, *Les saints rois*, p. 77. Two monks were also canonized shortly before the triple canonization, adding to the arsenal of national saints (see Klaniczay, "From Sacral Kingship," in *Uses of Supernatural Power*, p. 87).

[98] See Bartoniek, ed., *Legenda S. Emerici ducis*, in *Scriptores Rerum Hungaricarum*, 2:449–460; see Macartney, *Medieval Hungarian Historians*, pp. 170–171.

[99] For an account of his ascetic practices, see *Legenda S. Emerici ducis* c. 1, *Scriptores Rerum Hungaricarum*, 2:450–451.

tion was supposedly present from infancy. The only active, albeit indirect, governmental service that his hagiographer attributes to him is likewise a function of this preeminent virtue and demonstrates the symbiosis of familial sanctity. When Stephen and his son visited the monastery of St. Martin, the young prince measured the number of kisses he bestowed on individual monks in accordance with the degree of chastity he divined in each. His father shrewdly used this as a mechanism for ecclesiastical promotion: the purest monk (i.e., the most "osculated") became a bishop.[100]

Before he could succeed to the throne, Emeric died disappointingly in a hunting accident—a fact that is omitted by his hagiographer.[101] Although his *vita* asserts that Emeric's spiritual marriage came to light with his death, his chastity is not corroborated by any contemporary sources—even hagiographical ones. On the contrary, the more pragmatic foci of Stephen's *vitae* stress the king's concern for a regular succession—especially apparent in the active role he is said to have assumed in Emeric's education and his despondency resulting from Emeric's death.[102] There is nothing to suggest that Stephen could even begin to comprehend the anomaly of a spiritual marriage. Indeed, the laws remaining from Stephen's reign presuppose that all honorable laymen would, by definition, have wives and children.[103]

Emeric's cult added luster, but not stability, to Stephen's line. It was but a small consolation prize for a new and struggling nation— dependent on a regular succession, but prematurely deprived of its

[100] Ibid. c. 2–3, pp. 452–453.

[101] According to the Bollandist commentary, his death is reported in the *Annales Hildesheimenses* for the year 1031 (*AA SS*, November, 2:480).

[102] He commended Emeric to the Virgin Mary daily, praying for the survival of his sole heir to the throne: "hunc igitur fore superstitem, hunc regni eiusdem [heredem] votis omnibus desideravit." With respect to Emeric's untimely death, the author describes Stephen's grief in terms of the bleak prospects for posterity: "videns enim se solum sine spe posteritatis derelictum, pietatis affectu doluit" (see Stephen's *Legenda maior* c. 15, *Scriptores Rerum Hungaricarum*, 2:391; also see Hartvic's *Vita S. Stephani regis* c. 19, ibid., pp. 428–429). In the little book of instruction that Stephen allegedly wrote for Emeric, moreover, he at one point addresses the prince affectionately as the delight of his heart and his hope of future progeny: "fili mi amabilissime, dulcedo cordis mei, spes future sobolis" (Joseph Balogh, ed., *Libellus de institutione morum* c. 10, ibid., p. 627). It is by no means certain that Stephen was responsible for this work, although the *Legenda maior* and Hartvic refer to it when discussing Emeric's education. Scholars have attributed its composition to Bishop Gerard (see Kosztolnyik, *Five Eleventh Century Hungarian Kings*, p. 48). For an analysis of its contents, see Folz, *Les saints rois*, pp. 150–155.

[103] "Testes autem et accusatores clericorum sine aliqua sint infamia, uxores et filios habentes, et omnino Christum predicantes" (*S. Stephani regis Decretorum libri II* 1.3, ed. S. L. Endlicher, *Rerum Hungaricarum monumenta Arpadiana* [St. Gall, 1849; reprt. Leipzig, 1931], p. 313).

young prince.[104] But the eulogists of the German emperor Henry II (d. 1024)—Prince Emeric's maternal uncle—and of the Anglo-Saxon king Edward the Confessor (d. 1066), had even more potential indignation to assuage since the allegedly virginal unions of these monarchs resulted in the end of their respective dynasties.

The contemporary sources for Henry II's life are the chronicle of Thietmar of Merseburg and Bishop Adalbold of Utrecht's biography, which is derivative of the former.[105] Henry was a pious, but theocratic, ruler who applied the principle of *Eigenherr* to the church. Nevertheless, he was sympathetic to the spirit of reform: he made good ecclesiastical appointments, he felt a particular affinity to Cluny, and he was responsible for the ruling at Pavia in 1022 whereby the children of priests should be enslaved.[106]

Because Henry was an old-school representative of theocratic kingship, one would suppose that his chances of canonization in the wake of the Gregorian reform were virtually nil. As it happened, however, the bishopric of Bamberg (which he had founded and generously endowed) promoted his cult. Bishop Egilbert commissioned a new biography that not only gave a radically expurgated account of Henry's dealings with the church, it also falsely attributed new triumphs (such as the conversion of Hungary through the marriage of his sister Gisela) to Henry.[107] This biography, moreover, treated the subject of Henry's virginal marriage with his wife, Cunegund.[108] So ended the Ottonian dynasty, but at least it went out with glory. Such effort was not without effect. In response to the petitioning of the Bambergers, Henry II was canonized in 1146 by Eugenius III for basically two related reasons: that though an emperor, he did not live like one, and that this remarkable detachment from his office was epitomized by his absolute chastity. In other words, Henry had become monasticized.

---

[104] For the dissension following Stephen's death, see Kosztolnyik, *Five Eleventh Century Hungarian Kings*, pp. 56–71.

[105] *Die Chronik des Bischofs Thietmar von Merseburg*, ed. Robert Holtzmann, *MGH, Scrip. Rer. Germ.*, n.s., vol. 9 (Berlin, 1935). Thietmar's chronicle ends in 1018—six years before Henry's death. See bks. 5–8 for an account of his reign. Adalbold, *Vita Heinrici II*, ed. G. Waitz, *MGH, Scrip.*, vol. 4 (Hanover, 1841; reprt. 1925), pp. 683–695.

[106] Folz, *Les saints rois*, pp. 85–86.

[107] Ibid., pp. 86–89; also see Folz, "La légende liturgique de saint Henri II empereur et confesseur," in *Mélanges Jacques Stiennon* (Liège, 1982), pp. 245–246, 252–253. Note that Stephen was already a Christian at the time of his marriage. On the development of the imperial couple's cult, see Renate Klauser, *Der Heinrichs- und Kunigundenkult im mittelalterlichen Bistum Bamberg* (Bamberg, 1957).

[108] Adalbert of Bamberg, *Vita Heinrici II* c. 21 and 32, ed. G. Waitz, *MGH, Scrip.*, 4:805, 810.

No rumor of a chaste marriage was breathed during the imperial couple's reign or for a considerable time thereafter. On the contrary, one of Henry's charters of 1 November 1007 states that as he can no longer expect to have any future heirs, he makes God his heir.[109] Indeed, Humbert of Silva Candida attributed the couple's childlessness to Henry's misuse of church property, while Raoul Glaber presented it very matter-of-factly as the end of a dynasty.[110] The earliest mention of their pledge of chastity occurs at the very close of the eleventh century.[111]

The barren union of Edward the Confessor and Edith Godwin was an even greater disaster, as their failure to produce an heir led to the Norman Conquest. In this instance, however, rumors of the couple's chastity seem to date back to Edward's lifetime, although the motivation for their chastity has been called into question. Our most reliable source for Edward's life is a biography written between 1065 and 1067 and commissioned by Edith.[112] Unfortunately, the section of the book that would have dealt with their marriage is missing.[113] Nevertheless, there is sufficient evidence, even without the crucial section, to indicate that the anonymous writer promoted the idea that theirs was a chaste marriage, albeit in an understated way.[114] He tells, for example, of a vision experienced by Brihtwald, bishop of

---

[109] Folz, *Les saints rois*, p. 88.

[110] Humbert of Silva Candida, *Libri III adversus Simoniacos* 3.15, ed. F. Thaner, *MGH, Lib. de Lit.*, vol. 1 (Hanover, 1891), p. 217; Raoul Glaber, *Les cinq livres de ses histoires* 4.1, ed. Maurice Prou (Paris, 1886), p. 90.

[111] See Folz, *Les saints rois*, pp. 87–90. According to Georges Duby, the legend of the cult of the chaste emperor was deliberately intended to aggravate the emperors Henry IV and Henry V, who were still very far from a settlement with the papacy over the investiture struggle at the turn of the century. Moreover, Henry II had been instrumental in setting the reform movement in motion. The chaste union may also act as a metaphor for the fact that Henry was exceedingly pious and reform-minded, as he did not repudiate his barren wife although the crown passed to a distant cousin, Conrad II, who founded the Salian dynasty (*The Knight, the Lady, and the Priest*, pp. 57–59).

[112] For references to Edith's patronage (ranging from oblique to direct), see Frank Barlow, ed. and trans., *The Life of King Edward Who Rests at Westminster: Attributed to a Monk of St. Bertin* (London, 1962), pp. 2, 44, 59. Edith's commissioning of a biography, ostensibly to glorify her husband but also to clear her own name, bears a strong similarity to her mother-in-law, Emma's, motivation in commissioning the *Encomium Emmae reginae* (ed. Alistair Campbell, Camden Publications, 3d ser., vol. 72 [London, 1949]). Since Emma's marriage to the Danish Canute had the effect of disinheriting Edward the Confessor and his brother, it is not surprising that the encomiast suppresses all mention of her earlier marriage to Æthelred and even speaks of Emma as a virgin (2.16, p. 32). Both Edith and Emma fortified their positions by the misappropriation of chastity. For other possible parallels, see n. 146, below.

[113] This would have been chapter 2 of book 1 (Barlow, ed. and trans., *The Life of King Edward*, introd., p. xv).

[114] See ibid., pp. lxxiv–lxxviii.

Wiltshire, in which St. Peter consecrated a king and designated him for a life of chastity.[115] The couple's personal relationship is described as a father-daughter one (he was probably twenty years her elder), with Edith often seated adoringly at his feet.[116] With echoes of sacral kingship, Anonymous tells us that Edward was "consecrated to the kingdom less by men than, as we have said before, by heaven. He preserved with holy chastity the dignity of his consecration, and lived his whole life dedicated to God in true innocence."[117] Furthermore, recent scholarship has pointed out that Edward was unmarried at forty, his age of accession to the throne, and though plans for an heir should have been uppermost in his mind, yet he waited three years to marry.[118]

There were reasons other than sanctity for imputing chastity to Edward. Although William of Malmesbury used the anonymous life as his source, he gives quite a different coloring to both Edith's and Edward's chastity:

> Both in her [Edith's] husband's life-time, and afterwards, she was not entirely free from suspicion of dishonor; but when dying, in the time of king William, she voluntarily satisfied the by-standers of her unimpaired chastity, by an oath. When she became his wife, the king acted towards her so delicately, that he neither removed her from his bed, nor knew her after the manner of men. I have not been able to discover, whether he acted thus from dislike to her family, which he prudently dissembled from the exigency of the times, or out of pure regard to chastity: yet it is most notoriously affirmed, that he never violated his purity by connexion with any woman.
>
> But since I have gotten thus far, I wish to admonish my reader, that the track of my history is here but dubious, because the truth of the facts hangs in suspense.[119]

---

[115] "Uidet beatum Petrum, apostolorum primum, decentem hominis personam in regem consecrare, celibem ei uitam designare" (ibid., p. 9).

[116] Ibid., p. 60; cf. pp. 42, 76. Barlow notes the eleventh-century Goscelin's description of a citizen of Canterbury's chaste marriage as a brother-sister or a father-daughter relationship: "adiacent non ut coniugalia mancipia sed prorsus ut germanus et germana, aut pater et filia. Sponsa intacta ut nulli connubio obnoxia dormiebat; sponsus celebs quasi custos mutue integritatis totam noctem peruigilabat" (*Miracula S. Melliti*, London, British Library, MS Vespasian B XX, f.212; as cited by Barlow, p. lxxvi n. 3).

[117] "Ad regnum non tam ab hominibus quam, ut supra diximus, diuinitus est consecratus. Cuius consecrationis dignitatem sancta conseruans castimonia, omnem uitam agebat deo dicatam in uera innocentia" (ibid., pp. 60–61). See Rosenthal, "Edward the Confessor and Robert the Pious," pp. 8–19.

[118] Eric John, "Edward the Confessor and the Celibate Life," *AB* 97 (1979): 176.

[119] "Haec, et vivo marito et mortuo, probri suspicione non caruit; sed, moriens

In point of fact, the Godwin family, of which Edith was a part, had behaved treacherously during Edward's reign—so treacherously that Edward sent Edith away to a convent for a year.[120] It is even possible that he intended to divorce her.[121] Indeed, it has been convincingly argued that Edith was more the dutiful daughter, ever promoting the house of Godwin's interests, than the dutiful wife.[122] From this perspective, Edith may well have commissioned the biography to conceal Edward's dislike of her, and her own failure to produce an heir, behind an aura of sanctity.

At any rate, the cult of Edward was exceedingly slow to catch on. As in the case of Henry II and the patronage of the Bamberg diocese, Edward owes the success of his cult to the monks of Westminster, who, because they were rather short on relics and tradition, between 1138 and 1161 established the sanctity of their founder and chief benefactor.[123] Edward had been a pious monarch and generous to the church, hence the kind of ruler in line for a celestial reward. The anonymous *vita* abounds with his generous bequests, his promotion of monastic reform, and his kindness toward foreign abbots. Yet the cornerstone of Edward's claims to sanctity was, of course, his chastity. Osbert of Clare, prior of Westminster, who wrote a second life based on the anonymous account, realized this. Thus he introduced the theme of Edward's lifelong devotion to the Virgin, his determination to remain a virgin, the plot against his chastity on behalf of the kingdom, and finally a marriage in which God was said to have guarded Edward's chastity as closely as he had guarded that of St. Alexis.[124] He also wisely removed all the troublesome references to

---

tempore Willelmi, jurejurando astantibus de perpetua integritate ultro satisfecit. Nuptam sibi rex hac arte tractabat, ut nec thoro amoveret, nec virili more cognosceret: quod an familiae illius odio, quod prudenter dissimulabat pro tempore, an amore castitatis fecerit, pro certo compertum non habeo. Illud celeberrime fertur, nunquam illum cujusquam mulieris contubernio pudicitiam laesisse. Sed quia ad id locorum ventum est, lectorem praemonitum volo quod hinc quasi ancipitem viam narrationis video, quia veritas factorum pendet in dubio" (William of Malmesbury, *De gestis regum Anglorum* 2.13, ed. William Stubbs, Rolls Series, vol. 90 [London, 1887], 1:239; trans. J. A. Giles, *Chronicle of the Kings of England* [London, 1847], pp. 216–217).

[120] Barlow, ed. and trans., *The Life of King Edward*, pp. 23, 28.

[121] See Frank Barlow, *Edward the Confessor* (Berkeley and Los Angeles, 1970), pp. 115–116; Stafford, *Queens, Concubines, and Dowagers*, p. 76.

[122] See Kenneth E. Cutler, "Edith, Queen of England, 1045–1066," *Mediaeval Studies* 35 (1973): 222–231.

[123] On the development of Edward's cult, see Barlow, ed. and trans., *The Life of King Edward*, appendix D, pp. 112–133; also see Bernhard W. Scholz, "The Canonization of Edward the Confessor," *Speculum* 36 (1961): 38–60.

[124] Osbert of Clare, "La vie de S. Edouard le Confesseur" c. 14, ed. Marc Bloch, *AB* 41 (1923): 74–75.

foreign abbots and Godwins. But Osbert's efforts to get Edward offi-cially recognized in 1138 failed. Finally, Osbert's account was rewrit-ten by Aelred of Rievaulx in support of a new application for canon-ization. This *vita* is the most widely circulated version of the various accounts of his life and goes into the most detail regarding Edward's chastity. His devotion to the Virgin is even more developed.[125] Aelred also takes to task anyone who doubts the motives for Edward's pu-rity.[126] Alexander III issued a bull of canonization for Edward in 1161, while his relics were solemnly translated in 1163. The sermon, com-memorating Edward, was preached by Aelred.

Clearly the phenomenon of the virgin king is a convenient explana-tion for a disruption in succession—be it an awkward interregnum or the end of a dynasty. It also has the advantage of concealing disagree-able personal problems. But that this solution is only resorted to in the eleventh century is suggestive. Moreover, the fact that the reform-ing papacy singled out these royal cults for special favor at a time when it was just beginning to take an active interest in canonization seems at odds with its general tendency to enforce a strict separation between the clergy and laity on the basis of chastity.[127] It is doubtful that the papacy would extol such an extreme transgression of bound-aries unless there was much to be gained.

And in fact there was. Prior to the papal reform movement, there was a sacral quality to kingship:[128] a quality that was ecclesiastically

125 Aelred of Rievaulx, *Vita S. Edwardi regis*, PL 195, col. 747.

126 Aelred denounces carnally minded cynics who assume that Edward only re-sorted to chastity when he recognized that no heirs were forthcoming: "Et ne aliquis huic regis virtuti fidem deroget, sciat hoc temporibus illis per totam Angliam sic divulgatum et creditum, ut de facto certi plerique de intentione certarent. Quidam namque nihil nisi carnem et sanguinem sapientes, simplicitati regiae hoc imponebant, quod compulsus generi se miscuerit proditorum, et ne proditores procrearent, operi supersederet conjugali" (ibid., col. 748).

127 Both Henry's and Edward's canonizations, moreover, were not simply local af-fairs, performed by the bishop in response to popular pressure, but pontifical. The only other pontifical canonization of this period was Canute Laward, a type of the early martyr-king (Folz, *Les saints rois*, pp. 113–115). Gregory VII also approved the triple Hungarian cult of Stephen, Emeric, and Gerard.

128 I am using this term to imply a kind of *numen* that inheres in royalty itself, which is relatively distinct from actual sanctity. The concept of "sacred kingship" is not without problems. Certain scholars have assumed that the "saint-king" was sim-ply a continuation of the pre-Germanic idea of the king as sacred (see, for example, William A. Chaney, *The Cult of Kingship in Anglo-Saxon England: The Transition from Paganism to Christianity* [Berkeley and Los Angeles, 1970], esp. pp. 7–42; cf. Friederich Prinz, "Aristocracy and Christianity in Merovingian Gaul: An Essay," in *Gessellschaft, Kultur, Literatur: Rezeption und Originalität im Wachsen einer euro-päischen Literatur und Geistigkeit*, ed. Karl Bosl, Monographien zur Geschichte des Mittelalters, vol. 11 [Stuttgart, 1975], pp. 153–165). F. Graus, however, denies the

confirmed when the double ritual of coronation and anointing was introduced in the eighth century.[129] In the course of the reformers' attack on lay investiture, the sacral quality of kingship was likewise vigorously denied: hence the whole basis of royal theocracy was undermined.[130] Marc Bloch notes that the cult surrounding the English kings' powers to heal scrofula, introduced from France ca. 1100, was, in part, promoted in an effort to counteract the reformers' disclaimers.[131] Gregory VII was especially adamant that the lay state could in no way equal the supernatural powers of the priesthood and was possessed of no gifts for healing or for performing other miracles. This mentality spawned William of Malmesbury's heated denial that Edward the Confessor's ability to heal was hereditary, and his insistence that this was an aspect of the king's personal sanctity.[132]

The church's prerogative to pronounce officially upon the sanctity of an individual king is a much different matter from sacral kingship.

---

presence of sacral kingship in the pre-Christian West and stresses the role of the church in the cult of early medieval saint-kings (*Volk, Herrscher und Heiliger im Reich der Merowinger* [Prague, 1965]). An intelligent middle ground is proposed by Janet L. Nelson, who attempts to distinguish between sacral and sacred. According to Nelson, sanctity (which connotes sacredness) is something achieved as opposed to automatically ascribed (see "Royal Saints and Early Medieval Kingship," in *Sanctity and Secularity: The Church and the World*, ed. Derek Baker, Studies in Church History, no. 10 [Oxford, 1973], esp. pp. 41–42; cf. Ridyard, *Royal Saints*, pp. 74–78). K. J. Leyser effectively defends the use of the designation "sacral kingship" and cautions against an oversharp distinction between a living sacral ruler and the dead saint-king (*Rule and Conflict in an Early Medieval Society: Ottonian Saxony* [Bloomington, Ind., 1979], p. 75; cf. Vauchez, *La sainteté*, pp. 187–188, 192–193). For an analysis of how this nebulous sacral quality operated in Saxony prior to the reform of the church, see Leyser, *Rule and Conflict*, pp. 77–90; also see Carozzi, "Le roi et la liturgie," pp. 418–421.

[129] See especially Walter Ullmann, *The Carolingian Renaissance and the Idea of Kingship* (London, 1969). Also see Marc Bloch's discussion of this rite's evolution in *The Royal Touch: Sacred Monarchy and Scrofula in England and France*, trans. J. E. Anderson (London and Montreal, 1973), pp. 33–41. Of course, as many have noted, anointing and coronation cut both ways, as they imply that the priesthood confers royal power. This was probably in Charlemagne's mind at the time when Leo III placed the crown on his head—hence his displeasure about his coronation (Einhard, *Vie de Charlemagne* 3.28, ed. Louis Halphen [Paris, 1947], p. 80).

[130] See Vauchez, *La sainteté*, pp. 194–196. According to R. W. Southern's analysis, around the year 1100: "Even men with very little ability suddenly knew that the religious pretensions of kings had no foundation. . . . [The] chief result was to emphasize the superiority of the sacerdotal element in society which could not be cut down to human proportions. The spiritual nakedness of the lay ruler only disclosed more fully the indefeasible claims of the spiritual hierarchy. Moreover, with the secularization of the lay ruler, that whole broad stratum of society which he particularly represented—the laity—suffered a corresponding demotion" (*Western Society*, p. 37).

[131] Bloch, *Royal Touch*, pp. 47–48.

[132] Ibid., pp. 71–73; Nelson, "Royal Saints," p. 42.

A king who happens to become a saint is only recognized as such posthumously. Such an elevation clearly does nothing to augment his power in this life, while the act of recognition enhances the power and control of the church considerably. This is especially true with respect to the augmentation of papal power when canonization becomes centralized through the papacy in the time of Innocent III.[133]

A king, then, at least from the reformed clergy's perspective, is nothing more than a layperson with governmental responsibilities. (One reformer went so far as to compare a king to a swineherd who could be dismissed if he failed to acquit himself adequately.)[134] There had been many saintly kings in the past: but these had died in the saddle, as it were. They were martyrs for the faith, as opposed to royal confessors who spurned their most obvious responsibilities.[135] The cult surrounding martyr-kings was especially compelling because it drew a distinct parallel between Christ's sacrifice and the monarch in question, as well as betraying possible links with the non-Christian past.[136]

The cult of the virginal king, on the other hand, conveyed a distinct political message to the lay world on behalf of the reformed papacy. The message was twofold: first, that in order for a layperson to be considered truly holy, he must attain a monastic level of purity, and second, that the monarchy was in no way exempt from this imperative. In other words, kings, who had more of a responsibility to reproduce than the average person since a country's stability depended on a regular succession, were commended and elevated for becoming eunuchs for God. Although it is frequently argued that the saintly confessor kings play an important role in stabilizing the developing feudal monarchies and indicate church-state collaboration, the criterion of chastity nevertheless bespeaks ambivalence.[137] The cults of these "royal lemmings" show considerable hostility to the imperative of lineage, generally, and royal houses in particular. They may also underline the level of asceticism that the laity was coming to expect from their saints. It is but another sign of the times that Reginald of

[133] See Vauchez, *La sainteté*, pp. 25–37, 39–67. Nelson points out that the church could dictate models of idealized kingship to royal descendants. Moreover, the example of the king's sanctity, by serving as a yardstick and raising the expectations of his subjects, might even work as a means of social control on the successors who live in the shadow of the saint ("Royal Saints," pp. 43–44).

[134] Bloch, *Royal Touch*, p. 70.

[135] See Vauchez, *La sainteté*, p. 188; Ridyard, *Royal Saints*, pp. 243–246.

[136] See Folz, *Les saints rois*, pp. 55, 62–63; Chaney, *The Cult of Kingship*, pp. 86–120.

[137] See esp. Gorski, "Le roi-saint," pp. 370–371; Graus, "La sanctification du souverain," pp. 559–561.

Durham's mid-twelfth-century account of St. Oswald of Northumbria (d. 642), Bede's prototype of the royal saint, alleges that Oswald and his wife took a vow of chastity after the birth of their son.[138] Nor is it surprising that in the twelfth century, Bishop Pelagius of Oviedo (1109–1129) brought Alfonso II's puzzling bachelorhood into line with what was becoming a standard model of kingly sanctity by providing him with a wife.[139]

But these chaste kings were also implicated in the church's kerygma on marriage. If the virginal queens of the early Germanic kingdoms underscored the fragility and dissoluble nature of the marriage bond, their male counterparts indicated the opposite. In the eleventh

[138] Reginald of Durham, *Vita S. Oswaldi* c. 11, in Symeon of Durham's *Historia ecclesiae Dunhelmensis*, ed. Thomas Arnold, Rolls Series, no. 75, vol. 1 (London, 1882), appendix 3, p. 349. Cf. Bede, *Ecclesiastical History* 3.7, pp. 232–233. Note that this would have run counter to Bede's apparent opposition to excessive asceticism in kings (Ridyard, *Royal Saints*, p. 92).

[139] According to Pelagius, Alfonso's wife, Bertinalda, was a Frankish princess, but Alfonso never saw her: "Habuit tamen in Galliis sponsam Bertinaldam nomine orta ex regali genere, quam numquam vidit" (*Historia de Arcae Sanctae translatione, deque Sanctorum Reliquiis, quae in ea asservantur*, in Florez, *España Sagrada*, vol. 37, appendix 15, p. 357). Later chronicles would claim that her name was not Bertinalda but Bertha—the sister of Charlemagne (see Ramón Menéndez Pidal, "La Historiografía medieval sobre Alfonso II," in *Estudios sobre la Monarquia Asturiana*, pp. 22–25; Barrau-Dihigo, "Recherches sur l'histoire politique du royaume Asturien," pp. 285–286). Pelagius's intervention in Alfonso's personal life was not uncritically accepted by all. The thirteenth-century chronicle written under the direction of Alfonso X of Castile only reports that he never aligned himself with a wife or any other woman: "e seyendo omne de grand vertud et de castidad et de piedad, nunqua quiso en toda su vida aver companna nin allegança con mugier; mas todo su tiempo quiso bevir limpia-mientre; e por ende merescio de seer llamado don Alffonsso el Casto" (*Estoria de España: Antologiá*, ed. R. Ayerbe-Chaux [Madrid, 1982], c. 612, p. 257). Yet by the sixteenth century, Juan de Mariana's influential *Historia general de España* accepts uncritically the legend of Alfonso's spiritual marriage, claiming that he remained aloof from his queen, Bertha: "Tiénese por cierto que con deseo de vida mas pura y santa por todo el tiempo de su vida no tocó à la Reyna Berta su muger, que fué la causa de ponelle el sobrenombre de Casto" (7.9 [Madrid, 1818], 5:68).

On the other hand, Alfonso did build a church to SS. Julian and Basilissa, who, as discussed in chapter 1, themselves participated in a spiritual marriage. Mauro Gomez Pereira is inclined to link Alfonso's devotion to these saints with the legend of his own unconsummated marriage—even though this argument ignores the earliest and most reliable accounts of his marital status ("Alfonso II el Casto, y el Monasterio de Samos," in *Estudios sobre la Monarquia Asturiana*, pp. 247–258; esp. 250–251). But it should also be noted that the extent of Alfonso's patronage of Julian and Basilissa may have been exaggerated. He most certainly did build a church to them and, according to the Oviedo version of the *Crónica de Alfonso III*, dedicated a chapel to St. Julian in the church of St. Mary Ever-Virgin (Ubieto Arteta, ed., pp. 42–43). The 811 confirmation of the monastery of St. Julian of Samos is, however, suspect (see L. Barrau-Dihigo, "Actes des rois Asturiens," *Revue Hispanique* 46 [1919]: 115).

century, the church was attempting to impose an implacably indissoluble model of marriage upon the restive nobility[140]—somewhat ironically, perhaps, considering the reformers' savage dismissal of marriage among their own ranks. Maybe the clergy was even manifesting their superiority to the male nobility by the ease with which they broke their own marriages—leaving the kings to fume in their own sterile unions. The message of indissolubility was most powerful where the stakes were highest: a queen could not be repudiated, even if the stability of the kingdom depended on it. And so, while women were the "matter" out of place in the reformers' vision of a purified clergy, they were fast becoming the resented but protected "matter" that could not be displaced in noble marriages. The solemn elevation of Richardis's relics in 1049 by Leo IX,[141] the first of the reforming popes, may be significant in this context: eternal reward for a cruelly repudiated queen? But the cults of the virginal kings went still further in confirming this position.

If these cults are to be interpreted as a strong statement of the indissolubility of marriage, this statement was made at the expense of other messages that spiritual marriage had traditionally been entrusted with. Mutual sanctification through the marriage bond is absent even as the consensual nature of the bond is downplayed. These glaring omissions are accompanied by a curious gender reversal that is a marked feature of all these legends.

When saintly kings made their painful transition from martyrs to confessors, in the process they appropriated the virginal marriage model, hitherto the exclusive preserve of their regal consorts. Moreover, the virginal queens of an earlier age became saints under very different conditions. They preserved their virginity against their husbands' wishes, and their crowning act of defiance and ultimate triumph was dependent on an escape to the cloister. The objecting spouse could not and did not participate in a shred of her glory. But the situation is totally altered in the eleventh-century models. The virginal kings were presumed to have followed their peculiar vocation with the consent of their queens and amid the splendor of court life. This scenario would seemingly lend itself to the development of a double cult of virginal consorts. And yet this is not usually the case. Although the posthumous burden of proof for Emeric's chastity putatively resided in the testimony of his intact spouse, and only secondarily in that of his confessor, Emeric's hagiographer does not

---

[140] See Brundage, *Law, Sex, and Christian Society,* pp. 183–184; Duby, *The Knight, the Lady, and the Priest,* pp. 5–19.

[141] See *AA SS,* September, 5:793 (editor's preface).

even disclose the wife's name.[142] The description of Emeric's virginal union is instructive here:

> O the marvelous continence of the youth. How by a fountain of tears, he restrained the fires of passion, and, carrying the flame in his lap, was not burned by its fire. For it is great, and almost beyond mortal nature, to put bodily lust to sleep and to extinguish the flame of concupiscence, burning with the torches of adolescence, with the virtue of the spirit, and to shut out the strength of a twin delight by a spiritual endeavor: to live against the manner of the human race by despising the solaces of wives, and scorning the sweetness of children. . . . Great indeed is the labor of chastity, but greater the reward; temporal restraint, but eternal remuneration.[143]

This is a solitary chastity. Emeric plays a lone hand. The wife, never referred to in the lengthy panegyric, of which the above is only an excerpt, is simply instrumental in raising her husband to a higher level of asceticism. She, however, remains earthbound.

Likewise, it was Edith who was the impetus behind her husband's cult, yet she had to be content to bask in derivative glory. Clearly, anti-Godwin sentiment would allow her to do no more in her lifetime. And yet none of the twelfth-century promoters of Edward's cult attempted to restore Edith to her celestial husband's bosom—she was seemingly supplanted by the Virgin Mary. Only the empress Cunegund managed to rise to glory in the wake of her husband's sanctity, eventually becoming the object of veneration at the end of the twelfth century. She was officially canonized by Innocent III in 1200.[144]

The appropriation of this female pattern of sanctity by males betrays a confusion in gender roles that seems to confirm Jo Ann

---

[142] *Legenda S. Emerici ducis* c. 5, *Scriptores Rerum Hungaricarum*, 2:456. She was probably the daughter of Cresimir III, king of the Croats (1000–1030; see Bartoniek's comment, p. 451n.1).

[143] "O miranda iuvenis continentia, quam fonte lacrimarum restrinxit amoris incendia, flammamque portans in gremio, non urebatur eius incendio. Grande est enim, et pene ultra mortalem naturam, corpoream sopire luxuriam et concupiscentie flammam adulescentie facibus accensam animi virtute extinguere et spirituali conatu vim gemine oblectationis excludere, vivere contra humani generis morem, despicere solatia coniugum, dulcedinem contempnere liberorum. . . . Magnus quidem est pudicitie labor, sed maius premium, temporali custodia, sed remuneratio eterna" (ibid., p. 455).

[144] The bull of canonization is printed in *AA SS*, March, 1:280; it has recently been reedited by Jürgen Petersohn, "Die Litterae Papst Innocenz' III. zur Heiligsprechung der Kaiserin Kunigunde (1200)," *Jahrbuch für fränkische Landesforschung* 37 (1977): 1–25; see esp. pp. 21–25. For the significance of this bull for the papal reservation of canonization, see Vauchez, *La sainteté*, p. 31.

McNamara's supposition of a crisis in masculinity. In fact, both the virgin king topos and the drive for clerical celibacy reveal masculine efforts to monopolize chastity—this former bastion of female virtuosity. The reluctance to extol female chastity is also in line with the general insensitivity to female spirituality in this period, which corresponds to the further decline in the number of female saints over the course of the eleventh and twelfth centuries.[145] And yet, there is possibly something even more sinister at work. The resurfacing of the trial motif bespeaks an unmistakable hostility to these inconvenient wives. Edith was permitted to clear herself of charges of adultery by her own oath.[146] But Cunegund had to walk barefoot over hot plowshares as a proof of her purity. The hagiographic precedent for this is, of course, the trial of Empress Richardis. In this earlier scenario, however, the charges came from her presumably carnally minded and sexually disappointed husband. Cunegund's trial was required by Henry—her saintly partner in chastity.[147] Henry's false position was not lost on posterity: some declared him a tyrant as opposed to a saint. Jacobus de Voragine's *Golden Legend* depicts Henry as striking

---

[145] Schulenburg, "Sexism and the Celestial Gynaeceum," pp. 124–126.

[146] The *Winchester Annals* (ca. 1200), however, claim that a queen was accused of fornication with a bishop and required to prove her chastity by walking over hot plowshares (Henry Richards Luard, ed., *Annales Monasterii de Wintonia*, in *Annales Monastici*, vol. 2, Rolls Series, no. 36 [London, 1865], ann. 1043, pp. 20–24; also see Bartlett, *Trial by Fire and Water*, pp. 17–18). Although the trial is assigned to Emma, Edward's mother, Stafford thinks that the ordeal was originally associated with Edith's name and relates to the crisis of 1051 when Edith was sent away from court (*Queens, Concubines, and Dowagers*, pp. 82, 94). This seems likely, considering that the accuser was Robert of Jumièges, who was especially keen on Edward's divorcing Edith (see Barlow, *Edward the Confessor*, pp. 115–116). On the other hand, the confusion is not surprising considering Emma's speckled marital career.

[147] Adalbert of Bamberg does not lay the blame for Cunegund's trial directly at Henry's door, but makes it clear that Henry was presiding at the trial (*Vita Heinrici II* c. 21, in *MGH, Scrip.*, 4:805). Both Cunegund's *vita*, which was produced at the time of her canonization (see *AA SS*, March, 1:271), and Innocent's bull attempt to conceal Henry's role in the ordeal. The latter gives a circumspect account, attributing Cunegund's trial to diabolical instigation but failing to mention that it was Henry who was chiefly incited: "cum aliquando instigante humani generis inimico suspicio quedam contra eam fuisset exorta, ipsa, ut suam innocentiam demonstraret, super ignitos uomeres nudis planctis incessit et processit illesa" (Petersohn, ed., "Die Litterae Papst Innocenz' III.," p. 24); cf. the equally guarded language of the thirteenth-century liturgy for Henry in "La légende liturgique de saint Henri II," ed. Folz, in *Mélanges Jacques Stiennon*, p. 253. For a more forthcoming account, see the later additions to Adalbert's *Vita Heinrici II* that describe how the Devil, disguised as a knight, kept going in and out of Cunegund's bedroom, until the matter was brought to Henry's notice. Cunegund offered to clear herself by ordeal and Henry sat in judgment (*Additamentum* c. 3, *MGH, Scrip.*, 4:819).

Cunegund at the time of the trial; his death raises expectations in a multitude of demons, who think they have a good shot at his soul.[148] Even so, Cunegund's cult was destined to become a powerful vehicle for the reaffirmation of the consensual nature of marriage. Much of the familiar rhetoric of consensuality and mutual sanctification resurfaces in the *vita* that was written at the time of Innocent III's bull of canonization.[149] But the trial remains a popular feature of her legend—a grim reminder of earlier tensions. The conflation of two rather contradictory traditions is underlined by the fact that there are two moments of revelation of the couple's chastity in the various versions of the legend. The first follows the model of Richardis's trial. Empress Cunegund declares her chastity at the time of the ordeal. The second occurs on Henry's deathbed, where—in compliance with the gentler consensual model, exemplified in the writings of Gregory of Tours—Henry consigns his virgin queen to God.[150]

[148] Henry is saved only through the intervention of St. Lawrence (Ryan and Ripperger, trans., *Golden Legend*, p. 444). Likewise, Mutius in his *Chronicum Germaniae* denounces those who consider Henry a tyrant as opposed to a saint: "Qui scribunt, ex impulsu Sathanae hoc excogitatum ab Henrico, ut cogeret uxorem suam, quam numquam cognoverat, nec cum illa consuetudinem se habiturum decreverat, non sequitur, quod illi inferunt (paene dixerim calumniatores) esse satis indicii Henricum tyrannum potius fuisse, quam sanctum Regem" (as cited by *AA SS*, March, 1:267).

[149] The following panegyric from her *vita* emphasizes that the marriage was based on will as opposed to lust. It thus initiated the couple into so unified and intimate a participation in the virtues that husband and wife became indistinguishable: "O conjugium non voluptate, sed bona voluntate copulatum! O sanctum matrimonium, ubi una fides inviolatae castitatis, ubi unus spiritus misericordiae ac veritatis; ubi idem velle in virtutibus, idemque nolle in vitiis: ubi nec primus, nec alter discerni potuit, dum alter, quod primus, voluit: ubi par animus, in multifariis operum effectibus, pares in duobus ostendit affectus. Quales has nuptias dixerim, nescio. Unum scio: quia nescit nostra modo regio tales, dum illi propter regnum coelorum se castrantes, nec prolem terrenae foecunditatis exspectantes, coelibem a DEO generationem receperunt: a quorum ore laus Dei numquam deficiet" (*AA SS*, March, 1:272). Cf. Aelred of Rievaulx's description of the royal couple as husband and wife in mind, not flesh, who therefore abode in conjugal affection and in the embrace of a chaste love: "Convenientibus igitur in unum, rex et regina de castitate servanda paciscuntur, nec huic fidei alium quam Deum testem aestimant adhibendum. Fit illa conjux mente, non carne; ille nomine maritus, non opere. Perseverat inter eos sine actu conjugali conjugalis affectus, et sine defloratione virginitatis castae dilectionis amplexus" (*Vita S. Edwardi regis*, PL 195, col. 748).

It is of interest that Cunegund's sister, Achachildis or Atzin, is purported to have had a spiritual marriage. Hers was not a virginal marriage, however, as she and her husband took a vow of chastity only after she gave birth to five children on one occasion! (Dunbar, *Dictionary of Saintly Women*, 1:2). This cult began with the discovery of her tomb in the fifteenth century.

[150] In Cunegund's revelation, as reported by Adalbert, she calls on God to bear witness to the fact that she has never known a man sexually, including her husband:

Both Cunegund's and Edith's ordeals place the burden of proof of chastity on the wife, even as the burden of blame for sterility was undoubtedly laid at a woman's door by the angry male nobility. If the clergy already seemed disinclined to celebrate female chastity in the eleventh and twelfth centuries, they were even less inclined to suggest that there was anything particularly efficacious in prolonged contact with a woman. Moreover, the male nobility was certainly not prepared to celebrate a woman's barrenness. Mutual sanctification in marriage had no place in the earliest versions of the legends. And thus women were relegated to an ancillary role in these spiritual marriages.

"'Domine Deus, creator coeli et terrae, qui probas renes et corda, iudica iuditium meum et eripe me; te enim testem et iudicem hodie invoco, quia nec hunc praesentem Heinricum nec alterum quemquam virum carnali commertio umquam cognovi'" (*Vita Heinrici II* 1.21, *MGH, Scrip.*, 4:805). Henry's declaration on his deathbed runs as follows: "'Hanc ecce . . . michi a vobis, immo per Christum consignatam, ipsi Christo domino nostro et vobis resigno virginem vestram'" (1.32, p. 810). Cf. Cunegund's *vita* in *AA SS*, March, 1:271, 272; also see Innocent III's bull (Petersohn, ed., "Die Litterae Papst Innocenz' III.," p. 24).

FOUR

THE CONJUGAL DEBT AND VOWS OF CHASTITY:
THE THEORETICAL AND PASTORAL DISCOURSE
OF THE HIGH AND LATER MIDDLE AGES

THE FIGHT against nicolaitism had been won, at least nominally, by the early twelfth century: celibacy was the coat of arms that distinguished the clergy from the mass of humanity which formed the base of the pyramid. Now was the time to complete the work that was tentatively begun in the eleventh century: to structure the laity around the less laudable, but nevertheless worthy, institution of marriage.

Marriage urgently needed the attention, provided that it was benign. The twelfth century gave rise to a number of competing sexual discourses, which generated considerable confusion. A new literary persona emerged on the scene: that of the goddess Nature.[1] Bernard Silvestris was the first to evoke this vital deity, whom he succinctly describes as the *mater generationis* in his work *The Universe of the World*. Indeed, he concludes with a celebration of the five senses and a panegyric on the sexual organs.[2] The immediate successor to this tradition was Alan of Lille, who in *The Complaint of Nature* firmly emphasizes nature and heterosexual sexuality, including desire, as a part of the divine plan.[3] Marriage would ultimately benefit from this

---

[1] See M.-D. Chenu, *Nature, Man, and Society in the Twelfth Century*, ed. and trans. Jerome Taylor and Lester K. Little (Chicago and London, 1968; reprt. 1983), esp. pp. 1–48. For a good introduction to the tension between the ascetical and the natural stream, see the introduction to Nicole Grévy-Pons, ed., *Célibat et Nature: Une controverse médiévale*, Centre d'histoire des sciences et des doctrines, Textes et études, no. 1 (Paris, 1975), pp. 9–58.

[2] Bernard Silvestris, *De mundi universitate libri duo sive Megacosmus et Microcosmus* 2.14, ed. C. S. Barach and J. Wrobel (Innsbruck, 1876), pp. 65–71, esp. lines 151–162. Brian Stock, *Myth and Science in the Twelfth Century: A Study of Bernard Silvester* (Princeton, N.J., 1972), pp. 63–87; George D. Economou, *The Goddess Natura in Medieval Literature* (Cambridge, Mass., 1972), pp. 58–72.

[3] Alan of Lille, *De planctu Naturae* lines 199–246, ed. Nikolaus M. Häring (Spoleto, 1978), pp. 839–841. This celebration of Nature and its works moves out of the scholarly world into the vernacular and is pushed to extremes in Jean de Meun's extremely popular *Roman de la Rose*. In this anticourtly satire, chastity is entirely rejected as a positive value and the laws of nature are presented as a kind of "pop" religion (see

validation of nature. Yet other perspectives vied to upset the pivotal role that marriage had played in regulating heterosexual relations. Twelfth-century intellectuals, such as Heloise, drank deeply from the philosophical tradition, which was frankly misogamic.[4] The erotic ethos of the troubadours presented an extramarital model that celebrated passion as opposed to procreation. Because the alleged object of the poet's desire was usually unattainable, such relations were frequently described as remaining unconsummated—a feature connoting certain superficial similarities with spiritual marriage.[5] But

Grévy-Pons, ed., *Célibat et Nature*, introd., pp. 34–43). The remarkable figure of False Seeming (the son of Fraud and Hypocrisy, lover to Forced Continence who herself dresses like a Beguine and is a child of the Antichrist) has assumed the appearance of a friar (Jean de Meun, *Le Roman de la Rose*, lines 10952ff., ed. Ernest Langlois [Paris, 1921], 3:181ff.). Venus flies to the defense of the God of Love and declares war on Chastity (lines 15779–15890, 4:118–123). Nature makes a lengthy confession to her priest, Genius, during which she complains bitterly against humanity's refusal to live according to her laws. She is especially insistent on the tribute humanity should pay for the gift of sexuality (lines 19021–19334, 4:252–265). The newfound appreciation of nature and nature's laws lent ammunition to those who, in reaction to the "unnatural vices" of the clergy, moved to abandon clerical celibacy at the Council of Constance and later at Basel (Grévy-Pons, ed., *Célibat et Nature*, introd., pp. 52–53; cf. John Boswell, *Christianity, Social Tolerance, and Homosexuality* [Chicago and London, 1980], pp. 303–330). See G. Saignet's treatise *Lamentacio humane nature adversus Nicenam constitucionem* in favor of clerical marriage (which bases many of its arguments on nature and natural order) intended for the fathers of Constance (Grévy-Pons, ed., *Célibat et Nature*, pp. 135–156) and Gerson's *Dyalogus de celibatu ecclesiasticorum* in defense of clerical celibacy (ibid., pp. 165–187).

[4] See Brooke's *The Medieval Idea of Marriage*, pp. 90–92, 106–107; Katharina M. Wilson and Elizabeth M. Makowski, *Wykked Wyves and the Woes of Marriage: Misogamous Literature from Juvenal to Chaucer* (Albany, N.Y., 1990), pp. 76–81.

[5] For an introduction to this phenomenon, see Diane Borstein's "Courtly Love" in *DMA*, 3:668–674; also see Roger Boase's introduction, ibid., pp. 667–668. Possible parallels between courtly love and spiritual marriage are compounded by the fact that in troubadour literature, the prolongation of desire is frequently described as a quasi-spiritual discipline. The spiritual marriage of the Provençal nobles Dauphine and Elzear may also seem to argue in support of this claim (see the section entitled "Internalization and Mutual Sanctification: Dauphine and Elzear" in chapter 6). On the other hand, all of the orthodox couples who participated in spiritual marriage are explicitly described as being inspired by hagiographical models: the case of Elzear and Dauphine is no exception. Moreover, the spiritual nature of courtly love has been seriously challenged. René Nelli analyses the *asag*, the troubadour test of love, and interprets it as an extended form of foreplay that stops short of consummation, reflecting female sexual desires (see "Love's Rewards," trans. Alyson Waters, in *Zone: Fragments for a History of the Human Body*, ed. Michel Feher et al. [New York, 1989], 2,4:218–235; this is an excerpt from his monograph *L'érotique des troubadours* [Paris, 1963]). Cf. Danielle Jacquart and Claude Thomasset, who see courtly love as a rediscovery of and a demand for clitoral stimulation (*Sexuality and Medicine in the Middle Ages*, trans. Matthew Adamson [Princeton, N.J., 1988], pp. 94–98). There is little doubt that the alleged longing of the troubadours has a sexual as opposed to a religious telos.

undoubtedly the greatest threat to the integrity of marriage was radical dualism as exemplified by the Cathars of southern France. To these fervent individuals, the physical world was evil; hence, any institution dedicated to procreation—thereby entrapping souls in vitiated matter—was an abomination. The Cathar elite were required either to separate from their spouses or live with them in ascetic chastity.[6] To some extent this ascetical backlash was to be expected. The fervor of the early eleventh-century heresies had temporarily been absorbed by the reform movement. But the anti-matrimonial rhetoric of reform had, undoubtedly, quickened certain lay sectarians' contempt for marriage. Thus the clergy were partially to blame for aggravating this lay revulsion to marriage. Justice required that they repair the damage.

The Defense of Marriage

Marriage was reconstituted along Augustinian contours.[7] A two-pronged line of defense was developed: the first justified its worth.

---

[6] For an introduction to Cathar beliefs, see Moore, *The Origins of European Dissent*, pp. 218–224, and Malcolm Lambert, *Medieval Heresy: Popular Movements from Bogomil to Hus* (New York, 1977), pp. 108–206. Efforts have been made to show a correlation between Catharism and courtly love. Although it is unlikely that the Cathar elite (*perfecti*) would have approved of the unshackled celebration of carnality that characterized many of the troubadours' works, still common ground may be found in the fact that both the troubadours and Cathars were hostile to procreation, that both were patronized by powerful women, and that both heretics and troubadours were thought to spend entirely too much time with women (Noonan, *Contraception*, pp. 181–183; also see Denis de Rougemont's *Passion and Society*, trans. Montgomery Belgion, rev. ed. [London, 1956], pp. 75–102). A number of writers have also noted certain Neoplatonic parallels between the respective spiritual yearnings of troubadours and Cathars (see Déodat Roché, "Les Cathares et l'amour spirituel [1]," *Cahiers d'études Cathares* 2d ser., 94 [1982]: 16–17; Simone Hannedouche, "L'amour Cathare," ibid. 2d ser., 43 [1969]: 23–29. For an alternative view on troubadour love, see n. 5 above). Recent studies, however, suggest that the extent of female participation in Catharism has been considerably overrated. See Richard Abels and Ellen Harrison, "The Participation of Women in Languedocian Catharism," *Mediaeval Studies* 41 (1979): 215–251, and John H. Mundy, "Le mariage et les femmes à Toulouse au temps des Cathares," *Annales ESC* 42 (1987): 117–134. Let it suffice to say that whether or not there is a direct relation between the two phenomena, from an orthodox standpoint the two threats rose up in the same place at the same time and their shared hostility (or at the very least, the indifference on the part of the troubadours) to procreation and contempt for the orthodox church would excite a parallel alarm.

[7] See, for example, Jean Gaudemet's analysis of Gratian's debt to Augustine in his formulations on marriage in "L'apport de la patristique latine au Décret de Gratien en matière de mariage," in *Sociétés et mariage* (Strasbourg, 1980), pp. 290–319, esp. appendix 1, pp. 311–315. Also see Noonan's chapter 6, "The Canonists, the Cathars, and St. Augustine," *Contraception*, pp. 171–199.

Canonists and theologians alike turned to the three goods—offspring, faith, and indissolubility—to demonstrate the morality and stability of the marriage bond. This was a clear rebuttal of dualist doctrine. But the second line of defense argued for the sanctity of marriage and for its inclusion on the shortlist of sacraments that was being developed over the course of the twelfth century.[8] Such a claim was considerably more ambitious than a simple affirmation of marriage's general merit. Although the orthodox clergy vigorously refuted the heretics' doubts about the procreative function of marriage, they shared in their misgivings that the conjugal act itself was hopelessly compromised.

This ambivalence is omnipresent in Peter Lombard's *Sentences* (between 1155 and 1158), the standard theological textbook that was both studied and commented on until well into the seventeenth century.[9] Although coitus is excused by the three goods (4.31.8.1), all three goods must be present for it to be entirely without blame. In the event that the good of seeking children is absent, and yet faith between the couple is preserved, they are guilty of a venial sin. If, however, both faith and the desire to beget children are lacking (i.e., if a man were so conquered by concupiscence that he would have had intercourse with his partner even if she had not been his wife), it is a mortal sin. At this point Peter sounds Jerome's ominous warning about the evils of excessive ardor for one's wife (4.31.5.1–2).

Indeed, Peter's reluctance to exonerate the conjugal act is especially revealed by his resurrection of a thorny question: whether sex was ever blameless—even when motivated by a desire for children. If it were, then why does it require Paul's indulgence (1 Cor. 7.6)? Although Peter does, in fact, resolve that sex for the purpose of having children or for rendering the debt is sinless (4.31.6–7), he resuscitates what was considered to be Gregory the Great's equation of sex and pleasure and points out that it is very rare for a person not to exceed the desire for begetting when actually engaged in intercourse (4.31.8.4).[10] To those who closely assimilated sex and pleasure, sex

---

[8] On the evolution of the sacrament, see esp. G. Le Bras, "La doctrine du mariage chez les théologiens et les canonistes depuis l'an mille," *DTC*, vol. 9, cols. 2196–2217, and Brooke, *The Medieval Idea of Marriage*, pp. 273–280. Even so, marriage's inclusion as a sacrament always occasioned some debate. Initially it was a matter of controversy for the canonists as they denied the collation of grace. In 1283, moreover, Peter John Olivi was censured for his denial that marriage conferred grace (Le Bras, "La doctrine du mariage," cols. 2208–2212). The Protestant Reformation aimed at wresting marriage away from church control through a similar denial.

[9] See the new edition *Sententiae in IV libris distinctae*, ed. the Fathers of the College of St. Bonaventure, 2 vols. (Rome, 1971–1981).

[10] Bede cited a letter, allegedly written by Gregory the Great though in all probability spurious, in response to a series of questions by Augustine of Canterbury. "Gre-

was never without sin. Certain theorists even speculated as to whether it was more sinful to fornicate with a beautiful young woman or an ugly old hag on the basis of the pleasure quota.[11] The severe canonist Huguccio (d. 1210), who saw sexual pleasure as strictly postlapsarian and positioned the sex act outside of natural law, posited that perhaps if the husband avoided orgasm, and hence pleasure, the act might be sinless.[12]

This extreme sexual pessimism was challenged over the course of the thirteenth century—particularly by Dominican theologians who, under the influence of Aristotelian thought, attempted to vindicate the good of matrimonial sex by restoring it to its rightful place in the order of nature. Albert the Great, for example, even suggests that sexual pleasure would have been greater and more authentic before

gory" 's answer makes a direct association between the concupiscence that Augustine of Hippo believed to be implicit in sexual relations and pleasure. Pleasure is, in turn, associated with sin (see Bede, *Ecclesiastical History* 1.27, pp. 94–99).

[11] James A. Brundage, "Carnal Delight: Canonistic Theories of Sexuality," in *Proceedings of the Fifth International Congress of Medieval Canon Law*, Salamanca, 21–25 September 1976, ed. Stephan Kuttner and Kenneth Pennington, Monumenta Iuris Canonici, Ser. C: Subsidia, vol. 6 (Vatican City, 1980), pp. 366–368. On the other hand, Alan of Lille instructs confessors to ask the penitent if the woman he sinned with was beautiful or ugly, the latter being considered worse as there is less compulsion (*Liber poenitentialis* 1.27, ed. Jean Longère, Analecta Mediaevalia Namurcensia, no. 18 [Louvain and Lille, 1965], 2:34).

[12] For an introduction to Huguccio's life and works, see Kenneth Pennington, *DMA*, 6:327–328. Only excerpts of Huguccio's important *summa* on Gratian's *Decretum* have been edited. In addition to J. Roman's edition ("*Summa* d'Huguccio sur le *Décret* de Gratien d'après le Manuscrit 3891 de la Bibliothèque Nationale. Causa 27, Questio 2 [Théories sur la formation du mariage]," *Revue historique de droit français et étranger*, ser. 2, 27 [1903]: 745–805), I have relied on medieval authorities that cite Huguccio as well as on secondary sources.

For Huguccio's affirmation that sexual intercourse was always, to some degree, sinful, see Roman, ed., "*Summa* d'Huguccio," for C.27 q.2 c.10 ad v. *non poterat*, ad v. *pudenda*, and ad v. *ex peccato*, pp. 757–758. Also see Brundage, *Law, Sex, and Christian Society*, pp. 262, 279, 281–283. Some canonists, such as John Teutonicus, author of the *Glossa ordinaria*, saw Huguccio's rigorism as extremely questionable (Elizabeth M. Makowski, "The Conjugal Debt and Medieval Canon Law," *Journal of Medieval History* 3 [1977]: 103). Thomas N. Tentler sees both Huguccio and his student Innocent III as following in the severe tradition of Gregory the Great's *Responsum ad Augustinum episcopum* (*Sin and Confession on the Eve of the Reformation* [Princeton, N.J., 1977], p. 166). Brundage, on the other hand, contrasts the hatred of sex represented by Jerome with the more moderate Augustinian view of sexuality ("'Allas! That Evere Love was Synne': Sex and Medieval Canon Law," *Catholic Historical Review* 72 [1986]: 1–13). The fear that sexual innovation might heighten pleasure is also at the root of canonists' prescribing the "missionary position" during intercourse—also considering it optimum for conception (see Brundage, "Let Me Count the Ways: Canonists and Theologians Contemplate Coital Positions," *Journal of Medieval History* 10 [1984]: 81–93, esp. pp. 85–86).

the Fall, and Thomas Aquinas concurs.[13] Yet medieval sexual theory is undoubtedly one area in which two streams can coexist without any danger of either's drying up.[14] Moreover, the reaffirmation of marriage on the grounds that it was natural caused neither Albert nor Thomas to question the traditional view that chastity was the higher path and that continence in marriage was an admirable thing.

During the twelfth century when matrimonial theory was being shaped, attitudes toward sex were sufficiently ambivalent to suggest, once again, the expedience of separating sex and marriage or, as Georges Duby would have it, to develop a "disembodied" definition of marriage.[15] One of the earliest exponents of this definition was the monk Hugh of St. Victor (d. 1142). In Hugh we find a full-fledged revival of the patristic-consensual vision that not only accords with the marriage of Mary and Joseph but uses their union as the purifying fire which proves all others.[16]

Hugh describes marriage as having been instituted in two different stages: the procreative office was established prior to the Fall, while the remedy to sin was established after the Fall.[17] Marriage can be further divided into two separate sacraments: as a compact of love and as an office for procreation. The office of marriage entails copulation, while the compact of love entails only consent.[18] The office of mar-

---

[13] For this new Dominican perspective, see especially Fabian Parmisano, "Love and Marriage in the Middle Ages," *New Blackfriars* 50 (1969): 599–608, 649–660. Also see Le Bras, "La doctrine du mariage," *DTC*, vol. 9, cols. 2174–2180, and Servais Pinckaers, "Ce que le moyen âge pensait du mariage," *La vie spirituelle*, Supp. 20 (1967): 422–437. The positive assessment of nature is to a large extent on a continuum with twelfth-century interest discussed above.

[14] Cf. Christopher N. L. Brooke, "Marriage and Society in the Central Middle Ages," in *Marriage and Society: Studies in the Social History of Marriage*, ed. R. B. Outhwaite (London, 1981), pp. 18–19, and Chenu, *Nature, Man, and Society*, p. 48.

[15] Duby, *The Knight, the Lady, and the Priest*, pp. 118–119, 163–164, 179–180.

[16] Hugh grapples with the problem of their marriage in the treatise *On the Virginity of Blessed Mary* as well as in his work *On the Sacraments*, both of which were written around 1134. In the former work, the question of how Mary could consent to marriage with Joseph without compromising her mental commitment to virginity, if not her physical integrity, is raised (*De B. Mariae virginitate* c. 1, PL 176, col. 858). By separating consent to the society of marriage from consent to the office, Hugh demonstrates that consent to marriage need not detract from a resolve to remain a virgin. Only the office implies the rendering of the conjugal debt (col. 859). In *On the Sacraments*, Hugh develops the same basic argument. The major difference, however, is that he is now addressing marriage in general and not just the extraordinary case of Mary and Joseph. For a detailed analysis, see Gold, "The Marriage of Mary and Joseph," pp. 102–117, 249–251; esp. pp. 107–113, for Hugh of St. Victor and Peter Lombard.

[17] *De sacramentis* 1.8.12, PL 176, col. 314.

[18] "Erant enim duo haec in conjugio ipso: conjugium ipsum, et coniugii officium, et utrumque sacramentum erat. Conjugium constabat in consensu foederis socialis, officium conjugii constabat in copula carnis. Conjugium sacramentum fuit cujusdam

riage signifies the union of Christ with the church, while the compact of love signifies that of God with the soul. This latter configuration is described as the greater sacrament and as sufficient unto itself, without consummation. Indeed, the couple's observance of only this latter, greater sacrament is preferable to their fulfilling both:

> Yet true marriage and the true sacrament of marriage can exist, even if carnal commerce has not followed; in fact the more truly and the more sacredly it can exist, the more it has nothing in it at which chastity may blush but has that of which charity may boast.[19]

Hugh is, however, careful to stress that if the consent to carnal union is a part of the marriage agreement, both parties are obliged to observe this agreement. Yet this does not stop him from optimistically speculating: "But if perhaps in the compact of marriage on both sides by equal vow the consent of flesh is remitted, thereafter those joined are not reciprocally bound as debtors for this."[20] Hugh is one of the very few authorities who countenance the idea of a marriage in which both parties were previously agreed to chastity. Furthermore, his formulations provide spiritual marriage, whether contracted as such from the outset or agreed upon after consent, with an approval which far exceeds that of its carnal counterpart.[21] Even as consent, representing the union of souls, is dissociated from any physical bond, so consent becomes the sole legal requirement for a contract. Witnesses,

---

societatis spiritualis quae per dilectionem erat inter Deum et animam in qua societate anima sponsa erat et sponsus Deus. Officium conjugii sacramentum fuit cujusdam societatis quae futura erat per carnem assumptam inter Christum et Ecclesiam" (ibid. 1.8.13; cf. 2.11.3, col. 481).

[19] "Conjugium tamen verum, et verum conjugii sacramentum esse, etiam si carnale commercium non fuerit subsecutum, imo potius tanto verius et sanctius esse, quanto in se nihil habet unde castitas erubescat, sed unde charitas glorietur" (ibid. 2.11.3, col. 482; trans. Roy J. Deferrari, *On the Sacraments of the Christian Faith* [Cambridge, Mass., 1951], p. 326).

[20] "Quod si forte in foederatione conjugii utrinque pari voto consensus carnis remittitur, pro eodem deinceps conjugati debitores adinvicem non tenentur" (Hugh of St. Victor, *De sacramentis* 2.11.4, *PL* 176, col. 485; trans. Deferrari, p. 329).

[21] Some of the chill is taken off this austere appraisal by Hugh's very positive representation of the mutual love between husband and wife. The substance of the "greater" sacrament, for example, is the love (*dilectio*) that unites the couple's souls and signifies God's union with the rational soul: "Et haec ipsa rursus dilectio, qua masculus et femina in sanctitate conjugii animis uniuntur, sacramentum est; et signum illius dilectionis una Deus rationali animae intus per infusionem gratiae suae et spiritus sui participationem conjungitur" (*De sacramentis* 2.11.3, *PL* 176, col. 482). Peter Lombard, though largely derivative of Hugh, unfortunately omits the points that underline the mutual love between spouses (Pinckaers, "Ce que le moyen âge pensait du mariage," p. 416).

the nuptial mass, or any sacerdotal blessing are all extraneous to the couple's mutual pledge.[22]

Peter Lombard by and large accepts Hugh's consensual and disincarnate vision of the bond, but simplifies Hugh's position.[23] Eventually, under Alexander III (d. 1181), present consent between legitimate parties, informed by the ineffable presence of marital affection, became the sole criterion of a Christian marriage. Alexander's position was essentially ratified by Innocent III.[24]

And so chaste marriage was once again at the center of matrimonial theory. But theoretical endorsement does not translate into actual encouragement of the practice. In fact, couples who attempted to preserve chastity in marriage were regarded with considerable anxiety for old reasons that were again advanced with a new urgency. From the standpoint of doctrine, lay chastity is uncomfortably like heretical chastity: one would have to investigate the intentions informing such inscrutable behavior before one could sanction it. Cathar couples, for example, abstained from sex for all the wrong reasons and yet might easily pass for orthodox exemplars. The German visionary Elizabeth of Schönau (d. 1164) emphasizes this problem, while playing the artfully naive "straight woman" to her angelic guide.

> Lord, as I have heard, certain ones among them [the Cathars] assert that there is no legitimate marriage except between two people who preserve their virginity for the duration of their legal union. . . . And he answered: where such a union is possible, it is pleasing to God. But it is very rare that it happens. Nevertheless with respect to those who do not

---

[22] *De sacramentis* 2.11.5, *PL* 176, cols. 485–488.

[23] Rather than positing two sacraments, as does Hugh, Peter Lombard maintains that marriage represents one sacrament (Christ and the church) which operates through will and nature. A spiritual union in which the conjugal debt is remitted represents the union of Christ and the church through the instrument of the will alone (4.26.6).

[24] See Donahue, "The Policy of Alexander III's Consent Theory of Marriage," pp. 259–277, and Brooke's re-creation of Alexander's two ground-breaking decretals (*The Medieval Idea of Marriage*, pp. 149–156). Also see Noonan, "Marital Affection," pp. 500–509, and Brundage, *Law, Sex, and Christian Society*, pp. 331–341. For the difficulties that arose from the consensual theory of marriage, especially clandestine marriage and bigamy, see Michael M. Sheehan, "The Formation and Stability of Marriage in Fourteenth-Century England: Evidence of an Ely Register," *Mediaeval Studies* 33 (1971): 228–263. Scholars such as John Noonan have pointed out that the twelfth-century emphasis on individual consent was particularly liberating for the individual at the expense of the family ("Power to Choose," pp. 432–434). Also note Steven Ozment's contention that the church's fear of unregulated sex is what ensured the sanction of the consensual theory of marriage insofar as it would make marriage easier to contract (*When Fathers Ruled: Family Life in Reformation Europe* [Cambridge, Mass., 1983], p. 41).

contain, many are acceptable to the Lord, having legitimate marriages and walking in the commandments of the Lord. . . . And I said: Lord, which or what kind of faith or life do they [the Cathars] have? He answered: Their faith is depraved, and their works are worse. Again I said: Nevertheless they seem just in the sight of people and are praised as if [possessed] of good works. So it is, he said. They give the appearance of being of just and innocent life, and through these things they seduce and draw many to themselves. Inwardly, however, they are full of the worst venom.[25]

As a corollary to this latter point, the age-old question regarding the couple's integrity arose: if their intentions were pure, why did they remain together? Bernard of Clairvaux, in a sermon of 1144 refuting Cathar doctrine, vigorously protests against the possibility of chaste cohabitation with the opposite sex and goes so far as to claim that "the Church forbids men and women who have taken a vow of chastity to live together."[26] Likewise, Eckbert of Schönau, Elizabeth's brother and amanuensis, writing about a decade after Bernard, refutes heretical arguments that married individuals who do not separate must abstain sexually by pointing out that Christ and the apostles would never have ordered such a couple to remain together because they knew human nature only too well.[27]

[25] "Domine, ut audivi, quidam ex eis asserunt, quod legitimum esse non potest coniugium, nisi inter eos, qui usque ad tempus legitime coniunctionis virginitatem ambo custodierunt. . . . Et repondens ait: Ubi tale coniugium esse potest, gratum est domino. Sed rarum est valde, ut ita contingat. Veruntamen et ex his, qui non continuerunt, multi sunt acceptabiles domino, legitima habentes coniugia, et in mandatis domini ambulantes. . . . Et dixi: Domine, que vel qualis est fides eorum aut vita? Respondit: Prava est fides eorum, et opera peiora. Rursus dixi: Videntur tamen in conspectu hominum iusti, et laudantur, quasi sint bonorum operum. Ita est, inquit. Facies suas simulant, quasi iuste et innocentis vite sint, ac per hec multos ad se trahunt et seducunt, intrinsecus autem pessima sanie pleni sunt" (F.W.E. Roth, ed., *Die Visionen der hl. Elisabeth* [Brünn, 1884], pp. 104–105).

[26] Serm. 65, *On the Song of Songs* c. 6, trans. Wakefield and Evans, *Heresies of the High Middle Ages*, p. 137. Although Wakefield and Evans suggest that this may have referred to the ruling against syneisaktism made at Nicaea (see p. 682n.61), it seems more likely that Bernard was vetoing a much wider range of living arrangements than just that of two unmarried ascetics of opposite sexes—especially if one considers that in the same sermon he lets fly his famous comment: "To be always with a woman and not to know her carnally, is not this more than to raise the dead?" (c. 4, p. 135).

[27] Eckbert of Schönau, *Sermones contra Catharos*, Serm. 5, *PL* 195, cols. 28–29; 36. On the other hand, he seems prepared to accept the testimony of his sources that a number of married heretics lived in continence. Indeed, even in this sermon intended to refute the heresy, Eckbert cannot conceal the fact that he actually admires couples who are capable of this kind of self-restraint. Likewise, the *summa* of the Franciscan writer James Capelli (ca. 1240) reports as follows: "Indeed, these most stupid of people, seeking the purity of virginity and chastity, say that all carnal coition is shameful, base,

The remarks of Eckbert and Bernard direct us to the obvious disciplinary problems that a revival in chaste marriage presents. It was impossible for the clergy to ensure that the couple in question held to their chaste resolve. And yet more subtle deterrents can also be discerned on the level of hierarchy. From the standpoint of societal structure, a clerical celibate elite requires a copulating laity. Indeed, the clergy's dearly bought chastity brought them into direct competition with pious women generally, who had been traditionally acknowledged to possess chastity as an innate gift. We have already seen the eleventh-century efforts to downplay or even obscure female initiative toward chastity. These efforts at obfuscation will be strengthened by the intellectual revival. Thus with the influx of medical and biological texts, canonists and theologians alike will continually emphasize women's greater sexual appetite.[28] Moreover, at the very heart of clerical misgivings about spiritual marriage was the old anxiety that intramarital chastity would undermine male superiority, which, as we shall see, was being asserted with unprecedented vigor.

In short, lay chastity, whether heretical or orthodox, had the potential to challenge the structure of Christian society. It was necessary to deflect the laity from too rigid an imitation of the theological model of marriage. This apprehension of intramarital chastity may partially account for the dramatic reassertion of the centrality of sexual intercourse in marriage, in both canonistic sources and the new genre of pastoral manuals that were composed to assist priests in the hearing of confession.[29] What follows is an assessment of how this new em-

---

and odious, and thus damnable. Although spiritually they are prostituted and they pollute the word of God, they are, however, most chaste of body. . . . Actually, the rumor of fornication which is said to prevail among them is most false" (Wakefield and Evans, trans., *Heresies of the High Middle Ages*, p. 305).

[28] Jacquart and Thomasset, *Sexuality and Medicine*, p. 81 and n. 105; pp. 143–144, 173–177. Brundage, "Carnal Delight," pp. 375–376; idem, *Law, Sex, and Christian Society*, pp. 350–351, 426–428. It is interesting to note that Hildegard of Bingen was one of the few writers who deviated from the prevailing view that women were, by nature, more sexually oriented (see Bernhard W. Scholz, "Hildegard von Bingen on the Nature of Woman," *American Benedictine Review* 31 [1980]: 376, and Joan Cadden, "It Takes All Kinds: Sexuality and Gender Differences in Hildegard of Bingen's *Book of Compound Medicine*," *Traditio* 40 [1984]: 168).

[29] For an introduction to this genre, see Pierre Michaud-Quantin, "A propos des premières *Summae confessorum*," *Recherches de théologie ancienne et médiévale* 26 (1959): 264–306; idem, *Sommes de casuistique et manuels de confession au moyen âge du XIIe au XVIe siècles*, Analecta Mediaevalia Namurcensia, 13 (Louvain, Lille, and Montreal, 1962); idem, "Les méthodes de la pastorale du XIIIe au XVe siècle," in *Methoden in Wissenschaft und Kunst des Mittelalters*, ed. Albert Zimmerman, Miscellanea Mediaevalia, vol. 7 (Berlin, 1970), pp. 76–91; Leonard Boyle, "*Summae Confessorum*," in *Les genres littéraires dans les sources théologiques et philosophiques*

phasis on sex was articulated in these sources, how it was played out in their treatment of gender relations, and how it ultimately came to impinge on female spirituality.

Consummation and the Conjugal Debt

The very emphasis on consent and its implicitly chaste paradigm simultaneously gave rise to its opposite in canonistic discourse. Never before were sexual relations so openly and even obsessively discussed in learned circles; never before were the legal consequences of sexual intercourse so profoundly felt. The bias in favor of consummation and the conjugal debt is true not only of canonical works; it passes from canon law back into the work of the theologians.[30]

The canonist Gratian had posited that marriage was begun with consent but ratified only by sexual intercourse (C.27 q.2 c.34 dpc; c.37; c.39 dpc; c.45 dpc). This concrete focus was contested by French theologians and some of Gratian's more consensually minded successors.[31] An unconsummated marriage was indissoluble—even if the marriage had been contracted privately and one party publicly contracted a subsequent marriage that was later consummated (X.4.3.2 and X.4.1.31). And yet, clearly ambivalent about so rarified a model, these same authorities permitted an important concession to

---

médiévales: définition, critique et exploitation, Actes du colloque international de Louvain-la-Neuve, 25–27 mai, 1981 (Louvain-la-Neuve, 1982), pp. 227–237. For England, see Jacqueline Murray, "The Perceptions of Sexuality, Marriage and Family in Early English Pastoral Manuals" (Ph.D. diss., University of Toronto, 1987). The emphasis placed on annual confession by Lateran IV's publication of *Omnis utriusque sexus* sped up the multiplication of confessors' manuals, especially of the more comprehensive variety known as the *summae confessorum.* While Boyle sees Lateran IV as enhancing a movement toward instructing the clergy that was already under way, Thomas N. Tentler sees Lateran IV as basically creating the genre of *summae confessorum* (Boyle, "Summae Confessorum," pp. 227–228, 230, 232–233; Tentler, "The Summa for Confessors as an Instrument of Social Control," in *The Pursuit of Holiness in Late Medieval and Renaissance Religion,* ed. Charles Trinkaus, Studies in Medieval and Reformation Thought, vol. 10 [Leiden, 1974], pp. 103–104; for Boyle's objections to Tentler's perspective, see p. 126).

[30] The authorities in Peter Lombard's section on the conjugal debt (4.32.2) are largely derived from Gratian, especially C.33 q.5.

[31] See especially Huguccio's attack on Gratian for C.27 q.2 c.45 dpc ad v. *sicut per fidem* and ad v. *sed concedatur;* cf. C.27 q.2 c.50 dpc ad v. *verum est* (Roman, ed., "Summa d'Huguccio," pp. 799–800, 803). Gold shows that Gratian's solution was rejected since he failed to account for the marriage of Mary and Joseph ("The Marriage of Mary and Joseph," pp. 103–107); also see Brundage, *Law, Sex, and Christian Society,* pp. 236–237, 274, 354–355.

remain. Prior to consummation, an entrance into religion could be undertaken unilaterally (X.3.32.2; X.3.32.7). This flagrant contravention of consensuality irked many and required elaborate justifications.[32] It was argued that saints such as St. Alexis, St. Macarius, and even St. John the Evangelist (who tradition held was called away from his marriage at Cana by Christ himself) paved the way for this exception.[33] Some urged that an unconsummated marriage drew its constitution from the church, while a consummated marriage was divinely instituted—a formulation which certainly called into question the perfection of Mary and Joseph's union.[34] Still others justified this exception by maintaining that an unconsummated marriage could be abandoned in favor of the higher life.[35] But whatever the rationale, the underlying message was clear. Prior to sexual intercourse, either party could act with autonomy in this one area. Thus Huguccio, who accepted Lombard's consensual view of marriage and vigorously denounced Gratian's distinction between *matrimonium initiatum* and *matrimonium ratum*, still raised no objection to the view that Mary was separated from Joseph and entrusted to John's care because the marriage was unconsummated.[36] But the door on this nebulous pe-

[32] Innocent III makes it clear that he is unhappy with this alternative, though he nevertheless does not want to deviate from the example of his predecessors (X.3.32.14. He presumably means Alexander III, who, though largely responsible for the rigidly consensual view of marriage, was also behind the decretals that carved out this exception). Robert of Flamborough's *Liber poenitentialis* (between 1208 and 1213), which was produced in the time of Innocent, seems to resist the idea that the abandoned spouse who remained in the world was free to remarry (ed. J. J. Francis Firth [Toronto, 1971], 2.33.56, p. 88; but for another reading, see pp. 88–89 n. 31. On Robert's work, see Michaud-Quantin, "A propos des premières *Summae confessorum*," pp. 276–278; idem, *Sommes de casuistique*, pp. 21–24; and John W. Baldwin, *Masters, Princes, and Merchants: The Social Views of Peter the Chanter and His Circle* [Princeton, N.J., 1970], 1:32–33, 2:23–24). Jean Gaudemet demonstrates that the inclusion of so marked an exception to the consensual theory was a kind of mistake or fluke ("Recherche sur les origines historiques de la faculté de rompre le mariage non consommé," in *Proceedings of the Fifth International Congress of Medieval Canon Law*, ed. Kuttner and Pennington, pp. 309–331).

[33] C.27 q.2 c.26 dpc. Huguccio notes disagreement over this issue: some argue that saints were special instances and that no general application can be drawn from their example (C.27 q.2 c.26 dpc ad v. *ecce*, Roman, ed., "Summa d'Huguccio," p. 779).

[34] See the *Glossa ordinaria* for X.3.32.7 ad v. *consummatum* (in the *Decretales D. Gregorii Papae IX* [London, 1584]), which notes the disagreement between canonists and theologians over the significance of consent.

[35] Hostiensis (d. 1271), *Summa aurea* (Lyons, 1537), *De conuersione coniugatorum* (X.3.32) ad v. *Et vtrum possit exire*, no. 7, p. 175. For a brief introduction to Hostiensis's life and work, see Elisabeth Vodola, *DMA*, 6:298–299.

[36] Huguccio for C.27 q.2 c.43 ad v. *nichil habentem*, Roman, ed., "Summa d'Huguccio," p. 797; cf. his gloss for C.27 q.2 c.10 (ad v. *divortium*, p. 757, where he somewhat feebly volunteers that Joseph separated from Mary so that he could better provide for

riod of opportunity did not remain ajar indefinitely for the average woman as it had for the Virgin Mary. It closed rather abruptly after two months, at which point the resisting party could be compelled by ecclesiastical authorities toward payment of the debt—willy-nilly.[37]

The possibility of a unilateral entrance into religion called into question the sexual content implicit in consent to the marriage contract. The inability to consummate a marriage was considered to be a permanent impediment.[38] Despite Hugh of St. Victor's unusual readiness to affirm the entrance into a marriage in which both parties were resolved to remain virgins, it was generally believed that there was no marriage without consent to carnal intercourse.[39] But it was by no means clear at what precise moment one was obliged to begin fulfilling that debt. Gratian and Huguccio maintained that the obligation of the debt arose only after the first coupling.[40] Although

---

her); also see C.27 q.2 c.29 dpc ad v. *divortium* and ad v. *fuisset*, pp. 784–786. Note that Huguccio and the *Glossa ordinaria* reject Peter Comestor's simpler solution that Joseph was dead at the time of the Crucifixion, preferring to trust to the authority of Ambrose and John Chrysostom. See *Glossa ordinaria* for C.27 q.2 c.43 ad v. *Si enim. Vxoris* (in *Decretum Gratiani; seu verius, decretorum canonicorum collectanea* [Paris, 1561]). Cf. Robert of Flamborough's view that if one party vowed never to exact the debt, the other could effect a unilateral entrance into religion (*Liber poenitentialis* 2.3.21, p. 70).

[37] X.3.32.7; Thomas of Chobham's *Summa confessorum* (ca. 1215) states explicitly that an unconsummated marriage can no longer be dissolved by a unilateral entrance into religion after six months (ed. F. Broomfield, Analecta Mediaevalia Namurcensia, 25 [Louvain and Paris, 1968], 4.2.7.6, p. 149. On Thomas, see Baldwin, *Masters, Princes, and Merchants*, 1:34–36, 2:25–26, and Michaud-Quantin, "A propos des premières *Summae confessorum*," pp. 284–290). It was not, however, entirely clear how the two months should be calculated: Innocent IV (d. 1254) points out that some say the clock starts ticking the moment the marriage is contracted, while others say it begins with the bishop's warning to the resistant spouse that he or she must consummate the marriage or enter religion (*Commentaria Innocentii Quarti pontificis maximi super libros quinque Decretalium* [Frankfurt, 1570], for X.3.32.6 ad v. *Duorum*, p. 426r).

[38] C.27 q.2 c.2 dpc, and c.29 and dpc; also see X.4.15 "De frigidis et maleficiatis, et impotentia coeundi." For the Decretists' views, see Brundage, *Law, Sex, and Christian Society*, pp. 236, 290–292. Also see idem, "The Problem of Impotence," in *Sexual Practices and the Medieval Church*, ed. Bullough and Brundage, pp. 135–140, 261–262, and Makowski, "Conjugal Debt," pp. 106–107.

[39] Huguccio says this explicitly with reference to C.27 q.2 c.3 ad v. *in carnalem copulam* (Roman, ed., "Summa d'Huguccio," p. 753). Following Gratian, he believed that the Virgin Mary made only a conditional vow of chastity and that she mentally consented to carnal union, if this was in accordance with God's will (C.27 q.2 c.3 ad v. *non expressit ore* and ad v. *nisi Deus aliter*, p. 752). Hugh of St. Victor would have been distressed by this view (see *De B. Mariae virginitate* c. 1, *PL* 176, col. 859).

[40] See C.27 q.2 c.18 dpc. Huguccio notes the disagreement between those who think the conjugal debt immediately pertains and those who think that it is only established with the first sex act. He opts for a middle ground, positing that, while consent carries

Raymond of Peñafort's important *Summa on Penance and Marriage* (begun ca. 1225) reiterates the usual remarks that, prior to sexual intercourse, either spouse can make a unilateral entrance into religion, it presents the additional observation that, after consent, a spouse is instantly bound to render the debt, thus implying that prevarication was out of the question and that the decision to enter a monastery must be immediate. If a wife claims she wishes to enter a monastery, but defers entrance, she should be compelled by the bishop to render after the allotted time.[41] Whether one was inclined to accept that the debt arose only with the first coupling, or that the debt arose simultaneously with consent, both options anticipated and accommodated a forced consummation. Most of the authorities agreed that if a woman was intercepted and violently penetrated by her husband while en route to the convent, she must by necessity adhere to him. The husband was only acting in accordance with his rights.[42] The influential theological casuist Peter the Chanter

---

with it the right to exact, one cannot seek immediate execution of this right (C.27 q.2 c.6 ad v. *a prima fide desponsationis*, Roman, ed., "*Summa* d'Huguccio," p. 755; cf. c.27 ad v. *eligere monasterium*, p. 779); see A. Esmein, *Le mariage en droit canonique*, 2d ed. (Paris, 1935), 2:10–11.

[41] *Summa sancti Raymundi de Peniafort de poenitentia, et de matrimonio* 4.2.9 (Rome, 1603), p. 516; 1.8.8, p. 66. A more recent edition of Raymond's work is also available (ed. Xavier Ochoa and Aloisius Diez, Universa bibliotheca iuris, vol. 1, pts. B and C [Rome, 1976 and 1978]). I have chosen to use the earlier edition for the benefit of the glosses of the Dominican William of Rennes, which were composed between 1240 and 1245 (note that they are erroneously attributed to John of Freiburg on the frontispiece). On Raymond's significance, see Michaud-Quantin, *Sommes de casuistique*, pp. 35–42. Also see A. Teetaert, "La doctrine pénitentielle de saint Raymond de Penyafort, O.P.," *Analecta Sacra Tarraconensia* 5 (1929): 121–182.

Cf. Hostiensis, *Summa aurea* bk. 3 (for X.3.32) ad v. *et vtrum possit exire*, no. 6, p. 175r. Innocent IV shows considerable concern that the two-month delay not be used maliciously: it was not intended for simple deliberation between marriage and religion but should be applied to the monastic period of probation. He also urges ecclesiastical judges to excommunicate individuals for dilatory entrances (for X.3.32.6 ad v. *Duorum*, *Commentaria*, p. 426r). John of Freiburg's *Summa confessorum* (ca. 1297), however, which incorporates the work of the more liberal Dominican theologians, cites those who think the obligation to render takes effect immediately, but also cites Thomas Aquinas's view that the woman can spend two months deciding whether she wishes to enter a monastery ([Rome, 1518], 4.2.34, fol. 219v). See Leonard Boyle, "The *Summa Confessorum* of John of Freiburg and the Popularization of the Moral Teaching of St. Thomas Aquinas and Some of His Contemporaries," in *St. Thomas Aquinas, 1274–1974: Commemorative Studies*, ed. Armand A. Maurer et al. (Toronto, 1974), 2:245–268; reprt. in Boyle, *Pastoral Care, Clerical Education, and Canon Law, 1200–1400* (London, 1981).

[42] See Hostiensis, *Summa aurea* bk. 3 (for X.3.32), ad v. *et vtrum possit exire*, no. 9, p. 175v; cf. John of Freiburg, *Summa confessorum* 1.8.42v, fol. 21, and William of Rennes, glossator of Raymond of Peñafort, in *Summa de poenitentia* 1.8.8, gloss e ad v. *ipsa*

(d. 1197) envisages a less violent but particularly pathetic scenario that smacks of realism considering the sparse religious options for women—particularly poor ones. A woman wishes to enter a religious community but is too poor. She bangs at the gates of the convent with tears and entreaties. At the end of two or three months, however, her husband can take her, if he still wishes to. In short, her commitment to chastity must be fulfilled within a convent.[43]

The focus on the ability to consummate was relentless. In the event that the woman could not be penetrated, surgery was recommended. William of Rennes also argues that the woman ought to be able to sustain a certain amount of violence in consummation.[44] Although Innocent III permitted the dissolution of a marriage due to gross disparity in the size of genitals, later pastoral advisers, such as John of Freiburg, cast doubt on the necessity of such a release clause—a wise woman told him, John claims, that never or, at least, very rarely was a man's penis so large that his bride could not accommodate it.[45]

The rhetoric of consummation placed additional pressures on male virility, and this, in turn, seems to have fostered a climate of sexual violence. Peter the Chanter noted (not without some dismay) that Alexander III permitted a man to remarry after he had damaged his wife on his wedding night so that neither he nor anyone else could have intercourse with her.[46] (On the other hand, if the groom was

---

ingrediatur, p. 66, and 4.2.8, gloss g ad v. *secuta,* p. 515. Panormitanus (d. 1445), writing much later, is the only source I have found which tentatively denies that forced consummation should inhibit a woman's entrance into religion (Panormitanus [= Nicolaus de Tudeschis], *Lectura in Decretales cum optimis glossis* [Turin, 1509], for X.3.32.2, no. 9, 5:156v). He does, however, permit forced cohabitation (for X.3.32.7, no. 2, p. 158r); see Esmein, *Le mariage,* 2:11; cf. Brundage, "Rape and Marriage in the Medieval Canon Law," *Revue de droit canonique* 28 (1978): 70–71; idem, *Law, Sex, and Christian Society,* p. 312. Note that the notion of intramarital rape did not exist in medieval times.

[43] Peter the Chanter, *Summa de sacramentis et animae consiliis* c. 314, ed. Jean-Albert Dugauquier, Analecta Mediaevalia Namurcensia, 16 (Louvain and Lille, 1963), 3,2a:367. Peter the Chanter and the practical orientation of his theological casuistry had an enormous impact on his contemporaries. See Baldwin, *Masters, Princes, and Merchants.* For a brief discussion of Peter's life and *summa,* see esp. 1:3–16, 2:1–8. Baldwin thinks the *summa* was written between 1191/2 and 1197.

[44] See Raymond of Peñafort, *Summa de poenitentia* 4.16.2, p. 559, and William of Rennes's gloss e ad v. *non potest cognoscere;* cf. John of Freiburg, *Summa confessorum* 4.16.22, fol. 236r.

[45] X.4.15.6; see Brundage, *Law, Sex, and Christian Society,* p. 339; John of Freiburg, *Summa confessorum* 4.16.21, fol. 236r. Finally, however, John resolves that in such a case, he would consult the pope.

[46] Peter the Chanter, *Summa de sacramentis* c. 291, 3,2a:325. Cf. the Talmudic tradition whereby a husband who damages his wife in intercourse is liable for assault (Samuel Morrell, "An Equal or a Ward: How Independent Is a Married Woman according to Rabbinic Law?" *Jewish Social Studies* 44 [1982]: 198).

castrated prior to the consummation of the marriage, the marriage was upheld.)[47] Hagiographical and devotional works offer still more lurid perspectives. The aspiring ascetic Christina of Markyate (d. after 1155) was forced into marriage by her parents. When she had momentarily convinced the groom to forgo consummation, the revelers outside of the nuptial chamber not only goaded him to attempt but were prepared to assist him in a forced consummation.[48] One of the miracles of the Virgin alleges that Mary cured a young woman who had been mortally wounded by her spouse. The husband, clearly crazed by his inability to penetrate his bride's hymen after half a year of nightly attempts, had thrust a knife into her vagina.[49]

Thus, although the church championed the freedom of consent, its

---

[47] Huguccio for C.27 q.2 c.39 dpc ad v. *separabile*, Roman, ed., "*Summa* d'Huguccio," p. 795; cf. Raymond of Peñafort, *Summa de poenitentia* 4.16.2, p. 560; John of Freiburg, *Summa confessorum* 4.16.12, fol. 234v; see Brundage, *Law, Sex, and Christian Society*, p. 456.

[48] Christina used the example of Cecilia and Valerian to convert her groom, Burthred, to chastity. When he left the chamber, however: "They joined together in calling him a spineless and useless fellow. And with many reproaches they goaded him on again, and thrust him into her bedroom another night, having warned him not to be misled by her deceitful tricks and naïve words nor lose his manliness (*ne infinitis ambagibus et candidis sermonibus fallentis effeminetur*). Either by force or entreaty he was to gain his end. And if neither of these sufficed, he was to know that they were at hand to help him: all he had to mind was to act like a man (*modo meminerit esse virum*)" (C. H. Talbot, ed. and trans., *The Life of Christina of Markyate* c. 10 [Oxford, 1959; reprt. 1987], pp. 50–53). The onlookers suggested that Burthred's behavior was unmanly, but they did not accuse him of impotence. Although it is possible that spiritual marriage could be used as a pretext for concealing male impotence, this use is not addressed in the sources. Couples such as Margery and John Kempe, whose vow was known by the community, were instead accused of unchastity. Others, such as Catherine of Sweden and her husband Eggard, were subjected to ridicule, but no aspersions concerning impotence were voiced. The absence of suspicion with respect to male impotence reflects the primarily hagiographical nature of the sources, which would be little inclined to undercut the merit of the saint or aspirant saint in question by such a possibility. But it also reflects a masculine prejudice, which is more inclined to attribute failure to produce children to the wife's deficiency. Dauphine of Puimichel, for example, was believed to be sterile. This prejudice is also reflected in the unequal treatment women receive when testifying to their husbands' impotence, as discussed later in this chapter. Sterility could and did, however, act as an impetus for a transition to chastity—a subject treated in chapter 5.

[49] Gautier de Coinci, *Les miracles de Nostre Dame*, ed. V. Frédéric Koenig (Geneva, 1970), II, Mir. 27 (D.76), lines 129–162, 4:300–301. For this motif, see F. C. Tubach, *Index Exemplorum: A Handbook of Medieval Religious Tales*, Folklore Fellows Communications, no. 204 (Helsinki, 1969), no. 3176. According to Abbot Poquet, the Virgin appeared to two jongleurs of Arras during the plague of 1105. This incident was soon followed by a number of parallel visitations, as is the case with the tale in question (*Les miracles de la Sainte Vierge* [Paris, 1857], editor's note, cols. 257–260). Note that Poquet's edition omits this grisly scene entirely (see the ellipsis in col. 264 after line 111; cf. his comments on cols. 261–262).

tolerance of forced consummation would suggest that this professed freedom was, in many ways, nominal.[50] And yet with consummation a woman's window of opportunity shut: thenceforth she was unremittingly subordinated to her husband. Ironically, consummation also inaugurated the one area of celebrated equality between husband and wife: the conjugal debt. But the rhetoric of equality that surrounds medieval and modern discussions of the debt is only convincing if all awareness of social mores and biological differences is suspended.[51] It is impossible that the debt alone should be free from all inequities built into the gender system.

Once the debt was established, inequities become even more apparent. Modern scholars have noted that the higher level of chastity expected of women was conspicuously at odds with their allegedly lascivious nature.[52] Such tensions become especially apparent over the question of adultery. In theory, the adultery of one party suspends his or her right to the conjugal debt. But Gratian himself puzzles over the sexual double standard of his day, asking why, if the husband and wife are equal with regard to the debt, a man's adultery is frequently tolerated while a woman's is not (C.32 q.5 c.22 dpc). He then goes on to cite a decretal of Innocent I that remarks on how women are more frequently accused of adultery but less inclined to accuse their husbands (c.23; cf. C.32 q.6 c.4–5). Canonistic refinement of procedure against adultery potentially compounds this inequity: if the adulterous husband exacts the debt, the wife is still bound to render until the case has been tried before an ecclesiastical court. On the other hand, were the wronged wife to exact, she would probably be guilty of

[50] This intransigent emphasis on consummation, favoring deed over intention, goes against the general tenor of Gratian's pronouncements. With regard to the rape of nuns, for example, he maintains that, since virginity is primarily a state of mind, they do not lose their chastity—although he does acknowledge that they may no longer dare to follow the virgins in the procession of the Lamb (C.32 q.5 c.13 dpc; cf. c.14 and dpc). The difference between consecrated women and the victims of a forced consummation is that the latter were trapped by verbally consenting to marriage.

[51] Modern scholars tend to take medieval professions of equality of the debt and, even more significantly, the assumption that such an "equality" benefits both parties in the same way, at face value. See particularly Brundage, "Sexual Equality in Medieval Canon Law," in *Medieval Women and the Sources of Medieval History*, ed. Joel T. Rosenthal (Athens, Ga., 1990), pp. 66–79; cf. Makowski, "Conjugal Debt," p. 111, and René Metz, "Le statut de la femme en droit canonique médiéval," *Recueils de Société Jean Bodin pour l'histoire comparative des institutions* 12 (1962): 88–89. Only occasionally does one get a more realistic sense of the many inequities. See especially Eleanor McLaughlin, "Equality of Souls, Inequality of Sexes: Woman in Medieval Theology," in *Religion and Sexism*, ed. Ruether, pp. 225–228.

[52] See McLaughlin, "Equality of Souls," p. 226, and Brundage, *Law, Sex, and Christian Society*, pp. 350–351, 426–427.

a mortal sin.[53] The tendency to turn a blind eye to male infidelity was endorsed by practical rationales as well as by speculative exercises aimed at exculpating male adultery and even polygamy.[54]

At the end of the twelfth century particularly, the excruciatingly technical focus on ability to render the debt seems to have been unabated by more humane concerns. Peter the Chanter's casuist speculation is particularly chilling: a woman suffers damage from a recent birth. If she becomes pregnant again she will die,. and yet her husband exacts the debt. Must she render? Before attempting to answer this difficult question, Peter does his best to dredge up a similarly life-threatening situation for a man (the hypothetical man will become insane if he has sex again) but in fact there is no parallel situation. Peter admits the predicament is a perplexing one, and likens the individual from whom the debt is exacted to a debtor who will die of indigence if he pays what he owes. On the basis of this analogy, he tentatively posits that the fragile party is justified in refusing, but he is by no means certain. In fact, once the debt is established, the individual's right of sexual refusal in life-threatening situations does not seem to have been clearly articulated by canonistic or pastoral sources until the fifteenth century.[55]

---

[53] Raymond of Peñafort, *Summa de poenitentia* 4.2.11, p. 517; Raymond omits the part about mortal sin, but his glossator, William of Rennes, following Huguccio, adds it (gloss o ad v. *si vir*). William also includes the cheerless reflection that a prelate can order one to render the debt to the other. Although the prelate should not order his penitent to do anything illicit, if he does, the penitent is bound to obey (gloss p ad v. *debet reddere*, pp. 517–518); cf. John of Freiburg, *Summa confessorum* 4.2.48, fol. 221r.

[54] Brundage cites Innocent IV's rationale that men represent Christ, who was first married to the synagogue and later to the church, but women represent the church, which is always virgin ("Carnal Delight," p. 377). Peter the Chanter notes that wives sicken and, as one can glean from the Old Testament, multiple wives would be a convenience to men (*Summa de sacramentis*, c. 321, 3,2a:381). Cf. Thomas Aquinas's equally pragmatic view that adultery is more serious in the wife than in the husband due to the threat to the family (McLaughlin, "Equality of Souls," pp. 227–228). According to Esmein, this bias is confirmed practically by the fact that a husband can criminally prosecute a wife's adultery, while the wife can only civilly prosecute her husband's in order to obtain a *divortium quoad torum* (Le mariage, 2:3–4).

[55] Peter the Chanter, *Summa de sacramentis* c. 350, 3,2b:463; the editor, Dugauquier, cites Panormitanus's answer to this problem, namely, that charity is inseparable from self-love: "Doctores [dicunt] communiter quod non, quia charitas incipit a se ipso" (for X.4.8.2, no. 3 n. 1); Esmein also turns to Panormitanus for a solution (Le mariage, 2:13 n. 1). Likewise, in the fifteenth century, Jean Gerson admits denial of the debt when intercourse would result in certain physical harm—either to the solicited party or to the fetus: "Nullus coniugum tenetur reddere debitum in detrimentum notabile et certum sui corporis vel foetus nascituri" (Op. 434, *Regulae mandatorum*, no. 154, in *Oeuvres complètes*, ed. Mgr. Glorieux [Paris, 1973], 9:132; see Tentler, *Sin and Confession*, p. 171). Aquinas anticipated this refusal (*Summa Theologica* pt. 3 [Supplement] Q. 64, art. 1, rep. obj. 2). Cf. the Jewish tradition whereby all of the

In a period when the paradigm of chastity was permanently enshrined in matrimonial theory, as exemplified in the union of Mary and Joseph, the debt swelled to unwieldy proportions. The traditional periods of abstinence to a large extent receded: although Gratian dutifully lists these restricted times, he nevertheless sweeps them to one side with the following *dictum*: "These [periods of abstinence] should be observed if the wife wishes to furnish consent; but without her consent, continence should not be observed for the sake of prayer."[56] With this landmark qualification, the debt pursues the couple everywhere. If the party seeking the debt is in danger of falling into adultery, holy seasons and even holy places are now fair game.[57]

Just as the penitential periods became "open season," so the ancient taboos around the woman's biological cycle were often suspended.[58] Rendering the debt during pregnancy was deemed licit by Dominican authorities provided that the fetus was not imperiled.[59] The taboos surrounding childbirth and, to a lesser degree, during menstruation were likewise mitigated. Either party exacting the debt during these times sinned—but the degree of their sinfulness var-

---

authorities permitted the use of a cervical contraceptive sponge in the event that pregnancy could endanger the life of the woman (Kenneth R. Stow, "The Jewish Family in the Rhineland in the High Middle Ages: Form and Function," *American Historical Review* 92 [1987]: 1103).

[56] "Hec autem seruanda sunt, si uxor consensum adhibere uoluerit; ceterum sine eius consensu nec causa orationis continentia seruari debet" (C.33 q.4 dpc. 11); see Brundage, *Law, Sex, and Christian Society*, p. 242.

[57] Thomas of Chobham has considerable qualms about rendering the debt on holy days, comparing it with giving a sword to a madman. He finally resolves, however, that one must render but that the one rendering would be absolved of sin (*Summa confessorum* 7.2.2.3, p. 337; also see p. 336, and 4.2.7.24, pp. 188–189; cf. Raymond of Peñafort, *Summa de poenitentia* 4.2.10, p. 516); William of Rennes adds the practical consideration that if you render in a holy place when another one is available, you sin mortally (gloss k ad v. *abstinendum*, p. 517). John of Freiburg, citing Albert the Great, says that if no other place can be found, one should submit with sorrow in one's heart. Even the one exacting (if he or she is in danger of falling into illicit fornication) does not sin mortally, unless another place is available (*Summa confessorum* 4.2.43, fol. 220v). See Tentler, *Sin and Confession*, pp. 171–173.

[58] As a rule of thumb, the sources become more lenient as time progresses. Some of the pre–Lateran IV manuals, such as Robert of Flamborough's *Liber poenitentialis*, have not yet thrown off the bondage of the old-style penitentials. Robert has considerable apprehensions concerning such matters as the reception of communion after sexual intercourse, thus incorporating many of the prohibitions of "Gregory the Great" that appear in the letter to Augustine of Canterbury (see esp. 4.6.285–288, pp. 236–238). Even in the section which stresses that a spouse cannot contain without the other's consent, Robert still maintains that the couple should abstain on Sundays (4.7.289, p. 239; also see 4.13.296, p. 243 regarding Lent).

[59] John of Freiburg, *Summa confessorum* 4.2.44, fol. 220v.

ied from venial to mortal, depending on which authority was consulted.[60] Most authorities were agreed that the one rendering the debt did not sin, but not all. Thomas of Chobham, for example, writing ca. 1215, believed that women who permitted their husbands to know them after childbirth sinned mortally. He suggests a way in which such sin could be expeditiously avoided, however. If the husband were to exact the debt, the wife should go instantly to the church and seek purification so that she could accommodate him—a painful and even dangerous solution for the woman.[61]

Yet while the female body was rendered more available, it was by no means less dangerous. The myths around the dangers of menstruation in this period were legion. It was widely believed that the blood from menstruation or afterbirth produced leprosy, elephantiasis, and epilepsy in the offspring.[62] The woman was placed in an ambiguous

[60] With regard to the individual exacting during menstruation, William of Rennes lines up two different sets of authorities (the first group describing the action as mortal sin, the second as venial) but concludes by favoring the first: "prima tamen opinio videtur verior, et magis consonat auctoritatibus sanctorum" (*Summa de poenitentia* 4.2.10, gloss k ad v. *abstinendum*, p. 516). Exacting during pregnancy or prior to purification is only a venial sin; cf. John of Freiburg, who follows William here (*Summa confessorum* 4.2.45–46, fol. 220v).

[61] "Similiter turpissimum est iacere cum muliere iacenti in puerperio dum laborat profluvio menstrui sanguinis, quia puerpera diu habent fluxum immundi humoris. Peccant autem mortaliter mulieres que in tempore illo viros suos recipiunt, et viri qui in tali tempore debitum exigunt, et debet eis iniungi penitentie multo maior quam pro simplici fornicatione. . . .

"Verumtamen sciendum est quod si vir petat debitum ab uxore sua puerpera et ipsa timeat de lapsu viri, consilium est ut statim accedat ad purificationem et statim reddat debitum" (Thomas of Chobham, *Summa confessorum* 7.2.2.3, pp. 338–339). Thomas seems to differ from the others in expressing more abhorrence over sex prior to purification than during menstruation. With regard to the latter he mentions only the threat of leprosy to potential offspring: "Similiter periculosum est dormire cum menstruata, quia inde nascitur partus leprosus" (7.2.2.3, p. 338). Thomas's compatriot Robert of Flamborough, on the other hand, only assigns ten days on bread and water for the same offense (*Liber poenitentialis* 4.14.296, p. 243).

[62] See Robert of Flamborough, *Liber poenitentialis* 4.8.226, p. 198, and 5.6.288, p. 238, and Thomas of Chobham in the above note. The same anxieties are reiterated in John of Freiburg's later, and more sexually liberal, collection (*Summa confessorum* 4.2.46, fol. 220v). Cf. Innocent III's powerful statement of this dread in his literary tour de force—*On the Misery of the Human Condition*: "But notice what food the fetus is fed in the womb: with menstrual blood of course, which ceases in the woman after conception so that with it the fetus is fed inside the woman. The blood is said to be so detestable and unclean that 'on contact with it crops do not germinate, orchards wither, plants die, trees drop their fruit; if dogs eat of it, they are transported into madness.' Conceived fetuses contract the defect of the seed, so that lepers and elephantiacs are born from this corruption" *De miseria condicionis humanae* 1.4, ed. and trans. Robert E. Lewis, Chaucer Library [Athens, Ga., 1978], p. 100). Also see Jacquart and Thomasset, *Sexuality and Medicine*, pp. 71–78, 129, 186, 191–192.

position, with regard to both her own body and her husband. Her position was unique. Although any unconsenting body could be the occasion of sin—Christ himself had said that one can be an adulterer simply through mentally coveting, while according to Christian theologians, the same act of intercourse could be meritorious for one partner and sinful for the other on the basis of intention—the menstruous wife, whether rendering or exacting, was now a licit source of pollution.

This "opening up" of the female body was complemented by a new emphasis on female appearance and even adornment, which was likewise gender specific.[63] Although women's finery was roundly condemned both in Scripture and by the church fathers, women were at first begrudgingly permitted and later expected to adorn themselves in order to arrest potentially truant male interest and focus it on the nuptial chamber. At first, this emphasis does not exceed patristic counsel. Gratian cites the passage in Augustine's letter to Ecdicia which stipulates that as long as her husband is alive, she should dress like Susanna as opposed to Anna.[64] But the confessors' manuals expand on this responsibility. Thomas of Chobham, for example, although often peculiarly sensitive to his married female penitents—arguing against the assignment of any extraordinary penance that the husband might interfere with or that might alert him to a secret offense—buttresses these considerations by the wife's singular responsibility of appearing attractive for rendering the debt. "Indeed she ought to nourish and cherish [her body] so it is suitable for manly uses, because fleshy members befit the office of the flesh."[65] No like

---

[63] See Dyan Elliott, "Dress as Mediator between Inner and Outer Self: The Pious Matron of the High and Later Middle Ages," *Mediaeval Studies* 53 (1991): 279–308.

[64] C.33 q.5 c.4. Biblical references are to the apocryphal history of Susanna and to Luke 2.36–37. The canonical *Glossa ordinaria* simply observes that Anna is a widow (ad v. *Anna*) and Susanna a married woman (ad v. *Susanna*). The *Summa Parisiensis* (ca. 1160) went into considerably more detail recounting how Anna the prophetess lived in virginity with her husband for seven years, while Susanna ornamented herself with precious clothing and unguents. Augustine is saying that even if Ecdicia dressed like the latter in compliance with her husband's wishes, she would not displease God (ad v. *indueris non sicut Anna sed sicut Susanna*, *The "Summa Parisiensis" on the "Decretum Gratiani,"* ed. T. P. McLaughlin [Toronto, 1952], p. 253).

[65] "Immo debet illud nutrire et fovere ut sit idoneum ad usus viriles, quia carnis ad officium carnea membra placent" (Thomas of Chobham, *Summa confessorum* 7.2.9.3, p. 363; cf. 4.2.7.11, p. 157, and 7.12.3, p. 560). His concern that the penance of married penitents (particularly matrons) not attract the attention of their mates echoes local conciliar legislation. The Statutes of Canterbury I (between 1213 and 1214) warn against the assignation of a penance that would alert the husband to his wife's hidden crimes: "et ut penitentia talis iniungatur uxori unde non reddatur marito suo suspecta de aliquo occulto crimine et enormi. Idem de marito observetur" (c. 40, in F. M. Powicke and C. R. Cheney, eds., *Councils and Synods with Other Documents Relating*

requirement is ever placed upon the husband. The assimilation of Dominican theology into pastoral literature pushes the emphasis on female appearance the furthest. Well aware of the ambivalence of female adornment, John of Freiburg (writing ca. 1297), following Aquinas's lead, raises the question of whether women sin mortally in self-adornment. He resolves, however, that they are permitted to adorn themselves in order to please their husbands—casually misappropriating Paul's regretful comment (that wives think first of pleasing their husbands) as a justification. John also cites Albert the Great's advice that if a man has difficulty consummating his marriage, the woman should be warned to dress more provocatively, while the man should be instructed on how a more lovable woman can be fashioned.[66]

The progressive interest in making women both more available and more appealing for rendering the debt corresponds to certain shifts in medical discourse that theoretically rendered women entirely passive and instrumental in the sex act. As Galenic solicitude for the "ejaculation" of female "seed" gave way to the Aristotelian emphasis on masculine agency in conception, female pleasure was, accordingly, excised from medieval theories of conception.[67] On the other hand, the increased emphasis on women's passive availability is complemented by efforts to explain or even justify male sexual defection. Innocent III's monumental statement that husbands could embark on a Crusade without their wives' permission is undoubtedly the most flagrant example of this.[68] But this double standard was apparent in multiple contexts. If the woman claimed that the man was incapable of consummating the marriage but he denied it, his word held, as he was her lord. Only a virgin could be certain of proving her

---

to the English Church [Oxford, 1964], 2,1:32). This is reiterated by many other councils. Cf. the Statutes of Salisbury I (between 1217 and 1219; c. 34, ibid., p. 71); the Statutes of Exeter I (between 1225 and 1237; c. 32, p. 236); the Statutes of Salisbury II (between 1238 and 1244; c. 11, p. 370), etc.

[66] John of Freiburg, Summa confessorum 3.34.284, fol. 214r; 4.16.23, fol. 236r. Cf. Elliott, "Dress as Mediator," pp. 288–289. Certain members of the clergy, most notably the Franciscan Bernardino of Siena, strenuously resisted this Dominican liberalization. See, for example, Serms. 17 and 18 in Opera omnia, ed. Fathers of the College of St. Bonaventure (Florence, 1950), 1:204–226. I have discussed Bernardino's resistance in a paper entitled "The Conjugal Debt and Female Spirituality" at the conference on "Sex and Sexuality in the Middle Ages and Renaissance," Centre for Reformation and Renaissance Studies, University of Toronto, 22–24 November 1991.

[67] See Jacquart and Thomasset, Sexuality and Medicine, pp. 57–60, 128–130, 154; cf. Thomas Laqueur, Making Sex: Body and Gender from the Greeks to Freud (Cambridge, Mass., 1990), pp. 40–43, 255n.36.

[68] X.3.34.9. See James Brundage, "The Crusader's Wife: A Canonistic Quandary," Studia Gratiana 12 (1967): 427–441, esp. pp. 434–435.

allegation by insisting on a physical examination.[69] Gender-specific limitations on penitential practices could also disparage female sexual rights. While neither spouse was, in theory, permitted to undertake so rigid a program of asceticism that it would impede ready payment of the debt, the husband was permitted to interfere with his wife's pious practices (be they prayers, fasts, vigils, or other forms of devotion), while the reverse was not true.[70] Even so, pastoral advisers were aware that abstinence from food, drink, and sleep was much more inclined to affect a man's potency than a woman's. Thus William of Rennes says explicitly that a man cannot afflict himself with fasting to the extent that he cannot render the debt. But John of Freiburg later resolves that a husband who renders himself incapable of rendering by permitted fasting does not sin.[71]

John's work was shaped by Dominican Aristotelianism, which, through its invocation of the natural order, simultaneously redeemed the sex act and more securely subordinated wife to husband. This twofold process results in a benign paternalism that further erodes the equality of the debt. Thomas Aquinas maintained that women are more concupiscent by nature and also, somewhat contradictorily, more bashful about seeking payment of the debt.[72] Hence John, following Thomas, urges that a husband should render the debt when the wife was not explicitly seeking, but he cautions that the reverse does not hold true for the woman. John also permits a husband to

---

[69] See C.33 q.5 c.1. An oath supported by seven witnesses is an alternative way of presenting an allegation of impotence for the nonvirgin, but the husband has the opportunity of swearing first. See Huguccio, for C.27 q.2 c.29 ad v. *probare*, Roman, ed., "*Summa* d'Huguccio," pp. 782–783; cf. *Glossa ordinaria* ad v. *probare*; Raymond of Peñafort, *Summa de poenitentia* 4.16.6, pp. 562–563, and John of Freiburg, *Summa confessorum* 4.16.16, fol. 235r–v. Both Raymond and John agree, however, that if the man claims he has never known the woman and she denies it, her word should be taken over his, as many men would incur perjury in order to rid themselves of their wives. Time constraints impose additional pressures: if a woman waits for half a year before she charges her husband with impotence, and he denies it, her case should be dismissed because she waited too long to complain (X.4.15.1; also see William of Rennes's gloss in *Summa de poenitentia* 4.16.5, gloss q ad *cap.i.*, p. 561). Jacqueline Murray's article "On the Origins and Role of 'Wise Women' in Causes for Annulment on the Grounds of Male Impotence" (*Journal of Medieval History* 16 [1990]: 235–249) shows how an examination of the husband was probably a practice that began in England in the thirteenth century and then spread elsewhere. Whether the husband of a nonvirgin who denied his impotence was obliged to submit to such an examination, however, would depend on the whim of the ecclesiastical court.

[70] See *Glossa ordinaria*, for C.33 q.5 c.11 ad v. *nisi auctor*.

[71] William of Rennes, *Summa de poenitentia* 1.8.8, gloss i, ad v. *praeiudicium*, p. 67. On William, see n. 41, above. John of Freiburg, *Summa confessorum* 4.2.36, fol. 220r.

[72] See *Summa Theologica* pt. 3 (Supplement) Q. 64, art. 2, and Brundage, *Law, Sex, and Christian Society*, pp. 426–427.

deflect the wife's exaction of the debt, provided there is a reasonable cause.[73]

Admittedly, many of these innovations might be welcomed by the average married couple. But it is equally true that as every pretext for sexual refusal was inexorably removed from the woman, the potential for division between husband and wife widened. The distinction between the spouse exacting the debt (who, depending on the extent of his or her transgression, was guilty of sin that could range from venial to mortal) and the spouse rendering (who was credited with the good of continence) was reiterated in all of the sources.[74] The obligation of the debt was only removed by adultery or by a mutual vow of chastity.

The Wife's Vow versus Vows of Chastity

Gratian did not invent female subordination. And yet he was responsible for assembling a devastating array of sources that had the effect of consolidating the husband's authority over his wife and ensuring the wife's consequent submission. The wife's loss was the husband's gain.

Of particular importance from the perspective of female autonomy was the authority the husband was granted over his wife's vow (C.33 q.5 c.11). A wife's vow had to be authorized by her husband. Although this was not new—the bulk of Gratian's most damaging sources were from Augustine, particularly his comments on woman's legal limitations in the Book of Numbers—it was powerfully articulated.[75] Moreover, Gratian expanded the husband's competence so that he could even revoke vows that he had formerly authorized. Although the husband might sin by revoking the vow, the wife must nevertheless obey *propter condicionem seruitutis.*[76]

[73] "Utrum vir teneatur aliquando debitum reddere vxori etiam non petenti. Respondeo secundum Thomam et Petrum et Albertum dicendum quod non solum quando expresse petit debitum vxori vir tenetur reddere: sed etiam quando per signa apparet eam hoc velle. Non tamen idem iudicium est de petitione viri: quia mulieres magis solent verecundari petendo debitum quam viri.

Utrum vir debeat vxorem auertere ne petat debitum. Respondeo secundum Thomam dicendum quod non debet hoc facere nisi propter aliquam rationabilem causam: et tunc etiam non debet cum magna instantia auerti propter pericula imminentia. Idem Albertus" (John of Freiburg, *Summa confessorum* 4.2.40–41, fol. 220r).

[74] C.33 q.5 c.1 and c.5; Raymond of Peñafort, *Summa de poenitentia* 4.2.13, p. 519; John of Freiburg, *Summa confessorum* 4.2.37 and 39, fol. 220r.

[75] See Gaudemet, "L'apport de la patristique latine," in *Sociétés et mariage*, appendix 1, p. 314.

[76] C.33 q.5 c.11 dpc. This latter point is already implicit in the passage cited in c. 11

The temporal implications of these pronouncements are obvious. They not only corresponded to, but rapidly advanced, women's legal impoverishment in this period. Gratian's presentation of the husband's absolute lordship was sufficiently comprehensive that civil lawyers looked to him to justify the husband's control over his wife's dowry.[77] Thus at a time when Europe was alive with new possibilities, and all important undertakings were sealed by the vow, women were sunk into a humiliating minority. This message was reinforced not only in confessors' manuals but through local councils as well. The English canonist Lyndwood (d. 1446), for example, cites a local piece of legislation that draws particular attention to the wife's vow. The statute exhorts priests to warn continually their parishioners, especially women, against making hasty vows. The reason that women are singled out is given in the gloss: "*Women*: Who are accustomed to emit vows more readily than men, especially when they are placed in some sort of tribulation and distress. And you should understand that this is said concerning married women, as is clear below."[78]

The husband's ascendancy over the wife also made considerable inroads into the wife's spiritual autonomy. According to Christian theory, men and women were equal before God according to the order of grace. But, as René Metz has implied, Gratian achieved the wife's total submission by sacrificing the spiritual to the natural, the invisible to the visible.[79] The husband's position is powerfully bolstered by references to natural order, building particularly on the order of cre-

---

from Augustine's *Questions on Numbers*. Gratian heightens the wife's subjection by omitting Augustine's preceding text from Numbers 30.11–16, which states that if the wife emits a vow in her husband's hearing and he remains silent, the vow stands (*Quaest. Num.* 59.2–3, in Augustine, *Quaestionum in Heptateuchum*, ed. I. Fraipont, *CCSL*, vol. 33 [Turnholt, 1958], pp. 271–272).

[77] Susan Mosher Stuard, "From Women to Woman: New Thinking about Gender c. 1140," *Thought* 64 (1989): 208–219, esp. pp. 213–215.

[78] "*Mulieres*. Quae facilius solent Vota emittere quam viri, maxime cum sunt in aliqua Tribulatione, et Angustia positae. Et intelligas, quod hic dicitur, de mulieribus conjugatis, ut infra patet" (William Lyndwood, *Provinciale [seu constitutiones Angliae]* [Oxford, 1679], bk. 3, tit. 18, gloss e, p. 204). Lyndwood cites Archbishop Edmund Rich as his source, but the Statutes of Salisbury I (between 1217 and 1219) seem more likely. (c. 89, *Councils and Synods with Other Documents Relating to the English Church*, ed. Powicke and Cheney, 2,1:89). For the husband's control over the wife's vow in pastoral manuals, see Robert of Flamborough, *Liber poenitentialis* 2.3.29, p. 68; Peter the Chanter, *Summa de sacramentis* c. 224, 3,2a:201; Thomas of Chobham, *Summa confessorum* 4.2.7.11, p. 157; Raymond of Peñafort, *Summa de poenitentia* 1.8.8, pp. 64–65; John of Freiburg, *Summa confessorum* 1.8.35–37, fol. 21r.

[79] Metz, "Le statut de la femme en droit canonique médiéval," pp. 81–82; cf. Stuard "From Women to Woman," p. 216.

ation (man in God's image) and the order of governance (man as the head of woman) (C.33 q.5 c.12–20). In short, the husband was presented as God's vicar: God preferred female obedience to her husband over the fulfillment of sworn acts of devotion. Furthermore, the husband was permitted to enforce his will physically, as elsewhere in the same *causa* Gratian upholds his right of correction (C.33 q.2 c.10).

The only vow that the husband could not revoke was a vow of chastity, which had to be made mutually—hence husband and wife were equally bound. And yet a vow of chastity would not, in theory, undermine the natural hierarchy between the sexes. All the authorities agreed that such a vow suspended the right to the conjugal debt alone: if the couple intended to pursue their chaste resolve in their home, as opposed to separating to enter a religious community, the husband's authority remained intact. Even so, where intramarital chastity was at stake, the authorities clearly sensed that male dominance needed reinforcement because everywhere—embedded in language, in law, and in practice—is the association between heterosexual intercourse and the subordination of women. The expression in English common law that connotes a married woman's legal disabilities, *feme coverte*, has an explicitly sexual derivation.[80] The biblical *Glossa ordinaria* on Ephesians 5 relays the express anxiety that female subjection may end with a dissolution of the carnal bond, as might male affection.[81] Canonists are hard pressed to explain why women who resolve to live chastely with their husbands are frequently called widows.[82] Gratian cites a passage from an Augusti-

[80] For the sexual derivation of the term *coverture*, see F. Pollock and F. W. Maitland, *The History of English Law*, 2d ed. (Cambridge, 1952), 2:406–407; esp. p. 407 n. 1. A sexual etymology may also pertain to the legal expression *sub virga*, usually translated "under the rod" (i.e., under the husband's discipline) since *virga* is a common word for penis (see J. F. Niermeyer, *Mediae Latinitatis Lexicon Minus* [Leiden, 1954–1956], p. 1110). *Virga* appears frequently in the pastoral manuals in matters of impotence (see Robert of Flamborough, *Liber poenitentialis* 2.2.15, p. 65; John of Freiburg, *Summa confessorum* 4.16.19, fol. 236r). At the very least, the term conveys a double entendre when applied to husband and wife.

[81] The following gloss on Eph. 5.22–24 (i.e., "Let women be subject to their husbands, as to the Lord . . ."), attributed to the sixth-century Primasius, makes this association explicitly. It also anticipates the potential danger of a transition to chastity being understood as a sanction for divorce: "Non eos sicut Corinthios lactabat incontinentes, sed perfecto cibo continentiae nutriebat, timet ne in plerisque cessante carnis officio aut in mulieribus subiectio, aut in viris cessaret charitatis affectus, et non tam continentiam quam divortium docuisse videretur" (*Glossa ordinaria*, in Nicolaus de Lyre et al., *Biblia sacra cum Glossa ordinaria*, vol. 6 [Paris, 1590], col. 562). Primasius seems to be taking it for granted that masculine love is based on carnality and dominance.

[82] This is among the many meanings for the word *widow* that Huguccio cites,

nian sermon which rebukes husbands for their moral laxity, arguing that if women precede them in chastity, this imperils masculine leadership (C.32 q.6 c.5). Robert of Flamborough posits that if one spouse vows never to exact the debt, the other can unilaterally enter religion and never be recalled.[83] It is partly the corrosive effect of chastity on male authority that directs the strange elision of Gratian's celebrated C.33 q.5, which begins with a discussion of vows of continence and concludes with the canonization of male supremacy in the order of nature.[84]

The medieval doctrine of vows takes as its starting point the uncompromising words of the Old Testament: vow and render (Ps. 75.12–76.11). Even so, with most vows there was a certain amount of flexibility: a pilgrimage, for example, could be commuted for other kinds of penance, such as almsgiving or fasting, if poor health impeded fulfillment.[85] The vow of chastity alone could not be commuted for the simple reason that there was nothing better than chastity.[86] One who failed to fulfill a vow of chastity was, arguably,

---

although he maintains it is a misnomer: "Item multer [sic] improprie dicitur vidua que a marito vivente divisa est quoad carnalem commixtionem, promissa continentia ab utroque, ut sunt uxores presbyterorum apud nos . . . et unde uxores apostolorum vidue dicebantur, et uxores David vocantur istoria vidue, quia carnaliter cum eis non commiscebatur" (for C.27 q.2 c.29 dpc ad v. *item sponsa*, Roman, ed., "*Summa* d'Huguccio," p. 784).

[83] Robert of Flamborough, *Liber poenitentialis* 2.3.21, p. 70; cf. the *Glossa ordinaria* for X.3.32.3 ad v. *non exigere*, where it is debated as to whether a recalled spouse—reentering the world from a monastery after a unilateral entrance and thus enjoined to render but not exact the debt—can recall his or her spouse if he or she enters unilaterally.

[84] The evolution is of interest: the first few canons begin by insisting that a vow of continence be mutual (c. 1–4), but midway in canon 4 we get tangled up in the plight of Ecdicia who, associating freedom from the debt with the restoration of autonomy, began to dress like a widow and manage her property independently. Probably to ensure that other husbands do not blindly let go of the reins by vowing continence, Gratian then assures couples that mental continence and a pious rendering of the debt are perfectly acceptable, although virginity is undoubtedly superior (c. 5; c. 7–9). Moreover, an overly hasty vow is invalid (c. 6). Canon 10 insists on the simultaneity of conversion, while canon 11 launches into the Augustinian passage regarding the husband's authority over the wife's vow (also see dpc). This leads directly into the uncompromising passages regarding male headship and female inferiority in the order of creation (c. 12–30 and dpc 30).

[85] For the theory of the vow, see Gratian C.17 q.1 c.1–4 and esp. c.4 dpc. The possibility of dispensation and commutation emerges somewhat later, toward the end of the twelfth century. See James Brundage, *Medieval Canon Law and the Crusader* (Madison, Wis., 1969), pp. 39–43.

[86] Robert of Flamborough, *Liber poenitentialis* 2.3.30, p. 75; Peter the Chanter, *Summa de sacramentis* c. 224, 3,2a:201; also see Joseph Goering, ed., "The *Summa de penitentia* of Magister Serlo," *Mediaeval Studies* 38 (1976): c. 30, p. 44. Raymond of

committing spiritual suicide. It is little wonder that the clergy concluded that intramarital chastity could be every bit as threatening as extramarital sex, and thus redoubled its efforts at supervising it. Thus, over the course of the twelfth century, rules surrounding vows of chastity were considerably elaborated and refined. What emerged were essentially two kinds of vows: a solemn vow and a simple vow.[87] With respect to married individuals, both vows required mutual consent in order to be valid. The chief difference, however, was ultimately in the degree of enforceability.

The solemn vow was made publicly, into the hands of a church official, and was thus enforceable by the church.[88] It was more often than not indecipherable from an entrance into religion, which, for husband and wife, should be mutual and simultaneous.[89] Such a vow

---

Peñafort raises the question of whether the pope can release one from a vow of continence but ultimately decides that if one vows expressly and without condition, he cannot (*Summa de poenitentia* 1.8.3, pp. 56–57; 1.8.9, pp. 67–68). Cf. his glossator, William of Rennes (gloss m ad v. *abdicatio proprietatis*, p. 68; 1.8.17, gloss m ad v. *non excusat*, pp. 77–78). William's second gloss addresses whether the pope can dispense vows of continence, poverty, or obedience, and it is exceptionally detailed. Because of the problems surrounding this question, William posits that no vow should be emitted without the condition that the pope can dispense it. John of Freiburg also cites a number of conflicting opinions, including Hostiensis's controversial view that the pope, in plenitude of power, can dispense with any vow (*Summa confessorum* 1.8.70, fol. 24r).

[87] For a cogent summary of the evolution of vows of chastity over the course of the twelfth and into the early thirteenth century, see Brundage, *Medieval Canon Law and the Crusader*, pp. 39–65. Also see Esmein, *Le mariage*, 2:22–29; Makowski, "Conjugal Debt," pp. 109–110; and Gabriel Le Bras's review of two doctoral theses, one by René Le Picard, "La communauté de la vie conjugale, obligation des époux. Etude canonique" (Faculté de droit de Paris, 1930), and the other by Hubert Richardot, "Les pactes de séparation entre époux. Etude historique, comparative et critique de la séparation de corps par consentement mutuel" (Faculté de droit de Dijon, 1930), in "Comptes rendus," *Revue historique de droit français et étranger* 10 (1931): 743–757.

[88] With respect to the solemn vows of married individuals, the bishop's permission was strongly recommended, but this counsel was seemingly difficult to enforce; see C.27 q.2 c.23 and Huguccio's gloss, ad v. *sine conscientia*, Roman, ed., "Summa d'Huguccio," p. 777. Cf. John Andreas, *In tertium Decretalium librum nouella commentaria* (Venice and Siena, 1581), for X.3.32.8 ad v. *conspectu ecclesiae*, p. 162. Panormitanus notes that although a bishop's permission is recommended, if it is not solicited, this does not invalidate a profession (*Lectura*, for X.3.32.8, no. 7, 5:159).

[89] Yet if an individual was considered to be above suspicion, that is, if he or she *senex est et sterilis*, that person might remain in the world (X.3.32.4). This does not apply to the bishop's wife, however, who must enter a monastery before her husband's elevation (X.3.32.6), undoubtedly for the same propertied reasons that partially informed the policy of the Gregorian reformers. The spouse intending to remain in the world was expected to make a public declaration of chastity *in conspectu ecclesiae* (X.3.32.8). A similar vow was required if a husband was going to be admitted to major orders. The

created a permanent impediment; hence any marriage contracted subsequent to a solemn vow would be invalid.

William of Rennes remarks that the solemn vow was instituted by the church so that publicity could act as a safeguard, not only against deception but against whatever scandal might ensue from the breaking of the vow.[90] But when the intentions of not one but two individuals are at stake, the situation often goes awry. One problem that frequently arose was that of a spouse who gave permission for the other to enter a monastery, but did not enter him or herself and subsequently complained.[91] Or suppose that the uncloistered spouse resorted to fornication, as a vignette in 1329 from the diocese of Exeter suggests. Beatrice, the wife of Ralph Stronge, aspired to become an anchoress and had obtained her husband's consent to her purpose. And yet the bishop had heard rumors of the husband's incontinence and felt that he could not in good conscience permit her to be permanently enclosed as an anchoress while her husband persisted in his offense.[92]

---

following quotation is the formula by which a wife would free her husband to enter the priesthood or become a monk, as utilized in the archbishop's court of Rheims (ca. 1284). It places particular emphasis on the mutuality of the vow and the wife's uncoerced consent—presumably to forestall future complaints: "Littera de voto continencie inter virum et uxorem. Universis, etc. Noverint universi, quod in nostra presencia, propter hoc personaliter constituti, *Talis* [sic] et Berta ejus uxor, zelo devocionis accensi, votum castitatis de communi eorum assensu coram nobis solenniter emiserunt, Deo continenciam promittentes, ut ipsi sic vivendo valeant Domino complacere; dictaque mulier professa continenciam, affectans promocionem dicti *Talis* mariti sui clerici, dedit spontanea sua voluntate ipsi *Tali* clerico plenam potestatem, facultatem, et liberam licenciam, intrandi religionem, et faciendi se ad sacros ordines promoveri, in religione, vel extra religionem, ubi, quando, et prout, anime sue saluti viderit expedire. Nos autem officialis predictus, judex ordinarius dictorum conjugum, vota sua et eorum bonum propositum in Domino approbantes, consideratis et plenius intellectis statu et condicione personarum predictarum, et aliis eciam consideratis que in talibus solent et debent considerari, inspici, et attendi, in hiis premissis omnibus juste et rite actis consensu nostro interveniente, auctoritatem nostram prebuimus et prebemus. In cujus, etc. Datum, etc." (Pierre Varin, ed., *Archives administratives et législatives de la ville de Reims*, pt. 1, *Coutumes* [Paris, 1840], c. 293, pp. 232–233). As a further safeguard, the English church attempted to institute the custom that the names of individuals who had made such vows be read out loud twice a year as a reminder (Lyndwood, *Provinciale* bk. 3, tit. 18, p. 203).

[90] William of Rennes, *Summa de poenitentia* 1.8.17, gloss m, ad v. *non excusat*, p. 79.

[91] X.3.32.1; cf. C.27 q.2 c.20–22, C.33 q.5 c.2–4, X.3.32.5, X.3.32.8. Also see R. H. Helmholz, *Marriage Litigation in Medieval England* (Cambridge, 1974), pp. 67–68. There is a certain amount of controversy as to how long the abandoned party could wait before recalling the other from a monastery: some say a year and a day, others say within three years, but the *Glossa ordinaria* states that this can be done at any time (for C.33 q.5 c.2 ad v. *coniugium*).

[92] All the same, the bishop gave the wife permission to enter a cell for a time and

That Ralph had no right to be fornicating is clear. Yet it is nevertheless unclear what Ralph's consent to his wife's vocation implied. Was
an individual, such as Ralph, bound by a tacit vow, or did a vow of
chastity have to be expressed?[93] Certain authorities held that the
spouse who remained in the world, if ignorant of the law, was not
bound.[94] Hence the spouse who had solemnly vowed chastity could
be recalled from the monastery with the understanding that he or she
should render, but not exact, the conjugal debt.[95] But whether recalled spouses should be compelled to return to the monastery after
the deaths of spouses who had petitioned for their restitution was a
question of some debate.[96] Rigorists, like Huguccio, insisted that

---

temporarily excused her from the conjugal debt, hoping for her eventual perpetual vow
and the conversion of her husband. The local vicar was instructed to assist and not to
hinder her (F. C. Hingeston-Randolph, ed., *The Register of John Grandisson, Bishop of
Exeter* [London and Exeter, 1894], 1:535).

[93] X.3.32.1 explicitly denies that a tacit vow is sufficient. Huguccio makes note of
this decree, but is nevertheless a strong proponent of the binding force of the tacit vow.
He denies that a spouse can be recalled from a monastery once the other has given
permission, and maintains that the one remaining in the world should be forced to
enter (C.27 q.2 c.21 ad v. *voluntate* and ad v. *nec quondam*, Roman, ed., "Summa
d'Huguccio," p. 771; cf. *Glossa ordinaria* for X.3.32.8 ad v. *nullatenus recipiatur*).
William of Rennes requires an expressed vow, thus differing from Huguccio (*Summa de
poenitentia* 1.8.8, gloss c ad v. *promittit*, p. 65). According to William, Huguccio pushes
the tacit vow much too far by arguing that, prior to consummation, if one spouse agrees
to the other's entrance into religion, he or she likewise is bound by a vow of chastity
(gloss f ad v. *poterit aliam ducere*, p. 66). Innocent IV invokes the controversy over the
question of whether consent to another's vow is equivalent to a tacit vow (*Commentaria*, for X.3.32.1 ad v. *servare*, pp. 424v–425r). He later resolves that not only is the one
who has remained in the world permitted to recall the other, but the one who entered
religion is even permitted to seek the one remaining in the world. His or her vow is
ratified only by an explicit vow or by the death of the spouse remaining in the world (for
X.3.32.3 ad v. *votum non tenuit*, p. 425v; cf. for X.3.32.10 ad v. *dirimendum*, pp. 426r–
426v).

[94] See *Glossa ordinaria* for C.27 q.2 c.21 ad v. *vel ipsa*, and for X.3.32.9 ad v. *consentiente vxore*; cf. Panormitanus, *Lectura*, for X.3.32.9, no. 4, 5:159r. All the same, not
everyone concurs: hence Thomas of Chobham tells priests to warn women that she
who permits her husband to receive monastic garb on his deathbed is herself bound to
observe perpetual chastity (*Summa confessorum* 7.2.14.3, p. 373). See William of Rennes's objection to this view in n. 93, above. Also see Brundage, *Law, Sex, and Christian
Society*, pp. 375–376).

[95] For the bishop's right to recall a spouse from the monastery, even if the one who
remained in the world agreed to his or her profession, see X.3.32.1 and 9. The *Glossa
ordinaria* resolves that though a wife may have theoretically relinquished her rights
over her husband, nevertheless the bishop can recall him to save the wife from fornication (for X.3.32.8 ad v. *nullatenus recipiatur*; cf. Panormitanus for X.3.32.8, *Lectura*
nos. 5 and 6, 5:159r). For the concept of rendering and not exacting the debt, see
X.3.32.3, X.3.32.12; also see Huguccio for C.27 q.2 c.21 ad v. *conjugii*, Roman, ed.,
"Summa d'Huguccio," p. 775.

[96] X.3.32.9 and 12 seem to take opposing views on this question.

they should be; others were inclined to think that they were not, but that they must forgo the right to remarry.[97] If they did remarry, most authorities felt that the marriage was valid, but that the one who had formerly been recalled from the monastery should render but not exact the debt.[98]

The simple vow, on the other hand, was made by those who wished to remain in the world and was usually made without any particular formalities. Since publicity was often lacking, it eluded close monitoring or enforcement by the church, even though it was considered binding before God. Not only did the simple vow imply the same obligation as the solemn vow, in theory, but it was even maintained that the vow was binding from the moment the resolve was shaped in the heart.[99] But such a vow could not be proven, and the clergy rightly agonized over the false position that this placed them in. Thomas of Chobham says that if one vowed privately and subsequently married,

[97] John Andreas thinks the recalled spouse's obligation to chastity is equivalent to that of a simple vow (*In tertium Decretalium librum nouella commentaria*, for X.3.32.12 ad v. *promisit*, p. 163). Alexander III resolves that the recalled spouse need not reenter after his wife's death, but that he cannot remarry, as he has promised not to exact the debt (X.3.32.3). Huguccio, not surprisingly, disagrees with Alexander's ruling, even doubting the authenticity of the decretal. His view is that now that the impediment to the monk's vow is removed by the wife's death, he is bound to fulfill it (C.27 q.2 c.21 ad v. *conjugii*, Roman, ed., "*Summa* d'Huguccio," p. 775; cf. Robert of Flamborough, *Liber poenitentialis* 2.3.21, p. 69). The *Glossa ordinaria* points out that a number of canons contradict Huguccio on this point (C.27 q.2 c.21 ad v. *tonsuratus*). The later gloss on the *Decretales*, however, strikes a middle ground: once the impediment is removed, he sins in refusing to enter the monastery, but he should not be compelled (for X.3.32.3 ad v. *non tenetur*). Innocent IV vigorously opposes Huguccio's view that a recalled spouse is bound to enter after his or her partner's death (*Commentaria*, for X.3.32.3 ad v. *votum non tenuit*, p. 425v). His efforts to bolster this position and reduce the seeming conflict between X.3.32.9 and 12 lead to a somewhat slanted reading of the former (for X.3.32.9, p. 426r).

[98] As the *Glossa ordinaria* notes, some authorities maintain that such a marriage is not legitimate and that the couple should be made to separate. Some even allege that the wife could unilaterally enter religion, as the husband has already relinquished his right to the debt. But the majority uphold the marriage and counsel the husband to render, but not exact (for X.3.32.3 ad v. *non exigere*). Raymond of Peñafort concurs: the recalled individual's obligation to chastity is parallel to the simple vow, and he should exact from neither his first nor his second wife (*Summa de poenitentia* 1.8.12, p. 72). Raymond readily acknowledges, however, that others claim the husband can exact since the simple vow has been destroyed by the good of marriage ("Plures alii Doctores dixerunt quod licite poterit exigere; quia licet peccauerit contrahendo, tamen tantum est bonum matrimonii, quod tollit totaliter obligationem illam"). He also recommends that the individual do penance (1.8.3, p. 57).

[99] C.22 q.5 c.11; X.4.6.6; cf. *Glossa ordinaria*, for C.27 q.2 c.3 ad v. *ore*. Thomas of Chobham notes that an unexpressed vow cannot be enforced by the church, but if it is firmly proposed in the heart, it is binding before God (*Summa confessorum* 7.12.1, p. 559).

the church would uphold the marriage, although it is not a marriage. Master Serlo, writing sometime after 1234, concurs with this but adds the grim reflection that time does not diminish but increases the extent of the sin.[100] According to the most inflexible letter of the law, the guilty party could not even do penance until the death of his or her spouse.[101] A breach of a vow of chastity between spouses was no less egregious. Innocent IV's mature thinking on vows stressed that whether a couple had vowed publicly or privately, any children born subsequently were illegitimate.[102] Thus, individuals who wished to maintain chastity in their homes were likewise urged to make their vow into the hands of a bishop. And yet it is by no means clear that such a precaution would raise it to the level of a solemn vow. Some held that a solemn vow necessarily implied retreat to a cloister.[103]

The simple vow presents additional dangers for female chastity insofar as the husband's overall authority must inevitably intrude, even in this area of theoretical equality. John of Freiburg, for example, presents a wide spectrum of opinions that serve to demonstrate the free reign given to the husband's dominance: Peter of Tarentaise (d. 1276) believes that if the husband gave his consent to the vow *in facie ecclesiae*, he cannot recall it. If it was pledged in private, however, he can renege before the actual exercise of the vow (*usus*) has been estab-

---

[100] Thomas of Chobham, *Summa confessorum* 4.2.7.11, p. 156; Goering, ed., "*Summa de Penitentia* of Magister Serlo," c. 30, p. 45.

[101] C.27 q.1 c.43 dpc. In practice, however, the later ecclesiastical courts were forced to come to terms with broken vows. C. H. Cooper cites two examples of couples who were assigned penance for the wife's broken vow. The wife of John Godnay (married in 1444) was only a consecrated widow, but Elizabeth of Juliers, widow of John, earl of Kent (d. 1352), was actually a professed nun. See "The Vow of Widowhood of Margaret, Countess of Richmond and Derby," *Communications to the C.A.S.* (Cambridge Antiquarian Society) 1 (1851–1859): 73–74, 77.

[102] Innocent is very much in favor of a vow's not being judged solemn unless certain solemnities intervene (*Commentaria*, for X.3.32.20 ad v. *castitatem*, p. 427v). Even so, he developed a considerably more stringent standard for those who had vowed. When raising the question of whether spouses who have vowed chastity are not obliged to render the debt in order to avoid the greater sin of adultery, his answer is uncompromising: "Licet hoc aliquando sic tenuerimus, tamen postea visum est nobis aliter in aliquibus, et maxime in hoc, quia credimus in coniugatis aliquod speciale, quia ex quo coniuges, siue in priuato, siue in publico, siue solenniter, siue non vouerint, continentiam illam seruare tenentur, et si commiscentur, illicita est commistio et filii inde nati sunt illegitimi" (p. 428r).

[103] William of Rennes cites opinions on both sides but ultimately resolves that one can vow solemnly and still remain in the world (*Summa de poenitentia* 1.8.2, gloss h ad v. *priuatum, seu simplex*, p. 55; 1.8.8, gloss h ad v. *compelli potest*, p. 67). Likewise, John of Freiburg cites Peter of Tarentaise's view that even an explicit vow into the hands of a public person need not dissolve a subsequent marriage (i.e., it does not equal a solemn vow), but John disagrees with this position (*Summa confessorum* 1.8.10, fol. 18v).

lished. Thomas Aquinas and Albert the Great agree that if the husband expressly gave permission for the vow, then he himself has vowed chastity and cannot retract it. And yet both Albert and Thomas claim that if the husband pretends to go along with the vow at the time (*dissimulat*) but later has a chance to deliberate, he can then recall the vow, and the wife need not feel bound to fulfill it. Finally, Innocent IV (d. 1254) and Hostiensis (d. 1271) say that, even if a husband gave permission for a vow, he can retract it provided he did not expressly vow himself. John does not offer any resolution to this complex problem of the husband's power over his wife's vow.[104] On the other hand, he believes that even a simple vow of chastity, to be pursued in the couple's home, is binding and that they would sin mortally in breaking it.[105]

An exemplary case brought before Pope Celestine III (d. 1198) by the king of Sweden helps to elucidate the dangers of the private vow. We only know of the royal couple's marital problems through the pope's letter to the archbishop of Uppsala. Evidently, they had a number of detractors who may have thought their marriage was invalid because of the many years that the queen had spent in a convent. At any rate, the king seems to have prefaced his petition to the pope by a defense of his marriage, asserting that his wife had been placed in the convent for safekeeping during a series of wars. But a more recent crisis had arisen that had, once again, set the court gossip-mill in motion. The queen, oppressed by illness and fear of death, vowed continence, and the king had agreed to her vow—allegedly on a temporary basis (*ad tempus*). Now that she had recovered, however, he wanted to return to her bed, claiming that he had had no intention of swearing perpetual chastity. He wanted the pope to order his wife to

---

[104] "Utrum coniunx si dederit licentiam coniugi vt voueat castitatem possit illam licentiam postea reuocare. Respondeo secundum Petrum aut dedit in facie ecclesie quasi in iudicio et tunc non potest reuocare: aut in priuato et tunc ante vsum licentie potest reuocare. Sed postea reuocare non potest. Thomas dicit quod si expresse consensit coniugi et licentiam dedit vt voueret castitatem non potest votum illud a coniuge emissum reuocare vnde propter periculum talia vota occulta non sunt approbanda. Cum Thoma concordat Albertus. Si autem vir ad tempus dissimulat et post habita plena deliberatione reuocat mulier non tenetur implere vt dicunt Thomas et Albertus. Innocentius . . . dicit quod qui dat licentiam vouendi non impeditur propter hoc exigere debitum nisi et ipse voueat hoc . . . . Idem Hostiensis" (John of Freiburg, *Summa confessorum* 1.8.45, fol. 21v–22r). This confusion was not restricted to the later, more scholastic pastoral manuals either. Robert of Flamborough is opposed to the husband's retraction of a mutual vow of chastity but discusses others who hold the contrary view (*Liber poenitentialis* 2.3.19, p. 68 and n. 26, which points out that two decretals used elsewhere by Flamborough could be interpreted as supporting the husband's right to recall a vow of chastity that he also partook in; X.3.32.1 and 11).

[105] John of Freiburg, *Summa confessorum* 1.8.46, fol. 22r.

treat him with marital affection, in spite of her vow.[106] The pope was ready to oblige, after having made some discreet inquiries in order to ensure that the king's representations were accurate (X.3.32.11).

If the queen regretted her vow, her frame of mind at the time it was made could provide an antidote. Fear of death could be construed as a form of flawed consent, which would invalidate the vow.[107] The source of contention is clearly the nature of the king's resolve. Panormitanus's discussion of this decretal walks us through some of the options. If we accept the surface representation of events, namely, that the king agreed to his wife's vow on a temporary basis, the main area of uncertainty would be whether or not the king was attempting to exact during the specified period of continence. Suppose he were. Panormitanus is prepared to push the husband's control even beyond Gratian by assimilating a temporary vow of chastity with any other vow of abstinence: the husband is within his rights to recall it, although he sins in doing so. Another possibility is that the king gave permission for his wife to vow perpetually but did not vow himself. Panormitanus again asserts the king's right to recall such a vow. The queen would be justified in resisting her husband's advances only if both had expressly and perpetually vowed.[108]

[106] For Gratian, marital affection signifies the essential quality informing consent to marriage (see Noonan, "Marital Affection," pp. 489–499; also see Michael Sheehan, "*Maritalis Affectio* Revisted," in *The Olde Daunce*, ed. Edwards and Spector, pp. 32–43, 254–260). By the late twelfth century, however, in response to an abandoned spouse's petition for the restitution of conjugal rights, popes began to order the truant spouse's return and enjoined him or her to treat the other with marital affection (Noonan, "Marital Affection," pp. 500–505; Helmholz, *Marriage Litigation in Medieval England*, pp. 101–102).

[107] C.33 q.5 c.6 is an excerpt from Augustine's letter to Armentarius and Paulina, already discussed in chapter 2, which treats the invalidity of a hasty vow. The *Glossa ordinaria* also cites trickery and excessive anger as possible reasons for invalidation (X.3.32.16 ad v. *captiose asseruit*; X.3.32.20 ad v. *calore iracundiae*). An earlier case (ca. 1185–1187) in the time of Urban III has striking parallels to this one. A sick husband assumes the habit with his wife's consent. When he recovers, however, he is permitted to return to his wife (X.3.32.9). It should be noted that commentators were puzzled as to why the wife had not also vowed chastity (see esp. *Glossa ordinaria* ad v. *consentiente vxore* and ad v. *de iure ad religionem*; cf. John Andreas, *In tertium Decretalium librum nouella commentaria*, ad v. *et in fine*, p. 162, and Panormitanus, *Lectura* no. 4, 5:159r). Note that Thomas of Chobham permits a sick man who vows chastity to break it, provided that the vow was not undertaken with sure deliberation. Such an individual, however, should first consult a priest to ensure that he is not deluding himself (*Summa confessorum* 4.2.7.11, p. 159).

[108] "No. 4 [Regarding an ordinary vow of abstinence] Quin imo si maritus consensisset potest nihilominus reuocare. Et licet ipse peccet reuocando ex quo licentiam prebuit: vxor tamen potuit non resistere nec peccat desistendo: quia tenetur in hoc lege divina et humana obedire marito. . . . No. 5 [Regarding a husband who consents to a temporary vow and then seeks the debt during the stipulated time] Aut vxor emisit

Panormitanus was working from a shorter version of Celestine's letter, such as was circulated in the *Decretales* of Gregory IX. The letter seems to end with the complacent expectation that the king's representations would be vindicated by the inquiry. But a longer version, included in an earlier but lesser-known compilation, indicates that the pope was also prepared for less comfortable revelations.

> But if you [the archbishop of Uppsala] were to know that the matter itself is to be characterized otherwise and the man vowed perpetually and it was witnesssed by you, another [solution] ought to be decreed by canon law, which should be justly assuaged by you—disregarding [the king's] appeal, you should resolve and do what you determine is to be observed. Because, however, we heard that the same king is a lover of the Christian religion and always fights for the growth of the holy church with an army against pagans and he asserts that for their total expulsion an alliance with his wife's relatives is necessary, we wish to concur with his petition in grateful affection and to avert the oppression of the kingdom— inasmuch as we can with respect to God and the health of his soul. Therefore, if in the course of discussion about this business, your consideration discerns such a thing which perhaps, from the point of view of canonical justice, ought not to be done, but a deed that can be reasonably tolerated by the dispensation of mercy, we, from apostolic indulgence, concede such a thing and grant that your discretion may overlook it.[109]

---

votum continentie et tunc valet in sui preiudicium scilicet vt non exigat debitum quia non exigere nullum preiudicium irrogat marito . . . si autem simpliciter vouit et maritus consensit aut ad tempus et potest indubie lapso tempore debitum exigere et isto modo intelligendo indubie procedit hac littera. Aut queritur nunquid pendente tempore possit maritus exigere debitum et sic reuocare votum cui consensit et est magis dubium. [He then presents the position that the husband and wife are equal with respect to the conjugal debt.] . . . Tamen puto contrarium quia votum continentie est votum abstinentie. . . . Cum ergo iura diuina et humana dant marito plenam facultatem in voto abstinentie: ergo videtur quod votum continentie possit reuocare [He goes on to say that the same rule pertains if the wife vows perpetually and the husband agrees to her vow, but does not vow himself.] . . . Peccat tamen maritus veniendo contra id quod semel consensit. Vxor tamen non potest resistere. . . . No. 6 [If both vow perpetually] Tunc vterque tenetur servare continentiam nec vxor tenetur obedire marito volenti contra votum venire" (Panormitanus, *Lectura* for X.3.32.11, 5:159v). Also see Esmein, *Le mariage*, 2:23–25.

It is useful to compare the situation of the queen of Sweden with that presented in another decretal: in this instance we also have a husband suing for the restitution of his conjugal rights, but the woman's situation is this time more secure: she has insisted that her husband renounce his conjugal rights publicly, and that he publicize his resolve to live and work in a hospital, while she simultaneously entered a religious community (X.3.32.20).

[109] "Si vero aliter rem se habere cognoveritis et virum perpetuam vovisse continentiam visumque vobis fuerit aliud de iure canonico statuendum, quod vobis iuste re-

The pope was prepared to go to extraordinary lengths to satisfy the king: the queen's vow gets buried in high politics even as spiritual values are sacrificed to temporal ones. But in this instance, papal power had overreached itself, for a vow of continence was incommutable—even after the concept of the pope's *plenitudo potestatis* was formulated, most authorities were doubtful of his competence in this area. Small wonder that the disturbing conclusion of this letter was excised in later canonical works.[110]

Vows of Continence and Channels to the Laity

The laity were the objects of a mixed and conflicted discourse. Even as the paradigm of the chaste marriage had stimulated an unprecedented concern over the conjugal debt, the elaboration of a theory of vows coincided with efforts to discourage simple vows. Efforts at dissuasion were rather marked. Thomas of Chobham held that all simple vows should essentially be future vows: I will enter religion, or I will contain; thus, if a person subsequently married, he or she would not be guilty of a mortal sin. Similarly, William of Rennes argued for a safety valve: every vow should contain the condition that the pope could dispense it. John Andreas regarded the simple vow as a transitional stage that every couple must needs go through before vowing solemnly but, on contemplating Innocent IV's uncompromising view that all children born subsequent to any vow be considered illegitimate, urged that all vows be taken solemnly.[111] Others were

---

sederit, appellatione postposita decernatis et faciatis quod decreveritis observari. Quia tamen eundem regem Christiane religionis amatorem existere et pro amplification sancte ecclesie semper exercicio contra paganos decertare audivimus, ad quos etiam expugnandos omnino sibi necessariam esse asserit societatem consanguineorum uxoris sue, petitioni eius, quantum cum Deo et salute anime sue possumus, grata volumus affectione concurrere ac regie oppressioni providere. Proinde si in presentis negocii discussione consideratio vestra tale quid forte perspexerit, quod de iusticia quidem canonica fieri non debuerat, sed iam factum ex dispensatione misercordie rationabiliter tolerari queat, hoc tale et nos de apostolica concedimus indulgentia et ut vestra discretio dissimulet annuimus" ("La *Collectio Seguntina* et les décrétales de Clément III et de Célestine III," c. 95, Walter Holtzmann, ed., *Revue d'histoire ecclésiastique* 50 [1955]: 445).

[110] The pope's advice is sufficiently daring that in the last line of the letter, he foresees the possibility that the archbishop may wish to ignore it. He graciously sanctions this option: "Quod si omnes his exequendis nequiveritis interesse, tu, frater archiepiscope, cum duobus vel tribus suffraganeis tuis aut abbatibus, quos elegeris, ea nichilominus exequaris" (ibid.). For the debate regarding the pope's competence over vows of continence, see n. 86, above.

[111] Thomas of Chobham, *Summa confessorum* 4.2.7.11, p. 156; William of Rennes,

adamant in their denunciation of the simple vow. Peter the Chanter, although historically aware that such vows between the married were honored in the early church, nevertheless concluded that they should no longer be tolerated. His invocation of clerical discipline as justification strongly identifies chastity with clerical prerogative and further communicates that there was no room for such amorphous relations among the laity. Likewise, John of Freiburg, after an examination of the perilous distinction between public and private, expressed and tacit, concludes that hidden vows should not be approved by the church.[112]

Nor should we expect to find open exhortations to chastity in marriage in sermon literature and catechetical works. In the Dominican *Somme le roi*, an exceptionally detailed manual for lay instruction that was written in 1279 at the request of the French king Philip III, chastity is described as an important condition in a sevenfold path toward knowledge of God. In this context, seven degrees of chastity are discerned. Marital chastity—fidelity to the marriage contract and observance of church guidelines for marital usage—figures third in this reckoning. Absolute continence in marriage, however, is not discussed.[113] D'Avray's examination of sermons directed to the married laity reveals that they are likewise more concerned with regulating the sexual relations of the many than with promoting acts of singular asceticism in the few.[114] Only Jacques de Vitry in his discussion of

---

Summa de poenitentia 1.8.17, gloss m ad v. *non excusat*, p. 77; John Andreas, *In tertium Decretalium librum nouella commentaria*, for X.3.32.20 ad v. *castitatem*, p. 165a. John cites X.1.17.14 (regarding the illegitimacy of a child born subsequent to the husband's ordination, even if the child is a product of a licit marriage) and D.81 c.19 (which states that a priest who sleeps with his wife cannot approach the altar) in support of Innocent's assertions. John also cites Hostiensis's view that no vow should be judged binding unless certain solemnities intervene.

[112] Peter the Chanter, *Summa de sacramentis* c. 376, 3,2b:573; Peter cites D.77 c.6 from the Council of Agde (506), requiring that the wife of a priest occupy a separate chamber and make a promise of religion. See n. 111, above for John Andreas's parallel attempts to curb lay chastity by appealing to clerical disasters, as well as John of Freiburg, *Summa confessorum* 1.8.45, fol. 22r.

[113] See the fourteenth-century English translation of this work, entitled *The Book of Vices and Virtues*, ed. W. Nelson Francis, EETS, o.s., no. 217 (London, 1942), pp. 245–249. The *Somme le roi* has not been edited, but C.-V. Langlois provides a systematic discussion of its contents (see *La vie spirituelle*, vol. 4 of *La vie en France au moyen âge de la fin du XIIe au milieu du XIVe siècle* [Paris, 1928], pp. 123–198, esp. 193–195). The author's omission of absolute chastity in marriage is rather odd, considering that the Virgin's participation in marriage is evoked. The lowest order of chastity comprises those who are undedicated virgins—especially children who are chaste by necessity, not by choice. After this come unmarried fornicators who repent. The highest degree is monastic chastity.

[114] The recent studies undertaken by D. L. d'Avray concentrate on *ad status* collections and on sermons delivered on the second Sunday after Epiphany. The *ad status*

fides seems to engage briefly the idea of perpetual chastity in marriage. "Faith in this [respect] is considered, so that one should render the debt to the other, unless by mutual consent they were to wish to be continent; [and] they would merit far more were they to live in continence and abstain from carnal union on account of God."[115] It is appropriate that such a recommendation should come from Jacques insofar as his spiritual mentor, Mary of Oignies, had convinced her own husband to forgo the conjugal debt permanently, as will be seen in the next chapter. But Jacques's remarks are little more than an aside. In truth, Jacques, like most preachers, shows considerable timidity about publicly broaching the question of even moderate sexual abstinence. Although he is seemingly explicit about abstaining for fasts, great feasts, and during menstruation, and even mentions that the wife is permitted to exhort her husband to chastity, provided she render the debt, yet he is extremely cautious about how this information is conveyed. Ultimately, he advises that sexual restrictions should be discussed from the pulpit only in very general terms, calling for restraint on the husbands' part.[116] It was generally presumed

---

collections consist of a series of sermons intended to show other preachers how to address groups of individuals according to their station in life; thus, the laity is addressed directly about their married state. The second Sunday after Epiphany commemorates the wedding at Cana, and the sermon delivered on this occasion traditionally treated marriage. See especially "The Gospel of the Marriage Feast of Cana and Marriage Preaching in France," pp. 207–224, and d'Avray and Tausche, "Marriage Sermons in *ad status* Collections," pp. 71–119. As Michaud-Quantin points out, prior to the twelfth century, most sermon cycles seem to have been written for primarily monastic audiences ("Les méthodes de la pastorale du XIIIe au XVe siècle," pp. 76–77). Increased concern with lay instruction coincides with the growth of heresy.

[115] "Fides in hoc attenditur, ut unus alii debitum reddat, nisi ex consensu voluerint (*cod.* noluerint) continere, ut longe magis mereantur, si continenter (*cod.* continentur) vivant et a carnali commixtione propter deum abstineant" (Paris BN lat. 17509, fol. 137 vb), as cited by d'Avray and Tausche, "Marriage Sermons in *ad status* Collections," p. 92.

[116] Ibid., pp. 97–98. Alan of Lille likewise discusses sexual taboos only in the most general terms, maintaining that marriage should be undertaken for procreation—even though it excuses the voluptuousness of carnal union. Marital usage must be tempered by considerations of time, place, and religious duty. Jerome's condemnation of excessive marital lust is also fleetingly evoked: "Sed quamvis a peccato excuset carnale commercium, celebratur tamen ad susceptionem prolis, non ad voluptatem carnis. Temperet ergo se connexa communio carnalis, ratione loci, ratione temporis, ratione religiosi officii. Observet etiam homo spirituale conjugium inter carnem et spiritum, ut caro tanquam mulier spiritui obediat, spiritus tanquam vir, carnem ut uxorem regat. "Sit ibi fides tori . . . juxta illud quod dicitur, quod 'vehemens amator uxoris adulter est'" (Alan of Lille, *Summa de arte praedicatoria* c. 45, "Ad coniugatos," *PL* 210, col. 193); see d'Avray and Tausche, "Marriage Sermons in *ad status* Collections," pp. 79–80. Compare the following jingle that lists five ways in which a husband abuses his wife sexually ("time, mind, place, condition, way"). Prayer and caution are advanced as the best prophylactics: "Quinque modis peccat uxore maritus abutens / Tempore,

that more detailed instructions should be relegated to the confessional.[117]

And yet, victims of their own discourse, the clergy were forced by their canonistic casuistry to entertain uncomfortable possibilities. Thus John of Freiburg reasoned that one could contract a marriage with the resolve of never exacting, in accordance with the example of the Virgin, provided one did not deny to the other the use of his or her body. William of Rennes pushes such speculation to the limit when he asks whether one could contract a marriage with the resolve of neither exacting nor rendering the debt. He determined that it was possible, provided such a resolve was unexpressed at the time of the wedding.[118] But speculative hypotheses aside, vows of chastity were everywhere present in the interstices. They were silently evoked by discussions of consent and the debt. The Anglo-Norman *Manuel des péchés* (ca. 1260), translated into English and much enlarged in 1303 under the name *Handlyng Synne*, is one of the best-known of lay catechetical works.[119] The consensual theory of marriage is related as follows:

> ȝyf þou plyghtyst trouþe to any lyghtly
> To be at holy cherchys cry,
> But þou dedyst with her no foly dede
> þat ys fleshly felaurede,
> þou gost and ȝyfst þy trouþe anouþer
> As þou dedyst byfore þe touþer,
> And lyst by here, and ys þy wyfe,
> yn hordam boþe þan ys ȝoure lyfe,
> Þe ferst womman þat þou ches
> Ys þy wyfe, with-outë les.[120]

Although doubtlessly intended to mediate against the evils of clandestine marriage, which resulted in innumerable cases of bigamy, the text makes it clear that marriage is not contingent on consumma-

---

mente, loco, condicione, modo, / Ille minus peccat, qui caute precat et ampla / Est virtus vicium scire jacere suum" (*Le Speculum laicorum* c. 15, ed. J. Th. Welter, Thesaurus exemplorum, fasc. 5 [Paris, 1914], p. 22). This latter work was probably produced between ca. 1279 and 1292 by an anonymous Franciscan compiler.

[117] A. Lecoy de la Marche, *La chaire française au moyen âge*, 2d ed. (Paris, 1886), p. 434.

[118] John of Freiburg, *Summa confessorum* 4.2.55, fol. 221v; William of Rennes, *Summa de poenitentia* 4.2.12, gloss q. ad v. *non apponant conditionem*, p. 518.

[119] Jean Leclerq et al., *The Spirituality of the Middle Ages*, vol. 2 of *A History of Christian Spirituality* (New York, 1968), p. 344.

[120] Robert of Brunne, *Handlyng Synne*, ed. F. J. Furnivall, *EETS*, o.s., no. 119 (London, 1901), pt. 1, lines 1647–1656, pp. 59–60.

tion. The author's point is further illustrated by his invoking the sexless union of Mary and Joseph ("Pere was verry matrymony, / with-outë fleshly dede of any").[121] The emphasis on consensuality is subsequently balanced with a discussion of the conjugal debt, which the author sagely places at a distance of two hundred lines—possibly to mute the implicit tensions in contemporary matrimonial theory.[122]

Similarly, the standard marriage ceremony *in facie ecclesiae*, which crystallized in either Normandy or England in the twelfth century, was loaded with allusions to chastity. With an exchange of vows through *verba de praesenti*, the couple was deemed truly married; this bespeaks the triumph of a spiritualized, consensual view of marriage.[123] The ceremony at the church door was generally concluded with the prayer of Toby—a reminder of the most vivid condemnation of marital lust in Scripture. Moreover, in certain liturgies the priest recommended that the couple practice the three nights of sexual abstinence attributed to Tobias.[124] One of the oldest and most common blessings for the nuptial chamber was, even more significantly, from the apocryphal *Acts of Thomas*. As was seen in chapter 1, this was the prayer Thomas used when he was asked to bless King Gundaphorus's daughter and her groom on the eve of their wedding. But the suppressed climax to this extremely popular work, in which the couple convert to chastity and vehemently revile the conjugal act, could not fail to resonate as an implied subtext. Finally, the blessing

[121] Ibid., lines 1659–1660.

[122] "ȝyf þou wendest oute of cuntre, / Aȝens þy wyuys wyl to be, / But she mow wonë yn þat stede / To haue þy fleshly felawrede, / ȝyf þou do hyt aȝens her' wyl / Certeynly þou synnyst ful yl. / ȝyf þou hyt do to holde þe chaste / Wyþ-oute here wyl, þou werchyst waste" (ibid., lines 1877–1884, pp. 67–68). Likewise, *The Lay Folks' Catechism* (1357) was little more than a rhymed translation of Archbishop Peckham's constitutions from Lambeth Council (8 July 1287, "Injunctions for the Parish Clergy of the Diocese of Canterbury," in Powicke and Cheney, eds., *Councils and Synods with Other Documents Relating to the English Church*, 2,2:1078–1080). Even so, the brief entry on marriage concisely describes it as a sacrament administered by mutual consent (T. F. Simmons and H. E. Nolloth, eds., *Lay Folks' Catechism*, EETS, o.s., no. 118 [London, 1901], introd., p. xv; p. 68).

[123] Jean-Baptiste Molin and Protais Mutembe, *Le rituel du mariage en France du XIIe au XVIe siècle*, Théologie historique, 26 (Paris, 1974), pp. 32–37, 102–106, 116–117. For a discussion of the triumph of the consensual definition of marriage and its impact on ecclesiastical architecture, see Brooke, *The Medieval Idea of Marriage*, pp. 248–257.

[124] Molin and Mutembe, *Le rituel du mariage*, pp. 123, 202, 248. The blessing is in the apocryphal Book of Tobit 7.15. Tobias was the eighth man to marry Sara. The preceding seven had been torn apart on their wedding nights in punishment for their lust and their failure to remain mindful of God. Tobias avoided this fate by spending the first three nights in prayer and not consummating the marriage until this period had elapsed (6.18–22).

of bread and wine that the couple is supposed to share—either in the church or in the nuptial chamber—is supposedly representative of their common life and of the miracle at Cana.[125] But Cana itself, so often used by those championing the dignity of marriage, is an ambiguous symbol because of the widely held belief that the groom was the apostle John and that he was called away from his wedding to a higher vocation, prior to consummation.[126]

Sermons and devotional literature were likewise peppered with short instructive narratives or *exempla*, often drawn from saints' lives or the *Vitae patrum*, in which chastity in marriage is frequently highlighted.[127] Chaste marriages are periodically evoked to demonstrate that "religious should not despise the secular state," as the early fourteenth-century *Alphabet of Tales* succinctly puts it.[128] We have already met with the popular motif that accompanies this heading. It concerns a hermit to whom, in response to his prayers, God

[125] Molin and Mutembe, *Le rituel du mariage*, pp. 265–266, 250–253, 262.

[126] Cf. Nicolaus de Lyre's commentary on John 2 (*Glossa ordinaria*, vol. 5 [London, 1545], p. 192r). This tradition, already mentioned in passing, became widely known in the high and later Middle Ages. Jacobus de Voragine makes note of, but ultimately denounces, the popular claim that the bride was none other than Mary Magdalene, who, upon being spurned, gave herself over to a life of pleasure. He cites with greater approval Albert the Great's view that John's abandoned bride became a consecrated virgin who lived out her days in the entourage of the Virgin Mary (Ryan and Ripperger, trans., *Golden Legend*, p. 363—discussed on Magdalene's feast day, 22 July). Wilson and Makowski also point out that the misogamic angel named John is John the Evangelist in one popular rendering of the motif of the cleric who is wrested away from his marriage by the Virgin Mary (*Wykked Wyves and the Woes of Marriage*, pp. 125–126). Also see the fourteenth-century life of Cuthburga (one of the virgin queens discussed in chapter 2): when the groom, Alfrid, attempts to counter Cuthburga's exhortation to chastity with the example of Cana as evidence of matrimony's worthiness, she cites the tradition of John's timely escape as evidence to the contrary (Fletcher, ed. and trans., "The Marriage of St. Cuthburga," pp. 176–179).

[127] For this genre, see J. Th. Welter, *L'exemplum dans la littérature religieuse et didactique du moyen âge* (Paris and Toulouse, 1927); Claude Bremond, Jacques Le Goff, and Jean-Claude Schmitt, *L'"Exemplum,'* Typologie des sources du moyen âge occidental, fasc. 40 (Turnholt, 1982). For chastity in marriage as a motif, see Stith Thompson, *Motif-Index of Folk-Literature*, rev. ed. (Bloomington, Ind., 1958), T315, 5:376.

[128] "Religiosi non debent statum secularium contempnere" (M. M. Banks, ed., *An Alphabet of Tales*, EETS, o.s., no. 127 [London, 1904; reprt. 1972], no. 677, 2:453). This work, often attributed to Etienne of Besançon (d. 1294), is now thought to have been written by the fourteenth-century Arnold of Liège. The collection also contains two other instances of spiritual marriage. The story of Alexis is retold, wherein his parents renounced sex in return for a child. Likewise in the tale of Amicus and Amelius, the couple renounced sex out of gratitude for the life of their children (no. 600, pp. 399–401; EETS, o.s., no. 126, no. 55, 1:38–41). This hagiographical motif is discussed in chapter 2 in the section entitled "Consummated Marriage: The Transitional Model and the Clergy."

reveals either one or several individuals of great sanctity who happen to be laymen. After he asks these men in what way they could possibly have distinguished themselves (the holy laymen often seem as genuinely puzzled as the hermit), it eventually turns out that their main claim to sanctity is that they have lived in virginal chastity with their wives for thirty years or more. The moral behind this particular topos is potentially damaging: these tales imply not only that abstention from sex is necessary for sanctity, but, reversing the rubric, that the members of the laity who engage in normal marital relations are still deserving of scorn—no matter how worthy of admiration the couples are who secretly abstain.[129]

A common theme which emerges from these *exempla* is that chastity works wonders—more specifically, chastity triumphs over death. Caesarius of Heisterbach (d. 1240), for example, tells of a knight who was deathly ill. Both he and his wife "gladly acquiesced" in the abbot's advice to enter religious orders, and as soon as the knight took the vow of profession, he was cured.[130] This anecdote, of course, associates marriage with illness and death and chastity with spiritual and physical health. In the *Speculum laicorum* ("The Mirror of the Laity," between ca. 1279 and 1292), on the other hand, our married royal virgins of the previous chapter are evoked to present situations that require a still more spectacular suspension of nature's laws. Edward the Confessor's body did not corrupt after his death, while Cunegund walked over the burning plowshares unharmed.[131]

In *The Golden Legend* of Jacobus de Voragine (d. ca. 1298)—undoubtedly one of the period's most popular collections of saints' lives—the cumulative representation of chaste marriage numerically reinforces the association between chastity and both spiritual and physical salvation. Only twelve days are dedicated to saints who

[129] In another collection from the first half of the thirteenth century, the same motif appears under the title "De concordia viri et uxoris," Joseph Klapper, ed., *Erzählungen des Mittelalters*, Wort und Brauch, no. 12 (Breslau, 1914), no. 5, p. 233. For the dating of this work, see the introduction, pp. 4–5. Also see Tubach, *Index Exemplorum*, no. 3175. As is evident from the rubric, this kind of *exemplum* suggests that a sexless union is the key to perfect harmony between the couple.

[130] Caesarius of Heisterbach, *Dialogus miraculorum* 1.25, ed. J. Strange (Cologne, Bonn, and Brussels, 1851), 1:30–31.

[131] Welter, ed., *Speculum laicorum* c. 15, nos. 96–97, p. 23; see Tubach, *Index Exemplorum*, no. 2525, for the motif of Henry's suspicions. The example of their chaste marriage is also employed occasionally (no. 2524). The legend circulated in a lengthy Middle High German poem (ca. 1400) that remains in only one manuscript (Ebernand von Erfurt, *Heinrich und Kunegunde*, ed. Reinhold Bechstein [Quedlinburg and Leipzig, 1860; reprt. Amsterdam, 1968]), see esp. verse 14, lines 897–903, in which Henry initiates the move to chastity (pp. 39–40). Cunegund's trial is described in verse 22, lines 1487–1580 (pp. 61–64).

were married to Christians and whose spouses are explicitly mentioned. Of the twelve, six had spiritual marriages.[132] It is also interesting to note that all of those who partook of normal marital relations were martyred, with the single exception of St. Elizabeth of Hungary (d. 1231). Jacobus, however, does not fail to tell us of how she was unwilling to marry and of the vow of perpetual chastity she took on condition that she survived her husband.[133] Four of the six couples engaging in spiritual marriage, on the other hand, were spared a violent death and lived out their lives as confessor saints.[134]

Popular representations of spiritual marriage were by no means confined to devotional works but also made inroads into the romance tradition. Periodically we find a hero using the idea of a temporary commitment to chastity to save him from at least technical infidelity

---

[132] The author names both spouses only when both are venerated as saints. The saints who enjoyed normal conjugal relations are: Peter the Apostle and his wife (Jacobus de Voragine, *Golden Legend*, trans. Ryan and Ripperger, 29 June, pp. 330–341); Vitalis and Valeria (28 April, pp. 245–246); Hadrian and Natalia (8 September, pp. 531–535); Eustace and his wife (20 September, pp. 555–561); Elizabeth of Hungary and her husband (19 November, pp. 675–689); James the Dismembered and his spouse (27 November, pp. 716–720).

The spiritual marriages are: Hilary of Poitiers and his wife (13 January, pp. 90–92); Julian the Hospitaller and his wife (27 January, pp. 130–131); the Virgin Mary and Joseph (esp. the Annunciation, 25 March, pp. 204–208, and the Nativity of the Virgin, 8 September, pp. 519–530); Germanus of Auxerre and his wife (31 July, pp. 396–400; though in point of fact Germanus probably separated from his wife upon his ordination, as seen in chapter 2); Chrysanthus and Daria (25 October, pp. 631–633); Cecilia and Valerian (22 November, pp. 689–695). With respect to Julian, we are told that after he inadvertently slew his parents, he and his wife lived as penitents, which implies total chastity. Hence, they are included in this count. In addition to the saints who are given their own feast day, five spiritual marriages are noted in passing. These are St. Nicholas's parents, Epiphanius and Joanna (p. 17); St. Alexis's parents, Euphemianus and Aglae (p. 348); Cunegund and Henry (pp. 444, 763); the noblewoman and her husband for whom Francis of Assisi predicts a conversion to chastity (p. 600; this passage is cited as an epigraph for chapter 5), and Theodora and Sisinnius, a couple converted by St. Clement (pp. 703–704).

[133] Ibid., p. 677. Marc Glasser stresses the importance of Jacobus's inclusion of Elizabeth of Hungary, a contemporary matron, in *The Golden Legend* ("Marriage in Medieval Hagiography," pp. 24–25). As we will see below, the thirteenth century marks a change in perceptions of sanctity whereby marriage and saintliness are not necessarily incompatible. Note, however, that Elizabeth's *vita* may not have been included in the earliest versions of *The Golden Legend*. See Vauchez, "Jacques de Voragine et les saints du XIIIe s. dans la *Légende dorée*," in *"Legenda Aurea": Sept siècles de diffusion*, published under the direction of Brenda Dunn-Lardeau, Actes du colloque international sur la *Legenda aurea*, Université du Québec à Montréal, 11–12 mai 1983 (Montreal and Paris, 1986), pp. 29–30.

[134] These are Hilary, Julian, Germanus, and their respective spouses, and, of course, the Virgin Mary and Joseph.

to an earlier love.[135] Absolute vows of chastity also make their appearance. In Gerbert de Montreuil's continuation of Chrétien de Troyes's *Perceval*, for example, the hero's marriage to Blancheflor is chaste from its inception. This is in spite of the fact that Perceval's marriage is represented as essential to the quest—presumably for purposes of lineage.[136]

The most carefully delineated portrayal of spiritual marriage in this genre is, however, *Blanquerna*—Ramon Lull's late thirtccnth-century romance.[137] Blanquerna begins by describing the union of an extremely pious married couple, Evast and Aloma. After having lived a long and productive life in the world, and having brought up their only child, a son, Blanquerna, in all the virtues, Evast announces to his wife that it is time they gave up the world and entered separate religious orders.[138] He is taken by surprise when his usually docile wife defies him for the first time: though it pains her greatly to disagree with him, she refuses to abandon the state of matrimony in which she has lived her entire life. Instead, she proposes that they live

---

[135] The knight Zifar, for example, was forced to remarry before he was certain that his first wife was dead. Because of the youth of his bride, they were required to live chastely for two years anyway. When the time came to consummate the marriage, however, the woman found the knight weeping. When she asked why, he told her that he must continue in penitential chastity for another two years, or commit a mortal sin. At the end of this period she conveniently died (*The Book of the Knight Zifar* bk. 2, c. 80–81 and 118, trans. Charles L. Nelson [Lexington, Ky., 1983], pp. 101–103, 147–148).

[136] At the moment that their decision to live chastely is expressed, a voice from the sky predicts that the knight of the Swan and the Deliverer of the Holy Sepulcher will descend from Perceval's line—however little, in this respect, Perceval did to help (Gerbert de Montreuil, *La continuation de Perceval*, ed. Mary Williams [Paris, 1922], lines 6809–6934, 1:209–213). The impact of monastic spirituality on the Grail legend is especially apparent in *La Queste del saint Graal*, where the virginal Galahad replaces Perceval, the original hero of the quest. For the parallels between Christ and Galahad and the emphasis on the latter's virginity, see *La Queste del saint Graal*, ed. Albert Pauphilet (Paris, 1923), esp. pp. 77–79. Regarding the influence of Cistercian spirituality on *La Queste*, see Etienne Gilson, "La mystique de la grâce dans *La Queste del saint Graal*," in *Les idées et les lettres* (Paris, 1932), pp. 59–91. Jessie L. Weston thinks that Perceval's anomalous spiritual marriage in *La continuation* results from the conflation of two conflicting traditions—the originally earthy Welsh hero with the monasticized Galahad (*The Legend of Sir Perceval: Studies upon Its Origin, Development, and Position in the Arthurian Cycle* [London, 1906], 1:117–121).

[137] *Blanquerna* was written sometime in the 1280s or 1290s. For more precise dating, see J. N. Hillgarth, *Ramon Lull and Lullism in Fourteenth-Century France* (Oxford, 1971), pp. xxiv n. 12, 47 n. 4, 124 n. 320.

[138] This is quite a common motif. Cf. Marie de France's lay of *Eliduc*, lines 1151–1158 (in *Les lais de Marie de France*, ed. Jeanne Lods, Les classiques français au moyen âge, 87 [Paris, 1959], pp. 179–180). Also note the inclusion of the tale of Abelard and Heloise in Jean de Meun's *Roman de la Rose*, lines 8759–8832, 3:94–97.

chastely in the world, while submitting to as disciplined and as ascetic a life as if they had entered religion. Evast eventually agrees
since he is presented with no other alternative.[139]

Admiration versus Imitation: The Case of the Virgin Mary

However one assesses the net impact of these depictions of spiritual
marriage, it is obvious that *Blanquerna* is in a class of its own. The
didactic work of a pious layman, *Blanquerna* is thoroughly imbued
with Franciscan spirituality and Lull's own idiosyncratic vocation to
penitence.[140] But of particular interest is the fact that the work seems
to invite real-life imitation—Lull even offers up Avast and Aloma's
short rule of life as a possible model for pious laypersons.[141] The other
instances of chaste marriage—the *exempla*, the saints' lives, and the
romance couples—were probably introduced with a very different
purpose and calculated to produce an entirely different effect. They
may have been told with a view to inspiring admiration, not imitation.

By emphasizing the distinction between admiration and imitation,
I in no way mean to diminish the significance of imitation for lay
piety. It was certainly one of the essential components in the religious
revival of the twelfth century. The example of Waldo, who upon hearing the story of St. Alexis, was inspired to leave both his business and
his wife, is only one of the more extravagant instances of this.[142]

Even so, from the beginning of the thirteenth century, when the
clergy took its first major initiative toward lay instruction, the distinction between admiration and imitation—though always present
—began to be stressed even as the ascetical feats of the saints become
more flamboyant.[143] It is certainly no coincidence that this precision

[139] For the fascinating disagreement between Evast and Aloma, see Ramon Lull,
Blanquerna 1.4, trans. E. Allison Peers (London, 1926), pp. 44–52. It happens, however,
that Blanquerna refuses to take responsibility for the estate, as his parents had intended
he should, driven by a love for poverty (1.5, pp. 53–60).

[140] On Lull's spiritual vocation, see Mark D. Johnston, "Ramon Llull's Conversion
to Penitence," *Mystics Quarterly* 16 (1990): 179–192. For further insight into Lull's
character and spirituality, see Hillgarth, *Ramon Lull and Lullism*, pp. 27–45.

[141] Lull, *Blanquerna* 1.9.1, pp. 77–78. Lull also intended for the work to be widely
disseminated by jongleurs (see Hillgarth, *Ramon Lull and Lullism*, pp. 39–40).

[142] I chose Waldo as an example because his subsequent heresy ensures that the
sources are not concerned with idealizing him. It is equally important that the early
chronicles do not vilify Waldo either. See *Chronicon universale anonymi Laudunensis*, in Wakefield and Evans, trans., *Heresies of the High Middle Ages*, p. 201.

[143] André Vauchez remarks on the tendency for saints to become more extraordinary in the later Middle Ages, but tends to perceive this as a fourteenth-century trend

corresponds not only to the radical "democratization" of sanctity, whereby the clerical and aristocratic hegemony was weakening, but to an equally marked "feminization" of sanctity.[144] More women, especially laywomen, were being recognized as saints. The clergy sharpened the distinction between admiration and imitation in order to channel and contain the worst excesses of lay piety. From this perspective, the *exempla* concerning chaste marriage may have been generated with the conservative expectation that the hierarchy of merit (i.e., chastity over marriage) would be reinforced, and nothing more.

The delicate balance between singularity and commonalty, between admiration and imitation, is nowhere more apparent than in the cult of the Virgin Mary.[145] The union of Mary and Joseph was undoubtedly the most celebrated of virginal marriages: however, all of the circumstances around their union, particularly their divinely inspired fulfillment of the Augustinian goods, were beyond imitation. And yet, as we have seen, their marriage was the touchstone for determining the norms of Christian marriage.

Did the marriage of Mary and Joseph act as a celestial advertisement prompting satellite experiments in conjugal purity? Certainly, we will see that it seems to have had this effect on some. There was an undoubted increase in the number of spiritual marriages in the thirteenth century, which, from a chronological standpoint, appears to

---

("L'influence des modèles hagiographiques sur les représentations de la sainteté, dans les procès de canonisation (XIIIe–XVe siècle)," in *Hagiographie, Cultures, et Sociétés*, pp. 585–587; cf. Kieckhefer, *Unquiet Souls*, pp. 1–3, 118–121). A focus on women's *vitae* indicates that this tendency is well under way in the thirteenth century. See, for example, the life of Christina the Astonishing, *AA SS*, July, 5:650–660, esp. pp. 651–654.

144 On these two trends, see especially Vauchez, *La sainteté*, pp. 243–249, 412–413; idem, *Les laïcs*, pp. 79–82, 189–195. It is equally significant that Jacques de Vitry is one of the first to outline this distinction in depth in the life of Mary of Oignies—who initiated a chaste marriage with her husband. For his distinction between *admiranda* and *imitanda*, see *AA SS*, June, 5:550. The passage is translated in Kieckhefer's *Unquiet Souls*, p. 13; also see Kieckhefer's discussion on pp. 12–14 and 200. Cf. William R. Cook, who points out that Bonaventure also relies on this distinction in his later life of St. Francis. See "Fraternal and Lay Images of St. Francis in the Thirteenth Century," in *Popes, Teachers, and Canon Law in the Middle Ages*, ed. J. R. Sweeney and S. Chodorow (Ithaca, N.Y., 1989), p. 267. Canon lawyers are possibly even more aware of this distinction. See n. 33, above, for Huguccio's comment on saints such as Macharius, Alexis, et al. who unilaterally withdrew from the marriage bed.

145 For a discussion of this problem in understanding Mary's example, see Penny S. Gold, *The Lady and the Virgin: Image, Attitude, and Experience in Twelfth-Century France* (Chicago and London, 1985), pp. 68–72; for the challenges that Mary presented on a physiological level, see Charles T. Wood, "The Doctor's Dilemma: Sin, Salvation, and the Menstrual Cycle in Medieval Thought," *Speculum* 56 (1981): 717–722.

follow in the wake of Mary's flourishing cult. On the other hand, the clergy did its best to diminish such an effect through appeals to Mary's singularity. The *Glossa ordinaria*, for example, maintained that a chaste marriage was considerably holier, but that a couple should contract with a very different desire: namely, procreation.[146] Because of human weakness it would be folly to contract with the resolve of never exacting—the Virgin Mary was in a special category, as her chaste resolve was directed by divine revelation.[147]

Nevertheless, the Virgin's presumed vow of chastity (it is nowhere mentioned in Scripture) was sufficiently problematical that it required some toning down. Thus Gratian, in an effort to explain how Mary could consent to marriage and remain true to her vow of chastity (C.27 q.2. c.2 dpc), strings together a series of Augustinian sentiments and comes up with the following:

> The Blessed Mary proposed that she would preserve a vow of virginity in her heart, but she did not express that vow of virginity with her mouth. She subjected herself to divine disposition when she proposed that she would preserve virginity, unless God revealed to her otherwise. Therefore, committing her virginity to divine disposition, she consented to carnal union, not by seeking it, but by obeying divine inspiration in both the one case and the other. But it was after she bore a son that she expressed with her lips what she had conceived in her heart, together with her husband, and each remained in virginity.[148]

Although Gratian's theory of the formation of marriage was not successful, his Augustinian-inspired explanation of the Virgin's vow was immensely so. Peter Lombard adopted the passage wholeheartedly (4.30.2.2), as did Raymond of Peñafort and John of Freiburg.[149] Thus

[146] *Glossa ordinaria* for C.33 q.5 c.4 ad v. *sanctiora*.

[147] *Glossa ordinaria* for X.3.32.3 ad v. *non exigere*. The gloss goes on to state that a minority of authorities think that such a resolve, even if unexpressed, would invalidate a marriage. Cf. n. 39, above.

[148] "Beata Maria proposuit se conseruaturam uotum uirginitatis in corde, sed ipsum uotum uirginitatis non expressit ore. Subiecit se diuinae dispositioni, dum proposuit se perseueraturam uirginem, nisi Deus ei aliter reuelaret. Conmittens ergo uirginitatem suam diuinae dispositioni consensit in carnalem copulam, non illam appetendo, sed diuinae inspirationi in utroque obediendo. Postea uero filium genuit quod corde conceperat simul cum uiro labiis expressit, et uterque in uirginitate permansit" (C.27 q.2 c.3).

[149] Raymond of Peñafort, *Summa de poenitentia* 4.2.15, p. 522; John of Freiburg, *Summa confessorum* 4.2.64, fol. 222v. John includes additional refinements: namely, that, according to Thomas Aquinas and Peter of Tarentaise, she consented to carnal union not explicitly but implicitly, and that, according to Ulrich Engelbrecht (d. ca. 1278), Joseph had prior knowledge through divine revelation that the marriage would never be consummated.

Mary's potential as a role model for women aspiring to chastity was seriously undercut by the conditional nature of her vow. Canonists attempted to bring Mary's behavior even further in line with female submission, however. The *Glossa ordinaria* embroiders the conditional nature of her vow with some entirely temporal considerations: unless the law prohibited or her parents compelled her.[150] Such qualifications could easily be wielded against women in order to force them to submit to parental or social pressures.

When the Virgin's commonalty is explicitly invoked, it is almost invariably to reinforce socially prescribed roles for women. Thus the thirteenth-century wives' manual *The Goodman of Paris* presents Mary's obedience and humility to God as prescriptive for how a wife should behave to her husband.[151] The cult of the lactating Virgin is one of the more graphic manifestations of Mary's female mentorship.[152] Indeed, the example of Mary's motherhood arguably made more obvious inroads into the spirituality of female celibates than did her virginity into that of the married. Cloistered female visionaries suckled and even bore the infant Jesus, while some religious communities developed elaborately staged Nativity rituals that were focused on the crèche.[153]

The wife's approved submission to her husband was reinforced through the late introduction of the cult of Joseph. The apocryphal tradition had given Joseph bad press, portraying him as an elderly and rather cantankerous widower. This began to change in the high and later Middle Ages. Belief in his perpetual virginity was already widespread in the twelfth century.[154] But it is only in the fourteenth and

---

[150] *Glossa ordinaria* for C.27 q.2 c.2 dpc ad v. *voti virginalis.*

[151] Eileen Power, trans., *The Goodman of Paris (Le ménagier de Paris)* (New York, 1928), 1.6, p. 140.

[152] See Marina Warner, *Alone of All Her Sex: The Myth and the Cult of the Virgin Mary* (London, Melbourne, and New York, 1978), pp. 192–205, 251; Wood, "Doctor's Dilemma," p. 721.

[153] See Rosemary Hale, "*Imitatio Mariae*: Motherhood Motifs in Devotional Memoirs," *Mystics Quarterly* 16 (1990): 193–203. Hale also described painstaking reenactments of aspects of Mary's maternal career in a recent paper, entitled "*Mariennachfolge*: The Imitation of Mary in Late Medieval German Spirituality" at Fordham University's Conference on Medieval Spirituality (1–2 March 1991). These rituals were practiced by cloistered and lay devotees alike. The idealization of motherhood seems to have grown especially intense in the fifteenth century. Pamela Sheingorn points to some of the negative consequences this had with regard to narrowing options for women—especially in Protestant Europe ("The Holy Kinship: The Ascendency of Matriliny in Sacred Genealogy of the Fifteenth Century," *Thought* 64 [1989]: 268–286, esp. pp. 278–284).

[154] According to Francis L. Filas, Peter Damian was pivotal in establishing Joseph's perpetual virginity, which ran counter to the apocryphal tradition (*Joseph: The Man*

especially the fifteenth century that Joseph truly came into his own, at least in part through the stimulus of a handful of powerful churchmen.[155] Different reasons have been posited for the relatively sudden emergence of this hitherto shadowy figure. Marina Warner contends that the emphasis which the mendicants placed on Mary's humility reinforced society's vision of woman's passive and submissive role. This emphasis, in turn, stimulated the cult of Joseph, so that Mary would submit to the head of the household.[156] David Herlihy thinks the cult may well be a conscious ecclesiastical reaction to the feminization of sanctity, but also remarks that a strong paternal figure would be a comfort in this period of chaos.[157] But there is little question that the cult of Joseph stimulated the development of a meeker, humbler, and more submissive Mary.

Thus while Mary's double capacity as virgin and mother exerted considerable influence on chaste celibates, she remained, for the married, rather one-dimensional, reinforcing the general mores of married life. When she is acting as special patroness of chastity, a cleric is often the beneficiary. The *Miracles de Nostre Dame* of Gautier de Coinci (d. 1236) frequently depict Mary acting in this capacity. The common motif of Mary as substitute bride for celibate men shows her jealously plucking a cleric away from his wedding.[158] On the one

---

Closest to Jesus [Boston, 1962], p. 99). Note, however, that this position had already been anticipated by Jerome (*Adversus Helvidium* c. 19, *PL* 23, col. 213; cf. Filas, *Joseph*, p. 92). Peter Lombard credited Joseph with a tacit wish to preserve his virginity, parallel with Mary's (4.30.2.1). Bernard of Clairvaux compares Joseph to his namesake, the Old Testament patriarch, as both were noted for their chastity and their association with dreams (*In laudibus virginis matris* Hom. 2.16, ed. J. Leclercq and H. Rochais, *S. Bernardi opera* [Rome, 1966], 4:33–34. This comparison would become something of a commonplace). In fact, Bernard comes close to tampering with the Gospel tradition in order to redeem Joseph's reputation. Thus when Joseph discovered Mary's pregnancy, he never for a moment doubted her chastity, but only thought to send her away as he believed himself unworthy to be her consort (c. 14–15, pp. 31–33). Because of the growth of interest in Joseph, a feast day had to be inserted for him in the Usuard martyrology ca. 1150 (Filas, *Joseph*, p. 493).

[155] Filas, *Joseph*, pp. 495–543; David Herlihy, *Medieval Households* (Cambridge, Mass., 1985), pp. 127–128.

[156] Warner, *Alone of All Her Sex*, pp. 182–191. Warner is assuming, however, that the cult of the Virgin in its earlier stages reflected and to some extent fostered a positive role for women. For some of the difficulties in drawing a direct parallel between positive female imagery and an improved situation for women, see Caroline Bynum, "Jesus as Mother and Abbot as Mother: Some Themes in Twelfth-Century Cistercian Writing," in *Jesus as Mother: Studies in the Spirituality of the High Middle Ages* (Berkeley and Los Angeles, 1982), pp. 136–144.

[157] Herlihy, *Medieval Households*, pp. 128–130; cf. idem, "The Family and Religious Ideologies in Medieval Europe," *Journal of Family History* 12 (1987): 13–14.

[158] Gautier de Coinci, *Les miracles de Nostre Dame*, ed. Koenig, II Mir. 29 (D.78),

occasion in Gautier's collection of a relationship that closely resembles the virginal union of Mary and Joseph, the circumstances are not auspicious. The unfortunate woman whose husband had deflowered her with a knife was a devotee of Mary's and had even made a private vow of chastity at Mary's behest. Although Mary ultimately healed her, she did nothing to spare her the forced marriage or the blade. When the woman's case was brought before the bishop of Arras, moreover, he decided against granting the couple a divorce (although grounds for either a divorce or an annulment were hardly lacking), instead bidding the man to remain with the young girl as her guardian.[159]

But Gautier also reports another miracle of the Virgin that is much more in line with pastoral considerations and underscores many of the clergy's worst apprehensions.[160] A knight (*preudom*) and his wife made a mutual vow of chastity, having already raised what they perceived as an adequate number of children (lines 12–19). They held to their pious resolve for a long time until one night, on the eve of Easter, the husband broke the vow, despite the strenuous resistance of his wife. The aggrieved wife vowed that whatever child might have been conceived on that night belonged to the Devil (lines 33–55). A son was born to them who was beautiful and pious by nature. One day he found his mother weeping, and, in response to his questioning, she told him of her unfortunate words (lines 116–145). He set out on a series of travels to learn how to free himself of the Devil's claims. But neither the pope, nor the patriarch of Jerusalem, nor an exceptionally holy hermit had the power to absolve him (lines 163–303). The hermit, however, did advise him to trust in Mary's great power (lines

---

lines 101–528, 4:344–360. Gautier winds up this tale by citing Gregory the Great's example of the spiritual marriage in which a couple chastely cohabit for forty years, and yet the husband still finds the wife a threat to his chastity when he is on his deathbed (lines 643–700, pp. 365–367. This anecdote is discussed in chapter 2 in the section entitled "Consummated Marriage: The Transitional Model and the Clergy"). Cf. *An Alphabet of Tales*, ed. Banks, EETS, o.s., no. 127, no. 656, 2:438–439. Regarding the motif of a monk or priest as Mary's spiritual groom, see Warner, *Alone of All Her Sex*, pp. 156–159; Tubach, *Index Exemplorum*, no. 5148. Also note the experience of Hermann Joseph, who received the latter part of his name when he actually "married" the Virgin Mary—supplanting the historical Joseph (*BS*, vol. 5, cols. 25–28).

[159] Koenig, ed., *Les miracles de Nostre Dame*, II Mir. 27 (D.76), lines 27–56, 188–201, 4:296–297, 302.

[160] Ibid., I Mir. 22 (D.24), 2:205–223. I will refer to the poem by line references in the text. The identical story is included in Vincent of Beauvais's *Speculum historiale* 7.115 (in *Speculum quadruplex; sive, Speculum maius* [Douai, 1624; reprt. Graz, 1964–1965], 4:263–264). I am grateful to Robert L. A. Clark for bringing this material to my attention as well as for his illuminating comments.

304–329). The hapless child was nevertheless seized by the Devil at the very moment when he was attending the hermit's mass (lines 362–369), only to be rescued from hell by the Virgin herself (lines 399–408). The child lived out the rest of his life penitentially—as a hermit in service to Mary (lines 412–422, 456–457).

The tale of the child sworn to the Devil was immensely popular.[161] It was transmitted in many different forms—Latin, vernacular, prose, and verse—and even surfaces in the mid-fourteenth century as a miracle play.[162] Later treatments of this motif introduce a number of significant changes. In a fifteenth-century rhymed version in Old French, for example, the couple is reclassified as a bourgeois and his wife as opposed to a knight and his lady—a change that, not only reflects the leading role the bourgeoisie began to play in lay piety beginning in the thirteenth century, but also, as we will see, ushers in a number of nuanced business negotiations.[163] The troublesome vow of chastity is dropped entirely and the pivotal sexual transgression is the failure to contain on Holy Friday.[164] The wife's rash words result in a written contract with the Devil.[165] The resolution of the story is

[161] In A. Poncelet's "Index miraculorum B. V. Mariae quae saec. VI–XV latine conscripta sunt" (*AB* 21 [1902]), nos. 638, 657, and 1558 contain the same basic narrative as Gautier's story; nos. 300, 1436, 1517, and 1272 are related narratives. Also see Tubach, *Index Exemplorum*, no. 975b.

[162] See "Un miracle de Nostre Dame d'un enfant qui fu donné au dyable quant il fu engendré," in *Miracles de Nostre Dame par personnages*, ed. Gaston Paris and Ulysse Robert (Paris, 1876), 1:35–56. See Robert L. A. Clark's analysis of this play in his forthcoming dissertation entitled "The *Miracles de Nostre Dame par personnages*: Confraternity Drama as Socio-Cultural Text" (Indiana University).

[163] Paul Meyer, ed., "L'enfant voué au diable," *Romania* 33 (1904): 163–178. For a discussion of the way in which this poem differs from some of its analogues, see Meyer's introduction, pp. 164–166; the poem itself is on pp. 167–178. Although the husband is generally characterized as "le bourgeois," he is once called "uns preudons" (verse 3, line 12, p. 168), which evokes earlier renderings. The bourgeoisie's increasing role in popular piety will be discussed in chapter 5.

[164] Meyer, ed., "L'enfant voué au diable," verses 7–8, lines 25–32, p. 168. It should also be noted that, initially, the wife is represented as more sexually receptive: prior to her protests, the couple is described as lying together in great affection. She does not protest when he begins his sexual advances: "Se coucherent ensemble par mout grant amitié. / Le bourgois vers sa fame s'est maintenant glachié; / Il [l]a baise, il [l']acole: elle ne brait ne crie" (verse 7, lines 26–28). The miracle play is the poem's closest analogue (see pp. 166–167). In the play, however, the vow of perpetual chastity is retained and the woman's initiative in the vow is more pronounced. The woman appeals to the Virgin for strength in this undertaking and for help in converting her husband to chastity ("Un miracle de Nostre Dame d'un enfant," lines 1–47, in *Miracles de Nostre Dame par personnages*, ed. Paris and Robert, 1:3–4).

[165] The Devil is represented as being beside the bed. It would seem that the wife's words spontaneously result in a written contract, but the wording of the pertinent verse is rather obscure. "L'anemy si l'ouy qui a nul bien ne touche: / Une pensée

of particular interest. The doomed child, receiving little help from the various holy men he approaches, is eventually directed to a chapel of the Virgin Mary where both Christ and Mary are miraculously present. At Christ's request, the Virgin questions the Devil concerning his right to the child, eventually requiring to see the contract (verses 74–76). The child is saved when the Virgin triumphantly pronounces the contract void, as a woman's bequest is invalid without the husband's authorization. She tears it up with a flourish.[166]

Female Spirituality and the Two Fora

The wife who vowed her son to the Devil epitomizes many of the potential problems inherent in married chastity and also highlights aspects of the married woman's depleted position. It points to the dangers of the hidden vow—a vow that cannot be protected by the ecclesiastical authorities but is clearly binding before God. Masculine power is presented at its ugliest in a violent rape scenario, and the canonistic deterrent of illegitimacy for the breaking of a vow of continence (or a failure to observe a feast day) is dramatically heightened by the mother's tragic contract with the Devil. The church authorities are powerless at first to discern, and later to dispel, the couple's sin, which lived on in their progeny.[167] In the later versions of

---

tantost luy bouta en la bouche; / Puis print de sa salive, qui qu'en poit ne qui grouche, / Une lectre en a fait, tantost enprès la bouche" (verse 12, lines 45–48, Meyer, ed., "L'enfant voué au diable," p. 169).

166 "La dame print la lectre, que nous tenons a mere. / 'Certes,' se dit la dame, 'tu ne la seüs faire; / Et don ne peult valloir, puis qu'il ne vient du pere.' / . . . / La dame prant la lectre, errant l'a depieche" (verses 77–78, lines 305–309, Meyer, ed., "L'enfant voué au diable," p. 177). Cf. the similar ending in the miracle play when the Virgin attempts to refute the devils' claims (there are two devils in this account) with the counterclaim that they had no legal seisin in the child: " 'Avez vous trouvé en voz livres / Le droit, que vous cy demandez? / Biau tresdoulx filz, or m'entendez: / Ly enfes est vostres et miens. / Nul n'a que donner en voz biens, / S'il n'en est en propre saisine. / Ycelle preude femme fine / Qui porta cest valeton cy / N'avoit riens a donner en lui / Ou point que dès lors fist le don'" ("Un miracle de Nostre Dame d'un enfant," lines 1312–1321, in *Miracles de Nostre Dame par personnages*, ed. Paris and Robert, 1:47). The Virgin's legal acumen is corroborated by Christ's judgment (lines 1346–1349, 1368–1373, pp. 48–49).

Note, however, that William of Rennes contends that all subject people *can* bind themselves to the Devil with the liberty of free will, but not to God, as it may require some work they are not free to perform (*Summa de poenitentia* 1.8.17, gloss m ad v. *non excusat*, p. 79).

167 There are echoes of this in Robert Courson's scenario of a woman who repented for having introduced a spurious heir to her husband's estate. Her offense cannot be made known out of fear of scandal and possibly even war. The putative heir should,

the story, the situation is rectified by a reminder, from the Virgin Mary no less, of a woman's legal incapacity.

When this story first began to circulate in the twelfth century, Europe was only just evolving a mentality that could appreciate the problems it presented and a vocabulary which could describe them. In the first quarter of the twelfth century, the distinction between the inner and outer person was dramatically drawn into center stage by Abelard's *Ethics*, which maintained the primacy of intention over action in the assessment of sins.[168] Abelard's bold formulation acted as a powerful tonic on the development of a more subtle penitential system.[169] Toward the end of the twelfth century, a complementary distinction between the twofold capacity in which the church exercised judgment began to be distinguished: the external and internal

---

however, be told. Ideally, he is required to renounce his heritage in favor of the true heir, retreat to a cloister, and do penance for his mother's sin. His son, if he has one, is also supposed to withdraw from the world (V. L. Kennedy, ed., "Robert Courson on Penance," *Mediaeval Studies* 7 [1945]: 320–321, c. 10). According to Baldwin, Robert's *summa* was written between 1208 and 1212/13 (see *Masters, Princes, and Merchants*, 1:19–25, 2:9–15). Also note that a minority of theorists, such as Vincent of Beauvais (significantly, one of the many transmitters of this tale) still subscribed to the two-seed theory of conception, whereby a woman must "ejaculate" and thus experience pleasure in order to conceive (see Jacquart and Thomasset, *Sexuality and Medicine*, p. 64; Laqueur, *Making Sex*, pp. 43–45). Buried in this story may be the suggestion that the wife enjoyed the allegedly forced sex act, which amounts to a subtle vindication of rape. Cf. n. 164, above.

[168] See *Peter Abelard's "Ethics,"* ed. and trans. D. E. Luscombe (Oxford, 1971), esp. pp. 12–15, 22–23, 40–47. For his debt to Augustine and the school of Laon, see introduction, pp. xvii–xviii; xxxiii, and idem, "The *Ethics* of Peter Abelard: Some Further Considerations," in *Peter Abelard*, ed. E. M. Buytaert, Proceedings of the International Conference, Louvain, 10–12 May 1971 (Louvain and the Hague, 1974), pp. 80–84. For an explication of the relationship between intention and sin in Abelard's thought, see Robert Blomme, *La doctrine du péché dans les écoles théologiques de la première moitié du XIIe siècle* (Louvain and Gembloux, 1958), pp. 128–164. For its impact on twelfth-century thought (especially on Hugh of St. Victor, Gratian, and Peter Lombard) see Odon Lottin, *Psychologie et morale aux XIIe et XIIIe siècles*, 2d. ed. (Louvain and Gembloux, 1954), 4,1:310–321, and D. E. Luscombe, *The School of Peter Abelard: The Influence of Abelard's Thought in the Early Scholastic Period* (Cambridge, 1969), pp. 194–196, 217–222, 276–279.

The emphasis on intentionality is an aspect of the greater focus on the individual in this period. See Colin Morris, *The Discovery of the Individual, 1050–1200* (New York, 1972), esp. pp. 64–79; John F. Benton, "Consciousness of Self and Perceptions of Individuality," pp. 263–295, and Caroline Bynum's important qualifying remarks in, "Did the Twelfth Century Discover the Individual?" in *Jesus as Mother*, pp. 82–109.

[169] See especially Paul Anciaux, *La théologie du sacrement de pénitence au XIIe siècle*, Universitas Catholica Lovaniensis, ser. 2, vol. 41 (Louvain and Gembloux, 1949), pp. 176–179, 186–231; A. Teetaert, *La confession aux laïques* (Wetteren, Bruges, and Paris, 1926), pp. 85–89, 100–101, 116–118, 121, 124–125.

fora.[170] The external forum judged the outer person and his or her manifest deeds. Its business was handled through the increasingly sophisticated ecclesiastical courts; the internal forum was focused on the individual's progress toward salvation and thus judged the inner person. The church's jurisdiction over the internal forum was exercised through the sacrament of confession and penance. But this jurisdiction was limited and must ultimately be subservient to the forum's extrasacramental capacity, since God is the ultimate judge of human hearts.

The emphasis on intention and the emergence of two separate fora coincided with the married woman's progressive legal impoverishment. Her respective relations with the two fora were naturally more complex than a man's, even as they were more involuted. Church teaching bolstered patriarchal authority by strictly subordinating wife to husband. Gratian had reinforced this teaching through a canonistic piece of wizardry that assimilated the husband's will with God's will—an elision which carved deep inroads into the wife's spiritual autonomy. The husband's authority over the wife's vow, in particular, straddled both fora since she was bound internally to perform something externally.

Although the absolute quality of masculine authority was the dominant discourse, not all of Gratian's successors were quite so sanguine. Vows were an essential part of penitential expiation: it was generally held that the merit of a pious act was increased by a deliberate vow.[171] Naturally, this was an area in which the clergy would be most inclined to curtail the husband's authority for the sake of the wife's spiritual well-being. The canonist Huguccio showed precisely this kind of initiative. Hitherto I have emphasized Huguccio's suspicion of the flesh and his severity in sexual matters. But if we approach Huguccio's thinking from a broader perspective, we are forced to conclude that the uncompromising attitude which informs much of his thinking is linked to the fearsome responsibility he attributes to the individual. This severity has an enabling effect on female spirituality. His tendency to privilege the internal over the external forum caused him to perceive the tacit vow as binding. Likewise, an individual who was recalled from a monastery by a protesting spouse was

[170] For a basic definition see R. Naz, "For," *Dictionnaire de droit canonique*, vol. 5 (Paris, 1953), cols. 871–873; also see P. Capobianco, "De notione fori interni in iure canonico," *Apollinaris* 9 (1936): 364–374, esp. pp. 366–369; for the evolution of the concept, see idem, "De ambitu fori interni in iure ante Codicem," *Apollinaris* 8 (1935): 591–605. Also see Michaud-Quantin, who discusses Raymond of Peñafort's discernment of a penitential forum ("A propos des prèmieres *Summae confessorum*," p. 305).

[171] See, for example, John of Freiburg, *Summa confessorum* 1.8.7, fol. 18r–v.

held to fulfill his or her monastic vow whenever he or she was free to do so. Finally, Huguccio denied the husband's right to revoke a vow that he had at one time authorized, and maintained that if the wife independently made a harmless vow that did not incite scandal, she was bound to fulfill it, even as she was bound to please God over her husband.[172]

The movement away from Huguccio's severity, particularly at the hands of later Dominican theologians, is justly viewed as a benign concession to human frailty, generally, and as a major breakthrough for married sexuality.[173] Yet such liberalizing tendencies did not necessarily augur well for female spirituality. The revival of Aristotelian naturalism spawned a neopaternalism that invited husbands to interpose themselves benignly between their wives and God. As will become clearer in the next chapter, Huguccio's sexual rigor was probably more in line with pious matrons' own attitudes toward sex than with those of the Dominican liberalizers. Likewise, pious women did not necessarily share in canonists' and spiritual counselors' debilitating view of a woman's spiritual autonomy: they continued to feel bound by vows that were broken by fathers and husbands.

On the other hand, it would be wrong to exaggerate the extent of Huguccio's interference with the husband's authority. His invocation of scandal as the criterion for an illict vow confined female piety to a narrow register. Pastoral sources show increased concern with scandal per se and a corresponding sensitivity to the way in which outer manifestations of piety could scandalize the community.[174] Female

---

[172] Huguccio's views also made a considerable impression on Robert of Flamborough (*Liber poenitentialis* 2.3.19–20, pp. 68–69) and on William of Rennes (*Summa de poenitentia* 1.8.7, gloss t, ad v. *reuocet*, p. 63 and 1.8.8, gloss x, ad v. *possunt contrauenire, vel irritare*, pp. 65–66). Robert follows Huguccio more closely, thus denying that the husband can recall a vow he has consented to and maintaining that a recalled vow should still be fulfilled after the impediment is removed. William cites opinions on both sides but ultimately upholds the husband's right to recall any vow, authorized or not, and the corresponding nullity of a recalled vow. The husband's power over the wife's vow is at the center of Chaucer's *Franklin's Tale*. By refusing to recall his wife's unfortunate vow (which entailed committing adultery), the husband was unresistingly accepting disgrace as well as making his wife's life more difficult. On the other hand, he was keeping his private promise to her, made at the time of their marriage, that he would never exercise a husband's lordship.

[173] For the movement away from Huguccio's rigor, see Tentler, *Sin and Confession*, pp. 174–180, and Brundage, *Law, Sex, and Christian Society*, pp. 447–449.

[174] According to pastoral discussions, the source of scandal was not necessarily a sin in and of itself, but was a form of behavior that might cause others to sin. Thus it was immensely difficult to assign penance for scandal (Thomas of Chobham, *Summa confessorum* 7.13.1, p. 566; 7.13.4, p. 571). It is significant that Thomas ends his *summa* with an in-depth discussion of scandal. Peter the Chanter allows the commutation of penitential fasts on the assumption that it would scandalize the company if one of

piety generated particular concern. Peter the Chanter, for example, who makes numerous references to the dearth of religious options for women in his time,[175] nevertheless questions the wisdom of permitting women who cannot find accommodation in a monastery to pursue a vocation in the world; his fear is that such women, spurning marriage, will be taken for Cathars.[176] A wife's tether was considerably shorter. The *Glossa ordinaria*, following Huguccio, identifies a wife's scandalous vow as equivalent to lying in a thin nightshirt, fasting while the husband dines, or attending matins.[177] Trepidation over a woman's penitential practices was linked to and corroborated by the new solicitude spiritual advisers were showing for her physical appearance, purportedly as it enhanced her ability to render the debt.

Thus if the clergy's overt sponsorship of defiant female spirituality was already declining sometime prior to the eleventh century, it was moribund by the end of the thirteenth. And yet it would be wrong to say that the clergy abandoned their female penitents. Rather they forged a furtive coalition with them that was necessitated by the husband's control over the wife's person and was based on the woman's delicate balance between the hidden and the manifest, between the tacit and the expressed, between the inner and the outer, between the internal and external fora. Ultimately the confessional fostered a subtle subversion of masculine authority.[178]

The more limitations that the clergy placed around female penitential practices in the external forum, the more they sponsored her dependency on the internal forum for vindication before God. Part of this was inadvertent, but part was undoubtedly deliberate. Raymond of Peñafort's treatment of a husband's sinful retraction of a wife's vow is a case in point. He firmly puts to rest Huguccio's contention that a wife should serve God over a husband by reaffirming that a woman obeys God in obeying her husband. However, he adds that she should sorrow in her soul that she is unable to fulfill her vow, clearly

---

their number dined on bread and water while the rest ate meat (*Summa de sacramentis* c. 224, 3,2a:203). There was a general consensus that such pious acts should be restrained if they could be restrained without sin (Raymond of Peñafort, *Summa de poenitentia* 3.30.1–5, pp. 353–356).

[175] Peter the Chanter, *Summa de sacramentis* c. 314, 3,2a:367; c. 376, 3,2b:572.

[176] Ibid. c. 319, 3,2a:376. The clergy's hostility to extraregular single women will be discussed at greater length in chapter 5.

[177] *Glossa ordinaria* for C.33 q.5 c.11 ad v. *nisi auctor*; cf. William of Rennes's similar specifications (*Summa de poenitentia* 1.8.8, gloss x, ad v. *possunt contrauenire, vel irritare*, p. 65). Note that matins occurs in the middle of the night, hence the occasion's capacity for scandal.

[178] Cf. Elliott, "Dress as Mediator," pp. 302–306.

regarding her internal grief as a testimony to the purity of her intentions.[179]

Raymond's emphasis on the wife's intentions is by no means extraordinary: it is fully consonant with contemporary penitential theory, which, from the time of Abelard, had paid less attention to outer expiation and more to the crucial role of contrition in the forgiveness of sins.[180] Everywhere we see evidence of a new appreciation for the efficacy of the inner life. For each of the four forms of physical penitence that Raymond of Peñafort prescribes, for example, there is a spiritual or psychic level on which they can be performed.[181] Confessors' manuals, generally, were quick to reassure penitents that they would be credited for the good intentions that they were unable to realize in deeds.[182] But this tendency to look inward had a special pertinence for women. Spiritual advisers fostered this orientation, sometimes to such a degree that women were tacitly encouraged to

[179] "Sed adhuc obijcitur de vxore, quae potius obedit viro, quam Deo, dum ad mandatum viri frangit votum, quo se astrinxerat Deo. . . . Ad hoc dic, quod vxor in talibus obediendo viro, obedit Deo, quia Deus vult ipsam ita facere; dum tamen doleat in animo, quia votum non potest implere" (*Summa de poenitentia* 3.33.4, p. 383). Raymond's glossator, William, however, does not believe that the wife is required to grieve, since she did not sin: "non tamen credo, quod ad huius modi dolorem teneatur, si nullum sit eius in hac parte peccatum" (gloss y ad v. *doleat*). Cf. Raymond's more extensive treatment of the husband's power over the wife's vow in 1.8.8, pp. 64–65. John of Freiburg repeats Raymond's counsel (*Summa confessorum* 3.33.18, fol. 115r).

[180] In Q. 151 of *Sic et Non*, Abelard's emphasis on contrition leads him to raise the question of whether oral confession is necessary (Blanche B. Boyer and Richard McKeon, eds. [Chicago, 1976–1977], pp. 510–512). Thereafter, his successors must likewise grapple with this problem. Hugh of St. Victor reacts violently against Abelard's query and vigorously upholds the power of the priest to remit sins (*De sacramentis* 2.14.8, *PL* 176, cols. 564–570). Gratian lists the arguments both for the sufficiency of internal contrition (*De poen.* D.1 c.1–37) and for oral confession and external satisfaction (dpc 37–c.87), but arrives at no clear solution (dpc 87 and dpc 89). Peter Lombard analyzes both positions and ultimately concludes that God remits sins without confession and satisfaction, but the will to confess must be present (4.17.1). See Anciaux's analysis in *La théologie du sacrement de pénitence*, pp. 176–207, 223–231. Raymond of Peñafort proffers Peter's solution as the most celebrated view (*Summa de poenitentia* 3.34.11, pp. 446–447).

[181] Alms are described as threefold: through contrition of the heart, through compassion for one's neighbor, and through largesse, which can be manifested in either physical or spiritual assistance. Maceration of the flesh can be achieved in four ways: through prayers, vigils, fasts, and whips. Fasts are threefold: abstention from food, from temporal joy, or from mortal sin. Finally, flagellation can be practiced physically through ashes, hairshirts, genuflections, self-chastisement, and pilgrimages, or through tribulation and affliction (*Summa de poenitentia* 3.34.34–38, pp. 467–470).

[182] See, for example, Thomas of Chobham, *Summa confessorum* 7.2.9.2, p. 360. Thomas is quick to add, however, that evil works operate differently, since to do evil is much worse than to simply wish it.

dissociate themselves from their physical surroundings. The rules of life written for pious laywomen in the high and later Middle Ages are a case in point. The clerical advisers tended to superimpose an endless round of meditation and prayers on the woman's mundane life, making little or no reference to her physical surroundings or familial responsibilities. This would ultimately encourage these women to develop a detached or divided spirituality.[183]

The only form of outer expiation that the clergy advocated for their female penitents, even if it provoked the husband's disapproval, was almsgiving—significantly an activity that was presumed to contribute as much to the husband's spiritual good as it did to the clergy's material good.[184] But the resistance the clergy sponsored was discreet: it was limited to the confessional. Thus if the woman's insubordination was exposed, it would probably not be construed as clerical counsel. Raymond of Peñafort, for example, expressly affirms the husband's financial control over his wife. When raising the delicate ques-

---

[183] Geneviève Hasenohr, "La vie quotidienne de la femme vue par l'église: l'enseignement des 'Journées Chrétiennes' de la fin du moyen-âge," *Frau und spätmittelalterlicher Alltag*, Internationaler Kongress krems an der Donau 2. bis 5. Oktober 1984, Österreichische Akademie der Wissenschaften, Philosophisch-Historische Klasse, Sitzungsberichte, 473; Veröffentlichungen des Instituts für mittelalterliche Realienkunde Österreichs, no. 9 (Vienna, 1986), pp. 41–50, 66–67. At least one of these authors, Hernando de Talavera (ca. 1430–1507) is intensely aware of the limitations that a husband imposes on his wife's spiritual practices. He notes that he cannot fast without her husband's permission or perform vigils, and that he can even force her into sin or maliciously block her efforts to save her soul (pp. 47–48). Cf. Georges Duby's assessment of the twelfth-century clergy's sexual counsel to married women, discussed later in this chapter.

[184] Cf. Elliott, "Dress as Mediator," pp. 289–291. The example of the usurer's wife also indicates that the clergy was most inclined to curtail the husband's authority where money was concerned. Although the wife should make every effort to turn the usurious husband from his evil ways, if he is truly incorrigible, a number of spiritual advisers permit her to leave. See, for example, Robert Courson (Kennedy, ed., "Robert Courson on Penance," c. 10, p. 320). Thomas of Chobham cites opinions in favor of staying and going, but seems more inclined toward the latter response (*Summa confessorum* 7.6.11.3, pp. 506–507). Peter of Poitiers, writing shortly after 1215, seems to think that the wife should remain in order to make secret restitution to the despoiled (*Summa de confessione. Compilatio praesens*, ed. Jean Longère, CCCM, vol. 51 [Turnholt, 1980], c. 29, p. 32. On Peter of Poitiers, see Baldwin, *Masters, Princes, and Merchants*, 1:33–34, 2:23–24). To remain and make no effort toward restitution was to be complicit and could lead to the wife's damnation. Mary of Oignies had a pathetic vision of the damnation of her own mother, an otherwise pious woman, who made no effort to restore her husband's ill-gotten goods (see Thomas of Cantimpré, "Supplementum ad Vitam S. Mariae Oigniacensis," *AA SS*, June, 5:576). On the question of the usurer's wife, see Baldwin, *Masters, Princes, and Merchants*, 1:296–311, 2:204–211, esp. 1:305–306, and Sharon Farmer, "Persuasive Voices: Clerical Images of Medieval Wives," *Speculum* 61 (1986): 531–532.

tion of whether a wife can give alms against her husband's wishes, however, he concedes that she can distribute them from her paraphernalia, if she has one, or from the household provisions that are under her care, in accordance with her husband's resources and the needs of the poor. He justifies this breach in masculine authority as follows:

> And she should always shape her consciousness [*conscientiam*] so that she would not displease her husband in his heart, although perhaps he would sometimes prohibit [an act] by mouth: for husbands are accustomed to make a prohibition to their wives absolutely, so that they may thus restrain them from the excess which they suspect, but not entirely. Also she can shape her consciousness according to the condition and the misery of the poor, knowing that if her husband saw them, it would please him in every way that she made alms for him. If, however, consciousness should proclaim utterly and precisely to the wife that an act displeases her husband and thus would scandalize him, let her put aside that consciousness if she can; if not, however, she ought not to, and let her grieve that she cannot give [these alms].[185]

Others likewise resolve that a wife is entitled to give moderate alms, even if she knows that her husband would be displeased. Not equal to Raymond's bravery, however, they stipulate that she must not go against his *expressed* command.[186]

What the confessors are advancing is nothing less than an advanced course in deep reading. The distinction between tacit and expressed inaugurates the wife into the slippery distinction between blamelessness in the external forum and blameworthiness in the internal forum. Raymond's distinction between heart and mouth is, perhaps, the truer one, but more precarious still. The husband's expressed word condemns the wife's action in the external forum; but his heart ultimately vindicates her action in the internal forum. Raymond was thus empowering the wife to ignore the dross of outer verbiage and read the inner language of the heart, much as God does.

But the husband need not regard a wife's abilities in this area in so

---

[185] "Et debet semper sibi conformare conscientiam, quod non displiceat marito in corde, licet forte aliquando prohibuerit ore: solent enim mariti facere prohibitionem vxoribus absolute, vt sic temperent eas, non a toto, sed ab excessu, quem suspicantur. potest etiam formare sibi conscientiam ex qualitate, et miseria pauperis, cogitans quod si maritus illum videret, omnibus modis placeret ei, quod sibi faceret eleemosynam. Si autem omnino, et praecise dictat ipsi vxori conscientia, quod viro displicet, et scandelizatur inde, deponat conscientiam illam, si potest; sin autem, non debet, et doleat, quia non potest dare" (Raymond of Peñafort, *Summa de poenitentia* 2.8.9., p. 252).

[186] William of Rennes answers that a wife does not sin even if she knows her husband would be displeased at her alms, provided that she gives moderately, does not go against his expressed prohibition, and avoids scandalizing him (ibid. 2.8.9, gloss l, ad v. *displicet, et scandalizatur*, p. 252); cf. John of Freiburg, *Summa confessorum* 2.8.28, fol. 95r.

exalted a light, and probably did not. What looks like spiritual discernment from one vantage resembles female deception from another. Moreover, Thomas of Chobham, whom we have seen to be especially solicitous that female appearance be harnessed in favor of the debt, actively encourages his female penitents to use their sexuality in order to move their husbands to good works and to obtain alms.[187] This advice is in keeping with the time-honored tradition whereby wives were expected to effect the conversion of their husbands, a tradition already present in the earliest hagiographical treatments of spiritual marriage.[188] But Thomas's explicit sexualization of female influence would invariably strengthen antifeminist stereotypes, which become particularly rife from the thirteenth century onward.[189] Both the Wife of Bath and the seductive alms-seeking wife were seemingly prepared to mobilize their sexuality for cash.

Clerical efforts to blur the margins between a wife's spiritual efforts and her sexual duties further suggest that both are essentially perceived as appendixes to the full life: the life of the male. The secular wives' manuals, perhaps taking their lead from this prejudicial impulse in the confessors' manuals, show a marked tendency to recast female spiritual endeavors within the narrow margin of masculine sinfulness. Hence, *The Book of the Knight of the Tower* complacently states:

> The good that she dothe appeaseth the yre of god. . . . For the good that she dothe supporteth the euylle and mysdedes of her husbond. . . . And therfor it is good and necessary to an euyl man to haue a good wyf of holy lyf / And the more that the good wyf knoweth her husbond more felon and cruel / and grete synnar / the more she ought to make gretter abstynences and good dedes for the loue of god.[190]

[187] Thomas of Chobham, *Summa confessorum* 7.2.15, pp. 375–376.

[188] See chapter 2, esp. the section entitled "Virginal Marriages and Didactic Hagiography: The Affirmation of the Spiritual Bond." Pope Boniface's letter to Queen Æthelburh as cited by Bede, is one of the most famous and explicit statements of the church's expectations for the wife (*Ecclesiastical History* 2.11, pp. 172–175).

[189] For a more optimistic reading of Thomas of Chobham's advice and potential impact, see Farmer, "Persuasive Voices," pp. 538–542. For the growth of misogynistic literature in this period, see Wilson and Makowski, *Wykked Wyves and the Woes of Marriage*, chap. 4., pp. 109–161.

[190] William Caxton, trans., *The Book of the Knight of the Tower* c. 100, ed. M. Y. Offord *EETS*, supp. ser., no. 2 (London, 1971), p. 133. Also see Christine de Pisan, *The Treasure of the City of Ladies or the Book of the Three Virtues*, trans. Sarah Lawson (Harmondsworth, Middlesex, 1985), pt. 1, c. 12, pp. 63–64. The subordination of female spirituality to male needs is by no means restricted to married women. John Coakley analyzes the way in which the female charges of mendicant confessors made up for masculine inadequacies through certain supernatural services (see "Gender and the Authority of Friars: The Significance of Holy Women for Thirteenth-Century Franciscans and Dominicans," *Church History* 60 (1991): 445–460, esp. pp. 454–456.

As wives became progressively subordinated to their husbands and the potential gap between intention and action widened, women learned to identify with their intentions as the part they more truly owned. The conjugal debt had always served as a preliminary exercise in this kind of discernment. In theory, this would be true for men and women alike. The taint of conjugal sex was never entirely dissipated, and both canonists and theologians, in line with Augustinian thinking, were quick to reassure the party rendering the debt that he or she would be credited with the good of continence. But, as Georges Duby contends, spiritual directors encouraged their female charges particularly to dissociate themselves from the sex act and focus their *amor* on their spiritual bridegroom.[191] Yet even without such explicit counsel there is reason to suppose that married women from the twelfth century onward would draw more comfort from the distinction between rendering and exacting than their husbands did. As the taboos surrounding the female body progressively gave way to the exigencies of the debt and women were more frequently expected to adorn themselves in order to make themselves acceptable for rendering, neither their appearance nor even their actions were necessarily reliable representations of their spiritual state. Good intentions were the only bulwark against sin.

The increased emphasis on intentionality may have permitted a majority of wives to live peaceably with their sexual destiny. But for an ascetical minority, there is reason to believe that identification with their intentions actually renewed their commitment to chastity. The clue to such labyrinthine reasoning is close at hand. In this period of fervent lay asceticism when married women alone were, in theory, restrained from flamboyant acts of self-divestment, the inward-looking gaze would alert them to the one promise they could make to God that was unassailable: they could vow never to exact the debt.

We have already met with this one-sided effort at chastity in a number of different contexts. A person who unilaterally entered a monastery and was subsequently recalled by the abandoned spouse was generally advised to render and not exact the debt.[192] This same counsel was meted out to a penitent guilty of a secret sin such as incest or adultery.[193] But, although prescriptions for this kind of sex-

---

[191] Duby, "Que sait-on de l'amour en France au XIIe siècle?" *The Zaharoff Lecture for 1982–1983* (Oxford, 1983), esp. pp. 9–11.

[192] Cf. Panormitanus's advice to an individual who unilaterally vows chastity (*Lectura*, for X.3.32.1, no. 6; for X.3.32.3, no. 4, 5:156r and 157r).

[193] See Huguccio, for C.27 q.2 c.21 ad v. *nec quondam* and ad v. *dimittere*, Roman, ed., "*Summa* d'Huguccio," pp. 772 and 774; for C.27 q.2 c.30 dpc ad v. *licet ei vel adultere*, p. 787; cf. Thomas of Chobham's advice to the adulteress (*Summa confessorum* 7.2.9.3, p. 363).

ual reticence were frequently punitive, when the same behavior was cheerfully and voluntarily assumed, it generally ranked high in the hierarchy of merit. Indeed, one of the common theological understandings of Paul's admonition to have one's wife as if one had no wife was to render but not to exact the debt.[194] The merit would, of course, be increased if such a resolve was reinforced by a vow. But of even greater significance to the married woman is that it was widely maintained that this was the one vow that a husband could not recall.[195] Even so, by the time of John of Freiburg, the ethics of a one-sided vow had elicited a certain amount of criticism. According to John, while certain authorities (such as Peter of Tarentaise and Raymond of Peñafort) argued that the vow could be sustained without the consent of the other, as each spouse was autonomous with regard to exacting the debt, the later Dominican theologians were inclined to discourage one-sided vows and perhaps even doubt their validity on the grounds that it was onerous for the other spouse always to seek the debt. Albert the Great goes so far as to condemn the stupidity of such a vow, which he believes should be dispensed by the bishop.[196] And yet John refrains from condemning the one-sided vow and even seems to acknowledge its merit.[197]

[194] *Glossa ordinaria* for the Bible, vol. 6, regarding 1 Cor. 7.29 ad v. *tanquam non habentes sint*, col. 254: "Quod vtique facit qui habens vxorem reddit, non exigit debitum: et qui propter infirmitatem propriam ducit vxorem, plangens potius: quia sine vxore esse non potuit, quam gaudens, quia duxit, et maxime quia pari consensu continentiam seruant. Gratiora sane coniugia iudicanda sunt, quae siue filiis procreatis, siue prole contempta continentiam pari consensu seruare poterunt." As this passage suggests, such temperance is second only to absolute continence in marriage. Also cf. C.33 q.5 c.5.

[195] Robert of Flamborough, *Liber poenitentialis* 2.3.18, p. 67; 2.3.21, p. 70. Robert puts such a vow on the same level as an absolute vow of chastity, thus denying that it can be commuted. Panormitanus says that a wife can make this vow to her own prejudice because it does not harm the husband's rights (*Lectura* for X.3.32.11, no. 5, 5:159v).

[196] "Sed de petitione debiti quidam dicunt quod potest vnus vouere sine consensu alterius quod non peccat: quia in hoc vterque sui iuris est. Alii dicunt probabilius quod non: quia nimis onerosum fieret matrimonium semper alteri quem oporteret subire verecundiam in petendo debitum. Sed Petrus sentit cum prima opinione scilicet quod possit vouere quod non petat. Et idem sentit Raymondus. . . . Albertus dicit idem quod Thomas scilicet quod non debet aliquis hoc vouere. Addit etiam quod si vouerit: credo etiam quod per episcopum potest dispensari. Et tunc arguendus est de stultitia et penitentia iniuncta debet absolui a voti obligatione" (John of Freiburg, *Summa confessorum* 1.8.43, fol. 21v).

[197] This may be inferred from the following *quaestio* in which John asks whether it is a mortal sin to vow chastity without the permission of the other. He only cites Peter of Tarentaise, who distinguishes between a vow not to render and a vow not to exact. With respect to the latter, Peter not only attests to its licitness, but possibly perceives it as a strategy that could contribute to a person's salvation (although the verb "saluari" is somewhat ambiguous in this context): "quia saluari potest in eo quod est licitum scilicet in non exigendo" (*Summa confessorum* 1.8.44, fol. 21v).

And so, in a period when the extension of the husband's authority in conjunction with the new emphasis on the conjugal debt had potentially devastating ramifications for female spiritual autonomy, these very constraints stimulated spiritual creativity. The inward-looking gaze proved to be an important stepping-stone toward mysticism, while simultaneously discerning a new motive and meaning for chastity. Thus marriage incalculably acted as a powerful leaven for female spirituality, fostering a situation in which the spirituality of married women was to break through its boundaries and ravish the Christian world.

FIVE

SPIRITUAL MARRIAGE AND THE
PENITENTIAL ETHOS

Another time a certain noblewoman ran after him [St. Francis] as he was passing by, and he was moved by her weariness and her panting breath, and asked her what she desired. "Pray for me, father," she replied, "for my husband prevents me from carrying out my salutary resolutions, and hinders me much in the service of Christ!" "Go, daughter," he answered, "for thou shalt speedily have consolation of him; and tell him in the name of Almighty God and in my name, that now is the time of salvation, and later shall come the time of justice." Hearing these words from his wife, the husband changed his ways forthwith, and promised to live continently.[1]

JACOBUS DE VORAGINE'S dramatic condensation of this incident is derived from Thomas of Celano's second life of St. Francis. Thomas himself reports at greater length that, when the wife returned from her encounter with the saint, she found her husband a "changed man"—who gently volunteered: " 'Let us serve God and save our souls in our home.' " The wife promptly responded: " 'It seems to me that continence should be established in the soul as a kind of foundation and that the rest of the virtues should be built upon it.' " Thomas wraps up his tale with a bittersweet reflection:

Happy woman, who thus could soften her lord unto eternal life! In her is fulfilled the words of the Apostle: "The unbelieving husband is sanctified by the believing wife" (1 Cor. 7.14). But such people, if I may use a popular expression, can be counted on one's fingers today.[2]

---

[1] "Transeunti sibi aliquando mulier quaedam nobilis concitu gradu occurrit, cujus lassitudinem et interclusos auhelitus [sic] miseratus, quidnam requireret, inquisivit. Et illa: ora pro me, pater, quia salubre propositum, quod concepi, viro impediente non exsequor, sed in servitio Christi mihi plurimum adversatur. Cui ille: vade, filia, quia cito de eo sonsolationem [sic] recipies, et ex parte Dei omnipotentis et mea sibi denunties, quod nunc est tempus salutis, postmodum aequitatis. Qua denuntiante vir subito immutatur et continentiam pollicetur" (Th. Graesse, ed., Legenda aurea, 3d ed. [1890; reprt. Osnabrück, 1965], pp. 664–665; trans. Ryan and Ripperger, Golden Legend, p. 600).

[2] Thomas of Celano's second life of St. Francis, 9.38 Analecta Franciscana 10 (1941): 154–155; trans. Placid Hermann, St. Francis of Assisi: First and Second Life of St. Francis (Chicago, 1963; reprt. 1988), p. 171.

In spite of Thomas's forgivable cynicism, his anecdote brings home how deeply ingrained chastity was in female religious practice, albeit at a time when the pastoral kerygma was generally becoming more liberal. In the twelfth century, there were only two celebrated incidents of spiritual marriage, in both of which it was the chastity of the husband that was extolled. By the time that Thomas was writing, however, it was already clear that the motif of spiritual marriage had returned to women after centuries of exile. The canonization of Empress Cunegund in 1200, from this perspective, heralds its timely reintroduction. Not only does Innocent III's bull seem to signify a veritable celebration of the newly refurbished spiritualized view of marriage, but official recognition returns the slighted queen to the side of her celestial consort.

The Laity and Penitential Practices

If spiritual marriage is again depicted as figuring powerfully in female piety, it nevertheless arises from an entirely new and different ethos. Intrinsic to the question of lay chastity in the high and late Middle Ages is the spread of penitential practices that occurred largely through the influence of the mendicant orders. We have seen early indications of this orientation during the course of the reform of the church. At the end of the eleventh century, Bernold of Constance makes his tantalizingly brief reference to lay penitential communities in Germany. Meersseman and Adda also document a similar group in northern Italy that arose in the last quarter of the twelfth century.[3] But it is really not until the thirteenth century that the penitential movement comes to fruition.

The "carnality" or sexual activity of the laity was one of the major factors that had enabled the clergy to refuse them a more active and estimable role in the church. While this negative perspective was present throughout the Middle Ages, heretical pressure and, later, the naturalistic trend in mendicant theology wrested a certain number of conflicted concessions out of the church that reconciled lay life more fully with the life of the spirit. On the one hand, in 1175 Alexander III stated that sexual abstinence on the numerous fast days was a counsel as opposed to a precept.[4] On the other hand, after a few false starts

[3] Meersseman and Adda, "Pénitents ruraux," pp. 346–365.

[4] Vauchez, *La spiritualité*, p. 128. For the penances set by Burchard for nonobservance of periods of sexual abstinence, see *Decretorum libri viginti*, *Corrector* 19.5, under "De abusione conjugii," *PL* 140, cols. 959–960. All of these old prohibitions were still included by Gratian in C.33 q.4 c.1–11, but his dpc 11, discussed in chapter 4,

(as for example when Alexander III inadvertently pushed the unnervingly zealous, but essentially orthodox, Waldo into the heretical camp)[5] the papacy officially recognized and sanctioned certain pious lay movements. The Humiliati, who in twelfth-century papal documents were lumped together with the heretics, were reintegrated into the body of the faithful in 1197 by Innocent III, who wrote letters approving the various *proposita* that the different groups submitted for living in the world.[6] Especially significant is Innocent's approval of the Franciscan order. By this act, the pope elevated to institutional respectability a cluster of practices—such as mendicancy, manual labor, and the *vita apostolica*—that had arisen principally in lay penitential movements, both orthodox and heterodox. Moreover, the Franciscans were responsible for the diffusion of the *Memoriale propositi* (ca. 1221): a penitential rule of life intended for pious laypeople still living at home. Penitents—whether married, celibate, or widowed—were given a distinct dress, and were expected to observe strict regulations with regard to fasting and prayer. Entrance into the order, by a vow made to a priest and involving either tonsure or the imposition of a veil, was binding for life. Individuals adhering to such a rule, under supervision of either of the mendicant orders, became known as third-order penitents or tertiaries—the first two orders being the friars themselves and the female communities living by their rule.[7]

Women especially swelled the ranks of the third order, although married women required their husbands' permission to join.[8] But

---

anticipates Alexander III's relaxation of these regulations. Also see G. G. Meersseman, ed., *Dossier de l'ordre de la pénitence au XIIIe siècle*, Spicilegium Friburgense, vol. 7 (Fribourg, 1961), p. 280n.6.

[5] See the report from *The Chronicle of Laon* in Wakefield and Evans, trans., *Heresies of the High Middle Ages*, p. 203.

[6] These early *proposita* do not survive, but the papal letters do. Innocent divided the Humiliati into three orders: the first two were celibates (the first being clergy and the second laity) who lived in religious communities. Only the third order lived at home with their families. See Vauchez, *La spiritualité*, pp. 127–128; Brenda Bolton, "Sources for the Early History of the Humiliati," in *Materials, Sources, and Methods of Ecclesiastical History*, ed. Derek Baker, Studies in Church History, no. 11 (Oxford, 1975), pp. 126–127. The standard source regarding the Humiliati, with documents in the appendix, is still Luigi Zanoni's *Gli Umiliati nei loro rapporti con l'Eresia, l'industria della lana ed i Comuni nei secoli XII e XIII*, Bibliotheca historica italica, series altera, 2 (Milan, 1911; reprt. Rome, 1970).

[7] See Meersseman, ed., *Dossier*, introd., pp. 5–21. The *Memoriale* is printed on pp. 92–112 and translated in *St. Francis of Assisi: Writings and Early Biographies*, ed. Marion A. Habig, 3d rev. ed. (Chicago, 1973), pp. 168–175.

[8] "Mulieres viros habentes non recipiantur nisi de consensu et licentia maritorum" (*Memoriale* c. 33, in Meersseman, ed., *Dossier*, p. 110).

female initiative in instigating lay religious movements is more easily discerned in the development of the Beguine movement in the
Low Countries. These women, living either in communities or at
home, were likewise committed to the *vita apostolica*: they supported themselves by their own labor (which was very often hospital
work) and pledged themselves to lives of poverty and chastity without taking a solemn lifetime vow, as was required by the tertiary
orders. Jacques de Vitry (ca. 1160/70–1240), who was something of a
religious voyeur and has left us a number of eyewitness accounts of
certain alternative forms of religious expression that were developing
in his day, makes note of the early Humiliati, and of the Franciscan
movement. He was, however, particularly familiar with the primitive
Beguine movement that was centered on the charismatic figure of
Mary of Oignies (ca. 1177–1213) in the diocese of Liège. Jacques had
come to Oignies from his studies at Paris precisely because of Mary's
reputation, and, even though he eventually became her confessor,
Jacques continually referred to her as his *mater spiritualis*. Indeed,
Jacques saw the *mulieres sanctae* as a valuable tool against heresy as
well as a practical option for the "surplus" and, hence, unmarriage-
able woman who was becoming more of a factor in high and late
medieval society. Hence, his biography of Mary—an important work
from a historical standpoint, as it was the first biography of a female
mystic and thus inaugurated a new kind of hagiography—was intended as a propagandistic tool aimed at gaining official recognition
for these women as an independent female order. Because of Lateran
IV's prohibition against new orders, the most he received was verbal
approbation from Honorius III that the Beguines could continue to
live in common, assisting one another by mutual exhortation.[9]

---

[9] Verbal recognition was formally corroborated by Gregory IX (a friend of Jacques's)
in the bull *Gloriam virginalem*. This was not, however, equivalent to the rule that
Jacques had hoped for. The main source for the early Beguine movement is Jacques de
Vitry's *Vita Mariae Oigniacensis*, *AA SS* June, 5:547–572. Cf. Thomas de Cantimpré's
Supplementum, pp. 572–581. Also note Jacques's important letter of 1216 (describing
the Humiliati of Lombardy and Umbria), as well as his descriptions of contemporary
religious movements, such as the Franciscans (R.B.C. Huygens, ed., *Lettres de Jacques
de Vitry* [Leiden, 1960], Ep. 1, pp. 71–78; Jacques de Vitry, *Historia Occidentalis*, ed. J. F.
Hinnebusch, Spicilegium Friburgense, vol. 17 [Fribourg, 1972], esp. c.15, 28–29, 32, pp.
116–118, 144–148, 158–163). For his involvement with the Beguine movement, see
E. W. McDonnell, *The Beguines and Beghards in Medieval Culture, with Special
Emphasis on the Belgian Scene* (New Brunswick, N.J., 1954), pp. 20–39; Brenda Bolton,
"*Mulieres Sanctae*," in *Women in Medieval Society*, ed. Stuard, pp. 141–158, esp. 144–
149 (Bolton's article also provides an excellent overview of the difficulties that con-
fronted a woman with a religious vocation in this period); eadem, "*Vitae Matrum*: A
Further Aspect of the *Frauenfrage*," in *Medieval Women*, ed. Baker, pp. 253–273; and
Dennis Devlin, "Feminine Lay Piety in the High Middle Ages: The Beguines," in

What concerns us most nearly, however, is the role chastity plays among these diverse penitential groups—especially their married members. In the time of the early church, public penitents, who were generally guilty of a serious offense such as adultery, murder, or apostasy, were expected to observe absolute sexual continence.[10] Such rigors had given way to a milder practice in the high Middle Ages, although the tertiaries following the *Memoriale* upheld the traditional periods of sexual abstinence that had ceased to be compulsory for the average lay person. There was also the expectation that once a person was admitted to the order, even if married, he or she would not make a second marriage after the death of his or her spouse.[11] Other related groups, such as the Poor Catholics or the Poor Lombards, may have required a stricter sexual code.[12] Certainly, there are clear references to total continence among various pious lay movements. When tracing the earliest period of the Humiliati, for example, Zanoni describes how a natural family grouping with its bonds between husband and wife, parents and children, was transformed into a quasi-monastic unit. In one of the few remaining documents from the early

---

Distant Echoes, ed. Nichols and Shank, pp. 183–196. Most scholars stress the "spontaneous" emergence of the Beguine movement. Carol Neel, however, argues that this misconception was purposefully perpetrated by Jacques de Vitry's life of Mary, an interpretation that further emphasizes the work's originality. Neel analyzes the Beguine movement in terms of its natural evolution from Cistercian spirituality (see "The Origins of the Beguines," in *Sisters and Workers in the Middle Ages*, ed. Bennett, pp. 240–260).

[10] See chapter 2, n. 66, above.

[11] Meersseman, ed., *Dossier*, introd., p. 20. Cf. the *Regula* of the Militia of the Virgin (1261): "vivant . . . et in coniugali vel perpetua castitate, si non habentes uxores sine uxoribus volerint permanere" (c. 51, p. 302).

[12] The *Propositum* of the Poor Catholics (1208), stipulates that members should preserve virginity or continual chastity: "virginitatem et castimoniam continuam inviolabiliter conservando" (Meersseman, ed., *Dossier* c. 9, p. 283). The second *Propositum* of the Poor Lombards (1212) maintains the same standard of chastity, but also attempts to forbid (or, failing that, to monitor) all contact with women: "Continentiam perpetuam et castimoniam vel virginitatem inviolabiliter conservando suspectum mulierum consortium devitando, ut nemo nostrum solus ad solam, nec etiam ad loquendum, nisi audientibus aut videntibus legitimis testibus et certis personis accedat" (c. 9, p. 289). On the other hand, it is difficult to know what level of chastity is implied. In Duane Osheim's examination of the *conversi* and *conversae* of Tuscany, who continued to cohabit with their spouses, only three couples made explicit reference to chastity: one promised "castitatem honestam," a second felt it necessary to say that they had no intention of professing chastity ("non intendent per hec verba continentiam profiteri," did this imply that others did?), and a third promised "castitatem matrimonialem." Osheim concludes that it is almost impossible to know for certain what these words mean since the only other explicit references to chastity were made by widows or single persons ("Conversion, *Conversi*, and the Christian Life," pp. 382–383. Also see the discussion of this problem in the Introduction).

stages of the movement, a certain Marchesius and his wife Merida pledged perpetual continence, while their household likewise promised to live chastely under them.[13]

Chastity loomed particularly large in the Beguine milieu.[14] According to Jacques de Vitry, when Liège was attacked by Henry I, duke of Brabant (3–7 May 1212) women flung themselves in sewers and the river, choosing what they believed to be assured death, rather than risk being violated.[15] Moreover, in the prologue to Mary's *vita* he describes to Bishop Fulk of Toulouse, to whom the work is dedicated, the various groups of women who participated in the Beguine movement: virgins, matrons, widows, and married women pledged to chastity.

> You also saw holy women (and you rejoiced), serving the Lord devoutly in matrimony, raising their children in fear of God, guarding an honest marriage and an immaculate marriage bed . . . [F]or many, abstaining from licit embraces with the consent of their husbands, and leading a celibate and truly Angelic life were so much the more worthy of the greater crown, the more they were placed in the fire and did not burn.[16]

There is much in the lay spirituality of this period that is characteristically female: eucharistic devotion, mystical raptures, and extreme asceticism (of which a preoccupation with chastity was an important part) were areas in which women, especially laywomen, were leaders. Furthermore, as Caroline Bynum has remarked, masculine religious experience, which so frequently involved dramatic conversions and reversals (as, for example, the renunciation of power and wealth) also lent itself to a gender reversal. Thus in the act of renunciation, men tended to identify themselves with the weakness of the female in relation to God. This identification paved the way for a new appreciation of female spirituality. Women, in fact, came to represent a liminal state for men—femininity was perceived as a kind

---

[13] This document, dated 7 February 1218, is cited in full in Zanoni, *Gli Umiliati*, p. 56 n. 2. Because so few of the earliest records for the Humiliati remain, Bolton raises the question of whether there was a deliberate effort to suppress such traces, especially since Jacques de Vitry claims that most of them were literate ("Sources for the Early History of the Humiliati," pp. 127–128).

[14] McDonnell, *Beguines and Beghards*, pp. 130–131, 159.

[15] *AA SS*, June, 5:548. As it happened, God permitted none of them to die, according to Jacques.

[16] "Vidisti (et gavisus es) sanctas etiam mulieres, in matrimonio Domino servientes devote, filios suos in timore Dei erudientes, honestas nuptias et thorum immaculatum custodientes . . . multae enim ex maritorum consensu a liciti [*sic*] amplexibus abstinentes, caelibem, et vere Angelicam vitam ducentes, tanto majori corona dignae sunt, quanto in igne positae non arserunt" (ibid., pp. 547–548).

of "boundary" condition to which men might aspire.[17] This observation compares well with Vauchez's view that women, seen as weak and morally or physically inferior, were, because of the resurgence of the penitential ideal with its emphasis on suffering and self-mortification, in the best position to be saved.[18]

But despite this new appreciation of women on a spiritual plane (which was by no means universal), the institutional hierarchy was in constant anxiety about groups of pious laypeople—especially women. The Beguines as an unaffiliated group of laywomen, not bound by any rule, came in for more than their share of abuse. Jacques de Vitry speaks of "certain shameless men, hostile to all religion, maliciously defaming the religion of these . . . women."[19] Nor does the situation improve after his time. Efforts were made to legislate on private vows of chastity—one council in particular tried to insist that women who took private vows, to be fulfilled in their homes, should be at least forty.[20] Indeed the Beguines were frequently persecuted as heretics. The very fact that one possible derivation for their name is from *Albigensian* (another term for Cathar) attests to this.[21]

All of these pious lay movements sprang up spontaneously and

[17] For an insightful assessment of some of the central issues in female spirituality of the high Middle Ages, see Caroline Bynum's *Holy Feast and Holy Fast*. For the discussion of male renunciation and use of gender reversal, see pp. 282–288. Also see eadem, "Women's Stories, Women's Symbols," pp. 109–112, and ". . . And Woman His Humanity: Female Imagery in the Religious Writings of the Later Middle Ages," in *Gender and Religion: On the Complexity of Symbols*, ed. Bynum et al. (Boston, 1986) pp. 268–269, 277–280.

[18] Vauchez, *Les laïcs*, p. 254.

[19] "Quosdam impudicos et totius religionis inimicos homines, . . . mulierum religionem malitiose infamantes" (*AA SS*, June, 5:548).

[20] "Item, juxta prioris statuta Concilii prohibemus; ne mulierculae, quae votum continentiae emiserunt, mutantes habitum saecularem nec tamen aliter certae regulae se adstringentes, per vicos passim discurrant [it then goes on to outline the way such women should live and to insist on their submission to their parish priest] . . . quia juvencularum Beginarum lapsus frequens, et evidens, statum relgionis deformat, et plurimos scandalizat, statuimus, ut nulla de caetero in earum numerum admittatur, nisi XL aetatis suae annum excesserit" (Council of Mainz, 1261, in Mansi, ed., *Sacrorum conciliorum nova et amplissima collectio*, 23:1089). See McDonnell's discussion of this and other legislation surrounding private vows of chastity (*Beguines and Beghards*, pp. 95–96, 507–508).

[21] Lambert, *Medieval Heresy*, pp. 174–181, 204–205. An overliteral reading of the Beguine Marguerite Porete of Hainault's mystical work *The Mirror of Simple Souls* allowed the Inquisition to draw the wrongheaded conclusion that the Beguines were harboring an antinomian heresy which they christened "The Free Spirit." If a coherent heresy of the Free Spirit ever did exist, it was probably born at the Council of Vienne in 1312 where *Ad nostrum* was drawn up for the purpose of persecuting the Beguines. See Robert E. Lerner's study, *The Heresy of the Free Spirit in the Later Middle Ages* (Berkeley and Los Angeles, 1972).

generally had to fight for official recognition and pastoral care. Although the penitential movement among the laity proved irrepressible, the hierarchy was nevertheless riddled with profound misgivings. They especially looked askance at the female contingent, alarmed by the extremities to which their strict asceticism led them.[22] Consistent with the fact that the penitential movement was born at least partially out of a desire to transcend the mere lay state (which had so often been roundly despised) or even out of a sense of rivalry with the clergy, women undoubtedly went the extra mile. Female zeal in the spiritual realm allegedly placed considerable demands on the clergy, which the latter group met begrudgingly—if at all. Meersseman cites abundant legislation restricting the extent of association between mendicants and pious women. Beguines (a term that seems to be used as a catchall for any pious, extraregular woman) are especially singled out.[23] But the mendicant orders were also eager to divest themselves of all responsibility toward the third order. Bonaventure, though endorsing the view that the third order was specifically founded by Francis himself,[24] constructs an elaborate twelve-point justification supporting the Franciscans' efforts to disassociate themselves from the tertiaries. He particularly vituperates the time investment such lay charges require, the potential for sexual as well as other kinds of scandal, and the confusions and abuses arising from their quasi-clerical status.[25]

Apart from an ongoing concern that familiarity with women leads to scandal, a major difficulty which ecclesiastical authorities generally share with Bonaventure concerns just how to categorize penitents: were they members of the regular clergy or were they laity?[26]

---

[22] Caroline Bynum has recently suggested that the very extremity of female piety in this period was a reaction to mainstream theology and pastoral counsel that urged moderation (see *Holy Feast and Holy Fast*, pp. 237–244). Also note that the lives of St. Francis not only attempt to de-emphasize the extremities of Francis's own penitential practice, but downplay the Franciscans' mission of calling the laity to penance. See Cook, "Fraternal and Lay Images of St. Francis," pp. 266–268. For a discussion of penitential practices in the later Middle Ages, see Kieckhefer, *Unquiet Souls*, pp. 139–149.

[23] Meersseman, ed., *Dossier*, introd., pp. 21–22; appendix, pp. 118–122.

[24] Bonaventure, *Legenda maior S. Francisci* 4.6, in *Analecta Franciscana* 10 (1941): 573–574.

[25] Meersseman, ed., *Dossier*, pp. 123–125.

[26] Hostiensis also takes up this problem. He resolves that if a man makes a vow of chastity with his wife into the hands of a bishop, remains single after her death, and renounces his property, he does qualify as a religious (*Summa aurea* 3.2–3; Meersseman reproduces Hostiensis's argument in *Dossier*, pp. 308–309). Also see Osheim, who addresses the haziness of the quasi-regular status of *conversi* who remain in their own homes in mid-thirteenth-century Tuscany ("Conversion, *Conversi*, and the Christian Life," pp. 369–371, 385–386).

Were they sincere or were their motives for membership tainted by the desire to gain the valuable benefits of clergy? Certainly Bonaventure was not alone in attributing such mixed motives to them.[27] But many of the difficulties Bonaventure raises are prompted by the clergy's profound sense of superiority over the laity and a jealous desire to retain this advantage. The Franciscan movement was, for example, very quick to lose its lay character. Salimbene was admitted to the order in 1239 (only thirteen years after Francis's death) and immediately began railing against the proposition that laymen should ever have any authority over clerics. In fact, there was no lay minister general from the year 1239, and by 1260 the clerical contingent overwhelmed the lay contingent both numerically and ideologically.[28] If the Franciscans were unwilling to share their clerical privilege with their lay brethren, who at least had left the world and vowed celibacy, their aversion would be even more marked with respect to pious laypeople who were still living in the world and still paying the conjugal debt. The temptation to remake the threatening lay contingent in their own image was irresistible. In fact, this process of co-optation bore fruit: by the early fourteenth century there were cloistered religious communities adhering to the third order, reflecting the pressures exerted upon lay groups to become regularized.[29]

Despite the undercurrents of resistance from ecclesiastical authorities and elements of competition between lay and clerical piety,

[27] Hostiensis discusses the way in which "rustici" use their undeserved status as a tax dodge (Meersseman, ed., *Dossier*, p. 308).

[28] See Lawrence C. Landini, *The Causes of the Clericalization of the Order of Friars Minor, 1209–1260* (Ph.D. diss. ad Lauream in Facultate Historiae Ecclesiasticae Pontificiae Universitatis Gregorianae, Chicago, 1968), esp. pp. 103–107, 121, 123–126, 140–143.

[29] Vauchez, *Les laïcs*, p. 112. Angelina Corbara of Marsciano, who participated in a spiritual marriage, is purported to have founded the first enclosed order of Franciscan tertiaries—at least in Italy. See Luigi Jacobilli, *Die selige Angelina von Marsciano* c. 11, trans. into German by a sister of Ewigen Abbey (Dülmen, 1919), pp. 65–69. Daniela Rando's explication of a dispute that occurred between 1228 and 1229 within the hospital order of Ognisanti in Treviso indicates how divisive the question of chastity could be ("*Laicus religiosus* tra strutture civili ed ecclesiastiche: l'ospedale di Ognisanti in Treviso [sec. XIII]," *Studi medievali*, ser. 3, 24,2 [1983]: 617–656). The community was divided between two groups: the *fratres et sorores extrinseci* and the *dominae inclusae*. The former group was married but lived with their respective spouses *honeste* (the precise meaning of which is unclear; see p. 621). They seemed to take some of their meals at the hospital and some at home, and likewise divided their sleeping time between the two places. The female group of *inclusae*, on the other hand, lived on the premises but were not, as yet, a stable order with vows (pp. 635–636). The court case basically resulted from the efforts of the *inclusae* to subordinate the lay minister of the *extrinseci* (whom they accused of leading scandalous and irregular lives) to a religious prior. The case was resolved when the two groups were divided. Sometime between 1229 and 1248, moreover, the *inclusae* became a regular order with vows (pp. 639–644).

conceptions of sanctity changed under the pressure of increasing lay activity in the realm of religion. Penitential life laundered secular life, especially matrimonial sex, sufficiently that the laity was admitted into the hierarchy of saints in an unprecedented way. Until the end of the twelfth century, married individuals who partook of normal marital relations—who were not founders of monastic institutions and had missed out on martyrdom—had practically no chance of being considered saints. Most saints were of noble birth and drawn from the clergy: missionaries and bishops tended to figure largely in the church's reckoning. So clerical an orientation necessarily meant that women were grossly underrepresented as saints; they were barred not only from the priesthood, but also from distinguishing themselves through an active role in the church. Cloistered nuns generally lacked a vehicle for visibility: an obvious prerequisite for sainthood. Moreover, the Gregorian reform had had disastrous effects on the number of female saints.[30]

Patterns of sanctity underwent a dramatic change in the thirteenth century. Vauchez cites the canonization of the pious merchant St. Homebon of Cremona (d. 1197) as a sociological breakthrough on a number of different levels. Although Innocent III's bull of canonization made no mention of it, Homebon was married with two children.[31] Nevertheless, Innocent, who launched the Albigensian Crusade, initiated Lateran IV, and recognized the need for the two major mendicant orders, saw the expedience in officially approving the life of the average layperson in order to lessen the attraction of heretical validation.

There is an especially impressive surge in the number of female saints in this period. According to Weinstein and Bell, the percentage of female saints rose steadily from 11.8 in the twelfth century to 22.6 in the thirteenth, 23.4 in the fourteenth, and 27.7 in the fifteenth.[32] Although the overwhelming majority of saints, officially recognized or not, were still male, this was no longer the case among sanctified members of the laity, where female saints constituted the majority.[33]

[30] This relates to the reduction in number of female monasteries that resulted from the monastic reform over the eleventh and twelfth century as discussed in chapter 3. See Schulenburg, "Sexism and the Celestial Gynaeceum," esp. pp. 119–120, 124–127.

[31] Vauchez, *La sainteté*, pp. 412–413.

[32] Weinstein and Bell, *Saints and Society*, pp. 220–221; cf. Michael Goodich, "The Contours of Female Piety in Later Medieval Hagiography," *Church History* 50 (1981): 20–21; idem, *Vita Perfecta: The Ideal of Sainthood in the Thirteenth Century*, Monographien zur Geschichte des Mittelalters, vol. 25 (Stuttgart, 1982), p. 173.

[33] Vauchez's study of papal canonizations between 1198 and 1431 indicates that although the vast majority of processes undertaken were for men (81.7 percent male compared with 18.3 percent female), with respect to the laity, there are 58.8 percent

This development is largely owing to the rise of penitential practices and women's affinity for such practices. Furthermore, married
women, particularly those who had at one time been sexually active,
appear to have made the best penitents.

The Sources: The Confessor and His Charge

With the two exceptions of Margaret Beaufort and Margery Kempe,
the specific evidence concerning spiritual marriage is almost exclusively hagiographical in nature (see appendixes 5 and 6). As a result of
the centralization of canonization through the papacy in the thirteenth century, the sources for the high and later Middle Ages are
remarkably good when compared with those of earlier centuries. Official recognition required a *processus*—an elaborate inquiry into the
life of a prospective saint—and these frequently included testimonies of witnesses from among the individual saint's personal acquain-
tances.[34] Equally important, a prospective cult usually produced a
contemporary *vita*, and this was often written by the confessor or an
associate of the saint. Indeed the confessor frequently did double duty
on behalf of his penitent: not only was he entrusted with a potential
saint's posthumous reputation, but the task of recording the inspired
subject's revelations or teaching often fell to him.

As the saint becomes progressively more individualized, so does
the hagiographer. The symbiosis here is unmistakable: the confessor-
hagiographer who distinguished his penitent for veneration received
a certain amount of derivative glory himself.[35] But many of the hagiographers were learned and undoubtedly celebrated among their contemporaries, independent of their holy charges, and their separate
claims enhanced the credibility of the particular cult they were promoting. Just from the instances of spiritual marriage for the high and
late Middle Ages, a number of names stand out. Jacques de Vitry,
confessor and hagiographer of Mary of Oignies, studied theology at

processes for women compared with 41.2 percent processes for men. In the fourteenth
and first third of the fifteenth century, moreover, 71.4 percent of the processes were
undertaken on behalf of female saints. It is interesting, however, that female processes
have less chance of succeeding than male, underlining some of the tensions between
official sanctity and the *vox populi* (*La sainteté*, pp. 316–318).

[34] On the centralization of canonization, see ibid., pp. 25–39, 125–129; on the
processus, see pp. 50–67.

[35] See, for example, John Coakley's description of Raymond of Capua's relationship
with Catherine of Siena in "Friars as Confidants of Holy Women in Medieval Dominican Hagiography," in *Images of Sainthood in Medieval Europe,* ed. Renate Blumenfeld-
Kosinski and Timea Szell (Ithaca, N.Y., 1991), pp. 234–238.

Paris and was eventually made a cardinal in the Holy Land. Bridget of Sweden was surrounded by a shifting team of theologians, which included the retired bishop of Jaen, Alphonse of Pecha. These men were responsible for recording and assembling her revelations, as well as for writing her *vita*. John of Marienwerder, confessor, amanuensis, and ultimate hagiographer of Dorothea of Montau, was an eminent theologian.[36] Moreover, during her lifetime, he took the further caution of submitting her visions to the canonist John Reyman.

The high degree of theological sophistication among many of the hagiographers has particular bearing on the portrayal of married subjects. Although from the thirteenth century onward the manifestations of sanctity become more extraordinary—particularly from the standpoint of degrees of asceticism—hagiographers in general now felt constrained to depict their holy charges as complying with the norms of Christian marriage. Already in the twelfth century we can see this new solicitude projected backward to amend the possible errors of the past. Thus in later versions of St. Osyth's life, the presiding bishops require that she solicit her husband's consent before her consecration in religion.[37] The confessor's efforts to comply with current matrimonial norms was both programmatic and pragmatic. It was programmatic insofar as such efforts to dignify marriage complemented current pastoral trends. It was pragmatic in that it was essential for the hagiographer to address the individual saint's conduct during the dangerous years of sexual activity. If represented skillfully, such sexual minutiae could elicit modest plaudits for the part of a saint's career that was felt to be least distinguished, but in which the saint in question often spent a disproportionate amount of time.

The careful scrutiny to which the lives of the people in question were subjected provides us with more detailed information than ever before about sexual practice. But there are many difficulties in interpreting these sources. Pious behavior is inevitably realized within a larger discourse of sanctity with which the confessor would attempt

---

[36] On Jacques de Vitry's life and career, see Philipp Funk, *Jakob von Vitry: Leben und Werke* Beiträge zur Kulturgeschichte des Mittelalters und Renaissance, no. 3 (Leipzig and Berlin, 1909); on Bridget of Sweden's spiritual advisers and their role in producing the Brigittine corpus, see F. Vernet, "Brigitte de Suède," *DS*, vol. 1, cols. 1943–1958, esp. 1944–1946; also see Eric Colledge, "*Epistola solitarii ad reges*: Alphonse of Pecha as Organizer of Birgittine and Urbanist Propaganda," *Mediaeval Studies* 18 (1956): 19–49; on John of Marienwerder, see F. Hipler, "Johannes Marienwerder, der Beichtvater der seligen Dorothea von Montau," *Zeitschrift für die Geschichte und Altertumskunde Ermlands* 29 (1956): 1–92.

[37] Bethell, "The Lives of St. Osyth," pp. 87, 99.

to align his holy charge. Clerical advisers would be inclined to recast their subject's marriage into an exemplary mold, constructed around a veritable handbook of marital usage. But the confessor was hardly alone in these efforts. Action and narrative recital of action could not and did not exist independent of appropriate hagiographical structures. Female piety operated within this set of constraints. This is, perhaps, especially true with the heightened level of lay instruction that followed in the wake of Lateran IV, and with the increased dissemination of saints' lives. We can see both of these didactic influences at work in Margery Kempe's recital of her life. On the one hand, Margery and her husband, John, show an impressive familiarity with the church's teaching on sexuality. Margery draws some comfort (but clearly not enough) from the knowledge that God credits chaste intentions—a matter that will be discussed at greater length below. Both parties are aware of the implications of a vow of chastity and the proper method of making a solemn vow.[38] On the other hand, the impact of saints' lives, particularly the life of Bridget of Sweden, demonstrates the extent to which Margery strives to bring her own actions in line with a recognized model of sanctity. Margery attempts to elicit comparisons between herself and Bridget—not only in her visionary conversations with Christ, but also from the circle of individuals who had known the Swedish visionary.

This construction of sanctified behavior operates at every level and becomes more complex with the problem of repeated narration. Frequently, John of Marienwerder, confessor to Dorothea of Montau, will relate a particular mystical experience and then discuss the way in which Dorothea *later* came to understand it. One senses the conflation of many different stages in John's disclosure: the experience itself; Dorothea's discussion of its contents with John; her reconstruction of the initial experience as illuminated by this conversation and in conjunction with subsequent revelations; and John's written rendering(s) of the same experience.[39]

Certainly this is a rather impressive set of obstacles militating against an understanding of the original experience. There are, however, mitigating factors. Witnesses for the *processus* of canonization frequently provide intimate details about the subject's life. Even

---

[38] John's reticence about making such a vow is shaped by his recognition that subsequent sexual activity would be a mortal sin (Meech and Allen, eds., *The Book of Margery Kempe* 1.11, pp. 23–24).

[39] John wrote four lives of Dorothea all told. See Richard Stachnik, "Zur Veröffentlichung der grossen Lebensbeschreibung Dorotheas von Montau von Johannes Marienwerder," *Zeitschrift für Ostforschung Länder und Völker im östlichen Mitteleuropa* 17 (1968): 713–717.

though these individuals are responding to a carefully contrived set of articles, comments that would be better left unsaid do occasionally slip by. In Dauphine of Puimichel's process, for example, certain witnesses repeated remarks of hers that had an unsettling Encratite resonance, which may ultimately have cost her the canonization.[40]

Even so, it is ultimately unproductive to attempt a definitive separation of a saint's experience, its hagiographical representation, and its ultimate assimilation by the church as an exemplar of sanctity. If, however, we accept as an analytical postulate the fact that these women existed and struggled to live a holy life within marriage, this modest assumption is in itself enabling. For the first time since the late antique period, we can do more than simply measure the frequency and variations of saintly motifs against changing historical circumstance. We can at least attempt to reconstruct the ways in which marriage and chastity were understood to interact with and shape our subjects' spirituality.

Spiritual Marriage: A Woman's Choice?

No woman with a vocation to chastity "chose" spiritual marriage as a preferred calling. All the same, women's initiative in spiritual marriage, although effaced in the twelfth century, becomes marked from the thirteenth century. If we restrict ourselves to the twenty-two marriages in appendixes 5 and 6 that occur between 1200 and 1500, thus excluding the twelfth-century cults of Magnus of Orkney and Isidore the Laborer, this pattern becomes clearer. Women were the prime movers in sixteen of these cases. Two of the remaining six examples are described as mutual agreements, while men seem to have instigated four such unions.

Spiritual marriage continues to be peculiarly tailored to a woman's plight for old reasons that develop new meanings in the high and later Middle Ages. It remained a last resort for the pious female married against her will. The gendered patterns of flight or conversion of one's spouse, suggested by the two most famous hagiographical models for saints forced into unwanted marriages, St. Alexis and St. Cecilia, still pertain. The reasons for the continuity of these patterns are as one would expect. A timely flight from family and friends would be difficult for a male but almost unthinkable for a female. Even Christina of Markyate, a woman of iron nerves, chose flight only as a last resort.

---

[40] Dauphine's marriage is discussed at length in chapter 6. See particularly the section entitled "Internalization and Mutual Sanctification: Dauphine and Elzear."

Although Christina tried for the less stressful Cecilia model, she was forced to go the fugitive route of Alexis when her father stripped her and threw her out of the house:[41] it is no coincidence that the Psalter she acquired as an anchoress later in life featured the Old French romance of her male prototype.[42]

The undoubted constraints placed on the female vocation in this period from an institutional standpoint provided an additional incentive to spiritual marriage. Because of the sudden upswing in the female population, which ironically coincided with a narrowing of official religious options for women, competition for entering a religious community was very stiff indeed.[43] Caroline Bynum has recently put a more positive turn on these constraints, however, by pointing out that male spirituality operates most comfortably in an institutional setting, while women seem to thrive in a looser, more amorphous arrangement.[44] Hence, the less formal mode of spiritual affiliation, so typical of female spirituality in this period, is perhaps better understood in terms of women's affirmative choice than as a result of certain exclusionary trends in monasticism. Women's advocacy of spiritual marriage is undoubtedly a part of this larger picture: appendix 7 indicates that men play a much more prominent role in the move to separate to enter monastic communities than they do as initiators in spiritual marriage. Even with respect to male initiators in chaste cohabitation, for three out of the four men who provided the impetus for a vow of chastity, spiritual marriage was a transition to a more formal, institutionalized renunciation of the world.[45] A majority of the women initiators, on the other hand, never formally joined enclosed religious houses.

Again, the element of "choice" becomes muted here. As will become clearer in the course of this study, the transition to chastity

---

[41] Talbot, ed., *The Life of Christina of Markyate*, pp. 72–73.

[42] For a discussion of the aptness of this Psalter, see Christopher J. Holdsworth's "Christina of Markyate," in *Medieval Women*, ed. Baker, pp. 189–192.

[43] Bolton, "*Mulieres Sanctae*," esp. pp. 143–144, 149–152.

[44] Bynum, "Women's Stories, Women's Symbols," pp. 116–117; cf. Virginia Woolf's timeless refusal on behalf of women generally to join a society to prevent war, in *Three Guineas* (London, 1938), esp. pp. 188–261. There were, however, immense advantages in becoming institutionalized. Mary McLaughlin analyzes the rift in a late medieval female community that arose between those wishing to institutionalize and those who, allegedly, wished to respect the original intentions of their foundress. See "Creating and Recreating Communities of Women: The Case of Corpus Domini, Ferrara, 1406–1452," in *Sisters and Workers*, ed. Bennett, pp. 261–288.

[45] Of the four, Robert Malatesta died at an early age; John Colombini founded the Jesuati; James Oldo became a Franciscan tertiary and joined the priesthood; Chiarito del Voglia built a convent for his wife and served in it as a lay brother.

often took many years. Many husbands, having agreed to this step, would not have parted with their wives even had the wives proposed it. But it is equally true that by the time the husband died, many of the women in question had become inured to living out their vocations in the world, in keeping with the penitential philosophy of the day. Moreover, while male sanctity was still to some extent assessed in terms of strict separation from women, women—dependent on male priests for the sacraments—never had the luxury of this yardstick.[46] Yet here again we run the risk of assessing the anti-institutional quality of female spirituality solely in terms of women's necessary dependence on a male priesthood—an unnecesssarily negative and narrow perspective. A number of authors have recently pointed out that the spiritual discourse generated by women tended to present the sexes as complementary rather than opposing. Not only does this balanced perspective emerge in the writings of someone like Hildegard of Bingen, a cloistered woman coming from a traditional Benedictine background, but it is also evident from the symbolism used by female mystics, who were either aligned with the newer orders or were altogether uncloistered.[47]

In the final analysis, predilection and predetermination are still inseparable in female spirituality. Spiritual marriage as a "compromising vocation" provides a unique opportunity to understand how the two interact.

The Early Inception of the Female Vocation to Chastity

In one of Bridget's many revelations that touches on child rearing, she overhears Christ tell his mother: What children learn in youth, they retain in their old age.[48] Bridget is living proof of this proverb. She had

[46] This was certainly the image of sanctity that Thomas Celano tried to evoke for St. Francis. See especially Thomas of Celano's *Vita secunda S. Francisci* 78.12, 155.204–157.207, in *Analecta Franciscana* 10 (1941): 196–197, 247–249.

[47] See Bynum, ". . . And Woman His Humanity," p. 274. For discussions of Hildegard's vision of the sexes as complementary, see Barbara Newman, *Sister of Wisdom: St. Hildegard's Theology of the Feminine* (Berkeley and Los Angeles, 1987), pp. 93–99; Cadden, "It Takes all Kinds," pp. 155–156; Scholz, "Hildegard von Bingen on the Nature of Woman," pp. 374–377. Also see Prudence Allen's *The Concept of Woman: The Aristotelian Revolution, 750 BC–AD 1250* (Montreal and London, 1985), pp. 292–315, 408–409.

[48] "Prouerbium antiquum est, quod 'illud, quod iuuenis discit in iuuentute, hoc retinet in senectute'" (*Revelaciones. Bk. I, Rev.* 20, ed. Carl-Gustaf Undhagen, Samlingar utgivna av Svenska Fornskrifsällskapet, ser. 2, Latinska Skrifter, vol. 7,1 [Uppsala, 1978], p. 294 = *Rev.*1.20). Only bk. 1, bk. 5 (ed. Birger Bergh, Kungl. Vitterhets Historie och Antikvitets Akademien Stockholm [Uppsala, 1971]; also appears in Sam-

an ardent desire to preserve her virginity by the time she was seven, but she was married against her will at thirteen.[49] Even so, she never forgot her early instinct for chastity. Not only is she said to have managed to convince her husband to delay consummation for either one or two years, but after twenty-six years of marriage and eight children, she finally convinced him to make a permanent vow of chastity.[50] An early vocation to chastity that is thwarted by a coerced marriage is typical of the women in this study. Indeed, in fourteen of the sixteen cases in which spiritual marriage was initiated by a woman, the individual in question had a childhood desire to remain chaste. The only two exceptions, Margery Kempe and Margaret Beaufort, are both from England, where the penitential movement had less of a hold. Margery Kempe, however, although experiencing her conversion to continence as an adult, manifests many of the same patterns as her Continental counterparts. Lady Margaret Beaufort (d. 1509), countess of Richmond and Derby and mother of Henry VII, on the other hand, was the veteran of three marriages (four if one counts the one that was contracted on her behalf when she was six, and annulled when she was nine). She conforms with the time-honored pattern of *conversio* late in life.[51]

---

lingar . . . , ser. 2, Latinska Skrifter, vol. 7,5), bk. 7 (ed. Bergh, Samlingar . . . , ser. 2, Latinska Skrifter, vol. 7,7 [Uppsala, 1967]), and the *Extravagantes* (ed. Lennart Hollman, Samlingar . . . , ser.2, Latinska Skrifter, vol. 5 [Uppsala, 1956]) have as yet appeared in a modern critical edition. For the remaining books (2, 3, 4, 6, and 8) I have used *Revelationes*, ed. Florian Waldauf von Waldenstein (Nuremburg, 1500), which is unpaginated. These revelations will be cited by book and chapter number alone.

[49] At seven, she had a vision of the Virgin Mary, who offered her a crown. The *vita* that was used toward her canonization, drawn up by her two confessors (both confusingly named Peter Olaf), is contained in her process. See *Acta et Processus Canonizacionis Beate Birgitte*, ed. Isak Collijn, Samlingar . . . , ser. 2, Latinska Skrifter, vol. 1 (Uppsala, 1924–1931), *Vita b. Brigide prioris Petri et magistri Petri*, p. 76. The life will henceforth be referred to as *Vita Brig.*, and the actual articles and testimonies from the process will be referred to as *Acta . . . Birg.* This life has been recently translated by Albert Ryle Kezel along with some of Bridget's revelations in *Birgitta of Sweden: Life and Selected Revelations*, ed. Marguerite Tjader Harris (New York, 1990). A second contemporary life, written by Birger, archbishop of Uppsala, who had known Bridget during her years in Sweden, is printed in *AA SS*, October, 4:485–495.

[50] Although Bridget's life alleges only that she postponed consummation by one year (*Vita Brig.*, p. 77), her daughter, Catherine, testifies that they contained for two (*Acta . . . Brig.*, p. 305). For the vow of chastity, see *Vita Brig.*, p. 80; also see *Acta . . . Brig.* art. 23, pp. 19–20.

[51] Margaret's piety and vow of chastity are immortalized by an oration preached by her confessor, John Fisher, a month after her death. See "Month's Mind of the Lady Margaret," in *The English Works of John Fisher, Bishop of Rochester*, ed. John E. B. Mayor, *EETS*, e.s., no. 27, pt. 1 (London, 1876; reprt. Millwood, N.Y., 1973), pp. 289–310. On Margaret, also see Michael K. Jones and Malcolm G. Underwood, *The King's*

But the general pattern of a childhood predilection for chastity corresponds with Weinstein and Bell's observations that a female's vocation to higher spirituality frequently begins at an earlier age than is true for a male—seven years of age seems significant, probably because this period coincides with the child's dawning awareness of her biological destiny as wife and mother. Hence, the first glimmering of a girl-child's vocation is invariably linked with a rejection of sexuality, sometimes marked by an infantile vow of chastity.[52]

It is tempting to see the rejection of the mothering role as a rejection of the mother herself.[53] If we accept this explanation, however, it nevertheless requires careful qualification: many of the girl-child's earliest manifestations of piety arise out of her desire to emulate

---

Mother: Lady Margaret Beaufort, Countess of Richmond and Derby (Cambridge, 1992). For the vow itself, see Fisher, *English Works*, p. 294. Jones and Underwood seem to think that there is something uncanonical about a wife's making a vow of chastity during her husband's lifetime. The evidence of the present study clearly shows that this is not the case—despite the apprehensions of many clerical advisers. Margaret's establishment of a separate household is, perhaps, more questionable (see Jones and Underwood, *The King's Mother*, pp. 153–154, 160). She reconfirmed this vow after her husband's death, and the text of her vow is reproduced by Cooper, "The Vow of Widowhood of Margaret," p. 72. Regarding Margaret's various marriages, see Jones and Underwood, *The King's Mother*, pp. 35–38, 93–96, 138–150; Brooke, *The Medieval Idea of Marriage*, pp. 34–38; cf. C. H. Cooper, *Memoir of Margaret, Countess of Richmond and Derby* (Cambridge, 1874), pp. 6–9, 12–13, 18 (note that there are a number of inaccuracies, especially with regard to dating, in this latter work). Cooper cites the rumor that the third marriage was never consummated, but points out that the authority for this is late and seems to have been derived from a misreading of Fisher's funeral oration (see Cooper, *Memoir of Margaret*, n. on p. 233 regarding p. 18, line 13). Also see *The Dictionary of National Biography*, ed. George Smith et al. (Oxford, 1921–1922), 2:48–49. This entry wrongly states that Margaret took a monastic vow during her husband's lifetime, a confusion which seems to arise from a misunderstanding over the nature of an intramarital vow of chastity. It may also be, as Jones and Underwood's description of her costume would suggest, that later generations mistook the traditional widow's garb in depictions of Margaret for a religious habit (*The King's Mother*, p. 188).

[52] Note, however, that seven also corresponds with the church's notion of the age of reason, so the frequent association of this age with a spiritual calling in saints' lives could be a hagiographical flourish. Males, on the other hand, are represented as more prone to adolescent crises (Weinstein and Bell, *Saints and Society*, pp. 42–44, 234–235, and the section in this chapter entitled "Masculine Motives for Spiritual Marriage"). Also, 64 out of a sample of 151 (42 percent) female saints had conflicts arising from their sex lives, compared with 137 out of 713 (19 percent) male saints (Weinstein and Bell, *Saints and Society*, p. 97). Cf. Kieckhefer, *Unquiet Souls*, pp. 142–143. On the basis of Weinstein and Bell's figures (*Saints and Society*, pp. 123–137), Bynum estimates that 31 percent of these female saints converted as children, compared with 15 percent of the male saints, while 55 percent of the male saints converted as teenagers compared with 34 percent of the females (*Holy Feast and Holy Fast*, p. 317 n. 50).

[53] See, for example, Weinstein and Bell, *Saints and Society*, p. 46.

maternal piety. The fact that the daughter developed a vocation for chastity when she was clearly intended for marriage marks the difference between conventional and extraordinary piety, although the two sorts could be said to drink at the same trough.

The experience of Dorothea of Montau (d. 1394), who aspired to virginity but instead waited many years to convert her husband to chastity, helps us to explore this difference. Dorothea's mother, Agatha, was an extremely pious woman—indeed many of those who had known Agatha believed that Dorothea was a saint because her mother had been.[54] Agatha attended vigils and kept all of the fasts of the church. Although she initially tried to forestall Dorothea's imitation owing to her tender youth, she finally gave in when Dorothea was ten and the daughter shared more completely in Agatha's ascetic regime.[55] After the death of her husband, Agatha lived for forty years in chastity and developed so satisfying and close a relationship with her confessor that they agreed to die at the same time (Agatha predeceased him by a few hours, but when he heard the funeral bells ringing, he too died). They were even, as they had agreed ahead of time, buried in the same tomb—a decision that might imply no very warm feelings for her late husband, although it is impossible to be sure.[56] The local bishop describes Agatha as something of a walking

---

[54] The priest Otto of Montau claims this in *Die Akten des Kanonisationsprozesses Dorotheas von Montau von 1394 bis 1521*, Forschungen und Quellen zur Kirchen- und Kulturgeschichte Ostdeutschlands, vol. 12, ed. Richard Stachnik (Cologne and Vienna, 1978) = *Akten . . . Dorotheas*, p. 349; John Reyman, a doctor of canon law in Marienwerder, says that Dorothea's pious habits came from imitating her mother (pp. 194–195). The sources for Dorothea's life are excellent. John of Marienwerder, her confessor, produced three Latin lives as well as a German one. (He also testified at some length at her process and wrote a short treatise on her virtues that is included in the process). The "Deutsches Leben" has been edited by Max Toeppen (*Scriptores rerum Prussicarum*, vol. 2 [Leipzig, 1863; reprt. Frankfurt am Main, 1956], pp. 179–350). The two shorter Latin lives are printed in *AA SS*, October, 13:493–560. I will be working from the last and most comprehensive of her lives: *Vita Dorotheae Montoviensis Magistri Johannis Marienwerder*, ed. Hans Westpfahl, Forschungen und Quellen zur Kirchen- und Kulturgeschichte Ostdeutschlands, vol. 1 (Cologne and Graz, 1964) = *Vita Dorotheae*.

[55] *Akten . . . Dorotheas* art. 5, pp. 19, 196, 411; also see *Vita Dorotheae* 2.8, p. 73.

[56] A number of witnesses, including Dorothea's confessor John of Marienwerder, were familiar with this story, even though Agatha died in 1401, seven years after her daughter (see *Akten . . . Dorotheas*, pp. 195, 301–302). With regard to burial customs, Gratian cites the canons listed in Burchard of Worms and Ivo of Chartres which ordain that spouses and relatives be buried in the same tomb (C.13 q.2 c.2–3)—a practice concordant with some of the earliest hagiographic treatments of spiritual marriage discussed in chapter 2. But in C.13 q.2 c.3 dpc he concludes by saying that there is nothing legally binding in this practice; thus each individual can be buried where he or she chooses. Also see Michael Sheehan, "The Wife of Bath and Her Four Sisters:

prayer wheel: from her youth she said one thousand Our Fathers a day.[57]

And yet this same mother made her daughter marry against her will—indeed, according to Dorothea's rather surprising testimony, " 'My mother, who bore me and educated me bodily, today judges that she had educated me in great joy and sweetness for the conjugal bed, nor does she agree with the bitterness of my multiple affliction and suffering.' "[58] Some of their differences came to the fore when Dorothea was about to enter the reclusorium in which she spent the last year of her life. According to the testimony of one witness at Dorothea's canonization, Agatha exclaimed in grief: " 'Oh wretched mother that I am! You [Dorothea] are [so] agitated that you cannot do penance in the world. . . . Do you think that in the world you cannot be nourished in any other way than through priests and Canons?' " Dorothea answered mildly but firmly: " 'My most beloved mother, while I was in the world married to a husband and dressed in precious clothes, you were very joyful. But now you should be able to rejoice more and in a better way because I will now be the spouse of the highest King, our Lord Jesus Christ.' "[59]

When Dorothea was asked by her confessor why she agreed to marry, one of the several reasons that she gave was that it was not the custom for a woman of marriageable age to remain a virgin in her town.[60] This extenuates Agatha's seeming insensitivity: perhaps she

---

Reflections on a Woman's Life in the Age of Chaucer," *Medievalia et Humanistica*, n.s., 13 (1985): 34–35.

[57] When the interrogator, clearly taken aback, asked how Agatha could accomplish this feat of piety when occupied by so many domestic responsibilities, he answered that these prayers had become so habitual that they could be recited while milking the cows or performing other chores: "quod ex continua consuetudine devenit ad istum usum, quod etiam faciendo negotia sua domestica, scilicet mulgendo vaccas et alia opera domus, eque bene non dimisit dicere orationes" (*Akten . . . Dorotheas*, p. 411).

[58] " 'Mater mea, que me genuit et corporaliter educavit, hodie estimat se me educasse in magno gaudio et dulcedine usque ad thorum coniugalem, nec sibi constitit de amaritudine multiplicis afflictionis et passionis mee' " (*Vita Dorotheae* 2.16, p. 78).

[59] " 'O, me miseram matrem! Tantis es convoluta, quod in mundo non potes penitere! . . . Credis, quod in mundo non poteris nutriri aliter, quam per presbiteros et Canonicos?'. . . . 'Mater mea dilectissima, dum fui in mundo nupta viro et vestita vestimentis pretiosis, multum gavisa fuisti! Nunc vero melius et potius gaudere poteris, quia ero nunc sponsa altissimi Regis Domini nostri Jhesu Cristi!' " (*Akten . . . Dorotheas*, p. 188). Dorothea's sister-in-law, Gertrude, likewise testifies to the rift between Agatha and Dorothea's spirituality. Once when Dorothea asked her mother if God ever spoke to her, Agatha promptedly replied, " 'How could it happen that God would speak to a sinner like me?' " When she put the same question to her daughter, the latter put her finger mysteriously to her lips (pp. 355–356).

[60] Ibid., p. 272.

assumed that the single-minded attention to God to which Dorothea aspired was an indulgence that was only earned through marriage and enjoyed in widowhood. And yet even chaste-minded relatives were frequently unreliable advocates for a young girl's chastity. Despite her own thwarted vocation for virginity, Bridget of Sweden did not interfere with the marriage of her unwilling daughter Catherine. Salome, princess of Galicia in Poland (d. 1268), who lived in virginal purity with her spouse Caloman, worked hard to bring about the marriage between her brother Boleslaus and the resisting Cunegund of Poland. She actually smuggled Cunegund out of Hungary in a basket.[61]

The effect of familial examples in shaping a vocation for chastity makes its impact in both an immediate and a dynastic way. Bridget of Sweden was perhaps inspired by the example of her aunt, Lady Ramborg, who is said to have lived out her life in a virginal marriage.[62] Bridget's example undoubtedly inspired her daughter, Catherine, who succeeded in remaining a virgin for the duration of her six years of marriage, although her predilection for virginity was further corroborated by her convent education.[63] The eastern European saints are particularly noted for their saintly lineage.[64] Hedwig of Silesia (d. 1243), also the product of a conventual school, was herself from a long line of saints and was aunt to the illustrious Elizabeth of Hungary. Hedwig took a vow of chastity with her husband after twenty-eight

[61] Bridget did, however, unsuccessfully oppose the marriage of her eldest daughter, Mereta, because she did not trust the character of the future husband (see Johannes Jørgensen, *Saint Bridget of Sweden*, trans. Ingeborg Lund [London and New York, 1954], 1:73–75.) It is uncertain if Salome knew of Cunegund's vocation to chastity at this point, but there is little doubt that she learned of it during the course of Cunegund's marriage. Hence it is no surprise that when Brother Rinerus of the Franciscan order questioned Salome in a vision two years after her death as to whether Cunegund and Boleslaus would have children, the blessed apparition at first refused to answer but then said, circumlocutiously, " 'perhaps they will have children,' " (ed. W. Kętrzyński, *Vita sanctae Salomeae, MPH*, 4:788). Salome's life was written by her confessor, the Franciscan Stanislaus.

[62] Jørgensen, *Saint Bridget of Sweden*, 1:24.

[63] *AA SS*, March, 3:504. Catherine of Sweden's near-contemporary life was written up by a Brigittine monk, Ulphonsus (d. 1433), who collected evidence from individuals who had known Catherine.

[64] See especially André Vauchez, "*Beata Stirps*: Sainteté et lignage en occident aux XIIIe et XIVe siècles," in *Famille et parenté dans l'occident médiéval*, ed. Georges Duby and Jacques Le Goff, Collection de l'Ecole Française de Rome, 30 (Rome, 1977), pp. 397–407. Klaniczay points out that women in particular were entrusted with dynastic sanctity ("Legends as Life-Strategies for Aspirant Saints in the Later Middle Ages," in *Uses of Supernatural Power*, pp. 95–110, esp. pp. 100–103; cf. "The Cult of Dynastic Saints in Central Europe: Fourteenth-Century Angevins and Luxembourgs," ibid. pp. 111–128).

years of marriage.[65] Cunegund, princess of Poland and great-niece to Hedwig, refused to consummate her marriage with Boleslaus, thus following in the footsteps of her much-admired cousin and sister-in-law, Salome, who was married to the brother of St. Elizabeth of Hungary and kept her virginity through seventeen years of marriage.

But the actual format for spiritual marriage was also absorbed through traditional saints' lives. Vauchez and other scholars have noted that in the later Middle Ages there was a greater tendency among the laity to internalize hagiographical models due to the increased circulation of saints' lives.[66] Certainly this seems to be especially evident with the subjects of virginal marriages. Dauphine of Puimichel consistently answered her husband's demands for the debt with examples of spiritual marriage from the lives of the saints, as did Jeanne-Marie of Maillac.[67] Catherine of Sweden was said to have consciously imitated the marriage of Mary and Joseph.[68] Contemporary saints were also compelling models. Bridget of Sweden's career and revelations had a considerable impact on Dorothea of Montau and on Margery Kempe. Margery was also influenced by Mary of Oignies, and may well have known and emulated the example of her contemporary Dorothea of Montau. Margery had actually visited Dorothea's hometown of Danzig; the two women were from the same class and had parallel religious experiences, and both had many children.[69]

The undeniable impact of saintly paradigms on the lives of these women may seem to undercut my earlier contention that the clergy was inclined to discourage intramarital chastity by developing the distinction between admiration and imitation—but I think not. The discouragements were present, but the women were not listening.

---

[65] Hedwig's anonymous life was written by a contemporary monk. See the coeval treatise on Hedwig's genealogy that follows the *vita* in *AA SS*, October, 8:265–270.

[66] Vauchez, "L'influence des modèles hagiographiques," pp. 585–592, esp. pp. 589–590.

[67] Dauphine's marriage is discussed in chapter 6; for Jeanne-Marie, see *AA SS*, March, 3:735. Jeanne-Marie's life was written by her confessor.

[68] See *AA SS*, March, 3:504.

[69] Regarding Bridget's influence on Dorothea, see Hans Westpfahl, "Dorothée de Montau," *DS*, vol. 3, col. 1665. For Bridget's and Mary of Oignies's influence on Margery, see Meech and Allen, eds., *The Book of Margery Kempe* 1.17, 20, 39, 58, 62; pp. 39, 47, 94–95, 143, 152–153. For her visit to Danzig, see 2.4, pp. 231–232. Regarding Dorothea's possible influence on Margery, see Atkinson, *Mystic and Pilgrim*, pp. 179–181. Also for Bridget's influence in England, see Roger Ellis, " 'Flores ad Fabricandam . . . Coronam': An Investigation into the Uses of the Revelations of St. Bridget of Sweden in Fifteenth-Century England," *Medium Aevum* 51 (1982): 163–186, and F. R. Johnson, "The English Cult of St. Bridget of Sweden," *AB* 103 (1985): 75–93.

Certainly with respect to Elzear and Dauphine, whose union was arguably the most extraordinary of spiritual marriages, the *vitae*—and, perhaps more significantly, Dauphine's process of canonization—lean very heavily on this distinction. But one can judge even more clearly from the responses of the parents and often the spiritual advisers that they had in no way calculated that a conventionally pious upbringing would stimulate so great an aversion to the marriage bed. Dauphine, for example, the sole heir to immense estates in Provence, who was orphaned at seven and thenceforth brought up by her uncles, was especially recommended to the care of two relatives: the nun Sibille de Puget, who had refused to marry and became a nun, and the Friar Minor Philippe de Riez. Both of these individuals are reported to have urged Dauphine to keep her virginity and bolstered their counsel with examples from saints' lives.[70] And yet the uncles were clearly infuriated and surprised at her refusal to marry.[71]

Philippe's active encouragement of Dauphine's vocation to chastity is rather unusual and supports Vauchez's contention that spiritual marriage was often linked to a Franciscan ambiance.[72] More often, however, we see members of the clergy stepping in to reinforce pressures to marry or to consummate the marriage.[73] Thus, as a counterpart to Dauphine's good Franciscan guide, the uncles import a "bad" friar, William of S.-Martial, to argue in favor of solemnizing the marriage. William's line of argument is of the highest interest for us. He first praises the goods of marriage and takes advantage of current trends in sanctity by mentioning how many married people have

---

[70] Jacques Cambell, ed., *Vies occitanes de saint Auzias et de sainte Dauphine*, Bibliotheca Pontificii Athenai Antoniani, 12 (Rome, 1963), 1.2, pp. 134–137 (the two different lives will henceforth be indicated by *Vie . . . Dauphine* and *Vie . . . Auzias*). The double lives of Dauphine and her husband, Elzear (Auzias), were translated from the Latin lives shortly after 1370. Elzear's Latin life reached its final form between 1361 and 1363 and has been printed in *AA SS*, September, 7:539–555. Dauphine's original Latin life has been lost. For dating, see Cambell, *Vies occitanes*, introd., pp. 17–18. Processes of canonization were undertaken for both husband and wife. See Jacques Cambell, ed., *Enquête pour le procès de canonisation de Dauphine de Puimichel, Comtesse d'Ariano* (Turin, 1978) = *Canonisation de Dauphine*. Unfortunately, Elzear's process remains only in summary form: see Cambell, ed., "Le sommaire de l'enquête pour la canonisation de Elzéar de Sabran, TOF (d. 1323)," *Miscellanea Francescana* 73 (1973): 438–473.

[71] *Vie . . . Dauphine* 2.1, pp. 138–141; cf. *Canonisation de Dauphine* art. 6, p. 33.

[72] Vauchez, *Les laïcs*, pp. 220–221, 227.

[73] This is strikingly evident in the life of Christina of Markyate. See especially her conversation with the prior Fredebert (Talbot, ed., *The Life of Christina of Markyate*, pp. 58–65). Cf. the experience of Paula Gambara-Costa (d. 1515), *BS*, vol. 6, cols. 28–29; A. Butler, *Lives of the Saints*, ed. and rev. H. Thurston and D. Attwater (New York, 1956), 1:216–217; and the example of Melania the Younger, p. 56, above.

recently been canonized by the church.[74] This clearly made little headway with Dauphine, as he immediately changed his approach. He finally suggested to her that God, who does not deceive, had foreseen that she would convert her spouse to chastity in the manner of St. Cecilia. It was this argument that moved her to give her consent.[75]

And thus if a stubborn young woman perversely imagined she could evade consummation by following the holy model of spiritual marriage, the model could be used against her in a coercive way—a snare both baited with and triggered by the same capacity for *imitatio* that had made her strive for chastity in the first place. Occasionally, one finds that the women themselves are apprised of the risks. Lucia Brocadelli of Narni, for example, received a visitation from the Virgin, St. Catherine of Siena, and St. Domitilla, who encouraged her to marry, but to keep her virginity intact. Yet Lucia was apprehensive, knowing that Lucifer could appear as an angel of light.[76] Lucia was one of the lucky ones who remained a virgin: one can only wonder vainly how many others were caught. The women who allegedly pursued a program of wedding-night proselytism for chastity were invariably the ones who were successful.[77] The hagiographer was no

[74] "E amb aysso espauzan e declaran los grans bes que so en matremoni, en lo cal motas personas son sanctas e per la Glieya canonizadas" (*Vie . . . Dauphine* 2.3, p. 144). Cf. Cunegund of Poland's later life by John Dlugos, completed in 1475, in which her confessor uses the example of the saintly matrons in her family in an attempt to get her to consummate her marriage (*AA SS*, July, 5:683). In addition to Dlugos's life, there is also an anonymous one that was composed about a hundred years earlier. See W. Kętrzyński, ed., *Vita et miracula sanctae Kyngae ducissae Cracoviensis, MPH*, 4:682–744. Note that Kynga is another name for Cunegund.

[75] *Vie . . . Dauphine* 2.2, pp. 144–147.

[76] "E se bene non era affatto sicura, che non potesse esser qualche inagnno dell' Angelo delle tenebre trasformato in angelo di luce; nondimeno confidatasi nella Bontà Divina" (G. Marcianese, *Narratione della nascita, vita, e morte della B. Lucia da Narni* [Ferrara, 1616], c. 10, p. 50; henceforth cited as *Narratione . . . Lucia*). The earliest extant treatment of Lucia's life, by Serafino Razzi—a short epitome written some thirty years after her death—does not mention this episode. In fact it suppresses her marriage altogether (see *Vite dei santi e beati così del Sacro Ordine de' frati predicatori* [Florence, 1577], pp. 179–183). Razzi's account is based on a near-contemporary life by Arcangelo Marcheselli di Viadana (now lost) and on the testimony of people who had known Lucia. Marcianese's more prolix life draws on both of these earlier accounts as well as on what he claims to be Lucia's own written account of her visions (these are no longer extant). For Marcianese's detailed discussion of his sources, see *Narratione . . . Lucia* c. 23, pp. 101–103. Also see Gabriella Zarri, *Le sante vive: Cultura e religiosità femminile nella prima età moderna* (Turin, 1990), pp. 97 and 134 n. 65.

[77] The only exception is Christina of Markyate, but the point still holds. Although she failed to convert Burthred to a spiritual marriage, she did manage to preserve her virginity, while her bewildered husband eventually released her of her marriage vows (Talbot, ed., *The Life of Christina of Markyate*, pp. 50–51, 108–109).

more likely to report an aborted effort in this direction than he was likely to describe a failed attempt to raise someone from the dead. And so the enviable parallel with saints like Cecilia was the preserve of the virgin, although the main difference between the virgin wife and her plainer sisters, who lived to become sexually active and conformed to the late and relatively unspectacular transitional model of spiritual marriage, was probably only on the level of success rather than that of intention or desire.

A Broken Vow, a Broken Heart

Despite efforts to contain a subject woman's power to vow chastity, there is little doubt not only that women made these technically invalid vows, but that they perceived them as binding. Angela of Foligno made a unilateral vow of chastity directly to Christ. Her husband died before he could challenge her resolve.[78] With respect to Elzear and Dauphine, who had lived in virginal purity since the time of their wedding in 1299, no formal vow was made until 1316. But Dauphine herself anticipated this vow by four years through a private vow of her own. Although she was aware that she should have consulted her husband, she was equally certain that if she broke that vow she would be guilty of a mortal sin.[79]

The sense of female autonomy and responsibility to vows can also be discerned in childhood and adolescence, but such vows are again veiled by the hagiographer's customary caution: the only childhood vows of chastity we ever hear of are voiced by the women who succeeded in guarding their virginity until death. This observation may act as a reminder that the vow of a subject woman was something of a spiritual mare's nest. Although it served the purposes of most canonists and theologians to dismiss such a vow as not binding, hagiographers reveal a more mixed perspective on its status.[80] They are pecu-

---

[78] Angela of Foligno, *Le livre de l'expérience des vrais fidèles* 1.11–12, ed. M.-J. Ferré (Paris, 1927), pp. 8–10.

[79] *Canonisation de Dauphine* art. 12, pp. 38–39; *Vie . . . Dauphine* 5.1–2, pp. 164–166. The author of the *vita*, however, attempts to cover Dauphine's lapse in judgment by maintaining that the Holy Spirit moved Elzear toward the resolution of formally swearing chastity at the same moment (6.1, pp. 168–169).

[80] The canonical dismissal of a minor's vow is still riddled with ambiguities, however. According to Raymond of Peñafort, if a child enters religion willingly prior to the age of majority and later regrets the decision, though the entrance is not technically binding, the individual in question may not leave until the age of majority is achieved. Both Raymond and William of Rennes refer frequently (and rather nervously) to Huguccio's uncompromising *dictum* that if a prepubescent child is capable of deceit (*doli*

liarly sensitive to the unsettling truth that what may be null in the external forum may still be binding in the internal forum. Thus the young girl's vow, although theoretically requiring the approval of a parent or guardian, is nevertheless represented as a serious undertaking.

Dauphine's hagiographer plays for dangerously high stakes by placing the emphasis on intention as opposed to a formal act. Apparently at ten years old, Dauphine was so inflamed by the inspiration of the Holy Spirit that she firmly proposed in her heart that she would preserve her virginity, though the author is careful to emphasize that she does not vow.[81] The lack of a formal vow is, from a certain standpoint, a technicality: it does not prevent Philippe de Riez from reproaching her, when she contracted marriage, with the words " 'You had firmly proposed to serve God in virginity' " and aligning her with other lost souls.[82] But his courage goes no further than this reproach: frightened of the family, he hangs back from visiting her. When she asks for his assistance in fleeing to a monastery before the marriage is solemnized, he tells her not to move but assures her that he will ask for the prayers of all the good people of the region.[83]

Both Angelina Corbara of Marsciano (d. 1435) and Lucia Brocadelli of Narni (d. 1544) vowed their virginity at twelve—significantly the age at which a woman allegedly achieved the majority that supposedly corresponded to puberty and marriageability. And yet, while girls were theoretically nubile at twelve, the age of majority had

capax est), his or her entrance into religion should be considered binding. Raymond acknowledges that a father can reclaim a minor from a religious community if he or she has entered without his permission, but warns that this must be done immediately (Summa de poenitentia 1.8.7, pp. 62–63; cf. John of Freiburg, Summa confessorum 1.8.30, fols. 20v–21r). Note that in the entry on Elena dall'Olio, the Bollandist Stilling is reluctant, due to her subsequent marriage, to credit the contemporary claim that she made a solemn vow of virginity (AA SS, September, 6:658).

[81] "Fo de tan gran fervor del Sanh Esperit enlhumenada e enflammada, que fermamen prepauzec en son coratge, ces tot autre vot, no cossentir en matremoni ni en plazer carnal, mas tostemps vieure en virginitat e am l'ajutori de Dieu gardar" (Vie . . . Dauphine 1.3, p. 136).

[82] " 'O Dalphina, que es fach; que t'es endevengut? Tu, que fermamen avias prepauzat a Dieu servir en virginitat, has consentit en matremoni! Davan hieu pregava Dieu per tu ayssi devotamen e per ton sanh prepauzamen; empero d'aquesta hora enan hyeu pregariey per tu ayssi coma per perduda!' " (Vie . . . Dauphine 2.2, p. 142).

[83] Compare the experience of Christina of Markyate, who made a private vow of virginity when she was somewhere between the ages of thirteen and sixteen. This was later confirmed by her friend Sueno, a canon at Huntingdon. When he heard of Christina's marriage, not knowing that Christina was in the custody of her parents, he abandoned her, assuming that she had deceived him (Talbot, ed., The Life of Christina of Markyate, pp. 36–41, 54–57).

escalated for the purposes of a religious profession. Already in the thirteenth century, a young girl had to be fourteen or even fifteen to pledge the solemn vow that marked her entrance into religion.[84] One can adduce a number of possible effects from this change. A young girl of twelve would be increasingly dependent on the private vow to solidify her relationship with God since her minority had been artificially extended. The higher age requirement for the solemn religious vow may well have undermined the efficacy of the already fragile simple vow in the eyes of certain authorities, especially if undertaken without the consent of the young girl's guardian. Moreover, the difference between age of marriage and age of entering religion must inevitably tilt the odds in favor of the former.

Angelina vowed directly to God, while Lucia seems to have taken the additional precaution of vowing to her confessor, the Dominican prior Martin of Tivoli.[85] Certain modern hagiographers have improvised scenes in which Lucia reassures Martin when she is obliged to accept what she has been miraculously assured would be only a nominal husband,[86] but earlier sources make no such claims. It is entirely possible that Martin was prepared to forget about the earlier vow and yield to expediency by not challenging her right to marry. Yet this is by no means certain. Four years after the marriage, the same man risked veiling the virgin spouse as a nun without the permission of her husband.[87] The gravity of this move becomes even more apparent when one considers that four years was long past the point at which even the party to an unconsummated marriage could unilaterally retreat to the cloister. This may suggest that Martin was simply giving precedence to the earlier vow. In fact, he paid dearly for this trespass against the husband's authority, as the latter, failing in his efforts to murder Martin, vented his frustration by burning down his monastery. But ultimately, the husband resigned himself to Lucia's decision, joined the Franciscans, and gained a reputation as a fine

[84] See Johnson, *Equal in Monastic Profession*, p. 106.

[85] The earliest source for Angelina is Luigi Jacobilli's seventeenth-century account (*Die selige Angelina von Marsciano* c. 1, trans. into German by a sister of Ewigen Abbey, p. 14). For Lucia's vow, see *Narratione . . . Lucia* c. 7, p. 38. Marcianese does not state explicitly that Martin was present at the time, but the vow is described in a chapter treating his active sponsorship of Lucia's devotions. Moreover, Marcianese suggests a degree of formality when he speaks of Lucia's desire to change the simple promise that she made when she was seven into a vow. On her earlier promise, see c. 6, p. 33.

[86] See, for example, M. C. de Ganay, *Les bienheureuses Dominicaines* (Paris, 1924), p. 440.

[87] *Narratione . . . Lucia* c. 20, pp. 92–95. Note that although the couple had been married for four years, they only cohabited for the last three.

preacher.[88] His options were decidedly limited since, in theory, he could not remarry.

Hagiographers and spiritual advisers were insecure about even the most successful of informal vows or propositions, especially when they were externally jeopardized by a subsequent marriage. Despite Lucia's sterling record of virginity against all odds, it is no accident that the earliest account of her life forestalls cynical doubts by suppressing all mention of prenuptial vow and marriage alike. The various persecutions she endured from her husband were, hagiographically, shouldered by her brothers.[89] If such trepidation surrounded a redeemed vow, a broken vow would be, presumably, a gray zone to which the hagiographer dared not allude.

The women who had made explicit vows frequently became ill when they thought that their chastity was imperiled. The illnesses in question are generally not of the marathon type through which female sanctity is so frequently proven—or as Bynum has characterized it, something "to be endured" as opposed to "cured."[90] These illnesses are generated by the crisis of marriage and tend to recede when they have served their specific function. For virgin wives such as Christina of Markyate, Lucia Brocadelli of Narni, and Jeanne-Marie of Maillac, illness can be interpreted as a form of pious stonewalling.[91]

A similar pattern is apparent for the women who were forced to consummate their marriage when no explicit vow is reported. And yet a suppressed vow can be inferred from the psychological devastation, illness, and, perhaps most important, the deep sense of guilt following in the wake of many of these marriages—a guilt that is in

---

[88] Ibid. c. 21, pp. 96–97; c. 22, p. 101. Peter managed to salvage something from the ruin of his marital life since, according to Marcianese, he later used domestic proofs of his wife's sanctity as *exempla* in his sermons (c. 13, p. 67). The seventeenth-century Luigi Jacobilli omits Peter's rather unedifying fit of pique from his account and moves right to his entrance into the Franciscans (*Vite de' santi e beati dell'Vmbria* [Foligno, 1647–1661; reprt. Bologna, 1971], 3:40).

[89] Razzi, *Vite dei santi*, p. 180.

[90] See Caroline Bynum, "The Female Body and Religious Practice in the Later Middle Ages," in *Zone: Fragments for a History of the Human Body*, ed. Michel Feher et al. (New York, 1989), 1,3:166–167; Kieckhefer, *Unquiet Souls*, pp. 57–58. For the greater frequency with which women are afflicted with illness, see Weinstein and Bell, *Saints and Society*, table 18, p. 234.

[91] Talbot, ed., *The Life of Christina of Markyate*, pp. 54–55. Lucia Brocadelli of Narni was cured when the Virgin and her attendant saints proposed the solution of a spiritual marriage (*Narratione . . . Lucia* c. 10, p. 50). Jeanne-Marie of Maillac was struck by illness just after her wedding, which may indicate that she, as yet, mistrusted her husband's alleged agreement to remain chaste (*AA SS*, March, 3:735). Also cf. Dauphine's feigned illness, discussed in chapter 6.

proportion to what they suffered with the loss of their virginity. These women suffer penitential, purgative illnesses. Thus in the case of Frances of Rome, for whom we hear of no explicit vow, we can sense the presence of a withheld one. According to her confessor John Mattiotti's account of her life, Frances's commitment to chastity was in evidence as an infant, when she allegedly objected to her father's touch. She was nevertheless married against her will at the age of thirteen and, almost as soon as she arrived at the home of her in-laws, was stricken with a paralyzing illness that lasted a year. At this point, she was cured by a vision of St. Alexis.[92] Her father could scarcely doubt that the illness resulted from her inability to be true to her vocation.[93] There seems to be a redemptive element in the fact that it was none other than St. Alexis who came to cure her, not only evoking Frances's lifelong yearning for the eremitic life,[94] but perhaps symbolically absolving her from all blame in not having fled her nuptials as he did his, once she had done her penance through illness. Likewise, at the age of thirteen Catherine of Genoa had attempted to join the convent in which her sister was a member, but was rejected on the basis of her youth.[95] Married at sixteen against her will, she fell into a deep depression that lasted for the first ten years of her married life. It is significant that her condition seems to have reached a crisis point on the vigil of St. Benedict, at which time she asked for a sickness that would confine her to her bed for three months—both as expiation for her broken monastic resolve and as an externalization of her inner despondency.[96]

---

[92] AA SS, March, 2:93–94; cf. Placido Tommaso Lugano, ed., I processi inediti per Francesca Bussa dei Ponziani (1440–1453), Studi e Testi, 120 (Vatican City, 1945), art. 1, pp. 8–10 (= Processi . . . Francesca). In addition to her confessor's vita (which includes an account of her visions in bk. 2) and the process, there is the 1641 Italian life of Maria Magdalena Anguillaria—a member of the order of oblates that Frances founded. Bks. 3 and 4 are translated into Latin and also appear in AA SS, March, 2:178–215. For an account of Frances's life and food asceticism, see Rudolph M. Bell, Holy Anorexia (Chicago and London, 1985), pp. 133–140.

[93] See the later life of Anguillaria, AA SS, March, 2:179.

[94] See Processi . . . Francesca, p. 226.

[95] Umile Bonzi da Genova, ed., Edizione critica dei manoscritti Cateriniani, vol. 2 of S. Caterina Fieschi Adorno (Turin, 1962). Biografia c. 2, pp. 109–110 (= Caterina. Biog.). This edition contains the most authoritative manuscripts for the entire corpus of Catherine's life and revelations, assembled after her death by her followers. MSS D and Dˣ are undoubtedly the earliest and most reliable (see introduction, pp. 50–59). I have relied on MS D in this study.

[96] Ibid. c. 3, pp. 113–114; cf. Dorothea of Montau, who resisted consummation for two weeks and then, after eight weeks of marriage, fell into so grave an illness that she received last rites. It is also significant that with marriage, her gaping wounds, which she had borne since childhood and later learned to associate with God's love, were

Consummated Marriages: Attitudes toward Sex

From the moment a marriage is consummated, the women in the transitional type of spiritual marriage decidedly part company with those adhering to the virginal model—in both experience and self-perception. The virgin wives have retained their "seal" with Christ (as the author of *Hali Medenhad* would describe it), which affords them not only physical autonomy but a sense of continuity with their past.[97] The implications of this continuity will be discussed at greater length in chapter 6. Women who submitted to consummation, however, are more closely aligned with pious matrons, generally. They had to work very hard to reestablish their identity and their relationship with God. These two pressing needs help to explain their marked predisposition to penitence and mysticism—two forms of religiosity that help them to relax their former grip on chastity in favor of obedience and humility. Ultimately, the extent to which they have successfully carved out a new vocation is perhaps most clearly evoked by the fact that by the end of their marital career, they are no longer fit for the cloister.

For the fifteen consummated marriages listed in appendix 6, four hagiographical sources are particularly prolific in their description of the sexual lives of these women: the lives of Hedwig of Silesia, Bridget of Sweden, Dorothea of Montau, and Frances of Rome. In addition to these, one should also add Margery Kempe's unique account of her life. As was mentioned earlier, Margery's spiritual odyssey runs somewhat against the general current of these women's lives insofar as she experienced a conversion to chastity late in life; even so, her conversion initiated her into a set of concerns that were common to all these women.

Most of the women in this study assume a rigorous stance in sexual matters that matches or outstrips Huguccio's mistrust. The conjugal debt almost invariably brings on an increase in ascetic austerities.[98]

---

reopened, while just prior to marriage they had, for the most part, closed (*Vita . . . Dorotheae* 2.30, p. 92). On Dorothea's wounds, see Kieckhefer, *Unquiet Souls*, p. 27.

[97] F. J. Furnivall, ed., *Hali Meidenhad*, EETS, o.s., no. 18; rev. ed. by Oswald Cockayne (New York, 1969), p. 14. Karma Lochrie discusses the concept of the "sealed body" in *Margery Kempe and Translations of the Flesh* (Philadelphia, 1991), pp. 23–27. On the contrast between the anatomical vision of virginity of the early Middle Ages, which persists in this thirteenth-century text, and virginity as a state of mind, see Clarissa Atkinson, " 'Precious Balsam in a Fragile Glass': The Ideology of Virginity in the Later Middle Ages," *Journal of Family History* 8 (1983): 131–143, esp. p. 138.

[98] For Mary of Oignies, see *AA SS*, June, 5:550; for Bridget of Sweden, *Vita . . . Brig.*, p. 78, and *AA SS*, October, 4:488; for Dorothea of Montau, *Akten . . . Dorotheas*, p. 204, and *Vita . . . Dorotheae* 2.4–6, pp. 68–72. Also note that Dorothea confessed more

But toward the debt itself, two particular attitudes can be discerned. There are those who are represented as adopting a perfunctory attitude toward married relations, holding pleasure at arm's length by carefully subscribing to the regimen of the *continentes*. For the second group, although equally imbued with the penitential ethos, the debt itself is the most horrible of penances, and one that makes deep inroads into the woman's sense of self.

Both Hedwig of Silesia and Bridget of Sweden fall into the first category.[99] Although Hedwig (d. 1243) convinced her husband to abstain from sex permanently only after twenty-eight years of marriage and six children, while sexually active, Hedwig distinguished herself by her moderate use of sex—a fact that her hagiographer details with zeal and upholds for imitation:

> Oh, how fortunate are the matrons hitherto subjected to matrimonial chains, if they try to imitate the example of this blessed woman, who not only, as it was said before, [once] she had conceived offspring strove otherwise to live continently, but also by salubrious counsels and exhortations inclined her own noble husband, so that he together with her would voluntarily observe continence every year through Lent and all of Advent, all of the Ember Days and Fridays, on the vigils of the saints and their solemnities, and on the Lord's days.[100]

Despite his admiration, the hagiographer is quick to remind us that as praiseworthy as such behavior might be, it is contingent on the consent of the husband. Fortunately, Henry himself seems to have had something of a vocation to penitence.[101]

Even by the most modest calculations, Hedwig's regimen limited sexual activity to less than half of the year, yet this reckoning does not take pregnancy or menstruation into account.[102] Indeed, her hagio-

---

frequently once married (*Vita . . . Dorotheae* 2.7, p. 73); for Frances of Rome, see *Processi . . . Francesca*, pp. 240–241. This pattern is typical for most pious matrons who were forced to marry. See Gerardesca of Pisa's life, *AA SS*, May, 7:162.

[99] Vauchez also uses Hedwig to demonstrate the penitential influence, in a chapter entitled "Un nouvel idéal au XIIIe siècle: la chasteté conjugale" (*Les laïcs*, pp. 203–209).

[100] "O quam felices sunt matronae matrimonialibus adhuc vinculis subjugatae, si hujus beatae foeminae imitari conantur exemplum, quae non solum, ut praedicitur, concepta sobole continenter de cetero vivere studuit, verum etiam salutaribus consiliis et exhortationibus suum ad hoc generosum maritum inflexit, ut una secum voluntarie continentiam observaret singulis annis per totum Adventum et per Quadragesimam, omnibus diebus Quatuor Temporum et sextis feriis, in Sanctorum vigiliis ac solemnitatibus eorundem et in diebus dominicis" (*AA SS* October, 8:225).

[101] After Hedwig's removal to the monastery of Trebnicz, Henry wore a beard (a nicely trimmed one) and a tonsure, and was said to have lived a monklike existence, while continuing to govern (ibid., p. 227).

[102] For a more comprehensive view of just what this level of continence would

grapher tells us that the noble couple went as many as eight weeks without sex, although they shared the same bed. After Hedwig and Henry made a solemn vow of chastity before the bishop, she was as parsimonious with visual contact as she had been with sexual contact. She met with him only for the purpose of doing charitable acts and then, to still the potentially vicious gossip of others, only in the presence of witnesses. Even when Henry was sick, she would go to see him only in the presence of her daughter-in-law.[103]

A similar kind of ethic permeates the life of Bridget of Sweden (d. 1373). The year or so during which Bridget had convinced her husband, Ulf Gudmarrson, to postpone consummation was spent in prayer; they asked God to grant that if they were to have sex, it would be performed totally without lust and the resulting children would be pious and God-fearing. They continued to pray thus after they became sexually active.[104]

This gingerly approach to sex could still accommodate pleasure—at least, Bridget's experience certainly implies this. Bridget probably scandalized some of her contemporaries a few days after her husband's death by removing the keepsake ring he had given her on his deathbed. The explanation she volunteered was that when she buried her husband, she buried all carnal love. The ring reminded her of earlier pleasures.[105] But even during Ulf's lifetime, her attitude to sex was tinged with the perfunctory Augustinian view of the world: "uti non frui"—use but do not enjoy. Thus when Bridget was once admiring an extravagant bed that she and Ulf had commissioned, she was knocked over the head by Christ. From this point on, she slept on a straw mat alongside the bed whenever she was permitted.[106]

Bridget had a vivid sense of the way in which sexuality informed an individual's salvation history. In one revelation, Ulf appeared to her from purgatory to report on the various things that had hastened and hindered his progress to heaven: the fact that he abstained sexually from his wife once she had conceived worked heavily in his favor.[107] On the other hand, the denizens of hell suffer horribly for lust: one

---

amount to in terms of days of the year, see Flandrin, *Un temps pour embrasser*, pp. 20–40.

[103] *AA SS*, October, 8:226. Clement IV's bull of canonization for St. Hedwig likewise made a virtue out of her judicious use of sex, mentioning her strict observance of all the penitential periods, and her participation in the Augustinian goods of marriage (p. 220). Cf. Vauchez, *Les laïcs*, pp. 207–208.

[104] *Acta . . . Birg.* art. 23, pp. 19–20, 305, 504–505; cf. *Vita Brig.*, p. 77.

[105] *Acta . . . Birg.*, p. 479; cf. Christ's corroborating words in *Rev.* 5.11, pp. 162–163.

[106] *Acta . . . Birg.*, p. 480; *Rev. ext.* 53, p. 175.

[107] *Rev. ext.* 56, pp. 178–179.

woman, for example, is luridly depicted as being torn apart by her own viperous arms, while a sharp stake has been driven into her vagina.[108]

Bridget also projects her sexual diffidence onto various celestial worthies in her visions. Anne and Joachim, parents to the Virgin Mary, are portrayed as actually hostile to the thought of sexual intercourse, only conceiving Mary "against their will and out of divine love."[109] Occasionally, her discussion of the generation of children teeters dangerously on the brink of a postlapsarian perception of sexuality—the tendency to regard human reproduction as a consequence of original sin.[110] Even after the Fall, when concupiscence has broken loose, Adam and Eve are presented as too terrified to initiate sexual intercourse (much like Bridget and Ulf), awaiting God's explicit permission before attempting it. The death of Abel instigates another sexual setback, and the pious couple mournfully abstain for a long period until God again makes it clear that it is his will for them to continue to procreate.[111] Although Bridget had loved her husband, she voices her disgust for her earlier sexual enjoyment and claims that she would rather die than return to her fleshly marriage.[112]

Women such as Hedwig and Bridget demonstrate the impact of the penitential movement in liberalizing attitudes toward sex. Its success was so marked that married relations actually became grist for the hagiographical mill. A second group of women, however, seems to dramatize how this very liberalization—particularly the new emphasis on payment of the debt—was torturous for others. For Dorothea, Frances, and postconversion Margery Kempe, the conjugal debt was horrific and the supreme act of penance. Margery's response

---

[108] "Venter eius sic miserabiliter torquetur: ac si naturali membro eius palus esset acutissimus infixus: et toto conamine fortissime impelleretur: vt amplius ingrederetur" (Rev. 6.16).

[109] "Tamen pro certo dico tibi, quod ex caritate diuina et ex verbo angeli annunciantis conuenerunt carne, non ex concupiscencia aliqua voluptatis sed contra voluntatem suam ex diuina dileccione" (Rev. 1.9, p. 261).

[110] Rev. 1.26 (pp. 312–313) describes sinless sex in Eden. After the Fall, however, Bridget's vision suggests that God distanced himself from the sex act by putting the child's soul into the parents' seed as opposed to more actively implanting it in the mother, as he did earlier. On the other hand, Christ's speech in Rev. 5. (int.12 q.1 resp., p. 136) could imply that, with the onset of concupiscence and the disobedience of the genitalia, God mercifully instigated procreation so that the sexual impulse would not be wasted. Cardinal Torquemada, however, successfully defended Bridget against this reading at the Council of Basel (see Kezel's comments in Birgitta of Sweden, ed. Harris, p. 262 n. 279).

[111] Rev. 1.26, p. 313.

[112] " 'Pudor est in corde meo cogitare de illa carnis delectacione priori et est michi nunc quasi venenum et eo amarior nunc, quo prius dilexi eam feruencius. Mallem enim mori quam umquam in illam redire' " (Rev. 1.32, p. 332).

is of particular interest in that her revulsion to sex was focused on the debt alone and, even after her conversion, she continued to be attracted to other men.[113] This seems to imply an unconscious awareness of the relation between the debt and the husband's authority—a matter that will be taken up below. The responses of Frances of Rome and Dorothea of Montau, however, were much more categorical. All physical contact was something of a trial for Frances, who was said to have covered her hand with a cloth, which she carried about with her, before touching other individuals.[114] Sex represented an extreme heightening of this revulsion. She was invariably ill after sexual intercourse and even vomited blood. Indeed, it was only in compliance with the orders of her confessor that she fulfilled the conjugal debt in the first place. Before sexual intercourse, she would drip molten grease or wax on her flesh until her skin was so charred that she could scarcely move in bed.[115] Frances was also prone to frequent demonic visions and was periodically tortured by being forced to watch these demons engaging in all manner of sexual offenses.[116]

Despite occasional instances of husbandly sympathy and support, the primary message inscribed in many of these women's lives is that submission to the marriage debt, hateful as it is, is but a microcosm for the greater burden of submission to the husband. Here we sense an important difference that reflects certain changes in marriage laws. While pious matrons from an earlier period were more likely to be physically martyred by their husbands, in the lives of their later counterparts the husband himself becomes a more subtle instrument of torture who creates the context through which the wives can display their exemplary virtues of submission and obedience.[117] As the Middle Ages draw to a close, the husband's dominance and brutality seem to increase in proportion with the wife's long-suffering obedience in female saints' lives. This motif is by no means restricted to spiritual marriage but provides a backdrop for the lives of many pious matrons.[118]

---

[113] Meech and Allen, eds., *The Book of Margery Kempe* 1.3–4, pp. 11–16; 1.59, pp. 144–146.

[114] *Processi . . . Francesca* art. 15, p. 39.

[115] Ibid.; Anguillara's later life, *AA SS*, March, 2:183.

[116] *Processi . . . Francesca* art. 26, pp. 57–58; *AA SS*, March, 2:162, note u.

[117] Cf. Kieckhefer, *Unquiet Souls*, p. 55.

[118] See especially the lives of Paula Gambara-Costa (*BS*, vol. 6, cols. 28–29, and Fr. Leon, *Lives of the Saints and Blessed of the Three Orders of Saint Francis*, translation of *Aureole Seraphique* [Taunton, 1885], 1:534–536), and Gentile of Ravenna (d. 1530; *AA SS* January, 3:525–529, esp. p. 526). Gentile's life shows a number of parallels with that of Dorothea of Montau, not only in the brutality of her husband, but also in the way in which her mystical raptures infuriated him. Also cf. Rita of Cascia (d. 1447;

The lives of Catherine of Genoa and Dorothea of Montau are especially compelling in this respect. Catherine's biography says explicitly that divine goodness gave her a difficult husband so that her suffering would free her from all earthly loves.[119] On the other hand, Dorothea's confessor and biographer, the skilled theologian John of Marienwerder, tends to temporize. He does try to make a case for marriage as an honorable state and for Dorothea's participation in its three goods,[120] but this effort is overshadowed by what he clearly construes as the main function of her marriage: that "she could be more fully commended in the holiness of her life the more she was humbled in suffering the burdens of marriage."[121] Dorothea's process and *vita* are especially detailed in their treatment of her attitude toward sex. She was married against her will at seventeen to Adalbert, a rich armorer in Danzig and many years her senior, who had little sympathy or patience for his wife's pious disposition. A number of witnesses at her process attest to the difficulty in consummating the marriage—hence she remained a virgin for about two weeks after the wedding.[122] The married Dorothea's increased austerities and the orientation of her asceticism are further evidence of a blighted sexual rapport. She bound sharp nut shells to her loins as well as placing them in open wounds so that during intercourse she would be guilty of no lustful feelings; she wept whenever her husband tried to remove her clothing.[123] Both process and *vita* make the Augustinian distinc-

---

AA SS, May, 5:226–234, esp. p. 226). Although Ivetta of Huy (d. 1228) converted to a more devout life only after the death of her husband, her *vita* is of interest because of her hatred of marital usage. The author of her contemporary life tells us that her aversion to sex was not prompted by piety but by a natural aversion: "sed naturali quodam mentis impulsu agitabatur interius complexio munda cordis, quo dedignabatur foris caro carnis delectationi subesse, et curis secularibus intricare animum prout expetebat et expetit usus, et ordo conjugii" (AA SS, January, 2:147).

119 "Ma la Bontà Divina, la quale sempre provede a tutti, massime a quelli de quali vuole havere speciale cura, acciò che non mettesse lo suo amore in terra da alcuna parte, li diedero un marito il quale le fu tanto diforme circa lo vivere humano, che la faceva tanto patire, che a pena sostentava la vita" (*Caterina. Biog.* MS D, c. 3, p. 112).

120 *Vita Dorotheae* 2.27, p. 90.

121 "Hec Sponsa Deo dilecta homini sponso copularetur, ⟨ut in⟩ statu matrimonii, sicut per ecclesiam approbatus est, per vite sanctimoniam amplius approbaretur, in sufferendo onera matrimonii plus humiliaretur" (ibid.).

122 *Akten. . . Dorotheas*, pp. 107, 187; *Vita Dorotheae* 2.27, p. 91. For a review of her life, see Kieckhefer, *Unquiet Souls*, pp. 22–33.

123 *Akten . . . Dorotheas*, pp. 272–273. Dorothea would occasionally make dark references to female friends about how certain people would afflict themselves for God, although she was careful never to specify herself. A certain Katherina, a widow who was a nun in the order of Teutonic Knights, testified that Dorothea spoke of certain people who wounded themselves (and strategically placed nutshells in their wounds)

tion between rendering and exacting the conjugal debt, stressing, perhaps with little need, that Dorothea was never guilty of the latter.[124] Often, Dorothea would pierce her feet with needles until she could not walk, significantly using this as an excuse for not attending marriage feasts.[125] Her experience of motherhood seems to have been equally grim. She apparently burned her nipples in a flame so that she would derive no pleasure from nursing her children;[126] nor did she relax her penitential observances, which included vigorous fasts, during pregnancy or lactation.[127] Indeed, her pitiful state is encapsulated in her mixed feelings about the ritual of purification that a woman had to undergo before entering the church, after she had given birth.

> When the days of her purgation were completed, she visited the church for that most Christian rite with the little child to which she had given birth. She was equally rejoicing and sorrowing. She was rejoicing, because she was able to visit the church and be present for the divine solemnities. But she was also sorrowing and grieving because she was diverted from church a little due to care for the infant and was forced to return to her husband's bed—from which she gladly absented herself, whenever she could conveniently do so.[128]

Nor did she mind her cold work around the cradle on winter nights, when she was purposefully thinly clad, since she was grateful for pretexts that kept her out of her husband's bed.

But Dorothea was not simply martyred by her antipathy to the married state: her husband Adalbert's active cruelty is often evoked in process and *vita* alike to demonstrate the saint's patience.[129]

---

so that they would experience no pleasure in rendering the debt: "se audivisse ab ipsa Dorothea, quod homines essent in mundo, qui, quando intellexerunt et sciverunt, se debere reddere debitum, se vulneraverunt et in vulnera testa de avellanis et nucibus posuerunt, ut ex isto actu libidinem carnis non sentirent, sed cum tali dolore libidinem fugarent et delectationem carnis" (p. 141).

[124] Ibid., pp. 204, 309; *Vita Dorotheae* 2.30, p. 92.

[125] *Vita Dorotheae* 2.12, pp. 75–76.

[126] *Akten . . . Dorotheae*, pp. 273, 306. The bishop of Pomerania, however, testifies that the burning of the nipple actually distracted her from the more horrible pain of the wound which had spontaneously arisen between her breasts (p. 413; cf. *Vita Dorotheae* 2.32, p. 95).

[127] *Vita Dorotheae* 2.6, 2.31; pp. 72, 93.

[128] "Diebus vero sue purgacionis impletis cum parvulo, quem genuit, ritu christianissmo ecclesiam visitabat. Gaudens erat tunc pariter et dolens. Gaudens, quia ecclesiam poterat visitare et divinis sollempniis interesse, dolens vero et merens erat, quia propter curam circa infantulum ab ecclesia aliquantulum retrahebatur et ad mariti thorum redire cogebatur, a cuius thoro libenter se absentaverat, quando convenienter poterat" (ibid. 2.31, p. 93).

[129] Nicolaus de Hoenstein, who was Dorothea's confessor for twelve years during her married life, cites Adalbert as Dorothea's first and principal persecution (*Akten . . .*

Adalbert interpreted Dorothea's unresponsiveness during mystical rapture as rebellion, not grace: twice he poured water on her and he often kicked her when she was in this state. On several occasions his beating resulted in internal bleeding or other serious injury.[130] Deep resentment over his wife's periodic absences from his bed (which according to John of Marienwerder were always motivated by piety) and her frequent attendance at church led Adalbert to chain Dorothea up for three days. When she endured this bondage with her usual equanimity and patience, he interpreted this as yet another instance of insolence and gave her a powerful blow on the head with a chair. For this indignity, as with others, we are told that she was rewarded with a sweet, inner consolation from God.[131]

Marriage, Sex, and the Refinement of a Religious Vocation

The point of all of this is not to prove that husbands could be very brutal or that sex could be very nasty, but to explore how these essential experiences shaped the spirituality of these women. A female saint's marriage is often perceived as an interruption in her spiritual career: not only by the hagiographer, but by modern scholars, and perhaps even by the woman herself.[132] This perception, however, frequently overshadows the fact that for the woman who was obliged to marry and later to consummate her marriage, both sexual activity and subordination to the husband were the sine qua non which shaped her mature religious vocation.

Despite the prevailing wisdom of canon law, which tends to amalgamate the husband's will and God's will, the lives of married women very often turn on the disparity between the two. The tension is already implicit in the *sponsa Christi* metaphor, used for single and married women alike. When married women are concerned, however, Christ and the husband are frequently presented as rivals for the

---

Dorotheas, p. 84). On the importance of patience as a motif in fourteenth-century lives, see Kieckhefer, *Unquiet Souls*, pp. 50–88.

[130] "Unde sepius a marito vocata, cum esset in raptu, inscia rei non respondit, quod ille rebellioni, non gracie imputavit" (*Vita Dorotheae* 2.40, p. 106; cf. 3.9, 3.13; pp. 124–125, 130). It is interesting to note that when the couple's respective confessors finally intervened on Dorothea's behalf and told Adalbert that she was not responsible during her rapture, he was obliged to forgo his "will." This sacrifice is described as provoking a grave illness: "Ex hiis dictis et aliis maritus sic correptus et coactus est suam dimittere voluntatem. Et ob hoc in gravem incidit infirmitatem" (3.13, p. 130).

[131] Ibid. 2.41, p. 107.

[132] See, for example, Weinstein and Bell, *Saints and Society*, p. 235; cf. the way in which the *vitae* of Frances of Rome and Bridget of Sweden attempt to separate their sexual from their spiritual activity—a maneuver discussed later in this section.

woman's affection and obedience. One of the more flamboyant instances of this conflict is Margery Kempe's calling on Christ in order
to prevent her husband from having sex with her during Holy Week.
John becomes impotent, as a result.[133] But these tensions are often
playfully enacted through less confrontational miracles that are ubi-
quitous in the lives of all married women. The women in question are
typically indulging in unauthorized charities or feats of asceticism,
which are miraculously concealed when the disapproving husband is
on the brink of discovery. Frequently a romantic triangle is enacted to
dramatize the conflict between the husband's will and God's. Christ
is often presented as the ardent wooer of the married women in question, which sets up an interesting quasi-adulterous situation. Sometimes the husband is presented as lurking in the shadows like a
jealous King Mark, hoping to catch the lovers together. Hedwig, for
example, continually practiced austerities such as walking barefoot
in winter—a fact that she had to conceal from her husband. One day,
however, she met Henry unexpectedly. Christ, anxious to hide his
lover's indiscretion, caused her sandals to appear miraculously.[134]
Hedwig's nocturnal vigils are generally depicted as clandestine meet-
ings with a lover.[135]

Miracles of divine concealment especially cluster around
clothes.[136] Pious matrons were constantly trying to divest themselves of sumptuous garments, clearly rejecting the newly sexualized
kerygma of the church whereby women were expected to be more
sexually available to their husbands and indeed were often expected

[133] Meech and Allen, eds., *The Book of Margery Kempe* 1.9, p. 21. A similar situation occurs in Lucia Brocadelli of Narni's life when the sensual husband was terrified
by the appearance of an angel (*Narratione . . . Lucia* c. 12, p. 61).

[134] *AA SS*, October, 8:232. These tensions are played out in the lives of virgin wives
as well. In the life of Cunegund of Poland, for example, Hedwig's great-niece, the focus
is on food. Cunegund's husband insisted that she eat normally, and stop tampering
with her food in order to make it as unpleasant as possible. When he surprised her by
eating some of her adulterated fare, it miraculously tasted delicious (*AA SS*, July,
5:696–697). Such miracles do occur, albeit less frequently, in the lives of men. See the
section entitled "Masculine Motives for Spiritual Marriage" in this chapter.

[135] The *vita* describes her as lying awake while others slept so that her ear could
receive secretly the "venas" of Christ's whisper—a word suggesting many possible
translations from pulse to penis (though the latter meaning is probably clearest in the
singular, it echoes in this plural usage). His amorous words light a flame in her heart:
"Istius verbi suavitate quia perfrui desiderabat, sollicite vigilabat, ut caeteris dormien-
tibus quasi furtive susciperet auris sua venas susurri ejus. Dilectus vero hanc ei reddebat vicissitudinem, ut excubantem in tam vigilanti custodia non transiret nec decli-
naret ab ipsa, sed stabat et loquebatur amatoria inflammabatque cor ejus ita, ut in
flamma amoris ipsius eum praesentem cognosceret ac in immutativa virtute ipsum
adesse intelligeret, quem amabat" (*AA SS*, October, 8:234).

[136] See Elliott, "Dress as Mediator," pp. 292–300.

to express their availability through dress. Generally, the women's response to clothing was in proportion to their revulsion toward the sex act. The women who subscribed to the more moderate form of penitential sex could generally allay some of their qualms with a hair shirt and renewed penitence. But to women such as Dorothea of Montau, Frances of Rome, and postconversion Margery Kempe, clothing took on a heightened significance. Margery, acting under divine inspiration, was constantly struggling to manifest her newly won purity through white clothes.[137] The sight of fine materials and pleated garments nauseated Dorothea: she imagined that they sent stinging darts at her eyes.[138] Frances went on veritable crusades against finery in her native Rome.[139] Her aversion is forcefully presented in her visions of hell. The single women who beautified themselves had headfuls of biting serpents, and hot swords penetrated every inch of their bodies, while taunting demons looked on.[140] Married women who were guilty of vanity fared considerably worse:

> The handmaid of Christ saw . . . the souls of married women who on account of the sin of vanity suffered such things as were described above concerning women ornamenting or beautifying themselves. But on account of the evil desires they [the married women] were guilty of, they were ripped by demons from head to foot, and in this wound the demons placed many worms, which were the penalty for their filthy thoughts and overabundant carnal delights. Many serpents surrounded those souls, biting them principally in those members in which they took delight. And because of the sin of excessive care in adorning themselves they were cast down and lacerated by these demons at the end of a certain mortar. And because of their excessive thoughts, they were placed in a bed full of serpents, toads, and other horrible wild animals.[141]

[137] Meech and Allen, eds., *The Book of Margery Kempe* 1.15, 30, 43–44; pp. 32, 76, 103–104; also see Gunnel Cleve, "Semantic Dimensions in Margery Kempe's 'Whyght Clothys,'" *Mystics Quarterly* 12 (1986): 162–170.

[138] *Vita Dorotheae* 3.17, p. 135.

[139] *Processi . . . Francesca*, pp. 23, 26, 161–163, 238–339.

[140] *AA SS*, March, 2:170.

[141] "Vidit . . . Christi ancilla animas foeminarum conjugatarum, quae propter peccatum vanitatis tales patiebantur poenas, quales superius dictae sunt de foeminis ornatis seu se venustantibus: sed propter mala desideria ab eis commissa, erant scissae a daemonibus a capite usque pedes: et in tali vulnere daemones eis imponebant multos vermes: quae quidem poena eis dabatur propter foedas cogitationes, et propter superfluas carnales delectationes: et multi serpentes circumdabant ipsas animas eas mordentes principalius in illis membris, in quibus se magis delectarant. Insuper propter peccatum superfluae sollicitudinis ad se ornandum erant ab ipsis daemonibus ad modum cujusdam pilae projectae et dilaceratae. Insuper propter nimias cogitationes ponebantur in uno lecto pleno serpentibus et bufonibus et aliis horribilibus feris" (ibid., p. 172).

The conflicts these women experienced as sexually active wives required that they develop a new vocation for themselves, and, as suggested above, penitence and mysticism were the tools they employed.[142] The propensity toward penitence is clear. We have already seen that sexual initiation provokes an increase in austerities. It is little wonder that a number of these women felt a deep affinity with Mary Magdalene.[143]

If the propensity for penitence in marriage is apparent, the mystical vocation is harder to establish. It is generally agreed that mysticism was very much the preserve of laywomen, who were much more likely to distinguish themselves through mystical raptures and related phenomena—such as visions, levitation, or stigmata—than were men, whether lay or clerical.[144] Vauchez points out how many of the well-known female mystics of the high and later Middle Ages were actually married at one time, and many were likewise mothers of families.[145] But a mystical vocation is generally seen as antithetical to traditional conceptions of either wife or mother. In her study on Margery Kempe, Clarissa Atkinson underlines the essential "incompatibility of sexual activity and sacred power"[146]—nor is this contradiction exclusive to medieval Christianity, but seems common to other cultures as well. According to Anita Spring and Judith Hoch-Smith: "To communicate with divinity, or the supernatural, a person

[142] Cf. Weinstein and Bell, *Saints and Society*, pp. 234–235.

[143] In one vision, Christ tells Margery Kempe explicitly that he knows that, next to the Virgin Mary, she puts the most trust in Mary Magdalene's power (Meech and Allen, eds., *The Book of Margery Kempe* 1.86, p. 210; cf. Margery's "Prayers of the Creature," p. 253); also see Bridget of Sweden, *Rev.* 6.119. Frances of Rome and Catherine of Genoa's identification will be discussed later in this chapter. Cf. Angela of Foligno's association with the Magdalene in *Livre de l'expérience* 1.48, pp. 84–86. Though the Magdalene was generally not a favorite with the virgin wives, there are exceptions. Lucia Brocadelli of Narni added her to the roster of the usual saints she invoked after someone commented on how, when her hair was loose, Lucia herself resembled the Magdalene (*Narratione . . . Lucia* c. 13, pp. 64–65). On Mary Magdalene's cult in the Middle Ages, see Ruth Mazo Karras, "Holy Harlots: Prostitute Saints in Medieval Legend," *Journal of the History of Sexuality* 1 (1990): 3–32, esp. pp. 17–28.

[144] For an introduction to the subject of mysticism, see Jesús López-Gay, "Le phénomène mystique," *DS*, vol. 10, cols. 1893–1902; Albert Deblaere, "La littérature mystique au moyen âge," ibid., cols. 1902–1919. For an excellent discussion of different kinds of mystical experiences, see Kieckhefer, *Unquiet Souls*, pp. 150–179. Regarding the prominence of women in this area, see Vauchez, *La sainteté*, pp. 435–446; Elizabeth Petroff, *The Consolation of the Blessed* (New York, 1979), pp. 39–82; and Bynum, "Women Mystics in the Thirteenth Century: The Case of the Nuns of Helfta," in *Jesus as Mother*, pp. 170–262 (esp. pp. 172–186, 258–262).

[145] Vauchez, *La sainteté*, p. 442.

[146] Atkinson, *Mystic and Pilgrim*, p. 176; cf. Elizabeth Petroff, *Medieval Women's Visionary Literature* (New York and Oxford, 1986), introd., p. 5.

must direct her life toward this pursuit. For a woman to devote her attention to spiritual concerns, she must not be hindered by physical fertility but comes to develop instead the potential of symbolic motherhood."[147]

Not surprisingly, many women had to wait until the death of their husbands or a parallel liberation from familial responsibilities to realize their mystical gifts. Angela of Foligno is a case in point. With the death of her entire family, an occurrence that she represented as a celestial windfall, she was free to engage in an intense mystical rapport with God. In the case of Gerardesca of Pisa, once it was clear that she and her husband were incapable of having children, she won her husband's consent to separate and enter religious communities. But she was fearful that he would renege, so she immediately rushed him down to the abbot before he could change his mind (because, according to her hagiographer, he had been inclined to evil since youth). Thereafter, she embarked on a career as a visionary.[148]

But the line between sexual activity and the possibility of mystical experience cannot be firmly drawn. Mysticism played an important part in the spirituality of eight out of the nine women who convinced their husbands to make a gradual transition to chastity, compared with probably only two out of seven of their virgin counterparts; this fact invites an examination of the relationship between sexual intercourse and spirituality.[149] Certainly the saints themselves felt limited in their rapport with God while they were still obliged to render the debt, particularly, or were subordinated to their husbands generally.[150] Margery Kempe undoubtedly felt constrained by her sexual

[147] Hoch-Smith and Spring, eds., *Women in Ritual and Symbolic Roles*, introd., p. 15. See Lois Paul, "Careers of Midwives in a Mayan Community," ibid., pp. 129–149. Midwives are seen as intermediaries with the supernatural in Mayan culture and are officially confirmed in this ritual function by the shaman. Pregnancy inhibits their important rapport with the supernatural. In the case of the twentieth-century Mayan midwife Juana, she was told of her vocation to midwifery in a dream and followed her profession despite her husband's objections. At the time of Paul's study, they were occupying separate rooms (pp. 134–137). This compares well with Atkinson's description of Margery Kempe as a shaman (*Mystic and Pilgrim*, pp. 213–215).

[148] Angela of Foligno, *Le livre de l'expérience* 1.12, pp. 10–12; for Gerardesca, see *AA SS*, May, 7:162–163.

[149] Margaret Beaufort was the only woman initiator in appendix 6 who was not reputed to be a mystic. I am including Hedwig in the count because, even though we know nothing substantive about the content of her mystical experiences, we are told that she experienced raptures from which it took her a long time to return and during which she was insensible to her surroundings (see *AA SS*, October, 8:234–235). Jeanne-Marie of Maillac and Lucia Brocadelli of Narni, on the other hand, both managed to keep their virginity through marriage and also became mystics.

[150] Atkinson, *Mystic and Pilgrim*, pp. 175–176, 194; also see Hoch-Smith and Spring's introduction to *Women in Ritual and Symbolic Roles*, esp. pp. 15–16.

duties, and many of her visionary conversations with Christ represent chastity as the occasion for a more complete union with him.[151] And yet, as Nancy Partner points out, the narrative of Margery's book is structured around her entering and leaving the marriage bed.[152] Her mystical vocation arose directly out of the experience of marriage (specifically childbirth and the conjugal debt),[153] and, while sexually active, she still enjoyed considerable intimacy with Christ. The same is undoubtedly true of Dorothea of Montau. Although she did experience a certain deepening in her relationship with Christ that coincided with the mystical extraction of her heart in 1385, this did not closely coincide with her conversion to chastity but occurred five years later.[154] Sometimes the hagiographer is responsible for a certain amount of obfuscation in this area. John Mattiotti, for example, presents Frances of Rome's transition to chastity as especially cathartic.

> Blessed Frances . . . lived with her husband for twenty-eight years and six months: for twelve years she lived with him separated from carnal union by the common consent of the parties: and then marvelously she was changed, and began by word and example to approach the number of the perfect, and whose life was found as admirable as it was incomprehensible.
>
> For by such sweetness of the soul and delight of the mind she took part in supernal things, and freed from all earthly things she was united to Christ so that very frequently even in the use of her hands she remained almost immobile or insensible: and frequently after such meditations and prayers she was seized in ecstasy.[155]

In fact, Frances experienced visions and ecstasies long before her conversion to chastity.[156] Perhaps Mattiotti's confusion derived from

---

[151] Meech and Allen, eds., *The Book of Margery Kempe* 1.11, 65, 76; pp. 24, 161, 180.

[152] See Nancy Partner, " 'And Most of All for Inordinate Love': Desire and Denial in *The Book of Margery Kempe*," *Thought* 64 (1989): 254–267, esp. pp. 257–259.

[153] Her first vision of Christ was when he came to relieve the despair resulting from postpartum depression. Likewise, her vocation to chastity arose when she heard a sweet celestial music while in bed with her husband (Meech and Allen, eds., *The Book of Margery Kempe* 1.1, 3; pp. 8, 11).

[154] On the extraction of her heart, see *Vita Dorotheae* 3.1, pp. 112–114.

[155] "Vixit . . . B. Francisca cum viro suo annis viginti octo, et sex mensibus: duodecim annis habitavit cum eo a carnis copula separata de communi partium voluntate: et tunc mirabiliter commutata est, coepitque verbo et exemplo aggregari numero perfectorum, ejusque vita tam admirabilis quam incomprehensibilis extitit.

"Nam tanta animi suavitate, et mentis oblectatione supernis intererat, et a cunctis erat exuta terrenis et Christo unita, ut saepius in ipsis etiam exercitiis manuum, quasi immobilis et velut insensibilis remaneret: et frequenter post tales meditationes et orationes in extasi rapiebatur" (*AA SS*, March, 2:96). John's comment regarding the immobility of Frances's hands marks the contrast with some of her ecstasies in which her hands twitch and move in a distorted way (vis. 65, p. 147).

[156] See the Bollandists' introduction to Frances's visions, ibid., p. 91.

the fact that he was Frances's confessor only for the last ten years of her life, first assuming this office about six years after the couple's transition to chastity. On the other hand, it seems more likely that Mattiotti consciously attempted to put distance between Frances's sexual activity and her visions in order to increase her credibility.[157] It is also clear that, to his mind, the synchronization of the visions and the vow made a more satisfying social drama.[158]

The women who enjoyed a mature mystical relationship during their marriage are precisely those whose aversion to the debt was greatest and who needed the most reassurance about the way that this impinged on their spiritual state. This is particularly true for women like Frances of Rome and Dorothea of Montau. Frances, the competent manager of an important household is, as Rudolph Bell points out, something of an anomaly for being able to retain a superficially banal exterior while she was engaged in such intense ascetic practices and was possessed of so vivid an interior life.[159] But, in fact, the mystical experience often arises precisely out of this kind of rupture between inner and outer selves. This is especially clear in the case of Dorothea:

> "When I was in secular state, having glory and joy on the outside, gazing on the honor that was exhibited, and showing a face as much cheerful as affable, then God was wont to press down on me inwardly with sadness and awareness. . . . For this reason, when I was seen at dances rejoicing outwardly in the entertainments, I was all the more grieving inwardly because God pressed down on me and inflicted sadness on my heart."[160]

Dorothea came to see this kind of rift as an essential feature in her life, which she characterized as a kind of "doubleness." God further revealed to her that her secular life should be perceived as a kind of

---

[157] Likewise in the Prologue to Bridget's first book of revelations, the theologian Mathias of Linköping, one of her earlier confessors, cites Bridget's initiation of chastity as evidence for the authenticity of her vocation: "Talia de sponsa Christi, quam sibi in huiusmodi gracie ministerium elegerat, suspicanda non sunt. Que, adhuc in coniugio viuens, maritum suum ad continencie perfeccionem adduxit, ut multis annis simul sine exaccione et reddicione debiti coniugalis viuerent" (*Rev.* 1. Prol., p. 233).

[158] Cf. Bynum's comments on the way male hagiographers shaped female experience to coincide with male experience or expectations in "Women's Stories, Women's Symbols," pp. 111–112.

[159] Bell, *Holy Anorexia*, p. 140.

[160] "'Quando fui in statu seculari, habens gloriam aut letitiam exteriorem, inspiciens honorem, qui exhibebatur, et vultus tam hylaritate quam affabilitate ostendens me gaudere, tunc Dominus solebat me interius tristitia et agnitione deprimere. . . . Ob hoc, quando in conviviis ad coreas videbar gaudens ad extra, eram plus merens ad intra, quia Dominus me depressit et in cor meum tristitiam ingessit'" (*Akten. . . Dorotheas*, p. 303).

veil that had the function of hiding her sanctity from the world.[161] Her raptures could be perceived as the point at which the more potent spiritual life tears through the secular veil, freeing her not only from the tedious aspects of her daily existence, such as marketing and cooking, but from some hateful ones as well. Her raptures doubtless helped her to disengage herself during the sex act.

> The Lord wounded her instantly with the arrows of love, and inflaming her with burning love he said: "You are capable of loving me exceedingly well. For frequently I seized [rapui] you from your husband when he still lived and thought he possessed you."[162]

All of these women partook, in varying degrees, of a sense of "doubleness" during their husbands' lifetime,[163] but the husband's authority was often perceived as the rivet that held these two lives in place, and his death would be presented as provoking a spiritual crisis. It is significant, for example, that Bridget was agonizing about her change in status and its bearing on her service to God when Christ first addressed her.[164] Christ is said to have told Bridget that her love for her husband and the world had eroded her love for God: " 'And when at your husband's death your soul was gravely shaken with

[161] "Consequentur Domino eius sensum et intellectum apperiente ad intelligendum vidit circa vitam suam quandam duplicitatem ex statu seculari, in quo extitit in vita spirituali, quam salubriter duxit. Status secularis velabat vitam eius spiritualem tali modo, quo duo panni simul complicati ostenderentur, quorum superior inferiorem absconderet et velaret" (Vita Dorotheae 2.18, p. 80). God even goes on to suggest that Dorothea's life is likewise a mystery to herself. Chapter 19 further associates her with the many saints who are never recognized in their native land (pp. 80–81). Also see 2.20, in which God commands Dorothea to tell her confessor that, while she was compelled to wear silken robes in her secular state, she was untouched by any of the vices that might attend this (pp. 81–82). Cf. the disclosure that Christ made to Margery Kempe in a vision: " '& þe Deuyl knowith not þe holy thowtys þat I ʒeue þe ne no man in erde knowyth how / wel & holily þu art ocupijd wyth me, ne þi-self can not tellyn þe gret grace & goodnes þat þu felist in me. And þerfor, dowtyr, þu begilyst boþe þe Deuyl & þe worlde wyth þin holy thowtys, and it is ryth gret foly to þe pepil of þe worlde for to demyn þin hert þat no man may knowyn but God a-lone' " (Meech and Allen, eds., The Book of Margery Kempe 1.84, p. 206).

[162] "Illico eam Dominus spiculis amoris vulneravit, et eam incendens caritate ferventer ardente dicebat: 'Tu potes me bene magnifice diligere. Nam frequenter a viro rapui te, quando adhuc vixit et estimavit te possidere' " (Vita Dorotheae 3.13, p. 131).

[163] Baron Friedrich von Hügel significantly describes the coexistence of Catherine of Genoa's outside work at the hospital and her avid interior experience as a kind of "double life" (The Mystical Element of Religion as Studied in Saint Catherine of Genoa and Her Friends [London and New York, 1923], 1:142–143).

[164] A few days after Ulf's death, "cum sponsa Christi solicita esset de mutacione status sui ad seruiendum Deo et super hoc stabat orando in capella sua" (Vita Brig., p. 80; Rev. ext. 47, pp. 162–163; also see Rev. 5.11, pp. 162–163).

disturbance, then the spark of my love—which lay, as it were, hidden and enclosed—began to go forth, for, after considering the vanity of the world, you abandoned your whole will to me and desired me above all things.'"[165] And yet the "crisis" of her husband's death, although central in the development of a public prophetic vocation, may not have been nearly so pivotal vis-à-vis the mystical experience as Bridget and her confessors would later suggest. After the *vita's* dramatic narration of Bridget's first encounter with Christ, the next rubric adds, rather anticlimactically, "How even before the death of her husband she saw certain things."[166]

The mystical relationship was essential for providing both sexually active matrons and widows with reassurance about their state and guidance toward a new vocation. On the other hand, the reassurances the women received, by necessity, displaced the primary hold that the cult of virginity had on their lives. Vocational development often entailed moderate tampering with the celestial hierarchy. In Frances of Rome's visions, for example, Mary Magdalene is consistently presented as leading the choir of virgins; Cecilia, on the other hand, is represented as leading the married.[167] Periodically, the hagiographer assumes sole responsibility for similar interventions on behalf of his subject. Jacques de Vitry, for example, tells us that Mary of Oignies, who managed to convert her husband to chastity within a very short time of their wedding, was restored to the hundredfold reward of virginity—an allegation that has led some to assert that she remained a virgin throughout her marriage.[168]

Bridget of Sweden and Margery Kempe, who to some extent modeled herself after Bridget, relied both on explicit affirmations and on intentionality to exculpate their married status. Christ frequently reassured Margery, for example, not simply for her own sake but on

---

[165] *Rev.* 5.11, p. 163; trans. Kezel, *Birgitta of Sweden*, ed. Harris, p. 148.

[166] "Quomodo eciam ante obitum viri sui vidit quedam" (*Vita Brig.*, p. 81).

[167] *AA SS*, March, vol. 2, vis. 21, 31, 38, 40, 43; pp. 118, 125, 131–132, 132, 135.

[168] "Tu [i.e., God] vero centuplum reddidisti ei in hoc seculo" (*AA SS*, June, 5:550). The Bollandist commentary mentions that Mary is called a virgin in certain legendaries. Although there is no contemporary evidence for this claim, the commentator does not rule out the possibility entirely (p. 545). B. A. Windeatt's recent translation of *The Book of Margery Kempe* seems to accept that Mary was a virgin ([Harmondsworth, Middlesex, 1985], notes to 1.9, p. 304 n. 1). I, however, have treated her as a matron because of the unlikelihood, had she remained intact, that her confessor, Jacques de Vitry, would not have known it. Nor would he have failed to make the most of it. On the other hand, if she did remain a virgin, this might account for the couple's easy transition to chastity and the complementary nature of their respective spiritual vocations. See the section entitled "Synchronization of Vocations: The Transition from Carnal to Spiritual Marriage" later in this chapter.

behalf of all spiritually ambitious matrons, that he loved wives as well as maids, that chaste intentions were as meritorious as chastity, and that a pious rendering of the debt deserved merit.[169] Bridget received parallel assurances. Christ is at one point compared with King David, who desired Saul's daughter when she was a virgin, married her as a widow, and then subsequently pursued Uriah's daughter—a married woman.[170] But Bridget also uses intentionality to undermine the virgin state, deriding virgins who are only technically so. The vision in which the virginal Agnes addresses Bridget, but also speaks on her behalf, is one of the more elaborate engagements of this theme.

> You may marvel that a woman coming into favor was corrupted. I respond to you that there are certain women who have continence but do not love; for them there is neither great delight nor great temptation. If honorable marriages were offered to them, they would indeed accept. But because they are not offered great things, they look down on the small. Thus nothing ever comes of their continence but pride and presumption. Therefore it happens that, with divine permission, [they] fall, as you already heard. Yet if someone were of the intention that they would not for the whole world, if it were offered to them, wish to be stained, it would be impossible that such a one would abandon herself to filthy things. But indeed if God were to permit from his hidden justice that such a one should fall, it would be more a crown than a sin for her: as long as it were against her will.[171]

Thus Bridget sculpts her own "fall" from her pristine chaste resolve into a position of personal strength. Dorothea touches the same chords, but the tune produced is, perhaps, less self-congratulatory. God said to her, " 'I might very well have kept you outside of marriage,

---

[169] Meech and Allen, eds., *The Book of Margery Kempe* 1.21, 86; pp. 48–49, 212.

[170] *Rev.* 4.53; cf. the similar tropes in 4.71–72, in which Christ addresses the question of Cecilia, Bridget's youngest child, who had been dedicated as a nun by Bridget and had left the convent to marry with the assistance of her brother, Carl (Jørgensen, *Saint Bridget of Sweden*, 1:131, 2:75). On the basis of Bridget's early vocation to virginity and the likelihood of a broken vow, it is also possible to read these visions in terms of her fears for her own as well as her daughter's soul.

[171] " 'Quod vero mirabaris de domina que ad indulgentias veniens corrupta est. Repondio [sic] tibi. Sunt quedam mulieres qui [sic] continentiam habent sed non diligunt: quibus nec delectatio magna est nec temptatio violenta: quibus si nuptie honorande preberentur susciperent quidem; sed quia non offeruntur magna: dedignantur parua. Et ideo ex continentia aliquando oritur superbia et presumptio: propter quam [sic] contingit ex permissione diuina cadere sicut iam audisti. Si vero aliqua talis esset intentionis: quod nec propter totum mundum si ei preberetur vellet semel maculari: impossibile est talem relinqui ad turpia. Veruntamen si deus permitteret ex occulta iusticia sua talem cadere: plus fieret ei ad coronam quam ad peccatum: dummodo esset contra eius voluntatem,' " (*Rev.* 4.20).

and thus drawn you from every transitory good. But this I did not do, so that my praise and glory should be enlarged and extended that much more.'" Dorothea understood this as meaning that divine goodness would be more evident if it worked through marriage than if she had been preserved in virginity and innocence.[172]

And so, out of the debris of a childhood vocation to chastity, a new vocation is formed. The emphasis on anatomical chastity is necessarily deflected toward its spiritual counterpart. Moreover, this shift is complemented by an emphasis on obedience and, as a kind of corollary, humility: the first being the virtue that accounts for the loss of physical chastity, and the second being the abjection arising from its loss.[173] For this new penitential topos to work, it is essential that the priority of anatomical virginity, though tested, is never seriously doubted.

The orientation of Frances of Rome's visionary life in particular exemplifies those exculpating and liberating qualities of humility and obedience. On the feast of All Saints, Mary Magdalene counsels Frances concerning the various virtues she needs in order to join their company: the first she mentions is humility, the last obedience.[174] The column of virgin saints that follows Mary Magdalene and St. Agnes proclaims, " 'We are sisters of the Mother of God on account of our humility.'"[175] In a later vision God himself reassures Frances, " 'All the things you did, you did out of obedience, and nothing stained you because I gave you a guardian and preserved you in my blessing, nor did you ever displease me.'"[176]

Most striking of all is the last vision that her confessor, John Mattiotti, records and which is meant to symbolize holy obedience. In

---

[172] " 'Ego bene te conservassem extra matrimonium, et sic attraxissem te ab omni bono transitorio. Sed hoc non feci, ut laus mea et gloria eo plus maioretur et dilatetur'" (Vita Dorotheae 2.20, p. 82; cf. Akten . . . Dorotheas, p. 272).

[173] Richard Kieckhefer rightly points out how frequently patience and humility are evoked as complementary virtues, manifesting themselves simultaneously in the same incident in a saint's life. He chooses to focus on patience for its narrative capacity, while "humility was a matter of inward disposition" (Unquiet Souls, pp. 64–65). My emphasis on humility is for precisely this inward quality, which replaces physical chastity.

[174] AA SS, March, vol. 2, vis. 43, p. 134.

[175] " 'Sumus Matris Dei Sorores propter suam humilitatem'" (ibid., p. 135; also cf. the discourses of various saints on obedience and humility in vis. 55, p. 143; vis. 59, p. 144; and vis. 62, p. 145).

[176] " 'Omnia fecisti per obedientiam, et nulla res te maculavit, eo quod ego te sustinui et custodiam tibi dedi, et in mea benedictione te semper conservavi, neque mihi umquam displicuisti'" (ibid. vis. 41, p. 133). "Guardian" refers to the various guardian angels, assigned to Frances throughout most of her life, which only she could see (p. 96; Processi . . . Francesca, arts. 46–47, pp. 89–94).

the midst of a square stands the column of fortitude, which is flanked by four wheels. The wheels are securely chained to the column. On each of the wheels a text appears. The writing on the first wheel has unfortunately been omitted by the scribe; the second wheel proclaims that it wishes to turn in the shadow of its own judgment; the third represents a kind of self-absorbed vanity—a wheel that finds itself extraordinary; while the fourth wheel represents vain desires for the things that one does not have. None of the wheels is permitted to turn: the first is chained by humility, the second by purity, the third by hope, the fourth by wisdom.[177]

The vision of holy obedience carries with it an implicit rejection of Frances's childhood vocation to virginity and the eremitic life. Nor is it surprising that once, when St. Onuphrius appears before her and attempts to lure her to the desert, Frances immediately recognizes him as a demon and answers: " 'Oh, most wretched one, how vile you are!. . . I want to remain where it pleases my Lord, and I desire nothing beyond that which is pleasing to him.' "[178]

Frances's vision of Onuphrius occurred sometime between 1430 and 1434, during the trying years when her domestic responsibilities were focused on constant attention around her husband's sickbed—a period in which her desire for escape must have been particularly

[177] "Et vidit ipsa Beata quatuor rotas in quodam loco quadrato positas, in quarum medio erat [columna, et singulae rotae erant] ligatae cum una catena ad praedictam columnam: quae quidem catenae erant insimul insertae. In prima rota tales erant litterae scriptae. . . . [missing] In secunda vero rota istae litterae scriptae erant: Ego desidero [manere] in meo apparere, et in meis tenebris semper me volvo. In tertia vero rota sic erat scriptum: Vado quaerendo quod habeo, et semper me revolvo et inusitatam . . . invenio. In quarta vero erant hae litterae: semper desidero quod habere non possum, frustra me revolvo in temporis perditione. In prima vero catena sic erat scriptum: Ego sum humilitas nobilis et perfecta, refraeno primam rotam, ut teneat veritatem, nec se rumpat in vili apparere. In secunda vero catena hae erant litterae: Ego sum puritas constans et firma, non permitto secundam rotam volvi, teneo eam, nec permitto submergi. In tertia vero catena sic erat scriptum: Spes sum cum oculis firmis, teneo tertiam rotam, nec eam permitto in mari suffocari. In quarta catena hae erant litterae: Ego sum sapientia in bonis propositis tenendis, teneo quartam rotam, nec permitto eam impediri. In columna vero hoc erat scriptum: In columna ista denotatur vera fortitudo, quae est stabilita cum potentia tenendi, et sic teneo ligatas istas catenas et cum Deo firmatas" (*AA SS*, March, vol. 2, vis. 97, p. 154). For Frances's rather idiosyncratic use of *apparere* in the sense of "will" or "caprice," see Dom. Du Cange et al., *Glossarium mediae et infimae Latinitatis* (Paris, 1937), 1:324.

[178] " 'O miserrime quantum es vilis! . . . Ego volo manere ubi placet meo Domino, et nihil aliud desidero praeter id, quod sibi placet' " (*AA SS*, March, 2:161). Her relations with Onuphrius are not always negative, however. See vis. 84, pp. 151–152, where he warns Frances against earthly love and instructs her on the proper way to love God.

acute.[179] But early on in her marriage, she had already received divine assurance that physical retreat to a desert hermitage was not technically necessary. Once when Frances and her sister-in-law, Vanessa, were longing for the eremitical life, two figs dropped from heaven—the concrete fruits of intentionality.[180] Her rejection of Onuphrius's offer of escape, either to a desert or to a cloister, held good for all time. Frances founded an order of oblates that was affiliated with the Benedictine convent of Monte Oliveto.[181] Bound by no vows, she ended her days working among the poor.

Catherine of Genoa's vocation underwent a similar process of redefinition. It will be remembered that when Catherine's misery in marriage reached a crisis point, she appealed to St. Benedict, the most auspicious representative of her shattered monastic dream, asking him for an illness. The following day, she received an infusion of divine love in the course of her Lenten confession.[182] During the next four years, Catherine undertook a harsh program of asceticism, especially remarkable for her extensive fasts.[183] She also received divine instruction on how to conduct herself in her new penitential life: of particular interest is the command that she should never excuse but always accuse herself.[184] From this time on, Catherine appealed to no more saints—a decision not prompted by disaffection, but by her desire to embrace the full austerity of divine justice.[185] Her acceptance of her new vocation was already complete when she attended a sermon on the Magdalene's conversion and said within her heart, " 'I understand you.' "[186] As noted by the most influential modern biographer of Catherine, Baron von Hügel, all traces of Catherine's monastic vocation vanished in the wake of her conversion, to the extent that she did not even affiliate herself with one of the tertiary orders, although her husband became a Franciscan tertiary.[187] She spent the remainder of her life in hospital work.

[179] The editor's introduction to Frances's visions points out that Mattiotti recorded visions only for these years (AA SS, March, 2:91). It is unclear why he stopped at this point.

[180] Processi . . . Francesca art. 111, p. 176.

[181] AA SS, March, 2:96.

[182] Caterina. Biog. c. 4, p. 114.

[183] Caterina. Biog. c. 7–8, pp. 122–131. On the significance of Catherine's fasting and her use of food metaphors, see Bynum, Holy Feast and Holy Fast, pp. 182–185.

[184] Caterina. Biog. c. 10, p. 135.

[185] Von Hügel, The Mystical Element, 1:124, 127. See in particular Il Dialogo Spirituale, when the Soul proclaims that it alone wishes to atone for all the evil it has done (Bonzi da Genova, ed., Edizione critica, 2:399).

[186] Caterina. Biog. c. 8, p. 131.

[187] Von Hügel, The Mystical Element, 1:130.

The piety of all these women reveals a general anti-institutional orientation. Having struggled against the powerful odds of marriage and consummation to develop a vocation, they were no longer suited to a conventional-conventual religious life. This distinguishes them from a number of their virgin counterparts, for whom the cloister was still an option. But the different alternatives that the formerly sexually active women turned to varied widely. Mary of Oignies lived an uncloistered life in a Beguine milieu. Although Bridget of Sweden founded a religious order, she never entered, instead embarking on a prophetic career in Rome. Margery Kempe chose the peripatetic life of pilgrimage. Dorothea of Montau became a recluse (an almost unheard-of vocation in Prussia) attached to the church at Marienwerder. Even Margaret Beaufort, who followed the more traditional pattern of latter-day conversion, remained in the world, continuing to take an active part in her own brand of religiopolitical patronage.[188]

The women who were most directly implicated in the monastic life were Humility of Faenza and Hedwig of Silesia. But the fit was never quite right. The noble Humility's desire to enter a convent was thwarted at the age of fifteen when she was forced to marry. She was married for nine years and produced two children before her husband's failing health made him yield to his wife's lifelong desire for chastity. They remained in the world only another year before they separated in favor of the monastic life. But Humility had, to some extent, outgrown her childhood dream. She found that the community life at the monastery of St. Perpetua left her insufficient time for prayer. One night she was led out of the convent to the Poor Clares by an invisible being, but this was only a temporary refuge. Soon after, she attached herself to the church of St. Apollinaris as an anchoress, where she engaged in great austerities for twelve years. Eventually, at the request of the rector of the Vallombrosan order, she emerged from her hermitage, and lived to found two convents.[189]

Hedwig of Silesia, on the other hand, resided primarily at her monastic foundation of Trebnicz after her permanent conversion to chastity. She never took the veil, much to the bewilderment of her daughter Gertrude, who was a member of the community. After the death of Henry, Gertrude continually harassed her mother about taking her religious vows. Hedwig answered only, " 'Are you not aware,

---

[188] For an overview of Margaret's patronage and charities, and their political ramifications, see Malcolm G. Underwood, "Politics and Piety in the Household of Lady Margaret Beaufort," *Journal of Ecclesiastical History* 38 (1987): 39–52; also see idem, "Lady Margaret and Her Cambridge Connections," *Sixteenth Century Journal* 13 (1982): 67–81.

[189] *AA SS*, May, 5:208–209, 210.

daughter, how great are the merits that alms bestow?'"[190] In fact, her penitential way of life was considerably more severe than if she had been bound by a rule.[191] A good part of Hedwig's resistance to religious vows, however, seems to be rooted in her profound sense of "otherness" from the nuns: a sense that stimulated and reinforced her vocation to penitence. Hedwig kissed the places in the choir where the sisters placed their feet and the towels on which they dried their feet. She also dunked her head in their dirty water and even bathed her grandchildren in it, so strong was her sense of the sisters' sanctity.[192]

Masculine Motives for Spiritual Marriage

Canonists and theologians alike feared that the transition from a carnal to a spiritual marriage might threaten the husband's authority, and did what they could to guard against this possibility. The husbands in question were no strangers to this fear and likewise took precautionary measures: thus we find men like John Kempe insisting that his wife still continue to eat and sleep with him before he will agree to chastity. Frances of Rome's husband, on the other hand, stipulated that she must continue to obey him and that she must promise never to leave him.[193] Given these masculine qualms, which we will find are by no means unjustified, it becomes especially interesting to see under what circumstances the men in question were prepared to concede their wives' desire for chastity.

Almost invariably, the husband has been brought low through some reversal of fortune. They were frequently afflicted by ill health, old age, or a combination of the two. Certainly this is true of Humility of Faenza's husband: Ugolotto, although a young man, was warned by his doctors after a severe illness that death was certain unless he gave up sex.[194] Bridget of Sweden's husband, Ulf, was clearly respectful of chastity and relatively sympathetic to his wife's vocation, as his delay in consummating their marriage suggests. And yet he agreed to chastity only after the marriage had produced eight children and after

---

[190] "'Num ignoras filia, quanti sit meriti eleemosynas elargiri?'" (*AA SS*, October, 8:227).

[191] Her hagiographer says this explicitly (ibid.), as well as detailing her numerous penances, particularly fasting. See especially pp. 230–233.

[192] Ibid., p. 228.

[193] Meech and Allen, eds., *The Book of Margery Kempe* 1.11, p. 24; for Frances, see the later life of Anguillaria, *AA SS*, March, 2:183.

[194] *AA SS*, May, 5:208.

his health had failed him on the return home from a pilgrimage to Santiago de Compostella.[195] Ulf was probably around forty-six at the time of the vow, while his wife was forty-two. A similar pattern is apparent with respect to Dorothea of Montau and her husband. In 1380, after seventeen years of marriage and nine children—only one daughter, Gertrude, had survived the ravages of the plague—Adalbert finally released Dorothea from the conjugal debt, and they spent the last ten years of their marriage in chastity.[196] Although Dorothea was only thirty-three at the time, we know that Adalbert was considerably her senior and that her petition was probably assisted by his indifferent health, and perhaps by the deaths of their children. Frances of Rome's husband, Lorenzo Ponziano, also fits into this pattern: during the last twelve of their forty years of married life they abstained sexually. Lorenzo had always been supportive of his wife's vocation and was proud of her piety. Even so, he waited until she had borne him six children or so. Moreover, Lorenzo was a sick man, having suffered exile at the hands of Ladislaus of Naples, during which time he was imprisoned and severely wounded.[197]

But other crises, besides ill health, could turn men to chastity. Catherine of Genoa's husband, Giuliano Adorno, for example, underwent a crisis as a result of bankruptcy. This paved the way for a conversion to chastity that occurred within about a year.[198] The sudden death of a child continues to be a common impetus toward chastity for either sex. The children of Ugolotto and Humility of Faenza, for example, died just after baptism, which may have shaped their decision to renounce the world formally.[199]

[195] *Acta . . . Birg.* art. 23, pp. 20, 305, 505; *Vita . . . Brig.*, pp. 79–80. They left for Compostella in 1341, and Ulf sickened on the return home and died in 1344. Thus they may have lived chastely for three years prior to a formal vow, if one considers the theoretically mandatory chastity undertaken by participants on a pilgrimage. Although after his vow of chastity Ulf had intended to take the Cistercian habit, he did not live to do so.

[196] *Vita Dorotheae* 2.30, p. 92; *Akten . . . Dorotheas*, pp. 108, 309. Gertrude became a nun and Dorothea dictated a short spiritual treatise for her. See Richard Stachnik, ed., "Die Geistliche Lehre der Frau Dorothea von Montau an ihre Tochter im Frauenkloster zu Kulm," *Zeitschrift für Ostforschung Länder und Völker im östlichen Mitteleuropa* 3 (1954): 589–596.

[197] *Processi . . . Francesca*, pp. 39, 46–47; *AA SS*, March, 2:96; later life by Anguillaria, p. 183.

[198] *Caterina. Biog.* c. 24, p. 230; Bynum, *Holy Feast and Holy Fast*, p. 181.

[199] On the death of Humility and Ugolotto's children, see *AA SS*, May, 5:209, note g. The death and miraculous resuscitation of a child probably prompted the mutual vow of chastity of Isidore the Laborer (d. 1130) and his wife Mary Torribia (*AA SS*, May, 3: 549). Details concerning their married life, however, are quite late. Isidore's *vita* was written in 1275, while Mary's *vita* was written as late as 1615. The tale about their son is from the later *vita*, which was a part of the process conducted for Isidore in 1615.

When no explicit crisis can be identified, the husbands still agreed to chastity only after the requirements of posterity had been met. Henry and Hedwig had six or seven children; Margery Kempe and John had fourteen. The major exception to this pattern is Mary of Oignies's husband, John, who agreed to chastity soon after their marriage and before the birth of any children.[200]

The few husbands who actually initiated the movement toward chastity, on the other hand, reflect the gender differences in patterns of conversion outlined by Weinstein and Bell. Women generally possess a religious vocation that can be traced back to their childhood; men experience a more sudden conversion as an adolescent or adult. The husband's chaste resolve is not freestanding or so absolute a standard as is the wife's, but is entangled with a series of renunciations that are set in motion by remorse over their past lives. In the case of the twelfth-century noble Magnus of Orkney, who wasted much of his youth in a pirate's life of booty and bloodshed, his commitment to chastity seems penitential in the old-fashioned, functional sense. Until he was treacherously murdered, Magnus lived with his bride for ten years in unsullied, but not undisturbed, virginity (he took frequent icy baths to slake his lust), seemingly in atonement for his past sins, as would a public penitent.[201] James Oldo of Lodi (d. 1404) was an Italian bourgeois who led a life of singular frivolity during the grim period of the Black Death. His sudden conversion occurred when he lay down in the cave of the local church of the Holy Sepulcher, in jest, to see whether he was taller than Christ. But he was also doubtless affected by the sudden loss of his two young daughters during the plague, who both died on the same day. Because his mother was concerned that his wife, Catherine, was too young to give up sex, it took James seven years before he finally made his break with his past life, becoming a Franciscan tertiary and entering the priesthood. His last three years with his wife were spent in total continence, although they continued to share the same bed.[202] John Colombini (d. 1367) was a rich Sienese merchant, who was converted while reading the life of St. Mary of Egypt. His call to a life of extreme poverty also occurred around the time of the Black Death, which probably had some influence. But of undoubted importance were his

[200] AA SS, June, 5:550. Mary, who had been married at fourteen, was still a young woman.

[201] G. W. Dasent, trans., "Magnus' Saga the Longer," in Icelandic Sagas: The Orkneyingers' Saga, Rolls Series, no. 88 (London, 1894), 3:247, 251–252, 254–255. Also see the hymns from the Aberdeen Breviary that eulogize his virginal marriage, AA SS, April, 2:436–437.

[202] AA SS, April, 2:598. James's life was written in 1448 by his confessor.

general misgivings about his substantial commercial success. Furthermore, his conversion followed fast on the heels of a political reversal. The Sienese Nine, of whom John was one, fell from power in 1355. A few months after this event, John experienced his conversion.[203] He lived in total chastity with his wife, Biagia, for eight years before he was able to win her permission to be entirely free to live an itinerant life of poverty.[204] A possible exception to this pattern of male remorse may be Chiarito del Voglia of Florence (d. between 1350 and 1356), but the sources for his life are poor and not much is known of his disposition prior to his conversion. It seems that he converted as a result of a vision of St. Zenobius, took a vow of chastity with his wife, and began to organize groups of female virgins in the religious life. Chiarito eventually founded a convent over which he made his wife abbess, and from then on served the nuns in the lowly position of lay brother.[205]

All of the men who initiated chaste marriages were fortunate in their choice of a spouse; none of these women seems to have placed any obstacle in the way of her husband's wish to live chastely. This is all the more remarkable when one considers the relative youth of these wives, which we can roughly approximate on the basis of their husbands' ages. Robert Malatesta was eighteen when he lived virginally with his wife for the first year and a half of their marriage; Magnus of Orkney was approximately twenty-five at the time of his marriage, hence thirty-five at the time of his death; James Oldo was approximately twenty-six at the time of his conversion and thirty by the time that he and his wife Catherine decided to live chastely; Chiarito del Voglia was twenty-eight at the time of his conversion. John Colombini, on the other hand, married as late as thirty-nine and was converted at fifty-one. We know from his biographer, however, that his wife was considerably his junior and still young when she agreed to a vow of chastity.[206]

[203] F. Belcari, *Vita del beato Giovanni Colombini da Siena* (Verona, 1817), pp. 25–27. Belcari, the Florentine poet, wrote this life in 1449. For an interesting discussion of the church's ambivalence toward the merchant, see Jacques Le Goff, *Your Money or Your Life: Economy and Religion in the Middle Ages*, trans. P. Ranum (New York, 1988), and idem, "Merchant's Time and Church's Time in the Middle Ages," in *Time, Work, and Culture in the Middle Ages*, trans. A. Goldhammer (Chicago and London, 1980), pp. 29–42, 289–293. Also see Vauchez, *La sainteté*, pp. 234–243, and Diana M. Webb, "A Saint and His Money," in *The Church and Wealth*, ed. W. J. Sheils and Diana Wood, Ecclesiastical History Society (London, 1987), pp. 61–73. See William M. Bowsky, *A Medieval Italian Commune: Siena under the Nine, 1287–1355* (Berkeley and Los Angeles, 1981), p. 262.

[204] Belcari, *Giovanni Colombini*, p. 38.

[205] *AA SS*, May, 6:160–161; Weinstein and Bell, *Saints and Society*, p. 80. The entry in *Acta Sanctorum* is based on the 1653 Italian life of Antonius Maria.

[206] Belcari, *Giovanni Colombini*, p. 27.

Of course, it would be wrong to exaggerate the docility of these women. But the worldly wife's resistance is only a pale reflection of that of the worldly husband, since, in point of fact, she was not empowered to interfere with his charities. Her objections are frequently presented as nagging; like Noah's querulous "Uxor," she provides a humorous secular backdrop that illuminates her holier husband. Generally, the wife's opposition is swept away by a miraculously full cupboard.[207] A rather more nuanced treatment of this subject, however, occurs in the life of John Colombini, since it was his wife, Biagia, who had been constantly trying to move her husband to greater piety and was responsible for putting the pivotal book of saints' lives in his hands. Yet Biagia was in no way prepared for the extravagant acts of self-denial that followed in the wake of her husband's midlife crisis. To use her own analogy, she had asked only for a little rain—not a deluge.[208] She scolded him for his excessive alms, the extent of his self-abasement, and the lepers he placed in their bed.[209] Nevertheless, John's request for chastity was readily met.

Gender-specific patterns, however, are by no means inalterable. Some men undoubtedly had an early vocation to chastity, while some women just as surely underwent an adult conversion. Women were more vulnerable to pressures to marry, but men also yielded to such pressures.[210] The career of Robert Malatesta, born to succeed to the

---

[207] This story is told in the life of Blessed Lucchese, though it is common to many saints of either sex. His wife, Bona Dona, was initially hostile to his conversion, but this miracle convinced her to join her husband in his vocation (AA SS, April, 3:605–606). They were, according to tradition, the first Franciscan tertiaries to receive the habit from Francis himself. Lucchese's conversion is typical in that he was a member of the bourgeoisie who was totally engrossed in politics and moneymaking. He had a midlife conversion, sometime between the ages of thirty and forty, brought on partially by the death of his children. The couple may also have had a spiritual marriage, but the sources are unclear on this score, so they are not included in my reckoning. It should be noted that although food is more central to female than to male piety, miracles involving food multiplication are found with relative frequency in the lives of men as well (Bynum, *Holy Feast and Holy Fast*, pp. 76, 192–193).

[208] Belcari, *Giovanni Colombini*, p. 32.

[209] Ibid., pp. 30–37.

[210] See, for example, the case of Maurice Czasky (d. 1336), crown prince of Hungary. As a child, Maurice was especially influenced by the story of St. Alexis and was thus inclined from his childhoood to enter a monastery. He was, however, forced to marry Catherine, daughter of the palatine prince Amadeus, a woman of similar spiritual aspirations. After three years of marriage, the young couple mutually agreed to separate and enter religious institutions. The external opposition was immense: Maurice was imprisoned for half a year and both parties were questioned closely, but they were equally firm in their resolve and eventually had their way (AA SS, March, 3:252). It is possible, perhaps even probable, that the marriage between this pious couple was never consummated, but if this was the case, it was a well-kept secret. At any rate, Maurice was intent on separation and was lucky that his wife was of the same mind.

governorship of Brescia, is a poignant reminder not only of the limitations of a gendered model but, indeed, of how fragile gender constructions are, in general.

Robert is an exception in many ways. From among the twenty-four cases of spiritual marriage listed in appendixes 5 and 6, five of which were instigated by males, Robert is the only one who was the victim of a forced marriage. He did not resort to the time-honored masculine model of flight from the marriage bed. In this, and in practically every other way, Robert's piety corresponds to a characteristically female profile. Robert was possessed of a religious vocation by the time he was five. In response to his uncle's queries as to what gift he would like, he asserted that he wanted to be poor—much to the disgust of the rest of the company, who derided him for requesting vile and feminine things.[211] Robert practiced secret austerities in his youth: unauthorized vigils and a discreet avoidance of delicacies. He married reluctantly, out of obedience, but failed to consummate the marriage for a year and a half. His confessors eventually intervened and forced him to pay the debt. Apparently Robert claimed that he would rather be tortured most bitterly than render the debt, and deeply believed that God was offended by the sex act.[212] A later life adds that he wept after the experience.[213] Robert had been married in November of 1427; he assumed the governorship in September of 1429. His earliest *vita* reports that, freed from the surveillance of his paternal uncle, he was now able to increase his austerities. The assumption of rule also coincided with the beginning of visions and ecstasies that culminate in Robert's reception of the stigmata. But it is also significant that the increased austerities and the mystical experience coincide almost exactly with his reluctant sexual initiation.[214]

Robert was scarcely twenty-two when he died, so it is impossible to know whether his later matrimonial life would have been marked by

[211] Constantino Bartolucci, ed., *Legenda B. Galeoti Roberti de Malatestis* c. 5, *Archivum Franciscanum Historicum* 8 (1915): 540. This is considered to be the earliest life; it was first redacted by 1433.

[212] "Et audio quod dicebat, quod prius vellet asperrime torqueri quam ad carnalem devenire copulam; tantum enim sanctissima castitas ei placebat, quod etiam putabat offendere Deum in matrimoniali copula" (ibid. c. 19, p. 545). On his youthful fasts, see c. 7, pp. 540–541; on his forced marriage, see c. 9, p. 541.

[213] See the Latin life by Mariano of Florence (before the end of the fifteenth century), "Vitae duae B. Galeoti Roberti de Malatestis" c. 9, ed. Gregorio Giovanardi, *Archivum Franciscanum Historicum* 21 (1928): 70.

[214] For the increased austeries, see Bartolucci, ed., *Legenda B. Galeoti Roberti de Malatestis* c. 11–12, pp. 541–542; for his mystical experiences, see c. 13–16, pp. 542–544; on the dating of his marriage and accession to power, see p. 541 nn. 1 and 2. Also see Gregorio Giovanardi, "Il B. Galeotto Roberto Malatesta," *Miscellanea Francescana* 35 (1936): 287–297, esp. pp. 287–288.

a return to chastity. This option would probably have been available, since Robert, though perhaps having little in common with the men described above, did share in the good fortune that brought them wives who were genuinely pious, or, at the very least, reasonably tractable. Robert's wife, Margaret d'Este, had been raised with Catherine of Bologna (d. 1463) and was of a pious disposition from youth. During Robert's lifetime, she had collaborated with him in his charities;[215] after his death, she resisted pressure to remarry, in spite of her youth, and lived out her life as one of Catherine's companions.[216]

Synchronization of Vocations: The Transition from Carnal to Spiritual Marriage

The inequitable spiritual capacities of husband and wife is an old story. Even when a couple separated immediately in order to enter religious institutions, by far the easier solution, there were innumerable pitfalls. Conrad of Piacenza (d. 1351), who inadvertently caused a fire while flushing out quarry during a hunting expedition, was forced to pay damages with his wife's dowry. She entered the Poor Clares, and he became a hermit under the direction of the Franciscans. But Conrad obviously suffered profound guilt over his wife's rather forced vocation, which his hagiographer chooses to record in the form of demonic temptations. For example, demons told him that his wife had wanted to follow him, had left her cloister, that her chastity was in danger.[217] The Spaniard Gonsalvo Sancii (d. 1361), on the other hand, convinced that he was dying, gained his wife's permission to join the Franciscans. When he recovered, his wife appealed to the bishop to restore him, as was her right. Gonsalvo, however, un-

---

215 See, for example, Bartolucci, ed., *Legenda B. Galeoti Roberti de Malatestis* c. 26, p. 547.

216 Catherine of Bologna's life, written about fifty years after her death, narrates how she was raised with Margaret (*AA SS*, March, 2:36; on Catherine's career, also see McLaughlin, "Creating and Recreating Communities of Women," pp. 279–285). Catherine also intervened through her prayers to ensure that Margaret, who had been unwillingly betrothed to a second husband, not be forced to remarry. On the day that the solemnization was to occur, a messenger arrived to announce that the groom was dead. That night, Margaret had a vision of Robert, who told her that he alone was her spouse ("'Scito Margarita me tuum esse sponsum, ac nolle ut alii viro jungaris'"), and married her for a second time. From that point she lived in chaste widowhood (*AA SS*, March, 2:38).

217 *AA SS*, February, 3:167–168 (from the life of Vincent Littara Netino of 1593) and notes d, h, and o, which present information concerning his wife, drawn from a later life of 1614.

canonically but adamantly refused to return and eventually convinced his wife to enter a convent, and to put their two daughters and one son into religious communities as well.[218] A similar story is told of Lucia Bartolini and her husband Ridolfo Rucellai. As Florentines in the time of Savonarola—himself a zealous advocate of chastity at all costs who seems even to have encouraged wives to withhold the debt without their husbands' permission—they mutually agreed to give up the world, once they had ascertained that they could have no children. Hence, they formally drew up an article of separation in the presence of a notary. Although this move had been made primarily on Ridolfo's initiative, and Lucia required considerable persuasion, he was nevertheless fed up with monastic life within seven months. When he attempted to reclaim her, she refused to comply and the furious husband vented his rage financially by leaving her nothing but her dowry.[219]

At least with regard to separation to enter religious communities, there is a time-honored social blueprint to be followed. Spiritual marriage had no clear blueprint. Very rarely do we hear of a transition to chastity that is allegedly mutual, as was the case with the pious comb-maker Peter Pettinaio (d. 1289) and his wife. But chastity presented itself as an alternative only after they knew that there were no children forthcoming.[220] More often, the move to a spiritual marriage was initiated by one party. With a male initiator, the transition tended to be friction-free; with a female initiator, the movement to chastity was frequently painful. Because spiritual marriage often followed a physical or psychic collapse in the male, while ushering in new freedom for the female, it could entail a radical break with former norms that made the transition especially traumatic for the husband. Moreover, both parties eventually became aware that a vow of chastity created certain reverberations that set a wider circle of changes in motion. For some women, spiritual marriage was a first step to a permanent separation. After Humility of Faenza and her

---

[218] The Fathers of the College of St. Bonaventure, eds., *Vita fratris Gonsalvi Sancii*, in *Chronica XXIV generalium Ordinis Minorum, Analecta Franciscana* 3 (1897): 549–552.

[219] *AA SS*, October, 13:204–205. The emphasis on chastity is in keeping with Savonarola's millenarian vision. See Donald Weinstein, *Savonarola and Florence: Prophecy and Patriotism in the Renaissance* (Princeton, N.J., 1970), esp. chap. 5.

[220] See Peter of Montarone, *Vita del beato Pietro Pettinajo* (Siena, 1802), c. 1, pp. 9–10. This life, composed by a fellow Franciscan and the main font for Peter, was originally written in Latin ca. 1330. All that remains is the sixteenth-century Italian translation of the original. For an analysis of contemporary and later references to the saint, see Francesco Cristofani, "Memorie del B. Pietro Pettinagno da Siena," *Miscellanea Francescana* 5 (1890): 34–52.

husband, Ugolotto, converted to chastity, things happened very quickly. In about a year, though weeping bitterly, Ugolotto permitted his wife to enter the Vallombrosan order, where he became a lay brother. Humility's entrance into religion at the early age of twenty-four was the start of a new life for her: we are told that she "suddenly began to be changed into a new woman."[221] She never agreed to see her husband again, but his attachment to her was the center of his existence. When she moved first to the Poor Clares and then to an enclosed cell, her husband followed. Furthermore, he took a vow of obedience first to the abbot of his monastery, but next to his wife.[222] A vow of chastity was, likewise, the first in a series of steps taken by Dorothea of Montau to escape her husband's control. In 1397, seven years after Adalbert had pledged chastity, she almost won his permission to remain behind on a pilgrimage and live as a mendicant, while he would return home to Prussia with their daughter. They were waiting in a church for the priest, who was to have drawn up the document of separation, when her excessive joy (she could not help crying " 'bread on behalf of our Beloved Lord!' " in preparation for her mendicant life) caused Adalbert to rethink his position.

> While she sat in such jubilation awaiting the parish priest with her husband, her husband changed his mind. For he began to grieve that he had given the permission to Dorothea. On that account when the priest arrived, he [Adalbert] launched a complaint against his wife that she wished to desert him and to remain in that spot, and he began pleading with the priest to induce her to return home with him.[223]

Even without a formal agreement to separate, the altered position of women in spiritual marriage is especially demonstrated by a much more flexible situation and greater freedom of movement for the wife. With regard to Mary of Oignies and her husband John, after spending a number of years tending the lepers at Nivelles, Mary received a revelation that she should move to Oignies and proceeded to do so alone.[224] Hedwig and Henry only met at intervals that Hedwig determined.[225] After their vow of chastity, Margery Kempe continued to make a pious tour of England in the company of her husband. They

---

[221] "Subito coepit in feminam alteram transmutari" (AA SS, May, 5:208).

[222] Ibid., p. 209.

[223] "Ea in tanta iubilacione sedente et marito plebanum expectante mutata fuit voluntas viri. Cepit enim dolere, quod licenciam dederat Dorothee. Idcirco veniente plebano querelam deposuit contra conparem suam, quod vellet eum deserere et ibi in loco permanere instititque precibus apud plebanum, ut eam induceret ad partes secum remeandum" (Vita Dorotheae 3.10, p. 127).

[224] AA SS, June, 5:568.

[225] AA SS, October, 8:226.

separated when she went to the Holy Land and lived apart on her return, but she went back home to nurse him in his last illness.[226] Dorothea of Montau likewise made independent pilgrimages, since at the time of Adalbert's death in Prussia in 1390 she was in Rome for the Jubilee year.[227]

In view of some of these vexed histories, it is not surprising that references to the deepening of the bond between spouses, implicit in the spiritualized definition of marriage, are generally absent. The only exception is Jacques de Vitry's eulogy of the marriage of Mary of Oignies and her husband John. It is worth emphasizing that John is something of an exception among husbands since he readily agreed to chastity early on in the marriage, graciously bypassing the usual prerequisite of children. Jacques's rhetoric of the enhanced spiritual bond is corroborated by a vision in which the wife psychically honors her husband's generosity.

> Indeed, the more he [John] separated himself from her in carnal affection, the more he was joined to her by the bond of spiritual marriage through love [dilectionem]. Whereupon, the Lord, afterward appearing to his handmaid in a vision, promised that her companion, who out of love of chastity had withdrawn himself from carnal commerce on earth, would be restored to her in heaven, as if in reparation for the marriage.[228]

But it is equally clear that many of these marriages, even happy ones like the marriage of Bridget and Ulf, were too burdened by the flesh and would stagger under the weight of such lofty constructions. Dorothea of Montau and Adalbert are the only ones who are explicitly compared to Mary and Joseph, but the allusion is to the holy couple's apocryphal avatars. One priest at the church of Pomerania said, " 'It is a marvel that so pretty a woman, devoted and courteous, should sustain reproaches and blows so patiently from that old Joseph!' "[229]

[226] Meech and Allen, eds., *The Book of Margery Kempe* 1.15, 26, 76; pp. 32, 60, 79–80.

[227] *Vita Dorotheae* 3.26, p. 147; see the chronological chart, p. 414. Adalbert also undertook pilgrimages alone. Dorothea was especially appreciative of his absences, as they provided opportunities for her to increase her austerities and church attendance (2.28, p. 91).

[228] "Quanto autem affectu carnali ab ea divisus est, tanto magis matrimonii spiritualis nexu ei per dilectionem conjunctus est. Unde et ancillae suae Dominus postea in visione apparens promisit, ut socium suum, quasi reparato matrimonii, ei redderet in coelis, qui castitatis amore a carnali commercio se subtraxerat in terris" (*AA SS*, June, 5:550).

[229] " 'Mirum est, quod tam pulchra mulier, devota et faceta, obprobria et verbera sustinet tam patienter ab illo antiquo Joseph!' " (*Akten . . . Dorotheas*, p. 390); cf. the incident on a pilgrimage when some passing jokers asked her if she were carrying Joseph to the fountain of youth (*Vita Dorotheae* 3.9, pp. 124–125).

As the spiritualized bond recedes, the didactic thrust of these stories becomes progressively focused on the conversion of the unbelieving spouse.[230] The husband's conversion to chastity is frequently the most apparent symbol of the wife's success. But since most of the husbands in question were insensible to the gentle "Cecilian" nudge, the "carrot-and-stick" ethic—a message clearly directed to women—is unmistakable: chastity is most effectively purchased through female submission. Indeed, in the later Middle Ages, both inside and outside of hagiographical genres, the story of the long-suffering wife most completely fulfills Paul's expectations by achieving more than a nominal conversion of her husband.

Catherine of Genoa's life reads like a stellar application of this rather punitive program. For the first ten years of marriage to Giuliano Adorno, she was either abused or neglected, and subjected to the shame of his flagrant adultery (we know of at least one illegitimate daughter). As a result, she suffered, purportedly by her own and her biographer's admission, intense mental anguish. It was the wretched state produced by her husband's behavior that seems to have precipitated a kind of conversion experience. Indeed, her marriage is presented as part of the divine plan to free her from all earthly love.[231] Giuliano's own conversion came several years later, undoubtedly prompted by the bankruptcy brought on by his own reckless spending, as suggested above. But Catherine's biography, by placing two key statements in quick succession, suggests an even more important causal rhythm: during all the years of her marriage she was totally obedient to her husband; then God put it into his heart to pledge chastity.[232] Giuliano joined his wife in the care of the poor at the hospital of Pammatone, where they spent the last eleven years of

[230] See Vauchez, *La sainteté*, pp. 444–445.

[231] *Caterina. Biog.* c. 3–4, pp. 114–115; cf. Bonzi da Genova, ed., *Il Dialogo Spirituale*, in *Edizione critica*, 2:399–400, in which the Soul describes its despair. See von Hügel, *The Mystical Element*, 1:102. Also see Bynum, *Holy Feast and Holy Fast*, pp. 181–182. Note Bynum's important cautionary statement that argues against the tendency to regard Catherine's conversion as a sudden crisis, conforming to masculine patterns of conversion. As was seen above, Catherine was possessed of a vocation to chastity from childhood.

[232] After describing his bad disposition, it reads: "Nientedimeno questa santa anima sempre le fu obediente in tutto quello che era secondo la conscienza, etiam in quelle cose che erano contro sua volontà, et era patientissima al suo volere, il quale era spesso disordinato.

"Il Signore le fece questa gratia, che pose in cuore al marito di stare insieme come fratello e sorella" (*Caterina. Biog.* MS D, c. 24, p. 230). Also see Catherine's unhappy reflections on her married life after her husband's death. When her friend responded that now Catherine was free from a great subjection, however, Catherine answered that she had no will apart from God's (pp. 233–234).

Giuliano's life in one small room.[233] Their mysterious spiritual inter-dependence continued until Giuliano's death. His exasperation with his last illness caused Catherine to fear for his salvation. She left the room and began crying upon divine love on behalf of Giuliano's soul. (This is in spite of the fact that Catherine was so reluctant to interfere with the divine will that she rarely prayed for others—at the most she would offer certain people up to God—and asked no one to pray for her.)[234] She eventually received divine assurance that Giuliano would be saved, and when she returned to the room, his whole attitude had changed.[235] Giuliano behaved generously toward Catherine in his will, naming her as executrix and leaving her, in addition to her dowry, a sizable amount of his own money, as well as all the precious metals, cash, furniture, and fabric in his estate. According to the wording of the testament: "[He] knows and recognizes that the said Catherine, his beloved wife and heiress, has ever behaved herself well and laudably toward himself. . . . [and he] wants to provide the means for her continuing to lead, after his death, her quiet, peaceful, and spiritual mode of life."[236] Catherine, like a good wife in a wives' manual, personally undertook the support of his illegitimate daughter.[237]

Submission and Subversion

The transitional model of spiritual marriage enabled women to participate more fully in the penitential ethos that dominated their spiritual horizons and, as such, is an important cog in the contemporary profile of female sanctity. But what is the net impact of this profile? Scholars, such as Elizabeth Petroff, have pointed to the way that vi-

---

[233] Bonzi da Genova, ed., *Il Dialogo Spirituale*, in *Edizione critica*, 2:427; von Hügel, *The Mystical Element*, 1:142.

[234] Catherine said: "'Amore, ti domando questa anima, damela, ti prego, tu me la puoi dare!'" (*Caterina. Biog.* MS D, c. 24, p. 231). On Catherine's reticence regarding prayer, see von Hügel, *The Mystical Element*, 1:127.

[235] *Caterina. Biog.* MS D, c. 24, pp. 231–232. She performed a similar service for the husband of Argentina de Sale, her later spiritual companion, dispelling his impatience and despair on his deathbed (c. 25, pp. 236–245).

[236] As cited by von Hügel, *The Mystical Element*, 1:152. He also left money to his natural daughter and to a woman in the third-order Franciscans who von Hügel thinks was probably the mother (p. 151).

[237] See ibid., pp. 153–154; cf. the anecdote in *The Goodman of Paris* wherein a pious wife, learning of her husband's illegitimate child, privately seeks her out and pays to have her apprenticed and married without ever a word of reproach to the husband (Power, trans., 1.8, pp. 186–187).

sions could be personally empowering for individual women.[238] Nevertheless, the manner in which the lives and revelations of these women entered the public domain and how this should be interpreted is clearly a more complex matter: so complex, in fact, that David Herlihy's inclusion of the "charismatic sector" in his assessment of whether women experienced a Renaissance is, to my mind, ultimately problematical.[239] And yet the extent to which women's growing spiritual presence affects medieval power relations remains a tantalizing question. Luce Irigaray, for example, suggests that female mysticism eluded patriarchal control by constituting a uniquely female discourse which, in turn, created the first public forum for women.[240] Karma Lochrie confirms this insight by examining the power of abjection and transgression within mystical discourse.[241] Alternatively, Sarah Beckwith points to the way in which mystical discourse reifies and secures social gender constructions, ultimately confirming patriarchy.[242]

There is little doubt that the patterns of piety described above had considerable potential for liberating a specific woman from restrictive gender constructions. A scenario that is often taken as representing a new level of female prestige is that of the illiterate female visionary dictating to her confessor.[243] (The potential for a role reversal is, however, debatable, depending on whether one sees the woman as

[238] Petroff, *Medieval Women's Visionary Literature*, introd., pp. 6, 32; cf. eadem, the chapter entitled "Women's Visons, the Path to Power," in *The Consolation of the Blessed*, pp. 39–82.

[239] David Herlihy, "Did Women Have a Renaissance? A Reconsideration," *Medievalia et Humanistica*, n.s., 13 (1985): 1–22, esp. pp. 15–16.

[240] Luce Irigaray, *Speculum of the Other Woman*, trans. Gillian C. Gill (Ithaca, N.Y., 1985), p. 191; see "La mystérique," pp. 191–202, generally.

[241] Karma Lochrie, "The Language of Transgression: Body, Flesh, and Word in Mystical Discourse," in *Speaking Two Languages: Traditional Disciplines and Contemporary Theory in Medieval Studies*, ed. Allen J. Frantzen (Albany, N.Y., 1991), pp. 115–140, 253–264; cf. eadem, *Margery Kempe and Translations of the Flesh*, pp. 38–47. On the ways in which mystical discourse, and Margery's in particular, challenges the church hierarchy, see esp. pp. 86–88, 105–108, 114–127, 148–154. There is little doubt that out of the sources discussed in the present chapter, Margery's book comes closest to eluding and, possibly, subverting the kind of ecclesiastical monitoring I describe in the following pages. On the other hand, as Lochrie shows, Margery's text was soon "contained" by posterity, and her raucous voice edited out (pp. 220–224).

[242] Sarah Beckwith, "A Very Material Mysticism: The Medieval Mysticism of Margery Kempe," in *Medieval Literature: Criticism, Ideology, and History*, ed. David Aers (Brighton, 1986), pp. 34–57.

[243] For a brief description of the writing process for various female mystics, all dependent to some degree on a male amanuensis, see Katharina M. Wilson, ed., *Medieval Women Writers* (Athens, Ga., 1984), p. 113 for Hildegard; p. 154 for Mechtild of Magdeburg; pp. 229, 233 for Bridget of Sweden; p. 297 for Margery Kempe.

propelled to the narrative "driver's seat" or as taking the backseat to male mediation.) Lay piety, generally, but female piety, in particular, is riddled with undercurrents of dissent that frequently test the limits of pastoral counsel or even ecclesiastical control. Recently, Caroline Bynum has pointed out that the very extremism of female asceticism surrounding food in the high and late Middle Ages was a reaction to the religious authorities who were urging moderation.[244] Certainly, the impulse toward a spiritual marriage represents another instance of the extreme asceticism that could be construed as vigorously rejecting the church's liberalization of sexual mores. The church still preferred cloistered continence; thus spiritual marriage goes against its marked apprehension concerning intramarital chastity. Practically speaking, the transition to chastity, for the most part, loosened the husband's control over his wife, and this in itself posed a threat to the correct hierarchy of the sexes.

But do these factors add up to a subversion or at least a reconfiguration of gender and power relations? The potential for such a disruption appears to be present in these women's lives. And yet if it were truly present, the question arises as to why many of these women, robbed of their virginity, and thus embarking on a compensatory way of life that bore all the hallmarks of female extremism or even rebellion, were frequently honored as saints after their death, or even in their lifetime. Some even attained the ultimate public laurel of official canonization.

The answer becomes clearer if we remember that the laity was told to imitate a saint's virtues, not her actual deeds—a counsel that became more self-evident with the dramatic increase in austerities in the lives of later medieval saints. The operative virtues in this case are obedience and humility: the backbone of exemplary female behavior that has the potential for reinforcing female submission to masculine authority.

No hagiographer misses an opportunity to tell us that the female victim of a forced marriage consents only out of obedience to her parents. In the cases of Frances of Rome and Dorothea of Montau, we are additionally told that they pay the conjugal debt out of obedience to their confessors. Obedience to the husband, however, although absolutely central to this construct, could present a problem for the hagiographer and the promoters of a matron's cult alike. For some of these women, the tension between the husband's will and God's will is minimal. Even so, the sources convey a marked attempt to underline the correct hierarchy of the sexes. Although John, the husband of

[244] Bynum, *Holy Feast and Holy Fast*, pp. 237–244.

Mary of Oignies, "did not contradict the holy proposition of his wife as is the practice of other men," he still remained the titular head of the marriage. Long after their conversion to chastity, Jacques de Vitry stresses that she solicited the permission of her husband and of her confessor before her removal to Oignies. The fact that her confessor was actually John's brother possibly increases the degree of patri-archal control.[245] Likewise, although Frances of Rome's husband re-joiced "that that lady involved herself in divine matters and prayers," yet her obedience to her husband was never in doubt.[246] In fact, her numerous demonic visitations frequently turned on attempts to fore-stall her immediate compliance with her husband's needs. Thus, Frances was suspended over the balcony outside the bedroom when she was required at her husband's sickbed; a huge serpent prevented her from going to the kitchen in search of hot cloths for her hus-band.[247] The strain between her obedience to her husband and the demands of spiritual life is impossible to conceal. Therefore, her ha-giographer's interpretive strategy, and perhaps her own, was to divide and conquer. Every potentially rebellious impulse is aligned with diabolical forces; instant compliance with marital and familial re-sponsibilities strikes a blow on the side of the angels. Frances's an-gelic domesticity is especially apparent in one celebrated miracle. After she had been repeatedly interrupted in her recitation of the office of the Virgin by various household duties, she finally returned to find that the passage at which she had left off had been illuminated by an angelic hand.[248]

In the case of Dorothea of Montau, the attempt to produce a sem-blance of perfect obedience would present a greater challenge to the hagiographer. Her husband, Adalbert, clearly perceived his wife's mystical raptures as a way of escaping household duties. Dorothea would often forget certain essential chores, would confuse other ones—as, for example, going to church when she had intended to go to the market—and, not surprisingly, would consistently make mis-takes marketing.[249] Adalbert complained freely about his wife's in-

---

[245] "Sancto conjugis suae proposito, sicut mos est aliorum virorum, non contra-dicebat" (AA SS, June, 5:550); also see p. 568 for Mary's petition to move to Oignies.

[246] "Et quod audiverunt dici ab ea et a suo viro quod ambo bene gaudebant quod ipsa domina se implicaret in rebus divinis et orationibus" (Processi . . . Francesca art. 15, p. 39).

[247] AA SS, March, 2:156, 163.

[248] Processi . . . Francesca, pp. 88–89.

[249] Once she was so abstracted that she could not recognize an egg, much to the mirth of the surrounding women (Vita Dorotheae 2.40, p. 106). There are many occa-sions on which Dorothea forgets to purchase essentials or ruins a meal. See, for exam-ple, 3.10, 3.13; pp. 126, 130; see also Akten . . . Dorotheas, pp. 188–189, pp. 276–277.

subordination and seems to have found a ready audience among his fellow husbands.[250] In fact, they advised Adalbert to curb his wife's piety, since her excessive churchgoing would induce other wives to do likewise, and they would rebel and no longer obey their husbands.[251] One wonders whether his criticism did not play a part in the local authorities' persecution of Dorothea. The husband of Gentile of Ravenna (d. 1530) had mistaken her ecstasies for corruption and denounced her as a heretic to the local bishop.[252] Likewise, two local priests threatened to burn Dorothea.[253] Did Adalbert's obstreperousness play a denunciatory role?

On the other hand, aspects of Dorothea's mystical rapport actually reinforced submission to appropriate authorities. This is put to the test once when Dorothea and Adalbert were engaged in one of their many pilgrimages. Dorothea was communing with the Lord when their cart stopped at a hospice. She heard her husband order her to step down, but was reluctant to obey, prepared to place God's will above her husband's.

> And because she deferred descending, her angry husband, seized with fury, raved on account of his wife's disobedience. Seeing this, she asked the sweetest Lord Jesus Christ whether she ought to remain where she was and ignore the order of her husband. Christ responded fittingly, saying: "For the time being, you should withdraw yourself from my discourse and acquiesce obediently in your husband's command!"

John of Marienwerder winds up this anecdote with an appropriate moralization:

> And so it behooved her often to abandon the Lord . . . , and instead to follow her husband and to minister to him faithfully and to sustain hard words and blows in his service on account of the good of obedience, through which she was bound to her husband, *for obedience is better than sacrifices*.[254]

---

[250] "Hinc maritus eius querulabatur apud alios, quod Dorothea uxor sua esset sompnolenta, pigra necnon otiosa, quia nollet sibi ad acquirendum necessaria deservire" (*Akten . . . Dorotheas*, p. 277).

[251] "Vicini sui induxerunt maritum suum, quod non deberet tollerare, quod Dorothea, uxor sua, ita frequentaret ecclesias, quia esset occasio, quod uxores eorum similiter facerent et fierent rebelles et non obedirent suis viris" (ibid., p. 188).

[252] *AA SS*, January, 3:526. The bishop found Gentile innocent. This life is a Latin translation of an Italian original, written by a contemporary who received his information from her confessor of twenty-one years.

[253] This is not something that John of Marienwerder chooses to include in his biography. It emerges in the course of various witnesses' testimonies, however. See *Akten . . . Dorotheas*, pp. 84, 108–109; cf. 473–474.

[254] "Et quia distulit descendere, maritus irascens cepit furore furere propter inobedienciam mulieris. Quo viso consuluit Dominum Ihesum dulcissimum, si pocius sibi

Nor is Dorothea's experience rare. Although mystical raptures may impede a woman's ready submission, the content of visions frequently reinforces it. Thus Bridget's revelations tend to support the hierarchy of sexes by ridiculing men who are ruled by women, or women who attempt to gain mastery over men.[255] Even the extremely independent Margery Kempe is occasionally reminded by Christ of her responsibilities to her husband: not only does he implicitly reproach her for desiring her confessor in heaven rather than her husband, but he sends her home to tend John in his last illness.[256] One could even claim that the miracles of pious concealment, in which the conflict between God's will and the husband's will are repeatedly enacted, indirectly reinforce the terrestrial chain of command. The fact that God or one of his agents intervenes to cover up these women's acts of piety does not ultimately subvert, but reinforces, the seemliness of complying with the husband's will.[257]

Generally with the husband's death, but sometimes even before, the relationship with the confessor becomes the new arena in which the woman's virtuosity for obedience is most insistently demonstrated. With the triumph of auricular confession and the rise of penitential life, obedience to one's confessor naturally becomes an important component in the later medieval profile of sanctity. But this seems to have been especially true of female mystics.[258] If these women brought their confessors closer to God, the confessors were not only charged with the posthumous reputations of their female penitents, but were frequently all that stood between them and charges of heresy in their lifetime. The level of obedience evinced is

---

deberet conmanere et viri mandatum preterire. Qui dignanter respondit dicens: 'Ad tempus a colloquio meo te abstrahe et iussioni mariti tui obedienter acquiesce!' . . .

"Et ita oportuit eam sepe Dominum suaviter loquentem ac blande consolantem delinquere, maritum vero sequi, et ei fideliter ministrare duraque in eius ministerio verba et verbera sustinere propter bonum obediencie, qua erat alligata viro suo, *quia melior est obediencia quam victima* [1 Kings 15.22 = 1 Sam.]" (*Vita Dorotheae* 3.14, p. 132).

255 See *Rev.* 1.40, p. 359; *Rev.* 4.84 and 8.12. Bridget's revelations, in particular, tend to support the church hierarchy, furthering papal politics and bolstering the corrupt system of indulgences. See Barbara Obrist, "The Swedish Visionary: Saint Bridget" in *Medieval Women Writers*, ed. Wilson, pp. 230–235.

256 Meech and Allen, eds., *The Book of Margery Kempe* 1.8, 76; pp. 20, 180.

257 Cf. Elliott, "Dress as Mediator," p. 306.

258 While Thomas of Celano's first life of St. Francis, completed in 1229, stressed Francis's obedience to the priesthood and emphasized each of the friars' obedience to his superior, Francis's personal obedience to one spiritual adviser is not mentioned (17.45, *Analecta Franciscana* 10 [1941]: 35–36). Celano's second life, however, completed in 1247, dedicates a chapter to how Francis always submitted himself to the direction of another for the sake of obedience. Yet there is no mention of a vow (111.151, ibid., p. 218).

proportional to this additional degree of dependency, which, as we will see, is totally at odds with the less mystical, more independent spirituality of the virgin wives. In fact, the contrast between the two groups may suggest an additional way in which the conjugal debt and submission to the husband affected female spirituality.

Practical demonstrations of obedience range from the banal to the extraordinary. Thus, Bridget was many times released from different ascetic practices under holy obedience—practices that she could not observe without danger to her health.[259] Frances of Rome, however, delivered her son as hostage to Ladislaus of Naples under the direction of her confessor.[260] She would also immediately respond to any of her confessor's commands, even when insensibly caught up in rapture. This sometimes entailed answering questions about her visions while in this state—questions that she was otherwise unwilling to answer—all under the imperative of holy obedience.[261]

Frequently, the desire to bind oneself in obedience to one's confessor finds expression in an explicit vow. This gesture becomes more common in the fourteenth century, but, as Elizabeth of Hungary's vow of obedience and subsequent slavish subjection to Conrad of Marburg would suggest, such vows were already a possibility in the early thirteenth century.[262] The vow of obedience had striking nuptial overtones.[263] When Dorothea of Montau first met John of Marien-

---

[259] *Acta . . . Brig.*, pp. 490–491; *Rev.* ext. 61, pp. 183–184. Note, however, that Christ himself at times released Bridget from her fasts. See *Acta . . . Brig.*, pp. 495–496; *Rev.* ext. 99, p. 220. Cf. Meech and Allen, eds., *The Book of Margery Kempe* 1.66, pp. 161–162.

[260] Frances was attempting to hide her son when she ran into her first confessor, Anthony of Monte Savello, who ordered her to hand him over (*Processi . . . Francesca*, pp. 28–29; later life of Anguillaria, *AA SS*, March, 2:187).

[261] *Processi . . . Francesca* arts. 9–11, pp. 26–32; *AA SS*, March, vol. 2, vis. 76, p. 150. Mattiotti also constrained her under holy obedience to speak of how the demons appeared to her (pp. 158–159; also see the later life of Anguillaria, p. 187).

[262] Ludwig, Elizabeth's sympathetic husband, permitted her to vow obedience to Conrad during his own lifetime, provided it did not interfere with his authority. See the testimony of Elizabeth's handmaids in *Quellenstudien zur Geschichte der hl. Elisabeth*, ed. A. Huyskens (Marburg, 1908), p. 115. After Ludwig's death, she was totally under her stern confessor's power, who did everything possible to break her will: "multipliciter temptavit eius constantiam, frangens eius in omnibus voluntatem et sibi contraria precipiens" (p. 126). In particular, he sent away her beloved handmaids who had been with her from childhood. The explicit vow of obedience that these matrons make to their confessors emulates the parallel monastic vow. See Johnson's discussion of monastic obedience and infractions against this vow (*Equal in Monastic Profession*, pp. 130–133).

[263] Margery likewise seems to have made such a vow, although we learn this only when Christ releases her from it so that she can follow his higher authority (Meech and Allen, eds., *The Book of Margery Kempe* 2.2; cf. 2.10, pp. 227, 247). Margaret Beaufort

werder, her soul was glued to him in immense *amicitia*.[264] God then enjoined that Dorothea make two vows to John. For the first, she promised that she would never leave him: "And . . . it appeared to her, just as God afterward said to his Spouse, that through this vow he bound her to remain with her confessor in the same manner as if he had united them matrimonially." The second vow subjected her to the yoke of full obedience, which she wished to be interpreted strictly so she would be entirely without a will. While making this vow, she humbly prostrated herself at his feet.[265] Thereafter, she would do and say nothing without her confessor's permission.[266] Likewise, Bridget of Sweden's supporters claimed that she would not go out of the house or even look at anyone without her confessors' prior permission. She further refused to hold any of her own property but placed it all under her confessors' control.[267]

The question of where the power lies in these relationships is, of course, a complex one, since many of the confessors were prepared to recognize the spiritual ascendancy of their penitents. Moreover, as John Coakley has persuasively shown, these women possessed the charisma that the men in question often lacked; thus the men, in a certain sense, could be construed as spiritual dependents. Coakley cites a number of instances in which the woman's spiritual enlightenment is demonstrated at the confessor's expense.[268] Similarly,

---

also made an explicit vow of obedience to her earlier confessor, Richard Fitzjames, and later, as John Fisher records, to him (Mayor, ed., *English Works*, pp. 295–296). Catherine of Genoa is somewhat of an exception to this pattern. Like Dorothea of Montau, she seems to have spent many years of her spiritual life without any spiritual direction, taught by divine love alone (*Caterina. Biog.* c. 10, pp. 134–138, also see von Hügel, *The Mystical Element*, 1:117–121, but against this view see Bonzi da Genova's comments in *Caterina. Biog.*, p. 276 n. 8). Late in life, however, Don Marabotto became her spiritual director, bringing her more closely in line with the experiences of the other women. Marabotto is not treated in the earliest version of the Caterina corpus but has a chapter dedicated to him in the 1550 version (see Pierre Debongnie, trans., *Sainte Catherine de Gênes: Vie et doctrine et Traité du Purgatoire* [Brussels, 1960], *Vie et doctrine* c. 44, pp. 139–144). Also see Umile Bonzi da Genova, *Teologia Mistica di S. Caterina da Genova*, vol. 1 of *S. Caterina Fieschi Adorno* (Turin, 1960), pp. 53ff.

[264] *Vita Dorotheae* 3.27, p. 149.

[265] "Et . . . apparuit sibi, prout eciam Dominus postea Sponse dixit, quod per hoc votum taliter eam ad commanendum Confess⟨ario⟩ astrinxisset, ac si eas [*sic*] matrimonialiter copulasset" (ibid. 3.28, p. 151). John was stupified by these vows but did not want to go against the divine word. He did share the responsibility of directing Dorothea with the canon lawyer John Reyman. Both carefully scrutinized her faith before her withdrawal into the reclusorium.

[266] *Akten . . . Dorotheas* art. 19, pp. 22, 118, 281.

[267] *Acta . . . Birg.* art. 18, pp. 17, 260, 312, 370, 489–490; *Vita . . . Brig.*, p. 100.

[268] See Coakley, "Gender and the Authority of Friars," pp. 453–456; also see idem, "Friars as Confidants of Holy Women," pp. 236–237.

Frances of Rome once failed to bow to her confessor or ask for his blessing when he entered her chamber (as she was wont to do) because he was accompanied by a demon—an overt manifestation of the anger he retained from an argument he had just waged. The demon was dispelled by her prayers.[269] Dorothea of Montau miraculously gleaned certain episodes of incontinence that John of Marienwerder had experienced in his adolescence, and even told him when they began and at what point he conquered these urges.[270] Even so, the woman's spiritual authority is, arguably, contained by the priest's sacerdotal power, even as it had been effectively checked by the husband's authority.[271]

Having said all this, I once again should emphasize that the move to chastity in particular, or a higher level of asceticism in general, undoubtedly had an empowering effect on the women in question. How their life experiences and revelations would be read and applied is another matter. Margery Kempe certainly used the lives of Mary of Oignies, Bridget of Sweden, and possibly Dorothea of Montau as stepping-stones to freedom. On the other hand, it is equally possible, as Sarah Beckwith suggests, that the cults of these women merely provided an outlet for female discontent, while ultimately reinforcing social norms.[272] Their lives could be used coercively, even as the ancient lives of virgin wives could be used to pressure a young girl into marriage. From a sexual standpoint, consummation is presented as the supreme act of obedience. The transition to chastity is presented as an eventual reward for the sacrifice of their pristine virginity. The toll paid en route to this end was abject humility and unquestioning obedience. Since these virtues were identified with the path to sanctity, the husband's authority, even in its most brutal form, was lionized as an extension of God's will. This compelling paradigm produced an echo in secular letters in the shape of the Patient Griselda motif, which first emerged in the mid-fourteenth century in Boccaccio's *Decameron*. The clergy showed restraint in not incorporating it into sermon literature.[273] On the other hand, the kindly

---

[269] *AA SS*, March, 2:158.

[270] *Vita Dorotheae* 2.33, p. 96.

[271] Cf. Coakley, "Gender and the Authority of Friars," pp. 449–450, 459; idem, "Friars as Confidants of Holy Women," p. 238; Bynum, *Holy Feast and Holy Fast*, pp. 227–237.

[272] Beckwith, "A Very Material Mysticism," pp. 46–47, 52.

[273] On the various versions of this story, see Ann Middleton, "The Clerk and His Tale: Some Literary Contexts," *Studies in the Age of Chaucer* 2 (1980): 124–125. Middleton notes "the absence of any comparable and explicit life within clerical tradition. It does not figure in this period in writings of ecclesiastical origin or sponsorship: in homiletic, confessional, or exemplum literature, or pulpit speech." Even so, I think

"Goodman of Paris" included it in the manual of instruction he wrote for his child bride; it stands as the veritable tour de force in his section entitled "To Be Humble and Obedient to Your Husband." He appended the following afterword:

> Dear sister, this story was translated [into Latin] by master Francis Petrarch, crowned poet at Rome, in no wise only to move good ladies to be patient in the tribulations that they suffer from their husbands for the love of those same husbands alone, but 'twas translated to show that since God and the church and reason will that they be obedient and since their husbands will that they have much to suffer, and since to escape worse things it behoves them of need to submit them in all things to the will of their husbands and to suffer patiently all that those husbands will . . . by how much the greater reason behoveth it for men and women to suffer patiently the tribulations which God . . . sendeth unto them.[274]

Submission inevitably overshadows subversion in the hands of a skilled narrator.

---

the clergy played a large role in shaping the paradigm of sanctity that made such a story possible.

[274] Power, trans., *The Goodman of Paris* 1.6, pp. 136–137.

SIX

VIRGIN WIVES

THE CANONIZATION of Empress Cunegund not only anticipated the return of the spiritual marriage motif to women, but it also signaled the resurfacing of the completely unconsummated marriage as a distinct and well-publicized model of the married state. Conjugal chastity as a practice within a previously consummated marriage tended to emerge haphazardly: often (though not invariably) late, in response to other life-events, and without restriction to any one social level or situation. Virginal marriage, by contrast, is more coherent with regard to pattern, motivation, and social level. Of the nine unconsummated unions I have studied (appendix 5), two couples are from royal families and seven are members of the nobility.[1] Among the fifteen unions that were at one time consummated (appendix 6), one is royalty, seven are nobility or urban patrician, six are members of the bourgeoisie, and one is from the peasantry. Moreover, female initiative is considerably more pronounced in unconsummated unions: women initiated the commitment to chastity in seven of these marriages, while in an eighth the decision was described as mutual. The exception is the twelfth-century Magnus of Orkney, a reformed pirate, whose continence was contingent on his role as public penitent. Among those consummated marriages in which the chaste initiative is attributable to one party, however, female agency is apparent in only nine out of thirteen cases (appendix 6).

---

[1] I am excluding the example of Elena dall'Olio (d. 1520), a member of the bourgeoisie, since I was unable to examine the unedited sources concerning her life. The story of her virginal union, which allegedly lasted for thirty years, was publicized by her zealous followers, as were the contentions that she was the daughter of the emperor of the Turks and was related to the Virgin Mary and Catherine of Alexandria. These and other assertions (for example, that she could see the divine essence whenever she wished and that she lived for many years without a heart) probably jeopardized her claims as a serious mystic vis-à-vis the church hierarchy, though she was considered a saint during her lifetime. See the Bollandist summary of and commentary on a contemporary life, *AA SS*, September, 6:655–659. Also see Zarri's "L'altra Cecilia: Elena Duglioli dall'Olio (1472–1520)," in *Le sante vive*, pp. 165–196, for a detailed examination of her cult and its relation to Raphael's painting of the rapture of St. Cecilia. The Bollandists tend to dismiss Elena's claims to virginity. Zarri, however, seems inclined to credit them.

The uniform class makeup of the virginal marriage is undoubtedly a reminder that, despite changes in patterns of sanctity, the nobility continued to dominate as the exemplary class due to its superior visibility, connections, and funding.[2] It is nevertheless curious that the virginal marriage motif, traditionally the property of royals and nobles in the West, was resistant to tendencies toward democratization.[3] But this conservative quality, implicit not only in the number of noble constituents but even in the evidence of heightened female initiative is, in fact, an early indication that the unconsummated marriage might be a repository for more archaic conceptions of chastity. The resistant and uncompromising aspect of female chastity, so successfully muted in the transitional model, is the one that immediately presents itself. Indeed, from the point of view of the nobility as a caste, there can be no greater form of rebellion than the refusal to replace itself.

Despite ample evidence of the wife's initiative in these unions, one should not forget the complicity of the husband: obviously, it takes two "not to tango" and the male can likewise be understood to be rebelling against familial and class pressure. His chaste resolve, in particular, places considerable emphasis on secrecy, which is not present in the latter-day conversions to chastity. But it is significant that the virginal husband has not taken the more usual route of refusal to marry or total renunciation of his noble heritage. He has, instead, followed a more typically female pattern of rebellion under the influence of his wife.

The Spirituality of the Virgin Wives and Their Hagiographical Representation

All of the women in this study who lived in the high and later Middle Ages, virgin and matron, were affected by the penitential movement: all of them fasted, all of them kept vigils, most of them shunned finery, and many of them flagellated their bodies. What distinguishes the outer religious practices of these two groups of women is often just a question of degree. The women who had experienced normal conjugal relations were almost invariably presented as more extreme in their penances. The wives who managed to keep their virginity

[2] See Vauchez, La sainteté, p. 324, table 27.
[3] Note that this is not the case in the East. There are a number of virginal unions attributed to peasants (see appendix 1). Also cf. the efforts of Elena dall'Olio's followers to attribute the appropriate pedigree to her, as well as aligning her with the virginal marriage tradition. See n. 1, above.

throughout their marriage, on the other hand, appear to have effectively realized their childhood dreams. Perhaps because their physical integrity assured them of a time-honored union with God, they were not under the same compulsion as the would-be virgins to forage for new spiritual sustenance. Thus, their penitential practices were, accordingly, more moderate. Other differences, however, are more concrete. Only two out of eight of these women became mystics, while a total of six eventually became cloistered nuns—which further underlines the continuity with their earliest vocation and traditional ascetic values.[4] The sexual hierarchy within marriage likewise seems to have made fewer inroads into their spirituality: they appear to be considerably less subservient to their husbands and to their confessors.[5]

The arcane sanctity of the virgin state and the heroic vigilance of the women who preserved their virginity in marriage tended to make the hagiographer's task easier in a certain sense: the subject's claims to sanctity could be anchored on seemingly secure moorings. There are, of course, exceptions. Jeanne-Marie of Maillac's claims to sanctity were based primarily on her charity, penitence, and mysticism, and only secondarily on her virginity. Likewise, Lucia Brocadelli of Narni became a celebrated mystic in her day, acting as private prophetess for the court of Ercole d'Este of Ferrara.[6] But for many of these women,

---

[4] Jeanne-Marie of Maillac and Lucia Brocadelli of Narni were both mystics. Moreover, only Jeanne-Marie and Dauphine of Puimichel lived their entire lives outside the cloister. The ninth virgin wife is the nameless bride of Magnus of Orkney. Since we are told nothing about her, except that she was a virgin of noble birth, she is not included in this count.

[5] Catherine of Sweden did take a vow at the bequest of her mother, Bridget, as will be seen below. When Cunegund of Poland became a member of the third order, she was allegedly placed under obedience to a confessor ("sub obediencia confessoris constituta" [Kętrzyński, ed., *Vita et miracula sanctae Kyngae* c. 11, *MPH*, 4:697]). But this appears to be the hagiographer's rather cosmetic move to counteract her flagrant disobedience to her husband and confessor with regard to consummating the marriage. The argument for obedience makes a poor showing: the only way it was exercised was when the confessor attempted to interfere with some of her penances, such as making her eat meat or wear sandals—the soles of which she repeatedly cut out (c. 13–14, p. 698).

[6] Mysticism and charity seem to have been related in Jeanne-Marie's life. On one occasion a fiery globe fell upon her while she was at prayer and she felt inflamed by the Holy Spirit. This experience strengthened her spiritually, and it was then that she began her more active ministry to the poor (*AA SS*, March, 3:736). Lucia Brocadelli of Narni's mystical experiences culminated in her reception of the stigmata (see Razzi, *Vite dei santi*, p. 181; Marcianese, *Narratione . . . Lucia* c. 26, 37; pp. 113–125, 169–181). The correspondence between Ercole and Lucia, prior to her arrival in Ferrara, has been published (see Luigi Alberto Gandini, ed., *Sulla venuta in Ferrara della beata suor Lucia da Narni* [Modena, 1901]). On her career in Ferrara, see *Narratione . . . Lucia* c.

virginity remained at the heart of their cult and possibly their spirituality. With regard to the latter question, there is, of course, a wide margin for doubt. The drama of Dauphine of Puimichel's struggle to preserve her virginity tends to eclipse the arduous life of apostolic poverty that she undertook after her husband's death, and the hagiographer and promoters of her cult must, to some extent, be held accountable for that. No fewer than twelve of the forty-eight articles that described her life in her process were related to her virginity, while article 1, regarding her *fama* as a virgin and holy woman (in that order), was the most widely attested.[7]

On the other hand, the hagiographer's prejudice in favor of virginity may not be as distorting as it seems. Certainly in the cases of Dauphine and Cunegund of Poland, who met with the most resistance from their families and husbands alike, we can readily believe that this level of opposition would make them cling more desperately to their pristine ideal. Many of these women might well consider virginity to be their most notable spiritual asset. But whether the hagiographer is fabricating plausible motives or whether he is attempting to represent the views of his subject accurately, it is precisely in this area that he is most likely to run into difficulties. If the merit of physical autonomy was self-evident, the expression of this ideal was becoming progressively problematical since it was impossible to keep the rejected alternative of a standard marriage out of the picture. The women are presented as not attacking, but undoubtedly belittling, the celebrated goods of marriage by emphasizing their temporality and uncertainty. Thus when Elzear attempts to convince his virginal wife, Dauphine, that a number of holy people marry and have children, she answers uncompromisingly:

> "There are many married people who cannot have children, as well as many who, if they have children, live badly, die, and end just as badly. And for such people, it would have been preferable not to have had them. Because of this—the uncertainty of heirs and deceiving and treacherous riches, which are the cause of death and eternal damnation—it is not safe to put oneself in peril. But the state of virginity, which is firm and sure and very pleasing and agreeable to God, is to be embraced above all.

32, pp. 144ff., Edmund G. Gardner, *Dukes and Poets in Ferrara* (New York, 1904), pp. 368–467, and Zarri, *Le sante vive*, pp. 51–62. Zarri's study emphasizes the ways in which Renaissance rulers appropriated the charisma of women like Lucia in order to buttress their regimes.

[7] See arts. 1 and 6–16 in *Canonisation de Dauphine*. Also note that on the basis of the chart at the end of her process, article 1 had a total of twenty-four witnesses (p. 596). The next most widely supported claim was art. 35, which addressed her ability to inspire individuals toward a change of life. It had twenty witnesses.

For such people accompany the Lamb of God, Jesus Christ, and the Virgin Mary, his Mother, as their familiars."[8]

Dauphine's answer echoes the saints' lives that she learned in her youth, repeated to her husband on their wedding night, recited to her household after meals, and lectured about to wondering listeners in her widowhood.[9] Similar arguments against the married state are attributed to Angelina Corbara of Marsciano and Cunegund of Poland, and they correspond to the sentiments of the twelfth-century Christina of Markyate.[10] But the tendency to de-emphasize virginity as an anatomical state was already apparent in twelfth-century monastic literature, and this was corroborated by aspects of the church's pastoralia on marriage, as well as by the phenomenon of the penitential matron.[11] In former times, a passionate commitment to virginity was considered heroic. But these new factors conspired to make Dauphine's retort seem fanatical, willful, and ultimately antiquated.

The women who had rebuilt their religious vocation in the context of marriage and childbearing became exemplars of a broadly based penitential ethos that reinforced obedience and humility. The virgin wives seem to have drawn inspiration from a more ancient but ultimately more rebellious model. Some actually became active proselytizers for purity. Occasionally, we only get hints of this: Bridget of Sweden's daughter, Catherine, for example, was accused by her brother Carl of attempting to turn his wife into a Beguine.[12]

The countess Dauphine's exhortations to chastity are much more blatant and extend far beyond her immediate household.[13] Although

---

[8] " 'Granre son en matrimoni que no podo aver efans; yssamen que si an efans, vivo mal e mal moro e mal finissho; e ad aytals fora melhs que non aguesso; e per amor d'aysso, per la no certanetat dels hereties e per las dessebens riquezas e enganablas, que so causa de mort e de dampnacio eternal, no es cauza segura si metre en perilh; mas majormen l'estamen de virginitat, lo cal es ferm e segur, e mot a Dieu plazen e acceptable, es tenedor. Car aytals familiarmen acumpanho l'anhel Jhesu Crist e la sua Mayre verges; per aquest estamen es per tu, savi jovensel, elegidor' " (Vie . . . Dauphine 3.2, p. 148).

[9] For Dauphine's youth, see ibid., 1.2, pp. 134–135; for her wedding night, see 3.1, pp. 148–149; for the discussion of saints' lives after meals, see Vie . . . Auzias 7.1, pp. 78–79; for her preaching, see Canonisation de Dauphine, pp. 184, 226, 231, 267, 385, 482.

[10] Jacobilli, Die selige Angelina c. 6, pp. 37–38; AA SS, July, 5:684; Talbot, ed., The Life of Christina of Markyate, pp. 60–63.

[11] See Thomas Renna, "Virginity in the Life of Christina of Markyate and Aelred of Rievaulx's Rule," American Benedictine Review 36 (1985): 79–92, esp. pp. 79–80; Atkinson, " 'Precious Balsam,' " pp. 138–140.

[12] " 'Non es contenta, quod te beguinam feceras, quin etiam uxorem meam tecum beguinam faceres et fabulam populorum?' " (AA SS, March, 3:505).

[13] See Vauchez, Les laïcs, p. 214.

the secret of her virginity was kept among a circle of intimates during her husband's lifetime, their court nevertheless became a locus of chastity and people emulated their chaste rule of life. The holy couple even assumed a kind of cult status. Their very bed was believed to be possessed of thaumaturgical powers: on more than one occasion individuals beset by lust would, in secret, kneel before their bed and their temptation would subside.[14] After Elzear's death, when Dauphine liquidated her holdings and began a life of mendicant poverty, her chaste kerygma extended even further. A number of prostitutes were reformed by her example.[15] Several prosperous merchants gave up the world and lived in chastity with their wives.[16] She won a signal coup with seven rich young widows, who, gripped by her preaching, relinquished their prospects of remarriage and pledged chastity into the bishop's hands.[17] Dauphine's position as a hierophant of chastity was so deeply acknowledged that an old friend of hers felt compelled to apologize for his second marriage, pleading the desirability of children. This inspired one of Dauphine's more memorable comments: that she would not for all the world be a mother, even if her children were the apostles themselves.[18]

[14] *Vie . . . Dauphine* 16.1, pp. 226–229; *Canonisation de Dauphine*, pp. 73–75; *AA SS*, September, 7:546.

[15] *Vie . . . Dauphine* 17.8, pp. 242–243. After her death, prostitutes were allegedly reformed by touching the feet of her corpse (*Canonisation de Dauphine* art. 50, p. 64; pp. 411, 470).

[16] *Canonisation de Dauphine* art. 35, pp. 53–54. Two couples are reported to have taken vows of chastity: Bartholomew de Perthusio, a rich draper of Apt, and his wife Beatrice, and Raymond Chieusa and his wife Huga (pp. 401–402). The conversion of Bartholomew is mentioned a number of times in the process and seems to have made an impression on the townsfolk (see pp. 226–227, 335, 476). The widow Alsacia de Mesellano says that as a result of Dauphine's preaching Bartholomew made restitution for all ill-gotten goods and gave away his property. It was only later that his wife was likewise converted (p. 442). Clearly Bartholomew conforms to the pattern of John Colombini and other guilt-stricken merchants who underwent a midlife crisis. Other couples also changed their way of life, but it is unclear if this entailed a transition to chastity (see, for example, p. 335).

[17] *Vie . . . Dauphine* 14.2, pp. 210–213. There are eight widows, according to the process (*Canonisation de Dauphine*, p. 384). One of these widows, Cecilia Baxiana, was gripped by sexual temptation after her vow and in danger of lapsing. Dauphine intuitively sensed this and removed this temptation through her pious conversation (*Canonisation de Dauphine*, pp. 384–385; *Vie . . . Dauphine* 15.2, pp. 220–223).

[18] " 'Bene fecistis contrahere matrimonium propter liberos procreandos; tamen in bona constancia vobis dico quod nolo fuisse matrem alicuius ex apostolis Ihesu Christi!' " (*Canonisation de Dauphine*, p. 364). According to Vauchez, quips like these may ultimately have cost Dauphine a successful canonization (*Les laïcs*, p. 216). But Dauphine did graciously predict that her friend would have a child and asked to stand godmother. When she asked the father what he wished to name the child, he answered,

Parallel proselytizing maneuvers on behalf of the countess of Civitella, Angelina Corbara of Marsciano (d. 1435), actually brought her into conflict with secular authorities. Angelina lived in virginal chastity with her husband for two years.[19] After her husband's death, she took the habit of a tertiary Franciscan and lived a life of itinerant mendicancy, preaching virginity. In the course of her travels, she attracted many female followers from all walks of life, but especially from the nobility. She converted these women to a life of virginity, and it was in this capacity, as an advocate of chastity, that she attracted the unfavorable attention of the secular ruler. Angelina was arraigned before Ladislaus, king of Naples, who, acting on the complaints of the men of the area, had resolved to have her burned as a heretical despiser of marriage. Angelina was said to have appeared before him bearing hot coals in her mantle—a by-now-familiar motif—allegedly as an indication that she was not afraid of fire. Ladislaus, overwhelmed by this miraculous testimony to her innocence, released her.[20] The pressure of continued complaints nevertheless caused him to exile her from his land.

The earliest remaining life for Angelina was written more than two hundred years after her death. The miracle of the coals may have been a hagiographical flourish to reinforce her claims of virginity. But it serves as a reminder that since these women's claims to sanctity are frequently grounded on their virginity, the *vitae* themselves must likewise be oriented toward vindicating these claims. This could be a difficult task. Virginal marriages were almost invariably shrouded in secrecy: even the best testimony to the couple's purity was hearsay, frequently dependent on the disclosures of the subject herself. Dauphine was rather unusual in the pleasure she derived from talking about her virginity, frequently bringing it up in the course of her confession.[21] Occasionally, the women made veiled allusions to their

---

"Francis." This answer both pleased and disappointed her because she, though deeply influenced by the Franciscan movement, had rather touchingly hoped that he would name it after her late husband, Elzear (*Canonisation de Dauphine*, pp. 366–367).

[19] Jacobilli, *Die selige Angelina* c. 3–4, pp. 19–28.

[20] Ibid. c. 5–7, pp. 32–41. Margery Kempe was clearly understood to be engaged in similar proselytism on account of her white clothes. When she was apprehended in Leicester, the mayor, acting as her accuser at the trial, said: " 'I wil wetyn why þow gost in white clothys, for I trowe þow art comyn hedyr to han a-wey owr wyuys fro us & ledyn hem wyth þe' " (Meech and Allen, eds., *The Book of Margery Kempe* 1.48, p. 116). At a subsequent examination, the archbishop of York asked her if she was a virgin and charged her with encouraging Lady Greystoke to leave her husband (1.52, p. 124; 1.54, p. 133). For a look at Margery from the point of view of her disruptive influence, see Anthony Goodman, "The Piety of John Brunham's Daughter, of Lynn," in *Medieval Women*, ed. Baker, pp. 347–358.

[21] *Canonisation de Dauphine*, pp. 242–244, 193, 205.

state. When Cunegund of Poland entered religion, for example, she was allegedly entitled to the auspicious consecration that befits a virgin. She nevertheless accepted the lesser consecration of a widow out of humility, much to the annoyance of her confessor.[22] But she compensated in other ways. She always told the other sisters at the convent that she preferred virginity to all the other virtues; she bragged that she only ever saw the hands and face of her husband, from which the sisters drew their own conclusions. Moreover, once, rather touchingly, she attempted to win the confidence of an angry nun by revealing her secret.[23] We also find the resurfacing of the graveside revelation: Elzear reveals his wife's virginity at the time of his death. Cunegund's confessor is entrusted with this task, but Cunegund later seconds his revelation by praising God on her deathbed for having kept her immaculate.[24]

The mystique of virginity only rarely furnished clinical proof. Dauphine, for example, due to an internal ailment late in life, was subjected to a physical examination that verified her integrity.[25] But, failing that degree of exactitude, miracles continued to be the most conclusive route. The secrecy of Elzear and Dauphine's purity was supernaturally communicated to the pure: a Franciscan friar and a holy woman had visions of Elzear and Dauphine sleeping together, with Christ looking on benignly from the head of the bed.[26] The bishop of Avignon claimed that a sweet redolence issued from their chamber.[27] Catherine of Sweden's hagiographer invoked the bestiary tradition of the pure maiden who could tame a unicorn, claiming that a wild beast nestled in her lap.[28] We also find the resurfacing of accusations of unchastity, no longer as a mechanism for repudiation, but simply as an occasion for the revelation of the chaste condition. Cunegund was accused of fornication with her confessor, after her husband's death. Her chastity was reaffirmed when a concealed friar saw her bathed in celestial light.[29] The body of the saint was likewise a

---

[22] Kętrzyński, ed., *Vita et miracula sanctae Kyngae* 45.2, 57, *MPH*, 4:719–720, 724.

[23] Ibid. c. 55, p. 723; cf. 45.4, p. 720.

[24] Ibid. c. 58, 63, pp. 724, 727. Dauphine and Elzear's union is discussed at greater length at the end of this chapter.

[25] *Canonisation de Dauphine*, p. 244.

[26] *AA SS*, September, 7:544.

[27] *Canonisation de Dauphine*, p. 527.

[28] *AA SS*, March, 3:504. See T. H. White, trans., *The Bestiary: A Book of Beasts* (New York, 1960), pp. 20–21.

[29] Kętrzyński, ed., *Vita et miracula sanctae Kyngae* 39.1, *MPH*, 4:713. She did not levitate, as Klaniczay suggests (see "Legends as Life Strategies," *Uses of Supernatural Power*, p. 107). He may have misread the cynical reflections of her new confessor, who believed the gossip and thought that levities, as opposed to devotion, made her perspire ("conspicatur ipsam levitatibus pocius quam devocioni insudare"). Cf. *AA SS*, July, 5:710.

locus for miraculous phenomena, frequently appearing incorruptible or exuding a sweet odor after the woman's death.[30]

The miracles are a reminder that the anatomical purity of these women effortlessly aligns them with a supernatural order, which is timeless. Virginity had always short-circuited temporality: to the Encratites, it recalled the pristine purity of prelapsarian humanity; to the more orthodox cult of virginity, it anticipated the resurrection and the *vita angelica*. Not surprisingly, the sheer magnitude of this tradition had greater potential for overpowering and depersonalizing the virginal subject than is the case with her matronly counterpart.[31] But there is a fine line between timeless and static. As Jacques Le Goff has shown, in the later Middle Ages time was becoming rationalized and secularized under the pressures of urbanization and commercialization.[32] The story of sanctification, working within these constraints, was becoming more compelling than the ancient story of women who automatically had access to celestial privilege. Perhaps this was true democratization. Certainly the conception of sanctity was changing: victimized by their hagiographers' archaism (and perhaps their own), the virgin wives were being left behind.

Husbands and Wives

If the hagiographers of virginal marriages had greater cause to emphasize the superiority of the spiritual bond than is true with the transitional model, the risks were also greater. Jacques de Vitry had sung the praises of Mary and John's union around 1215—fast on the heels of Innocent III's bull of canonization for Empress Cunegund and the contemporaneous *vita* that eulogized the virgin union. But since

[30] See, for example, Kętrzyński, ed., *Vita sanctae Salomeae* 5.1, *MPH*, 4:782; cf. *Vita et miracula sanctae Kyngae* c. 58, ibid., p. 729; and the diocesan inquest for Jeanne-Marie of Maillac, *AA SS*, March, vol. 3, art. 10, p. 745. Note that one of the reasons for the failure of Elena dall'Olio's cult was the accelerated corruption of her body, at least according to some accounts. Her supporters claimed that she had miraculously received milk in her breasts at an advanced age, as proof of virginity and out of devotion to the Virgin. After her death when her body was examined, however, some of the examiners claimed it was pus (see Zarri, "L'altra Cecilia," in *Le sante vive*, pp. 182–183).

[31] This is particularly true of Cunegund of Poland's hagiographers, who, working at a distance of one hundred and two hundred years respectively, engage in numerous strained comparisons between their subject and greater luminaries like Cecilia and the Virgin Mary. See Kętrzyński, ed., *Vita et miracula sanctae Kyngae* c. 4 and 5–6, *MPH*, 4:687, 690; *AA SS*, July, 5:677.

[32] Le Goff, "Merchant's Time and Church's Time in the Middle Ages," pp. 29–42, 289–293.

then, the imperial marriage had been put to more sinister uses. In the latter part of the thirteenth century, for example, a Pseudo-Joachimist apocalyptic treatise describes their union as a kind of realized eschatology, projecting it beyond the grave: "The glorious rulers of the earth loved each other in life not in a carnal way, but spiritually, so that in death they were not separated nor divided by burial."[33]

And so this tremulous hope of the early church was again abroad in quasi-orthodox circles but was now more categorically identified as dangerous. Thus, the majority of hagiographers show considerable restraint in their praise of virginal unions, undoubtedly reluctant to be perceived as promoting, as opposed to simply eulogizing, such behavior.[34] Instead, the hagiographer usually contented himself with placing his holy subjects in a venerable, but elite, tradition. When petitioning on behalf of Elzear's canonization, Raymond Bot, bishop of Apt, sets up a scale with gradations of chastity that measures the way in which Elzear and Dauphine, who cohabited chastely for twenty-four years, outstripped both John the Evangelist and Alexis (who both left their spouses) as well as Cecilia and Valerian (whose union was of short duration). He concludes by saying that the closest parallel is Mary and Joseph.[35] Likewise, the seventeenth-century Jacobilli carefully aligns figures like Angelina Corbara of Marsciano and Lucia Brocadelli of Narni with an almost comprehensive list of chaste unions.[36]

This kind of alignment occasionally facilitated the glossing over of some notable disasters. The exemplar of the defiant queen of the Germanic kingdoms, who nobly resisted consummation, had long since lost its currency. And yet she was still in circulation. To create

---

[33] "Gloriosi principes terre, quomodo in vita sua non carnaliter, sed spiritualiter dilexerunt se, ita quod in morte non sunt separati nec sepultura divisi" (Franz Pelster, ed., "Ein Elogium Joachims von Fiore auf Kaiser Heinrich II. und seine Gemahlin, die heilige Kunigunde," Liber Floridus, mittellateinische Studien: Paul Lehmann, ed. Bernhard Bischoff and Suso Brechter [St. Ottilien, 1950], p. 350). The author of this treatise also suggests that children are an impediment to God's work (p. 345) and compares Cunegund with the woman in the Apocalypse who is crowned with twelve stars (p. 350). See Vauchez, Les laïcs, p. 222. Joachim of Fiore's eschatological works were interpreted by some of his followers as indicating the imminent end of the world. On his influence, see especially Marjorie Reeves, The Influence of Prophecy in the Later Middle Ages: A Study in Joachimism (Oxford, 1969).

[34] The two exceptions are the hagiographers of Dauphine and Elzear and of Catherine of Sweden and Eggard, as will be seen below.

[35] Libellus Supplex, in AA SS, September, 7:522; cf. Vauchez, Les laïcs, pp. 214–215.

[36] Jacobilli, Die selige Angelina c. 3, p. 24; idem, Vite de' santi e beati, 3:37. Marcianese, on the other hand, is content to compare Lucia to Edward the Confessor and move on (Narratione . . . Lucia c. 11, p. 52).

the semblance of mutual consent to chastity, the hagiographer attempted to transform a spiritual Amazon into a suppliant wife. Such experiments have mixed results. Cunegund, daughter of the king of Hungary and wife of the prince of Sandomierz (grand prince of Poland), was a very determined woman. Her hagiographers had the unviable task of pitting personal sanctity against potential national disaster. The royal couple are flatteringly compared with Cecilia and Valerian on their wedding night.[37] But soon pretensions to mutual consent give way and the less esteemed hagiographical model begins to reassert itself. Boleslaus was piously tricked into an agreement of chastity: he haplessly offered to give his bride anything she wanted, intending to make her a material present. He would only agree to postpone consummation by a year, however.[38] A second year's delay was elicited under the pretext of reverence for the Virgin Mary.[39] When Cunegund pressed for a third year on behalf of John the Baptist, Boleslaus lost patience. He appealed to Cunegund's confessor, who, although sympathetic to his plight, was nevertheless incapable of convincing Cunegund to consummate the marriage. In the middle of the third year of their marriage, the desperate husband was driven to adultery for solace (although Cunegund's biographers tactfully claim he only pretended to be unfaithful in order to force his wife to pay the marriage debt).[40] Eventually, however, through the intercession of John the Baptist, Boleslaus conceded his wife the freedom to preserve her virginity.[41] In the earlier life, Boleslaus makes no vow, but eventually grants Cunegund permission to accept the habit of the tertiary Franciscans.[42] The author of the later life, however, works harder to show that Boleslaus underwent a real conversion. The results of his

[37] See especially the later life completed in 1475 by John Dlugos, in *AA SS*, July, 5:677; cf. the anonymous life edited by Kętrzyński, *Vita et miracula sanctae Kyngae* c. 6, *MPH*, 4:690. Dlugos also discusses the couple's chastity in his chronicle (see *Annales seu Cronicae incliti regni Poloniae* anno 1239, ed. D. Turkowska (Warsaw, 1973), 6:285. The reign of Boleslaus is described in bks. 6 and 7.

[38] Kętrzyński, ed., *Vita et miracula sanctae Kyngae* c. 6, *MPH*, 4:690. The later life by John Dlugos reverses the order slightly: Boleslaus agrees freely to a first year of chastity but is tricked into the second year (*AA SS*, July, 5:677–678).

[39] Kętrzyński, ed., *Vitae et miracula sanctae Kyngae* c. 7, *MPH*, 4:692; cf. the later life that credits Cunegund with winning a third year on the basis of this pretext (*AA SS*, July, 5:678).

[40] Kętrzyński, ed., *Vita et miracula sanctae Kyngae* c. 8, *MPH*, 4:693; cf. *AA SS*, July, 5:683.

[41] In the earlier life, John promises that Boleslaus will eventually yield, but is unclear as to when this will occur (Kętrzyński, ed., *Vita et miracula sanctae Kyngae* c. 8, *MPH*, 4:694). In the later life, John clearly predicts that Boleslaus will submit in three days (*AA SS*, July, 5:685–686).

[42] Kętrzyński, ed., *Vita et miracula sanctae Kyngae* c. 11, *MPH*, 4:697.

efforts are again mixed. Although he reports that Boleslaus began to share in his wife's love of chastity so completely that he earned the name "The Chaste" ("Pudicus"), he also states that the duke had by no means abandoned all hopes of heirs. Boleslaus certainly recognized that Cunegund's decision to remain chaste was immutable, yet it seems to have occurred to him that she might predecease him. For this reason, he withstood for many years her entreaties that they both take vows of perpetual chastity.[43]

Cunegund may have realized the virginal integrity that had only been strategically attributed to her Ottonian namesake. While the stories of eleventh-century virgin monarchs were generated after the fact to hold a kingdom together, the latter-day Cunegund seems to have internalized a model that could potentially wrench apart a struggling kingdom that was beset by external foes.[44] The anonymous author of the earliest *vita* alludes to these ramifications only once, but in an evocative way that traces the evolution from a private incident to a public drama. One night, Cunegund's ripped nightgown (*camisia foraminosa*) accidentally touched Boleslaus's body in bed, and when Cunegund attempted to move it, Boleslaus awoke and began to upbraid her with "sinistra intencione." Cunegund created enough of a disturbance that each seemed obliged to render some account to their followers in the morning. The women thought: "What kind of wife is this who does not want to see either the foot or the least naked bit of body of her own duke?" while "a confusion arose for the sake of future offspring"[45] among the soldiers.

But virginal marriage presented other more subtle problems as well. Catherine of Sweden's hagiographer, perhaps oblivious to certain heretical strains further south, was one of the few who eulogized the strength of the spiritual bond.

[43] According to Dlugos's life, they made their vow into the hands of the bishop of Cracow, who, at the time, was a man named Prando (*AA SS*, July, 5:700).

[44] On the increase of external dangers, see Aleksander Gieysztor, *History of Poland*, 2d ed. (Warsaw, 1979), pp. 93–97; W. F. Reddaway et al., eds., *The Cambridge History of Poland* (Cambridge, 1950), 1:98. In 1259, Boleslaus's lands experienced a devastating defeat at the hands of Mongol invaders.

[45] "Quadam vice cum inopinate corpus ducis camisia foraminosa tetigisset, albugineam amovere cupiens, ipsum excitavit. Qui sinistra intencione dominam increpavit. Quo facto turbata statim in mane dominabus patefecit, que dixerunt ad invicem: O qualis ista coniunx est, que nec pedem nec minimam particulam nudam corporis ducis sui vult videre. Que omnia indicant castitatis observanciam pleniorem. Et cum eandem materiam dux militibus suis in mane referret, turbacio exoritur racione prolis future, qua carere opinabantur" (Kętrzyński, ed., *Vita et miracula sanctae Kyngae* c. 8, *MPH*, 4:694); cf. the later account, which more explicitly describes the hostility that Cunegund's chastity evoked in the kingdom as well as Boleslaus's fears for the resurgence of civil war (*AA SS*, July, 5:684).

Happy, therefore, was this marriage, because neither the petulance nor the lasciviousness of the flesh made the two hearts one. But love, which is in Christ Jesus, bound [the marriage] by the glue of charity with chaste embraces. Happy was the marriage of them, who tried to imitate as much as possible the most holy virginal union of Mary and Joseph out of respect and love of divine compassion.[46]

Although Catherine of Sweden had no trouble converting her young husband, Eggard, to chastity, the strength of the *glutinum caritatis* that Catherine's hagiographer claimed for their union was in many ways deficient. Ultimately, Catherine's affection for her mother far outweighed a sense of responsibility to her husband—though consummation of the marriage would not necessarily have ameliorated this situation. All the trappings of a mutual vocation were present: together they undertook an ascetic regimen and endured the mockery and humiliation of being spied upon in their bedroom, which allegedly served only to reinforce their chaste resolve. And yet, after six years of marriage, Catherine began to miss her mother, Bridget, so terribly that she could no longer eat or sleep.[47] She insisted on leaving at once for Rome, although Eggard had fallen seriously ill. When her older brother, Carl, wrote to Eggard, threatening his life if he permitted his wife to go, Catherine managed to intercept the letter.[48]

Once in Rome, Catherine was totally under her powerful mother's influence, and Bridget adamantly refused to part with her. Catherine begged to return to her husband, but Bridget had a revelation in which Christ ordered Catherine to remain in Rome through a metaphor that mobilized the *sponsa Christi* motif in an unexpected way.[49] Christ describes himself as a father who has to choose between two suitors for his daughter, both of whom the daughter loves. He naturally chooses the richer one and dismisses the poorer one with a gift. Catherine is the daughter. Her husband is the poor suitor who is sacrificed in favor of the celestial bridegroom, Christ. The gift the poor suitor receives is death.[50] Thus Christ warns Bridget that Eggard will soon

---

[46] "Felix ergo fuit hoc conjugium, quod non carnis petulantia et lascivia duo corda unum fecerat, sed dilectio, quae est in Christo Jesu, castis amplexibus contrinxerat glutino caritatis. Felix eorum conjugium, qui sanctissimum Mariae et Joseph virginale conjugium, quantum possible fuit, conabantur imitari, ob divinae miserationis respectum et amorem" (*AA SS*, March, 3:504).

[47] Ibid., p. 505; Jørgensen, *Saint Bridget of Sweden*, 2:57–58.

[48] *AA SS*, March, 3:505.

[49] Ibid., p. 506. The vision was initially recorded in *Rev.* 6.118.

[50] "'Ideo quia ditior sum et dominus omnium prouidere ei volo de donis meis vtilioribus sibi ad animam: quia placet mihi cito vocare eum: et infirmitas qua laborat signum est exitus sui'" (*Rev.* 6.118).

die. The next time Catherine attempted to leave, Christ appeared again to Bridget in order to disclose that her daughter was already a widow.

Behind Christ's double role as father-suitor to Catherine stands Bridget as the mother-suitor: rival to Eggard's claims on Catherine. Johannes Jørgensen, a modern biographer of Bridget, assumes that Catherine's virginal union would have earned Bridget's high esteem, presumably because she would recognize in it a realization of her own childhood aspirations.[51] Certainly, Catherine attempted in all ways to emulate her mother's piety, and her virginal union is doubtlessly evidence of this.[52] But Bridget's vocation had been altered, in certain ways unrecognizably, over her many years of marriage. While still prizing chastity over marriage to the extent that she converted her husband to chastity just prior to his death, Bridget, the penitential matron, was by no means an unthinking advocate for intramarital chastity. King Magnus of Sweden and his wife, Blanche, had attempted such an experiment, and, as far as we can discern from Bridget's urgent attempts at dissuasion and her later visionary denouncements of Magnus's alleged homosexual activity, this was an unmitigated disaster.[53] When Bridget married Catherine to Eggard, she clearly expected that Catherine, like herself, would engage in normal married relations and develop a religious vocation in that context. When the marriage remained unconsummated, Bridget's attitude in Rome perhaps suggests that she regarded the marriage as a

[51] Jørgensen, *Saint Bridget of Sweden*, 1:151–152.

[52] Regarding Catherine's early imitation of Bridget, see *AA SS*, March, 3:504; this is also underlined in Rome when Urban VI remarks that Catherine clearly imbibed her mother's milk ("'Vere filia tu biberas de lacte matris tuae'" [p. 506]).

[53] In *Rev.* 8.11, Bridget describes how a certain king and queen had two children and then decided to take a vow of continence. When Bridget prays about this, Christ appears before her and denounces their vow as ill-considered. The husband was impelled by the indiscreet zeal of a novice; the wife, desirous of pleasing, gave way to sudden impulse: "'quia altera pars consentit voto continentie ex feruore nouicio: et ex zelo indiscreto: et leuitate animi. Alia vero pars ex quadam placentia et impulsu subito.'" He urges the royal couple to return to the first law of marriage: "'Immo tutius est et laudabilius: redire ad primam legem: matrimonialis copule.'" In a later vision, the Virgin Mary addresses Magnus, declaring that his unnatural relations with men have given him the worst reputation in the entire kingdom: "'Vos habetis pessimam famam in toto regno, dicentem vos habere et exercere naturalem commixtionem et turpitudinem cum masculis contra naturalem disposicionem,'" (*Rev.* ext. 80, p. 202). Also see Jørgensen, *Saint Bridget of Sweden*, 1:86–87. For Bridget's influence on Magnus, also see Birger Bergh, "A Saint in the Making: St. Bridget's Life in Sweden (1303–1349)," in *Papers of the Liverpool Latin Seminar*, ed. Francis Cairns, vol. 3, *ARCA* Classical and Medieval Texts, Papers and Monographs, 7 (Liverpool, 1981), pp. 375–376.

nonmarriage. Although Bridget was an ardent supporter of the sexual hierarchy, she clearly saw her maternal claims (admittedly, divinely endorsed) as preempting those of a virginal husband.

Bridget's subsequent behavior in Rome further suggests that if she regarded her daughter's marriage as a nonmarriage, she also saw the "virgocentric" vocation she had evolved therein as a nonvocation. Bridget immediately set about remodeling the young widow's vocation into a semblance of her own penitential image. Catherine's near-contemporary hagiographer reports that in Rome, she "was struck with a certain horror of the unaccustomed life, mindful of her past liberty."[54] Although she accepted her mother's word that God had willed her to remain in Rome, she longed for Sweden, even after Eggard's death, and applied to her mother for a remedy.

> Her venerable mother, already the victor over all such temptations, provided a healthful remedy for the daughter who was wounded by carnal affection. Calling her master confessor, she asked with supplication and devotion that he should cast out the disease of her [Catherine's] mind by a beating with branches. . . . And when she [Catherine] was beaten by the confessor, she said to the master: do not spare me, but rather strike harder, because as yet you do not reach the hardness of my heart. The master continued the scourgings, until the moment when she said with a cheerful face: this suffices me. For I feel that my heart has changed and that all the movement of that temptation has inwardly departed.[55]

In fact, Catherine had only begun the process of submission. Because there were riots and plagues in Rome, Catherine was forced to remain indoors. She became sullen and pale, refusing to speak to her mother. But the Virgin Mary came to Catherine in a dream and told her to obey Bridget and her confessor. The next day Catherine went to Bridget, sought her forgiveness, and "then promised to obey her willingly to death, and remain with her steadfastly in her exile abroad."[56] But Bridget yet required something more:

> Blessed Bridget wished for her daughter to be bound more tightly by the yoke of obedience and humility so that she would not live remissly on

[54] "Horrore quodam inconsuetae vitae concussa, memorque libertatis praeteritae" (AA SS, March, 3:506).

[55] "Venerabilis mater ejus, omnium talium tentationum jam triumphatrix, filiae sauciatae carnali affectione, remedium providit salutare, vocans magistrum Confessorem suum, rogando suppliciter et devote, ut caede virgarum mentis incommodum excutiat. . . . Et quandoque cum a Confessore caederetur, dixit magistro: Non parcas, imo fortius percute, quia adhuc duritiam cordis non attingis. Continuante igitur magistro flagella, una vice hilari vultu dicebat: Sufficit mihi: sentio enim cor meum mutatum, et omnem tentationis illius motionem penitus abscessisse" (ibid.).

[56] "Promisit deinde se usque ad mortem libenter ei velle obedire, et secum stabiliter in peregrinationis ejus exilio remanere" (ibid.).

the path of holy penitence due to the indulgence of maternal compassion. Thus she called her master Lord Peter . . . urgently requesting that he would accept the obedience of her daughter. . . . Lady Catherine humbly promised obedience, and held to it so efficaciously that she would not presume to do the least thing without his permission.[57]

Perhaps Bridget went rather far with Catherine even by her own rigorous standards. The Virgin Mary had come to remind Catherine of her obligation of obedience. Likewise, she later performed a similar function for Bridget, urging her to maternal kindness (she tells Bridget to sew Catherine's tunic) and reminding her of the way in which Catherine sacrificed her marriage and her homeland for God.[58]

The penitential life into which Bridget initiated her daughter was a heavier yoke than Catherine had ever borne under the light rule of her husband. Catherine's circle continued to narrow. She was too young and too uniquely Scandinavian in appearance to wander around Rome unaccompanied, and she was equally preyed upon by her own anxious fears for her chastity. After an aborted abduction by a local count, from which she was released through her mother's prayers, she resolved her dilemma by remaining mostly within the four walls of her mother's house.[59] Catherine did not return to Sweden until twenty-five years later, when she accompanied her mother's funeral procession.[60]

Internalization and Mutual Sanctification: Dauphine and Elzear

If the virginal unions closely simulate the most highly esteemed of models for a Christian marriage, they also magnify some of the dangers of intramarital chastity generally: unilateral denial of the debt, wifely insubordination, husbands straying into adultery or, worse still, "unnatural vice"—in short, the clerical advisers' worst-case scenario. The tensions between Bridget and Catherine further suggest that a penitential matron might regard a virginal spouse as a mere spiritual "lightweight" in need of more ponderous definition.

---

[57] "Volens igitur B. Birgitta filiam suam humilitatis et obedientiae jugo arctius obligari, ne ex maternae compassionis indulgentia in via sanctae poenitentiae remissius viveret, vocat magistrum suum Dominum Petrum . . . suppliciter efflagitans ab eo, ut filiae suae obedientiam acceptaret. . . . Domina Catharina humiliter obedientiam promisit, et tenuit adeo efficaciter, quod nec minimam rem absque ejus licentia facere praesumeret" (ibid., p. 507).

[58] *Rev.* ext. 69, pp. 191–192.

[59] *AA SS*, March, 3:507–508.

[60] Ibid., p. 511.

Virginal marriages nevertheless possessed advantages. When the formula actually takes hold, not only is there less friction between husband and wife than is true of the transitional model, but husband and wife occasionally act as deliberate spiritual helpmates to one another. Some of these more joyous unions were relatively short-lived: John, the husband of Angelina Corbara of Marsciano, died after two years of marriage, leaving her a widow at seventeen; Sperandeo of Gubbio (d. ca. 1261) and his wife Gennaia parted after a few years to enter separate religious institutions.[61] But the marriages of Jeanne-Marie of Maillac and Salome of Galicia certainly ran a more than average term by contemporary standards since the two couples were married sixteen and seventeen years respectively.

These unions present harmonious pictures. Jeanne-Marie of Maillac (d. 1414) and her husband Robert (d. ca. 1362) were two nobles living in the ravaged France of the Hundred Years War. Prayer and pious acts took the place of sexual relations and offspring.[62] According to Jeanne-Marie's *vita*, Robert knew in advance of his future wife's desire for chastity, while Jeanne-Marie had been advised by the Virgin that she would be able to keep her virginity. This may be an oblique way of indicating that each was acquainted with the other's pious leanings: Jeanne-Marie had supposedly known her husband, Robert, from childhood and had saved him from drowning through her prayers. At any rate, she allegedly convinced him to pledge virginity by reciting saints' lives on their wedding night. They not only engaged in the usual charitable works, such as giving alms to the poor, but further cemented their union by becoming adoptive parents to three abandoned orphans. Indeed, Jeanne-Marie's hagiographer relates that when Robert was imprisoned by the English, and Jeanne-

---

[61] Jacobilli, *Die selige Angelina* c. 4, pp. 27–28. For Gennaia and Sperandeo, see Jacobilli, *Vite de' santi e beati*, 1:78–80; *BS*, vol. 11, cols. 1346–1347; also see the brief notice in *AA SS*, September, 3:892. As is often the case, the example of Gennaia and Sperandeo inspired other couples: Santuccia Terrabotti (d. 1305) and her husband likewise renounced the world (see *AA SS*, March, 3:361–363, and Jacobilli, *Vite de' sancti e beati*, 1:297–298).

[62] Both André Vauchez (*La sainteté*, p. 445 n. 506) and Caroline Bynum (*Holy Feast and Holy Fast*, p. 215) have characterized Jeanne-Marie's marriage as unhappy, but I have never understood on what basis they made this judgment. It is true that the hagiographer's claims for their contentment are no real proof of happiness, but if we judge from external circumstances, I find no clearer answer. The couple both suffered from ill health and bad luck during Robert's lifetime (see esp. *AA SS*, March, 3:735), but there is no appreciable change in Jeanne-Marie's overall felicity after Robert's death. In fact, with the added persecution of her relatives and the mockery of strangers, her problems seem to increase (see esp. pp. 735–737, 739). For an examination of the Franciscan influence on her life, see Vauchez, *Les laïcs*, pp. 225–236.

Marie's efforts to collect ransom failed, she released him through her prayers alone.[63]

Salome, the princess of Galicia (d. 1268), likewise knew her husband-to-be from childhood. Daughter of the king of Poland, Salome was taken to the Hungarian court, where she was betrothed to Caloman (d. 1241), the son of the Hungarian king, at three, took a vow of chastity with her husband at nine, and married at thirteen.[64] Eventually Caloman acceded to the throne of Galicia, where the couple led a life of exemplary piety. Although, on the basis of her *vita*, it would seem that Salome had the greater appetite for self-mortification and penance, her husband appears to have been quite sympathetic to her penitential practices.[65] After seventeen years of married life, but twenty-five years since she had first arrived at the Hungarian court, Caloman died and Salome returned to her homeland where she entered a convent at Sandomierz and lived as a Poor Clare for an additional twenty-eight years.[66]

But nowhere is the deep internalization of a spiritual construct so apparent as in the marriage of the remarkable Provençal nobles Dauphine and Elzear, whose union Vauchez has fittingly characterized as something out of *The Golden Legend*.[67] Their marriage can best be described as a holy collaboration or even a symbiosis wherein mimetic action is rewarded by St. Paul's paradigmatic, but elusive, concept of mutual sanctification.

Dauphine's passionate commitment to virginity is represented as the central feature of her piety, and she is portrayed as erecting a whole modus vivendi based on this commitment. A practiced reader of saints' lives would recognize that Dauphine was destined for chastity from the womb. Her mother, also named Dauphine, had been unable to carry a child full-term and had experienced a number of miscarriages. Dauphine's birth was the answer to a prayer. But like all

---

[63] *AA SS*, March, 3:735.

[64] Kętrzyński, ed., *Vita sanctae Salomeae* 1.1–2, in *MPH*, 4:776–777. For the chronology of her life, *BS*, vol. 11, cols. 589–590.

[65] Caloman is presented as making only gentle remonstrances against his wife's penitential excesses. He tells her when her labors seem sufficient, and begs her to desist lest she fall ill: "Mox Colomanus misertus voce compassionis eam sincerius rogabat, dicens: Amica mea, sufficiunt tibi labores iam pro domino Deo facti; desiste amodo, ne fatigata labore infirmitate preocuperis" (Kętrzyński, ed., *Vita sanctae Salomeae* 1.2, *MPH*, 4:777–778). He was also supportive of her virginal resolve. After one occasion on which Salome ornamented herself like a woman of the world in order to please him, a gesture that brought them perilously close to consummation, Caloman even encouraged her to dress like a widow during his lifetime (1.3, p. 778).

[66] Ibid., c. 2, p. 779.

[67] Vauchez, "L'influence des modèles hagiographiques," p. 590.

gifts of fertility, Dauphine was simply on loan. The only appropriate return for the gift was the young girl's chastity.[68] We have already seen that at the age of seven, Dauphine was orphaned and moved to her uncles' house, where she fell under the influence of two relatives—a nun and a friar—who both urged Dauphine to guard her virginity. One of her confessors, testifying at her process of canonization, said that he had often heard from Dauphine that virginity was so established in her heart by the time she was eight that she would rather be broken piecemeal than sacrifice it.[69] She ardently wished that all of her châteaus would burn, or that she would develop a physical deformity to deter all suitors.[70] Despite her protests, however, Dauphine was taken to Marseilles in 1296, when she was about twelve, to be betrothed to Elzear, who was about ten years old. This was done at the behest of Charles II of Sicily. At first Dauphine adamantly withheld her consent. She was subjected to a certain amount of physical abuse at the hands of her relatives, but it was only when the Virgin Mary appeared to her and promised to protect her virginity that she would agree to the betrothal.[71] The contract seems to have been made in the presence of the king in *verba de praesenti*. Dauphine had been wrongly informed by the friar who had been introduced by the family to win her consent to marriage that she could repudiate the union five years later, and she shrewdly asked if this were so. To facilitate matters, the king assured her that it was.[72]

The marriage was celebrated three instead of five years later, in 1299. Although she outwardly consented to its solemnization, she inwardly resolved to follow Cecilia's example.[73] On her wedding night, she preached the beauty of virginity and entertained her young

[68] Every night during her pregnancy, the elder Dauphine's sister-in-law would read the Symbol of Athanasius over her womb (*Canonisation de Dauphine* art. 4, pp. 31–32; *Vie . . . Dauphine* 1.1, pp. 130–133).

[69] See the testimony of Bertrand Iusbert, *Canonisation de Dauphine*, p. 205; cf. art 7, p. 34. Aycardus Boti, a priest from Apt, also testifies that when he consulted Dauphine regarding a relative whom the family wished to make a nun against her will, Dauphine counseled against it. She said it would be dangerous since she knew from her own experience that when she was nine or ten she would sooner have died than change her mind about her vocation (p. 294).

[70] Ibid. art. 6, p. 33; *Vie . . . Dauphine* 1.3, pp. 136–137.

[71] *Canonisation de Dauphine* art. 7, p. 34; *Vie . . . Dauphine* 2.1, pp. 138–141. Regarding Elzear and Dauphine's exact ages see Cambell, *Vies occitanes*, introd., pp. 31–32, 48 n. 14.

[72] *Vie . . . Dauphine* 2.1, pp. 140–143; *Canonisation de Dauphine* art. 8, p. 35 deals with the friar William of S.-Martial's misinformation. Also see the testimony of Dauphine's confessor, Durandus Andreas, p. 247.

[73] *Vie . . . Dauphine* 2.3, pp. 146–147.

husband with saints' lives, until he fell asleep. Indeed, this was the pattern for some time: Dauphine, like a Christian Sheherazade, bought time with stories,[74] while Elzear, although enjoying the stories very much, would in no way consent to pledge perpetual virginity.

After about a year of marriage, Elzear's desire to have sexual relations became more insistent. At this point, according to Dauphine's Occitan life, she became so ill that the doctors feared she would die. She called Elzear to her bedside, told him of her forced marriage and of her intention to preserve her virginity, and concluded with the threat that she would never rise from the bed alive unless he respected her wish. Elzear, who loved her tenderly, promised her a two-year reprieve.[75] But Dauphine's process for canonization tells a slightly different story, suggesting that Dauphine employed some pious subterfuge to expedite her negotiations for chastity. According to Durandus Andreas, canon of Apt, former confessor to Dauphine and a member of her household for ten years, when Elzear began to demand payment of the conjugal debt, Dauphine consulted Garsende Alphante, a pious widow who had helped to raise Elzear from childhood and acted as a companion and teacher to Dauphine. Not only was Garsende personally committed to the cause of chastity, having formerly taken a vow of chastity with her husband, but she was also one of the few people who knew that the marriage had not been consummated and continually encouraged the young couple to persevere in their pious abstinence.[76] Garsende comforted Dauphine, perhaps recommending the sickbed stratagem:

> And a little after she [Dauphine] pretended that she was gravely ill; and remaining in bed, she kept to the diet of sick people. Then after a short interval fever truly seized [her] with a certain kind of inflamed throat.

Clearing the room, she called Elzear to her and said:

> "O Elzear, I have a secret to tell you, because I feel that you love me quite tenderly. And on that account you should know that I cannot escape this grave illness unless you promise me one thing: because if you will comply, in a short time, God granting, I will get better; otherwise I will not escape." To which the aforementioned Elzear, smiling, said: "What is it

---

[74] Ibid. 3.1–2, pp. 146–149; 3.4, pp. 152–153; *Canonisation de Dauphine* art. 9, p. 36.

[75] *Vie . . . Dauphine* 3.6, pp. 154–155; see n. 146.

[76] Ibid. 3.5, pp. 152–155; regarding Garsende, see *Vie . . . Auzias* (i.e., Elzear) 6.1, pp. 70–71. Later when Elzear and Dauphine solemnly pledge chastity in Garsende's presence, her son, Isnard—a noble knight—would do likewise (*Vie . . . Dauphine* 6.2, pp. 170–171; *AA SS*, September, 7:551).

that you wish?" She said to him: "Promise me and I will tell you." And he said: "I promise."

The smile suggests that Elzear was not unduly alarmed by her illness, and that her predictable request to keep her virginity was anticipated. In fact, Dauphine admitted to others later that she was not so gravely ill, but thought that her pious pretense would hasten Elzear's consent to chastity. Yet Elzear's eyes filled with tears when he responded to her petition.

> "I agree, but how shall we manage with my relatives, since they expressly wish that we should endeavor to have children?" To which she said: "Do not doubt, because God agrees with this decision and will appoint a remedy."[77]

From this time onward, Elzear never again troubled Dauphine for the conjugal debt: indeed on the feast of the Assumption of the Virgin Mary in the next year (1302), Elzear experienced a mystical rapture, after which he allegedly lost all carnal desire.[78] Even so, it was not until fourteen years later that Elzear relinquished all possibility of progeny by taking a formal vow of chastity.[79]

Dauphine and Elzear went on to develop a profound spiritual rapport in marriage, the very cornerstone of which was their mutual commitment to chastity. During the first eight years of their common life, while living in the house of Elzear's paternal grandfather, the necessity of keeping their virginity a secret forged a link between

---

[77] "Et paulo post simulavit se graviter infirmari; et stans in lecto, dietam tenuit infirmorum, quam post modicum temporis intervallum febris veraciter arripuit cum quadam specie squinancie. . . .

'O Elziari, habeo secretum tibi dicere, quoniam sencio quod tenerrime me diligis. Et ideo credas non me evasuram de hac gravi infirmitate, nisi promittas michi unum: quod, si consesseris, breviter, Deo dante, convalescam; aliter non evadam.' Cui dictus Elziarius subridens, ait: 'Quid hoc est quod vis?' Cui illa: 'Promittas michi, et dicam.' Ac ille: 'Promitto.' . . .

'Michi placet, sed quomodo faciemus de parentibus, cum ipsi omnino cupiant quod pro prole habenda laboremus?' Cui illa dixit: 'Non dubites, quoniam Deus super hoc conveniens apponet remedium'" (*Canonisation de Dauphine*, pp. 242–243). This story is told by Durandus Andreas, physician and confessor to Dauphine and onetime member of their household. Dauphine's admission that she exaggerated the extent of her illness is disclosed in the testimony of Bertrand Iusbert, a Franciscan in Apt (p. 212).

[78] *Vie . . . Dauphine* 3.6, pp. 156–157; *Vie . . . Auzias* 2.3, pp. 56–57; *AA SS*, September, 7:541.

[79] *AA SS*, September, 7:550–551; *Vie . . . Auzias* c. 10, pp. 96–101; *Vie . . . Dauphine* c. 6, pp. 168–173; *Canonisation de Dauphine* art. 13, pp. 39–40. On Dauphine's precipitous vow, see chapter 5, p. 219, above.

them that certainly would have rivaled a carnal bond for strength. They were subjected to a number of trials. The family was ambitious for heirs and Dauphine's piety troubled them. Dauphine was made to sing and dance, and was decked out in sumptuous clothes. The candles, which Dauphine used for vigils, were likewise removed from her chamber.[80] The grandfather questioned Dauphine closely, worrying that her prayer and weeping inhibited conception. He ordered doctors to prescribe various potions and ointments for her—all of which she privately threw out.[81] As a final desperate measure, he sent the young couple to Marseilles to see the renowned Arnold of Villanova—who, as luck would have it, was himself an ardent Joachimist and very much in favor of virginity from an eschatological standpoint.[82] The remarkable doctor collaborated with the holy couple by contriving a bogus list of explanations as to why they were temporarily sterile.[83] But the relatives were still suspicious. They eventually resorted to planting spies in their bedroom—worldly women who were supposed to report on anything unusual that they saw and to encourage them (one wonders just how) in conjugal relations. Finally, Elzear's relatives decided that Dauphine was permanently sterile and apparently made attempts on her life by trying to poison her food.[84]

In 1307 Elzear came of age and they were permitted to live at Dauphine's estate at Puimichel. This was a blessed release for the couple. Only then did they have the opportunity to shape a household in accordance with their private ideology. The result was a strict rule of life in which chastity dominated as a kind of absolute value.[85] No sexually active persons, whether married or single, were allowed.[86]

Certainly one of the keys to this virginal success story is Elzear's mysticism that corroborated Dauphine's promptings in favor of chastity. As with Robert Malatesta, who was constrained by the conjugal debt and the accession to power, the various pressures that secret

[80] *Vie . . . Dauphine* 3.3, pp. 150–151.

[81] Ibid. 4.2, pp. 158–161.

[82] See John F. Benton, "Arnald of Villanova," *DMA*, 1:537–538. Indeed, as Vauchez points out, Arnold was responsible for writing a commentary on the Ps.-Joachimist treatise on the chaste marriage of Henry II and Cunegund mentioned earlier in this chapter (*Les laïcs*, p. 222).

[83] *Vie . . . Dauphine* 4.3, pp. 160–163.

[84] Ibid. 4.4, pp. 162–165.

[85] Cf. Vauchez, *Les laïcs*, p. 212.

[86] *Vie . . . Auzias* 7.1, pp. 76–77; *AA SS*, September, 7:546. The Occitan life is slightly more blatant than the Latin original. Not only does it put chastity as the first rule of the household, ahead of church attendance, but it explicitly excludes married women. The Latin simply insists that everyone should lead a chaste and clean life ("omnes tenerent vitam castam et mundam").

chastity imposed on Elzear likewise initiated him to that peculiar "doubleness" which is so characteristic of female spirituality and, as with the mystical matrons described above, would eventually open up a direct channel to God.[87]

The path to mysticism began from the moment he was united with Dauphine. Throughout their marriage, Dauphine and Elzear slept in the same bed, although they remained dressed. During the first year of marriage, however, Elzear was still troubled by sexual feelings. While the onset of sexual activity has been seen to provoke increased asceticism in the women who were forced to marry, delay and frustration may have produced the same effect in Elzear. He undertook a harsh program of self-mortification which included a fast that lasted throughout all of Lent. According to his hagiographer, this ascetic feat changed his appearance permanently.[88] On the other hand, Elzear could in no way betray his frustration to the world. When some ribald associates urged him to join in their womanizing, Elzear prudently answered that he had a beautiful and gracious wife, and that was sufficient for him.[89] Elzear's hormonal turmoil receded with his first ecstasy, at which point he began to collaborate more actively in Dauphine's chaste vision.[90] But because of Elzear's position in the world, the sense of "doubleness" grew in proportion to the need for secrecy. While preserving chastity at home, and making their familiars swear to keep their chastity a secret, the couple publicly posed as worldly society types.[91]

On the whole, Elzear was the source of this split existence. The author of Elzear's Occitan life implicitly presents this doubleness as essential to his spirituality by claiming that Christ ordered Elzear to

[87] The content of Elzear's mystical experience is also characteristically female. Particularly worthy of note are the burning sensations that accompany his ecstasies, his personal witnessing of the Crucifixion, his tears, and his emphasis on divine love (see *AA SS*, September, 7:542–543, 547; *Vie . . . Auzias* 3.2–3, pp. 58–61; 5.1, pp. 62–67). Also note his desire for frequent communion (*Vie . . . Auzias* 5.1, pp. 64–65; *AA SS*, September, 7:546–547).

[88] *AA SS*, September, 7:540; *Vie . . . Auzias* 1.4, pp. 50–51. The second life adds that Elzear's great desire was to be a hermit, but God had chosen to draw him to himself in another way. Elzear's extensive fasting is especially characteristic of female spirituality. See Bynum, *Holy Feast and Holy Fast*, pp. 78–79.

[89] *AA SS*, September, 7:540; *Vie . . . Auzias* 1.4, pp. 50–51.

[90] He felt no carnal lust when awake, and if he was tempted in his sleep, he not only resisted but found the experience unpleasant (*AA SS*, September, 7:541; *Vie . . . Auzias* 2.3, pp. 56–57).

[91] *Vie . . . Dauphine* 4.1, pp. 156–157. On the vow of secrecy, see 8.1, pp. 174–175; *AA SS*, September, 7:551; *Canonisation de Dauphine* art. 15, p. 41. Bertranda Bartholomea, a member of the household who had lived with Dauphine for forty-seven years, said that she was required to swear into the hands of Dauphine's confessor and that she had heard that the knights were made to swear as well (p. 319).

change nothing in his external activities.[92] As with Dorothea of Montau, Elzear's mysticism not only functioned within but flourished under these constraints. Although worldly distractions annoyed him, dancing, singing, and the sound of musical instruments tended to induce his raptures.[93] Dauphine, on the other hand, was more clearly in favor of their withdrawing from the world together in order to pursue a private life of prayer—a step that he was finally prepared to take just before he met his death.[94]

The shapes of Elzear and Dauphine's respective spiritualities are in many ways markedly different. There is no evidence that virginity ever held the same symbolic value for Elzear as it did for Dauphine. It rather served as a catalystic means to a mystical end. Dauphine, on the other hand, was no mystic but was deeply drawn to the Franciscan ideal of apostolic poverty, as her radical divestment of property after Elzear's death would suggest.[95] And yet the balanced and complementary nature of the couple's spiritual progress is, indeed, striking. Dauphine started Elzear on his path to perfection, and perhaps her slight seniority facilitated her initial dominance. She also played a central role in his intellectual development, teaching him first to read, then to recite the hours of the Virgin and finally the divine office.[96] Dauphine's physical presence was a spiritual assist to her

[92] *Vie . . . Auzias* 5.3, pp. 68–69.

[93] "Insuper, quando erat in colloquio cum diversis, et confabulabatur cum iisdem, ejus spiritus minime longabatur a Deo; imo, quod plus est, quando erat in choreis, cantus et instrumenta musica audiendo, mens ipsius mirabili et maximo excessu rapiebatur in Deum" (*AA SS*, September, 7:547; cf. p. 544; *Vie . . . Auzias* 5.3, pp. 68–69).

[94] Elzear waited until all the debts on his land had been paid. He also told Dauphine that he had had a premonition that he would not live long (*AA SS*, September, 7:554; *Vie . . . Auzias* 13.1, pp. 118–119). My assumption that the impulse to withdraw from the world was generated by Dauphine is not based just on Elzear's greater secular responsibilities but on the fact that Elzear offered this possibility up as consolation before he went away on his last mission ("Et antequam recederet, ut suam consortem virginem dimitteret consolatam, dicebat sibi . . ." [*AA SS*, September, 7:554]). Also, after Elzear's death, Dauphine divests herself of her property (see *Canonisation de Dauphine* arts. 20–23, 25, pp. 44–49). Her process also makes mention of how, during her husband's lifetime, she was often impeded from serving God as she ought to (pp. 43, 219).

[95] *Vie . . . Dauphine* c. 10–11, pp. 182–193, and n. 94, above. After a life of mendicancy, she returned to Provence and lived as a recluse for a number of years (*Vie . . . Dauphine* 13.1, pp. 198–201; *Canonisation de Dauphine* art. 26, p. 49). This seems to have been a relatively popular ascetic alternative for women in southern France. See, for example, Paulette L'Hermite-Leclercq, "Reclus et recluses dans le sud-ouest de la France," in *La femme dans la vie religieuse du Languedoc (XIIIe–XIVe s.)*, ed. E. Privat, Cahiers de Fanjeaux, 23 (Toulouse, 1988) pp. 281–298.

[96] *Vie . . . Auzias* 7.3, pp. 82–83; *Vie . . . Dauphine* 4.1, pp. 156–157. This is not unusual in the lives of female saints. Bridget of Sweden, for example, taught Ulf to read (*AA SS*, October, 4:489). Noblewomen were often better educated than their husbands.

husband. He claimed that the closer he was to her, the more secure he was in his chaste resolve—a feature that the sources never mention without sounding the "more admirable than imitable" alarm.[97] Even in his prayers and mystical raptures, he felt freer when his wife was present.[98] Nor was Elzear backward in acknowledging his spiritual debt to his wife. On his deathbed, in the presence of witnesses, he alludes to Paul's most ambitious expectations for the married (1 Cor. 7.14): "'A wicked man is saved through a good woman, whom, just as I received a virgin, so I relinquish a virgin in this mortal life.'"[99] The revelation of virginity at the death of one of the spouses is, by now, a familiar motif. The only element that is different in this case is that the incident is probably true.[100]

But the debt was by no means entirely on his side. When Elzear was absent on a diplomatic mission, the prescient Dauphine was miraculously apprised of his death and fell to weeping. The queen of Sicily tried to comfort her, saying that Dauphine had, after all, never known the love of a husband, but Dauphine responded, "'My lord husband was the father of my soul, its pastor, guardian, and governor.'"[101] Unlike many holy matrons who grieve little or even welcome their husbands' death, Dauphine was inconsolable for over a year. Indeed, her grief subsided only when Elzear appeared to her and gently reproached her, reminding her that now he was delivered from the body and that she was free to pursue her apostolic vocation. "Since that hour he instructed her like an uncreated clarity," her *vita* reports.[102]

[97] *AA SS*, September, 7:541; *Vie . . . Auzias* 2.3, pp. 54–55; *Canonisation de Dauphine* art. 14, p. 40; *Vie . . . Dauphine* 4.1, pp. 158–159.

[98] *AA SS*, September, 7:547.

[99] "'Salvatus est homo malus per mulierem bonam, quam sicut virginem accepi, ita in hac vita mortali virginem relinquo'" (*AA SS*, September, 7:554). Cf. the following version from his Occitan life: "'Hyeu, dysh el justa lo dig del apostol sanh Paul, peccador enfizel, per ma espoza Dalphina fizel e drechurieyra, la qual en comensamen e tostemps me ha promogut e singularmen a observar virginitat; e soy fag fizel e sals, la qual laysi en aquesta vida peregrina vergis, no tocada'" (*Vie . . . Auzias* 13.2, p. 120).

[100] There were witnesses present at Elzear's deathbed. See, for example, *Canonisation de Dauphine*, p. 205. Cf. the wording of Innocent III's bull of canonization for the empress Cunegund in which Henry is attributed with the same formula: "'Qualem eam michi assignastis, talem eam uobis resigno. Virginem eam dedistis et uirginem reddo'" (Petersohn, ed., "Die Litterae Papst Innocenz' III.," p. 24). Also see Gregory of Tours's story of Injuriosus and Scholastica, discussed in chapter 2.

[101] "'Mossen mo marit era payre de la mia arma, e pastor, e garda, e governador'" (*Vie . . . Dauphine* 9.2, p. 180); cf. similar comments in *AA SS*, September, 7:541; *Vie . . . Auzias* 2.3, pp. 54–55.

[102] "E d'aquela hora la essenhava aysi coma clartat no creada" (*Vie . . . Dauphine* 9.2, p. 182); also see *Canonisation de Dauphine* art. 19, pp. 43–44. Cf. Robert Malatesta's parallel appearance to his young widow in which he confirms her vocation to chastity, in chapter 5, n. 216, above. When Dauphine was on the point of abandoning

Finally, Dauphine was the chief witness at Elzear's process for canonization, attesting to both his sanctity and the miracles he wrought.[103] Sure of his goodness, however, she had already begun to venerate him as a saint in private. Nor is this balanced and trusting reliance on one another limited to the spiritual sphere alone, but it also translates to the practical level. When, for example, Elzear was claiming his father's estate in Lombardy, Dauphine was placed in charge and Elzear vigorously defended her rule to dissatisfied relatives who threatened to seize the land.[104]

Their remarkable, but carefully circumscribed, intimacy was the basis of their complementary spiritualities. They lived together for just under twenty-five years, never separating chamber or bed, though always sleeping fully clothed and carefully avoiding physical contact.[105] But one scene, in particular, illustrates the interaction of spiritual and physical closeness. Once when Dauphine was washing her husband's hair, the latter warned her that he could feel the approach of a vision. He spent the rest of the night in prayer.

> And when dawn came, he called his spouse, who immediately came in with a light, and she found him totally inflamed. For she saw that a certain brightness proceeded from his face, more beautiful and bright than the light of the candle, which rendered his face and the surrounding area beautiful and bright. And at a suitable time, he revealed to her, namely, to his holy spouse, what he had seen through that entire night.[106]

---

the world, she called her household together and said some apologetic, self-deprecatory words about how badly she had spent her time since her lord's demise and her difficulty in obeying God's will—comments that suggest some kind of breakdown occasioned by the loss of her husband: "'Scitis eciam quomodo, ex quo dominus meus sanctus migravit de hoc seculo, male et negligenter expendi tempus meum. Scitis eciam quod frequenter Deus inspiravit michi quod dimitterem mundum. . . . Et ego propter meam sensualitatem . . . non curabam hoc facere, sed totum neglexi et in tantum neglexi quod iusto Dei iudicio penitus amiseram omnem bonam voluntatem'" (*Canonisation de Dauphine* art. 23, p. 46).

[103] See Cambell, ed., "Le sommaire de l'enquête pour la canonisation de Elzéar de Sabran," esp. pp. 448–449 (on arts. 10, 12, and 15), and 455 (on arts. 36–37).

[104] *Vie . . . Dauphine* 5.3, pp. 168–169. They complained that she lived in the company of religious who were inept at worldly business and were thus wasting Elzear's property.

[105] *Canonisation de Dauphine* art. 11, pp. 37–38; pp. 213, 316, 462.

[106] "Cumque esset aurora, vocavit sponsam, quae statim accessit cum lumine, et invenit eum totaliter inflammatum. Videbat enim, quod de ejus facie quaedam claritas procedebat, luce candelae clarior et pulchrior, quae faciem ipsius et spatium convicinum reddebat speciosum et clarum. Et congruo tempore revelavit sibi, scilicet suae sacrae sponsae, quod tota illa nocte viderat" (*AA SS*, September, 7:543; cf. *Vie . . . Auzias* c. 4, pp. 60–61).

The pivotal role of the confessor in a mystic's life recedes in the face of so extraordinary a level of conjugal confidence.

When Elzear reappeared to Dauphine after his death, he recited the following line from Psalm 123.7: "The snare is broken; and we are delivered." Dauphine's hagiographer says that she took this to mean that he was now totally liberated from the bondage of the flesh, while she, released from the rule of her husband and the matrimonial tie, was also free, in part.[107] This seems to comply with the commonly held orthodox view that marriage ended with death. And yet, as Vauchez points out, there are some very real reasons for arguing that Elzear and Dauphine perceived their relationship as a kind of realized eschatology, not simply in the singular and individualistic way of virgins living the *vita angelica*, but insofar as the spiritual union that they experienced on earth would endure in paradise. This is indicated by Elzear's own reflection on their union. When Dauphine was expressing shock and grief that the duke of Calabria would be so quick to remarry after the very recent death of his wife, and—worse— would actually be elated by her demise, Elzear answered:

> "Between husbands and wives who love the world, it often happens that the carnal love which is between them fails like the flesh. But between me and you, there is a spiritual and pure love and such love, just like the spirit, will last forever and not fail."[108]

Dauphine and Elzear represent a high watermark in realized hagiography, actualizing practically every motif that has been touched on in the course of this study. Dauphine was the product of a barren union who was destined for chastity. A forced marriage made her resort to the wedding-night stratagem exemplified in the Cecilia legend. The couple's chastity elided the many gendered divisions that were once so lamented in the early church. Not only is this demonstrated by their frictionless intimacy and consummate friendship, but by Elzear's mysticism, which suggests a limited gender reversal. They vindicated Augustine's claims to the superior strength of a spiritual bond; indeed, they injected new meaning into the Pauline hopes for mutual sanctification. Their purity was divulged in the tradi-

---

[107] *Vie . . . Dauphine* 9.2, pp. 180–183. Ps. 123 is numbered as 124 in modern versions of the Bible.

[108] " 'Entre motz maritz e molhers amadors del mon soven s'endeve que la amor carnal, que es entre lor, ayssi coma la carn, tost defalh; mas entre mi e tu es amor spiritual e pura; e aytal, ayssi coma l'esperit, tostemps dura e no defalh ni ·s marfezish'" (*Vie . . . Dauphine* 8.2, p. 178). Vauchez points out that this view compares well with the Ps.-Joachimist treatise on Henry and Cunegund, cited above (see *Les laïcs*, p. 221).

tional graveside formula, through which Elzear expressed his debt to his wife. Finally, they perceived their union as withstanding the grave.[109]

To this already impressive list of exemplification, we can add one more mimetic item that was undoubtedly beyond our holy couple's control but nevertheless evokes certain eleventh-century patterns. Elzear posthumously outstripped his holy partner in the race for official sanctity. Although Dauphine's process for canonization was undertaken in 1363, only three years after her death, her case foundered, in spite of the fact that many witnesses confirmed that Elzear himself attributed his virginity and purity of life to his wife's influence.[110] André Vauchez rightly points out that Dauphine's petition was jeopardized by the very virginity around which her claim to sanctity was constructed. The force of her commitment to virginity and the eschatological possibilities of their chaste union were open to a heretical construction.[111] Elzear's bull of canonization tended to stress his

[109] It is also possible that Elzear internalized and then realized certain more secularly conditioned formulas. The question of courtly love, theoretically an unconsummated love, which certain scholars perceive as a method of simultaneously increasing and refining passion, immediately comes to mind. Most assuredly Provence, as home of the troubadours, would be the right place to look for such a phenomenon, if it was ever realized in a cogent system of beliefs and practices, which I am inclined to doubt (see chap. 4, n. 5, above). Moreover, as Vauchez points out, the sources make it abundantly clear that their chastity was grounded in mainstream hagiography (see Les laïcs, pp. 217–218). On the other hand, I would not cancel out the possible influence of the kind of spiritualized chivalric ethos alluded to earlier. It is probably no coincidence that Elzear experienced his first ecstasy when he was present for the making of a knight and that the rapture he experienced on the vigil of his own knighting prompted him to send for Dauphine in order to make the permanent vow of chastity (AA SS, September, 7:540, 550; cf. Vie . . . Auzias 10.1, pp. 96–99). Even if Elzear did not deeply identify with such a model, there is little doubt that others projected it onto him. In 1307, the noble widow Mabilla de Simiane experienced an ecstasy in which she saw a knight on a vast field dressed in a resplendent habit. He carried a great white banner, and a multitude of men and women, of every age and class, followed. When she asked the meaning of this vision, it was divinely revealed to her that it concerned the virginity of Count Elzear, whose holy example would lead many people to lead a chaste and holy life (Vie . . . Auzias 6.2, pp. 72–75). Perhaps Mabilla was familiar with Peter John Olivi's Provençal treatise "Lo cavalier armat." See Raoul Manselli's edition and comments, and M.-H. Vicaire's translation of this text in La religion populaire en Languedoc du XIIIe siècle à la moitié du XIVe siècle, ed. E. Privat, Cahiers de Fanjeaux, 11 (Toulouse, 1976), pp. 203–216, esp. p. 209 regarding the cuirass of purity, which enables the mystical marriage with Christ. On Olivi's significance, see chap. 4, n. 8, above and n. 111, below.

[110] See especially Canonisation de Dauphine arts. 10 and 14, pp. 36–37, 40, 249, 251, 318; cf. Vie . . . Auzias 1.4, pp. 48–49.

[111] Vauchez, Les laïcs, pp. 211–224. Vauchez suspects the influence of the Franciscan theologian Peter John Olivi, who was associated with what came to be considered the heretical camp of the Spiritual Franciscans. Olivi argued that marriage was not a sacrament and that it actually impeded spiritual growth. He promoted chastity for

mysticism and his charity. But Dauphine, as initiator and hierophant of the virginal union, was too profoundly implicated in a vision of perfection that had fallen out of favor.

One wonders if the failure of Dauphine's process did not inspire the promoters of Jeanne-Marie of Maillac's cult to proceed with a certain amount of caution. No official process of canonization was undertaken on behalf of Jeanne-Marie. A diocesan inquiry was, however, conducted immediately after her death in 1414; interestingly enough, this document makes no explicit mention of her virginity. Article 1 describes her early piety but does not even refer to her desire to remain a virgin. The second article is even more oblique.

> Item and after the Lord of Silleye, her spouse [sponsus], had been released from the bonds of the flesh, that same Lady, then having lived thirty years, continued the same contemplative life and dedicated the intention of her widowhood to God. She inwardly gave up all empty and superfluous words and macerated her body with vigils and prayers from that time to the day of her death.[112]

Only the use of the word "sponsus" as opposed to "conjunx" could conceivably give the game away. Likewise, although article 10 mentions that her body became white and pure after her death, it does not

---

eschatological reasons and had a particular impact on certain Beguines in southern France, who were later deemed heretical. On his writings and influence, see Pierre Péano, "Olieu," *DS*, vol. 11, cols. 751–762; Le Bras, "La doctrine du mariage," *DTC*, vol. 9, cols. 2208–2212; Raoul Manselli, "Les opuscules spirituels de Pierre Jean-Olivi et la piété de béguins de Langue d'Oc," in *La religion populaire en Languedoc*, ed. Privat, pp. 187–201. His writings on marriage and virginity have been excerpted from his *De perfectione evangelica* and edited by A. Emmen as "Verginita' e matrimonio nella valutazione dell'Olivi," *Studi Francescani* 64 (1967): 11–57; see esp. pp. 32–50. Cambell tends to downplay the eschatological influences that Vauchez highlights, however (see *Vies occitanes*, pp. 110–111 n. 84). Certainly Dauphine wholeheartedly embraced the doctrine of apostolic poverty associated with the Spiritual Franciscans. Nor could she have picked a more unpopular time for it. John XXII pronounced against the Spiritual Franciscans in 1322; Dauphine divested herself of her property shortly thereafter (see *Vie . . . Dauphine*, p. 186 n. 199). On the condemnation of the Spiritual Franciscans, see Malcolm Lambert, *Franciscan Poverty: The Doctrine of the Absolute Poverty of Christ and the Apostles in the Franciscan order, 1210–1323* (London, 1961), esp. pp. 225–245. Also see David Burr, *Olivi and Franciscan Poverty: The Origins of the 'Usus Pauper' Controversy* (Philadelphia, 1989), esp. pp. 57–87.

[112] "Item et quod Domino de Seilleyo, ejus sponso a carnis vinculis absoluto, eadem Domina, tunc tricesima annorum existente, eamdem vitam contemplativam continuando, et Deo viduitatis suae propositum dedicando, verba inania et otiosa a se penitus abdicavit, et corpus suum vigiliis et orationibus ab illo tempore usque ad diem sui transitus maceravit" (art. 2 in *AA SS*, March, 3:745).

pursue the implications of this miraculous rejuvenation.[113] Who would ever have thought that virginity could become a liability for women?

None of the late medieval virgin wives was canonized, although a number of them were beatified several centuries after their deaths.[114] Dauphine stands alone in being the subject of an official process.[115] Since processes became progressively more expensive and political in the later Middle Ages, not too much should be made of this point.[116] On the other hand, it is significant that figures such as Angelina Corbara of Marsciano and Cunegund of Poland even failed to engage the interest of a contemporary hagiographer.

In comparison, the women who made the transition from early sexual activity to spiritual marriage, and thus did less to advance the argument for lay chastity, enjoyed more illustrious posthumous careers. Each of the women who initiated the move to chastity in the course of her marriage attracted the attention of a contemporary hagiographer. Hedwig of Silesia, Dorothea of Montau, Bridget of Sweden, and Frances of Rome all inspired processes for canonization immediately after their deaths. Not only were all four of these women eventually canonized, but Hedwig and Bridget were canonized within a hundred years of their deaths.[117]

---

[113] Ibid. The point is not lost on all of the witnesses, however. A certain Joanna la Quarree attests that many thought the body resembled that of a young girl who had retained virginal purity: "et quod majus est omnibus, claustrum virgineum, purum, integrum et intactum repertum est" (p. 759); cf. the testimony of Richeta, wife of Oliver Tranchant (p. 760).

[114] Dauphine was eventually beatified at the end of the seventeenth century (see Cambell, *Canonisation de Dauphine*, introd., p. viii). A process for the beatification of Cunegund was undertaken in 1628; her cult was confirmed in 1690 (*BS*, vol. 4, col. 400). Salome of Galicia's process for beatification was begun in 1650 and confirmed in 1672 (*BS*, vol. 11, cols. 589–590). Angelina Corbara of Marsciano's cult was confirmed in 1825, but no formal process of beatification seems to have occurred (*BS*, vol. 1, cols. 1231–1232). Lucia Brocadelli of Narni's popular cult was likewise confirmed by the papacy in 1710 (*BS*, vol. 3, cols. 547–548). The inquiry into Jeanne-Marie of Maillac's sanctity was held up by the schism. Her cult was confirmed only in 1871 (*BS*, vol. 6, cols. 589–590). With respect to Gennaia of Gubbio and her husband, Sperandeo, the latter was the focus of attention, but he seems to have failed to inspire a cult after his death (*BS*, vol. 11, cols. 1346–1347).

[115] A process for canonization was attempted on behalf of Catherine of Sweden. But this occurred between 1466 and 1489, more than eighty years after her death, and was never completed. Papal permission was obtained for a solemn translation of relics (*BS*, vol. 3, cols. 994–996).

[116] See Vauchez, *La sainteté*, pp. 71–90.

[117] Hedwig was canonized in 1267 (*BS*, vol. 4, cols. 933–934). Although Bridget was canonized in 1391, the papal schism was sufficiently problematical and her revelations were sufficiently controversial that her canonization needed to be reconfirmed in 1415

Of course this fits into the larger pattern of the church's more positive pastoral teaching on marriage and the corresponding extension of sainthood to the married. Although modern scholars have generally considered this trend to be progressive, one must still take stock of all that this implies. Virginity had continued to be a matrix for the production of insubordinate acts, and the virgin wives were not submissive. They failed in their first marital responsibility, namely, rendering the debt, and frequently balked at others. Lucia Brocadelli of Narni fled her husband's company dressed like a man.[118] Catherine of Sweden intercepted her husband's correspondence so she could travel unaccompanied to Rome to join her mother. Dauphine took a unilateral vow of chastity during her husband's absence. A list of their collective transgressions could go on and on. On the other hand, chastity that had been gradually achieved in the course of a marriage had been hagiographically reconditioned to correspond with normative conceptions of female submission. Thus, while the rise of the penitential matron undoubtedly reflects the liberalized sexual kerygma of the church, it also signifies more constricting gender constructions for women: wives who are sexually active in spite of themselves, an unquestioning obedience to unworthy masters, fine material subjected to coarse ends.

---

and again in 1419. See James A. Schmidtke, " 'Saving' by Faint Praise: St. Birgitta of Sweden, Adam Easton, and Medieval Antifeminism," *American Benedictine Review* 33 (1982): 149–161; also see *BS*, vol. 3, cols. 515–517. Other canonizations were not so expeditious: Frances was not canonized until 1608 (see *BS*, vol. 4, cols. 1011–1021), while Dorothea was not canonized until 1978. For the political problems that plagued her case for canonization, see Ute Stargardt, "The Political and Social Backgrounds of the Canonization of Dorothea von Montau," *Mystics Quarterly* 11 (1985): 107–122.

[118] After three years of chaste cohabitation, Lucia's flight was inspired by the example of St. Euphronisia. When she was led back in the company of SS. Dominic and Peter the Martyr of Verona (who ungallantly disappeared when they reached her husband's home), she was imprisoned and fed on a diet of bread and water for all of Lent. Upon her release, she immediately fled her husband's house and unilaterally took the veil (*Narratione . . . Lucia* c. 19, pp. 87–91). This, as we have seen, prompted her husband to burn down her confessor's monastery.

CONCLUSION

> MARIA: But they say chastity is a thing most pleasing to God.
>
> PAMPHILUS: And therefore I want to marry a chaste girl, that I may live chastely with her. It will be more a marriage of minds than of bodies. We'll reproduce for the State; we'll reproduce for Christ. By how little will this marriage fall short of virginity! And perhaps some day we'll live as Joseph and Mary did. But meantime we'll learn virginity; for one does not reach the summit all at once.
>
> (Erasmus, "The Wooer and the Maiden")[1]

PAMPHILUS'S SUASIONS are merely strategic ploys for seduction. Although superficially similar in tenor to many of the panegyrics we have been considering, the context exposes the ideal of intramarital chastity to light derision.

Spiritual marriage could probably have withstood the jibes of a crusty old humanist like Erasmus, but it could not withstand the changes brought on by the Reformation and Counter-Reformation. The Protestant reformers' depreciation of the practice of chastity, if not the theory, led to the rejection of sacerdotal and monastic celibacy alike. Mariology and the cult of saints inspired profound mistrust and were peremptorily abandoned. These changes soon rendered the concept of intramarital chastity incomprehensible. In Catholic countries, the changes were more subtle but no less real. The Council of Trent and the post-Tridentine reformers affirmed and even accentuated the differences between clergy and laity. This growing emphasis on clerical authority, in turn, escalated suspicions against lay piety. Female piety, in particular, was closely monitored. Strict claustration was rigorously imposed on convents, and female initiative toward an active lay apostolate was ultimately suppressed or redirected into a cloistered milieu. A proportionate decline in female sanctity was inevitable, while instances of spiritual marriage accordingly disappeared from view. There are rare mentions of unconsummated unions: Sebastian Aparicio (d. 1600), for example, married twice in order to afford the women in question financial security.[2]

---

[1] *Ten Colloquies of Erasmus*, trans. Craig R. Thompson (New York, 1957), p. 32.

[2] On Sebastian Aparacio, see *BS*, vol. 11, cols. 773–776. A possible exception is the English martyr Anne Line (d. 1601), who lived in chastity with her husband, Roger.

And yet, divorced as these unions were from theological and hagiographical tradition alike, they bore more in common with the modern marriage of social or economic convenience.

Although the history of spiritual marriage presents an intriguing and often seamless symbiosis of theory and practice, one distinction representing differential access along gender lines is nevertheless clear: women were only its most celebrated practitioners. They were never its theorists and only rarely the direct transmitters of the tradition in which they partook. The limitations of their role had important consequences.

As practitioners, women reaped immediate benefits from intramarital chastity. The fact that spiritual marriage repeatedly coincided with or facilitated a collapse in the husband's authority and enabled a relative suspension of the gender hierarchy might imply that the relation between sexual intercourse and masculine authority is permanent and historically invariable. Yet the wives who participated in (or were believed to have participated in) spiritual marriage must be understood to have gained only a limited and situationally defined—rather than invariable or historically transcendent— agency. These women undoubtedly inspired imitation, and this frequently had an enabling effect on later female emulators. On the other hand, since women were neither hagiographers nor chroniclers, the tradition could play strange tricks on them.

The topos of the virgin monarch illustrates such diversified application. Queens such as Æthelthryth may well have preserved their virginity by a unilateral refusal to pay the marriage debt. But this heroic precedent could also be put to other uses. In the later Germanic kingdoms, spiritual marriage could mask the brutal repudiation of a queen. During the eleventh-century reform when chastity was a contested locus of power, kings were eulogized at the expense of queens, who were temporarily excluded from a tradition in which they had ostensibly pioneered. Clerical disciplinarians, for a time, looked to spiritual marriage in their struggle to achieve a ritually pure clergy—one that was untainted by women. And so spiritual marriage was directly implicated in a movement that would ultimately marginalize women and limit their influence in the church. Even the invocation of this superficially "timeless" ideal had temporal appli-

---

Even so, the marriage was contracted shortly after Anne had been disinherited by her parents for her conversion to Catholicism, and seems to have been a marriage of convenience (see John Gerard, *The Autobiography of an Elizabethan*, trans. Philip Caraman [London, New York, and Toronto, 1951], pp. 82–86). I am indebted to Sandra Meisel for drawing this instance to my attention.

cations that frequently worked against female autonomy. Reluctant young girls could be cajoled into making a marriage on the presumption that they would imitate the saints and convince their husbands to forgo the debt. Indeed, the virgin wives of the later Middle Ages, by either aligning themselves or, more surely, being aligned with this tradition, ironically forfeited their claims to sanctity, which, in turn, limited their historical influence.

Of greater gravity, perhaps, is female exclusion from the theological tradition. Augustine was the undoubted architect of the theoretical framework for spiritual marriage in the West. He was probably inspired by the spontaneous practice of intramarital chastity in contemporary Christian circles that already bore the imprint of female initiative. And yet, in his delineation of the spiritual bond, he did not look to the experiences of these couples who had made the difficult transition to chastity but to the hypothetical marriage of Mary and Joseph, whose marriage had been recently upheld as entirely virginal. He also enlisted the Roman concept of consensus to demonstrate that the essence of the marriage bond was in no way contingent on physical relations. However, sensitive to the challenge that intramarital chastity presented to masculine authority and having made his peace with temporal hierarchies, Augustine attempted to consolidate the husband's authority by making it as enduring as the spiritual bond itself. Indeed, he interrupted previous tradition by associating female chastity with subjection to the husband—an equation facilitated by the Virgin's malleable and supple persona.

Augustine's formulations were extended in the high and later Middle Ages, which saw the triumph of the spiritualized definition of marriage and the concomitant flourishing of the Virgin's cult. But this later period also appealed to natural order. Woman, as the less perfect of the species, was relentlessly subordinated to man. This emphasis lent quasi-scientific weight to the traditional gender hierarchy, ultimately extending the power of the husband over the wife far beyond mere temporal considerations into the sensitive realm of the conscience. The Virgin, accordingly, began to emerge as a compelling amalgam of both chastity and submission. While the circumstances surrounding the Virgin's chastity placed her beyond the reach of real women, her exemplary submission, a virtue that was further refined with the introduction of the cult of St. Joseph, made an immense impression on normative prescriptions for female behavior. Furthermore, the consensual and nonphysical definition of the marriage bond—in conjunction with the new ascendancy of the realm of nature, the threat of dualism, and the desire to buttress masculine authority—stimulated a backlash among these same theorists. Con-

summation and the attendant obligation of the conjugal debt received unprecedented deference; the ancient appreciation for female
chastity was consequently undercut. Moreover, despite the much-
vaunted equality of the conjugal debt, dear to medieval theorists and
modern scholars alike, social and biological considerations would
suggest that the husband was the overwhelming benefactor of this
emphasis, while the wife was potentially relegated to an exaggerated
sexual servitude.

On the other hand, it is precisely these vexed developments that are
intrinsic to the new toleration for married sexuality and a general
democratization of sanctity. And these novel conditions are, in turn,
reflected in the growing attention given to the penitential matron,
who made a gradual transition to chastity in the course of her marriage. The competing demands of a spiritual vocation and married
life, of her inner and outer selves, produced a creative tension that
was a powerful leaven for mysticism—a potential source of female
empowerment. Yet this avenue, too, was closed almost as soon as it
appeared. The lives of these mystical matrons, and perhaps even the
content of their mystical experiences, were renarrated by skilled
theologians in such a way as to reinforce submission to appropriate
authorities. The submissive matron was more zealously promoted by
the ascendant powers than her virginal counterpart, but only in this
revised and less challenging form. It is also probable that this more
naturalistic and accessible transitional model of intramarital chastity, so implicated in the demands of the world, was more compelling
than the ancient story of elite virginal privilege. But the net result was
that female suffering and endurance came to overshadow trenchant
female heroism. Furthermore, the hardship that these matrons were
depicted as enduring in the course of their gradual transition to chastity and the ineffaceable conflict between husband and wife undermined the Augustinian rhetoric of the deepening bond between
spouses accompanying the transition to chastity. Rather, the emphasis on the virtues of humility and obedience seemingly buttressed
a contention alternatively available in his writings: that the more
subject a woman is, the more chaste she is.

Once the quintessential penitential virtues of humility and obedience had been isolated and hypostatized, they were no longer dependent on the institution within which they were frequently fostered. Future generations would be content to stress the virtues, and
to cut loose the problematical setting in which they were manifested.

In the later Middle Ages, when a tactical separation between the
practice of intramarital chastity and the theoretical idealization of
the purer consensual bond was admitted, spiritual marriage had al-

ready turned its last critical corner. Hagiographers had become apprehensive about praising the superior and transcendent nature of a
chaste bond. Those who did risked exposing their pious subjects to
suspicions of heresy. Moreover, as the example of Dauphine indicates, the virginal marriage, formerly one of the most powerful symbols of Augustine's vision of consensus, was rendered particularly
suspect. Thus, it was bequeathed to subsequent centuries as a severely attenuated ideal, severed from the sustaining theological discussions that had given it continuing life. In the abandonment of this
potential matrix for female defiance, however, a powerful image of
mutual sanctification in marriage was also relinquished. The double
cults of Henry and Cunegund and of Elzear and Dauphine are the only
instances in the entire Christian tradition in which both husband
and wife are officially recognized objects of veneration; this is a reminder of what was, and of what has been lost.

Women dominated spiritual marriage for a millennium and a half
without ever really mastering it. And yet, despite powerful interventions and manipulations, clerical theorists were equally incapable of
controlling the tradition. The virgin queen of the Germanic kingdoms, to name but one example, proved less tractable than the Virgin
Mary. Though frequently manipulated to suit male expedience, the
virgin queen nevertheless presented a model of heroic female spirituality that continued to inspire and, to some extent, validate female
defiance long after the political and social conditions that she inhab-
ited had disappeared. Female mystical propensities that were stimulated as a result of the penitential ethos presented an undeniable
challenge to the husband's authority as well as to the orthodox hierarchy, despite clerical efforts to contain them. Finally, the very long-
evity of spiritual marriage as a model that inspired emulation demonstrates the clergy's failure to impress the distinction between
admiration and imitation on pious laywomen. It also bespeaks the
clergy's ultimate inability to either monopolize or control the charismatic gift of chastity.

APPENDIXES

THE APPENDIXES list the couples discussed in this study who participated in spiritual marriages. They are alphabetized according to the name of the spouse who was the center of the cult or is most likely to be known.

The following abbreviations pertain to Appendixes 1–7:

A = Contemporary source for spiritual marriage

B = Source treating spiritual marriage over 100 years after alleged death of individual

C = Source treating spiritual marriage over 200 years after alleged death of individual

a/a = Contemporary source for individual with tradition of spiritual marriage added within 100 years of alleged death

a/b = Contemporary source for individual with tradition of spiritual marriage over within 100 years of alleged death

a/c = Contemporary source for individual with tradition of spiritual marriage added over 200 years of alleged death

Only one of the above codes is assigned per couple, except when there is an appreciable difference between the historical traditions of husband and wife.

Some of the individuals included in Appendixes 1–4 are probably hagiographical fabrications. A "yes" under the category "Historical Figure" denotes that the person in question in all probability existed.

The individuals in Appendixes 5–7 are all historical figures who received some contemporary notice. Their source typology refers to the first *detailed* source that discusses the marriage.

APPENDIX 1

Spiritual Marriage and the Laity: ca. 300–900
(including Eastern lives that circulated in the West)

Couple	Country	Rank	Died	Forced Marriage	Children	Initiator of Chastity	# of Years of Chaste Cohabitation	Religious Affiliation	Historical Figure	Source
Amon of Nitria	Egypt	wealthy	ca. 350	yes	unconsummated	husband	18	hermit	yes	A
unknown	"	"	"	no				nun	"	
anonymous rustic of Cassian	Egypt	peasantry	late 4th century?	yes	unconsummated	husband?	12	—	yes	A
unknown	"	"	"	unknown				—	"	
Aper	Gaul	nobility	after 400	unknown	unknown	wife	unknown	hermit	yes	A
Amanda	"	"	"	"				—	"	
Armentarius†	North Africa	nobility	after 410	unknown	unknown	wife	unknown	—	yes	A
Paulina†	"	"	"	"				—	"	
Aye	Frankish kingdom	nobility	691?	unknown	unconsummated	mutual	many	founder/ nun	yes?	C
Hidulph	"	"	prior	"				abbot/ bishop?	"	
Bertilia	Frankish kingdom	nobility	ca. 687	unknown	unconsummated	wife	many	anchoress	yes	C?
Guthland	"	"	prior	no				—	"	
Cecilia	Rome	nobility	3d century	yes	unconsummated	wife	1?	martyr	no	C
Valerian	"	"	before wife	no				"	"	

Chrysanthus	Rome	nobility	3d century	yes	unconsummated	husband	unknown	martyr	no	C
Daria	"	"	"	no				"	"	
Ecdicia	North Africa	nobility	after 418	unknown	1	wife	unknown	—	yes	A
unknown††	"	"	"	"				—	"	
Epiphanius	Greece	nobility	4th century	no	1	mutual	unknown	—	no	C
Joanna (parents of Nicholas)	"	"	"	"				—	"	
Eucharistos	Egypt	peasantry	between 4th and 6th century	unknown	unconsummated	mutual	unknown	—	?	B or C
Mary	"	"	"	"				—	"	
Euphanius	Rome	nobility	5th century	no	1	mutual	many	—	no	C
Aglae (parents of Alexis)	"	"	"	"				—	"	
Euphraxia	Lycia (Asia Minor)	nobility	late 4th or early 5th century	unknown	1	mutual	1	—	yes	A
Antigonus (parents of St. Euphraxia)	"	"	before wife	"				—	"	

(continued)

APPENDIX 1 (Continued)

Couple	Country	Rank	Died	Forced Marriage	Children	Initiator of Chastity	# of Years of Chaste Cohabitation	Religious Affiliation	Historical Figure	Source
Gumbert	Frankish kingdom	nobility	late 7th century	yes	unconsummated	mutual	unknown	founder/monk/martyr	yes	B
Bertha	"	"	after husband	"				founder/nun/martyr?	"	
Hilary, senator of Dijon	Gaul	nobility	6th century	no	yes	mutual	unknown	—	yes	B
Quitta?	"	"	after husband	unknown				—	"	
Julian	Egypt	nobility	304?	yes	unconsummated	mutual	unknown	founder/monk/martyr	no	C
Basilissa	"	"	prior	"				founder/nun/martyr	"	
Lucinus	Spain	nobility	ca. 398	unknown	unknown	mutual	unknown	—	yes	A
Theodora (correspondent of Jerome)	"	"	after	"				—	"	

Name	Region	Status	Date							
Malchus	Syria	captive	after 375	yes	unconsummated	wife	unknown	monk	yes	A
unknown	"	"	"	"				nun	"	
Martinian	North Africa	captive	458	no	unconsummated	wife	unknown	monk/martyr	yes	A
Maxima	"	"	after	yes				nun	"	
Perpetua	unknown	nobility	fl. 1st part of 5th century	unknown	unknown	wife	unknown	unknown	yes	A
unknown (mentioned by Sedulius)	"	"	"	"				"	"	
Phairaildis	Frankish kingdom	nobility	ca. 745	yes	unconsummated	wife refused debt	unknown	—	yes	C
Guy	"	"	prior	no				—	"	
Rusticus†	Gaul	nobility	after 407	no	unknown	wife?	unknown	—	yes	A
Artemia† (correspondent of Jerome)	"	"	"	unknown				—	"	
Scholastica	Gaul	nobility	4th century after wife	yes	unconsummated	wife	unknown	nun	no?	C
Injuriosus	"	"	"	no				monk	"	
Serena of Spoleto	Italy	unknown	late 3d century	unknown	unconsummated	wife?	unknown	nun/martyr	yes	C
unknown	"	"	"	"				unknown	?	

(continued)

APPENDIX 1 (*Continued*)

Couple	Country	Rank	Died	Forced Marriage	Children	Initiator of Chastity	# of Years of Chaste Cohabitation	Religious Affiliation	Historical Figure	Source
Sigolena	Frankish kingdom	nobility	7th century before wife	unknown	unconsummated?	wife	10?	deaconess/ nun	yes	A
Gislulf	"	"		no				—	"	
Singenia Ampelius (inscription)	Gaul	nobility	496	unknown	unknown	wife	20	—	yes	A
	"	"	472	"				—	"	
Turcius Apronianus	Italy	nobility	after 405	unknown	2	wife	unknown	—	yes	A
Avita	"	"	"	"				—	"	
Wandrille	Frankish kingdom	nobility	668	yes	unknown	mutual	unknown	hermit/ founder/ abbot	yes	A
unknown	"	"	?	"				nun	"	

†Relapsed into carnal relations.
††Lapsed into adultery.

Clerical Couples Who Remained Together after Ordination: ca. 300–600

Couple	Country	Rank	Died	Forced Marriage	Children	Initiator of Chastity	# of Years of Chaste Cohabitation	Religious Affiliation	Historical Figure	Source
Amator of Auxerre	Gaul	nobility	418	yes	unconsummated	husband	a few days	bishop	yes	C
Martha	"	"	prior	no				nun	"	
anonymous bishop (reported to Gregory of Tours by Felix of Nantois)	Frankish kingdom	nobility?	6th century	no	unknown	chaste upon ordination	unknown	bishop	yes	A
unknown	"	"	"	unknown				—	"	
Arnoul of Tours	Frankish kingdom	nobility	early 6th century	unknown	unconsummated	mutual	many years of intermittent cohabitation	bishop	no	C
Scariberge	"	"	after husband	"				—	"	
Casaria Valens of Avignon (inscription)	Gaul	nobility	586 or 587 ca. 591	unknown	1?	mutual?	unknown	anchoress bishop	yes	A
	"	"		"					"	
Cassius of Narni	Italy	nobility?	538	unknown	unconsummated?	unknown	unknown	bishop	yes	a/c
Fausta	"	"	prior	"				—	"	

(continued)

APPENDIX 2 (Continued)

Couple	Country	Rank	Died	Forced Marriage	Children	Initiator of Chastity	# of Years of Chaste Cohabitation	Religious Affiliation	Historical Figure	Source
Eucher of Lyons	Gaul	nobility	ca. 449	unknown	2?	mutual	unspecified intermittent cohabitation	hermit/bishop	yes	A
Galla	"	"	prior	"				anchoress	"	
Hilary of Poitiers	Gaul	nobility	368	no	1	chaste upon ordination	unknown	bishop	yes	A
unknown	"	"	prior	unknown				—	"	
Melania	Rome	nobility	439	yes	2	wife	29	—	yes	A
Pinian	"	"	432	no				priest	"	
Paulinus of Nola	Gaul	nobility	431	no	1	wife	unknown	bishop	yes	A
Therasia	Spain	"	unknown	unknown				—	"	
Riticius of Autun	Gaul	nobility	314	unknown	unconsummated	mutual	many	bishop	yes	a/c
unknown	"	"	prior	"				—	"	
Senator Nectariola (mentioned briefly in Germanus's life)	Gaul	nobility	5th century	unknown	unknown	unknown	unknown	priest	yes	A
	"	"	"	"				—	"	
Severus of Ravenna	Italy	artisan	ca. 390	no	1	chaste upon ordination	many	bishop	yes	a/c
Vincentia	"	"	prior	"				—	yes?	
Simplicius of Autun	Gaul	nobility	ca. 420	unknown	unconsummated	mutual	many	bishop	yes	C
unknown	"	"	unknown	"				—	yes?	

APPENDIX 3

Royal Virginal Unions: ca. 650–1100

Couple	Rank	Died	Forced Marriage	Initiator of Chastity	# of Years of Chaste Cohabitation	Religious Affiliation	Historical Figure	Source
Æthelthryth	queen of Northumbria	679	yes	wife refused debt	unknown	founder/abbess	yes	A
Tonbert	prince of South Gyrvii	655	no	"	3	—	"	
Egfrid	king of Northumbria	685	no	"	12	—	"	
Alfonso II	king of Asturias	842	unknown	unknown	unknown	secular founder	yes	a/c
Bertha†	queen	unknown	"			—	no	C
Cuthburga	queen of Northumbria	ca. 725	yes	wife probably refused debt	unknown	founder/abbess	yes	a/c
Aldfrid?	king	705	no			monk?	"	
Cyneburga††	princess of Northumbria	7th century	yes	wife probably refused debt	unknown	founder/abbess	yes	a/c
Alfrid	prince	"	no			—	"	
Cyneswitha	queen of E. Saxons	7th century after 709	yes	wife probably refused debt	unknown	nun	yes	a/c
Offa	king		no			monk	"	
Edward the Confessor	king of England	1066	yes?	husband?	21	secular founder	yes	A
Edith	queen	1075	no?			—	"	

(continued)

Couple	Rank	Died	Forced Marriage	Initiator of Chastity	# of Years of Chaste Cohabitation	Religious Affiliation	Historical Figure	Source
Emeric	prince of Hungary	1031	yes?	husband?	unknown	—	yes	a/a
unknown	princess	after	unknown			—	"	
Henry	Holy Roman Emperor	1024	unknown	mutual	ca. 26	secular founder	yes	a/a
Cunegund	empress	1033	"			"	"	
Osyth	queen of E. Saxons	ca. 700	yes	wife refused debt	1?	founder/ abbess/ martyr	?	C
Sigerius	king	unknown	no			—	yes	a/c
Richardis	empress	ca. 895	unknown	wife?	10–12	founder/abbess	yes	A
Charles the Fat	king of E. Franks, emperor of the Franks	888	no			—	"	

† Although a Bertha, the sister of Charlemagne, did exist, she never married Alfonso.
†† Also note that the belief arose in the twelfth century that Oswald, king of Northumbria, and his wife, a different Cyneburga, took a vow of chastity after the birth of their son.

APPENDIX 4

Eastern Lives That Did Not Circulate in the West: 300–900

Couple	Country	Rank	Died	Forced Marriage	Children	Initiator of Chastity	# of Years of Chaste Cohabitation	Religious Affiliation	Historical Figure	Source
Conon	Isauria (Asia Minor)	unknown	1st century	unknown	unconsummated	husband	unknown	martyr	yes	C
Anna	"	"	"	"				—	"	
Galaction	Syria	nobility	n.d.	yes	unconsummated	husband	unknown	hermit/martyr	no	C
Episteme	"	"	"	no				nun/martyr	"	
Gorgonia	Cappadocia (Asia Minor)	nobility	after 374	unknown	5	wife	unknown	—	yes	A
Vitalianus?	"	"	unknown	"				—	"	
Magna	Galatia (Asia Minor)	unknown	after 420	yes	unconsummated	wife refused debt	unknown	nun	yes	A
unknown	"	"	before wife	no				—	"	
Olympias	Thrace	nobility	ca. 410	yes	unconsummated	wife refused debt	1	—	yes	A
Nebridius	"	"	ca. 387	no				—	"	
Pelagius of Laodicea	Syria	nobility?	after 381	yes	unconsummated	husband	unknown	bishop	yes	A
unknown	"	"	unknown	unknown				—	"	

(continued)

APPENDIX 4 (Continued)

Couple	Country	Rank	Died	Forced Marriage	Children	Initiator of Chastity	# of Years of Chaste Cohabitation	Religious Affiliation	Historical Figure	Source
Theophanus the Chronographer	Thrace	nobility	817	yes	unconsummated	mutual	2	abbot	yes	A
unknown	"	"	?	unknown				nun	"	
Theophilus	Syria	nobility	6th century	yes	unconsummated	husband	24+	—	yes	A
Marie	"	"	"	unknown				—	"	
Theoctista Photinus (parents of Theodore Studite)	Thrace	nobility	before 826	unknown	4	wife	5+	nun	yes	A
	"	"	"					monk	"	

Unconsummated Unions: ca. 1100–1500

Couple	Country	Rank	Died	Forced Marriage	Age at Marriage	Initiator of Chastity	# of Years of Chaste Cohabitation	Religious Affiliation	Source
Angelina Corbara of Marsciano	Italy	nobility	1435	yes	15	wife	2	3d-order Franciscan (nuns)	C
John, count of Civitella	"	"	1395	no	unknown			—	
Catherine of Sweden	Sweden	nobility	1381	yes	12	wife	6	Brigittine	A
Eggard von Kuren	"	"	1350	no	unknown			—	
Cunegund	b. Hungary	princess	1292	yes	16	wife	40	Poor Clares	B
Boleslaus V (the Chaste)	Poland	prince of Sandomierz, grand prince of Poland	1279	no	18			3d-order Franciscan	
Elzear of Sabran	Provence	nobility	1323	no	13	wife	24	unofficial 3d-order Franciscan	A
Dauphine of Puimichel	"	"	1360	yes	15			3d-order Franciscan	

(continued)

APPENDIX 5 (Continued)

Couple	Country	Rank	Died	Forced Marriage	Age at Marriage	Initiator of Chastity	# of Years of Chaste Cohabitation	Religious Affiliation	Source
Jeanne-Marie of Maillac	Touraine	nobility	1414	yes	16	wife	14	Poor Clares	A
Robert of Silleyo	"	"	1362?	no	unknown			—	
Lucia Brocadelli of Narni	Italy	nobility	1544	yes	15	wife	3	Dominican	A
Count Peter di Alessio of Milan	"	"	unknown	no	unknown			Franciscan	
Magnus of Orkney	Scotland	nobility	1116	no	ca. 25	husband	10	martyr	A
unknown	"	"	unknown	unknown	unknown			—	
Salome	Poland	princess	1268	n/a†	13	wife?	17	Poor Clares	A
Caloman	b. Hungary	grand prince of Galicia	1241	n/a†	16			—	
Sperandeo of Gubbio	Italy	nobility	ca. 1261	unknown	unknown	mutual	unknown	Benedictine	C
Gennaia	"	"	1293?	yes	"			Augustinian	

† As in the case of Elizabeth of Hungary, the couple was betrothed while they were infants (she was three, he was six) and though they lived in the same court, I am dating length of chaste cohabitation from when the marriage was solemnized. Salome's *vita* (Kętrzyński, ed., *Vita sanctae Salomeae* 1.2, *MPH*, 4:777) only specifies puberty. *Vies des saints* (ed. J. L. Baudot and L. Chaussin [Paris, 1954], 11:588) says she was thirteen. They made a vow of chastity earlier, however, when she was nine and he was twelve (*BS*, vol. 11, col. 589).

APPENDIX 6

A Vow of Continence after Years of Normal Married Relations: ca. 1100–1500

Couple	Country	Rank	Died	Forced Marriage	Age at Marriage	Children	Initiator of Chastity	# of Years of Chaste Cohabitation	Religious Affiliation	Source
Bridget of Sweden†	Sweden	nobility	1373	yes	13 or 14	8	wife	ca. 4	secular founder of Brigittines	A
Ulf Gudmarrson	"	"	1344	no	18				unofficial Cistercian	
Catherine Fieschi of Genoa	Italy	nobility	1510	yes	16	no	wife	ca. 21	—	A
Giuliano Adorno	"	"	1497	no	unknown	1 (illegit.)			3d-order Franciscan	
Chiarito del Voglia	Italy	urban patrician	between 1350 and 1356	no	unknown	yes	husband	over 1	founded Augustinian convent/lay brother	C
Nicolasia	"	"	unknown	unknown	"				Augustinian nun	
Dorothea of Montau	Pomerania	bourgeois	1394	yes	17	9	wife	10	anchoress	A
Adalbert Swertfeger of Danzig	"	"	1390	no	unknown				—	

(continued)

APPENDIX 6 (Continued)

Couple	Country	Rank	Died	Forced Marriage	Age at Marriage	Children	Initiator of Chastity	# of Years of Chaste Cohabitation	Religious Affiliation	Source
Frances Bussa (of Rome)	Italy	nobility	1440	yes	13	6?	wife	12	founded lay order of Benedictine oblates	A
Lorenzo Ponziano	"	"	1436	no	unknown				—	
Hedwig	b. Bavaria	princess	1243	yes	12	6 or 7	wife	30††	founder/ unofficial Cistercian	A
Henry I (the Bearded)	Silesia	prince of Silesia, grand prince of Poland	1238	no	18				secular founder	
Humility of Faenza	Italy	nobility	1310	yes	15	2 or more	wife	ca. 1	Vallombrosan and Poor Clares Vallombrosan	A
Ugolotto Caccianemici	"	"	1256	no	unknown					
Isidore the Laborer	Spain	peasantry	1130	no	unknown	1	mutual	unknown	—	B
Mary Toribia	"	"	after	"	"				—	C

Name	Country	Class	Date	Consummated	Age	Children	Initiator	Years	Religious status	
James Oldo	Italy	bourgeois	1404	no	unknown	3	husband	3	3d-order Franciscan/ priest	A
Catherine Bocchone	"	"	before 1435	"	"	"	"	"	3d-order Franciscan	
John Colombini	Italy	bourgeois	1367	no	39	2	husband	8	founded Jesuati	A
Biagia Cerretani	"	urban patrician	1371	"	unknown				Benedictine nun	
Margaret Beaufort†††	England	nobility	1509	no	29 (3d marriage)	1	wife	5	—	A
Thomas Stanley	"	"	1504	"	ca. 37	10			—	
Margery Kempe	England	bourgeois	after 1438	no	ca. 20	14	wife	ca. 18 (intermittent)	—	A
John Kempe	"	"	ca. 1431	"	ca. 27				—	
Mary of Oignies	Brabant	bourgeois	1213	yes	14	no	wife	ca. 14	Beguine	A
John	"	"	after	no	unknown				—	
Peter Petinaio	Italy	bourgeois	1289	no	unknown	no	mutual	unknown	3d-order Franciscan	A
unknown	"	"	prior	unknown	"				—	
Robert Malatesta†	Italy	nobility	1432	yes	18	no	husband	1½	3d-order Franciscan	A
Margaret d'Este			1475	unknown	unknown				Poor Clares	

†Bridget and Robert Malatesta are somewhat peculiar cases in that they both postponed consummating their marriages for over a year. At Bridget's prompting, her husband also pledged chastity toward the end of his life and intended to enter a religious community.

††Although neither Hedwig nor Henry left the world in any formal way, after their vow of chastity, Hedwig avoided Henry's company unless there were witnesses. She also made lengthy stays at the monastery of Trebnicz.

†††Margaret's child, the future Henry VII, was a product of her first marriage to Edmund Tudor, earl of Richmond. Thomas's children were also from his first marriage. The couple's five-year period of chaste marriage was really an informal separation, although Margaret continued to keep separate rooms for Thomas at her estate.

Instance of Separation to Enter Religious Communities Discussed in Chapter 5

Couple	Country	Rank	Died	Forced Marriage	Age at Marriage	Children	Initiator of Chastity	# of Years of Marriage Prior to Conversion	Religious Affiliation	Source
Conrad of Piacenza Eufrosina	Italy "	nobility "	1351 unknown	no "	unknown "	no	husband	unknown	3d-order Franciscan Poor Clares	C
Gerardesca of Pisa Alferio di Bandino	Italy "	nobility "	1269 unknown	yes no	ca. 19 "	no	wife	ca. 2	Camaldolese "	A
Gonsalvo Sancii unknown	Spain "	nobility "	1361 unknown	no "	unknown "	3	husband	unknown	Franciscan —	A
Maurice Czasky Catherine Amadeus	Hungary "	prince princess	1336 unknown	yes unknown	20 unknown	no	husband	3	Dominican "	A
Lucia Bartolini Ridolfo Rucellai	Italy "	nobility "	1520 1498?	no "	19 unknown	no	husband	ca. 12	3d-order Dominican (nuns) Dominican	A
Santuccia Terrabotti of Gubbio unknown	Italy "	nobility "	1305 unknown	no? "	unknown "	1	mutual	unknown	Benedictine "	C

SELECT BIBLIOGRAPHY

PRIMARY SOURCES

Abelard, Peter. *Peter Abelard's "Ethics."* Ed. and trans. D. E. Luscombe. Oxford, 1971.

———. *Sic et Non.* Ed. Blanche B. Boyer and Richard McKeon. Chicago, 1976–1977.

Adalbero of Laon. *Poème au roi Robert.* Ed. Claude Carozzi. Paris, 1979.

Adalbert of Bamberg. *Vita Heinrici II.* Ed. G. Waitz. *MGH, Scrip.* 4:792–814. Hanover, 1841; reprt. 1925.

Adalbert of Prague. "Homilia in natale S. Alexii Confessoris." *PL* 137.897–900.

Adalbold of Utrecht. *Vita Heinrici II.* Ed. G. Waitz. *MGH, Scrip.* 4:683–695. Hanover, 1841; reprt. 1925.

Ado of Vienne. *Sancti Adonis Martyrologium.* *PL* 123.143–420.

Aelred of Rievaulx. *Vita S. Edwardi regis.* *PL* 195.737–790.

Alan of Lille. *De planctu Naturae.* Ed. Nikolaus M. Häring. Spoleto, 1978.

———. *Liber poenitentialis.* Ed. Jean Longère. 2 vols. Analecta Mediaevalia Namurcensia, nos. 17 and 18. Louvain and Lille, 1965.

———. *Summa de arte praedicatoria.* *PL* 210.111–198.

Alberigo, G., et al., eds. *Conciliorum oecumenicorum decreta.* Freiburg, 1962.

Amand, David, and M.-C. Moons, eds. "Une curieuse homélie grecque inédite sur la virginité adressée aux pères de famille." *Revue Bénédictine* 63 (1953): 18–69, 211–238.

Ambrose. *De virginibus.* Ed. Otto Faller. Florilegium Patristicum, fasc. 31. Bonn, 1933.

———. *De virginitate, Liber unus.* Ed. E. Cazzaniga. Corpus Scriptorum Latinorum Paravianum. Turin, 1954.

———. *Traité sur l'Evangile de S. Luc, Livres I–VI.* Ed. Gabriel Tissot. *SC,* no. 45. Paris, 1956.

Amiaud, Arthur, ed. and trans. *La légende syriaque de saint Alexis, l'homme de Dieu.* Paris, 1889.

Andreas, John. *In tertium Decretalium librum nouella commentaria.* Venice and Siena, 1581.

Andrew of Strumi. *Vita sancti Arialdi.* Ed. F. Baethgen. *MGH, Scrip.* 30,2:1049–1075. Leipzig, 1934.

Angela of Foligno. *Le livre de l'expérience des vrais fidèles.* Ed. M.-J. Ferré. Paris, 1927.

Aquinas, Thomas. *Summa Theologica.* Trans. Fathers of the English Dominican Province. 22 vols. 2d rev. ed. London, 1920–1922.

Arnulf of Milan. *Arnulfi gesta archiepiscoporum Mediolanensium.* Ed. L. C. Bethmann and W. Wattenbach. *MGH, Scrip.* 8:6–31. Hanover, 1848; reprt. Leipzig, 1925.

Athanasius. *Apologie à l'empereur Constance. Apologie pour sa fuite.* Ed. J.-M. Szymusiak. *SC*, no. 56. Paris, 1958.

———. *Historia Arianorum. PG* 25.696–796.

Athenagoras. *Legatio pro Christianis. PG* 6.889–972.

Attenborough, F. L., ed. and trans. *The Laws of the Earliest English Kings.* New York, 1963.

Augustine. *Commentary on the Lord's Sermon on the Mount.* Trans. Denis J. Kavanagh. *FC*, vol. 11. New York, 1951.

———. *Confessionum Libri XIII.* Ed. Martin Skutella and Lucas Verheijen. *CCSL*, vol. 27. Turnholt, 1981.

———. *Contra Julianum. PL* 44.641–874.

———. *De adulterinis coniugiis.* Ed. J. Zycha. In *Opera sancti Aureli Augustini. CSEL*, 41:347–410. Prague, Vienna, and Leipzig, 1900.

———. *De bono coniugali.* Ed. J. Zycha. In *Opera sancti Aureli Augustini. CSEL*, 41:187–231. Prague, Vienna, and Leipzig, 1900.

———. *De bono uiduitatis.* Ibid., 305–343.

———. *De civitate Dei.* Ed. B. Dombart and A. Kalb. 2 vols. *CCSL*, vols. 47 and 48. Turnholt, 1955.

———. *De haeresibus.* Ed. R. Vander Plaetse and C. Beukers. *CCSL*, 46:282–345. Turnholt, 1969.

———. *De nuptiis et concupiscentia.* Ed. C. F. Urba and J. Zycha. In *Opera sancti Aureli Augustini. CSEL*, 42:209–319. Prague, Vienna, and Leipzig, 1902.

———. *De sancta virginitate.* Ed. J. Zycha. In *Opera sancti Aureli Augustini. CSEL*, 41:235–302. Prague, Vienna, and Leipzig, 1900.

———. *De sermone Domini in monte. PL* 34.1229–1308.

———. *Epistolae.* Ed. A. Goldbacher and J. Divjak. *CSEL*, vols. 34 (pts. 1 and 2), 44, 57, 58, 88. Prague, Vienna, and Leipzig, 1895–1981.

———. *Letters.* Trans. Sr. Wilfrid Parsons. 5 vols. *FC*, vols. 12, 18, 20, 30, 32. New York, 1951–1956.

———. *Quaestionum in Heptateuchum.* Ed. I. Fraipont. *CCSL*, vol. 33. Turnholt, 1958.

———. *Retractationum Libri II.* Ed. A. Mutzenbecher. *CCSL*, vol. 57. Turnholt, 1984.

———. *Saint Augustin: Anti-Pelagian Writings.* Trans. Peter Holmes and Robert E. Wallis. *LNPNFC*, vol. 5. New York, 1887.

———. *Saint Augustine: Treatises on Marriage and Other Subjects.* Ed. R. J. Deferrari. *FC*, vol. 27. New York, 1955.

———. *Sermones. PL* 38 and 39.

Ayerbe-Chaux, R., ed. *Estoria de España: Antologiá.* Madrid, 1982.

Baker, A. T., ed. "An Anglo-French Life of St. Osith." *Modern Language Review* 6 (1911): 476–502.

Baldric of Dole. *Vita B. Roberti de Arbrissello. PL* 162.1043–1058.

Balogh, Joseph, ed. *Libellus de institutione morum. Scriptores Rerum Hungaricarum.* Ed. E. Szentpétery, 2:619–627. Budapest, 1938.

Banks, M. M., ed. *An Alphabet of Tales.* 2 vols. *EETS*. o.s., nos. 126–127. London, 1904; reprt. 1972.

Barlow, Frank, ed. and trans. *The Life of King Edward Who Rests at West-minster: Attributed to a Monk of St. Bertin.* London, 1962.

Bartholomew of Exeter. *Bartholomew of Exeter, Bishop and Canonist.* Ed. Adrian Morey. Cambridge, 1937.

Bartolucci, Constantino, ed. *Legenda B. Galeoti Roberti de Malatestis. Archivum Franciscanum Historicum* 8 (1915): 532–557.

Bartoniek, Emma, ed. *Legenda S. Emerici ducis. Scriptores Rerum Hungaricarum.* Ed. E. Szentpétery, 2:449–460. Budapest, 1938.

———., ed. *Legenda S. Stephani* (including the *Legenda maior* and the *Legenda minor*). Ibid. 2:377–400.

Basil of Caesarea. *Saint Basil: Letters.* Trans. Agnes Clare Way. Notes by R. J. Deferrari. 2 vols. *FC*, vols. 13 and 28. New York, 1951–1955.

———. *Saint Basile: Lettres.* Ed. and trans. Yves Courtonne. 3 vols. Paris, 1957–1966.

Ps.-Basil. *Sermo de contubernalibus. PG* 30.811–828.

Bede. *Ecclesiastical History of the English People.* Ed. and trans. Bertram Colgrave and R.A.B. Mynors. Oxford, 1969.

Belcari, F. *Vita del beato Giovanni Colombini da Siena.* Verona, 1817.

Bernard of Clairvaux. *S. Bernardi opera.* Ed. Jean Leclercq et al. 8 vols. Rome, 1957–1977.

Bernard Silvestris. *De mundi universitate libri duo sive Megacosmus et Microcosmus.* Ed. C. S. Barach and J. Wrobel. Innsbruck, 1876.

Bernardino of Siena. *Opera omnia.* Ed. Fathers of the College of St. Bonaventure. 7 vols. Florence, 1950–1959.

Bertrand of Pontigny. *Vita beati Edmundi Cantuariensis archiepiscopi.* In *Thesaurus novus anecdotorum,* ed. E. Martène and U. Durand, 3:1775–1826. Paris and Florence, 1717; reprt. 1968.

Bollandists, eds. *Vita S. Arnulphi.* In *Catalogus codicum hagiographicorum latinorum antiquiorum saeculo XVI qui asservantur in Bibliotheca Nationali Parisiensi,* 1:415–428. Brussels, 1889.

Bonaventure. *Legenda maior S. Francisci. Analecta Franciscana* 10 (1941): 557–626.

Bridget of Sweden. *Birgitta of Sweden: Life and Selected Revelations.* Trans. Albert Ryle Kezel. Ed. Marguerite Tjader Harris. New York, 1990.

———. *Revelaciones. Bk. I.* Ed. Carl-Gustaf Undhagen. Samlingar utgivna av Svenska Fornskriftsällskapet, ser. 2. Latinska Skrifter, vol. 7,1. Uppsala, 1978.

———. *Revelaciones. Bk. V: Liber questionum.* Ed. Birger Bergh. Kungl. Vitterhets Historie och Antikvitets Akademien Stockholm. Uppsala, 1971. (Also appears in Samlingar . . . ser. 2, Latinska Skrifter, vol. 7,5.)

———. *Revelaciones. Bk. VII.* Ed. Birger Bergh. Samlingar utgivna av Svenska Fornskriftsällskapet, ser. 2. Latinska Skrifter, vol. 7,7. Uppsala, 1967.

———. *Revelaciones Extravagantes.* Ed. Lennart Hollman. Samlingar utgivna av Svenska Fornskriftsällskapet, ser. 2. Latinska Skrifter, vol. 5. Uppsala, 1956.

———. *Revelationes.* Ed. Florian Waldauf von Waldenstein. Nuremburg, 1500.

Burchard of Worms. *Decretorum libri viginti. PL* 140.537–1058.

Caesarius of Heisterbach. *Dialogus miraculorum.* Ed. J. Strange. 2 vols. Cologne, Bonn, and Brussels, 1851.

Cambell, Jacques, ed. *Enquête pour le procès de canonisation de Dauphine de Puimichel, Comtesse d'Ariano.* Turin, 1978.

———, ed. "Le sommaire de l'enquête pour la canonisation de Elzéar de Sabran, TOF (d. 1323)." *Miscellanea Francescana* 73 (1973): 438–473.

———, ed. *Vies occitanes de saint Auzias et de sainte Dauphine.* Bibliotheca Pontificii Athenai Antoniani, 12. Rome, 1963.

Campbell, Alistair, ed. *Encomium Emmae reginae.* Camden Publications, 3d ser., vol. 72. London, 1949.

Cassian, John. *Conférences.* Ed. E. Pichery. 3 vols. *SC*, nos. 42, 54, 64. Paris, 1955–1959.

Catherine of Genoa. *Edizione critica dei manoscritti Cateriniani.* Vol. 2 of *S. Caterina Fieschi Adorno.* Ed. Umile Bonzi da Genova. Turin, 1962.

———. *Sainte Catherine de Gênes: Vie et doctrine et Traité du Purgatoire.* Trans. Pierre Debongnie. Brussels, 1960.

Caxton, William, trans. *The Book of the Knight of the Tower.* Ed. M. Y. Offord. *EETS*, supp. ser., no. 2. London, 1971.

Chadwick, Henry, ed. and trans. *The Sentences of Sextus.* Cambridge, 1959.

Chaucer. *The Works of Geoffrey Chaucer.* Ed. F. N. Robinson. 2d ed. Boston, 1957.

Christine de Pisan. *The Treasure of the City of Ladies or the Book of the Three Virtues.* Trans. Sarah Lawson. Harmondsworth, Middlesex, 1985.

Chrysostom, John. *A une jeune veuve. Sur le mariage unique.* Ed. G. H. Ettlinger. Introd., trans., and notes by B. Grillet. *SC*, no. 138. Paris, 1968.

———. *In epistola I ad Corinthios homilia XIX. PG* 61.151–160.

———. *Instruction and Refutation Directed against Those Men Cohabiting with Virgins.* Trans. Elizabeth Clark. In *Jerome, Chrysostom, and Friends: Essays and Translations,* 164–208. Studies in Women and Religion, vol. 1. New York and Toronto, 1979.

———. *On the Necessity of Guarding Virginity.* Ibid., 209–248.

———. *On Virginity. Against Remarriage.* Trans. Sally Rieger Shore. Introduction by Elizabeth Clark. Studies in Women and Religion, vol. 9. Lewiston, Lampeter, and Queenston, 1983.

———. *Saint Jean Chrysostome: Les cohabitations suspectes. Comment observer la virginité.* Ed. Jean Dumortier. Paris, 1955.

———. *La virginité.* Ed. Herbert Musurillo. Trans. B. Grillet. *SC*, no. 125. Paris, 1966.

Ps.-Chrysostom. *Ascetam facetiis uti non debere. PG* 48.1055–1060.

Clark, Elizabeth, trans. *The Life of Melania the Younger.* Studies in Women and Religion, vol. 14. Lewiston, Lampeter, and Queenston, 1984.

Clement of Alexandria. *Clemens Alexandrinus: Stromata.* Ed. O. Stählin. 2 vols. *GCS*, vol. 15 (rev. L. Früchtel). Berlin, 1960. Vol. 17. Leipzig, 1909.

———. *Le Pédagogue.* 3 vols. *SC*, no. 70 (introd. and notes, H.-I. Marrou; trans. M. Harl); no. 108 (notes by Marrou; trans. C. Mondésert); no. 158 (notes by Marrou; trans. Mondésert and C. Matay). Paris, 1960–1970.

———. *Stromata III.* In *Alexandrian Christianity,* trans. John E. L. Oulton and Henry Chadwick, 40–92. Library of Christian Classics, vol. 2. London, 1954.

———. *Les Stromates. SC*, bk. 1, no. 30 (introd. C. Mondésert; trans. and notes by M. Caster); bk. 2, no. 38 (ed. and trans. Mondésert; introd. and notes by Th. Camelot); bk. 5, nos. 278 and 279 (ed. with commentary by A. Le Boulluec; trans. P. Voulet). Paris, 1951–1981.

Ps.-Clement. *The Clementine Homilies*. Trans. Thomas Smith. In *Ante-Nicene Fathers*, 8:223–346. Ed. Alexander Roberts and James Donaldson. Buffalo, 1886.

———. *Die Pseudoklementinen I. Homilien*. Ed. Bernhard Rehm. *GCS*, vol. 42. Berlin and Liepzig, 1953.

———. "Two Epistles Concerning Virginity." Trans. B. L. Pratten. In *ANL*, 14:367–395. Ed. Alexander Roberts and James Donaldson. Edinburgh, 1869.

Collijn, Isak, ed. *Acta et Processus Canonizacionis Beate Birgitte*. Samlingar utgivna av Svenska Fornskriftsällskapet, ser. 2. Latinska Skrifter, vol. 1. Uppsala, 1924–1931.

Constantius. *Vita Germani Episcopi Autissiodorensis*. Ed. W. Levison. *MGH, Scrip. Rer. Merov.* 7:247–283. Hanover and Leipzig, 1920.

Courson, Robert. "Robert Courson on Penance." Ed. V. L. Kennedy, *Mediaeval Studies* 7 (1945): 291–336.

Cyprian. *S. Thasci Caecili Cypriani opera omnia*. Ed. W. Hartel. *CSEL*, vol. 3, pts. 1–3. Vienna, 1868–1871.

Ps.-Cyprian. *De singularitate clericorum*. Ibid. 3,3:173–220.

Damian, Peter. *Opera. PL* 144 and 145.

———. *Sermones*. Ed. John Lucchesi. *CCCM*, vol. 57. Turnholt, 1983.

Dasent, G. W., trans. *Icelandic Sagas: The Orkneyingers' Saga*, vol. 3. Rolls Series, no. 88. London, 1894.

Dionysius Exiguus. *Die Canonessammlung des Dionysius Exiguus in der ersten Redaktion*. Ed. A. Strewe. Berlin, 1931.

Dlugos, John. *Annales seu Cronicae incliti regni Poloniae*. Ed. I. Dabrowski et al. 10 vols. Warsaw, 1964–1985.

Dorothea of Montau. "Die Geistliche Lehre der Frau Dorothea von Montau an ihre Tochter im Frauenkloster zu Kulm." Ed. Richard Stachnik. *Zeitschrift für Ostforschung Länder und Völker im östlichen Mitteleuropa* 3 (1954): 589–596.

Drew, Katherine Fischer, trans. *The Lombard Laws*. Philadelphia, 1973.

Ebernand von Erfurt. *Heinrich und Kunegunde*. Ed. Reinhold Bechstein. Quedlinburg and Leipzig, 1860; reprt. Amsterdam, 1968.

Eckbert of Schönau. *Sermones contra Catharos. PL* 195.11–102.

Eddius Stephanus. *The Life of Bishop Wilfrid*. Ed. and trans. Bertram Colgrave. Cambridge, 1927; reprt. 1985.

Einhard. *Vie de Charlemagne*. Ed. and trans. Louis Halphen. Paris, 1947.

Elizabeth of Schönau. *Die Visionen der hl. Elisabeth*. Ed. F.W.E. Roth. Brünn, 1884.

Endlicher, S. L., ed. *Rerum Hungaricarum monumenta Arpadiana*. St. Gall, 1849; reprt. Leipzig, 1931.

Epiphanius. *Adversus octoginta haereses. PG* 41.173–1200; *PG* 42.9–832.

Erasmus. *Ten Colloquies of Erasmus.* Trans. Craig R. Thompson. New York, 1957.

Fathers of the College of St. Bonaventure, eds. *Vita fratris Gonsalvi Sancii.* In *Chronica XXIV generalium Ordinis Minorum. Analecta Franciscana* 3 (1897): 549–552.

Fisher, John. *The English Works of John Fisher, Bishop of Rochester.* Ed. John E. B. Mayor. *EETS.,* e.s., no. 27, pt. 1. London, 1876; reprt. Millwood, N.Y., 1973.

Fletcher, J.M.J., ed. and trans. "The Marriage of St. Cuthburga, Who Was Afterwards Foundress of the Monastery at Wimborne." *Proceedings of the Dorset Natural History and Antiquarian Field Club* 34 (1913): 167–185.

Flodoard of Rheims. *Historia Remensis ecclesiae.* Ed. J. Heller and G. Waitz. *MGH, Scrip.* 13:405–599. Hanover, 1881.

Florez, H., ed. *Chronicon Albeldense* (= *Epitome Ovietensis*). In *España Sagrada,* vol. 13, appendix 6, 417–464. Madrid, 1756.

Foreville, Raymonde, and Gillian Keir, eds. and trans. *The Book of St. Gilbert.* Oxford, 1987.

Fortunatus, Venantius. *Vita sancti Hilarii.* Ed. B. Krusch. *MGH, Auct. Ant.* 4, 2:1–7. Berlin, 1885.

Francis, W. Nelson, ed. *The Book of Vices and Virtues. EETS,* o.s., no. 217. London, 1942.

Furnivall, F. J., ed. *Hali Meidenhad. EETS,* o.s., no. 18. Rev. ed. by Oswald Cockayne. New York, 1969.

Gandini, Luigi Alberto, ed. *Sulla venuta in Ferrara della beata suor Lucia da Narni.* Modena, 1901.

Gautier de Coinci. *Les miracles de la Sainte Vierge.* Ed. Abbot Poquet. Paris, 1857.

———. *Les miracles de Nostre Dame.* Ed. V. Frédéric Koenig. 4 vols. Geneva, 1955–1970.

Geoffrey of Vendôme. *Epistolae. PL* 157.33–212.

Gerard, John. *The Autobiography of an Elizabethan.* Trans. Philip Caraman. London, New York, and Toronto, 1951.

Gerbert de Montreuil. *La continuation de Perceval.* Ed. Mary Williams and Marguerite Oswald. 3 vols. Paris, 1922–1975.

Gerson, Jean. *Oeuvres complètes.* Ed. Mgr. Glorieux. 10 vols. Paris, 1960–1973.

Glaber, Raoul. *Les cinq livres de ses histoires.* Ed. Maurice Prou. Paris, 1886.

Glossa ordinaria. See under Gratian, Gregory IX, and Nicolaus de Lyre.

Gorce, Denys, ed. and trans. *Vie de sainte Mélanie. SC,* no. 90. Paris, 1962.

Grant, Robert M., ed. and trans. *Gnosticism: A Source Book of Heretical Writings.* New York, 1961; reprt. 1978.

Gratian. *Decretum Gratiani; seu verius, decretorum canonicorum collectanea.* Paris, 1561 (containing the *Glossa ordinaria*).

———. *Decretum Magistri Gratiani.* Ed. A. Friedberg. In *Corpus Iuris Canonici.* Vol. 1. 2d ed. Leipzig, 1879; reprt. Graz, 1955.

Gregory of Nazianzus. *Epigrammata PG* 38.81–130.

————. "In laudem sororis suae Gorgoniae." *Oratio* 8. *PG* 35.789–818.

Gregory of Nyssa. *Ascetical Works.* Trans. Virginia Woods Callahan. *FC*, vol. 58. Washington D.C., 1967.

————. *Traité de la virginité.* Ed. and trans. Michel Aubineau. *SC*, no. 119. Paris, 1966.

Gregory of Tours. *The History of the Franks.* Trans. Lewis Thorpe. Harmondsworth, Middlesex, 1974; reprt. 1982.

————. *Liber in gloria confessorum.* In *Opera.* Ed. B. Krusch. *MGH, Scrip. Rer. Merov.* Vol. 1,2:744–820. Hanover, 1885.

————. *Liber vitae patrum.* Ed. B. Krusch. Ibid., pp. 661–744.

————. *Libri Historiarum X.* Ed. B. Krusch and W. Levison. *MGH, Scrip. Rer. Merov.* Vol. 1, pt. 1. Rev. ed. Hanover, 1951; reprt. 1965.

Gregory I. *Dialogues.* Ed. Adalbert de Vogüé. Trans. Paul Antin. *SC,* nos. 251, 260, 265. Paris, 1978–1980.

————. *Dialogues.* Trans. O. J. Zimmerman. *FC,* vol. 39. New York, 1959.

————. *Registrum epistolarum.* Ed. Dag Norberg. *CCSL,* vols. 140–140a. Turnholt, 1982.

————. *Registrum epistolarum.* Ed. P. Ewald and L. M. Hartmann. 2 vols. *MGH. Epist.* vols. 1–2. Berlin, 1891–1899.

Gregory VII. *Monumenta Gregoriana.* Ed. P. Jaffé. *Bibliotheca Rerum Germanicarum.* Vol. 2. Berlin, 1865.

Gregory IX. *Decretales D. Gregorii Papae IX* (containing the *Glossa ordinaria*). London, 1584.

Gregory IX et al. *Decretalium Collectiones.* Ed. A. Friedberg. In *Corpus Iuris Canonici.* Vol. 2. 2d ed. Leipzig, 1879; reprt. Graz, 1955.

Grévy-Pons, Nicole, ed. *Célibat et Nature: Une controverse médiévale.* Centre d'histoire des sciences et des doctrines. Textes et études, no. 1. Paris, 1975.

Grosseteste, Robert. *Templum Dei.* Ed. J. Goering and F.A.C. Mantello. Toronto, 1984.

Guibert of Nogent. *Histoire de sa vie (1053–1124).* Ed. Georges Bourgin. Collection de textes pour servir à l'étude et à l'enseignement de l'histoire, fasc. 40. Paris, 1907.

Habig, Marion A., ed. *St. Francis of Assisi: Writings and Early Biographies.* 3d rev. ed. Chicago, 1973.

Hartvic. *Legenda S. Stephani regis.* Ed. Emma Bartoniek. *Scriptores Rerum Hungaricarum.* Ed. E. Szentpétery, 2:401–440. Budapest, 1938.

Herimann of Laon. *De miraculis B. Mariae Laudunensis.* Ed. R. W. Wilmans. *MGH, Scrip.* 12:654–660. Hanover, 1856.

Herimann of Reichenau. *Chronicon.* Ed. G. H. Pertz. *MGH, Scrip.* 5:74–133. Hanover, 1844; reprt. Leipzig, 1925.

Herimann of Tournai. *Liber de restauratione S. Martini Tornacensis.* Ed. G. Waitz. *MGH, Scrip.* 14:274–327. Hanover, 1883.

Hermas. *The Shepherd.* Trans. Kirsopp Lake. In *The Apostolic Fathers,* vol. 2. Loeb Classical Library. London and New York, 1913.

Ps.-Hilary. *Epistola ad Abram filiam suam. PL* 10.549–552.

Hill, Rosalind M. T., ed. *The Register of William Melton: Archbishop of York,*

1317–1340. 2 vols. Canterbury and York Society Series, vols. 70, 71, and 76. Torquay, 1977–1988.

Hincmar of Rheims. *Annales Bertiniani.* Ed. G. Waitz. *MGH, Scrip. Rer. Germ. in usum scholarium.* Vol. 5. Hanover, 1883.

———. *De divortio Lotharii et Tetbergae. PL* 125.623–772.

Hingeston-Randolph, F. C., ed. *The Register of John Grandisson, Bishop of Exeter.* 2 vols. London and Exeter, 1894–1897.

Hirschfeld, Otto, ed. *Corpus Inscriptionum Latinarum.* Vol. 12. *Inscriptiones Galliae Narbonensis Latinae.* Berlin, 1888.

Holtzmann, Walter, ed. "La *Collectio Seguntina* et les décrétales de Clément III et de Célestin III." *Revue d'histoire ecclésiastique* 50 (1955): 400–453.

Hostiensis. *Summa aurea.* Lyons, 1537.

Hugh of St. Victor. *De B. Mariae virginitate. PL* 176.857–876.

———. *De sacramentis Christiani fidei.* Ibid., 183–618.

———. *On the Sacraments of the Christian Faith.* Trans. Roy J. Deferrari. Cambridge Mass., 1951.

Huguccio. "*Summa* d'Huguccio sur le *Décret* de Gratien d'après le Manuscrit 3891 de la Bibliothèque Nationale. Causa 27, Questio 2 (Théories sur la formation du mariage)." Ed. J. Roman. *Revue historique de droit français et étranger,* ser. 2, 27 (1903): 745–805.

Humbert of Silva Candida. *Libri III adversus Simoniacos.* Ed. F. Thaner. *MGH, Lib. de Lit.* 1:100–253. Hanover, 1891.

Huyskens, A., ed. *Quellenstudien zur Geschichte der hl. Elisabeth.* Marburg, 1908.

Ignatius. *Ignace d'Antioche. Polycarpe de Smyrne. Lettres. Martyre de Polycarpe.* Ed. and trans. Th. Camelot. 3d rev. ed. *SC,* no. 10. Paris, 1958.

Innocent III. *De miseria condicionis humanae.* Ed. and trans. Robert E. Lewis. Chaucer Library. Athens, Ga., 1978.

———. "Die Litterae Papst Innocenz' III. zur Heiligsprechung der Kaiserin Kunigunde (1200)." Ed. Jürgen Petersohn. *Jahrbuch für fränkische Landesforschung* 37 (1977): 1–25.

Innocent IV. *Commentaria Innocentii Quarti pontificis maximi super libros quinque Decretalium.* Frankfurt, 1570.

Irenaeus. *Contre les hérésies.* Ed. and trans. Adelin Rousseau et al. 10 vols. *SC,* nos. 100 (pts. 1 and 2), 152–153, 210–211, 263–264, 293–294. Paris, 1965–1982.

Jacobilli, Luigi. *Die selige Angelina von Marsciano.* Trans. into German by a Sister of Ewigen Abbey. Dülmen, 1919.

———. *Vite de' santi e beati dell'Vmbria.* 3 vols. Foligno, 1647–1661; reprt. Bologna, 1971.

Jacobus de Voragine. *The Golden Legend.* Trans. Granger Ryan and Helmut Ripperger. New York, 1941.

———. *Legenda aurea.* Ed. Th. Graesse. 3d ed. 1890; reprt. Osnabrück, 1965.

Jacques de Vitry. *Historia Occidentalis.* Ed. J. F. Hinnebusch. Spicilegium Friburgense, vol. 17. Fribourg, 1972.

———. *Lettres de Jacques de Vitry.* Ed. R.B.C. Huygens. Leiden, 1960.

James, M. R., trans. *The Apocryphal New Testament.* Oxford, 1924; reprt. 1966.

Jean de Meun and Guillaume de Lorris. *Le Roman de la Rose.* Ed. Ernest Langlois. 5 vols. Paris, 1914–1924.

Jerome. *Adversus Helvidium. PL* 23.193–216.

———. *Adversus Jovinianum.* Ibid. 221–352.

———. *Epistulae.* Ed. I. Hilberg. 3 vols. *CSEL,* vols. 54–56. Vienna and Leipzig, 1910–1918.

———. *St. Jerome: Letters and Select Works.* Ed. and trans. W. H. Fremantle. *LNPNFC.* 2d ser. Vol. 6. Oxford and New York, 1893.

———. *Vita Malchi monachi captivi.* Ed. and trans. Charles C. Mierow. In *Classical Essays Presented to James A. Kleist,* ed. Richard E. Arnold, 31–60. Saint Louis, Mo., 1946.

Ps.-Jerome. *Ad Oceanum. PL* 30.288–292.

John of Ephesus. *Lives of the Eastern Saints.* Ed. and trans. E. W. Brooks. *Patrologia Orientalis,* vol. 19, fasc. 2, pt. 3. Paris, 1925.

John of Freiburg. *Summa confessorum.* Rome, 1518.

John of Marienwerder. "Deutsches Leben." Ed. Max Toeppen. *Scriptores rerum Prussicarum,* 2:179–350. Leipzig, 1863; reprt. Frankfurt am Main, 1956.

———. *Vita Dorotheae Montoviensis Magistri Johannis Marienwerder.* Ed. Hans Westpfahl. Forschungen und Quellen zur Kirchen- und Kulturgeschichte Ostdeutschlands, vol. 1. Cologne and Graz, 1964.

Josephus. *The Jewish War, Books I–III.* Trans. H. St. J. Thackeray. In *Josephus,* vol. 2. Loeb Classical Library. London, 1927.

Justin Martyr. *S. Iustini Apologiae duae.* Ed. Gerhard Rauschen. Rev. ed. *Florilegium Patristicum,* fasc. 2. Bonn, 1911.

Margery Kemp. *The Book of Margery Kempe.* Ed. Sanford Brown Meech and Hope Emily Allen. *EETS.,* o.s., no. 212. London, 1940; reprt. 1960.

———. *The Book of Margery Kempe.* Trans. B. A. Windeatt. Harmondsworth, Middlesex, 1985.

Kętrzyński, W., ed. *Vita et miracula sanctae Kyngae ducissae Cracoviensis. MPH.* Ed. August Bielowski, 4:682–744. Lvov, 1884.

———, ed. *Vita sanctae Salomeae reginae Haliciensis.* Ibid. 4:776–796.

Klapper, Joseph, ed., *Erzählungen des Mittelalters.* Wort und Brauch, no. 12. Breslau, 1914.

Krusch, B., ed. *Vita S. Lupi Episcopi Trecensis. MGH, Scrip. Rer. Merov.* 7:295–302. Hanover and Leipzig, 1920.

Krusch, B., and W. Levison, eds. *Passiones vitaeque sanctorum aevi Merovingici. MGH, Scrip. Rer. Merov.* Vol. 5. Hanover and Leipzig, 1910.

Landulf the Senior. *Mediolanensis historiae libri quatuor.* Ed. Alessandro Cutulo. *Rerum Italicarum Scriptores,* Rev. ed. Vol. 4,2. Bologna, 1942.

Leibnitius, G. G., ed. *Vita comitissae Mathildis. Rerum Italicarum Scriptores,* 5:389–397. Bologna, 1724.

Leo I. *Epistolae. PL* 54.593–1218.

Luard, Henry Richards, ed. *Annales Monasterii de Wintonia.* In *Annales Monastici,* vol. 2. Rolls Series, no. 36. London, 1865.

Lugano, Placido Tommaso, ed. *I Processi inediti per Francesca Bussa dei Ponziani (1440–1453).* Studi e Testi, 120. Vatican City, 1945.

Lull, Ramon. *Blanquerna.* Trans. E. Allison Peers. London, 1926.

Lyndwood, William. *Provinciale (seu constitutiones Angliae)*. Oxford, 1679.

McLaughlin, T. P., ed. *The "Summa Parisiensis" on the "Decretum Gratiani."* Toronto, 1952.

McNeill, John T., and Helena M. Gamer, trans. *Medieval Handbooks of Penance*. New York, 1979.

Madzsar, E., ed. *Legenda sancti Gerhardi Episcopi* (includes *legenda maior* and *legenda minor*). *Scriptores Rerum Hungaricarum*. Ed. E. Szentpétery, 2:471–506. Budapest, 1938.

Mansi, G. D., ed. *Sacrorum conciliorum nova et amplissima collectio*. 31 vols. Florence, 1758–1798.

Marbod of Rennes. *Epistolae*. PL 171.1465–1492.

Marcianese, G. *Narratione della nascita, vita, e morte della B. Lucia da Narni*. Ferrara, 1616.

Mariano of Florence. "Vitae duae B. Galeoti Roberti de Malatestis." Ed. Gregorio Giovanardi. *Archivum Franciscanum Historicum* 21 (1928): 62–85.

Marie de France. *Les lais de Marie de France*. Ed. Jeanne Lods. Les classiques français du moyen âge, 87. Paris, 1959.

Meersseman, G. G., ed. *Dossier de l'ordre de la pénitence au XIIIe siècle*. Spicilegium Friburgense, vol. 7. Fribourg, 1961.

Methodius. *Le banquet*. Ed. Herbert Musurillo. Trans. V.-H. Debidour. *SC*, no. 95. Paris, 1963.

Meyer, Paul, ed. "L'enfant voué au diable." *Romania* 33 (1904): 163–178.

Michael the Monk. *Vita S. Theodori Studitae*. PG 99.113–232.

Minucius Felix. *Octavius*. Ed. and trans. Jean Beaujeu. Paris, 1964.

Mombrizio, Bonino. *Sanctuarium seu Vitae sanctorum*. 2 vols. Paris, 1910.

Monoñedo, Munio, Hugo Porto, and Gerard the Presbyter. *Historia Compostellana*. PL 170.889–1236.

Munier, C., and C. De Clercq, eds. *Concilia Galliae*. *CCSL*, vols. 148 and 148a. Turnholt, 1963.

Nelson, Charles L., trans. *The Book of the Knight Zifar*. Lexington, Ky., 1983.

Nicolaus de Lyre et al. *Biblia sacra cum Glossa ordinaria primum quidem a Strabo Fuldensi collecta*. 7 vols. vol. 1: Paris, 1590; vol. 2: Venice, 1603; vol. 3: Paris, 1590; vols. 4 and 5: London, 1545; vol. 6: Paris, 1590; vol. 7 (index): London, 1590.

Odenkirchen, Carl J., ed. *The Life of St. Alexius, In the Old French Version of the Hildesheim Manuscript*. Brookline, Mass., and Leyden, 1978.

Olivi, Peter John. "Lo cavalier armat." Ed. with commentary by Raoul Manselli. Trans. M.-H. Vicaire. In *La religion populaire en Languedoc du XIIIe siècle à la moitié du XIVe siècle*, ed. E. Privat, 203–216. Cahiers de Fanjeaux, 11. Toulouse, 1976.

———. "Verginita' e matrimonio nella valutazione dell'Olivi." (Excerpts from Olivi's *De perfectione evangelica*.) Ed. A. Emmen. *Studi Francescani* 64 (1967): 11–57.

Osbert of Clare. "La vie de S. Edouard le Confesseur." Ed. Marc Bloch. *AB* 41 (1923): 5–131.

Palladius. *Dialogue of Palladius concerning the Life of Chrysostom*. Trans. Herbert Moore. London and New York, 1921.

———. *Lausiac History.* Trans. Robert T. Meyer. *ACW*, no. 34. Westminster, Md. and London, 1965.

———. *Lausiac History of Palladius.* Ed. C. Butler. 2 vols. Cambridge, 1898–1904.

———. *Paladii dialogus de vita S. Joannis Chrysostomi.* Ed. P. R. Coleman-Norton. Cambridge, 1928.

Panormitanus (Nicolaus de Tudeschis). *Lectura in Decretales cum optimis glossis.* 6 vols. Turin, 1509.

Paris, Gaston, and Ulysse Robert, eds. *Miracles de Nostre Dame par personnages.* 8 vols. Paris, 1876–1893.

Paulinus of Nola. *Letters of St. Paulinus of Nola.* Trans. P. G. Walsh. *ACW*, nos. 35 and 36. Westminster, Md., 1966–1967.

———. *Opera sancti Pontii Meropii Paulini Nolani.* Ed. W. Hartel. *CSEL*, vols. 29 and 30. Prague, Vienna, and Leipzig, 1894.

———. *The Poems of St. Paulinus of Nola.* Trans. P. G. Walsh. *ACW*, no. 40. New York, 1975.

Pauphilet, Albert, ed. *La queste del saint Graal.* Paris, 1923.

Pelagius and John, trans. *Verba seniorum. PL* 73.851–1062.

Pelagius of Oviedo. *Historia de Arcae Sanctae translatione, deque Sanctorum Reliquiis, quae in ea asservantur.* Ed. H. Florez. In *España Sagrada*, vol. 37, appendix 15, 352–358. Madrid, 1789.

Pelster, Franz, ed. "Ein Elogium Joachims von Fiore auf Kaiser Heinrich II. und seine Gemahlin, die heilige Kunigunde." In *Liber Floridus, mittellateinische Studien: Paul Lehmann*, ed. Bernhard Bischoff and Suso Brechter, 329–354. St. Ottilien, 1950.

Pertz, G. H., ed. *Chronicon Affligemense. MGH, Scrip.* 9:407–417. Hanover, 1851.

———., ed. *Vita Mahthildis reginae. MGH, Scrip.* 4:283–302. Hanover, 1841.

Peter Lombard. *Sententiae in IV libris distinctae.* Ed. The Fathers of the College of St. Bonaventure. 2 vols. Rome, 1971–1981.

Peter of Montarone. *Vita del beato Pietro Pettinajo.* Siena, 1802.

Peter of Poitiers. *Summa de confessione. Compilatio praesens.* Ed. Jean Longère. *CCCM*, vol. 51. Turnholt, 1980.

Peter the Chanter. *Summa de sacramentis et animae consiliis.* Ed. Jean-Albert Dugauquier. 3 parts in 5 vols. Analecta Mediaevalia Namurcensia, 4, 7, and 16. Louvain and Lille, 1954–1963.

Power, Eileen, trans. *The Goodman of Paris (Le ménagier de Paris).* New York, 1928.

Powicke, F. M., and C. R. Cheney, eds. *Councils and Synods with Other Documents Relating to the English Church.* 4 vols. Oxford, 1964–1981.

Raymond of Peñafort. *Summa sancti Raymundi de Peniafort de poenitentia, et matrimonio.* Rome, 1603.

Razzi, Serafino. *Vite dei santi e beati così del Sacro Ordine de' frati predicatori.* Florence, 1577.

Reginald of Durham. *Vita S. Oswaldi.* In Symeon of Durham's *Historia ecclesiae Dunhelmensis*, ed. Thomas Arnold, vol. 1, appendix 3, 326–385. Rolls Series, no. 75. London, 1882.

Regino of Prüm. *Chronicon*. Ed. G. H. Pertz. *MGH, Scrip.* 1:543–612. Hanover, 1876.

———. *De ecclesiasticis disciplinis et religione Christiana*. *PL* 132.185–400.

Robert of Arbrissel. "Lettre inédite de Robert d'Arbrissel à la comtesse Ermengarde." Ed. René Nidurst. *Bibliothèque de l'Ecole des Chartes* 3,5 (1854): 209–235.

Robert of Brunne. *Handlyng Synne*. Ed. F. J. Furnivall. *EETS*, o.s., nos. 119 and 123. London, 1901–1903.

Robert of Flamborough. *Liber poenitentialis*. Ed. J. J. Francis Firth. Studies and Texts, no. 18. Toronto, 1971.

Robinson, James M., ed. *The Nag Hammadi Library*. San Francisco, 1977.

Sedulius. *Sedulii opera omnia*. Ed. J. Huemer. *CSEL*, vol. 10. Vienna, 1885.

Serlo, Mgr. "The *Summa de penitentia* of Magister Serlo." Ed. Joseph Goering. *Mediaeval Studies* 38 (1976): 1–53.

Simmons, T. F., and H. E. Nolloth, eds. *Lay Folks' Catechism*. *EETS*, o.s., no. 118. London, 1901.

Siricius. *Epistolae*. *PL* 13.1131–1178.

Stachnik, Richard, ed. *Die Akten des Kanonisationsprozesses Dorotheas von Montau von 1394 bis 1521*. Forschungen und Quellen zur Kirchen- und Kulturgeschichte Ostdeutschlands, vol. 12. Cologne and Vienna, 1978.

Talbot, C. H., ed. and trans. *The Life of Christina of Markyate*. Oxford, 1959; reprt. 1987.

Tertullian. *A son épouse*. Ed. and trans. Charles Munier. *SC*, no. 273. Paris, 1980.

———. *De monogamia*. In *Tertulliani opera*, pt. 2, ed. E. Dekkers. *CCSL*, 2:1229–1253. Turnholt, 1954.

———. *Exhortation à la chasteté*. Ed. C. Moreschini. Trans. J.-C. Fredouille. *SC*, no. 319. Paris, 1985.

———. *Tertullian: Treatises on Marriage and Remarriage*. Trans. W. P. Le Saint. *ACW*, no. 13. Westminster, Md., 1951.

Theodore the Studite. *Laudatio funebris in matrem suam*. *PG* 99.883–902.

Thietmar of Merseburg. *Die Chronik des Bischofs Thietmar von Merseburg*. Ed. Robert Holtzmann. *MGH, Scrip. Rer. Germ.*, n.s., vol. 9. Berlin, 1935.

Thomas of Celano. *St. Francis of Assisi: First and Second Life of St. Francis*. Trans. Placid Hermann. Chicago, 1963; reprt. 1988.

———. *Vita prima S. Francisci*. *Analecta Franciscana* 10 (1941): 1–117.

———. *Vita secunda S. Francisci*. Ibid., 128–268.

Thomas of Chobham. *Summa confessorum*. Ed. F. Broomfield. Analecta Mediaevalia Namurcensia, 25. Louvain and Paris, 1968.

Ubieto Arteta, Antonio, ed. *Crónica de Alfonso III*. Textos Medievales, 3. Valencia, 1971.

Usuard. *Martyrologium*. *AA SS*, June, vol. 6.

Varin, Pierre, ed. *Archives administratives et législatives de la ville de Reims*. Pt. 1. *Coutumes*. Paris, 1840.

Victor of Vita. *Historia persecutionis Africanae provinciae*. Ed. M. Petschenig. *CSEL*, vol. 7. Vienna, 1881.

Vincent of Beauvais. *Speculum quadruplex; sive, Speculum maius.* 4 vols. Douai, 1624; reprt. Graz, 1964–1965.

Wakefield, Walter L., and Austin P. Evans, trans. *Heresies of the High Middle Ages.* New York and London, 1969.

Welter, J. Th., ed. *Le Speculum laicorum.* Thesaurus exemplorum, fasc. 5. Paris, 1914.

White, T. H., trans. *The Bestiary: A Book of Beasts.* New York, 1960.

William of Malmesbury. *Chronicle of the Kings of England.* Trans. J. A. Giles. London, 1847.

———. *De Gestis regum Anglorum.* Ed. William Stubbs. 2 vols. Rolls Series, vol. 90. London, 1887–1889.

William of Rennes. Glosses on *Summa sancti Raymundi de Peniafort de poenitentia, et matrimonio.* Rome, 1603. (The frontispiece of this edition wrongly attributes William's glosses to John of Freiburg.)

Saints' Lives and Commentaries Consulted from the Acta Sanctorum (Paris and Rome, 1863–)

Æthelthryth. June, 5:417–495.

Alexis. July, 4:238–270.

Amator. May, 1:51–61.

Andronicus and Athanasia. October, 4:997–1001.

Aye and Hidulph. April, 2:575–578; June, 5:495–496.

Bernard of Mount Joy. June, 3:547–564.

Bertha and Gumbert. May, 1:115–120; April, 3:627–632.

Bertilia. January, 1:155–158.

Bridget of Sweden. October, 4:368–560.

Cassius and Fausta. June, 7:445–450.

Catherine of Bologna. March, 2:35–89.

Catherine of Sweden. March, 3:501–529.

Chiarito del Voglia. May, 6:160–164.

Christina the Astonishing. July, 5:637–660.

Chrysanthus and Daria. October, 11:437–495.

Conrad of Piacenza. February, 3:162–170.

Cunegund (empress). March, 1:265–280.

Cunegund of Poland. July, 5:661–783.

Cuthburga. August, 6:696–700.

Cyneburga and Cyneswitha. March, 1:440–446.

Donatus of Besançon. August, 2:197–200.

Dorothea of Montau. October, 13:472–584.

Elena dall'Olio. September, 6:655–659.

Elzear de Sabran. September, 7:494–555.

Emeric. November, 2:477–491.

Euphraxia. March, 2:260–270.

Frances of Rome. March, 2:89–219.

Galaction and Episteme. November, 3:33–45.

Gangulf. May, 2:641–652.

Gentile of Ravenna. January, 3:525–530.
Genulph of Cahors. January, 2:445–471.
Gerardesca of Pisa. May, 7:161–176.
Hadeloga. February, 2:306–311.
Hedwig of Silesia. October, 8:198–270.
Humility of Faenza. May, 5:205–224.
Ida of Bologne. April, 2:139–150.
Isidore the Laborer and Mary Torribia. May, 3:509–546, 547–554.
Ivetta of Huy. January, 2:145–169.
James Oldo. April, 2:596–606.
Jeanne-Marie of Maillac. March, 3:733–762.
Julian and Basilissa. January, 1:570–588.
Lucchese. April, 3:600–616.
Lucia Bartolini. October, 13:202–207.
Magnus of Orkney. April, 2:434–437.
Mary of Oignies. June, 5:542–588.
Maurice Czasky. March, 3:250–254.
Nereus and Achilleus. May, 3:4–16.
Osyth. October, 3:942–944.
Phairaildis. January, 1:170–173.
Richardis. September, 5:793–798.
Rita of Cascia. May, 5:224–234.
Robert Malatesta. October, 5:145–149.
Santuccia Terrabotti of Gubbio. March, 3:361–363.
Serena of Spoleto. January, 3:642–644.
Severus of Ravenna. February, 1:78–91.
Sigolena of Albi, July, 5:628–637.
Simon of Crépy, count of Valois. September, 8:711–751.
Sperandeo and Gennaia of Gubbio. September, 3:890–913 (this couple is only
    mentioned in passing in the life of Sperandea of Gubbio, p. 892).
Theodoric. July, 1:53–75.
Theophanus the Chronographer. March, 2:210–225.

SECONDARY SOURCES

Abels, Richard, and Ellen Harrison. "The Participation of Women in Lan-
    guedocian Catharism." *Mediaeval Studies* 41 (1979): 215–251.
Achelis, Hans. "Agapētae." *Encyclopaedia of Religion and Ethics.* 1:177–
    180. New York, 1961.
———. *Virgines Subintroductae: ein Beitrag zum VII. Kapitel des I. Ko-
    rintherbriefs.* Leipzig, 1902.
Akeley, T. C. *Christian Initiation in Spain, c. 300-1100.* London, 1967.
Albanès, J.-H. "Inscription de sainte Casarie." *Revue des sociétés savantes* 1
    (1875): 158–163.
Allen, Prudence. *The Concept of Woman: The Aristotelian Revolution, 750
    BC–AD 1250.* Montreal and London, 1985.
Anciaux, Paul. *La théologie du sacrement de pénitence au XIIe siècle.* Uni-

versitas Catholica Lovaniensis, ser. 2, vol. 41. Louvain and Gembloux, 1949.

Atkinson, Clarissa. *Mystic and Pilgrim: The Book and the World of Margery Kempe.* Ithaca, N.Y., 1983.

————. " 'Precious Balsam in a Fragile Glass': The Ideology of Virginity in the Later Middle Ages." *Journal of Family History* 8 (1983): 131–143.

Bailey, Derrick Sherwin. *The Man-Woman Relation in Christian Thought.* London, 1959.

Baldwin, John W. *Masters, Princes, and Merchants: The Social Views of Peter the Chanter and His Circle.* 2 vols. Princeton, N.J., 1970.

Barlow, Frank. *Edward the Confessor.* Berkeley and Los Angeles, 1970.

Barrau-Dihigo, L. "Actes des rois Asturiens." *Revue Hispanique* 46 (1919): 1–191.

————. "Recherches sur l'histoire politique du royaume Asturien (718–910)." *Revue Hispanique* 52 (1921): 1–360.

Barstow, Anne Llewellyn. *Married Priests and the Reforming Papacy: The Eleventh-Century Debates.* Texts and Studies in Religion, vol. 12, New York and Toronto, 1982.

Bartlett, Robert. *Trial by Fire and Water: The Medieval Judicial Ordeal.* Oxford, 1986.

Baudot, J. L., and L. Chaussin, eds. *Vies des saints et des bienheureux selon l'ordre du calendrier, avec l'historique des fêtes.* 13 vols. Paris, 1935–1959.

Beckwith, Sarah. "A Very Material Mysticism: The Medieval Mysticism of Margery Kempe." In *Medieval Literature: Criticism, Ideology, and History,* ed. David Aers, 34–57. Brighton, 1986.

Bell, Rudolph M. *Holy Anorexia.* Chicago and London, 1985.

Benton, John F. "Consciousness of Self and Perceptions of Individuality." In *Renaissance and Renewal in the Twelfth Century,* ed. Robert L. Benson and Giles Constable, 263–295. Cambridge, Mass., 1982.

Bergh, Birger. "A Saint in the Making: St. Bridget's Life in Sweden (1303–1349)." In *Papers of the Liverpool Latin Seminar,* ed. Francis Cairns, 371–384. Vol. 3. *ARCA* Classical and Medieval Texts, Papers and Monographs, 7. Liverpool, 1981.

Bethell, Denis. "The Lives of St. Osyth of Essex and St. Osyth of Aylesbury." *AB* 88 (1970): 75–127.

Bishop, Jane. "Bishops as Marital Advisors in the Ninth Century." In *Women of the Medieval World: Essays in Honor of John Mundy,* ed. Julius Kirshner and Suzanne F. Wemple, 53–84. Oxford, 1985.

Bloch, Marc. *Feudal Society.* Trans. L. A. Manyon. 2 vols. Chicago, 1961.

————. *The Royal Touch: Sacred Monarchy and Scrofula in England and France.* Trans. J. E. Anderson. London and Montreal, 1973.

Blomme, Robert. *La doctrine du péché dans les écoles théologiques de la première moitié du XIIe siècle.* Louvain and Gembloux, 1958.

Blum, Owen J. *St. Peter Damian: His Teaching on the Spiritual Life.* Catholic University of America. Studies in Mediaeval History, n.s., vol. 10. Washington, D.C., 1947.

Bolton, Brenda. "*Mulieres Sanctae.*" In *Women in Medieval Society,* ed. Susan Mosher Stuard, 141–158. Philadelphia, 1976.

Bolton, Brenda. "Sources for the Early History of the Humiliati." In *Materials, Sources, and Methods of Ecclesiastical History*, ed. Derek Baker, 125–133. Studies in Church History, no. 11. Oxford, 1975.

———. "*Vitae Matrum*: A Further Aspect of the *Frauenfrage*." In *Medieval Women*, ed. Derek Baker, 253–273. Studies in Church History. Subsidia, 1. Oxford, 1978.

Bonzi da Genova, Umile. *Teologia mistica di S. Caterina da Genova*. Vol. 1 of *S. Caterina Fieschi Adorno*. Turin, 1960.

Boswell, John. *Christianity, Social Tolerance, and Homosexuality*. Chicago and London, 1980.

Bowsky, William M. *A Medieval Italian Commune: Siena under the Nine, 1287–1355*. Berkeley and Los Angeles, 1981.

Boyle, Leonard. "*Summae Confessorum*." In *Les genres littéraires dans les sources théologiques et philosophiques médiévales: définition, critique, et exploitation*, 227–237. Actes du colloque international de Louvain-la-Neuve, 25–27 mai, 1981. Université Catholique de Louvain, publications de l'Institut d'Etudes Médiévales. 2d ser. Textes, Etudes, Congrès, vol. 5. Louvain-la-Neuve, 1982.

———. "The *Summa Confessorum* of John of Freiburg and the Popularization of the Moral Teaching of St. Thomas Aquinas and Some of His Contemporaries." In *St. Thomas Aquinas, 1274–1974: Commemorative Studies*, ed. Armand A. Maurer et al., 2:245–268. Toronto, 1974; reprt. Leonard Boyle, *Pastoral Care, Clerical Education and Canon Law, 1200–1400*. London, 1981.

Bremond, Claude, Jacques Le Goff, and Jean-Claude Schmitt. *L'"Exemplum."* Typologie des sources du moyen âge occidental, fasc. 40. Turnholt, 1982.

Brooke, Christopher N. L. "Marriage and Society in the Central Middle Ages." In *Marriage and Society: Studies in the Social History of Marriage*, ed. R. B. Outhwaite, 17–34. London, 1981.

———. *The Medieval Idea of Marriage*. Oxford, 1989.

Broudéhoux, J. P. *Mariage et famille chez Clément d'Alexandrie*. Théologie historique, 2. Paris, 1970.

Brown, Peter. *Augustine of Hippo: A Biography*. Berkeley and Los Angeles, 1967.

———. *The Body and Society: Men, Women, and Sexual Renunciation in Early Christianity*. New York, 1988.

———. *The Cult of the Saints: Its Rise and Function in Latin Christianity*. Chicago, 1981.

———. *Religion and Society in the Age of Saint Augustine*. London, 1972.

———. *Society and the Holy in Late Antiquity*. Berkeley and Los Angeles, 1982.

Brundage, James A. "'Allas! That Evere Love was Synne': Sex and Medieval Canon Law." *Catholic Historical Review* 72 (1986): 1–13.

———. "'Better to Marry than to Burn?' The Case of the Vanishing Dichotomy." In *Views of Women's Lives in Western Tradition: Frontiers of the Past and the Future*, ed. F. R. Keller, 195–216. Women's Studies, vol. 5. Lewiston, Queenston, and Lampeter, 1990.

―――. "Carnal Delight: Canonistic Theories of Sexuality." In *Proceedings of the Fifth International Congress of Medieval Canon Law*, Salamanca, 21–25 September 1976, ed. Stephan Kuttner and Kenneth Pennington, 361–385. Monumenta Iuris Canonici. Ser. C: Subsidia, vol. 6. Vatican City, 1980.

―――. "The Crusader's Wife: A Canonistic Quandary." *Studia Gratiana* 12 (1967): 427–441.

―――. *Law, Sex, and Christian Society in Medieval Europe*. Chicago and London, 1987.

―――. "Let Me Count the Ways: Canonists and Theologians Contemplate Coital Positions." *Journal of Medieval History* 10 (1984): 81–93.

―――. *Medieval Canon Law and the Crusader*. Madison, Wis., 1969.

―――. "The Problem of Impotence." In *Sexual Practices and the Medieval Church*, ed. Vern L. Bullough and James A. Brundage, 135–140, 261–262. Buffalo and New York, 1982.

―――. "Rape and Marriage in the Medieval Canon Law." *Revue de droit canonique* 28 (1978): 62–75.

―――. "Sexual Equality in Medieval Canon Law." In *Medieval Women and the Sources of Medieval History*, ed. Joel T. Rosenthal, 66–79. Athens, Ga., 1990.

Brunner, Karl. *Oppositionelle Gruppen im Karolingerreich*. Vienna, Cologne, and Graz, 1979.

Buckley, Jorunn Jacobsen. *Female Fault and Fulfilment in Gnosticism*. Chapel Hill, N.C., 1986.

Bugge, John *"Virginitas": An Essay in the History of a Medieval Ideal*. Archives internationales d'histoire des idées, series minor, 17. The Hague, 1975.

Bullough, Vern L. "Medieval Medical and Scientific Views of Women." *Viator* 4 (1973): 485–501.

―――. "Transvestism in the Middle Ages." In *Sexual Practices and the Medieval Church*, ed. Vern L. Bullough and James A. Brundage, 43–54, 237–239. Buffalo and New York, 1982.

Bultot, Robert. *Christianisme et valeurs humaines*. A. *La doctrine du mépris du monde, en Occident, de S. Ambroise à Innocent III*. Vol. 4. *Le XIe siècle*. Vol. 1. *Pierre Damien*. Louvain and Paris, 1963.

Burr, David. *Olivi and Franciscan Poverty: The Origins of the 'Usus Pauper' Controversy*. Philadelphia, 1989.

Burrus, Virginia. *Chastity as Autonomy: Women in the Stories of Apocryphal Acts*. Studies in Women and Religion, vol. 23. Lewiston and Queenston, 1987.

Butler, A. *Lives of the Saints*. Ed. and rev. H. Thurston and D. Attwater. 4 vols. New York, 1956.

Bynum, Caroline Walker. ". . . And Woman His Humanity: Female Imagery in the Religious Writings of the Later Middle Ages." In *Gender and Religion: On the Complexity of Symbols*, ed. Bynum et al., 257–288. Boston, 1986.

―――. "The Female Body and Religious Practice in the Later Middle Ages." In *Zone: Fragments for a History of the Human Body*, ed. Michel Feher et al., 1,3:160–220. New York, 1989.

Bynum, Caroline Walker. *Holy Feast and Holy Fast: The Religious Significance of Food to Medieval Women*. Berkeley and Los Angeles, 1987.

———. *Jesus as Mother: Studies in the Spirituality of the High Middle Ages*. Berkeley and Los Angeles, 1982.

———. "Women's Stories, Women's Symbols: A Critique of Victor Turner's Theory of Liminality." In *Anthropology and the Study of Religion*, ed. Robert L. Moore and Frank E. Reynolds, 105–125. Chicago, 1984.

Cadden, Joan. "It Takes All Kinds: Sexuality and Gender Differences in Hildegard of Bingen's *Book of Compound Medicine*." *Traditio* 40 (1984): 149–174.

Camelot, Th. "Les traités *De virginitate* au IVe siècle." In *Mystique et continence*, 273–292. Travaux scientifiques du VIIe congrès international d'Avon. Les études Carmélitaines, 31. Bruges, 1952.

Capobianco, P. "De ambitu fori interni in iure ante Codicem." *Apollinaris* 8 (1935): 591–605.

———. "De notione fori interni in iure canonico." *Apollinaris* 9 (1936): 364–374

Carozzi, Claude. "Le roi et la liturgie chez Helgaud de Fleury." In *Hagiographie, Cultures, et Sociétés, IVe–XIIe siècles*, 417–432. Actes du Colloque organisé à Nanterre et à Paris (2–5 mai 1979). Centre de Recherches sur l'Antiquité tardive et le haut Moyen Age. Université de Paris-X. Paris, 1981.

Castelli, Elizabeth. "Virginity and Its Meaning for Women's Sexuality in Early Christianity." *Journal of Feminist Studies in Religion* 2 (1986): 61–88.

Chaney, William A. *The Cult of Kingship in Anglo-Saxon England: The Transition from Paganism to Christianity*. Berkeley and Los Angeles, 1970.

Chenu, M.-D. *Nature, Man, and Society in the Twelfth Century*. Ed. and trans. Jerome Taylor and Lester K. Little. Chicago and London, 1968; reprt. 1983.

Church, F. Forrester. "Sex and Salvation in Tertullian." *Harvard Theological Review* 68 (1975): 83–101.

Clark, Elizabeth. *Ascetic Piety and Women's Faith: Essays on Late Ancient Christianity*. Studies in Women and Religion, vol. 20. Lewiston and Queenston, 1986.

———. "'Adam's Only Companion': Augustine and the Early Christian Debate on Marriage." In *The Olde Daunce: Love, Friendship, Sex, and Marriage in the Medieval World*, ed. Robert R. Edwards and Stephen Spector, 15–31, 240–254. Albany, N.Y., 1991.

———. *Jerome, Chrysostom, and Friends: Essays and Translations*. Studies in Women and Religion, vol. 1. New York and Toronto, 1979.

———. "John Chrysostom and the *Subintroductae*." *Church History* 46 (1977): 171–185.

Cleve, Gunnel. "Semantic Dimensions in Margery Kempe's 'Whyght Clothys.'" *Mystics Quarterly* 12 (1986): 162–170.

Coakley, John. "Friars as Confidants of Holy Women in Medieval Dominican

Hagiography." In *Images of Sainthood in Medieval Europe*, ed. Renate Blumenfeld-Kosinski and Timea Szell, 222–246. Ithaca, N.Y., 1991.

———. "Gender and the Authority of Friars: The Significance of Holy Women for Thirteenth-Century Franciscans and Dominicans." *Church History* 60 (1991): 445–460.

Colledge, Eric. "*Epistola solitarii ad reges*: Alphonse of Pecha as Organizer of Birgittine and Urbanist Propaganda." *Mediaeval Studies* 18 (1956): 19–49.

Colman, Rebecca. "Abduction of Women in Barbaric Law." *Florilegium* 5 (1983): 62–75.

Congar, Yves. "Les laïcs et l'ecclésiologie des *ordines* chez les théologiens des XIe et XIIe siècles." In *I laici nella 'Societas Christiana' dei secoli XI e XII*, 83–117. Atti della terza Settimana internazionale di studio, Mendola, 21–27 agosto 1965. Pubblicazioni dell' Università Cattolica del Sacro Cuore, Miscellanea del Centro di Studi Medioevali, 5. Milan, 1968.

Cook, William R. "Fraternal and Lay Images of St. Francis in the Thirteenth Century." In *Popes, Teachers, and Canon Law in the Middle Ages*, ed. J. R. Sweeney and S. Chodorow, 263–289. Ithaca, N.Y., 1989.

Cooper, C. H. *Memoir of Margaret, Countess of Richmond and Derby*. Cambridge, 1874.

———. "The Vow of Widowhood of Margaret, Countess of Richmond and Derby." *Communications to the C.A.S.* (Cambridge Antiquarian Society) 1 (1851–1859): 71–79.

Corbet, Patrick. *Les Saints Ottoniens: Sainteté dynastique, sainteté royale, et sainteté feminine autour de l'an Mil*. Sigmaringen, 1986.

Corbett, P. E. *The Roman Law of Marriage*. Oxford, 1930.

Cowdrey, H.E.J. "The Papacy, the Patarenes, and the Church of Milan." *Transactions of the Royal Historical Society*, ser. 5, 18 (1986): 25–48.

Cristofani, Francesco. "Memorie del B. Pietro Pettinagno da Siena." *Miscellanea Francescana* 5 (1890): 34–52.

Crouzel, Henri. "Le célibat et la continence dans l'église primitive: leurs motivations." In *Sacerdoce et célibat: études historiques et théologiques*, ed. J. Coppens, 333–371. Bibliotheca ephemeridum theologicarum Lovaniensium, 28. Gembloux and Louvain, 1971.

———. *Virginité et mariage selon Origène*. Museum Lessianum, section théologique, no. 58. Paris and Bruges, 1962.

Cutler, Kenneth E. "Edith, Queen of England, 1045–1066." *Mediaeval Studies* 35 (1973): 222–231.

Dalarun, J. *Robert d'Arbrissel: fondateur de Fontevraud*. Paris, 1986.

———. "Robert d'Arbrissel et les femmes." *Annales ESC* 39 (1984): 1140–1160.

Daniélou, Jean. *The Theology of Jewish Christianity*. Vol. 1 of *The Development of Christian Doctrine before the Council of Nicaea*. Trans. John A. Barker. London, 1964.

Davies, Stevan. L. *The Revolt of the Widows: The Social World of the Apocryphal Acts*. Carbondale, Ill., 1980.

D'Avray, D. L. "The Gospel of the Marriage Feast of Cana and Marriage

Preaching in France." In *The Bible in the Medieval World: Essays in Memory of Beryl Smalley*, ed. Katherine Walsh and Diana Wood, 207–224. Studies in Church History. Subsidia, 4. London, 1985.

———. *The Preaching of the Friars: Sermons Diffused from Paris before 1300*. Oxford, 1985.

D'Avray, D. L., and M. Tausche. "Marriage Sermons in *ad status* Collections of the Central Middle Ages." *Archives d'histoire doctrinale et littéraire du moyen âge* 47 (1980): 71–119.

Deblaere, Albert. "La littérature mystique au moyen âge." *DS* 10.1902–1919.

De Gaiffier, Baudouin. "*Intactam sponsam relinquens* à propos de la vie de S. Alexis." *AB* 65 (1947): 157–195.

———. "Source d'un texte relatif au mariage dans la vie de S. Alexis, BHL. 289." *AB* 63 (1945): 48–55.

De Ganay, M. C. *Les bienheureuses Dominicaines*. Paris, 1924.

Delaruelle, Etienne. *La piété populaire au moyen âge*. Turin, 1975.

Delehaye, Hippolyte. *Etude sur le légendier romain: les saints de novembre et de décembre*. Subsidia Hagiographica, 23. Brussels, 1936.

———. *The Legends of the Saints*. Trans. Donald Attwater. New York, 1962.

De Rougemont, Denis. *Passion and Society*. Trans. Montgomery Belgion. Rev. ed. London, 1956.

De Tillemont, Lenain. "Notes sur saint Eucher." In *Mémoires pour servir à l'histoire ecclésiastique des six premiers siècles*, 15:848–857. Paris, 1711.

Devlin, Derek. "Feminine Lay Piety in the High Middle Ages: The Beguines." In *Distant Echoes*. Vol. 1 of *Medieval Religious Women*, ed. John A. Nichols and Lillian Thomas Shank, 183–196. Cistercian Studies Series, no. 71. Kalamazoo, Mich., 1984.

D'Izarny, Raymond. "Mariage et consécration virginale au IVe siècle." *La vie spirituelle* supp. 6 (1953): 92–118.

Dodds, E. R. *Pagan and Christian in an Age of Anxiety*. Cambridge, 1965.

Donahue, Charles. "The Policy of Alexander III's Consent Theory of Marriage." In *Proceedings of the Fourth International Congress of Canon Law, Toronto, 21–25 August 1972*, ed. Stephan Kuttner, 251–281. Monumenta Iuris Canonici. Ser. C: Subsidia, vol. 5. Vatican City, 1976.

Dooley, William Joseph. *Marriage according to St. Ambrose*. Washington D.C., 1948.

Dortel-Claudot, M. "Le prêtre et le mariage: évolution de la législation canonique des origines au XIIe siècle." *L'année canonique* 17 (1973): 319–344.

Douglas, Mary. *Purity and Danger: An Analysis of the Concepts of Pollution and Taboo*. London, 1966.

Duby, Georges. *L'An mil*. Paris, 1967.

———. *The Knight, the Lady, and the Priest: The Making of Modern Marriage in Medieval France*. Trans. Barbara Bray. New York, 1983.

———. "Les pauvres des campagnes dans l'occident médiéval jusqu'au XIIIe siècle." *Revue d'histoire de l'église de France* 52 (1966): 25–32.

———. "Que sait-on de l'amour en France au XIIe siècle?" *The Zaharoff Lecture for 1982–1983*. Oxford, 1983.

———. *The Three Orders: Feudal Society Imagined.* Trans. Arthur Gold-hammer. Chicago, 1980.

Duff, Nora. *Matilda of Tuscany: La gran donna d'Italia.* London, 1909.

Dümmler, Ernst. *Geschichte des ostfränkischen Reiches.* 3 vols. Leipzig, 1887–1888; reprt. Hildesheim, 1960.

Dunbar, Agnes B. C. *A Dictionary of Saintly Women.* 2 vols. London, 1904–1905.

Dupont-Sommer, A. *The Essene Writings from Qumran.* Trans. G. Vermes. Oxford, 1961.

Economou, George D. *The Goddess Natura in Medieval Literature.* Cambridge, Mass., 1972.

Elliott, Dyan. "Dress as Mediator between Inner and Outer Self: The Pious Matron of the High and Later Middle Ages." *Mediaeval Studies* 53 (1991): 279–308.

Ellis, Roger. "'Flores ad Fabricandam . . . Coronam': An Investigation into the Uses of the Revelations of St. Bridget of Sweden in Fifteenth-Century England." *Medium Aevum* 51 (1982): 163–186.

Esmein, A. *Le mariage en droit canonique.* 2d ed. 2 vols. Paris, 1929–1935.

Farmer, Sharon. "Persuasive Voices: Clerical Images of Medieval Wives." *Speculum* 61 (1986): 517–543.

Filas, Francis L. *Joseph: The Man Closest to Jesus.* Boston, 1962.

Fiorenza, Elisabeth Schüssler. *Bread Not Stone: The Challenge of Feminist Biblical Interpretation.* Boston, 1984.

———. *In Memory of Her: A Feminist Theological Reconstruction of Christian Origins.* New York, 1983.

———. "Justified by All Her Children: Struggle, Memory, and Vision." In *On the Threshold of the Third Millennium,* ed. P. Hillyer, 19–38. Special Issue of *Concilium.* London and Philadelphia, 1990.

———. "Word, Spirit, and Power in Early Christian Communities." In *Women of Spirit: Female Leadership in the Jewish and Christian Traditions,* ed. Rosemary Radford Ruether and Eleanor McLaughlin, 29–70. New York, 1974.

Flandrin, Jean-Louis. *Un temps pour embrasser: aux origines de la morale sexuelle occidentale (Ve-XIe siècle).* Paris, 1983.

Fliche, Augustin. "Alphonse II le Chaste et les origines de la reconquête chrétienne." In *Estudios sobre la Monarquia Asturiana,* 119–134. Instituto de Estudios Asturianos. Oviedo, 1949.

Florez, H. *España Sagrada.* 51 vols. Madrid, 1754–1879.

Folz, Robert. "La légende liturgique de saint Henri II empereur et confesseur." In *Mélanges Jacques Stiennon,* 245–258. Liège, 1982.

———. *Les saints rois du moyen âge en occident.* Brussels, 1984.

Fransen, Gérard. "La rupture du mariage." In *Il matrimonio nella società altomedievale,* 22–28 aprile 1976, 2:603–630. Settimane di Studio del Centro italiano di studi sull'alto medioevo, 24. Spoleto, 1977.

Frazee, Charles A. "The Origins of Clerical Celibacy in the Western Church." *Church History* 41 (1972): 149–167.

Funk, Philipp. *Jakob von Vitry: Leben und Werke.* Beiträge zur Kulturgeschichte des Mittelalters und der Renaissance, no. 3. Leipzig and Berlin, 1909.

Gager, John G. *Kingdom and Community: The Social World of Early Christianity*. Englewood Cliffs, N.J., 1975.

Gardner, Edmund G. *Dukes and Poets in Ferrara*. New York, 1904.

Gaudemet, Jean. "Recherche sur les origines historiques de la faculté de rompre le mariage non consommé." In *Proceedings of the Fifth International Congress of Medieval Canon Law*, Salamanca, 21–25 September 1976, ed. Stephan Kuttner and Kenneth Pennington, 309–331. Monumenta Iuris Canonici. Ser. C: Subsidia, vol. 6 Vatican City, 1980.

———. *Sociétés et mariage*. Strasbourg, 1980.

Geary, Patrick J. *Furta Sacra: Thefts of Relics in the Central Middle Ages*. Rev. ed. Princeton, N.J., 1990.

Gieysztor, Aleksander. *History of Poland*. 2d ed. Warsaw, 1979.

———. "*Pauper sum et peregrinus*. La légende de saint Alexis en occident: un idéal de pauvreté." In *Etudes sur l'histoire de la pauvreté*, ed. Michel Mollat, 1:125–139. Publications de la Sorbonne. Sér. "Etudes," vol. 8. Paris, 1974.

Gilson, Etienne. "La mystique de la grâce dans *La Queste del saint Graal*." In *Les idées et les lettres*, 59–91. Paris, 1932.

Giovanardi, Gregorio. "Il B. Galeotto Roberto Malatesta." *Miscellanea Francescana* 35 (1936): 287–297.

Glasser, Marc. "Marriage in Medieval Hagiography." *Studies in Medieval and Renaissance History*, n.s., 4 (1981): 3–34.

Godefroy, L. "Mariage." *DTC* 9.2044–2123.

Gold, Penny S. *The Lady and the Virgin: Image, Attitude, and Experience in Twelfth-Century France*. Chicago and London, 1985.

———. "Male/Female Cooperation: The Example of Fontevrault." In *Distant Echoes*. Vol. 1 of *Medieval Religious Women*, ed. John A. Nichols and Lillian Thomas Shank, 151–168. Cistercian Studies Series, no. 71. Kalamazoo, Mich., 1984.

———. "The Marriage of Mary and Joseph in the Twelfth-Century Ideology of Marriage." In *Sexual Practices and the Medieval Church*, ed. Vern L. Bullough and James A. Brundage, 102–117, 249–251. Buffalo and New York, 1982.

Gomez Pereira, Mauro. "Alfonso II el Casto, y el Monasterio de Samos." In *Estudios sobre la Monarquia Asturiana*, 247–258. Instituto de Estudios Asturianos. Oviedo, 1949.

Goodich, Michael. "The Contours of Female Piety in Later Medieval Hagiography." *Church History* 50 (1981): 20–32.

———. *Vita Perfecta: The Ideal of Sainthood in the Thirteenth Century*. Monographien zur Geschichte des Mittelalters, vol. 25. Stuttgart, 1982.

Goodman, Anthony. "The Piety of John Brunham's Daughter, of Lynn." In *Medieval Women*, ed. Derek Baker, 347–358. Studies in Church History. Subsidia, 1. Oxford, 1978.

Goody, Jack. *The Development of the Family and Marriage in Europe*. Cambridge, 1983.

Gorski, Karol. "Le roi-saint: un problème d'idéologie féodale." *Annales ESC* 24 (1969): 370–376.

Grafe, Eduard. "Geistliche Verlöbnisse bei Paulus." *Theol. Arbeiten aus dem rheinschen wissenschaftlichen Prediger-Verein* N.F. 3 (1899): 57–69.

Graus, F. "La sanctification du souverain dans l'Europe centrale des Xe et XIe siècles." In *Hagiographie, Cultures, et Sociétés, IVe–XIIe siècles*, 559–572. Actes du Colloque organisé à Nanterre et à Paris (2–5 mai 1979). Centre de Recherches sur l'Antiquité tardive et le haut Moyen Age. Université de Paris-X. Paris, 1981.

———. *Volk, Herrscher und Heiliger im Reich der Merowinger.* Prague, 1965.

Gryson, Roger. *The Ministry of Women in the Early Church.* Trans. Jean LaPorte and Mary Louise Hall. Collegeville, Minn., 1976.

———. *Les origines du célibat ecclésiastique du premier au septième siècle.* Gembloux, 1970.

Hachez, Félix. "Du culte de sainte Aye." *Annales du cercle archéologique de Mons* 7 (1867): 357–365.

Hale, Rosemary. "*Imitatio Mariae*: Motherhood Motifs in Devotional Memoirs." *Mystics Quarterly* 16 (1990): 193–203.

Hallinger, Kassius. "The Spiritual Life of Cluny in the Early Days." In *Cluniac Monasticism in the Central Middle Ages*, ed. Noreen Hunt, 29–55. Hamden, Conn., 1971.

Hannedouche, Simone. "L'amour Cathare." *Cahiers d'études Cathares* 2d ser., 43 (1969): 23–29.

Hasenohr, Geneviève. "La vie quotidienne de la femme vue par l'église: l'enseignement des 'Journées Chrétiennes' de la fin du moyen-âge." In *Frau und spätmittelalterlicher Alltag*, 19–101. Internationaler Kongress krems an der Donau 2. bis 5. Oktober 1984. Österreichische Akademie der Wissenschaften, Philosophisch-Historische Klasse, Sitzungsberichte, 473. Veröffentlichungen des Instituts für mittelalterliche Realienkunde Österreichs, no. 9. Vienna, 1986.

Heffernan, Thomas J. *Sacred Biography: Saints and Their Biographers in the Middle Ages.* Oxford, 1988.

Hellmann, Siegmund. "Die Heiraten der Karolinger." In *Ausgewählte Abhandlungen zur Historiographie und Geistesgeschichte des Mittelalters*, 293–391. Weimar, 1961.

Helmholz, R. H. *Marriage Litigation in Medieval England.* Cambridge, 1974.

Herlihy, David. "Did Women Have a Renaissance? A Reconsideration." *Medievalia et Humanistica*, n.s., 13 (1985): 1–22.

———. "The Family and Religious Ideologies in Medieval Europe." *Journal of Family History* 12 (1987): 3–17.

———. *Medieval Households.* Cambridge, Mass., 1985.

Hillgarth, J. N. *Ramon Lull and Lullism in Fourteenth-Century France.* Oxford, 1971.

Hipler, F. "Johannes Marienwerder, der Beichvater der seligen Dorothea von Montau." *Zeitschrift für die Geschichte und Altertumskunde Ermlands* 29 (1956): 1–92.

Hoch-Smith, Judith, and Anita Spring, eds. *Women in Ritual and Symbolic Roles.* New York and London, 1978.

Hohler, Christopher. "St. Osyth and Aylesbury." *Records of Buckinghamshire* 18 (1966): 61–72.

Holdsworth, Christopher J. "Christina of Markyate." In *Medieval Women*, ed. Derek Baker, 185–204. Studies in Church History. Subsidia, 1. Oxford, 1978.

Hunt, Noreen. *Cluny under Saint Hugh, 1049–1109*. London, 1967.

Hurd, John Coolidge. *The Origin of I Corinthians*. London, 1965.

Huyghebaert, Nicolas. "Les femmes laïques dans la vie religieuse des XIe et XIIe siècles dans la province ecclésiastique de Reims." In *I laici nella 'Societas Christiana' dei secoli XI e XII*, 346–389. Atti della terza Settimana internazionale di studio, Mendola, 21–27 agosto, 1965. Pubblicazioni dell'Università Cattolica del Sacro Cuore. Miscellanea del Centro di Studi Medioevali, 5. Milan, 1968.

Iogna-Prat, Dominique. "Continence et virginité dans la conception clunisienne de l'ordre du monde autour de l'an mil." *Academie des inscriptions et belles-lettres. Comptes rendus*, January–March (1985): 127–143.

Irigaray, Luce. *Speculum of the Other Woman*. Trans. Gillian C. Gill. Ithaca, N.Y., 1985.

Jacquart, Danielle, and Claude Thomasset. *Sexuality and Medicine in the Middle Ages*. Trans. Matthew Adamson. Princeton, N.J., 1988.

John, Eric. "Edward the Confessor and the Celibate Life." *AB* 97 (1979): 171–178.

Johnson, F. R. "The English Cult of St. Bridget of Sweden." *AB* 103 (1985): 75–93.

Johnson, Penelope D. *Equal in Monastic Profession: Religious Women in Medieval France*. Chicago and London, 1991.

Johnston, Mark D. "Ramon Llull's Conversion to Penitence." *Mystics Quarterly* 16 (1990): 179–192.

Jones, Charles W. *Saint Nicholas of Myra, Bari, and Manhattan: A Biography of a Legend*. Chicago and London, 1978.

Jones, Michael K., and Malcolm G. Underwood. *The King's Mother: Lady Margaret Beaufort, Countess of Richmond and Derby*. Cambridge, 1992.

Jørgensen, Johannes. *Saint Bridget of Sweden*. Trans. Ingeborg Lund. 2 vols. London and New York, 1954.

Jülicher, A. "Die geistlichen Ehen in der alten Kirche." *Archiv für Religionswissenschaft* 7 (1904): 373–386.

Karras, Ruth Mazo. "Holy Harlots: Prostitute Saints in Medieval Legend." *Journal of the History of Sexuality* 1 (1990): 3–32.

Kendrick, T. D. *St. James in Spain*. London, 1960.

Kieckhefer, Richard. *Unquiet Souls: Fourteenth-Century Saints and Their Religious Milieu*. Chicago and London, 1984.

Klaniczay, Gábor. *The Uses of Supernatural Power in the Middle Ages*. Trans. Susan Singerman. Cambridge, 1990.

Klauser, Renate. *Der Heinrichs- und Kunigundenkult im mittelalterlichen Bistum Bamberg*. Bamberg, 1957.

Klinck, Anne L. "Anglo-Saxon Women and the Law." *Journal of Medieval History* 8 (1982): 107–121.

Kosztolnyik, Z. J. *Five Eleventh Century Hungarian Kings: Their Policies and Their Relations with Rome.* East European Monographs, no. 79. New York, 1981.

Kraemer, Ross S. "The Conversion of Women to Ascetic Forms of Christianity." *Signs* 6 (1980): 298–307.

Kugelman, R. "1 Cor. 7:36–38." *Catholic Biblical Quarterly* 10 (1948): 63–71.

Labriolle, Pierre de. "Le 'mariage spirituel' dans l'antiquité chrétienne." *Revue historique* 137 (1921): 204–225.

Lambert, Malcolm. *Franciscan Poverty· The Doctrine of the Absolute Poverty of Christ and the Apostles in the Franciscan Order, 1210–1323.* London, 1961.

———. *Medieval Heresy: Popular Movements from Bogomil to Hus.* London, 1977.

Landini, Lawrence C. *The Causes of the Clericalization of the Order of Friars Minor, 1209–1260.* Diss. ad Lauream in Facultate Historiae Ecclesiasticae Pontificiae Universitatis Gregorianae. Chicago, 1968.

Langlois, C.-V. *La vie en France au moyen âge de la fin du XIIe au milieu du XIVe siècle.* 4 vols. Paris, 1924–1928.

LaPorte, Jean. *The Role of Women in Early Christianity.* Studies in Women and Religion, vol. 7. New York and Toronto, 1982.

Laqueur, Thomas. *Making Sex: The Body and Gender from the Greeks to Freud.* Cambridge, Mass., 1990.

Larson, Martin A. *The Essene Heritage; or the Teacher of the Scrolls and the Gospel Christ.* New York, 1967.

Lea, H. C. *History of Sacerdotal Celibacy in the Christian Church.* 2 vols. 3d rev. ed. London, 1907.

Le Bras, G. "Comptes rendus." *Revue historique de droit français et étranger* 10 (1931): 743–757. Review of two doctoral theses: René Le Picard. "La communauté de la vie conjugale, obligation des époux. Etude canonique." Faculté de droit de Paris, 1930; Hubert Richardot. "Les pactes de séparation entre époux. Etude historique, comparative et critique de la séparation de corps par consentement mutuel." Faculté de droit de Dijon, 1930.

———. "La doctrine du mariage chez les théologiens et les canonistes depuis l'an mille." *DTC* 9.2123–2317.

Leclercq, H. "Aoste." *Dictionnaire d'archéologie chrétienne et de liturgie,* 1,2.2489–2494. Paris, 1924.

Leclercq, Jean. *Monks on Marriage: A Twelfth-Century View.* New York, 1982.

———. "S. Pierre Damien et les femmes." *Studia Monastica* 15 (1973): 43–55.

Leclercq, Jean, et al. *The Spirituality of the Middle Ages.* Vol. 2 of *A History of Christian Spirituality.* London and New York, 1981.

Lecoy de la Marche, A. *La chaire française au moyen âge.* 2d ed. Paris, 1886.

Le Goff, Jacques. "Merchant's Time and Church's Time in the Middle Ages." In *Time, Work, and Culture in the Middle Ages,* trans. Arthur Goldhammer, 29–42, 289–293. Chicago and London, 1980.

Le Goff, Jacques. *Your Money or Your Life: Economy and Religion in the Middle Ages.* Trans. P. Ranum. New York, 1988.

Leon, Fr. *Lives of the Saints and Blessed of the Three Orders of Saint Francis.* (Translation of the *Aureole Seraphique.*) 4 vols. Taunton, 1885–1887.

Lerner, Robert E. *The Heresy of the Free Spirit in the Later Middle Ages.* Berkeley and Los Angeles, 1972.

Levin, Eve. *Sex and Society in the World of the Orthodox Slavs, 900–1700.* Ithaca, N.Y., 1989.

Leyser, K. J. *Rule and Conflict in an Early Medieval Society: Ottonian Saxony.* Bloomington, Ind., 1979.

L'Hermite-Leclercq, Paulette. "Reclus et recluses dans le sud-ouest de la France." In *La femme dans la vie religieuse de Languedoc (XIIIe–XIVe s.),* ed. E. Privat, 281–298. Cahiers de Fanjeaux, 23. Toulouse, 1988.

Lienhard, Joseph T. *Paulinus of Nola and Early Western Monasticism.* Cologne and Bonn, 1977.

Little, Lester K. "The Personal Development of Peter Damian." In *Order and Innovation in the Middle Ages: Essays in Honor of Joseph R. Strayer,* ed. William C. Jordan et al., 317–341. Princeton, N.J., 1976.

Lochrie, Karma. "The Language of Transgression: Body, Flesh, and Word in Mystical Discourse." In *Speaking Two Languages: Traditional Disciplines and Contemporary Theory in Medieval Studies,* ed. Allen J. Frantzen, 115–140, 253–264. Albany, N.Y., 1991.

———. *Margery Kempe and Translations of the Flesh.* Philadelphia, 1991.

López-Gay, Jesús. "Le phénomène mystique." *DS* 10.1893–1902.

Lottin, Odon. *Psychologie et morale aux XIIe et XIIIe siècles.* 5 vols. 2d ed. Louvain and Gembloux, 1948–1959.

Luscombe, D. E. "The *Ethics* of Peter Abelard: Some Further Considerations." In *Peter Abelard,* ed. E. M. Buytaert, 64–84. Proceedings of the International Conference, Louvain, 10–12 May 1971. Louvain and the Hague, 1974.

———. *The School of Peter Abelard: The Influence of Abelard's Thought in the Early Scholastic Period.* Cambridge Studies in Medieval Life and Thought, n.s., vol. 14. Cambridge, 1969.

Lynch, John E. "Marriage and Celibacy of the Clergy: The Discipline of the Western Church; an Historico-Canonical Synopsis." *The Jurist* 32 (1972): 14–38, 189–212.

Macartney, C. A. *The Medieval Hungarian Historians: A Critical and Analytical Guide.* Cambridge, 1953.

McCulloch, Florence. *Mediaeval Latin and French Bestiaries.* University of North Carolina, Studies in Romance Languages and Literatures, no. 33. Chapel Hill, N.C., 1960.

McDonnell, E. W. *The Beguines and Beghards in Medieval Culture, with Special Emphasis on the Belgian Scene.* New Brunswick, N.J., 1954.

McLaughlin, Eleanor. "Equality of Souls, Inequality of Sexes: Woman in Medieval Theology." In *Religion and Sexism: Images of Woman in the Jewish and Christian Tradition,* ed. Rosemary Radford Ruether, 213–266. New York, 1974.

McLaughlin, Mary Martin. "Creating and Recreating Communities of Women: The Case of Corpus Domini, Ferrara, 1406–1452." In *Sisters and Workers in the Middle Ages*, ed. Judith M. Bennett et al., 261–288. Chicago, 1989.

———. "Survivors and Surrogates: Children and Parents from the Ninth to the Thirteenth Century." In *The History of Childhood*, ed. Lloyd deMause, 101–181. New York, 1974.

McNamara, Jo Ann. "Chaste Marriage and Clerical Celibacy." In *Sexual Practices and the Medieval Church*, ed. Vern L. Bullough and James A. Brundage, 22–33, 231–235. Buffalo and New York, 1982.

———. "The *Herrenfrage*: The Restructuring of the Gender System, 1050–1150." In *Medieval Masculinities*, ed. Clare A. Lees. Forthcoming.

———. *A New Song: Celibate Women in the First Three Christian Centuries*. New York, 1983.

McNamara, Jo Ann, and Suzanne F. Wemple. "Marriage and Divorce in the Frankish Kingdom." In *Women in Medieval Society*, ed. Susan Mosher Stuard, 95–124. Philadelphia, 1976.

Makowski, Elizabeth M. "The Conjugal Debt and Medieval Canon Law." *Journal of Medieval History* 3 (1977): 99–114.

Manselli, Raoul. "Les opuscules spirituels de Pierre Jean-Olivi et la piété de béguins de Langue d'Oc." In *La religion populaire en Languedoc du XIIIe siècle à la moitié du XIVe siècle*, ed. E. Privat, 187–201. Cahiers de Fanjeaux, 11. Toulouse, 1976.

Mariana, Juan de. *Historia general de España*. Vol. 5. Madrid, 1818.

Meeks, W. A. "The Image of the Androgyne: Some Uses of a Symbol in Earliest Christianity." *History of Religions* 13 (1974): 165–208.

Meersseman, G., and E. Adda. "Pénitents ruraux communautaires en Italie au XIIe siècle." *Revue d'histoire ecclésiastique* 49 (1954): 343–390.

Menéndez Pidal, Román, ed. *España Cristiana, 711–1038*. Vol. 6 of *Historia de España*. 3d ed. Madrid, 1971.

———. "La Historiografía medieval sobre Alfonso II." In *Estudios sobre la Monarquia Asturiana*, 3–36. Instituto de Estudios Asturianos. Oviedo, 1949.

Menoud, Philippe-H. "Mariage et célibat selon saint Paul." *Revue de théologie et de philosophie* 1 (1951): 21–34.

Meslin, Michel. "Sainteté et mariage au cours de la seconde querelle Pélagienne." In *Mystique et continence*. Travaux scientifiques du VIIe congrès international d'Avon, 293–307. Les études Carmélitaines, 31. Bruges, 1952.

Metz, René. "Le statut de la femme en droit canonique médiéval." *Recueils de Société Jean Bodin pour l'histoire comparative des institutions* 12 (1962): 59–113.

Meyer, Kuno. "An Crīnōg: ein altirisches Gedicht an eine Syneisakte." *Sitzungsberichte der königlich preussischen Akademie der Wissenschaften: Sitzung der philosophisch-historischen Klasse* 18 (1918): 362–374.

Michaud-Quantin, Pierre. "A propos des premières *Summae confessorum*." *Recherches de théologie ancienne et médiévale* 26 (1959): 264–306.

Michaud-Quantin, Pierre. "Les méthodes de la pastorale du XIIIe au XVe siècle." In *Methoden in Wissenschaft und Kunst des Mittelalters*, ed. Albert Zimmerman, 76–91. Miscellanea Mediaevalia, vol. 7. Berlin, 1970.

———. *Sommes de casuistique et manuels de confession au moyen âge du XIIe au XVIe siècles*. Analecta Mediaevalia Namurcensia, 13. Louvain, Lille, and Montreal, 1962.

Middleton, Ann. "The Clerk and His Tale: Some Literary Contexts." *Studies in the Age of Chaucer* 2 (1980): 121–150.

Molin, Jean-Baptiste, and Protais Mutembe. *Le rituel du mariage en France du XIIe au XVIe siècle*. Théologie historique, 26. Paris, 1974.

Mölk, Ulrich. "La diffusion du culte de S. Alexis en France aux XIe et XIIe siècles et le problème de la genèse de la Chanson de S. Alexis." In *Littérature et société au moyen âge*, ed. Danielle Buschinger, 231–238. Actes du colloque des 5 et 6 mai 1978. Université de Picardie, Centre d'études médiévales. Paris, 1978.

———. "Saint Alexis et son épouse dans la légende latine et la première Chanson française." In *Love and Marriage in the Twelfth Century*, ed. W. Van Hoecke and A. Welkenhuysen, 162–170. Mediaevalia Lovaniensia. Ser. 1, studia 8. Leuven, 1981.

Moore, R. I. "Family, Community, and Cult on the Eve of the Gregorian Reform." *Transactions of the Royal Historical Society*, ser. 5, 30 (1980): 49–69.

———. *The Formation of a Persecuting Society: Power and Deviance in Western Europe, 950–1250*. Oxford, 1987.

———. *The Origins of European Dissent*. New York, 1977.

———. "The Origins of Medieval Heresy." *History* 55 (1970): 21–36.

Morrell, Samuel. "An Equal or a Ward: How Independent Is a Married Woman according to Rabbinic Law?" *Jewish Social Studies* 44 (1982): 189–210.

Morris, Colin. *The Discovery of the Individual, 1050–1200*. New York, 1972.

Morrison, Karl F. "The Gregorian Reform." In *Christian Spirituality*, ed. Bernard McGinn and John Meyendorff, 177–193. Vol. 16 of *World Spirituality*. New York, 1985.

Mundy, John H. "Le mariage et les femmes à Toulouse au temps des Cathares." *Annales ESC* 42 (1987): 117–134.

Murray, Jacqueline. "On the Origins and Role of 'Wise Women' in Causes for Annulment on the Grounds of Male Impotence." *Journal of Medieval History* 16 (1990): 235–249.

———. "The Perceptions of Sexuality, Marriage, and Family in Early English Pastoral Manuals." Ph.D. diss., University of Toronto, 1987.

Naz, R. "For." *Dictionnaire de droit canonique*. 5.871–873. Paris, 1953.

Neel, Carol. "The Origins of the Beguines." In *Sisters and Workers in the Middle Ages*, ed. Judith M. Bennett et al., 240–260. Chicago, 1989.

Nelli, René. "Love's Rewards." Trans. Alyson Waters (from *L'érotique des troubadours* [Paris, 1963]). In *Zone: Fragments for a History of the Human Body*, ed. Michel Feher et al. 2,4:218–235. New York, 1989.

Nelson, Janet L. "Royal Saints and Early Medieval Kingship." In *Sanctity and Secularity: The Church and the World*, ed. Derek Baker, 39–44. Studies in Church History, no. 10. Oxford, 1973.

———. "Society, Theodicy, and the Origins of Heresy: Towards a Reassessment of the Medieval Evidence." In *Schism, Heresy, and Religious Protest*, ed. Derek Baker, 65–77. Studies in Church History, no. 9. Cambridge, 1972.

Newman, Barbara. *Sister of Wisdom: St. Hildegard's Theology of the Feminine*. Berkeley and Los Angeles, 1987.

Nicholson, Joan. "*Feminae gloriosae*: Women in the Age of Bede." In *Medieval Women*, ed. Derek Baker, 15–29. Studies in Church History. Subsidia, 1. Oxford, 1978.

Noonan, John T. *Contraception: A History of Its Treatment by Catholic Theologians and Canonists*. Cambridge, Mass., 1966.

———. "Marital Affection in the Canonists." *Studia Gratiana* 12 (1967): 481–509.

———. "Power to Choose." *Viator* 4 (1973): 419–434.

———. *Power to Dissolve*. Cambridge, Mass., 1972.

Obrist, Barbara. "The Swedish Visionary: Saint Bridget." In *Medieval Women Writers*, ed. Katharina M. Wilson, 227–251. Athens, Ga., 1984.

O'Rourke, J. J. "Hypotheses regarding 1 Corinthians 7, 36–38." *Catholic Biblical Quarterly* 20 (1958): 292–298.

Osheim, Duane J. "Conversion, *Conversi*, and the Christian Life in Late Medieval Tuscany." *Speculum* 58 (1983): 368–390.

Ozment, Steven. *When Fathers Ruled: Family Life in Reformation Europe*. Cambridge, Mass., 1983.

Pagels, Elaine. *Adam, Eve, and the Serpent*. New York, 1988.

———. *The Gnostic Gospels*. New York, 1979.

Parmisano, Fabian. "Love and Marriage in the Middle Ages." *New Blackfriars* 50 (1969): 599–608, 649–660.

Partner, Nancy. " 'And Most of All for Inordinate Love': Desire and Denial in *The Book of Margery Kempe*." *Thought* 64 (1989): 254–267.

Parvey, Constance. "The Theology and Leadership of Women in the New Testament." In *Religion and Sexism: Images of Woman in the Jewish and Christian Traditions*, ed. Rosemary Radford Ruether, 117–149. New York, 1974.

Paul, Lois. "Careers of Midwives in a Mayan Community." In *Women in Ritual and Symbolic Roles*, ed. Judith Hoch-Smith and Anita Spring, 129–149. New York and London, 1978.

Payer, Pierre J. "Early Medieval Regulations concerning Marital Sexual Relations." *Journal of Medieval History* 6 (1980): 353–376.

———. *Sex and the Penitentials: The Development of a Sexual Code, 550–1150*. Toronto, 1984.

Péano, Pierre. "Olieu." *DS* 11.751–762.

Pereira, B. A. *La doctrine du mariage selon saint Augustin*. 2d ed. Etudes de théologie historique. Paris, 1930.

Petroff, Elizabeth. *The Consolation of the Blessed*. New York, 1979.

Petroff, Elizabeth. *Medieval Women's Visionary Literature*. New York and Oxford, 1986.

Pinckaers, Servais. "Ce que le moyen âge pensait du mariage." *La vie spirituelle*, Supp. 20 (1967): 413–440.

Pollock, F., and F. W. Maitland. *The History of English Law*. 2 vols. 2d ed. Cambridge, 1952.

Poncelet, A. "Index miraculorum B. V. Mariae quae saec. VI–XV latine conscripta sunt." *AB* 21 (1902): 241–360.

Poulin, Joseph-Claude. *L'idéal de sainteté dans l'Aquitaine carolingienne d'après les sources hagiographiques, 750–950*. Quebec City, 1975.

Prinz, Friederich. "Aristocracy and Christianity in Merovingian Gaul: An Essay." In *Gessellschaft, Kultur, Literatur: Rezeption und Originalität im Wachsen einer europäischen Literatur und Geistigkeit*, ed. Karl Bosl, 153–165. Monographien zur Geschichte des Mittelalters, vol. 11. Stuttgart, 1975.

Quasten, Johannes. *Patrology*. 4 vols. Westminster, Md., 1950–1988.

Rader, Rosemary. *Breaking Boundaries: Male/Female Friendship in Early Christian Communities*. New York, Ramsey, and Toronto, 1983.

Rando, Daniela. "*Laicus religiosus* tra strutture civili ed ecclesiastiche: l'ospedale di Ognissanti in Treviso (sec. XIII)." *Studi medievali*, ser. 3, 24,2 (1983): 617–656.

Reames, Sherry L. *The "Legenda Aurea": A Reexamination of Its Paradoxical History*. Madison, Wis., 1985.

Reddaway, W. F., et al., eds. *The Cambridge History of Poland*, vol. 1. Cambridge, 1950.

Reeves, Marjorie. *The Influence of Prophecy in the Later Middle Ages: A Study in Joachimism*. Oxford, 1969.

Renna, Thomas. "Virginity in the *Life* of Christina of Markyate and Aelred of Rievaulx's *Rule*." *American Benedictine Review* 36 (1985): 79–92.

Reynolds, Roger E. "*Virgines Subintroductae* in Celtic Christianity." *Harvard Theological Review* 61 (1968): 547–566.

Reynolds, Susan. *Kingdoms and Communities in Western Europe, 900–1300*. Oxford, 1984.

Ridyard, Susan J. *Royal Saints of Anglo-Saxon England: A Study of West Saxon and East Anglian Cults*. Cambridge, 1988.

Ringbom, Sixten. "Nuptial Symbolism in Some Fifteenth-Century Reflections of Roman Sepulchral Portraiture." *Temenos* 2 (1966): 68–97.

Ritzer, K. *Le mariage dans les églises chrétiennes du Ier au XIe siècle*. Paris, 1970.

Roché, Déodat. "Les Cathares et l'amour spirituel (1)." *Cahiers d'études Cathares* 2d ser., 94 (1982): 3–39.

Rollason, D. W. *The Mildrith Legend: A Study in Early Medieval Hagiography in England*. Leicester, 1982.

Rordorf, Willy. "Marriage in the New Testament and the Early Church." *Journal of Ecclesiastical History* 20 (1969): 193–210.

Rosenthal, Joel T. "Edward the Confessor and Robert the Pious: 11th Century Kingship and Biography." *Mediaeval Studies* 33 (1971): 7–20.

Ross, Margaret. "Concubinage in Anglo-Saxon England." *Past and Present* 108 (1985): 3–34.

Rossi, Mary Ann. "The Passion of Perpetua, Everywoman of Late Antiquity." In *Pagan and Christian Anxiety: A Response to E. R. Dodds*, ed. Robert C. Smith and John Lounibos, 53–86. Lanham, Md., 1984.

Rousselle, Aline. *Porneia: On Desire and the Body in Antiquity.* Trans. Felicia Pheasant. Oxford and New York, 1988.

Ruether, Rosemary Radford. "Misogynism and Virginal Feminism in the Fathers of the Church." In *Religion and Sexism: Images of Woman in the Jewish and Christian Traditions*, ed. Ruether, 150–183. New York, 1974.

———. *Sexism and God-Talk: Toward a Feminist Theology.* Boston, 1983.

Russell, Jeffrey Burton. *Dissent and Reform in the Early Middle Ages.* Berkeley and Los Angeles, 1965.

Salisbury, Joyce E. "Fruitful in Singleness." *Journal of Medieval History* 8 (1982): 97–106.

Schmidtke, James A. " 'Saving' by Faint Praise: St. Birgitta of Sweden, Adam Easton, and Medieval Antifeminism." *American Benedictine Review* 33 (1982): 149–161.

Schmitt, Emile. *Le mariage chrétien dans l'oeuvre de saint Augustin: une théologie baptismale de la vie conjugale.* Paris, 1983.

Scholz, Bernhard W. "The Canonization of Edward the Confessor." *Speculum* 36 (1961): 38–60.

———. "Hildegard von Bingen on the Nature of Woman." *American Benedictine Review* 31 (1980): 361–383.

Schulenburg, Jane Tibbetts. "Sexism and the Celestial Gynaeceum—from 500 to 1200." *Journal of Medieval History* 4 (1978): 117–133.

———. "Women's Monastic Communities, 500–1100: Patterns of Expansion and Decline." In *Sisters and Workers in the Middle Ages*, ed. Judith M. Bennett et al., 208–239. Chicago, 1989.

Scroggs, Robin. "Paul and the Eschatological Woman." *Journal of the American Academy of Religion* 40 (1972): 283–303.

Seboldt, Roland H. A. "Spiritual Marriage in the Early Church: A Suggested Interpretation of 1 Cor. 7:36–38." *Concordia Theological Monthly* 30 (1959): 103–119.

Shahar, Shulamith. *The Fourth Estate: A History of Women in the Middle Ages.* Trans. Chaya Galai. London and New York, 1983.

Sheehan, Michael M. "The Formation and Stability of Marriage in Fourteenth-Century England: Evidence of an Ely Register." *Mediaeval Studies* 33 (1971): 228–263.

———. "*Maritalis Affectio* Revisted." In *The Olde Daunce: Love, Friendship, Sex, and Marriage in the Medieval World*, ed. Robert R. Edwards and Stephen Spector, 32–43, 254–260. Albany, N.Y., 1991.

———. "Marriage Theory and Practice in the Conciliar Legislation and Diocesan Statutes of Medieval England." *Mediaeval Studies* 40 (1978): 408–460.

———. "The Wife of Bath and Her Four Sisters: Reflections on a Woman's Life in the Age of Chaucer." *Medievalia et Humanistica*, n.s., 13 (1985): 23–42.

Sheingorn, Pamela. "The Holy Kinship: The Ascendency of Matriliny in Sacred Genealogy of the Fifteenth Century." *Thought* 64 (1989): 268–286.

Smith, Jacqueline. "Robert of Arbrissel: *Procurator Mulierum.*" In *Medieval Women*, ed. Derek Baker, 175–184. Studies in Church History. Subsidia, 1. Oxford, 1978.

Southern, R. W. *Western Society and the Church in the Middle Ages.* Harmondsworth, Middlesex, 1970.

Stachnik, Richard. "Zur Veröffentlichung der grossen Lebensbeschreibung Dorotheas von Montau von Johannes Marienwerder." *Zeitschrift für Ostforschung Länder und Völker im östlichen Mitteleuropa* 17 (1968): 713–717.

Stafford, Pauline. "The King's Wife in Wessex, 800–1066." *Past and Present* 91 (1981): 3–27.

———. *Queens, Concubines, and Dowagers: The King's Wife in the Early Middle Ages.* Athens, Ga., 1983.

Stargardt, Ute. "The Political and Social Backgrounds of the Canonization of Dorothea von Montau." *Mystics Quarterly* 11 (1985): 107–122.

Stickler, A. M. "L'évolution de la discipline du célibat dans l'église en occident de la fin de l'âge patristique au Concile de Trente." In *Sacerdoce et célibat: études historiques et théologiques*, ed. J. Coppens, 373–442. Bibliotheca ephemeridum theologicarum Lovaniensium, 28. Gembloux and Louvain, 1971.

Stock, Brian. *The Implications of Literacy: Written Language and Models of Interpretation in the Eleventh and Twelfth Centuries.* Princeton, N.J., 1983.

———. *Myth and Science in the Twelfth Century: A Study of Bernard Silvester.* Princeton, N.J., 1972.

Stow, Kenneth R. "The Jewish Family in the Rhineland in the High Middle Ages: Form and Function." *American Historical Review* 92 (1987): 1085–1110.

Stuard, Susan Mosher. "From Women to Woman: New Thinking about Gender c. 1140." *Thought* 64 (1989): 208–219.

Taviani, H. "Naissance d'une hérésie en Italie du Nord au XIe siècle." *Annales ESC* 29 (1974): 1224–1252.

Teetaert, A. *La confession aux laïques.* Wetteren, Bruges, and Paris, 1926.

———. "La doctrine pénitentielle de saint Raymond de Penyafort, O.P." *Analecta Sacra Tarraconensia* 5 (1929): 121–182.

Tentler, Thomas N. *Sin and Confession on the Eve of the Reformation.* Princeton, N.J., 1977.

———. "The Summa for Confessors as an Instrument of Social Control." In *The Pursuit of Holiness in Late Medieval and Renaissance Religion*, ed. Charles Trinkaus, 103–126. Studies in Medieval and Reformation Thought, vol. 10. Leiden, 1974.

Theis, Laurent. "Saints sans famille? Quelques remarques sur la famille dans le monde franc à travers les sources hagiographiques." *Revue historique* 255 (1976): 3–20.

Thompson, Stith. *Motif-Index of Folk-Literature*. 6 vols. Rev. ed. Bloomington, Ind., 1955–1958.

Tubach, F. C. *Index Exemplorum: A Handbook of Medieval Religious Tales*. Folklore Fellows Communications, no. 204. Helsinki, 1969.

Ullmann, Walter. *The Carolingian Renaissance and the Idea of Kingship*. London, 1969.

Underwood, Malcolm G. "Lady Margaret and Her Cambridge Connections." *Sixteenth Century Journal* 13 (1982): 67–81.

———. "Politics and Piety in the Household of Lady Margaret Beaufort." *Journal of Ecclesiastical History* 38 (1987): 39–52.

Van Eijk, Ton H. C. "Marriage and Virginity, Death and Immortality." In *Epektasis: Mélanges patristiques offerts au Cardinal Jean Daniélou*, ed. Jacques Fontaine and Charles Kannengiesser, 209–235. Paris, 1972.

Vauchez, André. "*Beata Stirps*: Sainteté et lignage en occident aux XIIIe et XIVe siècles." In *Famille et parenté dans l'occident médiéval*, ed. Georges Duby and Jacques Le Goff, 397–407. Collection de l'Ecole Française de Rome, 30. Rome, 1977.

———. "L'influence des modèles hagiographiques sur les représentations de la sainteté, dans les procès de canonisation (XIIIe–XVe siècle)." In *Hagiographie, Cultures, et Sociétés, IVe–XIIe siècles*, 585–592. Actes du Colloque organisé à Nanterre et à Paris (2–5 mai 1979). Centre de Recherches sur l'Antiquité tardive et le haut Moyen Age, Université de Paris-X. Paris, 1981.

———. "Jacques de Voragine et les saints du XIIIe s. dans la *Légende dorée*." In *"Legenda Aurea": Sept siècles de diffusion*, 27–56. Published under the direction of Brenda Dunn-Lardeau. Actes du colloque international sur la *Legenda aurea*. Université du Québec à Montréal, 11–12 mai 1983. Montreal and Paris, 1986.

———. *Les laïcs au moyen âge: pratiques et expériences religieuses*. Paris, 1987.

———. *La sainteté en occident aux derniers siècles du moyen âge d'après les procès de canonisation et les documents hagiographiques*. Bibliothèque des Ecoles Françaises d'Athènes et de Rome, fasc. 241. Rome, 1981.

———. *La spiritualité du moyen âge occidental, VIIIe–XIIe siècles*. Collection Sup., L'historien, 19. Rome, 1975.

Verdon, Michel. "Virgins and Widows: European Kinship and Early Christianity." *Man*, n.s., 23 (1988): 488–505.

Vermes. Geza. *Jesus the Jew: A Historian's Reading*. New York, 1973.

Vernet, F. "Brigitte de Suède." *DS* 1.1943–1958.

Veyne, Paul. "The Roman Empire." In *History of the Private Life*, ed. Paul Veyne, trans. Arthur Goldhammer, 1:5–234. Cambridge, Mass., 1987.

Violante, C. "Hérésies urbaines et hérésies rurales en Italie du 11e au 13e siècle." In *Hérésies et sociétés dans l'Europe pré-industrielle, IIe–18e siècles*, ed. Jacques Le Goff, 171–197. Civilisations et Sociétés, 10. Paris, 1968.

Von Hügel, Baron Friedrich. *The Mystical Element of Religion as Studied in*

Saint Catherine of Genoa and Her Friends. 2 vols. London and New York, 1923.

Vööbus, Arthur. *History of Asceticism in the Syrian Orient.* 2 vols. Corpus Scriptorum Christianorum Orientalium. Vol. 184, subs. vol. 14. Vol. 197, subs. vol. 17. Louvain, 1958–1960.

Warner, Marina. *Alone of All Her Sex: The Myth and the Cult of the Virgin Mary.* London, Melbourne, and New York, 1978.

Webb, Diana M. "A Saint and His Money." In *The Church and Wealth,* ed. W. J. Sheils and Diana Wood, 61–73. Ecclesiastical History Society. London, 1987.

Weinstein, Donald. *Savonarola and Florence: Prophecy and Patriotism in the Renaissance.* Princeton, N.J., 1970.

Weinstein, Donald, and Rudolph M. Bell. *Saints and Society: The Two Worlds of Western Christendom, 1000–1700.* Chicago and London, 1982.

Welter, J. Th. *L'exemplum dans la littérature religieuse et didactique du moyen âge.* Paris and Toulouse, 1927.

Wemple, Suzanne F. *Women in Frankish Society: Marriage and the Cloister, 500 to 900.* Philadelphia, 1985.

Weston, Jessie L. *The Legend of Sir Perceval: Studies upon its Origin, Development, and Position in the Arthurian Cycle.* 2 vols. London, 1906–1909.

Westpfahl, Hans. "Dorothée de Montau." *DS* 3.1664–1668.

Williams, Norman Powell. *The Ideas of the Fall and of Original Sin: A Historical and Critical Study.* London, 1927.

Wilson, Katharina M., ed. *Medieval Women Writers.* Athens, Ga., 1984.

Wilson, Katharina, and Elizabeth M. Makowski. *Wykked Wyves and the Woes of Marriage: Misogamous Literature from Juvenal to Chaucer.* Albany, N.Y., 1990.

Wood, Charles T. "The Doctor's Dilemma: Sin, Salvation, and the Menstrual Cycle in Medieval Thought." *Speculum* 56 (1981): 710–727.

Zanoni, Luigi. *Gli Umiliati nei loro rapporti con l'Eresia, l'industria della lana ed i Comuni nei secoli XII e XIII.* Bibliotheca historica italica, series altera, 2. Milan, 1911; reprt. Rome, 1970.

Zarri, Gabriella. *Le sante vive: Cultura e religiosità femminile nella prima età moderna.* Turin, 1990.

Zema, Demetrius B. "The Houses of Tuscany and of Pierlone in the Crisis of Rome in the Eleventh Century." *Traditio* 2 (1944): 155–175.

INDEX